Bridging Social Psychology
Benefits of Transdisciplinary Approaches

Bridging Social Psychology
Benefits of Transdisciplinary Approaches

Edited by

Paul A. M. Van Lange
Free University, Amsterdam

2006

LAWRENCE ERLBAUM ASSOCIATES, PUBLISHERS
Mahwah, New Jersey   London

Copyright © 2006 by Lawrence Erlbaum Associates, Inc.

All rights reserved. No part of this book may be reproduced in any form, by photostat, microform, retrieval system, or any other means, without prior written permission of the publisher.

Lawrence Erlbaum Associates, Inc., Publishers
10 Industrial Avenue
Mahwah, New Jersey 07430
www.erlbaum.com

Cover design by Tomai Maridou

Library of Congress Cataloging-in-Publication Data

Bridging social psychology : benefits of transdisciplinary approaches / Paul A.M. Van Lange, editor.
    p. cm.
Includes bibliographical references and index.
ISBN 0-8058-5094-5 (cloth : alk. paper)
ISBN 0-8058-5095-3 (pbk. : alk. paper)
1. Social Psychology. I. Lange Paul A. M. Van.

HM1033.B75 2006
302—dc22   2005051231
                                                CIP

Books published by Lawrence Erlbaum Associates are printed on acid-free paper, and their bindings are chosen for strength and durability.

Printed in the United States of America
10 9 8 7 6 5 4 3 2 1

Contents

Part 3: Bridges With Biology, Neuroscience, and Cognitive Science

Part 4: Bridges With Personality, Emotion, and Development

Part 5: Bridges With Relationship Science, Interaction, and Health

Part 6: Bridges With Organizational Science, Culture, and Economics

Preface

$\mathbf{S}$ ocial influences are all around us—with friends and family, at work, in the various media, to name just a few domains to which we devote considerable time. From the moment we wake up, it is, if not the actual presence, then at least the imagined or implied presence of others that exerts important influences on what we do, what we think, and how we feel. However, despite the ubiquity of social influences in everyday life, it is my conviction that most people, scientists and nonscientists alike, tend to underestimate the impact of "social influences" on cognition, emotion, and behavior. For whatever reasons, factors other than social factors tend to catch the eye more rapidly, thereby leading to underestimates of social influences as a powerful source of explanation. Differences in lifestyle, differences in personality, and differences in salary are among the prominent variables that are often used to understand a variety of important issues. For example, health is often linked to unhealthy habits such as smoking and lack of exercise, rather than to social factors such as quality of one's social network of close partners and friends. And happiness, organizational commitment, and consumer decisions are often overexplained in terms of financial or material rewards—even though close others and friends are important to happiness, colleagues are essential to whether we stay or leave an organization, and peers, family, and "idols" often exert powerful effects on what we buy and what we would never even consider buying. Indeed, often "the social" matters to people at least as much or more than "the money" (or any other resource that is not inherently social).

Clearly, an underestimation of "social influences" may lead to an inaccurate and biased understanding of various urgent societal issues, such as terrorism, health, or a clean environment. Similarly, theoretical progress on basic questions is unlikely to be made if social influences are underestimated. In fact, a stronger recognition of social influences is crucial to getting grips on important theoretical problems, such as the person versus situation debate or the nature versus nurture debate. For example, an insufficient realization of the impact of social influences may lead one to think too strongly in terms of person-caused influences alone, as if the social situation does not matter for the expression of social behavior. Similarly, an insufficient realization of the impact of social influences may lead one to think in terms of nature-caused influences alone, as if the social situation does not matter for the expression and development of genetic influences. Thus, social influences are often necessary—although not sufficient—causes of cognition, affect, behavior, and social interaction.

The book *Bridging Social Psychology* is inspired by the belief that many people tend to underestimate the impact of social influences, and, as such, the relatively unique contribution that social psychology can make to understanding major scientific and societal problems. The *key objective* of this book is to exchange views on how to bridge social psychological concepts with other scientific fields and disciplines so as to increase our understanding of major scientific themes, major societal issues, or important social phenomena.

Clearly, by its very nature, the topic of bridging social psychology inevitably raises general questions about the field of social psychology. What are the key assumptions of social psychology? Where is social psychology heading? What is social psychology's unique contribution to basic theoretical questions? And how about broad societal questions? The first collection of nine essays deals with such questions, although the most important topic centers on the benefits and costs of bridging social psychology, and the various obstacles that are needed to overcome for bridging to be successful.

The four subsequent sections deal with four grand bridges. One such category deals with bridges with *biology, neuroscience,* and *cognitive science.* Indeed, there is increasing consensus that various biological and neurological processes influence social processes and that various social processes influence biological and neurological processes. Such empirical findings may touch on important scientific problems, such as the mind–body problem or the nature versus nature controversy. Bridges of social psychology and cognitive psychology have received particular emphasis in the early 1980s, with the emergence of social cognition as a new area of theory and research. Twenty years later we see that *social cognition* is not only a central area within social psychology, but also increasingly integrated with most areas of research in social psychology. Bridges between social psychology and neuroscience into *social neuroscience* may well be equally promising, or even more promising.

A second category addresses bridges with *personality, emotion,* and *development.* Indeed, much of personality, emotion, and development is truly social in nature. Although personality and social psychology have always had a sibling-like relationship, this is less true for emotion and social psychology. Yet this relationship is on its way to become more sibling-like, because many emotions—and shame and guilt are just examples—are inherently social, in that they would not, or could not, come into being and persist if there were no social environment. Also, social development appears to be central to understanding many aspects of human development, including biological development, cognitive development, and personality development.

A third category deals with bridges with *relationship science, interaction,* and *health.* Increasing evidence suggests that our thoughts, emotions, and habits are strongly shaped in the context of relationships, especially close relationships such as marriage, dating relationships, or parent–child relationships, which often are also essential for how people enter new interactions and relationships. Also, relationships are central to understanding mental and physical health, presumably because relationships serve important needs and desires that are essential to social psychology.

A fourth category deals with bridges with *organizational science, culture,* and *economics.* Often, the "social environment" consists of large groups and societal systems, which are important to understanding internal processes such as cognition and affect, interpersonal behavior, and societal trends. Individuals' thoughts, feelings, and behavior in organizations are hard to understand if we knew nothing about the mission, structure, and climate of the organization. Similarly, various processes—attitudes, discrimination, political views—are socially shaped by cultural influences, by economic fluctuations, as well as by institutes that serve to regulate individual and collective behavior. And finally, notions of fairness, cooperation, or happiness, as we shall see, may be as basic to economic transactions as they are to social psychology and to the psychological sciences more broadly.

To summarize, the focus of this book is on illustrating the benefits and costs of bridging social psychology with other fields of psychology—such as cognitive, developmental, and personality psychology—as well as other disciplines, such as biology, neurosciences, or economics. Because bridges involve at least two "islands," it is likely that the benefits (and costs) extend beyond a particular field or discipline—indeed, often bridging involves more than two islands. Bridging is addressed for the general field of social psychology (with an emphasis on bridges that seem especially promising), particular topics (e.g., attitudes, cooperation), or specific lines of research or models relevant to those topics.

Audience.   The anticipated audience consists of scientists and advanced students who are interested in understanding social phenomena, including not only social psychologists but also scientists and students working in other fields of psychology (in particular, personality, developmental psychology, cognitive psychology, biological psychology, health and clinical psychology, organizational psychology) or working in other disciplines, including economics, sociology, political science, management science, communication science, marketing, neuroscience, biology, and philosophy. While a basic knowledge about social psychology is assumed, knowledge about specific areas of research in social psychology is not needed. For that reason, most essays clarify and explain specific social psychological concepts, principles, or phenomena.

Bridging Social Psychology features prominent authors in the field as well as those whose experience and expertise have seen the ebbs and flows of social psychology. In addition, many have been prominent journal editors, textbook authors, and/or panelists for grant review. For this reason, the end of the book includes a brief biographical statement from each contributor, so that readers from different fields and disciplines may have a "frame" for reading and interpreting the essay.

ACKNOWLEDGMENTS

This book was inspired by the teaching and research activities of members of the Kurt Lewin Institute, and interuniversity graduate school of social psychology and its applications. I served as the scientific director for the Kurt Lewin Institute from 2001 through 2004, and organized a workshop on Bridging Social Psychology at a conference at which the 10th anniversary of the Institute was celebrated. Next I asked each participating institute to write an essay for this volume, which included institutes at the University of Amsterdam, University of Groningen, Leiden University, University of Nijmegen (now Radboud University), Utrecht University, and the Free University at Amsterdam. Also, many of the members of Kurt Lewin Institute served as ad hoc reviewers of the essays. And last but not least, the Kurt Lewin Institute was for me a source of inspiration to initiate this book.

More generally, I want to thank all authors for their contributions. The chapters they wrote require even more thought, energy, and time than a regular chapter that tends to focus more strongly on one's own lines of research. As such, I was genuinely impressed and inspired by the enthusiasm, commitment, and precision with which they responded to the invitation and the review process—all of which made editing a real pleasure. Second, each essay was reviewed by at least one external reviewer, so I am grateful to all members who served on the editorial board, who have all done a wonderful job in providing constructive comments and suggestions to the authors. Moreover, I am grateful to a long list of excellent scientists who devoted some of their valuable time to providing thoughtful comments on early drafts of the essays or other advice: Henk Aarts, Chris Agnew, Ursula Athenstaedt, Daniel Batson, Bram Buunk, David De Cremer, Carsten De Dreu, Naomi Ellemers, José Miguel Fernández Dols, Agneta Fischer, Mark Fine, Eli Finkel, Catrin Finkenauer, Marcello Gallucci, Rob Holland, Chester Insko, Jeffrey Joireman, Johan Karremans, Laura King, Eric Knowles, Sander Koole, Esther Kluwer, Jacques-Phillipe Leyens, Craig Parks, Ann Rumble, Caryl Rusbult, Gün Semin, Diederik Stapel, Wolfgang Stroebe, Toon Taris, Jan Theeuwes, Kees Van Den Bos, Eric Van Dijk, Wilco Van Dijk, Mark Van Vugt, Daniel Wigboldus, Nico VanYperen, Mark

Weber, Tim Wildschut, Natalie Wyer, and Vincent Yzerbyt. I also thank Esther Coalter-Wiersma, Carla Heldens, and Iris van der Mark for their secretarial and other support throughout this project.

Last but not least, I thank my wife Wilma Otten, who is trained as a social psychologist and conducts research on medical decision making with patients (often with very serious diseases) in an Academic Hospital in Leiden, the Netherlands. She has always encouraged and inspired me to think (and sometimes act) across the boundaries of social psychology by asking critical but constructive questions about social psychology—especially the relevance of social psychology for understanding "real problems" such as the ones that she faces in the hospital. In fact, I think that without her I would not have started this project in the first place. My son and daughter can take credit for the fact that this project took quite a bit longer than I thought it would take. Thus, it is only natural to dedicate this book to Wilma, Dion, and Sera.

EDITORIAL BOARD

Part I

Bridging Social Psychology

INTRODUCTION

This section discusses the cost and benefits of bridging social psychology with other fields of psychology and other academic disciplines. In chapter 1, Paul Van Lange argues and illustrates that social psychology underuses its neighbors, that social psychology is being underused by its neighbors, and that the benefits of bridging social psychology exceeds its costs. Social psychology is argued to be in a perfect position to bridge because "the individual and the social environment" are almost anywhere, and such bridging is argued to be important to understanding classic debates, such as the nature versus nature debate or the person versus situation debate, as well as to understanding broad societal issues.

Chapter 2, authored by Arie Kruglanski, complements and extends chapter 1 by focusing on the importance of theory development. In particular, Arie Kruglanski argues that the relative absence of broad theorizing in social and personality psychology is not only unwarranted on philosophical grounds but it hurts our efforts in the long run, undermining our ability to forge bridges to other social sciences and to have a meaningful voice in the general dialogue about societal issues. It is argued that although as a field social and personality psychology does well in terms of the ideal of Truth, the field is doing less well as far as the ideals of Abstraction (i.e., the gleaning of general principles) and scientific Progress are concerned. The chapter notes that the field is beginning to recognize that this state of affairs needs to change, and concludes that this growing awareness needs to be translated into programs, structures, and institutional policies aimed at encouraging broad theory construction by upcoming generations of social and personality psychologists.

1

Bridging Social Psychology

Paul A. M. Van Lange
Free University, Amsterdam

Why bridging social psychology? Are there benefits to connecting with other fields of psychology, such as cognitive or developmental psychology? And how about connecting with other disciplines, such as neurosciences, biology, or economics? Are the potential benefits theoretical, methodological, or both? Are the benefits mutual? Are there costs to bridging with other fields or disciplines? If so, what may be such costs? Why do most grant-giving agencies emphasize the benefits of transdisciplinary approaches, and is this how scientific progress is to be promoted?

Such questions come easily to mind when discussing *bridging social psychology*—that is, when discussing the cost and benefits of connecting social psychology with other fields of psychology or other scientific disciplines. This should not be too surprising because the topic of bridging social psychology is at the heart of social psychology. It relates to how social psychology is to be defined, it touches upon the history of social psychology, and most importantly, it gives direction to the future of social psychology. And because the field of social psychology is becoming increasingly intertwined with other fields and disciplines, it becomes important to discuss the benefits and costs of bridging social psychology. The volume does so both from a general perspective as well as from the perspective of bridges to (a) biology, neuroscience, and cognitive science, (b) personality, emotion, and development, (c) relationship science, interaction, and health, and (d) organizational science, culture, and economics.

INSPIRATIONS TO BRIDGING SOCIAL PSYCHOLOGY

The project *Bridging Social Psychology* is inspired by three broad, complementary beliefs. The *first* belief may be labeled as the *underuse of neighbors*. It states that insights and knowledge rooted in neighboring fields, disciplines, and domains of application are underused in social psychology. This claim seems to be especially true for some periods of insularity in the history of social psychology, and it is important to note that social psychology is increasingly seeking and using knowledge and insights outside of social psychology (e.g., the increasing use of psychophysiological measures, or the increasing attention for emotion). Yet many would agree that the broader questions for which social psychology may be essential (e.g., questions regarding the mind–body problem, questions regarding human nature) are best answered by attending to relatively broad and diverse literatures that complement each other. Perhaps closer to home, a topic such as social development (which is inherently social psychological because it deals with interactions of the individual with the social environment) certainly requires learning about behavior genetics, developmental psychology, personality psychology, and cultural psychology. Or largely social psychological topics, such as aggression or altruism, call for input from, for example, the biological sciences (including ethology), cognitive sciences, neurosciences (e.g., to understand the cognitions and emotions that may underlie it), and developmental psychology, as well as cultural and political sciences and economics (e.g., to understand the institutions that may be effective at sanctioning aggression). One could argue that the success of social cognition is to be partially explained by the fact that the neighbors are "used" (but in a neighborly sense) in ways that promote interesting questions at the interface of social psychology and cognitive psychology (as well as the realization that much cognition centers on social stimuli), the use of sophisticated methodology, and ultimately the fact that some subtle mechanisms underlying key phenomena (e.g., stereotyping) are well illuminated.

The *second* belief may be labeled as *being underused by neighbors*. It states that social psychological insights and knowledge are underused in neighboring fields, disciplines, and in various domains of application. Granted, there are several examples of existing bridges with other fields of psychology and other disciplines. For example, there are links and cross-references between social psychology and cognitive psychology, and between social psychology and economics, and there are several examples of fruitful use of social psychological knowledge in domains such as consumer psychology, health psychology, and organizational psychology. At the same time, given that "the individual" and "the social environment" are so central to our understanding of an individual's feelings, thoughts, and behaviors in these (and other) contexts, the social psychological literature is underused in related fields, disciplines, and domains of application. For example, a strong case can be made for the underuse of social psychology in understanding the determinants of mental health. As noted recently by Hazel Markus (2004, p. 1), "Almost everything in basic social psychology is relevant to mental health and illness but we are the only ones who know this, and even more to the point, we are almost the only ones who know what we do." Thus, understanding why social psychology seems to be underused is central to the discussion of bridging social psychology.

The *third* belief may simply be labeled as *benefits exceed costs*, which is assumed to be true for many bridges. It states that there are several important opportunities and benefits that accrue from bridging with other fields and disciplines that outweigh any risks or costs following from bridging. This belief acknowledges that there are risks and costs to bridging. For example, we need to read a greater variety of journals, need to enlarge research activities (because most fields have their own methodological traditions), and need to attend conferences outside of our own field. Also, it is important to do all of that with care and precision but without losing touch with the central mission of a research project (one is more likely to get lost if more fields or disciplines are involved), or with the strengths of the field of social psychology.

Other complications may be relatively enduring communication (and coordination) problems, because social psychology has a relatively brief but strong history in which concepts are advanced, traditions are created, and implicit norms and rules have been established. One needs only to compare an average journal article in a biology, economics, or health journal with a prototypical social psychological article, and some differences are immediately clear. For example, social psychology articles tend to have much longer introductions (and more references) with fairly detailed attention to prior research and theorizing, and are more likely to report multiple studies, in which convenience samples of university students and experimental studies are the rule rather than the exception. Last but not least, for many situations, costs precede benefits, thus calling for investment from individual researchers as well as from the universities. As to the latter, the universities at large need to provide some infrastructure for bridging to work. The first task is, of course, to think hard about a somewhat flexible infrastructure in which bridges are likely to be built. How exactly to do that is beyond the scope of this introduction, but as early research on acquaintance and friendship revealed (Newcomb, 1961), it takes interaction for acquaintance to develop. Thus, promoting possibilities for natural ways of interaction and intellectual exchange is perhaps most important.

Although there are important risks and/or costs associated with bridging social psychology, there may be actually good measures to reduce or overcome at least some of the risks and costs. For example, working with colleagues from other fields and disciplines, sharing expertise, and dividing tasks and labor may be an effective way to address topics from a transdisciplinary perspective (e.g., Kahneman, 2004; Taylor, 2004). I return to the benefits and costs later, but for now, it suffices to note that there is an increasing (although implicit) belief that the benefits of bridging social psychology with several other fields and disciplines outweigh the costs of bridging. National science foundations increasingly make it part of their policy to reward transdisciplinary activities, in the form of supporting interdisciplinary research, teaching programs, and interdisciplinary research centers. (Whether such policy is always translated into concrete practice, is a different matter, of course). Also, there is an increasing tendency to publish books and special issues of journals that address the issue of transdisciplinary approaches to various topics, such as intentionality, social development, or trust. Although the focus of social psychology may have been inward, there is certainly an increasing attention for linking own research to methods and insights that are rooted in other fields or disciplines. As noted by Brewer, Kenney, and Norem (2000, p. 2) in the introduction to a special issue of *Personality and Social Psychology Review* on new directions of interdisciplinary research:

> *The history of the field has been marked by periods of relative insularity and periods of relative expansiveness and outward focus. The last few years of the 20th century marked the beginning of a major shift in the direction of renewed interest in personality and social psychology as a central node in an interdisciplinary network with rich connections to other subdisciplines of psychology and to the life sciences and social sciences more broadly.*

BENEFITS OF BRIDGING SOCIAL PSYCHOLOGY

It may not be a rare event that people get together and work together, simply because "let's work together" sounds so great. However, such working together is unlikely to be very successful if there are no real benefits of working together. In the following, I briefly discuss four benefits of bridging.

Major Scientific Problems Call for Bridging. What are some of the most pervasive or "biggest" scientific problems that (social) psychology has faced in the past? One classic scientific problem centers on the *mind–body problem*, and the existence and functions of conscience and "free will" in relation to the brain and behavior. It subsumes topics such as awareness, automaticity, and intentionality, all of which have strong implications for theorizing at different levels of analysis. Although such issues can to some degree be illuminated with methods derived from disciplines such as neurosciences and cognitive sciences, the answers to such problems clearly require insights from several fields of psychology, including social psychology. Because so much of the brain, of the mind, and of free will is social in nature, as are the motivations (e.g., interpersonal attraction or interpersonal conflict) and emotions (e.g., shame and guilt) that accompany brain activity, it is should be clear that the mind–body problem cannot really be addressed without "input" from social psychology. For example, if biased judgment and deceit can occur without any conscience or awareness, but triggered by subtle activation (e.g., by activating some parts of the brain), then such interpersonal actions are not only part of the mind–body problem, they are largely social psychological as well. Moreover, the topic of lying and deceit has strong implications for several other disciplines, such as business (e.g., business ethics), law and justice, and political science. A complementary classic problem is the problem of *human nature* ("Are people good or bad by nature?"), which also benefits from input of all fields of psychology, with strong implications for theorizing in anthropology, economics, and political science (e.g., for the way in which effective groups, organizations, and governments should be structured, and for theories about effective leadership).

A major scientific problem that is perhaps more closely connected to psychology is the *nature versus nurture* controversy, which has inspired considerable debate, theory, and research, and involves expertise and knowledge from various fields, such as biological psychology, personality, developmental psychology, and social psychology, and disciplines such as biology (including ethology), medicine, and anthropology. As it turns out, promising solutions to this debate suggest that much of nurture can only be expressed and developed via social circumstances—nature *via* nurture. Indeed, there is increasing evidence that nature can only be revealed (or not) via nurture, that is, through circumstances that provide the opportunities (and constraints) for nature-based tendencies to express, grow, and develop.

A long-standing debate even closer to social psychology is the person–situation debate, the controversy of whether behavior is primarily caused by the person or by the situation. Solutions to this debate, too, emphasize that both the psychology of the person and the psychology of situation are important to understanding feelings, thoughts, and behavior (Mischel, 2004). As for the nature versus nurture debate, one needs to understand "the person" and "the social environment" if one seeks to understand various social psychological phenomena. Similarly, it is likely that contemporary scientific problems that touch on the interface of cognition and affect will benefit from the input from various fields and disciplines.

That major scientific problems call for bridging is not to imply that all researchers and theorists should direct our attention to major scientific problems. On the contrary, much of the success of social psychology is due to the fact that the field is strongly oriented toward experimental methods and rather specific questions. For example, one of the most influential papers in social psychology is Taylor and Brown's (1988) article on positive illusion and well-being. This articles provides a comprehensive review of specific laboratory studies (e.g., on social comparison, on social judgment processes) as well as large field studies (e.g., among cancer patients, among chronically depressed individuals). In combination, these studies provide support for the general notion that positive, illusory beliefs about the self, rather than realistic beliefs about the self, tend to be associated with mental health. (Incidentally, this article by Taylor and Brown may also serve as a perfect demon-stration of the utility of bridging social psychology, personality, and clinical and health psychology). Thus, focusing on specific questions (and specific procedures) is not bad at all, especially if it contributes to understanding the major (social) psychological problems.

But what exactly constitutes major social psychological problems? Here is where things are not very clear, and where consensus is in need of improvement. As noted by Zajonc (1999, p. 200), "In physics, geology, and other branches of natural sciences, there is a consensus as to the 'core subject matter of their inquiry'; in social psychology, no such consensus exists." Perhaps bridging social psychology may be helpful in obtaining a greater consensus about the core subject—or perhaps, the core subjects—of the field.

Major Scientific Theories Call for Bridging. Social psychology is organized around many topics, such as attitudes, impression formation, helping and altruism, group performance, and the like. Typically, each of these topics has generated theories, models, or broad hypotheses. In fact, it is quite challenging to think about a topic that is not related to any model, hypothesis, or even theory. Clearly, such organizing of knowledge serves important functions, and it is remarkable how well people who have only followed the course "Introduction to Social Psychology" recall several years later several of our major models or theories, with perhaps the theory of cognitive dissonance (Festinger, 1957) being the best recalled theory. Although this is much appreciated, some or perhaps many would argue that the field would be much better organized if there were a "grand theory" that guided most or nearly all of social psychological research—especially because many of the phenomena that social psychology examines are closely related to each other. This is an often heard criticism, and can be illustrated by the Steven Pinker's (2002, p. 241) description of social psychology in *The Blank Slate*:

> Social psychology, the science of how people behave toward one another, is often a mishmash of interesting phenomena that are explained by giving them fancy names. Missing is the rich deductive structure of other sciences, in which a few deep principles can generate a wealth of subtle predictions—the kind of theory that scientists praise as "beautiful" or "elegant."

The point is not so much that social psychology has too many theories or models. Rather, there seems to be some consensus that social psychology lacks a general theory (e.g., Kelley, 2000) or general model (e.g., set of assumptions) that one would call "the social psychology model"—similar to evolution theory in biology, or rational choice theory in economics. One suggestion has been advanced by Hazel Markus (2004): "The goal, however, would be to agree on a general model that would draw attention toward the structure and patterning of the *social world* [italics added]. Next, we could develop ways to communicate it and illustrate and then systematically use it to explain our selves and our worlds" (p. 4). Clearly, Markus was defining social psychology and "its potential model" in terms of the individual and the social world (or social environment), and it seems important (and timely) to work on a fairly comprehensive model that informed scientists from other fields and disciplines too immediately recognize as "social psychological."

Hence, there is much to be said about the desirability for social psychology to develop a general model or theory, which provides a broad organizing framework for predicting and explaining a lot of phenomena that are "social psychological." We would probably even more impressed (a) if the theory can do that on the basis of a parsimonious set of assumptions and principles, and (b) if the theory is of direct relevance to the reciprocal relationship between the individual and the social environment. Although there does not seem to be a theoretical framework that guides most research in social psychology, there is an increasing attention for broad theories. A strong case in point is evolutionary psychology, which increasingly serves as an explanatory framework for a number of phenomena, such as important needs (e.g., need to belong; Baumeister & Leary, 1995), relationship processes (Buss & Kenrick, 1998), and the benefits of helping (e.g., the tending instinct; Taylor, 2002). Examples of other integrative activities include the emergence of the entire fields such as social cognition ("bridging social and cognitive psychology"; e.g., Fiske & Taylor, 1984), models developed within the tradition of social cognition (e.g., dual process models of information processing), and the emerging field of social neuroscience ("bridging social psychology and neurosciences"; e.g., Cacioppo et al., 2002). Also, work in the tradition of attachment theory (which bridges developmental, personality, and social psychology; e.g., Mikulincer, & Shaver, 2003), emotion theory (Frijda, 1988; Zajonc, 1998), and attempts to design taxonomies of situations in social psychology (e.g., taxonomy derived from interdependence theory; Kelley et al., 2003) are inherently transdisciplinary and integrative.

   Major Scientific Problems and Theories Call for Methods That Call for Bridging. Over the past decades, social psychology has become richer and richer in terms of research methods and experimental procedures for studying social cognition, attitudes, interpersonal relationships, and group processes. A recent *Handbook of Research Methods in Social and Personality Psychology* illustrates the variety of methods that social psychologists have used, ranging from survey research to computer simulation, or from psychophysiological methods to narrative analysis (Reis & Judd, 2000). This is not to imply that social psychologists have always relied on diversity in methods—after all, self-report methodology and experimental methods in the laboratory summarize most research activities. But there is an increasing consensus that social psychology benefits from explicit measures and implicit measures, and, as noted earlier, social psychologists are increasingly using methods derived from the biological, cognitive, and neurosciences, such as variations in blood pressure, sophisticated priming techniques, and functional magnetic resonance imagery (fMRI) techniques. The result of all these efforts is that the list of research tools that have been used (and largely validated) is impressively long—and in many ways serves as an important toolbox for scientific progress.

   Clearly, major scientific problems and theories can often only be addressed by diversity and complementarity in methods. For example, to address aspects of the mind–body problem one needs to consider explicit and implicit measures, psychophysiological methods and self-reports, and so on. At the same time, the reverse is also true. The introduction and use of new methods often raise new questions that may get at aspects of larger scientific problems or theories. For example, the increasing use of implicit measures in social psychology (e.g., using response latencies to assess implicit associations between positive and negative features and ingroups and outgroups; the Implicit Association Test; Greenwald, Nosek, & Banaji, 2003) and the fact that the empirical relationship between implicit measures and self-report measures is often rather weak have led to further theorizing about implicit and explicit processes in stereotyping and social judgment. Perhaps, in the near future, we see a closer connection between animal studies and social psychology, as animals allow us to examine issues that can never be examined among humans (e.g., Gosling, this volume). Thus, transdisciplinary in research methods is likely to enhance the progress we make in addressing major scientific problems and contributing to broad psychology theories.

Societal Problems Call for Bridging.   Scientists may have somewhat different views on the societal problems that are considered most urgent or important—be it terror, health, race issues, or the environment. Yet there should be a fair amount of consensus that for most, if not all, pervasive societal problems it takes knowledge, skill, and expertise from more than one discipline to really understand them and make a contribution to resolving them. One pervasive societal issue is promoting public health. Reducing the addiction to smoking, for example, is an excellent example of a societal problem that requires knowledge, expertise, and skill from a variety of disciplines, such as behavior genetics and personality (e.g., for understanding the genetics involved), communication sciences (e.g., for designing public education campaigns), law (e.g., for designing and implementing new laws), and economics (e.g., for considering to increase taxes on cigarettes). And there seems a bit of social psychology in each of these—for example, in understanding the potential reactance to law and law enforcement, in understanding the persuasion principles underlying campaigns, or in understanding the modest influence of financial rewards and costs in altering unhealthy habits.

Another pervasive societal issue is the vitality of our environment. The massive use of scarce natural resources (e.g., catching too many fish for nature to replenish) and the pollution of the environment (e.g., dumping industrial waste) create large-scale and to some degree irreversible societal problems. Such complex problems call for the input of various fields and disciplines to effectively understand the magnitude of the problem (e.g., biologists and geologists should inform us about the state of affairs regarding environmental solution), whereas other disciplines may inform us about the boundary conditions for bringing about effective change in behavior and habits in individuals, groups, and social institutes (e.g., psychologists, sociologists, political scientists, and policymakers).

Perhaps the most important societal problem that has faced us throughout history is international conflict. For example, the Cold War was characterized by international friction and distrust, and it took expertise from at least biologists, economists, political scientists, historians, and psychologists (cognitive and social, in particular) to get at least some grip on the problem. The contemporary problem of terror clearly is to be defined in terms of largely social psychological topics such as intergroup relations, stereotyping, communication, and trust (or distrust). And as in the era of the Cold War, several disciplines need to be involved to really understand the problem of terror, and it seems that history and theology need to be added to the already long list of disciplines that are needed to understand the problem of terror, let alone contributing to solving it.

Thus, taken together, the ability of science to understand and contribute to solving societal problems is strongly dependent on knowledge and expertise from various disciplines. This realization is already widespread, especially if one thinks of the various interdisciplinary journals, associations, and research centers that address health issues, environmental issues, and international relationships. In each of these major societal problems, social psychology should play a key role, because virtually no societal problem is only a technical (or biological) problem—and virtually no large societal problem can be resolved by technology alone. Rather, it are often problems in which "the social" plays a key role, in terms of both the origins (e.g., people in part may start smoking for interpersonal reasons) and solutions (e.g., effective communication to reduce smoking).

COSTS OF BRIDGING SOCIAL PSYCHOLOGY

Bridging is not without costs. As noted earlier, there are several costs following from bridging—and several costs are discussed in the various essays. There are several practical issues, such as finding the time to keep informed about scientific progress in other fields and disciplines. This should not be underestimated, especially because bridging requires traveling the required route (e.g., with care and precision), rather than taking intellectual shortcuts that are likely to lead to unsteady bridges (see also Batson, this volume). Care and precision are also involved in bringing scientists from various disciplines together, and in providing the infrastructure that is effective for building bridges. Indeed, if only national science foundations are going to promote (and enforce) transdisciplinary research, then such "extrinsic" initiatives may undermine some of the main virtues of science—creativity and drive (see Stroebe, this volume). The current evaluation system for getting tenure and promotions at most universities does not reward investments in learning about other fields or disciplines—which is where bridging starts (see also Berscheid, this volume). Rather, the systems at universities reward number and quality of publications, irrespective of whether they are published in the author's own field or not. Therefore, it is "cost-effective" (and therefore understandable) to publish in a single field, because this requires "investing" in only a single field.

Perhaps an even more pressing problem may be communication problems among scientists working and socialized in different fields or disciplines. One could argue that as a consequence of "going their own ways," many scientific disciplines and fields have developed their own traditions, cultures, and concepts and assumptions. Differences in concepts and basic assumptions, in particular, may lead to some serious communication problems. For example, economists often use behavioral definitions of altruism (Fehr & Gächter, 2002), conceptualizing altruism in terms of behaviors that benefit others at some economic cost to self. In contrast, social psychology uses motivational definitions of altruism, conceptualizing altruism in terms of intentions of promoting reward for others (e.g., Batson, 1998). Also, if the assumption of self-interest (*homo economicus*) continues to be a basic assumption in economics, then some social psychologists may not even be interested in digging deep into the economics literature. These are real issues, just as real as biological psychologists approach the problem of aggression with a set of assumptions that are quite different from those common in social psychology.

At the same time, communication problems are there to be solved. Different assumptions, beliefs and models should yield competitive hypotheses—which should promote, rather than inhibit, scientific progress. That is, being informed about the different assumptions and models, and becoming more specific about the precise nature of differences, should be translateable into experimental tests that should promote the cumulation of knowledge. In fact, a promising solution has been suggested by a psychologist who just recently won the Nobel Prize in economics—hence, a clear expert in "building bridges." After conveying pessimism about the ways in which controversies are played out (e.g., in the reply–rejoinder formats), Daniel Kahneman (2003) decided to do something about it by suggesting a procedure of *adversarial collaboration*. This is defined as a "good-faith effort to conduct debates by carrying out joint research—in some cases an agreed-upon arbiter may be needed to lead the project and collect the data." (p. 729). There is anecdotal evidence reported by Kahneman that such collaboration (the precise procedures are summarized in Mellers, Hertwig, & Kahneman, 2001) yielded new facts that were accepted by all, narrowed differences in opinion, and considerable mutual respect. The challenge is, of course, to translate differences in basic beliefs into mutually agreed-on research, which should be an important step toward cumulative science—with all the benefits, such as addressing major questions, testing major theories, using agreed-on and complementary methods, and ultimately yielding an understanding that should be of great value to understanding and solving societal problems as well. Although many costs are pervasive and persuasive, the preceding example illustrates that at least some (perceived) costs may be transformed into real benefits.

THE MAINLAND OF SOCIAL PSYCHOLOGY

Metaphorically, one may think of the scientific landscape as the world, consisting of disciplines and fields of disciplines (i.e., continents and countries, respectively). In addressing the topic of bridging social psychology, it is essential that one make an attempt at characterizing the field of social psychology. Although this is not easy, I start with summarizing common definitions of social psychology, as they should at least illuminate the mainland of social psychology. (I am slightly comforted by the fact that early atlases were quite inaccurate in representing the size and location of countries.) So I first discuss a possible definition of social psychology, and I am more than slightly comforted by the fact that there is quite some consensus about the definition of social psychology.

Most definitions of social psychology describe it as the science of the individual and the social environment. Indeed, one of the pioneers of social psychology and its applications, Kurt Lewin (1936), emphasized the importance of an individual's goals and the social environment as essential toward understanding behavior. In doing so, he emphasized not only the power of the (objective) situation, but also the power of an individual's subjective interpretation of reality. Definitions of social psychology typically are related to Kurt Lewin's seminal work, in that they emphasize social influence and interpretation. For example, the well-known definition by Allport (1985) describes social psychology as the scientific study of the way in which people's thoughts, feelings, and behaviors are influenced by the real, imagined, or implied presence of other people.

Although constructs such as the "individual" and the "social environment" are present in most definitions of social psychology, these key constructs only make sense when they are related to each other. When specified, definitions of social psychology focus on the influence of the social environment on the individual—that is, his or her thoughts, feelings, and behavior. Indeed, the experimental paradigm centers on varying aspects of the social environment that are expected to influence individuals' thoughts, feelings, and behaviors. However, social psychology also entails the opposite causal relationship, whereby individuals themselves are the source of influence. Individuals often actively select or shape the social environment, changing it in ways that match their needs and goals. For example, many or most individuals may actually prefer—and actively seek out—working in small groups rather than very large groups so as obtain an pleasant interpersonal climate as well as an atmosphere that is instrumental in getting the job done efficiently. Thus, social psychology can be defined as the science of the *reciprocal influence of the individual and the social environment*. This definition stands at the basis of research on social cognition and attitudes, interpersonal relationships, and group processes—broad topics that are regarded as central to social psychology.

THE CENTRAL LOCATION OF SOCIAL PSYCHOLOGY

Social psychology, defined by the constructs of "individual" and "social environment," finds itself in an excellent position to be linked to other fields of psychology or other disciplines, for at least two broad reasons. The first reason is that social psychology operates in between the micro level of analysis (molecular level) and the macro level of analysis (molar level). The "meso position" at which much of social psychology is located can be easily linked to both

(a) the micro level of analysis, representing the processes that operate within the individual, including the biological, neurological, and cognitive processes (e.g., the effects of social stimuli on bodily responses), and (b) the macro level of analysis, representing the processes that operate at the level of the broader social environment, including the organizational, cultural, and economical processes (e.g., the effects of democratic vs. autocratic leadership on voting). Thus, given that social psychology operates in between the micro and macro levels of analysis, the field is an excellent position to "bridge" with either end of the continuum of the human sciences.

A second reason derives from the fact that social psychology can be regarded as a rather broad, multifaceted, and inclusive field of psychology. Although it sounds like a rather self-serving or ingroup-serving claim, there are at least two good arguments in support of this view. To begin with, social psychology is the study of *all people*. That is, it is not a science that focuses on a particular category of people—and hence social psychologists may include in their samples the young and the old, or the healthy and the sick, without an overall attempt to understand differences (or similarities) among these categories of people. Unlike most of child psychology focusing on children or clinical psychology focusing on individuals with psychological disorders and depression, the field of social psychology is oriented toward the study of all people. Moreover, social psychology is the study of *all social contexts*. Social psychology does not directly focus on particular roles we may have in the various contexts we encounter in everyday life. Unlike fields such as organizational psychology, consumer psychology, or sport psychology, the science of social psychology does not tend to focus on a particular societal context, in which we work, consume, or engage in sport activities.

Thus, social psychology takes a rather central position (the meso level) in between the micro and macro levels of the scientific landscape. Moreover, there are no inherent boundary conditions (in terms of people or situations) in the definition of social psychology that would render bridging with other fields or disciplines less feasible.

NEIGHBORING CONTINENTS AND COUNTRIES

As can be seen in Fig. 1.1, the essays in this book are categorized according to a landscape involving five distinct systems: the biological system, the individual system, the interpersonal system, the group system, and the societal system (see Higgins & Kruglanski, 1996). These systems vary on two broad and correlated dimensions. The first dimension ranges from micro, via meso, to macro levels of analysis. The biological system is located at the micro level, the individual system, the interpersonal system, and the group system are located at the meso level, and the societal system is located at the macro level. The second dimension focuses on a continuum that ranges from "the individual" with a strong focus on internal processes, such as personality, motivation, and emotion, to "the social environment" with a strong focus on interpersonal and group processes.

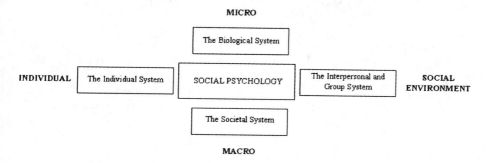

MICRO

The Biological System

INDIVIDUAL | The Individual System | SOCIAL PSYCHOLOGY | The Interpersonal and Group System | SOCIAL ENVIRONMENT

The Societal System

MACRO

FIG. 1.1. A spatial, two-dimensional representation of the field of social psychology being connected to four systems: the biological system, the individual system, the interpersonal and group system, and the societal system. Because social psychology bridges the micro level and macro level of analysis, as well as "the individual" and "the social environment," social psychology can be located at the heart of the four systems.

Although the individual and the social environment often are included in research, it is important to distinguish between the two ends of the continuum. The systems that emphasize the "individual" focus on how individuals think, feel, and act in their attempt *to effectively understand* the social environment and to regulate toward various goals. The systems that emphasize the social environment (i.e., interpersonal system and group system) focus on how individuals think, feel, and act in an attempt *to effectively interact* with the social environment, whether the social environment constitutes one person (dyads) or several persons (groups).

The individual system is, of course, inherently linked to the biological system, in that many of these internal processes, such as cognition, motivation, and affect, are intertwined with the biological system. The other systems are also closely interconnected, such that, for example, some aspects of the interpersonal system (e.g., a history of physical abuse) may be detected in the biological system. The biological and individual systems may underlie some behaviors that are societally relevant, such as need for affiliation (or need to belong). For example, in the Netherlands there is an active political debate about the increasing level of "individualism" (alienation from each other) in Western society, how it may (or may not) explain a variety of societal events (e.g., a believed increase in bystanders who do not help), and how eventually society needs to regulate itself.

CLASSIFICATION OF ESSAYS

Before and during the process of inviting authors to write essays on bridging social psychology, I sought to pursue two goals: (a) a scientific exchange of beliefs regarding the benefits and costs of bridging social psychology, and (b) a great variety of essays that illustrate the various bridges that seem especially promising. On the basis of the systems outlined above, I categorized the essays into five rubrics.

1. General essays (section 1): Each of these essays address the benefits and costs, opportunities and risks of bridging social psychology. The essays often make a strong point, thereby drawing on personal experiences, classic or recent research examples, or historical development. This section also contains essays that take a critical yet constructive look at social psychology, providing suggestions for how the field of social psychology could benefit from further progress.

2. Biology, neuroscience, and cognitive science (section 2): This section primarily focuses on biological system and areas at the interface of the biological and individual system. It includes essays addressing brain research, psychophysiology and neuroscience, cognitive science, and social cognition. Some essays also discuss interesting bridges involving the biological system and interpersonal system.

3. Personality, emotion, and development (section 3): This section primarily focuses on the individual system: that is, personality, motivation, emotion, and development. It includes essays addressing the interface of personality and social psychology, which represents a long-standing debate, emphasizing the central role of emotion in social psychology, and the close connection between important topics of developmental psychology and social psychology—which includes the individual system and the interpersonal system.

4. Relationship science, interaction, and health (section 4): This section primarily focuses on the social interactions of the individual with the social environment, thereby emphasizing the interpersonal system. It includes essays on relationships, social interaction, addressing issues such as the neuroscientific aspects of relationships or the linguistic and communicative aspects of interaction. It also includes essays on health, even though health is located at the interface of the individual system and the interpersonal system.

5. Organizational science, culture, and economics (section 5): This section primarily focuses on the social interactions of the individual with social environment (or parts thereof), thereby emphasizing the group and larger societal system. It includes essays on organizational processes and structure, thus addressing issues such as conflict, team innovation, and leadership. The section also includes essays on culture, larger societal or political issues, and economics, thereby addressing the bridges between economics

and social psychology, which are often discussed under emerging fields such as behavioral economics and microeconomics.

TAKE-HOME MESSAGE APPROACH

A project such as *Bridging Social Psychology* can easily lead to a series of essays conveying the same brief messages—such as "yep, working together is good"—that are not very helpful to understanding the benefits and costs of bridging social psychology.

Although it is not easy to discourage such "bridging is good" messages, the goal was, of course, to provide an overview of views or beliefs that are held by colleagues within and beyond social psychology. (I asked a much greater number of social psychologists than scientists working in other fields or disciplines, because the field is already broad and multifaceted, and it was considered "a must" that authors could effectively relate to social psychology.) I considered three "strategic" goals important.

First, I sought to promote the authors' own *points of view*. I deeply felt that an essay about one's own points of view could be accomplished with and without relying on the existing literature. I wanted the number of references to be relatively low (i.e., not exceeding two pages of references), and, more importantly, I sought to encourage authors to rely on their own feelings and beliefs. This is also why I used an "open formula" such that virtually none of the authors was asked to write an essay on a specific theme. Also, I selected authors on the basis of several grounds that are likely to promote one's views on bridging—indeed, many of the authors have been involved in integrative activities (such as writing textbooks), have held key positions (e.g., board members of associations), or have been very active in editing and reviewing (e.g., editorships of central journals in social psychology). Thus, some authors, more than usual, rely on sources other than scientific sources per se to make their point— indeed, personal experiences, and related forms of anecdotal evidence, are sometimes powerfully used.

Second, I sought to promote the exchange of *strong points of view*. As alluded to earlier, I felt it important to reduce tendencies toward simply concluding "bridging is good" and to promote tendencies toward enhancing a strong and clear point of view on bridging social psychology. To do so, the authors were told that the goal was to exchange clear points of view, and throughout the process were strongly encouraged to explicitly state and summarize their "take-home message" at the end of the essay under the heading "Conclusions." Often, I noted to authors that this is a perfect opportunity to let colleagues know how you think and feel about social psychology, and about their bridges with other fields and disciplines. Thus, I may advise readers to take a close look at the final conclusions at the end of the essay.

Third, I sought to promote the exchange of *many points of view*. It is, of course, undesirable to exert control over the contents of an essay. So throughout editing I deliberately did not evaluate the author's position in my editorial letters—even if I found myself in nearly perfect disagreement with the author's point of view. What I did do was invite scientists working in nearly all areas of social psychology, working in disciplines at both the micro side and the macro side of social psychology, and scientists working in different countries. Hence, a good number of social psychologists work in the areas of attitudes and social cognition, interpersonal relationships, and group processes. Also, because personality and social psychology are so intimately related, I invited quite a number of scientists working in those areas as well. Also, there is an emphasis on both micro sciences (e.g., cognitive science and neuroscience) and the macro sciences (e.g., anthropology, political science, and economics), and complementary sciences (philosophy). At the same time, several disciplines are not represented (e.g., mathematics, theology, or physics), not because they are not considered important to social psychology, but simply to avoid too much ambition. For the same reason, there are numerous areas that are strongly linked to social psychology but not represented in this volume, such as environmental psychology, consumer psychology, and educational psychology (even though several authors get at topics that are central to those fields as well). Finally, I wanted authors from a variety of different countries, because one maximizes differences by inviting authors being raised in different countries or working in different countries with often distinct intellectual traditions. Needless to say, I could only pursue this level of diversity if I asked authors to be brief and concise. Although not every author appreciated my (admittedly, somewhat inflexible) concern with brevity, and reader-friendliness at the same time, it is my hope that, collectively, we are better off by having many points of view expressed by many different scientists.

To conclude, given the diversity, I do not anticipate that the reader appreciates each and every essay. My advice to you as the reader is to be selective in reading (and perhaps start by reading the Conclusions), and to read essays with which you are likely to agree as well as those with which you are likely to disagree.

REFERENCES

Allport, G. W. (1985). The historical background of social psychology. In G. Lindzey & E. Aronson (Eds.), *Handbook of social psychology* (Vol. 1, 3rd ed., pp. 1–46). New York: Random House.

Batson, C. D. (1998). Altruism and prosocial behavior. In D. T. Gilbert, S. T. Fiske, & G. Lindzey (Eds.), *The Handbook of Social Psychology* (pp. 282–316). New York: McGraw-Hill.

Baumeister, R. F., & Leary, M. (1995). The need to belong: Desire for interpersonal attachment as a fundamental human motivation. *Psychological Bulletin, 117,* 497–529.

Brewer, M. B., Kenny, D. A., & Norem, J. K. (2000). Personality and social psychology at the interface: New directions for interdisciplinary research. *Personality and Social Psychology Review, 4,* 2.

Buss, D., & Kenrick, D. (1998). Evolutionary social psychology. In D. Gilbert & S. Fiske (Eds.), *Handbook of Social Psychology* (Vol. 2, 4th ed., pp. 982–1026). Boston: McGraw-Hill.

Cacioppo, J. T., Berntson, G. G., Adolphs, R., Carter, C. S., Davidson, R. J., McClintock, M. K., McEwen, B. S., Mearey, M. J., Schacter, D. L., Sternberg, E. M., Suomi, S. S., & Taylor, S. E. (Eds.). (2002). *Foundations in social neuroscience.* Cambridge, MA: MIT Press.

Fehr, E., & Gächter, S. (2002). Altruistic punishment in humans. *Nature, 415,* 137–140.

Festinger, L. (1957). *A theory of cognitive dissonance.* Stanford, CA: Stanford University Press.

Fiske, S. T., & Taylor, S. E. (1984). *Social cognition.* New York: Random House.

Frank, R. H. (1988). *Passions within reason: The strategic role of the emotions.* New York: Norton.

Frijda, N. H. (1988). The laws of emotion. *American Psychologist, 43,* 349–358.

Greenwald, A. G., Nosek, B. A., & Banaji, M. R. (2003). Understanding and using the Implicit Association Test: I. An improved scoring algorithm. *Journal of Personality and Social Psychology, 85,* 197–216.

Higgins, E. T., & Kruglanski, A. W. (Eds.). (1996). *Social psychology: Handbook of basic principles.* New York: Guilford Press.

Kahneman, D. (2003). Experiences of collaborative research. *American Psychologist, 58,* 723–730.

Kahneman, D., & Tversky, A. (1979). Prospect theory: An analysis of decision under risk. *Econometrica, 47,* 263–292.

Kelley, H. H. (2000). The proper study of social psychology. *Social Psychology Quarterly, 63,* 3–15.

Kelley, H. H., Holmes, J. G., Kerr, N. L., Reis, H. T., Rusbult, C. E., & Van Lange, P. A. M. (2003). *An atlas of interpersonal situations.* New York: Cambridge.

Ketelaar, T. (2004). Ancestral emotions, current decisions: Using evolutionary game theory to explore the role of emotions in decision making. In C. Crawford & C. Salmon (Eds.), *Evolutionary psychology, public policy, and personal decisions* (pp. 145–168). Mahwah, NJ: Lawrence Erlbaum Associates.

Lewin, K. (1935). *A dynamic theory of personality: Selected readings* (D. K. Adams & K. E. Zener, Trans.). New York: McGraw-Hill.

Markus, H. R. (2004). A social psychological model of behavior. *Dialogue, 19*(Suppl. 1), 1–4.

Mellers, B., Hertwig, R., & Kahneman, D. (2001). Do frequency representations eliminate conjunction effects? An exercise in adversarial collaboration. *Psychological Science, 12,* 269–275.

Mikulincer, M., & Shaver, P. R. (2003). The attachment behavioral system in adulthood: Activation, psychodynamics, and interpersonal processes. In M. P. Zanna (Ed.), *Advances in experimental social psychology* (Vol. 35, pp. 53–152). New York: Academic Press.

Mischel, W. (2004). Toward an integrative science of the person. *Annual Review of Psychology, 55,* 1–22.

Newcomb, T. M. (1961). *The acquaintance process.* New York: Holt, Rinehart, and Winston.

Pinker, S. (2002). *The blank slate: The modern denial of human nature.* New York: Viking.

Reis, H. T., & Judd, C. M. (Eds.). (2000). *Handbook of research methods in social and personality psychology.* New York: Cambridge University Press.

Taylor, S. E. (2002). *The tending instinct.* New York: Henry Holt.

Taylor, S. E. (2004). Preparing for social psychology's future. *Journal of Experimental Social Psychology, 40,* 139–141.

Taylor, S. E., & Brown, J. D. (1988). Illusion and well-being: A social psychological perspective on mental health. *Psychological Bulletin, 103,* 193–210.

Zajonc, R. B. (1998). Emotions. In D. Gilbert, S. Fiske, & G. Lindzey (Eds.), *Handbook of social psychology* (Vol. 2, 4th ed., pp. 591–632). New York: McGraw-Hill.

Zajonc, R. B. (1999). One hundred years of rationality assumptions in social psychology. In A. Rodrigues & R. V. Levine (Eds.), *Reflections on 100 years of experimental social psychology* (pp. 200–214). New York: Basic Books.

2

Theories as Bridges

Arie W. Kruglanski[1]
University of Maryland

In this volume devoted to the bridging of social psychology, I would like to argue for the importance of theory development. Theories are bridges that concatenate isolated domains of our discipline, connect us to our past, and forge links to other social sciences. Social psychology is like a fragmented archipelago that tore from its continent of origin (or its past) and is sequestered from other surrounding continents (other social science disciplines). Bridges are in order.

Science, as everyone knows, is an attempt to convert the "buzzing confusion" that surrounds us into neatly ordered regularities. Experience is infinitely varied. No two drops of water, no two persons, no two contexts, are exactly alike. We would be simply unable to budge unless we managed to classify somehow those multifarious objects and events and discover systematic relations between the categories. Such is the business of lay epistemics; such too is the business of scientific epistemics. At the heart of both lies the enterprise of theory construction. A metaphysical assumption that underlies it all is that lawful relations between categories do exist and can be discovered. Question that assumption in a given domain of study and you crash its hopes of ever being knowable. Most of us are assuming that human social behavior is systematically governed, and hence that its study constitutes a legitimate domain of science.

If we are a science, how can we be a good science? And what makes a science good, anyway? I would like to propose that good science is science that adheres to three regulatory ideals. These are guides that can be never attained, but can only be striven for in perpetuity.

---

[1]I am indebted to Harry Reis for insightful comments on an earlier draft.

ABSTRACTION

The first regulatory ideal is abstraction. Science is about generalizing and abstracting, replacing the particular by the general. From that perspective, the greater the abstraction (all else being equal), the better the theory. Indeed, Popper (1965, p. 217) characterized "as preferable the theory which tells us more, which contains the greater amount of empirical information or content." In short, we should be forever aiming for greater abstraction, for broader and broader laws. As a regulating ideal, the abstraction standard is never quite attained, for further abstraction is, in principle, possible and should be striven for.

TRUTH

The quest for abstraction is constrained by the concern with Truth. This concern too represents a regulatory ideal that guides all epistemic activity. This is what hypothesis testing is all about. Rats do it, lay people do it, and science as an institution does it in a much grander, explicit and rigorous manner.

As a regulatory ideal, Truth can be striven for but never securely attained. Why? Because science, quintessentially, is a conceptual activity. Our theories are constructions perennially susceptible to reconstructions. No theory, however successful, is secure, for alternative accounts of the same data are always possible. Moreover, the empirical facts themselves are constructions. When Popper talked about the "empirical basis" of a theory, or its "empirical content," he placed these in quotation marks to signal his profound awareness of their vulnerable nature. According to Popper (1959), the empirical basis of science is both conjectural and fallible as in the following quote:

> The empirical basis of objective science has nothing "absolute" about it. Science does not rest upon rock bottom. The bold structure of its theories rises, as it were, above a swamp. It is like a building erected upon piles. The piles are driven down from above into the swamp; and when we cease our attempt to drive our piles into a deeper layer, it is not because we have reached firm ground. We simply stop when we are satisfied that they are firm enough to carry the structure, at least for the time being. (p. 111)

Mind you, Popper isn't talking here about the empirical facts of such soft disciplines as psychology, sociology, or political science. He is referring primarily to physics, the "queen" of all the sciences. Thus, if our "facts" are ephemeral and vulnerable, at least we are in good company.

These properties permit one, in principle, to perennially avoid the conclusive testing of theories in the light of facts. The well-known Duhem–Quine thesis in the philosophy of science highlights this fundamental problem of undecidability, and the perennial possibility of defending a theory by denying or reinterpreting the facts. In practice, however, the scientific community typically gets tired of "limbo" and ultimately decides whether a theory (about which it cares) is or is not valid. As Tony Greenwald (2004) recently noted, "it is always an option for researchers to prolong or to resolve any competition between theories" (p. 278). In essence, the issue is sociopsychological (right down our alley): What will it take for a given scientist or a scientific community to be persuaded?

PROGRESS

Competition between theoretical positions naturally leads to a third regulatory ideal, that of scientific progress. A fundamental requirement of any scientific contribution is novelty. Science is not supposed to stagnate. It is expected to be incessantly on the move, to head for newer and better discoveries. Of course, progress is a relative term. It rests on a *comparison* between a present contribution and an existing body of knowledge. Assessing progress requires awareness of what has gone on before. In its absence, one risks "reinventing the wheel" and hence substituting fake progress for true progress. Comparison between divergent points of view, whether present and past ones, or disparate present ones, requires *choice*. Indeed, the history of scientific progress chronicles choices that the community of science has made over the centuries, declaring Galileo the victor over Aristotle, Newton over Descartes, and Einstein over Newton. Of course, no scientific "victory" is forever, for if Progress is to prevail, today's winners may expect to be tomorrow's losers.

SOCIAL AND PERSONALITY PSYCHOLOGY IN LIGHT OF THE THREE REGULATORY IDEALS

Truth.   If Abstraction, Truth, and Progress collectively are the hallmarks of successful science, how does social and personality psychology fare on these criteria? It certainly gets an A+ as far as the striving for Truth is concerned. Social/personality research is generally recognized as highly sophisticated and incredibly rigorous. We have earned the reputation of being one of the most self-critical and tough-minded communities of psychological scientists. It takes 2 to 3 years to amass enough evidence and courage (!) to submit a paper to our flagship journal, only to have it rejected in about 85% of the cases. Our grant panels, too, are known as extremely critical and conservative, significantly more so, according to some, than in other areas of psychology and in other social or life sciences. These critiques predominantly turn on whether the conclusions we would be able to reach through our research are likely to be valid. In short, we are second to none in worrying about the verisimilitude of our pronouncements, and we are faithful servants of that most exacting master called Truth. That we are such does not necessarily mean that we are getting closer to understanding real social circumstances in the world at large. Our preoccupation with Truth is no guarantee that we wouldn't be learning "more and more about less and less," however truthful and veridical.

Abstraction. We seem a bit less "on the ball" when it comes to the remaining two regulatory ideals, Abstraction and Progress. As far as abstraction is concerned, we are simply loath to engage in broad theorizing.

As I indicated elsewhere (Kruglanski, 2001, p. 871). "We are notoriously ill at ease about generalizing beyond our research findings, and we get quite anxious when invited to speculate beyond our data." Deutsch and Krauss (1965) commented that "social psychological theorizing is moving in the direction of 'theories of the middle range'" (p. 5), referring to theories by Lewin's students such as Festinger, Deutsch, Cartwright, Thibaut and Kelley, who, according to Deutsch and Krauss (1965), "unlike Lewin ... have not been theorists in the grand manner" (p. 62). It seems, however, that they were grand enough compared with much contemporary work. To borrow a metaphor from the world of fashion, if post-Lewinian theories were "middies," many subsequent formulations were more like "minis"—middi and mini theoretical skirts that is.

Progress. Our theoretical timidity may exact a price as far as scientific progress is concerned. Because our theories are narrow and phenomena centered, we often do not look beyond our immediate pale, nor are we comparing what we are doing to what others have done, or presently are doing. It is in this vein that Miller and Pedersen (1999, p. 150) commented on the "invention of new names for old concepts," which they considered "first on the list of impediments to scientific progress in contemporary social psychology," as a consequence of which "contemporary social psychology is rife with implicit, but unsubstantiated claims of discriminative construct validity."

Reasons and Causes for Our Theoretical Apprehensions

Why are social and personality researchers so apprehensive with regard to broad theorizing? There are explicit "ideological" reasons for this, and then there are causes that operate behind the scenes, at the level of the sociology of science, or the psychology of the scientist. Let me consider those first.

Risk Aversion. A major cause of our apprehensions seems to be the "risk aversion" that characterizes us as a field. Reis and Stiller (1992) traced such a conservative attitude to the "crisis" of the 1970s and the criticism that social psychology might not be a true science. This may have fostered what Tory Higgins (1992) called a "prevention focus." As he put it, "To avoid the perception of mistakes, it is best to work within traditional boundaries, use conventional paradigms and interpret results in accordance with established theories" (p. 491). Risk aversion and worries about being a "real science" may affect the reward structure confronting investigators at most academic institutions. Harry Reis expressed it compellingly (personal communication, July 2003):

Broad theorizing may earn the long-term respect of one's peers but it does not get one tenure, raises, or promotions (Just look at the advice in any of the new "how to" books for academic-psychology careers). For one thing, phenomenon-centered and "middling" theory research are much more likely to be funded and published. For another, broad theorizing takes time to develop and synthesize, something that career tracks (at most universities, in the US at least) do not encourage. A third reason is the "uniqueness" criterion of most tenure reviews: To achieve tenure, one must be described as the world's leading expert on something new and unique; something that no one else has studied successfully in the past ... this pressure pushes young scholars in the direction of ever greater specialization rather than broad theorizing (as John Kenneth Galbraith brilliantly satirized in his novel, "A tenured professor"). Piaget, Heider, Freud, Allport, and probably Darwin would not get tenure at my university.

Risk aversion on personal or institutional levels thus constitutes a motivational "cause" that "puts a damper" on our theorizing. Now you can hardly argue with a fear or an aversion. Mere words are unlikely to alleviate it, and enjoining one to "have no fear" does not necessarily inspire boldness. We stand a better chance, perhaps, by directly confronting the major "ideological" objections to broad theorizing. Let us see what these may consist of.

The Argument From Failure

"Nothing fails like a failure," and an often cited reason against grand theorizing is that we have tried it and failed. My reference here is to the disenchantment in the social sciences with the grand theoretical systems of the early and middle 20th century: Freud's psychoanalytic theory, Lewin's field theory, or the Hull–Spence learning theory in psychology; Parsons's theory of society in sociology, or Marx's theory of the economic order in economics. But is past failure reason enough to give up? The thumbnail sketch of science I presented earlier suggests that the answer is no. If progress is to prevail, theoretical systems of the past should be replaced by those of the present and these, in turn, by those of the future. Science consists of "conjectures and refutations" (Popper, 1965), and we learn through our mistakes. In a sense, then, "all theories are born false," but this is no reason to stop theorizing. From this perspective, it is better to have theorized and failed than not to have theorized at all.

Second, failure and disconfirmation do not apply uniquely or particularly to grand theories; narrow and highly localized mini theories are equally at risk. Because of the conceptual nature of all assertions, any assertion holds over an infinity of instances; for example, the concept "table" holds over an infinity of tables, the concept "swan" over an infinity of "swans" and so on. Any of those instances could falsify a conceptual assertion (about tables or swans), no matter how "narrow" or concrete its scope. Alas, then, theoretical timidity may not bring us epistemic peace of mind and (to twist an expression) there is no safety in small numbers (or "small" theories in this case).

The Argument From Testability

A kindred argument, articulated by Merton (1957), was that abstract or general formulations are notoriously difficult to verify, because they are so vast it would require a humongous amount of work to verify them in each and every instance over which they are assumed to apply. Of course, this assumption rests on an outmoded conception of science tied to the notion of verification. The problem vanishes if we accept the mechanism of falsification instead (e.g., Popper, 1959): A theory can be falsified by a single nonconforming instance, so the vastness of a theory is no impediment to its testability.

A different version of the testability argument has been that the grander the theory, the more stages of translation it requires, compounding the difficulty of its assessment. But note that abstractness or generality need not be mistaken for vagueness or complexity. You can have a narrow, highly localized theory that is vague, complex, or in need of multiple translation stages, and a highly general theory that is simple and readily testable. A general theory about mammals should be no more difficult to test than a more specific theory about dogs, assuming one could be clear about what constitutes a mammal, no less so than what constituted a dog. Darwin's evolutionary theory is extremely broad, yet its derivations are quite straightforward and apparently not all that difficult to test. Einstein's general relativity theory is extremely general, yet its testability is beyond question. All things considered, then, the various argument(s) from testability do not adduce particularly good reasons against broad theorizing.

The Argument From Impact

Occasionally one hears the argument that it is not the theories but rather the phenomena that really matter. Theories are "pallid" and boring. They leave people cold. Phenomena, by contrast, are vivid: They constitute the "discoveries" that shock you, surprise you, and jolt you out of your seat. It is the phenomena, not the theories, that make it to pages of the *New York Times*. It is they that lend a field of science visibility and prestige.

Now, there can be no denying that novel phenomena are exciting. Asch's conformity findings, Milgram's obedience results, Zimbardo's prison experiment, and Zajonc's mere exposure effects are milestones in the history of our field, and with excellent reasons. But it is a mistake to juxtapose theory and phenomena and force a choice between them, for the two are closely intertwined and any separation between them is artificial, for two reasons. First, new phenomena are exciting precisely because of their surprise value, that is, their deviation from prior theory. Such theory may often be rather implicit and take the form of lay wisdom. Asch's conformity results surprised Asch's own intuitions. Milgram's obedience findings contraverted the expectations of trained psychiatrists, and very few of us would have anticipated Zimbardo's prison study results.

Second, a surprising phenomenon isn't left there on a pedestal to bask in the glory of its surprisingness. To the contrary, it serves as a stimulus for theoretical activity aimed at its explanation. For instance, the illusory correlation effect fostered a flurry of theoretical activity by social cognition researchers. The "process loss" in brainstorming groups posed a similar challenge for group researchers. And the "enigmatic" anchoring effect elicited considerable theoretical creativity from social judgment researchers. In short, the interest in phenomena is theoretically driven. Phenomena are not exciting in a vacuum. They are exciting in the light of prior theory. And they are not put on a pedestal and left alone. As soon as they appear, they are put to work in an attempt to find out what "makes them tick," that is, to ground them in a theoretical explanation.

The Argument From Futility

Scientific progress can hardly be achieved without controversy and struggle between distinct theoretical positions. As Klaus Fiedler (2004) recently characterized it, "Creative theorizing means not only to be creative in a vacuum but to play an undesirable role, to break up with norms and conventions, to criticize old (and) established theories and to challenge fellow researchers, editors, and reviewers" (p. 166). One would think, thus, that the critical approach and the proposal of novel theoretical ideas are to be encouraged, even though facing majority opprobrium can be tough on one's nerves.

A counterargument to this view, recently articulated by Tony Greenwald (2004), was that "illusory theoretical disputes" are irresolvable and hence futile. Unfortunately, however, it is difficult to know in advance whether a given dispute will turn out to be illusory or not. The Duhem–Quine thesis asserts that, in principle, all theoretical disputes can be prolonged indefinitely, including disputes that are generally considered quite real. A theory can be defended come what may by incorporating multiple ad hoc assumptions and becoming extremely complex or "nuanced." Theoretical disputes, nonetheless, constitute the lifeblood of science, and if in the process of its defense a theory becomes too complex and convoluted, too "degenerative," to use Imre Lakatos's term, it will probably fall of its own "weight" and be abandoned by practicing researchers.

The Argument From Triviality

Finally, occasionally one hears the argument that "theories" are cheap and "a dime and dozen," whereas phenomena are precious. In this vein, Aronson and Carlsmith (1968) suggested that "where the ideas come from is not terribly important ... the important and difficult feat involves translating a conceptual notion into a tight, workable, credible, meaningful set of experimental operations" (p. 37). Presumably, thus, theories are "armchair" concoctions that one spins at will in the coziness of one's study, whereas the identification of empirical phenomena is lots of work drenched in veritable rivers of "blood, sweat and tears."[2] In fact, however, both empirical research and theorizing involve considerable craft, albeit of different kinds. Consider that a good theory needs to be not merely broad (embodying the abstraction ideal) but also innovative (embodying the progress ideal) and, above all, valid (embodying the Truth ideal). The conjunction of all three requirements is quite daunting, in fact. Possibly that is why we see relatively little theorizing in our field today. What one sees, instead, are two contrasting "strategies" to avoid genuine theorizing that, ironically, are polar opposites of one another. We see either the inordinate anchoring on, and insufficient adjustment to, old formulations, the "old theories never die" phenomenon that characterizes social and personality psychology (note the remarkable longevity of dissonance theory, balance theory, attribution theory, or social comparison theory) or, to the contrary, the complete denial of old theories' existence, and a reinvention of the wheel over and over again, as Miller and Pedersen (1999) decried.

THE ADVANTAGES OF BROAD THEORIZING: THEORIES AS BRIDGES

In short, not only are we risk averse, and prevention focused, but the fear of theorizing doesn't seem to have much of a leg to stand on and the various objections to theorizing seem at odds with contemporary understandings of science. Moreover, in being excessively "up tight" we may be "shooting ourselves in the foot." Broad theorizing may be just what the field needs to cure itself from its various "childhood ills" and advance to that next level of depth in understanding human social behavior.

Broad theories look beyond the "phenotype" and seek the underlying "genotype," they resist the allure of "surface structures" and insist on unearthing the "deep structures"; they transcend the specific context and escape the trap of context-bound formulations [of the "what you (empirically) see is what you (theoretically) get" variety]. Thus, they are bridges that connect us to our past, afford a clearer vision of our present, promise an integration of our fragmented field, and protect us from going around and around, experiencing that "déjà vu feeling over and over again."

But the bridging potential of broad theories does not stop here. For one thing, broad theories connect us to the "real world." To slightly amend Kurt Lewin's famous dictum, "There is nothing as practical as a good *broad* theory." Let me explain. A perennial critique of experimental social psychology hinged on the artificiality of our lab research, and on our use of college sophomores as subjects (cf. Sears, 1986). Because of the artificiality of our methods, so the criticism goes, social psychology is irrelevant to real-world concerns; instead, we should be performing field experiments and carrying out naturalistic observations. But the answer to the all-important issue of real

---

[2]Admittedly, reviewers and grant panels often make pleas for theoretical relevance. In many cases, however, the requested "theorizing" is little more than the provision of some kind of rationale for one's predictions.

world relevance is not to be found in field research or naturalistic observation. One could carry out naturalistic observations all one wanted and still come up short as far as a valid understanding of real-world phenomena is concerned. The answer lies not in replacing lab research by field research. Both are effective tools for *theory testing*. The answer lies in *theory generation*, that is, formulating broad enough frameworks and unabashedly applying them to real-world phenomena. If you have a theory about trust, apply it to the trust in government and its vicissitudes (Putnam, 1995); if you have a theory about the fear of death, apply it to international terrorism (as Pyszczynski, Solomon, & Greenberg, 2003, recently did); if you have a theory about judgment under uncertainty, apply it to the stock market; and so on.

How much interest there can be in what we have to say has been driven home to me by the diluvial public response that greeted a pair of papers on "political conservatism as motivated social cognition" that my colleagues and I published in the May 2003 issue of the *Psychological Bulletin* (Jost, Glaser, Kruglanski, & Sullaway, 2003a, 2003b). Once the press got wind of this news, there was no end to the excitement. Scores of e-mails appeared on our computer screens (not all of the "warm and fuzzy" variety). Major dailies (the *Wall Street Journal, Guardian, Washington Post, Boston Globe, Ha'aretz*, among many others) ran stories about it, syndicated columnists (Ann Coulter, Cal Thomas, George Will, William Raspberry) addressed it in print, and the BBC interviewed us on its *Nightnews* program, as did numerous other electronic media. Never mind that much of the reaction was prompted by a misapprehension of what our papers were all about. At the end of the day, the controversy engendered an appreciable amount of genuine interest in the gist of our message, and we had the opportunity to articulate our position at major media forums (including our Op Ed piece in the 8/28/03 issue of the *Washington Post*).

If we take our theories seriously, we should draw out their implications beyond the specific experimental paradigms where they may have been developed and tested. It would seem important to challenge them by confrontations with "real-world" phenomena and data, and to expose them to the reactions of others, including experts professionally immersed in these matters on an everyday basis.

A final bridge (but not "a bridge too far") is the bridge to other social science disciplines that real-world relevance may afford us. While we may have been waiting in the wings for "more data to come in," the other social sciences have been busily addressing the world at large, "rushing in" where we (the cautious "angels" that we are) "feared to tread," addressing issues of civil society, war, hunger, revolutions, or economic development. The last half century has seen a notable decline in the place of social/personality psychology among the social sciences. It is not that they do not respect us. They simply find us irrelevant to their concerns. This wasn't so 50 years ago, when social and personality psychologists like Gordon Allport and Henry Murray worked shoulder to shoulder with anthropologists and sociologists (the likes of Clyde Kluckhohn or Talcott Parsons) as part of the great "social relations" experiment at Harvard. At that time, social psychological findings and analyses, including the seminal works of Kurt Lewin, were widely known and cited across the social sciences. Now, it seems to me, the references to our works are notably fewer and farther between, proportionately speaking.

Our role in various social science institutions has correspondingly diminished. Social psychologists once played a dominant role at the Center for Advanced Study at Palo Alto; now, however, we typically constitute a rather underrepresented group among the Center's invitees. The same applies to other social science foundations like the Mellon Foundation, the Rockefeller Foundation, the Russell Sage Foundation, the Maison de Science de l'Homme in Paris, the Center at Upsala, Netherlands Institute for Advanced Study (NIAS) in Wassenaar, the College in Berlin, and on and on. These places are heavily populated by sociologists, political scientists, economists, or historians, whereas social and personality psychologists are hardly ever considered as appropriate candidates. Nor is this exclusively (or even principally) a matter of scientific power politics. Few are in principle prejudiced against us, or bent on keeping us out. Rather, our reluctance to speak on broad issues has redefined us outside the general conversation.

The focus on general processes transcending a variety of local effects is likely to pose questions of interest to other disciplines within the social sciences and the humanities. How do people think? Is human behavior rational? What is the nature of human goals? Of human personality? Of culture? Of groups? We as a discipline know a great deal about these topics, but our knowledge often is scattered, localized, and context specific. An attempt to distill a set of general principles from the plethora of facts and "mini theories" that fill the pages of our books and journals may forge a link between our science and related fields like philosophy, linguistics, sociology, political science, and economics. This is happening already to some extent (as witnessed by the recent Nobel Prize awarded to Daniel Kahneman); it should be happening considerably more, given the impressive conjunction of talent, rigor, and creativity present in social and personality psychology as a field. Broad theorizing touching on real-world social phenomena may be just the way to get us back into the dialogue.

Such theorizing, finally, may also make us a better science in terms of the ideals of *abstractness* (inherent in the very notion of *broad* theorizing), *truth* (inherent in exposing one's conceptions to a broader band of test situations), and *progress* (challenging one's theories to a broader set of comparisons with prior notions).

WHAT ABOUT THE FUTURE?

What about the future? Will the culture of social and personality psychology change toward bolder, broader theorizing? So far, at least, there is a "buzz" in this direction. Two symposia at major social/personality meetings (Society for

Experimental Social Psychology, 2000; Society for Personality and Social Psychology, 2002), were held on the topic of theorizing.

The relatively new *Personality and Social Psychology Review* provides an outlet for theoretical contributions that previously was lacking. Over the last decade, social and personality psychologists have been playing an increasingly prominent role as editors and as authors at such major theoretical outlets as the *Psychological Bulletin, Psychological Review,* and the new *Psychological Bulletin and Review.* Moreover, *Personality and Social Psychology Review* is coming out with a special issue on "theory construction" in which several conceptual thinkers in social and personality psychology divulge their ways and means of theorizing. A special project planned at the Center for Advanced Study and Columbia's new Institute for Motivation Science will bring together an interdisciplinary group of social psychologists, sociologists, linguists, and political scientists to collaboratively study the topic of social boundary construction. The Kurt Lewin Institute in Amsterdam is issuing the present volume devoted to bridging social psychology, and the graduate school of social psychology in Warsaw is planning a conference on integrating the micro and the macro approaches to social psychology. These are exciting developments. Yet they are few and the field is vast. Would the spark ignite a flame? "The future is not ours to see," but at least there is hope. This could be a truly important phase-transition for our discipline.

CONCLUSIONS

Although social/personality psychology is renowned for its rigor and toughness, and hence for adherence to the guiding scientific ideal of the quest for Truth, we may fall short where Abstraction (the gleaning of broad laws and principles from concrete observations) and Progress are concerned. Our field is phenomenon centered, and averse to broad theorizing in its various forms. Yet there are no compelling scientific reasons against broad theorizing. To the contrary, its relative absence undermines the significance of our contributions. As a consequence, we are isolated from other social sciences and have little voice in the general dialogue about societal issues. There are "rumblings" in our field of late attesting to a dawning awareness that this state of affairs needs to change. It is incumbent on us to make sure that these translate into concerted efforts to form concrete programs, structures, and institutional policies that encourage broad theorizing in social/personality psychology. We must do so to ensure that we fulfill our promise as a field of science, that our voice is heard, and that we have something of general interest to say to other social sciences and the world.

REFERENCES

Aronson, E., & Carlsmith, J. M. (1968). Experimentation in social psychology. In G. Lindzey & E. Aronson (Eds.), *Handbook of social psychology* (Vol. 2, pp. 1–79). Reading, MA: Addison-Wesley.

Deutsch, M., & Krauss, R. M. (1965). *Theories in social psychology.* New York: Basic Books.

Festinger, L. (1954). A theory of social comparison processes. *Human Relations, 7,* 117–140.

Fiedler, K. (2004). Tools, toys, tenure, truisms, and theories: Some thoughts on the creative cycle of theory formation. *Personality and Social Psychology Review, 8,* 164–172.

Greenwald, A. G. (2004). The resting parrot, the dessert stomach, and other perfectly defensible theories. In J. Jost, M. R. Banaji, & D. A. Prentice (Eds.), *The yin and yang of social cognition: Perspectives on the social psychology of thought systems.* Washington, DC: American Psychological Association, pp. 275–285.

Higgins, E. T. (1992). Increasingly complex but less interesting articles: Scientific progress or regulatory problem? *Personality and Social Psychology Bulletin, 18,* 489–492.

Jost, J. T., Glaser, J., Kruglanski, A. W., & Sullaway, F. J. (2003a). Political conservatism as motivated social cognition. *Psychological Bulletin, 129*(3), 339–375.

Jost, J. T., Glaser, J., Kruglanski, A. W., & Sullaway, F. J. (2003b). Exceptions that prove the rule: Using a theory of motivated social cognition to account for ideological incongruities and political anomalies, *Psychological Bulletin, 129*(3), 383–393.

Kruglanski, A. W. (2001). That "vision thing": The state of theory in social and personality psychology at the edge of the new millennium. *Journal of Personality and Social Psychology, 80*(6), 871–875.

Merton, R. K. (1957). *Social theory and social structure* (rev. ed.). Glencoe, IL: Free Press.

Miller, N., & Pedersen, W. C. (1999). Assessing process distinctiveness. *Psychological Inquiry, 10,* 150–155.

Popper, K. R. (1959). *The logic of scientific discovery.* New York: Harper. (Original work published as *Logik der Forschung,* 1935)

Popper, K. R. (1965). *Conjectures and refutations.* New York: Harper.

Putnam, R. D. (1995). Bowling alone: America's declining social capital. *Journal of Democracy, 6*(1), 65–78.

Pyszczynski, T., Solomon, S., & Greenberg, J. (2003). *In the wake of 9/11: The psychology of terror.* Washington, DC: American Psychological Association.

Reis, H. T., & Stiller, J. (1992). Publication trends in JPSP: A three decade review. *Personality and Social Psychology Bulletin, 18,* 465–472.

Sears, D. O. (1986). College sophomores in the laboratory: Influences of a narrow database on social psychology's view of human nature. *Journal of Personality and Social Psychology, 51,* 515–530.

PART 2

Social Psychology: General Views of Bridging

INTRODUCTION

By its very nature, the topic of bridging social psychology inevitably raises general questions about the field of social psychology. What are the key assumptions of social psychology? Where is social psychology heading? What is social psychology's unique contribution to basic theoretical questions? And how about broad societal questions? Many of these questions are at least implicitly raised in the essays in this section. The most important topic in the next chapters is a discussion of the potential benefits and costs of bridging social psychology with other fields and disciplines, or the various obstacles that are needed to overcome for bridging to be successful. The first essay, by Berscheid, notes that the desirability of bridging social psychology is beyond dispute, but discusses the various obstacles, often stemming from work conditions and career considerations, which may make bridging social psychology especially challenging. Greenberg illustrates the benefits of the various bridges of social psychology in the past decades, discusses how they have shaped contemporary social psychology, and recommends a greater traffic flow from other fields and disciplines to social psychology. Some essays discuss both benefits and potential costs. For example, Fiske's essay emphasizes the benefits of bridging, but does so while acknowledging some potential costs, indicating that bridging should occur with care and precision. Kerr makes a comparable point, noting that bridging may involve potential costs. In particular, he expresses caution concerning strategies that advocate better "packaging" of social psychology, loosening of evaluative standards, or major paradigm shifts. The essay by Batson expressed metaphorically the view that if we bridge with other fields and disciplines we should go by mainland. With some powerful research examples, he illustrates that care, precision, and "taking time in exploring" are exceptionally important, so that traveling through mainland seems more appropriate than "hopping islands." Two essays explicitly deal with assumed misunderstandings. The essay by Fiedler advances the argument that the contradiction between "science" and "societal practice" is a myth, and illustrates the benefits of bridging theories with societal practice in the context of judgment and decision making in the courtroom—based on personal experiences. The essay by Stroebe, on the other hand, seeks to correct another misunderstanding. Based on a combination of personal experiences and theories, he suggests that interdisciplinary efforts that primarily are "extrinsically" motivated by national science foundations may to some degree undermine creativity and innovation. In his experience, bridging is more likely to be fruitful when scientists from various disciplines work together without such extrinsic rewards. Two final essays address the theoretical benefits of bridging. Vallacher and Nowak advance a general dynamic model for pursuing an integrative psychological science, a model that they propose to explain various phenomena across various fields of psychology. They also suggest that the way in which social psychology makes theoretical progress adheres to a dynamic model, characterized by setbacks and incoherence as well as progress and coherence. Last but not least, Buunk suggests that social psychology has a "marketing problem," in that social psychology is underused in other scientific disciplines and societal practice. In particular, he argues that social psychology could do a better job by examining most or all applied areas, appreciating individual differences, and seeking greater embedding in evolutionary theory. Taken together, this section provides an overview of the various views that leaders in our field have about the benefits and costs of bridging social psychology, along with various other issues that they bring to bear on bridging social psychology.

3

The Difficulty of Getting From Here to There and Back

Ellen Berscheid

University of Minnesota

The noted biologist E. O. Wilson (1998) persuasively argued that the academic walls separating the disciplines searching for knowledge—many of which are as ancient, dilapidated, and now as purposeless as the Chinese Wall—and the specialization within disciplines that such compartmentalization fosters are hindering the advancement of knowledge. In *Consilience: The Unity of Knowledge*, Wilson contended that future major discoveries in science are most likely to emerge from seeing the natural world as an integrated whole and by integrating concepts and methodological and analytical tools across many disciplines. The word *consilience* is derived from two Latin words that mean "leaping together." Wilson used the term to refer to the advancement of knowledge by linking theory and facts across many disciplines to create a common groundwork of explanation.

Wilson's thesis is not new. In his classic essay *The Art of Scientific Investigation*, Beveridge (1950) observed that advances usually come when an individual trained in one field enters another. An early proponent of the thesis was August Comte (1798–1857). The great French philosopher of science believed that the six branches of knowledge of his time would form a pyramid whose base would be mathematics, with the other branches of knowledge (such as physics, astronomy, and physiology, within which psychology was then located) building on mathematics and then on each other in an orderly, integrative, and hierarchical fashion. The apex of the pyramid, Comte prophesied, ultimately would be a science he initially named "la système de morale positive" but in the last days of his life called "the science of humanity." Comte's "true, final science"—the pot of gold lying at the end of science's rainbow—

would address the "positive study of all the fundamental laws pertaining to social phenomena," according to his most recent intellectual biographer Pickering (1993, p. 615). All of the sciences would become parts of this last unified science, which Comte envisioned as a mixture of history, philosophy, political science, economics, anthropology, religion, aesthetics, international relations, biology, physiology, and the inorganic, material sciences (see Pickering, 1993, p. 708).

In the first edition of the *Handbook of Social Psychology*, Gordon Allport (1954), American social psychology's *éminence grise*, tendered the claim that Comte's true final science "parallels our present conception of modern psychology (especially social psychology)" (p. 7). I have contended elsewhere that Allport's argument was a mere gratis dictum offered in the political service of furthering acceptance of the then-fledgling field of social psychology by experimental psychologists and that the emerging multidisciplinary field of relationship science far more closely resembles Comte's idea of the capstone of the sciences (Berscheid, 2000). The experiment to decide the matter currently is in progress. Its outcome, I believe, will depend on the extent to which each field—social psychology or relationship science—is able to balance contemporary forces for specialization with the "systems" view of social phenomena that pervaded Comte's vision of a final science of humanity.

A systems view of human behavior views the individual as nested in a hierarchy of larger systems (e.g., a network of close relationships, nested in a society, nested in a culture) and encapsulating other systems (e.g., the human's biological systems, such as the cardiovascular system), themselves hierarchically arranged. As the physicist-philosopher of science Fritjof Capra succinctly put it, "An outstanding property of all life is the tendency to form multileveled structures of systems within systems.... Throughout the living world we find living systems nesting within other living systems" (1996, p. 28). Because each of the systems the human is nested in and encapsulates is "open"—they exchange information, energy, and material which influence their subsequent operation (see Reis, Collins, & Berscheid, 2000)—a full understanding of human behavior cannot be achieved without understanding these systems and their interfacial dynamics. Given their number and complexity, however, and given also that entire disciplines have been addressed to the understanding many of the systems involved, the task that confronts the student of human behavior is monumental. For most, there is neither time enough nor world enough to cultivate the knowledge necessary for a truly generalist stance in which useful alliances with other disciplines are forged and an integration and synthesis of even a small portion of the insights each discipline has won is accomplished. It is not surprising that, taking refuge in the doctrine of reductionism and comfort in its achievements, most of us simply follow our noses along familiar and well-traveled research paths within the discipline in which we were trained.

Historically, social psychologists have been somewhat of an exception to the rule of parochialism among students of behavior. A signal example of social psychologists' willingness to recognize the impact of context on behavior—including cognitive and affective behavior—is the formal classification of the properties of situations that are likely to influence and produce certain patterns of social interaction offered by Kelley et al. (2003). The contextualism theme in social psychology is, of course, a legacy of Kurt Lewin and the systems view of phenomena he inherited from his Gestaltist mentors and subsequently codified in his famous equation: $B = F(P,E)$, or the idea that behavior (B) is a function of the properties of the person (P) interacting with the properties of the physical and social environment (E) (see Berscheid, 2003; Marrow, 1969). Because social psychologists have maintained their awareness that each individual is nested in larger systems and encompasses internal systems that also influence the behaviors most psychologists wish to understand, they generally appreciate the need to understand and integrate behavior at several levels of analysis. Social psychology thus is in a prime position to provide the warp and woof of the "common groundwork of explanation" of which Wilson (1998) speaks and to serve as the catalyst for efforts to weave a tapestry of theory and facts across many disciplines in the biological, social, and behavioral sciences.

Often cited as evidence of the catholic value of social psychology and its theories, facts, and methods is the number of "applications" of these to problems in other disciplines. It should be noted, however, that application is not the same as integration. The term *application* connotes affixing something whole to the surface of an entity, as a Band-Aid on a cut, whereas the term *integration* means a mixing two or more things together such that the end product is not recognizable from the previous states of the things mixed. Social psychology, being theory rich and methodologically rigorous, is undeniably useful to less well-developed fields of inquiry in the social and behavioral sciences. The problem is that social psychologists who make the application rarely seem to come back with much of value to be integrated into social psychology; that is, although it is easy to think of many applications of social psychological theory to problems in other domains, it is not as easy to think of the contributions such applications have made to social psychological theory (which is not to depreciate their contributions to the human condition).

The ongoing attempt to integrate the biological and social approaches to behavior is illustrative of the difference between application and integration (e.g., see Cacioppo, Berntson, Sheridan, & McClintock, 2000; Cacioppo et al., 2003). The emergence of social neuroscience reflects the systems perspective that has been maintained by social psychology. For example, the subfield of social cognitive neuroscience attempts to understand psychological phenomena in terms of interactions between (a) the social level of analysis, which is concerned with the influence that others exert on an individual's behavior, (b) the cognitive level of analysis, which is concerned with the information processing mechanisms through which perceptions and thoughts about others influence the individual's behavior, and (c) the neural level of analysis, which is concerned with the brain mechanisms that underlie cognitive-level processes (see Ochsner & Lieberman, 2001). There is, of course, an equally compelling need for integration at the other end of the continuum—that is, to integrate psychological phenomena with interpersonal relationship, societal, and cultural phenomena.

CONCLUSIONS

Few scientists or philosophers are likely to quarrel with the premise that integration of theory, fact, and method across disciplinary boundaries not only is valuable but may be essential to the advancement of knowledge. As a consequence, one is led to the more interesting question of why the forces for compartmentalization and specialization now so brutally and consistently trump the forces of integration and synthesis. Answers to this question often refer to the tradition of reductionism in Western science and its admittedly impressive triumphs, as well as to the difficulty the systems perspective has had in translating into anything more than a metaphor (although a useful and influential one) in the social and behavioral sciences. I suspect, however, that it is largely a practical matter. If one believes that inter- and multidisciplinary research and integration depends not on putting two scholars from two different disciplines in the same room (as seems to be believed by funding agencies) but on getting two or more disciplines in one head, then one is forced to consider the training and employment conditions of psychologists. These virtually prohibit exploration of realms beyond those in which the individual was trained (too often, in a narrow subarea of that discipline).

The conditions of contemporary academic life are such that most young scholars have difficulty paddling fast enough to keep their noses above water; surfing sciences other than their own is not a possibility. Young scholars' survival depends on their publishing immediately and frequently and, often, redundantly (for bureaucrats can count but not read). Survival also depends on obtaining grant monies to support themselves, their students, and their institution, a time-consuming enterprise that too frequently is unsuccessful and even when not, results in crushing pressure for immediate empirical findings to post in 6-month progress reports, journals, and conference programs. Survival also depends on teaching more and more to increase tuition revenue for financially distressed universities and on performing numerous service and clerical duties to substitute for the staff these institutions can no longer afford to provide.

In sum, the desirability of cross-disciplinary intercourse and integration is not in question. The puzzle is how these can be accomplished under the conditions in which most contemporary scientists are trained and work. The solution is not clear, not the least because the puzzle itself has received little attention from society and even from scholars themselves.

REFERENCES

Allport, G. (1954). The historical background of modern social psychology. In G. Lindzey (Ed.), *Handbook of social psychology, Vol. 1: Theory and method* (pp. 3–56). Reading, MA: Addison-Wesley.

Berscheid, E. (2000). Foreword: Back to the future and forward to the past. In C. Hendrick & S. S. Hendrick (Eds.), *Close relationships: A sourcebook* (pp. ix–xxi). Thousand Oaks, CA: Sage.

Berscheid, E. (2003). Lessons in "greatness" from Kurt Lewin's life and works. In R. J. Sternberg (Ed.), *The anatomy of impact: What makes the great works of psychology great* (pp. 109–124). Washington, DC: American Psychological Association.

Beveridge, W. I. B. (1950). *The art of scientific investigation.* New York: Norton.

Cacioppo, J. T., Berntson, G. G., Adolphs, R., Carter, C. S., Davidson, R. J., Mc Clintock, M. K., McEwen, B. S., Meaney, M. J., Schacter, D. L., Sternberg, E. M., Suomi, S. S., & Taylor, S. E. (Eds.). (2003). *Foundations in social neuroscience.* Cambridge, MA: MIT Press.

Cacioppo, J. T., Berntson, G. G., Sheridan, J. F., & McClintock, M. K. (2000). Multilevel integrative analyses of human behavior: Social neuroscience and the complementing nature of social and biological approaches. *Psychological Bulletin, 126,* 829–843.

Kelley, H. H., Holmes, J. G., Kerr, N. L., Reis, H. T., Rusbult, C. E., & Van Lange, P. A. M. (2003). *An atlas of interpersonal situations.* Cambridge, UK: Cambridge University Press.

Marrow, A. J. (1969). *The practical theorist: The life and work of Kurt Lewin.* New York: Basic Books.

Ochsner, K. N., & Lieberman, M. D. (2001). The emergence of social cognitive neuroscience. *American Psychologist, 56,* 717–734.

Pickering, M. (1993). *August Comte: An intellectual biography* (Vol. 1). Cambridge, UK: Cambridge University Press.

Reis, H. T., Collins, W. A., & Berscheid, E. (2000). The relationship context of human behavior and development. *Psychological Bulletin, 126,* 844–872.

Wilson, E. O. (1998). *Consilience: The unity of knowledge.* New York: Knopf.

4

Traffic Flow During the Last Twenty-Five Years of Social Psychology

Jeff Greenberg
University of Arizona

The bridges between social psychology and other fields of inquiry flow in both directions, but I focus here primarily on the flow into social psychology. My own social psychological work has been greatly influenced by bridges with knowledge from many other disciplines. Among these are anthropology, biology, philosophy, sociology, and, within psychology, abnormal, cognitive, cross-cultural, developmental, and the psychoanalytic tradition. I suppose if I were going to focus in on any one of these, it would be the broad psychoanalytic tradition of Freud, Rank, Jung, Adler, Horney, Fromm, Lifton, and Yalom because so few social psychologists embrace this heritage explicitly and yet so much of their work has been either influenced or anticipated by this rich intellectual inheritance. But rather than promote any one bridge, in this brief essay, I'd like to offer a perspective on how social psychology has generally been doing with regard to building such bridges.

INCOMING TRAFFIC

Social psychology has always drawn extensively from other fields—traffic has flowed quite extensively in that direction. The traffic often flows rather slowly in that the field tends to draw on well-worn and some times antiquated contributions of these other disciplines rather than their latest advances, but late is generally better than never. However, during some time periods, this flow has been very narrow, with all of the traffic coming from only one of many possible sources. Let me begin by telling you a brief story of such a time.

Back around 1980, University of Kansas graduate students Sheldon Solomon, Tom Pyszczynski, and I spent a lot of time discussing the narrowness of social psychology. We were not alone, in that people like Edward Sampson (1978), Ken Gergen (1973), and Bill McGuire (1973) had written impressive critiques of the field on this very problem. Despite these cogent critiques, the field was dominated by the social cognition movement. The field's power figures of that period seemed to be obsessed with applying the methods, models, and constructs of cognitive psychology to social phenomena; the field seemed to be all about micro-level cognitive processes, with the assumption being that humans are essentially information processing machines. Indeed, in 1994 in the second *Handbook of Social Cognition*, Tom Ostrom proclaimed, "The ultimate destiny of social cognition as monarch of social psychology … it is easy to envision a future in which there is no longer a need for a separate *Handbook of Social Cognition*. The *Handbook of Social Cognition* will become the *Handbook of Social Psychology*" (Ostrom, 1994, pp. xi–xii).

Psychology and social psychology undoubtedly gained a lot from the "cognitive revolution" but it also paid a severe price, which is a bigger topic for another essay. In any event, because Sheldon, Tom, and I were motivationally oriented in our thinking about human behavior, we spent our earlier years in the field as salmon guppies, swimming upstream.

It probably didn't help that in the early 1980s Sheldon titled our first terror management talks "The Psychopathology of Social Psychology." He would begin by arguing that social psychology was an acultural, ahistorical, atheoretical, insulated discipline suffering from the worst kind of intellectual autism (with a touch of obsessive-compulsive disorder) in which the conceptual domain of the field had become narrowed to the point of focusing on findings about findings as an end in itself, dealing primarily with results from the latest experimental laboratory findings concerning reaction times and which numbers people were circling when judging hypothetical targets. He pointed out that this type of work was probably accounting for very little of the variance in real social behavior—what people were actually doing out in the world; social psychology lacked a broad theoretical framework to guide research questions and ignored little matters such as history, culture, social structure, and biology, matters critical to understanding why people behave the way they do. What we needed was an applied theoretical social psychology in which the conceptual focus of the field was the actual significant forms of social behavior occurring in the world. Adding insult to injury, he would then brashly offer up a broad theoretical framework to begin to rectify these deficiencies, building on the contributions of Kierkegaard, Marx, Freud, Rank, Becker, and other victims of the field's intellectual blockade … ah, those were fun times!

The reason I brought up this personal view of ancient history is to make two points. The first is that discussions of the issues of the narrowness of social psychology and the relationship between social psychology and other fields go back a long way, and may be a perpetually important component of a growth process for our field, for two reasons. The first is that this form of self-criticism is needed to counteract the human penchant for fads and for becoming enamored with specific methods and findings. The second is that, as Ernest Becker (1971) argued, the conceptual domain of social psychology renders it a field that should urgently welcome traffic from all disciplines of relevance to understanding social behavior, including other areas of psychology, anthropology, biology, sociology, philosophy, economics, and numerous other fields. In this light, the current book is a valuable continuance of a long, important tradition.

The second reason for my reminiscence is that it highlights how far the field has come since those dark days. Certainly, we are still prone to have tendencies toward hopping on fads, such as stereotype threat (Steele, 1997) or the Implicit Association Test (Greenwald, McGhee, & Schwartz, 1998). A few years ago, I headed a job search for a social psychologist, and it seemed like over a third of the applicants were studying stereotype threat. Don't get me wrong, it's a fascinating and important phenomenon. Indeed, one of my grad students is doing work on it now. But should one-third of the field's new PhDs be focused on it? No, but everyone wants to hop on the new hot finding or method in the field, and indeed, faculty positions and funding seem to reinforce such tendencies. These inclinations will inevitably exist to some extent in an empirically focused, highly competitive field, so perhaps a great deal of activity will always be tightly centered on the latest exciting laboratory findings.

However, even a casual glance at a recent issue of *Journal of Personality and Social Psychology* or *Personality and Social Psychology Bulletin* reveals a great deal of diversity in the topics, theoretical perspectives, research methods, statistics, and influences from other disciplines in the work being published. I believe that although it remains a human, and therefore fundamentally limited, endeavor, social psychology has truly come a long way in the last 25 years and has, as in its early formative years, become very open to influences from other disciplines and perspectives. The international growth of social psychology has been one major factor contributing to this welcome diversification; a field once dominated by North Americans is now a truly global product, with major contributions from Australia, Germany, Great Britain, France, the Netherlands, Poland, and other countries in Europe, Israel, and from Asia and Latin America as well. Social psychology has become a much broader discipline focused on a wide array of phenomena that is far more representative of the range of social behavior occurring in the world, and the international growth of the field is undoubtedly one of the factors leading to this broadening of the traffic into social psychology.

Obvious examples of this blossoming include work on cultural forces and differences (e.g., Markus & Kitayama, 1991; Nisbett & Cohen, 1996) evolutionary perspectives (e.g., Simpson & Kenrick, 1997), emotion (e.g., Fredrickson, 2001; Tangney, 2003), social identity (e.g., Hogg, 2003; Spears,

Doosje, & Ellemers, 1997), social psychophysiology (e.g., Winkielman & Cacioppo, 2001), human development and growth (e.g., Deci & Ryan, 2002), and the attachment theory perspective on close relationships (e.g., Hazan & Shaver, 1994). Other examples reveal a renewed, although only sometimes acknowledged, influence of the psychoanalytic tradition, reflected in the study of phenomena such as thought suppression (e.g., Wegner, 1994), projection (e.g. Schimel, Greenberg, & Martens, 2003), nonconscious goal activation (e.g., Fitzsimons & Bargh, 2003), ego depletion (Muraven & Baumeister, 2000) and self-disclosure of traumas (Pennebaker, 1990).

The breadth of the field's questions and approaches can also be seen in a book I recently coedited with Sander Koole and Tom Pyszczynski, the *Handbook of Experimental Existential Psychology* (Greenberg, Koole, & Pyszczynski, 2004) in which prominent social psychologists cover broad topics such as death, trauma, uncertainty, authenticity, culture, meaning, nature and animality, social connections, free will, and growth. Although perspectives such as positive psychology, evolutionary psychology, experimental existential psychology, social identity, social neuroscience, and implicit social cognition often run the risk of becoming rigid, insulated, imperialistic movements, as themes among many running through social and personality psychology, they clearly add useful richness and diversity to the field.

CONCLUSIONS

In sum, I believe the flow from other fields to social psychology, once a narrow stream letting only cognitive psychology through, has gradually burst wide open, a great development. However, in science, bridges between disciplines need to allow traffic to flow freely and broadly in both directions, so I would like to conclude these thoughts by suggesting that although continued construction to further diversify the bridges in the incoming direction is certainly warranted, even more work is needed to improve outbound traffic. That is, we need to better develop bridges from the discoveries of social psychologists outward to the rest of the disciplines concerned with understanding people.

REFERENCES

Becker, E. (1971). *The birth and death of meaning*. New York: Free Press.

Deci, E. L., & Ryan, R. M. (Eds.). (2002). *Handbook of self-determination research*. Rochester, NY: University of Rochester Press.

Fitzsimons, G. M., & Bargh, J. A. (2003). Thinking of you: Nonconscious pursuit of interpersonal goals associated with relationship partners. *Journal of Personality and Social Psychology, 84*, 148–164.

Frederickson, B. L. (2001). The role of positive emotions in positive psychology: The broaden and build theory of positive emotions. *American Psychologist, 56*, 218–226.

Gergen, K. J. (1973). Social psychology as history. *Journal of Personality and Social Psychology, 26*, 309–320.

Greenberg, J., Koole, S., & Pyszczynski, T. (Eds.). (2004). *Handbook of experimental existential psychology*. New York: Guilford Press.

Greenwald, A. G., McGhee, D. E., & Schwartz, J. L. K. (1998). Measuring individual differences in implicit cognition: The implicit association test. *Journal of Personality and Social Psychology, 74,* 464–480.

Hazan, C., & Shaver, P. R. (1994). Attachment as an organizational framework for research on close relationships. *Psychological Inquiry, 5,* 1–22.

Hogg, M. (2003). Social identity. In M. R. Leary & J. P. Tangney (Eds.), *Handbook of self and identity* (pp. 462–479). New York: Guilford Press.

Markus, H., & Kitayama, S. (1991). Culture and the self: Implications for cognition, emotion, and motivation. *Psychological Review, 98,* 224–253.

McGuire, W. J. (1973). The yin and yang of progress in social psychology: Seven koan. *Journal of Personality and Social Psychology, 26,* 446–456.

Muraven, M., & Baumeister, R. F. (2000). Self-regulation and depletion of limited resources: Does self-control resemble a muscle? *Psychological Bulletin, 126,* 247–259.

Nisbett, R. E., & Cohen, D. (1996). *Culture of honor: The psychology of violence in the South.* Boulder, CO: Westview Press.

Ostrom, T. M. (1994). Forward to R. S. Wyer & T. K. Srull (Eds.), *Handbook of social cognition: Vol. 1, Basic processes* (2nd ed., pp. vii–xii). Hillsdale, NJ: Lawrence Erlbaum Associates.

Pennebaker, J. (1990). *Opening up: The healing power of confiding in others.* New York: William Morrow.

Sampson, E. E. (1978). Scientific paradigms and social values: Wanted—A scientific revolution. *Journal of Personality and Social Psychology, 36,* 1332–1343.

Schimel, J., Greenberg, J., & Martens, A. (2003). Evidence that projection of a feared trait can serve a defensive function. *Personality and Social Psychology Bulletin, 29,* 969–980.

Simpson, J. A., & Kenrick, D. T. (1997). *Evolutionary social psychology.* Mahwah, NJ: Lawrence Erlbaum Associates.

Spears, R., Doosje, B., & Ellemers, N. (1997). Self-stereotyping in the face of threats to group status and distinctiveness: The role of group identification. *Personality and Social Psychology Bulletin, 23,* 538–553.

Steele, C. M. (1997). A threat in the air: How stereotypes shape intellectual history and performance. *American Psychologist, 52,* 613–629.

Tangney, J. P. (2003). Self-relevant emotions. In M. R. Leary & J. P. Tangney (Eds.), *Handbook of self and identity* (pp. 384–400). New York: Guilford Press.

Wegner, D. (1994). Ironic processes of mental control. *Psychological Review, 101,* 34–54.

Winkielman, P., & Cacioppo, J. T. (2001). Mind at ease puts a smile on the face: Psychophysiological evidence that processing facilitation elicits positive affect. *Journal of Personality and Social Psychology, 81,* 989–1000.

Building Bridges Inside and Outside Social Psychology: A Case for Lumping—Neatly[1]

Susan T. Fiske
Princeton University

LUMPERS AND SPLITTERS

Some people say there are two kinds of social psychologists: lumpers and splitters. Lumpers like to synthesize apparent differences under a few overarching principles, seeking similarities. Splitters like to analyze precise distinctions, distinguishing differences.

People also say there are another two kinds of psychologists: neats and scruffies.[2] Scruffies want to be interesting and take big leaps, even at the risk of being wrong and changing their minds (perhaps in midair). Neats want to be right, even at the risk of taking too-cautious incremental steps, building science one brick at a time.

I suspect these modes of science are correlated. Probably, lumpers tend to be scruffy, and splitters tend to be neat.[3] I will argue that it need not be this way.

---

[1] This essay is revised from two presidential columns in the American Psychological Society *Observer*, © American Psychological Society, and is adapted here by permission.

[2] Robert Abelson apparently used this distinction to differentiate two kinds of attribution theory, one viewing the process as more rough, heuristic, and not necessarily logical (e.g., Jones & Davis, 1965) and the other as logical and rational (e.g., Kelley, 1967). I recalled him as applying it even more broadly to styles of scientific thinking, and in any case, I have broadened the concept even farther by adding the elements of risk and caution, which I suspect are correlated with the ones originally identified by Abelson.

[3] I leave it to philosophers and historians of science to provide the derivations of these now-common distinctions, and I leave it to our colleagues in personality and individual differences to devise the appropriate psychometrics.

Some combination is beneficial: Social psychology finds some of its best insights in lumping—neatly. What I have in mind is the hyphenated research that finds similarities in problems investigated in seemingly different areas and sub-areas, and builds bridges of methods and theories to link the two. Finding common cause in apparently disparate domains requires a kind of mental lumping, but it is of course best done with considerable attention to neatness.

Note some of the most exciting bridge areas in current social psychology, efforts that operate at the boundaries between social psychology's subdisciplines and between social psychology and other disciplines. Among the hyphenated subdisciplines now lumping neatly are the fascinating and useful work in social-cognitive neuroscience, social-affective neuroscience, social behavior genetics, and social developmental psychobiology. Among the subdisciplines that happily hyphenated in the past are social cognition, social psychophysiology, social cognitive development, and clinical social neuropsychology. Among the hyphenated subdisciplines that collaborate outside of social psychology are new efforts in neuroeconomics, cultural psychology, and evolutionary psychology, all with strong social roots, as well as continuing work that links social psychology with political, health, and legal psychology (see Fiske, 2004b; Gilbert, Fiske, & Lindzey, 1998).

At this juncture in our broader field, constant centrifugal forces pressure us to fly apart at the seams, breaking apart the entire field of psychology. The forces are visible everywhere:

- Splitting psychology into separate departments, resulting in a number of bad divorces or enduring but tense and unhappy marriages.
- Difficulties in maintaining balance and broad commitment in our whole-field journals, such as *Psychological Science, Current Directions, Psychological Science in the Public Interest, Psychological Bulletin*, and *Psychological Review.*
- Keeping trust and loyalties across constituencies within our whole-field organizations, such as American Psychological Society and American Psychological Association and their European counterparts.
- Exposing students adequately to all of psychology in a single survey course.
- Representing psychology in the *Annual Review of Psychology* series, concurrent with more specialized companion volumes, such as the *Annual Reviews of Neuroscience* and *Clinical Psychology.*

In this context of splitting forces, which operate in the service of intellectual neatness and ingroup loyalty, organizations such as the American Psychological Society, the American Psychological Association, and other national and international psychology organizations have crucial roles in keeping us all together, but so do the individual scientists and collaborative teams who venture across boundaries. These cross-area efforts glue us together as a discipline, a nontrivial scientific contribution.

Some key challenges confront social psychologists who bridge boundaries. They typically start from a home area and bridge to a new area. The homies may view them as disloyal deserters. The new area may view them as alien invaders. So they are caught in between, fully adopted by no camp.

If they bridge from a more micro (biological, mathematical, or physical) home science to a more macro (social, clinical, or developmental) new science, their old colleagues view them as going soft in the head, being less rigorous, more scruffy, and too sloppy. If they bridge from home macro to new micro, they are scorned by their new, would-be colleagues, who may view their efforts as arrogant and ignorant. Essentially, of course, this is about status asymmetries, but that doesn't make the problem go away.

The problems of expertise are real. All the material learned in graduate school and beyond—methods, literature, and theoretical styles—is missing for the person expert in another area but neophyte in a new one.

Collaborations cure some of these problems. A willingness to admit ignorance and to tolerate naiveté together cure others. Subscribing less strictly to micro–macro (or hard–soft) hierarchies cures others. A genuine curiosity about what makes people tick, and doing whatever it takes to find out, got all of us into this business in the first place.

Lumpers and bridgers could be accused of having carpet-sweeper minds, gathering dusty bits and pieces, piling them together, but observers have to admit that it leaves the place neater than it began. Many of the hyphenators are taking their lumps, but they like it and lump it anyway. Consider these as highlights for now, but let's examine a more specific case in point, namely, social cognition.

SAVE THE HYPHENS: A CASE STUDY OF ONE SOCIAL-COGNITIVE PSYCHOLOGIST

As an assistant professor, I profited over several years from a small annual conference at Nags Head, NC, sponsored by Bibb Latané, at which we presented our research in t-shirts and shorts, talked psychology over bonfires and long beach walks, and rode the cognitive revolution in (social) psychology. The dozen or so regulars at this week-long conference on a variety of social-cognitive topics followed a dozen or so regulars at a conference on a topic more traditional to social psychology, namely, small groups. One year, we arrived to find the conference center's sole blackboard prominently bearing the international inscription of a circle with a diagonal slash, indicating prohibition. It was superimposed on the words *social-cognition.*

As a vulnerable junior colleague, I wondered if I was following the right path, working in an area that some people in my home field clearly hated. Social cognition (in its late 1970s, early 1980s form) was viewed as taking over the field. People in other areas had some reason for paranoia; most of the editors and associate editors of the field's primary journals at that time indeed were regulars at the Nags Head social-cognition conferences. People resented their editorial insistence on indicators of cognitive processes and their apparent preference for measures of recall, recognition, and reaction time, in stripped-down social settings. Even for someone sympathetic to these new bridges between cognitive and social psychology, it was a scary audience, beach sandals or no beach sandals.

Were the converts right to push their hyphenated agenda? Were the mainstream researchers right to resent the intrusion? Time would tell, and both the converts and the traditionalists have mellowed. Social-cognitive approaches soon did permeate the field, to such an extent that a reviewer once thought that our book *Social Cognition* (Fiske & Taylor, 1984, 1991) aimed to cover all of social psychology. It had no such aim, but the reviewer was not wrong to notice how many traditional areas were infected by the social cognition virus. Now it merits a standard chapter in textbooks, and a standard approach in many areas, including (gasp) the small-groups area, which has continued to thrive, itself bridging many adjacent areas (Fiske, 2004b; Gilbert et al., 1998). Social cognition is here to stay, but so is social psychology.

CONCLUSIONS

I started this chapter, whose theme has been bridging social psychology, with a discussion of lumpers and splitters, neats and scruffies. Tastes differ, and people are happiest with their accustomed level of borrowing. Nevertheless, I would advocate the advantages of lumping neatly, for the benefits both to the field (gluing together what threatens to split apart), to scientific insight (two or more perspectives are better than one), and to the individual scientist (nothing is more exciting). Social cognition, a field close to my heart, emerged in precisely this manner.

But to be credible, one must be rigorous and neat: One cannot merely dabble or drop in for a visit; one must take the other area seriously, learning from collaborators, gaining some significant expertise, dwelling for a while in the new territory. We spent a lot of time in the early days consulting with and learning from cognitive psychologists, who were only sometimes happy to talk with us. A similar process is going in social neuroscience at the present time.

The risks are real, and bridging boundaries is not for the faint-hearted or perhaps not even for the untenured (Fiske, 2004a). The more reductionist, micro, harder discipline questions the rigor, abilities, and expertise of the broader, macro, softer discipline. And the more macro discipline questions the realism, wisdom, and expertise of the more micro discipline. Either way, the traveler is seen as disloyal to the home discipline and as invading the receiving discipline. It's a high-risk but potentially high-gain research strategy.

Over the year I presided over the American Psychological Society, I recruited a series of *Observer* columns by colleagues about the sweet side of crossing boundaries, as well as the tough side, with examples from cognitive neuroscience, liberal arts psychology, organizational decision science, clinical emotions research, psychological sociology, and social neuroscience. Scruffy, lumpy adventurers have consistently fought the skeptics who have questioned the wisdom of borrowing. Sometimes the skeptics have been right, but sometimes the adventurers have been right. It would be well to remember this, as we confront this decade's new topics, and not too quickly to scrawl prohibitions over the newest hyphenated field. Take a few opportunities for intellectual adventure at the next conference, in the latest issue of our very own field-spanning journals, or as exemplified in this book.

REFERENCES

Fiske, S. T. (2004a). Developing a program of research. In C. Sansone, C. Morf, & A. Panter (Eds.), *Handbook of methods in social psychology* (pp. 71–90). Thousand Oaks, CA: Sage.

Fiske, S. T. (2004b). *Social beings: A core motives approach to social psychology*. New York: Wiley.

Fiske, S. T., & Taylor, S. E. (1984). *Social cognition*. New York: Random House.

Fiske, S. T., & Taylor, S. E. (1991). *Social cognition* (2nd ed.). New York: McGraw-Hill.

Gilbert, D. T., Fiske, S. T., & Lindzey, G. (Eds.). (1998). *Handbook of social psychology* (4th ed.). New York: McGraw-Hill.

Jones, E. E., & Davis, K. E. (1965). From acts to dispositions: The attribution process in person perception. In L. Berkowitz (Ed.), *Advances in experimental social psychology* (Vol. 2, pp. 220–226). New York: Academic Press.

Kelley, H. H. (1967). Attribution theory in social psychology. In D. Levine (Ed.), *Nebraska symposium on motivation* (Vol. 15, pp. 192–238). Lincoln: University of Nebraska Press.

6

Soft Versus Solid Foundations for Bridging Social Psychology

Norbert L. Kerr
Michigan State University

BRIDGING SOCIAL PSYCHOLOGY: HOW AND WHERE?

Before one embarks upon building a bridge (whether between the banks of a river or between disciplines), there are a number of questions that should be considered. One is how such a bridge might best be constructed. Another is precisely where such bridges ought to be built. In this essay, I consider each these two questions with regard to building bridges between my own scientific discipline, social psychology, and other fields (whether scientific, policy-making, service providing, or whatever).

How Best to Bridge?

Here, I am concerned less with the specific tactics of constructing such bridges and more with some general strategies. However, I begin with what I believe are poor strategies—that is, with how *not* to bridge.

One common suggestion for bridging is that social psychologists need to do a better job of disseminating what they do and know. There is a kernel of truth in this—like most scientists, most of us are more invested in doing our work than in disseminating it. However, I am doubtful that the "packaging" or public relations exercises recommended by such an approach—for example, establishing press offices in our professional associations, featuring charismatic spokespersons on public television series, declaring a "decade of social behavior"—will contribute very much to building lasting and productive bridges.

Another suggestion is that social psychologists undermine bridging by being too rigid and self-critical. Rejection rates at our journals and federal funding panels are high (relative to other disciplines), and intolerance of nontraditional methods of inquiry (e.g., qualitative methods) is common. Again, there is a kernel of truth here; too often, high critical standards (which can originate from ideals of rigorous theory and methodology) have verged into hypercriticality based on narrow and heuristically applied standards (see Abelson's, 1995, elegant dissection of the latter in statistical analyses). But the implied remedy—to loosen evaluative standards for theory and research—would undercut progress within our discipline and do little to build sturdy bridges to others.

Another suggestion is that social psychology must make fundamental changes in its standard paradigm (in the Kuhnian sense) before it can make major progress (with or without collaborative bridges). Advocates of this position may differ in their preferred new paradigm, but agree that the current dominant paradigm (essentially the standard hypothetico-deductive model with special emphasis on laboratory experimentation and mediation by few intrapsychic mediating variables) needs revision or replacement. Again, there is something to this argument, particularly when it advocates methodological diversity and convergence and greater receptivity to more macro units of analyses (cf. Steiner, 1986). But again, I doubt that sea changes in our paradigm are essential (or particularly useful) for bridging our field.

Having noted (and due to length constraints, dismissed with little explanation) a few ways in which *not* to bridge from social psychology, let me suggest some strategies for successful bridging. A bridge across a river requires a solid foundation on each end. Bridges from social psychology to other areas will be most durable if they are built on our discipline's bedrock—its distinctive strengths. To my mind, the most prominent strengths are (a) insistence on methodological rigor, (b) sophisticated techniques of experimentation on human social cognition, action, and interaction, (c) a strong commitment to theory development, and (d) the individual as the focal unit of analysis of social behavior (even when studying interpersonal or collective behaviors). Although some disciplines (e.g., cognitive psychology) share some of these, I believe that this particular mix of scientific perspectives is our discipline's unique and distinctive contribution to any fruitful collaboration. The best, most broadly useful knowledge we can offer to or will develop with potential collaborators is characterized by these perspectives. Rather than adopt the perspectives of other disciplines (e.g., to emphasize field research; to rely on qualitative methods; to stress a theoretical/descriptive work; to functionally become neuroscientists, cognitive psychologists, sociologists, or the like), I am convinced that we need to do more of what we do best, while keeping alert for opportunities to use our work to complement what others do and to use what others do best to enrich our own efforts.

We are, however, unlikely to recognize such opportunities unless we have at least an elementary understanding and appreciation of the corresponding strengths of those on the other sides of our bridges. It is not uncommon to confuse what is familiar with what is best. Similarly, one common trap that scientists fall into is assuming that the best (or only) way to make scientific progress is the way that they (usually for reasons of disciplinary tradition or training) chronically use. Runkle and McGrath (1972) make this point particularly well by locating generic methods of inquiry on a conceptual circumplex (i.e., at different points on a wheel). Each segment of the wheel is characterized by genuine strengths and inevitable weaknesses; one method's weakness is another method's strength. Ultimately, no method has any defensible claim to a general superiority over the others. Failure to recognize and appreciate this truth is all too common and a symptom of narrow methodological training and professional hubris. It is also a serious impediment to effective interdisciplinary bridging.

Finally, bridges do not magically spring up out of our conceptions or desires for them—they must be painstakingly constructed. Similarly, social psychologists cannot do their part in building useful interdisciplinary bridges without making painstaking efforts. These might include becoming familiarized with another area's jargon, methods, and literature; publishing one's own work in its journals; attending its professional meetings, hearings, and workshops; and actively nurturing interdisciplinary collaborations. Because such efforts must inevitably take time away from other, more intradisciplinary activities, they should also be recognized as valuable by social psychologists and their home institutions (or at the very least, not result in professional penalties).

Where to Bridge?

Of course, we should strive to build bridges between disciplines where there are the best prospects for mutually beneficial two-way intellectual traffic. Both intuition and history recommend that this will happen when the bridging partners have high overlap in their substantive interests. Many of the more successful extant links between social psychology and other areas have had such overlap. Examples include the following bridges: (a) social psychological work on attitude formation and change ↔ communication, advertising, and consumer behavior (e.g., Bagozzi, Gurhan-Canli, & Priester, 2002); (b) social psychological work on interpersonal attraction and prosocial behavior ↔ evolutionary psychology (e.g., Buss, 1999); (c) social psychology of aggression ↔ media studies (e.g., Anderson & Bushman, 2002); and (d) the social psychology of interpersonal influence ↔ behavioral medicine (e.g., Salovey & Rothman, 2003; Suls & Wallston, 2003).

Such substantive overlap, though, is not sufficient. Sometimes there are barriers on one side that will seriously interfere with bridging. Consider, for example, attempts to bridge social psychology and the law. On the social psychology side, these have originated primarily from substantive interest in two topics: eyewitness identification and jury behavior (Ellsworth & Mauro, 1998). However, there has been much greater utilization of social psychological knowledge by the law for the former topic than for the latter. There are a number of reasons for this (including some particularly effective bridge building by eyewitness researchers; Wells et al., 2000), but one significant reason is that the legal agents who must evaluate and utilize relevant jury research (e.g., the U.S. Supreme Court and lower appellate courts) are less receptive to making full use of this research than the corresponding agents for eyewitness research (e.g., investigating officers and prosecutors). Legal precedents or judicial belief on jury functioning, for example, may easily trump clear social psychological evidence (see Thompson, 1989, for a dramatic illustration). Recognition of such special difficulties can be a legitimate consideration in deciding where to attempt to build bridges from social psychology.

Social psychologists working within particular topical areas should be able to reach informed intuitions about where useful bridges might be built. As a social psychologist whose interests focus on small-group behavior, here are some of my own nominations for promising bridging sites:

- *Experimental economics.* Coincident with the growing interest within economics in the role of behavioral factors for economic phenomena (e.g., Thaler, 1993), a new subdiscipline has emerged within economics that is using experimental methods to explore economic behavior. There is a high level of overlap between this work and several lines of social psychological inquiry. There are, to be sure, strong institutional barriers within economics to the microeconomic empiricism that such a collaboration would entail, but the experimental economists are themselves laboring to lower these barriers.
- *Team research.* Work teams have grown dramatically in popularity in organizational settings. Paralleling this trend has been a burgeoning interest among organizational psychologists in the study of team behavior (e.g., Guzzo & Dickson, 1996). Social psychologists have been busy studying small-group performance since the start of the discipline. A more natural and productive bridging site is hard to imagine.
- *Group communication/support systems.* New technology has opened the door to a variety of innovative forms of group communication and work. A loosely connected set of scholars in a number of disciplines (e.g., computer science; organizational psychology; human factors; cognitive science) has begun to explore the potential of such technology to change (and hopefully improve) the way groups work. Again, social psychological studies of a number of topics (e.g., small-group performance and decision making; communication networks) provide natural bridgeheads.

CONCLUSIONS

I have argued that efforts to bridge from social psychology are most likely to be worthwhile where there are (a) reasonable overlap between bridging partners in substantive interests and (b) no strong opposing forces on either side of the bridge. The former suggests that the best bridging partners will be disciplines that share concern with the study of the core content of social psychology—attitudes, social cognition, pro- and antisocial behavior, interpersonal behavior and relations, intra- and intergroup dynamics. From the perspective of a social psychologist interested in group behavior, I have suggested three eligible and promising bridging partners (viz., experimental economics, research on teams, the use of technology in collaborative work).

I have also argued that we social psychologists should anchor our side of such bridges on the bedrock of our discipline, and not try—in our zeal to build bridges—to attempt to radically transform ourselves or our discipline. We social psychologists may (and often do) disagree about what the bedrock of our discipline is; here I suggest that our bedrock consists of a reliance on the individual as the basic unit of analysis, methodological sophistication and rigor in human experimental research, and strong commitment to theory development. On the other hand, we also need to better understand and value the bedrocks of those laboring on the other sides of these bridges.

An old proverb suggests that "good fences make good neighbors" (cf. "Mending Walls" in Frost, 1977). But to transform many good (but isolated) scientific neighbors into a vigorous scientific community, we may want to put as much thought and effort into building better bridges to our natural intellectual neighbors as we do to maintaining the sturdy fences between us.

REFERENCES

Abelson, R. F. (1995). *Statistics as principled argument.* Hillsdale, NJ: Lawrence Erlbaum Associates.

Anderson, C. A., & Bushman, B. J. (2002). The effects of media violence on society. *Science, 295,* 2377–2378.

Bagozzi, R. P., Gurhan-Canli, Z., & Priester, J. R. (2002). *The social psychology of consumer behaviour.* Buckingham, UK: Open University Press.

Buss, D. (1999). *Evolutionary psychology: The new science of the mind.* Boston: Allyn & Bacon.

Ellsworth, P. C., & Mauro, R. (1998). Psychology and law. In D. Gilbert, S. Fiske, & G. Lindsey. (Eds.), *The handbook of social psychology* (Vol. 2, 4th ed., pp. 684–732). New York, NY: McGraw-Hill.

Frost, R. (1977). *North of Boston.* New York: Dodd, Mead.

Guzzo, R. A., & Dickson, M. W. (1996). Teams in organizations: Recent research on performance and effectiveness. *Annual Review of Psychology, 47,* 307–338.

Runkle, P. R., & McGrath, J. E. (1972). *Research on human behavior: A systematic guide to method.* New York: Holt.

Salovey, P., & Rothman, A. J. (2003). *Social psychology and health*. New York: Taylor & Francis.

Steiner, I. D. (1986). Paradigms and groups. In L. Berkowitz (Ed.), *Advances in experimental social psychology* (Vol. 19, pp. 251–292). New York: Academic Press.

Suls, J., & Wallston, K. A. (2003). *Social psychological foundations of health and illness*. Malden, MA: Blackwell.

Thaler, R. H. (1993). *Advances in behavioral finance*. New York: Russell Sage.

Thompson, W. C. (1989). Death qualification after Wainwright v. Witt and Lockhart v. McCree. *Law and Human Behavior, 13*, 185–215.

Wells, G. L., Malpass, R. S., Lindsay, R. C., Fisher, R. P., Turtle, J. W., & Fulero, S. (2000). From the lab to the police station: A successful application of eyewitness research. *American Psychologist, 55*, 581–598.

7

Folly Bridges

C. Daniel Batson
University of Kansas

At risk of offending the editor, other contributors, and readers of a volume on interdisciplinary bridge building, I wish to suggest that building these bridges is, more often than not, folly. I raise this disquieting prospect not because I doubt that other disciplines have valuable insights to offer social psychology—or that social psychology has valuable insights to offer them. Quite the opposite. I raise it because I think a false assumption about geography of the intellectual enterprise underlies the call for bridges. The assumption is that different disciplines (e.g., psychology, biology, sociology, anthropology, and philosophy)—or even different areas within a discipline (e.g., clinical, cognitive, developmental, personality, physiological, and social psychology)—are islands of inquiry and insight in a sea of ignorance. Were this true, then bridge building would be wise indeed. Like connecting the islands in an archipelago chain, it would allow one to encounter new people and new ideas, to expand commerce and culture, to get someplace.

Disciplines and subdisciplines do not, however, suddenly rise out of the sea in volcanic eruptions of insight. Nor do they emerge gradually over eons, like coral islands, through the accumulation of zillions of hard little facts. Disciplines develop as peninsulas. These peninsulas extend out from the great mainland of everyday experience and our commonsense understanding of this experience. The origin of a discipline lies in focused attention on some aspect of everyday experience.

Almost always, the first extensions of awareness and understanding are made by philosophers, who give careful attention to the nuances of everyday experience and the order—and disorder—of commonsense explanations. This is why the most basic and profound questions one can ask in a discipline were usually posed long ago by philosophers. The sciences further extend our experience and our understanding, often through use of some new technology or instrument that provides a novel perspective. As new experiences and insights build, disciplines project farther and farther from the mainland out into the sea.

In time, disciplinary peninsulas extend so far that the mainland is no longer visible. They develop their own economy and culture. Inhabitants can live on the peninsula for years without ever returning to the mainland—or wanting to. There is an understandable tendency to focus on what is happening at the growing edge of the peninsula, where new insights are forming and life is full of zest and excitement. Why visit the mainland, where what happens is so mundane?

As these peninsulas grow, they send out fingers that reach toward other peninsulas. From the vantage point of such a finger, another peninsula—or even another part of one's own peninsula—may appear to be an island. Seeing the twinkling lights on the other shore, and hearing of exciting times there, it is natural to think of building a bridge.

WHY NOT BUILD A BRIDGE?

There are two good reasons to resist this impulse. One is pragmatic. Distances can be deceptive. It may be smarter to go around by way of the mainland—or take a boat or plane—than to build a bridge. This is especially true if one does not plan frequent trips, long stays, or extensive commerce. Building a bridge is both time-consuming and expensive, and the time and money may be better spent.

The second reason is more fundamental. Especially if one plans more than a brief visit, it is almost always unwise to move directly from one discipline to another without returning to the mainland. Without knowing the aspects of everyday experience that were focal in the original development of a discipline, the philosophical analysis of commonsense understanding of these aspects of experience, and how the discipline has grown out of and extended commonsense, one is likely to mistake the exotic features and fads of a discipline for its substance. Such features and fads are especially pronounced in those hot spots of the discipline that twinkle from afar and capture the attention of a visitor, whether a layperson from the mainland or an expert from another discipline. But trinkets from the tourist towns of a discipline are not the best it has to offer—or anywhere close. Often, they turn out to be junk.

If I am right that disciplines grow as peninsulas out of attempts to extend commonsense understanding of everyday experience, then it is important to recognize that one's own discipline is no island. It too is a peninsula extending out from this mainland. In social psychology, Fritz Heider (1958) built an impressive career on this recognition and on reminding his colleagues of it. It is also important to recognize that the wisest way to get from one discipline to another is not by bridge but by way of the mainland. Returning to the mainland of everyday experience, one is reminded of the aspects of experience that one's own discipline seeks to understand and of the philosophical issues involved in pursuing this understanding. One can then look to see what other disciplines have grown out of attempts to understand these same or related aspects of experience. And one can journey into one or more of these disciplines as a means to extend one's understanding. Even when a bridge exists, it is almost always best to take the long way around by the mainland.

AN IMPORTANT INSIGHT MISAPPLIED

To illustrate the distinction, consider the bridge between social psychology and evolutionary biology constructed by evolutionary psychology. This bridge has been the conduit for importing into social psychology explanatory models from evolutionary biology. These models are then used to explain human social behavior.

A prime example is William Hamilton's (1964) model of inclusive fitness (kin selection), which has been taken to provide a novel and exciting explanation of human helping of kin. It is said that helping kin developed through natural selection because, depending on the degree of relation, kin carry up to 50% of one's genes. (Identical twins are, of course, an even more extreme case.) Given this sharing, even if helping one's kin reduces the likelihood of directly placing one's own genes in the next generation (i.e., reduces personal reproductive fitness) it can increase the likelihood that one's genes will appear in the next generation (i.e., increase inclusive fitness). It can do this if it increases the likelihood that the helped kin will place the shared genes in the next generation. Indeed, if the proximal trigger for such helping is perceived similarity, then this naturally selected genetic impulse can explain helping for similar non-kin too (Rushton, Russell, & Wells, 1984).

In apparent support of the idea that human helping of kin is due to a genetic impulse to maximize inclusive fitness, it has been found that people report being more likely to help kin than to help strangers, especially close kin with a life-threatening need. But note that these findings reveal aspects of human experience to be explained; they do not provide evidence for one specific explanation. They provide no more evidence for an explanation in terms of inclusive fitness than for an explanation in terms of, for example, social norms and sanctions. To accept these findings as support for an inclusive fitness explanation is to fall victim to a confirmation bias. Yet most contemporary social psychology textbooks assume that these findings confirm the role of genetically based inclusive fitness in promoting human helping behavior. Textbook authors have traveled the bridge built by evolutionary psychology and returned to social psychology with inclusive fitness as an explanatory gem.

Contrast this approach to evolutionary biology with that of social psychologist Donald Campbell (1975). Campbell too was interested in taking advantage of insights from evolutionary biology to better understand human helping behavior. He, however, took the long way around.

Approaching biology by first returning to the mainland and attending to the aspects of everyday experience being explained, Campbell was well aware that Hamilton (1964) developed his model of inclusive fitness to account for a rather unique aspect of experience, the self-sacrificial behavior by members of worker castes among the social insects, including bees and wasps. These insects are different from humans in three conspicuous ways (other than body size, number of legs, and type of skeleton). First, they are unusually highly genetically related to others in the hive, sharing three-fourths of their genes with them. Second, they are sterile; they can have no offspring. Third, their behavior is limited to hard-wired stimulus-response patterns little modified by learning and experience.

Given these features of social insects, Campbell was quite willing to accept Hamilton's inclusive-fitness account of a honeybee's readiness to sting an intruder to the hive even though doing so costs the bee its life. Campbell was not, however, willing to accept an inclusive-fitness account of human helping behavior, even helping of close kin. Several characteristics of humans make them far less susceptible to natural selection based on inclusive fitness: (a) a lower level of genetic relatedness (except among identical twins, a case too rare to provide a basis for natural selection), (b) the rapid drop in relatedness as one moves from siblings to cousins and beyond, and (c) the ability of most humans to have children and so to place their genes in the next generation directly. In addition, the exceptional flexibility of human behavior and the sensitivity to social training and social rewards and punishments render social learning explanations of kinship patterns in human helping behavior highly plausible. Viewed in the light of the conspicuous differences between humans and social insects, to claim that human helping of kin is a product of inclusive fitness seems not only unfounded but also implausible.

It is not that Campbell was opposed to seeking insights from evolutionary biology. On the contrary, for many years he was probably the social psychologist most interested in doing so—and the best informed about developments in biology. But he was also aware of the basis and the context of biological insights; he knew their range of applicability. He had not traveled to evolutionary biology by bridge and stopped at the first curio shop. He had gone by way of the mainland.

In humans and other higher mammals, an impulse to care for offspring is almost certainly genetically hard-wired, although modifiable by circumstances. It is far less clear that an impulse to care for siblings, more remote kin, and similar non-kin—the behavior attributed to inclusive fitness—is genetically hard-wired. Ironically, attention given inclusive fitness has directed attention away from parental nurturance as a genetic basis for human caring. This is because inclusive fitness and other evolutionary accounts of "altruism" were developed explicitly to explain why one animal might help another who is not offspring. Only recently have researchers looking more closely at the unique features of human evolution begun to rediscover the importance of parental care (Bell, 2001, MacLean, 1990).

The bright lights of evolutionary biology are, of course, not the only ones that beckon from across the water. Neurophysiology fairly sparkles with new technology and measurement techniques. Computer science offers a steady stream of attractive information processing models—storage-and-retrieval, decision-tree, top-down, bottom-up, serial, parallel, spreading-activation, connectionist, and so on. Anthropology displays cultural differences that seem to suggest not only differences in what is thought and valued but also differences in how people in different cultures think and value. Bridges have been built. But beware. Approaching these exciting developments by way of the mainland, one is better able assess what is relevant and valuable rather than merely fashionable. One is better able to tell truths from trinkets.

CONCLUSIONS

We would be foolish not to take advantage of what other disciplines have to offer. Doing so is, however, not always easy. The case of inclusive fitness is but one example of a more general truth: Relying on bridges to import insights from another discipline is, more often than not, folly. There are important insights to be gained. But to gain them, we need to keep our feet on the ground and travel by way of the mainland. This means, first, that we need to be well aware of the aspects of everyday experience and commonsense understanding to which our own discipline is connected. We also need to be aware of the underlying philosophical issues. It means, second, that we need to approach other disciplines through awareness of their connection to everyday experience and commonsense understanding—and of the underlying philosophical issues.

As disciplines expand and become better established, they are seen not as perspectives on life but as life itself. They are seen as islands, not peninsulas. As a result, travel to other disciplines by way of the mainland becomes increasingly rare, and travel by bridge, increasingly common. Will travel by bridge get us where we really want to go?

ACKNOWLEDGMENT

Thanks to Lowell Gaertner for helpful comments on a draft.

REFERENCES

Bell, D. C. (2001). Evolution of parental caregiving. *Personality and Social Psychology Review, 5,* 216–229.

Campbell, D. T. (1975). On the conflicts between biological and social evolution and between psychology and moral tradition. *American Psychologist, 30,* 1103–1126.

Hamilton, W. D. (1964). The genetical evolution of social behavior (I, II). *Journal of Theoretical Biology, 7,* 1–52.

Heider, F. (1958). *The psychology of interpersonal relations.* New York: Wiley.

MacLean, P. D. (1990). *The triune brain in evolution: Role in paleocerebral functions.* New York: Plenum Press.

Rushton, J. P., Russell, R. J. H., & Wells, P. A. (1984). Genetic similarity theory: Beyond kin selection. *Behavior Genetics, 14,* 179–193.

8

On Theories and Societal Practice: Getting Rid of a Myth

Klaus Fiedler
University of Heidelberg

From the beginning of my career as a scientifically working psychologist, I felt I had to struggle with alleged opposites, calling for exclusive decisions between seemingly incompatible goals with no bridges between them. For example, there seemed to be an opposite relation between being a good teacher and being a good researcher, being interested in psychological contents or merely in methodological topics, quantitative and qualitative procedures, and realist or constructivist confessions. When applying for academic jobs, I learned that one should not try to have it both ways, being a social psychologist as well as a cognitive or non-social experimental psychologist. Working in two areas might be perceived like adultery. However, of all these opposition myths, one of the most persistent ones is the claim that theoreticians cannot be practitioners, and vice versa. In spite of Kurt Lewin's often cited phrase that there is nothing more practical than a good theory, the scientific community continues to presuppose that theories are largely detached from practical problem solving. Being concerned with refined theories—particularly, with formal or sophisticated ones that go way beyond common sense—is one thing. But being concerned with practical everyday problems is a completely different thing, fully out of reach from the theoretician's vantage point.

I'm afraid this perceived paucity or lack of bridges between nomological theorizing and practical applications holds in particular for the field of social psychology. For several reasons, social psychologists have shown little interest in competing for a number of applied domains that might be considered prototypical to a genuine social approach. Instead, they largely left decision making and risk management to mathematical psychologists and economists, political affairs to sociologists and political scientists, the family to clinical psychologists, language and the media to communication science, and aging to gerontology and lifespan developmental psychology. To be sure, there have always been notable exceptions (Janis, 1972; Osgood, 1962; Wegner, 2002). But even when my characterization may sound a bit exaggerated, I would defend my starting claim that social psychologists have been conspicuously uninfluential as practitioners, as political agents, economical advisors, entrepreneurs, or mediators of public opinion—*relative to their great potential*.

Social psychologists have been mainly in love with their theories and the experimental construction of the social world; outside the lab, they seem to lack self-confidence, political motivation, and leadership ambition. Having now participated in research, teaching, and peer reviewing over many years, in different subdisciplines, I know this reluctance to engage oneself in practical applications does not reflect a weakness of scientific standards in social psychology but, on the contrary, almost perfectionist standards that prevent us from applying imperfect expertise to real problems with serious consequences. Scientists in other disciplines—such as law, medicine, economics, or political science—are much less reluctant to apply, and sell, even imperfect competence in the course of important societal problems, feeling little scruples about the model or hypothesis they advance. The coping strategy of many social psychologists, instead, has been to refrain from practical problem solving and to concentrate on their flourishing field of research domain, which is a big success story.

SOCIAL PSYCHOLOGY FOR THE COURTROOM: A PERSONAL STORY

As to myself, I must confess that I have long defined my personal identity as a particularly pure exemplar of a theoretician who likes deep reflection on all kinds of theoretical and meta-theoretical issues, but who would leave it up to others to be concerned with practical applications. To be sure, I was always interested in politics, sports, justice, and many practical issues as a private person, but as a psychologist I felt fully committed to fundamental nomological research—at the highest and purest level of generality. Being interested in such abstract and uncommon approaches as connectionist computer simulation, sampling distributions in the environment, implications of statistical regression, Bayesian reasoning, and semiotic processes, my primary problem was even being understood by fellow theoreticians, let alone practitioners or clients asking for practical advice.

Nevertheless, in spite of my being a rather extreme exemplar of a theoretically minded social psychologist, about 5 years ago a bridge was erected between the island just depicted and the practical world. Working as an applied scientist has now become a substantial part of my identity. This aspect of my professional life is presumably unknown to my international colleagues, but within Germany the vast majority of telephone calls I get from journalists or potential users of psychological know-how do not refer to original research but ask for my practical advice in the area of deception, lie detection, manipulation, public opinion, criminality, and legal decision making. Although I still feel like a bloody novice in the domain of legal psychology—compared to established experts like Garry Wells (1993), David Lykken (1984), or Elizabeth Loftus (1993)—I have been pushed into a virtual expert role, quite similar to the paradigmatic nonexpert described by Thomas Kuhn (1970), who intrudes into an external paradigm and happens to make a contribution in spite of, or exactly because, he or she lacks expertise and too much knowledge. Let me briefly tell somewhat more about my personal story as an amateur legal psychologist, because I believe the story is quite telling about the many (alleged) gaps to be bridged between academic social psychology and applied domains. I then give up the (somewhat embarrassing) self-reference and end my essay with some conclusions concerning social psychology's role affordances in the modern information society.

As one of the very few social psychologists who had done some research on the intriguing topic of lie detection—and presumably because I was associated with a more critical attitude toward the mystical arts of lie detection than most legal practitioners—I received a telephone call in 1998 from one of the judges of the German Supreme Court, who were about to make a fundamental decision concerning the scientific value and the permissibility of polygraph lie detection in the courtroom. In spite of the dubious reputation of polygraph testing, its use had increased epidemically, due to lawyers' strategies and due to many popular publications about the alleged value of this diagnostic tool. Three other expert witnesses were involved, who could claim to be highly experienced legal practitioners and who also had vested interests in polygraph testing. The spectrum of opinions varied considerably, but I was clearly the one person with the most pronounced critical attitude. I never concealed being just a fundamental researcher and being fully inexperienced in legal affairs. But for several reasons, the court's decision followed my skeptical advice in virtually all respects, essentially denying any scientific basis of the Control Question Test (CQT; Iacono & Lykken, 1997) as a means of proving the defendant's guilt.

I cannot remember as similarly interested and open-minded an audience of students or conference attendants as the panel of judges in the Supreme Court, who were eager to learn as much as they could get from fundamental science. My repeated disclaimers that I am not expert in law and courtroom procedures and that all this is "merely" nomological science seemed to be disregarded, or even seemed to raise more curiosity. In my attempt to explain why the fancy statistics about the CQT's alleged accuracy rates must be misleading, I really had to resort to many abstract topics, such as incremental validity, Bayes's theorem, signal detection analysis applied to an emotional response model, or sampling biases intruding on validity studies that typically include all confirming cases but tend to exclude disconfirming cases that could invalidate polygraph results. It was my strong impression, and it was actually articulated explicitly by these intellectual opinion leaders among judges, that they were quite saturated with practitioners' advice and that they regarded the lessons they could take from theory-driven, fundamental science to be the enlightenment proper. Admittedly, other colleagues may not share this opinion, and a common experience may indeed be frustration with practitioners and applied domains. But here I want to highlight the less common experience that the opposite is also true and possible.

Since then, there have been several occasions for me to replicate and substantiate this impression. In another Supreme Court decision in which I was involved, the purpose was to develop and implement minimal criteria for scientifically based credibility assessment, as typically needed in rape or sexual abuse cases. Judges and legal experts were apparently intrigued by what psychology has to offer in terms of transparent psychometric rules, methods for checking interjudge agreement, reliability and aggregation, and the vicissitudes of verification biases in hypothesis testing. Again, it was an intellectually open-minded audience that let me forget the alleged gap between "mere theories" and "practical applications." Several seminars and workshops I have done for criminal lawyers and judges resulted in the same feedback. They were eager to learn systematically about the way human memory operates, about statistical artifacts and judgment biases, about lineups and face recognition, about linguistic influences in the courtroom (Schmid & Fiedler, 1998), or the role of judgment heuristics (Englich & Mussweiler, 2001) and attributional schemas in sentencing decisions.

In an extended court trial involving repressed memories and post hoc reconstruction of alleged severe child abuse, a physician was accused of having abused his daughter over more than 10 years. There was no physical evidence or original witness testimony whatsoever, and the daughter, who had committed suicide at the age of 25, had never really accused her father but merely yielded to all kinds of social influence to admit that she had really been the victim of extended abuse as a child. In the course of this trial, the participating persons would not only listen carefully to my refined distinctions of different types of reconstructive memory arising in individuals and groups. They would even attend to, and finally believe in the relevance of, a Gricean analysis of communication games, such as group therapy conversations around (alleged) abuse experiences that cannot be assumed to obey propositional truth values but follow the rules of cooperative communication.

To repeat, I simply no longer believe in the gap between theories and practice, between fundamental and applied research. The interest, patience, and readiness to learn about even technical and uncommon scientific insights are amazing. I think it is not a polemic exaggeration to pretend that the applied field of legal decision making that I have encountered is less conservative and more open-minded than a typical reviewing procedure in our major scientific journals supposed to publish creative and innovative research ideas.

CONCLUSIONS

Through my own recent story as an "amateur expert" in law, I have been sensitized for the need and for the affordance that social psychologists ought to cross the short bridge between research and urgent societal problems. There is no need to hesitate in offering what we know to politicians, administrators, and decision makers. In the modern information society of the new millennium, nobody can claim to be an ultimate expert. Those so-called applied experts who pretend to offer *practical solutions* to ill-understood modern problems may be needed less than the *models and methods* that scientists have to offer for dealing with the new challenges of globalism, ecology, economy, migration, education, religion and ethics, criminality, health, aging, new media, and international affairs. I think the time is ripe for social psychologists to take more public responsibility. Who else if not we social psychologists ourselves could tell decision makers and the public about the crucial dilemma structure of the global economy, about the ingenious idea of peer reviewing as a remedy against corruption, about the Internet as the major site of future political movements, about the wisdom of getting old in dignity, about the primitive and irrational rules of the stock market, or about the serious cognitive biases involved in risk management and health-related decisions? I dare to anticipate that political decision makers, authorities, and the public will not be resistant but will be as open-minded and actually grateful for all kind of serious social psychological input as the lawyers were in my personal story.

REFERENCES

Englich, B., & Mussweiler, T. (2001). Sentencing under uncertainty: Anchoring effect in the courtroom. *Journal of Applied Social Psychology, 31,* 1535–1551.

Iacono, W. G., & Lykken, D. T. (1997). The validity of the lie detector: Two surveys of scientific opinion. *Journal of Applied Psychology, 82,* 426–433.

Janis, I. L. (1972). *Victims of groupthink: A psychological study of foreign-policy decisions and fiascoes.* Boston: Houghton Mifflin.

Kuhn, T. (1970). *The structure of scientific revolutions.* Chicago: University of Chicago Press.

Loftus, E. F. (1993). The reality of repressed memories. *American Psychologist, 48,* 518–537.

Lykken, D. T. (1984). Polygraph interrogation. *Nature, 307,* 681–684.

Osgood, C. E. (1962). *An alternative to war or surrender.* Urbana: University of Illinois Press.

Schmid, J., & Fiedler, K. (1998). The backbone of closing speeches: The impact of prosecution versus defense language on juridical attributions. *Journal of Applied Social Psychology, 28,* 1140–1172.

Wegner, D. M. (2002). *The illusion of conscious will.* Cambridge, MA: Massachusetts Institute of Technology Press.

Wells, G. L. (1993). What do we know about eyewitness identification? *American Psychologist, 48,* 553–571.

9

Interdisciplinary Research and Creativity

Wolfgang Stroebe
Utrecht University

In most countries in which I have worked, granting agencies and university administrators have encouraged research to be interdisciplinary. Although the motives underlying this preference have never been clearly stated, I had the strong impression that it was based on the assumption that forcing researchers out of their "disciplinary ghettos" would somehow improve the quality of their research and increase the likelihood of innovative outcomes. I assume that this type of assumption also justified the foundation of interdisciplinary meeting places such as the Netherlands Institute for Advanced Studies or the Center for the Advanced Study in Behavioral Sciences. Because many of the chapters in this book will be similarly optimistic about interdisciplinary research, I would like to address the question of whether conducting research in an interdisciplinary setting is likely to stimulate the creativity of the researchers involved in such endeavors.

THE COMPONENTS OF CREATIVITY

Why should interdisciplinary research stimulate creativity? The three-component theory of creative performance developed by Amabile (1983, 1996) could offer a theoretical foundation for such a hypothesis. According to this theory, creativity is a function of *domain-relevant skills, creativity-relevant processes*, and *motivation*. Domain-relevant skills refer to the individual's expertise in his or her area. Thus, the domain-relevant skills of social psychologists would include their ability to think scientifically as well as their knowledge and technical ability in the field of social psychology.

Although a necessary condition for creativity, domain-relevant knowledge is not sufficient to ensure creative outcomes. People can produce good work if they are experts in their area, but they "will be incapable of producing work that will be considered creative if creativity-relevant skills are lacking" (Amabile, 1996, p. 83). Creativity-relevant skills refer to how people approach problems, their capacity to put existing ideas together in new combinations. They include a creative cognitive style characterized by a facility in understanding complexities and an ability to break set during problem solving. Problem solving is more likely to result in creative solutions when an old set of unsuccessful problem-solving skills is abandoned and the search, as a result, moves off in a new direction.

That the ability to abandon routine strategies of problem solving and to restructure problems in novel and unusual ways is an important characteristic of creative scientists has also been emphasized by Simonton (2002). He argued that "to attain scientific greatness ... may require the cognitive capacity to pursue unexpected, even contradictory trains of thought" (p. 140). Simonton even speculated that the decrease in productivity with increasing age observed in some scientists could be partly attributed to "the cognitive tendency for scientists to become increasingly ensnared by the ideas they themselves created. The creativity of their earlier years provides the chains for their later years" (p. 272).

Domain-relevant skills and creativity-relevant skills are the resources the individual needs to produce a creative product. But whether these resources will finally be used creatively depends on the individual's motivation, in particular on whether the individual is intrinsically motivated rather than responding to external pressures. Amabile (1996) defined as "intrinsic any motivation that arises from the individual's positive reaction to qualities of the task itself; this reaction can be experiences as interest, involvement, curiosity, satisfaction, or positive challenge" (p. 115). Extrinsic motivation comprises any motivation that arises from the sources outside the task itself, such as the expectation to be evaluated or that the task has been contracted for reward. Although Amabile (1996) still emphasized that intrinsic motivation is essential for creativity, she has abandoned her earlier hypothesis that extrinsic motivation is always damaging to the creative effort. Amabile (1996) now accepts that certain synergistic extrinsic motivators can increase intrinsic motivation. These synergistic motivators are factors that support one's sense of competence without undermining one's sense of self-determination (see also Deci, Koestner, & Ryan, 1999).

Amabile (1983, 1996) and Simonton (2002) considered creativity-relevant skills as an individual difference variable. It is conceivable, however, that environmental conditions can influence the extent to which individuals who already possess a high level of creative thinking skills will be challenged into applying them during problem solving. From an idealized image of how interdisciplinary research is conducted, one could easily imagine that the discourse among researchers from different disciplines approaching a common problem might help them to break the mold of their old disciplinary problem-solving strategies and motivate them to develop an innovative approach to tackle the problem. After all, seeing the different way in which a researcher from another discipline addresses a scientific problem might stimulate one to develop a new perspective and abandon the routine approach suggested by one's own discipline. However, in my experience, this idealized image does not reflect the everyday practice of interdisciplinary research.

THE EVERYDAY PRACTICE OF INTERDISCIPLINARY RESEARCH

Because most of my experiences with interdisciplinary research have been in the field of health psychology, I draw my examples from this area. Health psychology is an interdisciplinary field that integrates psychological knowledge relevant to the maintenance of health, the prevention of illness, and the adjustment to illness. It developed during the last half of the last century as a result of the growing recognition that lifestyle factors and psychological stress contribute substantially to morbidity and mortality from the chronic diseases that had replaced infectious diseases as major causes of death in industrialized countries. Social psychology is a major contributor to research in health psychology. In fact, health psychology has become one of the fastest growing areas of applied social psychology.

The conduct of research in health psychology is practically always an interdisciplinary endeavor, beginning with the choice of research questions and continuing with the execution of one's research. Thus, if it were true that interdisciplinary discourse stimulated creativity, health psychology should be one of the most innovative subdisciplines in psychology. Although there is no scientifically tenable test of this hypothesis, having twice reviewed research on social psychology and health during the last two decades (e.g., Stroebe, 2000), I am not convinced that the proportion of innovative research in health psychology is greater than in any other area of psychology.

In my experience, the type of interdisciplinary interaction that characterizes research in health psychology is no more likely to stimulate creativity-relevant processes than any interaction with colleagues from one's own discipline. In my frequent collaborations with medical colleagues, I never felt the need to break my (disciplinary) set or to adopt heuristics for generating new ideas. After all, these colleagues had chosen to collaborate with a social psychologist because they expected that knowledge of social psychological theories and research methods would contribute to a successful solution to the research problem they were confronting. Every member of the interdisciplinary team contributed their domain-relevant expertise to the project, and often there was no need for further meetings or interactions once the project had been set up.

Thus, there was rarely reason to cross the border into other disciplines. On the contrary: It was to avoid crossing the border into other disciplines that one had chosen certain experts in other fields to join the research project. Obviously, this division of labor of interdisciplinary teams, with every member contributing his or her own special knowledge, enables one to address problems that could not have been tackled *within* any of the disciplines involved. But it is probably also the main the reason why the normal practice of interdisciplinary research is unlikely to encourage the search for new problem-solving strategies. (Admittedly, such clear division of labor may be more typical for interdisciplinary collaborations between scientists from very different disciplines than for collaborations between neighboring areas.) A second reason is motivational. Most of my health psychological projects have been funded by outside funds and had to result in a successful dissertation and international publications. This external pressure is not helpful in nurturing the kind of intrinsic motivation that stimulates creative thought.

CAN INTERDISCIPLINARY COLLABORATION STIMULATE CREATIVITY?

I have also experienced interdisciplinary collaborations, which have been exceedingly stimulating. I have been a member of a small interdisciplinary group (Interdisziplinäre Sozialwissenschaftliche Arbeitsgemeinschaft, ISAG) formed with the aim to further the integration between different social sciences. The group consists of seven members, all from disciplines concerned with the study of human behavior: three economists, one sociologist, one philosopher, and three psychologists). The group meets twice a year and has done so for the last 30 years. There has never been any outside funding and there is no external pressure to produce. At each meeting half the members give talks and most of the discussions focus on the similarities and differences in how the different disciplines study human behavior.

Although there have been no joint products involving the whole group, there has been quite a bit of bilateral collaboration (in my case, Frey & Stroebe, 1980, 1981; Stroebe & Frey, 1980, 1982; Stroebe & Meyer, 1982). Furthermore, the group has left a deep impact on how each of us approaches his own discipline. Most often, this influence resulted in group members incorporating theoretical concepts from one of the other disciplines into their own theoretical thinking.

To give two examples, Bruno Frey, a political economist, began integrating the idea that extrinsic motivators can ruin intrinsic motivation into economic theory. Frey (1997) challenged traditional economic theory by arguing that people did not act in expectation of monetary gain alone, and that higher monetary compensation as well as regulations could make people less committed to their work. More recently, Frey and Stutzer (2002) demonstrated how economic and political institutions can affect human well-being and used ratings of life satisfaction and happiness as a measure to assess economic interventions.

In my own work, I have been greatly influenced by Olson's (1965) theory of collective action, and in particular his theoretical analysis of the reasons why the production of public goods increases the temptation to free ride (Stroebe & Frey, 1982). I used these theoretical ideas (of which I became aware at a meeting of ISAG) to account for motivation losses in group productivity (e.g., Arnscheid, Diehl, & Stroebe, 1987; Stroebe & Frey, 1982). It was this theory, which stimulated my interest in brainstorming as a collective action characterized by substantial productivity loss (e.g., Diehl & Stroebe, 1987). In my research in health psychology, the economic perspective motivated me to pay particular attention to changes in the incentive structure (e.g., price of alcohol and cigarettes; seatbelt laws) as a viable method to reduce health-impairing behavior patterns. I cannot judge whether this interdisciplinary interaction has increased the creativity of my research. However, the exposure to research and theories from other social science disciplines and from philosophy has certainly motivated me to question some of the preconceived notions of my discipline. Furthermore, some of the theories from these neighboring disciplines turned out to be extremely useful for the analysis of social psychological problems.

CONCLUSIONS

There are too many differences between my two examples of interdisciplinary collaboration to allow clear-cut conclusions. These examples do suggest, however, that interdisciplinary collaboration is no panacea for increasing creativity. In the normal course of interdisciplinary research, where the collaboration is often forced on researchers by granting agencies or university administrators, the interaction across disciplines is unlikely to result in a cross-fertilization of ideas.

Obviously, the absence of external pressures is not the only dimension on which my two examples differ. They also differ in the goals that motivated the interdisciplinary collaboration and in the similarity or dissimilarity of the disciplines involved. Thus, interdisciplinary collaboration in health psychology is often motivated by technical reasons. Psychologists collaborate with physicians because physicians have access to patient populations and to medical technology beyond the reach of most psychology departments. Although there are psychologists who are trained in the use of medical techniques, as there are physicians trained in psychology, more often than not in such collaborations each side collects its own data to combine the two data sets later for the analyses that form the basis of joint publications. Each discipline hopes that use of the techniques of the other discipline will help it to validate its own constructs and the ultimate goal of the interdisciplinary collaboration is the production of output which allows such cross-validation. Although collaboration of the latter type can result in a synergetic advance in knowledge, it is unlikely to lead to much interdisciplinary cross-fertilization.

In contrast, the collaboration of our interdisciplinary working group ISAG is motivated by conceptual and theoretical interests. We try to find out how constructs and theories from other social sciences can be integrated with our own theoretical approaches. We are aware of the fact that we (often) study the same social behavior, but focus on different determinants and use different theoretical approaches. Thus, we are in a question-finding rather than question-answering stage of research. The fact that our disciplines are "related but slightly dissimilar" is another likely reason why our collaboration has stimulated interdisciplinary cross-fertilization. Our curiosity (and the lack of external pressures) motivates us to be open to other approaches, and the similar nature of our disciplines makes it easy to relate to and to assimilate constructs and theories from other disciplines into our own theoretical thinking.

Thus, although the example of ISAG shows that interdisciplinary cross-fertilization is possible, it also suggests that such interdisciplinary stimulation may require unique circumstances: a group of researchers from related disciplines, motivated purely by curiosity, and who exchange ideas without the expectation of tangible rewards. The fact that such groups are likely to be rare probably accounts for the fact that interdisciplinary research is no more creative than any other type of research.

REFERENCES

Amabile, T. M. (1983). *The social psychology of creativity*. New York: Springer.

Amabile, T. M. (1996). *Creativity in context*. Boulder, CO: Westview Press.

Arnscheid, R., Diehl, M., & Stroebe, W. (1997). Motivationsverluste in Gruppen: Ein empirischer Test einer theoretischen Integration. *Zeitschrift für sozialpsychologie, 28,* 241–250.

Deci, E. L., Koestner, R., & Ryan, R. R. (1999). A meta-analytic review of experiments examining the effects of extrinsic rewards on intrinsic motivation. *Psychological Bulletin, 125,* 627–668.

Diehl, M., & Stroebe, W. (1987). Productivity loss in brainstorming groups: Towards the solution of a riddle. *Journal of Personality and Social Psychology, 53,* 497–509.

Frey, B. S., & Stroebe, W. (1980). Ist das Modell des Homo Oeconomicus "unpsychologisch?" *Zeitschrift für die gesamte Staatswissenschaft, 136,* 82–97.

Frey, B. S., & Stroebe, W. (1981). Der Homo Oeconomicus ist entwicklungsfähig. *Zeitschrift für die gesamte Staatswissenschaft, 137,* 293–294.

Frey, B. S. (1997). *Not just for the money: An economic theory of personal motivation.* Cheltenham: Edgar Publishing

Frey, B. S., & Stutzer, A. (2002). *Happiness and economics.* Princeton, NJ: Princeton University Press

Olson, M. (1965). *The logic of collective action.* Cambridge, MA: Harvard University Press.

Simonton, D. K. (2002). *Great psychologists and their times.* Washington, DC: APA.

Stroebe, W. (2000). *Social psychology and health* (2nd ed.). Buckingham: Open University Press.

Stroebe, W., & Frey, B. (1980). In defense of economic man: Towards an integration of economics and psychology. *Schweizerische Zeitschrift für Volkswirtschaft und Statistik, 116,* 119–148.

Stroebe, W., & Frey, B. S. (1982). Self-interest and collective action: The economics and psychology of public goods. *British Journal of Social Psychology, 21,* 121–137.

Stroebe, W., & Meyer, W. (Eds.). (1982). *Social psychology and economics.* Leicester: British Psychological Society.

Coherence in Human Experience and Psychological Science

Robin R. Vallacher
Florida Atlantic University

Andrzej Nowak
University of Warsaw

Social psychology is a highly diverse area of scientific inquiry that has left no stone unturned in its attempt to capture the nuances of human experience. The field's wide-ranging agenda is commendable, but it has had the unintended effect of promoting a highly fragmented discipline. With a topical landscape ranging from cardiovascular processes to inter-group relations, it's not surprising that the field is populated by an untold number of disconnected mini-theories and equally independent research strategies. The lack of theoretical and paradigmatic coherence has generated concern from several quarters in recent years. But lamenting this state of affairs is one thing, and fixing it is quite another. Is it possible to impose theoretical integration on the complexity and vagaries of human social experience? If so, what should such a theory look like?

CRITERIA FOR THEORETICAL COHERENCE

For a comprehensive theory of social psychology to "work," it must satisfy several requirements. To begin with the obvious, such an account must identify principles that are common to different topics and levels of personal and social reality. Are there processes common to, say, social judgment and societal transition? Can moods and groups be understood with respect to shared properties and investigated with similar methods and tools? Beyond finding common ground within psychology, a truly comprehensive theory would link social psychology with other areas of science. Bridges with sociology and neuroscience would be nice, but identifying clear links to distant domains—physics, chemistry, biology, and so forth—would be all the better. Do phenomena in the natural sciences operate in accord with principles that are manifest as well in human thought and action? Finally, a comprehensive account must retain sufficient precision to account for the variance in human social experience. Sweeping analogies and metaphors are fine for pop accounts and can serve as useful heuristics to jump-start research activity, but ultimately any theory lives or dies by its ability to predict and explain specific phenomena in specific contexts. Can an account sufficiently general to account for the behavior of fireflies and human brains capture the nuances and idiosyncrasies of subjective experience in diverse interpersonal and cultural contexts?

By these standards, constructing a comprehensive account of social psychology represents a daunting task, to say the least. Conventional wisdom has it, after all, that science necessarily entails a trade-off between generality and precision—grand theories are geared for illuminating the big picture, not specific instances, and the details of individual phenomena can often be framed in terms of mutually inconsistent higher order theories. And one could argue—as many have (cf. Gergen, 1994)—that the unique subject matter of social psychology requires a different approach from that employed in other areas of science, or even renders it opaque to scientific understanding altogether. Human functioning is certainly unique, even within the animal kingdom. We have much in common with other animals with respect to basic biological processes, but some of our psychological capacities and proclivities place us in a distinct category vis-à-vis other organisms. It's understandable, then, that theories in social psychology tend to be similarly unique, invoking constructs and principles that often have little overlap with those invoked to explain the psychology of other species. No one, for example, has looked for dog or chimp counterparts to self-esteem maintenance, mortality salience, thought suppression, or foot-in-the-door strategies. From this perspective, human social psychology is a distinctive enterprise with relatively few bridges to other disciplines.

THE RELEVANCE OF DYNAMICAL SYSTEMS

Until fairly recently, this resigned assessment might have been accepted by most people in the field as the final word on the matter. But recent adaptations of nonlinear dynamical systems to social psychological phenomena suggest that it is indeed possible to satisfy the parallel constraints of generality, precision, and human uniqueness in theory construction. A special issue of *Personality and Social Psychology Review* (Vallacher, Read, & Nowak, 2002), for example, developed the relevance of dynamical systems for diverse topics in the field and showcased a variety of specific methods for investigating this relevance. The dynamical perspective conceptualizes phenomena as sets of interconnected elements that evolve due to the mutual influences among the elements (cf. Strogatz, 2003). Research within this perspective focuses on describing the connections among a system's elements and investigating the system-level properties and behaviors that these connections promote.

Prior to the advent of the mathematical theory of nonlinear dynamical systems, the natural sciences typically assumed that the relations among elements could be approximately as linear. A linear relation simply means that a change in one element, represented as a variable, is directly proportional to changes in another element (variable). In causal terms, linearity means that the magnitude of the effect is proportional to the magnitude of the cause. The relations among variables in a linear system are also additive, so that one can decompose the system into separate and manageable parts, each of which can be analyzed independently. In a linear system, then, the whole is exactly equal to the sum of the parts.

The natural sciences were transformed in the 1980s by the realization that many phenomena do not conform to linear assumptions, but rather are more appropriately conceptualized as nonlinear dynamical systems. Nonlinearity means that the effects of changes in one variable are not reflected in a proportional manner in other variables. A variable may increase dramatically in magnitude with no corresponding change in the magnitude of another variable, for example, until a threshold is reached, beyond which even slight changes in the first variable can promote large changes in the second variable. In a nonlinear system, moreover, system-level behavior cannot be decomposed into separate additive influences. Rather, the relations among variables depend on the values of other variables in the system. So even if one's theoretical concern centers on the relation between two variables, one cannot ignore the influence of myriad other variables relevant to the phenomenon.

Because of these features, nonlinear systems are capable of far richer behavior than can be generated in linear systems. Even a system consisting of a few elements can display highly complex macro-level behavior when the interactions among elements are nonlinear as opposed to linear. Laser beams, fluid turbulence, the spread of infectious disease, stock-market cycles, epileptic seizures, and the synchronization of planetary orbits all derive from nonlinear relations among the respective elements in these systems. The spontaneous generation of macro-level properties and behavior from the internal workings of the system is referred to as *emergence* (cf. Holland, 1995; Strogatz, 2003). Emergence is reminiscent of pattern formation in Gestalt psychology and is captured by the familiar phrase, "the whole is greater than the sum of its parts." It reflects self-organization among system elements, such that each element adjusts to the current state of other elements without the influence of a higher order control mechanism.

A particularly interesting—and apparently quite ubiquitous—manifestation of emergence via self-organization is the spontaneous synchronization of elements that individually oscillate at different frequencies (Strogatz, 2003). Thousands of fireflies, for instance, will spontaneously synchronize their individual flashing rhythms, producing a single swarm-level rhythm that can last for hours, much to the delight of onlookers and the interest of scientists. The sudden and spontaneous coordination of individual elements into a coherent system-level pattern represents a universal property of nonlinear systems that underlies otherwise distinct phenomena, providing an important link between different areas of science (e.g., biology, physics, economics, neuroscience). The synchronized flashing of fireflies, for example, seems quite different from the synchronized firing of neurons that takes place during learning and that gives rise to conscious attention (cf. Tononi & Edelman, 1998), but in formal respects they both represent the tendency for the elements of a system to become coordinated and promote the emergence of system-level properties and behavior.

TOWARD A DYNAMICAL SOCIAL PSYCHOLOGY

In principle, it's easy to reframe social psychological processes in dynamical terms. Human experience qualifies as a complex system, in that any facet of experience can be analyzed with respect to myriad genetic, hormonal, familial, situational, dispositional, and cultural causes. And because these factors rarely operate as main effects but rather interact with one another over time to promote an ever-changing trajectory of experience, social psychological phenomena are open to investigation as nonlinear dynamical systems. The earliest formulations of social psychological issues were remarkably prescient in this regard. Such pioneers as James (1890), Cooley (1902), Mead (1934), Lewin (1936), and Asch (1946) all emphasized the multiplicity of interacting forces operating in individual minds and in social groups, the potential for sustained patterns of change resulting from such complexity, and the tendency for individuals and groups to strive for mental and interpersonal coherence.

The dynamical perspective, in fact, may prove *too* appealing for those seeking an integrative paradigm for social psychology. Such notions as self-organization, emergence, bifurcation, and chaos have an intuitive resemblance to many personal and interpersonal phenomena. It is tempting to note the penchant for spontaneous coordination of sentiments and actions in social groups, for example, or to suggest that attitudes emerge from the self-organization of specific thoughts. Although such intuitions are compelling, the success of the dynamical perspective will depend on the ability of this approach to go beyond metaphors to generate explicit theoretical statements and testable hypotheses. Because many of the methods developed to investigate the dynamic properties of complex systems were developed in other fields, it is not obvious how they should be adapted to the unique subject matter of social psychology.

This concern has abated in recent years as various research programs have generated means of implementing dynamical methods (see Vallacher et al., 2002). Some researchers use experimental methods to track the temporal trajectory of various processes, including social interaction, personality expression, mood, group dynamics, close relationships, attitude change, conformity, social judgment, and self-evaluation. These methods have been supplemented in some cases by analytical tools designed to identify the formal properties (e.g., complexity, equilibrium tendencies, coherence) of the observed dynamics.

For the most part, though, computer simulations provide the preferred means of investigating personal and interpersonal dynamics. Cellular automata and neural networks in particular have proven useful in modeling the emergence of global properties from the interactions of individual elements. With respect to intraindividual processes, elements typically represent components of the cognitive system (e.g., thoughts, items of information), and the global level represents such higher order phenomena as decisions, judgments, moods, and self-concepts. At higher levels of social reality, elements correspond to individuals or social groups that influence one another to promote the emergence of public opinion, social networks, cooperation in social dilemma situations, normative mating strategies, and societal transformation.

Some research programs have explicitly emphasized the commonality of formal properties across levels of social reality. The emergence and maintenance of self-concept (Nowak, Vallacher, Tesser, & Borkowski, 2000), for example, follow the same dynamical scenario as the emergence and stabilization of public opinion (Nowak, Szamrej, & Latané, 1990). In both cases, system-level coherence is achieved through the internal workings of the system without the need for a higher order control mechanism (e.g., a homunculus in the mind, a leader or an a priori value in society). Emergence via self-organization is a hallmark of nonlinear dynamics, and the expression of this tendency in mind and society cannot be modeled or observed within traditional approaches based on assumptions of additive relations and linear causality.

CONCLUSIONS

The promise of theoretical synthesis should be tempered with a note of caution. The dynamical perspective is new to social psychology and there are many topics and issues that have yet to be intensively investigated within this approach. In our own lab, such phenomena as self-regulation, emotion, personality, close relations, social influence, and social change have been analyzed in dynamical terms (cf. Nowak & Vallacher, 1998), but these attempts should be considered preliminary (and hopefully heuristic) forays at this point. The specific research strategies we and others have employed are certain to be modified to fit different agendas—and some may be supplanted by approaches that have yet to be envisioned—as the dynamical perspective gains ascendancy in the years to come.

Theory construction in social psychology can itself be viewed as a complex system, in which individual researchers influence one another over time in an attempt to achieve consensus on the nature of human experience. It is worth noting in this regard that despite the progressive coherence that evolves by virtue of self-organization, complex systems rarely attain complete integration. Cellular automata models of both society and self-concept tend to produce differentiated as opposed to unified structures, for example, and neural network models of mental and social dynamics often reveal multiple modes of satisfying parallel constraints, each providing a distinct equilibrium that vies for prepotency in mind and society. From this perspective, it is unreasonable to expect a field as multifaceted as social psychology to reach a stable equilibrium, with an immutable set of principles defining the diverse nuances of personal and interpersonal function. Complex systems are inherently dynamic, continually evolving and undergoing transformations in response to incoming information and outside influences. So although we anticipate dynamical principles and methods emerging as the paradigmatic foundation for social psychological science, the field is likely to display repeated episodes of disassembly and reconfiguration with respect to specific theories and research strategies in the years to come. Such a trajectory is ironic testament to the viability and generality of the dynamical perspective on human experience.

REFERENCES

Asch, S. E. (1946). Forming impressions of personalities. *Journal of Abnormal and Social Psychology, 41,* 258–290.

Cooley, C. H. (1902). *Human nature and the social order.* New York: Scribner.

Gergen, K. J. (1994). *Realities and relationships: Soundings in social construction.* Cambridge, MA: Harvard University Press.

Holland, J. H. (1995). *Emergence: From chaos to order.* Reading, MA: Addison-Wesley.

James, W. (1890). *Principles of psychology.* New York: Holt.

Lewin, K. (1936). *Principles of topological psychology.* New York: McGraw-Hill.

Mead, G. H. (1934). *Mind, self, and society.* Chicago: University of Chicago Press.

Nowak, A., Szamrej, J., & Latané, B. (1990). From private attitude to public opinion: A dynamic theory of social impact. *Psychological Review, 97,* 362–376.

Nowak, A., & Vallacher, R. R. (1998). *Dynamical social psychology.* New York: Guilford Publications.

Nowak, A., Vallacher, R. R., Tesser, A., & Borkowski, W. (2000). Society of self: The emergence of collective properties in self-structure. *Psychological Review, 107,* 39–61.

Strogatz, S. (2003). *Sync: The emerging science of spontaneous order.* New York: Hyperion Books.

Tononi, G., & Edelman, G. M. (1998). Consciousness and complexity. *Science, 282,* 1846–1851.

Vallacher, R. R., Read, S. J., & Nowak, A. (Eds.). (2002). The dynamical perspective in social psychology. *Personality and Social Psychology Review, 6*(special issue).

11

Social Psychology Deserves Better: Marketing the Pivotal Social Science

Abraham P. Buunk

University of Groningen

In modern terms, social psychology has a marketing problem. Social psychology deals with human social behavior, and with the cognitions, motivation, and emotions related with this behavior. As human behavior is to a large extent social behavior, in the ideal world, social psychology should be *the* pivotal social science, and should be widely known for its importance and relevance. But it is far from that. I have noticed that people in the media, business, politics, and in many other disciplines usually do not know what social psychology is. That the nonexistent discipline of mass psychology seems better known than social psychology tells something about the way we promoted our field. The fact that social psychology is so poorly known is the more noteworthy because in reality social psychology is already the pivotal social science that has made many bridges to other disciplines. Even many social psychologists may not know that in such seemingly remote fields—including movement science, marketing, leisure science, preventive medicine, geography, and gerontology—social psychological theories, in particular the theory of planned behavior (Ajzen, 1991), are often self-evidently used. To give just one example: When I was collaborating with economists, I discovered to my surprise that Caryl Rusbult's (1987) investment model—which I mainly knew from the relationship literature—was one of the major theories in the area of relationship marketing to explain consumer loyalty (Willenborg, 2001). This model assumes that commitment to a relationship, and therefore also consumer loyalty, are determined by three factors: high *satisfaction* (e.g., when the relationship has high rewards and low costs), low quality of *alternatives* (e.g., the perception of few attractive alternative partners), and high *investment size* (e.g., having invested time and energy in the relationship). In general, working in such divergent fields as organizational psychology and health psychology, I have been surprised over and over again by the applied value of basic, even simple, social psychological notions such as social exchange and social comparison (e.g., Buunk, Zurriaga, Gonzalez-Roma, & Subirats, 2003; Ybema, Kuijer, Buunk, DeJong, & Sanderman, 2001).

Why then, is social psychology so poorly known? One reason is that most people do not seem to have a natural and easy schema to grasp the meaning of social psychology. The concept of clinical psychology is much more easily grasped because it deals with disturbed people. The concept of gerontology is much more easily grasped than because it deals with "old" people. The concept of marketing is much more easily grasped because it deals with advertising. For someone not knowing what social psychologists do, a definition of social psychology may seem so all-encompassing that it would be hard to understand where social psychology begins and where it ends. Moreover, when people do understand what social psychology is, they are usually interested in precisely those issues that today's social psychologists often shun, such as how people behave in masses, what makes someone charismatic, why people want to commit suicide for political reasons, why people abuse close others, whether anorexia is caused by the media, and why people nowadays seem to be less polite and rule-abiding than in the past. Of course, social psychologists can say something on such issues on the basis of experimental findings, but others outside our discipline, and particularly journalists, usually like to hear how these processes work in the real world.

SOCIAL BEHAVIOR IN CONTEXT

Solving the marketing problem requires more than just "selling" social psychology better, as, in part, the marketing problem reflects an identity problem. Social psychology could make the bold claim of being the pivotal social science studying the nature and determinants of social behavior in a variety of contexts. However, it now seems that many aspects of social behavior— such as aggression, conflicts in groups, obedience, or the bystander effect— either have disappeared or have become identified with other disciplines, while social psychology has moved mainly in the direction of the cognitive perspective. One may wonder whether that is a real problem, and whether one could and should prevent it. But the risk is real that when the current trend continues, social psychology may eventually end up as a mere footnote in the neurosciences. If social psychologists want to market their discipline they need not only to focus more on social behavior, but also to study this behavior in what are usually referred to as "applied" fields. By doing this, people outside the field will find it easier to identify what social psychology's contributions may be.

That social psychology could be a completely different enterprise than the one we see today manifested in North America and Western Europe became very obvious to me when I recently visited for the first time the Spanish Conference on Social Psychology. It was as if I were visiting a conference of a different discipline. There were 18 themes at this conference, only one of which dealt with what would include most themes at a "standard" European Association of Experimental Social Psychology (EAESP), Society for Experimental Social Psychology (SESP), or Society for Personality and Social Psychology (SPSP) conference, that is, "basic psychosocial processes." Although 2 of the other themes, that is, group psychology, and prejudice, racism, and discrimination, would in part, although in a much more basic fashion, also be recognizable at a "standard" social psychological conference, all the other 15 themes would hardly be recognizable at such a conference. Among just the major examples are the psychology of politics, collective behavior, and social movements; the social psychology of communication and of new communication technologies; legal psychology; social psychology of the family; social psychology of education; community psychology; social psychology of tourism, sports, and consumption; social psychology of organizations; and environmental psychology. Although the *Handbook of Social Psychology* (Gilbert, Fiske, & Lindzey, 1998) may suggest otherwise, research in most of these areas is usually not considered to belong to the core of social psychology.

APPLIED IS BASIC

Of course, the big risk of expanding social psychology to all kinds of applied fields is that problem-oriented and descriptive approaches become dominant, and theoretical depth is lost. However, social psychology is unique in that it can combine—and often has combined—theoretical and methodological rigor with societal relevance. That is basically what Kurt Lewin envisaged. I am not arguing in favor of more applied or problem-oriented research. I think that an erroneous assumption in social psychology is that basic research is that what is done in the laboratory, and that what is done in the field is "applied." What I favor is to study social psychological processes in a variety of fields and populations other than undergraduate students, not primarily to solve social problems, but to understand better how such processes work. There is nothing more basic about how social exchange processes occur among undergraduates in a laboratory setting than social exchange in the relationships of cancer patients. There is nothing more applied in studying how social comparison processes influence the development of burnout than in studying how undergraduates react when they see another student performing better. It is even more basic to examine how couples face the threat of extramarital relationships than how undergraduate students who just have entered a relationship respond to an unattached attractive person of the opposite sex. In fact, research in applied settings may often lead to new theoretical insights. For example, it has been noted that so-cial comparison research has obtained a major impetus from "applied" re-search on social comparison processes occurring among people facing serious health threats (Buunk, Gibbons, & Reis-Bergan, 1997).

INDIVIDUAL DIFFERENCES

Although social psychology could be more firmly embedded in various "ap-plied" fields, it can only become the pivotal social science when it also incorpo-rates individual differences. Despite Kurt Lewin's notion that behavior is a function of the person and the environment, social psychology has always had a strongly situational bias. But people outside the field often spontaneously as-sume that individual differences exist in all types of social behavior, from ag-gression to conformity, from prosocial behavior to social comparison, and simply don't "buy" the often implicit message of social psychologists that the situation explains it all. And they are right: Social psychology cannot flourish without attention for individual differences. For example, through my collab-oration with personality psychologists I have learned that neuroticism, a vari-able social psychologists generally do not like, strongly affects many social psychological processes, such as jealousy (Buunk, 1981), the effects of social comparison (Buunk, Van der Zee, & Van Yperen, 2001; Van der Zee, Buunk, & Sanderman, 1998), and the effects of social exchange (Ybema, Kuijer, Buunk, DeJong, & Sanderman, 2001). Neuroticism seems to reflect largely a fear of being excluded from the group, and therefore is very relevant for social psy-chology (as are other personality factors such as extraversion). As another ex-ample of the importance of individual differences, recently, Rick Gibbons and I developed a scale for social comparison orientation (Buunk & Gibbons, 2005), and now we are finding not only that this moderates the effects of social comparison, but that various classic effects such as the effect of attitude-simi-larity on attraction (Michinov & Michinov, 2001) are very different, or even re-versed for those high in social comparison orientation.

AN EVOLUTIONARY META-THEORY

Last but not least, people outside the discipline are often confused by the plethora of theories and findings, and the marketing of social psychology would be much easier when it becomes an integrated science with the explicit metaperspective of the theory of evolution. That is not the same as just adapt-ing current evolutionary psychology, a discipline that has focussed too exclu-sively on sex differences, and has been severely criticized for many reasons. One of the most worrisome of these is erroneously applying the theory of evo-lution, and using simplistic adaptationist scenarios (e.g., De Waal, 2001). Nev-ertheless, the theory of evolution can teach us more about how to understand the background of many phenomena that we are observing. To give a few examples from the area of social comparison, an evolutionary perspective has the potential to provide a *meta-theory* specifying why social comparison would be important, and to integrate many seemingly contradictory findings. For example, as Gilbert and his colleagues have suggested, assessing one's status in the group would be the core goal of social comparison activity (e.g., Gilbert, Price, & Allan, 1995). We have tried to demonstrate that, for instance, the tendency of depressed people to view themselves as equal rather than superior to others may be interpreted from an evolutionary perspective that assumes that depression basically stems from a perception of an involuntary low status (Buunk & Brenninkmeijer, 2000). Beach and Tesser (2000) suggested that the mechanisms outlined in the self-evaluation model (SEM) developed as elaborated mechanisms to prevent competition in groups on the same dimensions and to enhance cohesion in the group. According to this perspective, the tendency to "bask in reflected glory" might have evolved to ensure that the self is drawn to others who are producing valuable products and resources.

CONCLUSIONS

Social psychology concerns what makes us essentially human: our social behavior. Although social psychology has influenced numerous disciplines, including health psychology, marketing, and movement science, even many academics, let alone the general public, do not know what social psychology is. A broad social psychology that again includes research in all "applied" areas, acknowledges individual differences, and explicitly adopts an evolutionary perspective could eventually become be recognized as the pivotal social scientific discipline.

REFERENCES

Ajzen, I. (1991). The theory of planned behavior. *Organizational Behavior and Human Decision Processes, 50,* 179–211.

Beach, S. R. H., & Tesser, A. (2000). Self-evaluation maintenance and evolution: some speculative notes. In J. Suls & L. Wheeler (Eds.), *Handbook of social comparison: Theory and research* (pp. 123–140). New York: Kluwer.

Buunk, B. P., & Gibbons, F. X. (2005). Social comparison orientation: A new perspective on those who do, and those who don't compare with others. In S. Guimond (Ed.), *Social comparison processes and levels of analysis.* Cambridge, UK: Cambridge University Press.

Buunk, B. P. (1981). Jealousy in sexually open marriages. *Alternative Lifestyles, 4,* 357–372.

Buunk, B. P., & Brenninkmeijer, V. (2000). Social comparison processes among depressed individuals: Evidence for the evolutionary perspective on involuntary subordinate strategies? In L. Sloman & P. Gilbert (Eds.), *Subordination and defeat: An evolutionary approach to mood disorders and their therapy* (pp. 147–164). Mahwah, NJ: Lawrence Erlbaum Associates.

Buunk, B. P., Gibbons, F. X., & Reis-Bergan, M. (1997). Social comparison in health and illness: An overview. In B. P. Buunk & F. X. Gibbons (Eds.), *Health, coping and well-being: Perspectives from social comparison theory* (pp. 1–23). Mahwah, NJ: Lawrence Erlbaum Associates.

Buunk, B. P., Van der Zee, K. I., & Van Yperen, N. W. (2001). Neuroticism and social comparison orientation as moderators of affective responses to social comparison at work. *Journal of Personality, 69,* 745–763.

Buunk, B. P., Zurriaga, R., Gonzalez-Roma, V., & Subirats, M. (2003). Engaging in upward and downward comparisons as a determinant of relative deprivation at work: A longitudinal study. *Journal of Vocational Behavior, 62,* 370–388.

De Waal, F. B. M. (2001). The inevitability of evolutionary psychology and the limitations of adaptationism: Lessons from the other primates. *International Journal of Comparative Psychology, 14*(1–2), 25–42.

Gibbons, F. X., & Buunk, B. P. (1999). Individual differences in social comparison: The development of a scale of social comparison orientation. *Journal of Personality and Social Psychology, 76,* 129–142.

Gilbert, D. T., Fiske, S. T., & Lindzey, G. (Eds.). (1998). *The handbook of social psychology* (Vols. 1 & 2). Boston: McGraw-Hill.

Gilbert, P., Price, J., & Allan, S. (1995). Social comparison, social attractiveness and evolution: How might they be related? *New Ideas in Psychology, 13,* 149–165.

Michinov, E., & Michinov, N. (2001). The similarity hypothesis: A test of the moderating role of social comparison orientation. *European Journal of Social Psychology, 31,* 549–556.

Rusbult, C. E. (1987). A longitudinal study test of the investment model: The development (and deterioration) of satisfaction and commitment in heterosexual involvements. *Journal of Personality and Social Psychology, 45,* 101–117.

Willenborg, G. (2001). *An integrated conceptual model of cooperative consumer relationships in services: development and test.* Capelle a/d IJssel: Labyrint.

Van der Zee, K., Buunk, B. P., & Sanderman, R. (1998). Neuroticism and reactions to social comparison information among cancer patients. *Journal of Personality, 66,* 175–194.

Ybema, J. F., Kuijer, R. G., Buunk, B. P., DeJong, G. M., & Sanderman, R. (2001). Depression and perceptions of inequity among couples facing cancer. *Personality and Social Psychology Bulletin, 27,* 3–13.

PART 3

Bridges With Biology,
Neuroscience,
and Cognitive Science

INTRODUCTION

Throughout the history of social psychology, we can witness continuity and change in the degree to which various bridges are being crossed. Changes are especially pronounced for bridges with biology and neuroscience. Although social psychology has been strongly connected to the study of biological systems, to animal research, and to the brain research, the popularity of these linkages fluctuated quite dramatically. However, in the past decade—sometimes referred to as "the decade of the brain"—we witness a remarkable increase in empirical studies that link socially shaped cognitions and emotions to the biological or neurological system, often using functional Magnetic Resonance Imaging (fMRI) techniques or physiological measures such as blood pressure or heart-rate variability. As a result of these studies, there is increasing consensus that various biological and neurological processes influence social processes and that various social processes influence biological and neurological processes. Such empirical efforts may touch on important scientific problems, such as the mind–body problem or the nature versus nurture controversy. Bridges with animal research hold promise but could be reenergized, because important questions that are hard to study with humans could perhaps be explored in animal studies. Bridges of social psychology and cognitive psychology have received particular emphasis in the 1980s, with the emergence of social cognition as a new area of theory and research. Twenty years later we see that social cognition is not only a central area within social psychology, but also increasingly integrated with most areas of research in social psychology. As the various essays show, social psychology is essential to cognition and biology ("mind and body") just as cognition and biology are essential to social psychology.

12

A Bridge Linking Social Psychology and the Neurosciences

John T. Cacioppo
University of Chicago

Gary G. Berntson
Ohio State University

SOCIAL NEUROSCIENCE

Social psychology is the scientific study of social behavior, with an emphasis on understanding the individual in a social context. Accordingly, social psychologists study a diverse range of topics ranging from *intrapersonal processes* shaped by or in response to others, such as the self, attitudes, emotions, social identity, normative beliefs, social perception, social cognition, and interpersonal attraction; to *interpersonal processes* such as persuasion and social influence, verbal and nonverbal communication, interpersonal relationships, altruism, and aggression; to group processes such as social facilitation, cooperation and competition, equity, leadership, outgroup biases, group decision making, and organizational behavior. The dominant dependent measure in social psychology has been verbal reports, an approach that placed an emphasis on clever experimental design and inductive inference (Reis & Judd, 2000). With the advent of social cognition several decades ago, chronometric measures, often used in conjunction with experimental techniques such as priming, were added to the methodological armamentarium. Importantly, social cognition also brought with it a conceptual framework for asking questions about the representation of and information processing components underlying social psychological phenomena.

Over the past decade, yet another approach, conceptual framework for asking questions, and family of measures which collectively fall under the heading of social neuroscience, have been added to the repertoire (Cacioppo & Berntson, 1992; Cacioppo et al., 2002; Ochsner & Lieberman, 2001). The emergence of social neuroscience is interesting in light of the fact that biological and social psychological approaches to human behavior began as allied areas at their outset. All human behavior, at some level, is biological, but this is not to say that biological reductionism yields a simple, singular, or satisfactory explanation for complex behaviors, or that molecular forms of representation provide the only or best level of analysis for understanding human behavior. Molar constructs such as those developed by the social sciences provide a means of understanding highly complex activity without needing to specify each individual action of the simplest components, thereby providing an efficient means of describing the behavior of a complex system (Cacioppo, Berntson, Sheridan, & McClintock, 2000). The vacuous application of overly simplistic and untestable biological causes (e.g., instincts) to explain every social behavior led, by the middle of the 20th century, to a deep schism and enduring suspicion (see review by Berntson & Cacioppo, 2000). Biopsychology began to emphasize cellular processes, neural substrates, and production mechanisms for behavior, largely ignoring or rejecting mentalist and functionalist theories, whereas social psychology emphasized multivariate systems, situational influences, and practical applications (see Allport, 1947). These divergences resulted in very different subject samples, research traditions, and technical demands, leaving what some regard as an impassable abyss between social and biological approaches (Scott, 1991).

Although autonomic and electromyographic measures appeared in the social psychological literature, they generally were used either as interchangeable indices of arousal or as a way of validating self-report measures. About half a century ago, for instance, Rankin and Campbell (1955) measured the electrodermal response of Caucasian participants to a Caucasian or African American experimenter as an index of arousal and thus, in this context, racial prejudice. Autonomic assessments of arousal in normal states is based on a theory in which autonomic activity ranges in a unitary fashion from low to high levels—a theory of autonomic organization and function that has been disconfirmed (Berntson, Cacioppo, & Quigley, 1991). On the other hand, when autonomic measures validated simpler social psychological measurements, the more difficult and costly autonomic assessments could be discarded in favor of the simpler, less expensive verbal assessments. Although somatovisceral measures occasionally were identified that provided information not easily available using self-reports (e.g., Cacioppo & Petty, 1981; Tomaka, Blascovich, Kelsey, & Leitten, 1993), outdated concepts of arousal remained the dominant biological constructs in social psychology, as is evident from a perusal of the subject indexes of the *Handbook of Social Psychology* (Gilbert, Fiske, & Lindzey, 1998; Lindzey & Aronson, 1985).

The past decade has seen something of a rapprochement between biological and social levels of analysis, in part because localized brain regions have been associated with social psychological processes (e.g., Cacioppo &

Berntson, 1992; Cacioppo et al., 2002; Klein & Kihlstrom, 1998; Ochsner & Lieberman, 2001). In past decades, studies of the neurophysiological structures and functions associated with psychological events were limited primarily to animal models, postmortem examinations, and observations of the occasional unfortunate individual who suffered trauma to or disorders of the brain. Developments in electrophysiological recording, brain imaging, and neurochemical techniques within the neurosciences have increasingly made it possible to investigate the role of neural structures and processes in normal and disordered thought in humans. Contemporary studies of racial prejudice, for instance, have utilized facial electromyography, event-related brain potentials, and functional magnetic resonance imaging (fMRI) to investigate specific, implicit cognitive and affective processing stages. Moreover, advances in ambulatory recording and its combination with experience sampling methodologies have removed the tether of the laboratory to permit in vivo investigations of biology and social behavior.

WHY TRY TO BRIDGE THE SOCIAL AND NEUROSCIENCES?

Contemporary work has demonstrated that theory and methods in the neurosciences can constrain and inspire social psychological hypotheses, foster experimental tests of otherwise indistinguishable theoretical explanations, and increase the comprehensiveness and relevance of social psychological theories. Several principles from social neuroscience further suggest that understanding social behavior requires the joint consideration of social, cognitive, and biological levels of analysis in an integrated fashion. The principle of *multiple determinism*, for instance, specifies that a target event specified at one level of organization, but especially at molar or abstract (e.g., social) levels of organization, can have multiple antecedents within or across levels of organization (Cacioppo & Berntson, 1992). At the biological level, for instance, we have identified the contribution of individual differences in cardiac sympathetic reactivity to people's susceptibility to illness, while on the social level, we have noted the important role of exposure to interpersonal stressors in daily life (Cacioppo et al., 1998). Both operate, and our understanding of immunity and health is incomplete if either a biological or a social perspective is excluded.

A corollary to this principle, termed the *corollary of proximity*, is that the mapping between elements specified across levels of organization becomes more complex (e.g., many-to-many) as the number of unspecified intervening levels of organization increases (Cacioppo & Berntson, 1992). An important implication of this corollary is that the likelihood of complex and potentially obscure mappings increases as one skips levels of organization. The effect of stress on health, for example, has been a heavily researched topic for over a century. Early studies were largely characterized by epidemiological approaches, and the outcomes correlational and probabilistic. This provided a somewhat fuzzy mapping at best, especially at the level of the individual. That fuzziness was attributable to a number of then-unknown intervening variables associated with intermediate levels of organization lying between the psychological (stress) and the health outcome. These variables include an individual's diathesis (genetic or constitutional predisposition for particular maladies), as well as the neuroendocrine and immunological responses to the stress, which serve as important mediators of the relations between stress and health outcomes. Understanding the more proximal mappings between psychological stress and physiological (neuroendocrine and immunological) states and between physiological states and health outcomes can sharpen and inform the broader mapping between stress and health. Similarly, cognitive neuroscience is an important companion to social neuroscience for numerous reasons, among them that it helps bridge intervening levels of organization.

The principle of *nonadditive determinism* specifies that properties of the whole are not always readily predictable from the properties of the parts (Cacioppo & Berntson, 1992). Consider an illustrative study by Morgan et al. (2002). The dopamine D2 family of receptor binding potential is related to cocaine's reinforcing effects. Morgan et al. (2002) examined the D2 receptors in dominant and subordinate male cynomolgus monkeys when they were individually housed and, later, when they were socially housed. No differences were found in D2 family receptor binding potential in the monkeys when they were individually housed. After only 3 months of being socially housed, however, a dominance hierarchy emerged, and those at the top of the dominance hierarchy showed a significant increase in D2 family receptor binding potential, whereas the submissive animals showed no change in dopaminergic characteristics. More interestingly, behavioral testing further showed that dominant animals self-administered cocaine at levels comparable to saline— that is, the dominant animals acted as if cocaine had no reinforcing value— whereas subordinate monkeys reliably self-administered more cocaine at doses of 0.01 and 0.03 mg/kg than saline. The importance of this study derives from its demonstration of how the vulnerability to the abuse-related effects of cocaine is not predictable from dopaminergic characteristics of individual animals nor of dominance hierarchies alone, but rather they become apparent only after a dominance hierarchy emerged in socially housed groups. A strictly physiological (or social) analysis, regardless of the sophistication of the measurement technology, may not have revealed the orderly relationship that exists.

Finally, the principle of *reciprocal determinism* specifies that there can be mutual influences between microscopic (e.g., biological) and macroscopic (e.g., social) factors in determining behavior (Cacioppo & Berntson, 1992). For example, the handling of rat pups alters maternal behavior toward the pups and affects the structure and reactivity of the hypothalamic pituitary adrenocortical system (Meaney, Sapolsky, & McEwen, 1985). These early influences on the stress-hormone system, in turn, affect the pups' reactions to stressors and in later life and promote similar maternal behavior toward *their* pups (Meaney et al., 1996). That is, the effects of social and biological processes can be reciprocal.

CONCLUSIONS

In the preceding paragraphs, we have discussed a few of the conceptual reasons for building bridges across the social and neurosciences. In many respects, we echo E. O. Wilson's (1998) argument that we are at a propitious moment in science where theoretical and empirical work to construct such bridges not only is possible but offers the possibility of more comprehensive theories of the human mind and behavior. In fact, the principles of multiple, nonadditive, and reciprocal determinism lead quite inextricably to the notion that interesting and complex aspects of the human mind and behavior may never be apparent by studying elements that are specified solely at the social (or biological) level of organization, as in scientific efforts that are limited to a single level of organization nonadditive and reciprocal effects slip away under the guise of error variance.

ACKNOWLEDGMENT

This research was supported by National Institute of Aging Program Project Grant No. PO1AG18911 and an award from the Templeton Foundation.

REFERENCES

Allport, G. W. (1947). Scientific models and human morals. *Psychological Review, 54,* 182–192.

Berntson, G. G., & Cacioppo, J. T. (2000). Psychobiology and social psychology: Past, present, and future. *Personality and Social Psychology Review, 4,* 3–15.

Berntson, G. G., Cacioppo, J. T., & Quigley, K. S. (1991). Autonomic determinism: The modes of autonomic control, the doctrine of autonomic space, and the laws of autonomic constraint. *Psychological Review, 98,* 459–487.

Cacioppo, J. T., & Berntson, G. G. (1992). Social psychological contributions to the decade of the brain: Doctrine of multilevel analysis. *American Psychologist, 47,* ·1019–1028.

Cacioppo, J. T., Berntson, G. G., Adolphs, R., Carter, C. S., Davidson, R. J., McClintock, M. K., McEwen, B. S., Meaney, M. J., Schacter, D. L., Sternberg, E. M., Suomi, S. S., & Taylor, S. E. (2002). *Foundations in social neuroscience.* Cambridge, MA: MIT Press.

Cacioppo, J. T., Berntson, G. G., Malarkey, W. B., Kiecolt-Glaser, J. K., Sheridan, J. F., Poehlmann, K. M., Burleson, M. H., Ernst, J. M., Hawkley, L. C., & Glaser, R. (1998). Autonomic, neuroendocrine, and immune responses to psychological stress: The reactivity hypothesis. *Annals of the New York Academy of Sciences, 840,* 664–673.

Cacioppo, J. T., Berntson, G. G., Sheridan, J. F., & McClintock, M. K. (2000). Multi-level integrative analyses of human behavior: Social neuroscience and the complementing nature of social and biological approaches. *Psychological Bulletin, 126,* 829–843.

Cacioppo, J. T., & Petty, R. E. (1981). Electromyograms as measures of extent and activity of information processing. *American Psychologist, 36,* 441–456.

Gilbert, D. T., Fiske, S. T., & Lindzey, G. (1998). *The handbook of social psychology* (4th ed.). Boston: McGraw Hill.

Klein, S. B., & Kihlstrom, J. F. (1998). On bridging the gap between social-personality psychology and neuropsychology. *Personality & Social Psychology Review, 2,* 228–242.

Lindzey, G., & Aronson, E. (1985). *The handbook of social psychology* (3rd ed.). New York: Random House.

Meaney, M. J., Bhatnagar, S., Larocque, S., McCormick, C. M., Shanks, N., Sharma, S., Smythe, J., Viau, V., & Plotsky, P. M. (1996). Early environment and the development of individual differences in the hypothalamic-pituitary-adrenal stress response. In C. R. Pfeffer (Ed.), *Severe stress and mental disturbance in children* (pp. 85–127). Washington, DC: American Psychiatric Press.

Meaney, M. J., Sapolsky, R. M., & McEwen, B. S. (1985). The development of the glucocorticoid receptor system in the rat limbic brain: II. An autoradiographic study. *Developmental Brain Research, 18,* 159–164.

Morgan, D., Grant, K. A., Gage, H. D., Mach, R. H., Kaplan, J. R., Prioleau, O., Nader, S. H., Buchheimer, N., Ehrenkaufer, R. L., & Nader, M. A. (2002). Social dominance in monkeys: Dopamine D2 receptors and cocaine self-administration. *Nature Neuroscience, 5,* 169–174.

Ochsner, K. N., & Lieberman, M. D. (2001). The emergence of social cognitive neuroscience. *American Psychologist, 56*(9), 717–734.

Rankin, R. E., & Campbell, D. T. (1955). Galvanic skin response to Negro and white experimenters. *Journal of Abnormal and Social Psychology, 51,* 30–33.

Reis, H. T., & Judd, C. M. (2000). *Handbook of research methods in social and personality psychology.* New York: Cambridge University Press.

Scott, T. R. (1991). A personal view of the future of psychology departments. *American Psychologist, 46,* 975–976.

Tomaka, J., Blascovich, J., Kelsey, R. M., & Leitten, C. L. (1993). Subjective, physiological, and behavioral effects of threat and challenge appraisal. *Journal of Personality and Social Psychology, 65,* 248–260.

Wilson, E. O. (1998). *Consilience: The unity of knowledge.* New York: Knopf.

13

The Emergence of the "Social" in Cognitive Neuroscience: The Study of Interacting Brains

Tania Singer

Institute of Cognitive Neuroscience, UCL, London

Chris D. Frith

Wellcome Department of Imaging Neuroscience, UCL, London

In the last few decades, cognitive neuroscience has considerably advanced our understanding of the relationship between the mind, the brain, and behavior. We now have a detailed picture of how our brain processes shape, color, and motion, recognizes objects, discriminates sounds, and process smells, as well as how the brain enables us to perform motor actions. Progress has also been made in the understanding of higher order cognitive functions, including short- and long-time memory processes, speech generation and recognition, and the executive functions involved in planning, multitasking, and self-monitoring. Neuroscientists, however, have tended to assume implicitly that understanding a single brain is sufficient to understand human behavior. Clearly, such an approach does not allow for the fact that humans are inherently social. Brains do not exist in isolation, and their basic function includes the expression of the social culture into which brains are born. It is likely that differences between our brains and the brains of apes and monkeys are associated with our outstanding skills in social cognition, such as our ability to represent and understand the beliefs, desires, and feelings of others.

THE EMERGENCE OF THE "SOCIAL" IN COGNITIVE NEUROSCIENCE

In the past few years the field of neuroscience has shown increased interest in the study of the affective and social brain. A new interdisciplinary field, *social-cognitive neuroscience*, has emerged from a union between classical cognitive neuroscience and social psychology. Its popularity is attested to by the number of conferences, special issues of journals, and books devoted to this topic (e.g., Adolphs, 2003; Frith & Wolpert, 2004; Ochsner & Lieberman, 2001).

The agenda of social cognitive neuroscience has been described as seeking to understand phenomena in terms of interactions between three levels: the social, the cognitive, and the neural (cf. Ochsner & Lieberman, 2001, p. 717 ff.).

Historically, the field of social psychology has focused on the investigation of one level, the influence of sociocultural factors on behavior. The level of cognitive processes was only added in the late 1970s, when the field of *social cognition* emerged as a subfield of social psychology. Strongly influenced by the information-processing approach in cognitive psychology, social cognition focused on the investigation of phenomena that could be studied with well-controlled laboratory experiments and explained by information-processing accounts. Person perception and stereotyping, causal attribution, and social inferences, as well as the study of the influence of emotion on cognition, represent typical topics.

The Scope of Social-Cognitive Neuroscience

Social-cognitive neuroscience has focused predominantly on the investigation of basic social abilities. Several functional imaging studies, for example, have investigated the neural correlates of attending, recognizing, and remembering *socially relevant stimuli* such as facial expressions of fear (Morris et al., 1996), attractiveness (O'Doherty et al., 2003), trustworthiness (Winston, Strange, O'Doherty, & Dolan, 2002), racial identity (Hart et al., 2000), and faces of fair and unfair players (Singer et al., 2004a), as well as more abstract cues indicative of biological motion in the form of body movements and gestures.

Another line of research has focused on our ability to have a *theory of mind* (e.g., Premack & Woodruff, 1978) or to *mentalize* (Frith & Frith, 2003), that is, to make attributions about mental states (desires, beliefs, intentions) of others based on complex behavioral cues. Recent imaging studies on normal healthy adults have used stories, cartoons, picture sequences, and animated geometric shapes that differed in the degree to which they represented the intentions, beliefs, and desires of others (for a review, see Gallagher & Frith, 2003). Another line of research has focused on the neural mechanism underlying our ability to imitate and represent the goals and intentions of others. Studies in humans and monkeys show that observing someone else's actions automatically activates neural systems underlying the production of our own actions (for a review, see Blakemore & Decety, 2001). Recently, this line of research has been extended to consider our ability to understand the *feelings and sensations* of others, that is, our ability to *empathize* (e.g., Gallese, 2003; Preston & de Waal, 2002). Thus, recent imaging studies investigated the brain activity associated with the imitation of and the mere observation of faces with different emotional expressions (Carr, Iacoboni, Dubeau, Mazziotta, & Lenzi, 2003), and the neural responses elicited by watching videos of faces with emotional expressions of disgust with responses induced by smelling aversive odors (Wicker et al., 2003), and have attempted to identify shared and unique networks elicited when feeling pain yourself or knowing that your partner (Singer et al., 2004b) or unfamiliar people whom you have learned to like or dislike (Singer et al., in press) are in pain.

Finally, social cognitive neuroscience has started to investigate moral and *social reasoning* in various ways. Moral reasoning is studied in *moral dilemma tasks* that involve situations in which all possible solutions to a given problem are associated with undesirable outcomes (Greene, Sommerville, Nystrom, Darley, & Cohen, 2001). Another line of research, closely linked to the emergent field of *neuroeconomics*, has focused on the study of social exchange and mutual cooperation using *social dilemma tasks*, such as the simultaneous and sequential Prisoners' Dilemma Game or the Ultimatum Game developed in the framework of game theory. These studies involve people playing games for monetary payoffs and elicit the use of different playing strategies, some selfish and some cooperative, and therefore allow for the investigation of social reasoning (working out what the other player will do; e.g., McCabe, Houser, Ryan, Smith, & Trouard, 2001), social emotions (emotional responses to fair and unfair play), and their interaction (e.g., Rilling et al., 2002; Sanfey, Rilling, Aronson, Nystrom, & Cohen, 2003; Singer et al., 2004a).

The Study of Social Interaction: From a Unidirectional to a Bidirectional Account

The importance of the studies on moral or social reasoning derives not so much from the results and insights they have produced as from the innovative paradigms that introduce realistic social interactions into the scanner environment. All of the studies using social dilemma paradigms involved subjects in the scanner playing interactive games with what they believed to be real persons situated outside the scanner. Similarly, the ability to mentalize as well as the feeling of social exclusion have been studied using other interactive games such as "rock, paper, scissors" (Gallagher, Jack, Roepstorff, & Frith, 2002) or a virtual ball-tossing game involving two virtual players in addition to the volunteer in the scanner (Eisenberger, Lieberman, & Williams, 2003).

Despite this introduction of "interactive mind paradigms," the present studies still adopt a unidirectional perspective. Thus, the goal of these studies has been to understand the effects of socially relevant stimuli on the mind of a single person. In contrast, the study of social interaction involves by definition a bidirectional perspective and is concerned with the question of how two minds shape each other mutually through reciprocal interactions. To understand interactive minds, we have to study how thoughts and feelings can be transferred from one mind to another. During communication we try to convey our thoughts and feelings so that someone else can build a representation of our thoughts and feelings in his or her own mind. The communication loop is closed when, in a second step, the person feeds back these representations to us. We can then compare our original thought with our representation of the other person's representation of our thought and attempt to correct that person's interpretation in case of a mismatch (neural hermeneutics; Frith, 2003). Delineation of these mechanisms is an important and promising goal for research in social cognitive neuroscience. This will have to be accompanied, however, by the development of new methods and paradigms, for example, force escalation (e.g., Shergill, Bays, Frith, & Wolpert, 2003), or the process of automatic "interactive alignment" during human dialogue (Garrod & Pickering, 2004). By recording simultaneously from two brains during dyadic verbal and nonverbal interactions of this kind it will be possible to measure the temporal interdependencies of brain activation and associated behavior (e.g., Montague et al., 2002).

CONCLUSIONS

We have sketched the development of the emerging field of social-cognitive neuroscience. There has already been rapid progress in terms of the range of different social phenomena that have been studied and in terms of the development of innovative experimental paradigms suitable for the scanning environment. However, this development needs to be grounded in established theories. Here social-cognitive neuroscience can profit from a closer collaboration with older neighboring disciplines, especially social and developmental psychology. Although the study of social interaction may be novel for the neurosciences, the social sciences have developed elaborated theories as well as reliable techniques for the study of dyadic interactions and their interdependencies. Moreover, social sciences with their complex theoretical accounts can help the field of social neuroscience to overcome its tendency for decontextualization and simplicity and, in the case of imaging research, to go beyond merely mapping the brain correlates of social phenomena. Theories about the role of controlled versus automatic as well as cognitive versus emotional processing for decision making can be tested by the use of sophisticated methods introduced by neuroscience, methods that permit new conclusions not easily drawn on the basis of self-report or other behavioral measures alone. For example, imaging methods can reveal automatic emotional activity elicited by the mere presentation of stimuli without the subject having to give any response (e.g., Singer et al., 2004a; 2004b; in press). In addition, knowledge about functional specialization of brain areas that primarily process social and emotional stimuli (amygdala, ventral striatum, orbito-frontal cortex) and others that primarily subserve cognitive operations (lateral prefrontal cortex) can help to answer questions about the relative contributions of cognitive and emotional processes for economic or social decision making. The understanding of two and more interacting brains with their emergent properties is clearly an endeavor in need of two and more interacting disciplines with the associated synergic effects.

ACKNOWLEDGMENTS

Preparation of this essay was supported by the German Academy of Natural Science Leopoldina Grant BMBF-LPD/9901/8-73 and the German Ministry of Education and Science as well as the Wellcome Trust.

REFERENCES

Adolphs, R. (2003). Cognitive neuroscience of human social behaviour. *Nat. Rev. Neurosci., 4,* 165–178.

Blakemore, S. J., & Decety, J. (2001). From the perception of action to the understanding of intention. *Nat. Rev. Neurosci., 2,* 561–567.

Carr, L., Iacoboni, M., Dubeau, M. C., Mazziotta, J. C., & Lenzi, G. L. (2003). Neural mechanisms of empathy in humans: A relay from neural systems for imitation to limbic areas. *Proceedings of the National Academy of Sciences, USA, 100,* 5497–5502.

Eisenberger, N. I., Lieberman, M. D., & Williams, K. D. (2003). Does rejection hurt? An fMRI study of social exclusion. *Science, 302,* 290–292.

Frith, C. D. (2003, June). *Neural hermeneutics: How brains interpret minds.* Presented at the 9th Annual Meeting of the Organization of Human Brain Mapping, New York.

Frith, U., & Frith, C. D. (2003). Development and neurophysiology of mentalizing. *Philosophical Transactions of the Royal Society, London, B, Biological Sciences, 358,* 459–473.

Frith, C., & Wopert, D. (2004). *The neuroscience of social interaction: Decoding, imitating, and influencing the actions of others.* Oxford: University Press.

Gallagher, H. L., & Frith, C. D. (2003). Functional imaging of "theory of mind." *Trends in Cognitive Science, 7,* 77–83.

Gallagher, H. L., Jack, A. I., Roepstorff, A., & Frith, C. D. (2002). Imaging the intentional stance in a competitive game. *Neuroimage, 16,* 814–821.

Gallese, V. (2003). The manifold nature of interpersonal relations: the quest for a common mechanism. *Philosophical Transactions of the Royal Society, London, B, Biological Sciences, 358,* 517–528.

Garrod, S., & Pickering, M. J. (2004). Why is conversation so easy? *Trends in Cognitive Science, 8,* 8–11.

Greene, J. D., Sommerville, R. B., Nystrom, L. E., Darley, J. M., & Cohen, J. D. (2001). An fMRI investigation of emotional engagement in moral judgment. *Science, 293,* 2105–2108.

Hart, A. J., Whalen, P. J., Shin, L. M., McInerney, S. C., Fischer, H., & Rauch, S. L. (2000). Differential response in the human amygdala to racial outgroup vs ingroup face stimuli. *Neuroreport, 11,* 2351–2355.

McCabe, K., Houser, D., Ryan, L., Smith, V., & Trouard, T. (2001). A functional imaging study of cooperation in two-person reciprocal exchange. *Proceedings of the National Academy of Sciences, USA, 98,* 11832–11835.

Montague, P. R., Berns, G. S., Cohen, J. D., McClure, S. M., Pagnoni, G., Dhamala, M., et al. (2002). Hyperscanning: Simultaneous fMRI during linked social interactions. *Neuroimage, 16,* 1159–1164.

Morris, J. S., Frith, C. D., Perrett, D. I., Rowland, D., Young, A. W., Calder, A. J., et al. (1996). A differential neural response in the human amygdala to fearful and happy facial expressions. *Nature, 383*, 812–815.

O'Doherty, J., Winston, J., Critchley, H., Perrett, D., Burt, D. M., & Dolan, R. J. (2003). Beauty in a smile: The role of medial orbitofrontal cortex in facial attractiveness. *Neuropsychologia, 41*, 147–155.

Ochsner, K. N., & Lieberman, M. D. (2001). The emergence of social cognitive neuroscience. *American Psychologist, 56*, 717–734.

Premack, D., & Woodruff, G. (1978). Does the chimpanzee have a theory of mind? *Behavioral and Brain Science, 1*, 515–526.

Preston, S. D., & de-Waal, F. B. M. (2002). Empathy: Its ultimate and proximate bases. *Behavioral and Brain Science, 25*, 1–72.

Rilling, J., Gutman, D., Zeh, T., Pagnoni, G., Berns, G., & Kilts, C. (2002). A neural basis for social cooperation. *Neuron, 35*, 395–405.

Sanfey, A. G., Rilling, J. K., Aronson, J. A., Nystrom, L. E., & Cohen, J. D. (2003). The neural basis of economic decision-making in the Ultimatum Game. *Science, 300*, 1755–1758.

Shergill, S. S., Bays, P. M., Frith, C. D., & Wolpert, D. M. (2003). Two eyes for an eye: The neuroscience of force escalation. *Science, 301*, 187.

Singer, T., Kiebel, S., Winston, J., Dolan, R. J., & Frith, C. D. (2004a). Brain responses to the acquired moral status of faces. *Neuron, 41*, 653–662.

Singer, T., Seymour, B., O'Doherty, J. P., Kaube, H., Dolan, R. J., & Frith, C. D. (2004b). Empathy for pain involves the affective but not sensory component of pain. *Science, 303*, 1157–1162.

Singer, T., Seymour, B., Stephan, K. E., O'Doherty, J., Dolan, R. J., & Frith, C. D. (in press). Empathic neural responses are modulated by the perceived fairness of others. *Nature.*

Wicker, B., Keysers, C., Plailly, J., Royet, J. P., Gallese, V., & Rizzolatti, G. (2003). Both of us disgusted in my insula: The common neural basis of seeing and feeling disgust. *Neuron, 40*, 655–664.

Winston, J. S., Strange, B. A., O'Doherty, J., & Dolan, R. J. (2002). Automatic and intentional brain responses during evaluation of trustworthiness of faces. *Nature Neuroscience, 5*, 277–283.

14

The Social Neuroscience of Empathy

Jean Decety
University of Washington

Sara D. Hodges
University of Oregon

Empathy is a complex psychological response in which observation, memory, knowledge, and reasoning are combined to yield insights into the thoughts and feelings of others (Ickes, 1997). There is broad agreement about two primary components of empathy: (1) an affective response to another person, which may (but not always) entail sharing that person's emotional state; and (2) a cognitive capacity to take the other person's perspective (e.g., Batson, 1991; Hodges & Wegner, 1997). Definitional variations on these general statements abound. However, virtually all empathy researchers agree that empathy requires making a link between the self and other, but without confusing the self and other. With this point in mind, our goal in this chapter is to bridge social psychological studies of empathy with findings from neuroscience in order to identify the fundamental neural mechanisms that could serve as the basis for empathy.

Our task is not to identify a single neural/cognitive module for empathy; no such simple module exists. A behavior as complex as empathy involves parallel and distributed processing in a number of dissociable mechanisms that are underpinned by distinct neural systems. We propose that empathy first relies on a system of shared neural representations that establishes the connection between the self and the target of empathy, but this shared representation network also necessitates regulatory mechanisms for distinguishing between the self and other.

SHARED REPRESENTATIONS BETWEEN SELF AND OTHER

At the core of our theoretical framework is the notion of *shared representations* between the self and other, which has been proposed as a possible neurophysiological basis for social cognition (Decety & Sommerville, 2003). Shared representations rely on the common neural coding associated with the *perception* and *performance* of actions. Perception of a given behavior in another individual automatically activates one's own representations of that behavior (Knoblich & Flach, 2003). However, the activation of that behavior is generally inhibited or occurs at a sub-threshold level. In neuroscience, evidence for shared representations ranges from electrophysiological recordings in monkeys to neuroimaging experiments in humans. These studies consistently demonstrate that similar brain areas (in the frontal and parietal cortices) are activated during imagining one's own action, imagining another's action, and observation of another's action (Jackson & Decety, 2004).

The shared representations model may also be applied to the processing of emotions, which are a key component of empathy. For instance, viewing facial expressions triggers expressions on one's own face, even in the absence of conscious recognition of the stimulus (Dimberg, Thunberg, & Elmehed, 2000). Further support for the role of shared representations in emotion processes is provided by reports of paired deficits of emotion production and emotion recognition. Damage within the right somatosensory related cortices (including the insula and anterior supramarginal gyrus) impairs people's ability to express emotions and judge the emotional states when viewing facial expressions (Adolphs, Damasio, Tramel, Cooper, & Damasio, 2000).

Moreover, there are several dramatic single case studies in favor of the idea that the same neural systems are involved both in the recognition and in the expression of a specific emotion. Lesions of the amygdala may cause paired deficits in both the recognition of fear in facial expressions as well as in the phenomenological experience of fear (Adolphs, Tranel, Damasio, & Damasio, 1995). There is also evidence of paired deficits in recognizing and experiencing disgust after lesion of the left insula (Calder, Keane, Manes, Antoun, & Young, 2000). Wicker et al. have demonstrated that the same regions of the insula and cingulate cortex are activated whether participants inhale odorants that produce disgust or watch video clips showing facial expressions of disgust (Wicker et al., 2003).

SHARED REPRESENTATIONS, THE EGOCENTRIC BIAS AND SOCIAL PROJECTION

Many social and developmental psychologists have documented that the default mode for understanding others is biased toward relying on one's own self-perspective. We see others through our own embodied cognition, and use our own knowledge (including beliefs and attitudes) as the primary basis for understanding others. Stated in other words, people are fundamentally ego-

centric and have difficulty getting beyond their own perspective when antici-
pating what others are thinking or feeling (Royzman, Cassidy, & Baron, 2003).
For instance, we are inclined to impute our own knowledge to others, and
overestimate what they know (Keysar, Lin, & Barr, 2003). In addition, recent
research indicates that people's predictions of how other people will feel in situations that arouse drive states (such as thirst) are based largely on their predictions of how they themselves would feel, which in turn are based on their
own current drive states (Van Boven & Loewenstein, 2003).

This projective tendency, which stems from the shared representations, is
very parsimonious and frequently useful in understanding and predicting the
behaviors of others. Yet it is far from perfect, as individual differences in people's thoughts and emotions abound. Errors in taking the perspective of others
stem from the inability to suppress the self-perspective (Hodges & Wegner,
1997) and many costly social misunderstandings are rooted in people's failure
to recognize the degree to which their perception of a situation may differ
from those of others.

ADOPTING THE SUBJECTIVE PERSPECTIVE OF THE OTHER

Fortunately, human empathic abilities are more sophisticated than simply
yoking of perceptions of the self and other. Furthermore, confusion of the self
and other is generally not considered a hallmark of empathy (Batson et al.,
1991; Ickes, 1997). The shared representations mechanism just described
lends credence to the idea that the same neural representational form is used
in coding embedded intentional actions, whether they involve the self as an
agent or another agent. Yet, although the self and other may be similar, we are
able to understand that they are separate. Perspective-taking allows us to adjust for differences in the way other individuals may, literally and figuratively,
see the world. Significantly, perspective-taking also plays a critical role in triggering empathy (Batson, 1991).

An essential aspect of empathy is to recognize the other person as like the
self, while maintaining a clear separation between self and other. When adopt-
ing the perspective of another individual, an adjustment must be performed
on shared representations. This ability to adjust further suggests that there is
an important role for regulatory mechanisms in the neural machinery of empathy that maintain this distinction. We argue that empathy requires some
form of executive inhibition (i.e., the deliberate suppression of cognitions or
responses to achieve an internally represented goal). The contributions of the
prefrontal cortex play an essential role in this regulation process.

A series of neuroimaging studies of healthy volunteers has investigated the
neural underpinning of perspective-taking in three different modalities (i.e.,
motoric, conceptual, and emotional) of self–other representations. Participants
were scanned while asked to imagine either himself or herself or another person performing a familiar action (Ruby & Decety, 2001), to judge the truthful-
ness of sentences (Ruby & Decety, 2003), to identify what emotion would be

elicited by a real life situation (Ruby & Decety, 2004), and to imagine painful situations (Jackson, Meltzoff, Brunet, & Decety, 2005). One of the most striking findings of these studies was the systematic involvement of two prefrontal cortex sub-areas (namely the frontopolar cortex and medial prefrontal cortex) when the participants adopted another person's perspective. Frontal damage in similar regions may result in impaired perspective-taking ability and a lack of cognitive flexibility. Interestingly, Anderson and colleagues (Anderson, Bechara, Damasio, Tranel, & Damasio, 1999) reported the cases of two patients with early damage to the anterior prefrontal cortex (encompassing the frontopolar cortex) who, when tested on moral dilemmas, exhibited an excessively egocentric perspective. We believe this inhibitory component is required to regulate the prepotent self-perspective (and disengage it in favor of another's perspective). This view is compatible with the role of the prefrontal cortex in top-down control of behavior. It is also congruent with Batson's (1991) empathy–altruism model, which postulates that concern for another person in distress is the more reliable predictor of the distressed person receiving help, rather than experiencing another person's distress as one's own.

SELF AND OTHER AWARENESS

In our view, self–other awareness is a vital component of human empathy. Indeed, it has been argued that self-awareness may have evolved for the specific purpose of allowing us to understand our own and others' behavior. This may help explain why humans are able to "feel for" and act on behalf of other people whose experiences differ greatly from their own. Behavior that constitutes rudimentary "empathy" in other species consists mainly of fixed action patterns that are engaged only for those recognized as kin. Self-reflexive capability may be a crucial difference between humans and other animals (Povinelli, 2001).

It is unlikely that self-awareness relies on one specific brain area; rather, it probably arises from the interaction of processes distributed in the brain. Regions of the right hemisphere, especially the prefrontal cortex and the inferior parietal lobule, play a prominent role. Notably, two recent fMRI studies have demonstrated a specific increased hemodynamic activity in the right medial prefrontal cortex and anterior cingulate during tasks that involved self-reflection (Gusnard et al., 2001; Johnson et al., 2002).

Clinical neuropsychological observations also support an important role of the right prefrontal cortex in self awareness. For instance, Keenan and his group (Keenan, Nelson, O'Connor, & Pascual-Leone, 2001) demonstrated that patients were temporarily desensitized in recognizing their own faces when their right hemispheres were anaesthetized as part of a diagnostic procedure. Right ventromedial prefrontal cortex damage can also be associated with impairments in autobiographical memory and self-evaluation. Interestingly, patients with lesions of this latter region exhibit empathy deficits (Shamay-Tsoory, Tomer, Berger, & Aharon-Peretz 2003).

Recent research indicates that the right inferior parietal cortex in conjunction with prefrontal cortex may be critical in distinguishing the self from the other, and is therefore important in modulating shared representations. The inferior parietal cortex is a heteromodal association area, and is well-situated to receive input from the lateral and posterior thalamus and prefrontal cortex, as well as from visual, auditory, somaesthetic, and limbic areas that plays a critical role in the sense of self-agency in distinguishing the perspective of the self from the other. Notably, when participants are asked to adopt another person's perspective to evaluate their beliefs or imagine their feelings or their pain, the right parietal cortex is also chiefly involved which is consistent with its role in self–other distinction required in our model of empathy (see Decety & Jackson, 2004).

CONCLUSIONS

Empathy denotes, at a phenomenological level of description, a sense of similarity between the feelings we experience and those expressed by others, without losing sight of whose feelings belong to whom. In this chapter, we have proposed a model of empathy that is grounded in shared representations between self and others, which produce a "self-bias" in the way we think and feel about others. By bridging social psychology and cognitive neuroscience, we have demonstrated how such a model, with its roots in social psychology, provides important guidelines for investigating the neural processes underlying empathy. For example, just as social psychologists have identified how multiple social stimuli may trigger empathy (e.g., the target person's emotion, kinship with the target, attempts to take the target's perspective), we suggest that within our model, there is no specific cortical site for shared representations. Instead, the neural substrate of shared representations is widely distributed and the patterns of activation (and also presumably deactivation) vary according to the processing domain, specific emotional responses, and stored information.

Furthermore, the bridge linking social psychology and neural explanations of empathy goes both ways. We have demonstrated how recent cognitive neuroscience findings have provided complementary and corroborating evidence of empathy mechanisms first proposed by behavioral scientists. Social psychologists (and philosophers before them) have distinguished empathy as more complex than mere projection and thus, the shared representations that form the basis of our model must be regulated and adjusted. Evidence of this adjustment is found in neural activity in the prefrontal cortex as well as in the neural structures involved in emotional regulation (anterior cingulate, orbitofrontal, and ventromedial prefrontal cortex). In addition, activity in the right hemisphere plays a predominant role in the way that the self is both connected to and distinguished from the other.

Further benefits of bridging the two disciplines may be accrued in future studies of empathy. For example, neural imaging studies of patient populations may provide a better understanding of, and possible treatments for, forms of psychopathology that are characterized by empathy deficits (e.g., autism and schizophrenia). Identifying how empathy behaviorally resembles other mental processes that link the self and other (e.g., social comparison) may suggest roles for additional neural structures in empathy. In a parallel manner, examining how the neural "signature" of empathy differs from that of other self–other processes may help us to further refine our definition of empathy. As our brief treatment here has demonstrated, neither the concept of empathy nor the mechanisms behind it are simple and thus, these investigations will not be easy. However, they will almost certainly be worth the effort in terms of understanding the uniquely human experience of empathy.

REFERENCES

Adolphs, R., Tranel, D., Damasio, H., & Damasio, A. (1995). Fear and the human amygdala. *Journal of Neuroscience, 15*(9), 5879–5891.

Adolphs, R., Damasio, H., Tranel, D., Cooper, G., & Damasio, A. (2000). A role for the somatosensory cortices in the visual recognition of emotion as revealed by three dimensional lesion mapping. *Journal of Neuroscience, 20*(7), 2683–2690.

Anderson, S. W., Bechara, A., Damasio, H., Tranel, D., & Damasio, A. R. (1999). Impairment of social and moral behavior related to early damage in human prefrontal cortex. *Nature Neuroscience, 2*, 1032–1037.

Batson, C. D. (1991). *The altruism question: Toward a social-psychological answer.* Hove, UK: Lawrence Erlbaum Associates.

Batson, C. D., Sager, K., Garst, E., Kang, M., Rubchinsky, K., & Dawson, K. (1997). Is induced helping due to self–other merging? *Journal of Personality & Social Psychology, 73*, 509.

Calder, A. J., Keane, J., Manes, F., Antoun, N., & Young, A.W. (2000). Impaired recognition an experience of disgust following brain injury. *Nature Neuroscience, 3*(11), 1077–1078.

Decety, J., & Jackson, P. L. (2004). The functional architecture of human empathy. *Behavioral and Cognitive Neuroscience Reviews, 3*, 71–100.

Decety, J., & Sommerville, J. A. (2003). Shared representations between self and others: A social cognitive neuroscience view. *Trends in Cognitive Science, 7*(12), 527–533.

Dimberg, U., Thunberg, M., & Elmehed, K. (2000). Unconscious facial reactions to emotional facial expressions. *Psychological Science, 11*, 86–89.

Gusnard, D. A., Akbudak, E., Shulman, G. L., & Raichle, M. E. (2001). Medial prefrontal cortex and self-referential mental activity: Relation to a default mode of brain function. *Proceedings of the National Academy of Sciences, USA, 98*(7), 4259–4264.

Hodges, S. D., & Wegner, D. M. (1997). Automatic and controlled empathy. In W. Ickes (Ed.), *Empathic Accuracy* (pp. 311–339). New York: Guilford.

Ickes, W. (1997). *Empathic Accuracy.* New York: Guilford.

Jackson, P. L., Brunet, E., Meltzoff, A. N., & Decety, J. (2005). Empathy examined through the neural mechanisms involved in imagining how I feel versus how you feel pain. *Neuropsychologia*, Epub ahead of print.

Jackson, P. L., & Decety, J. (2004, April). Motor cognition: A new paradigm to study self other interactions. *Current Opinion in Neurobiology, 14*, 259–263.

Johnson, S. C., Baxter, L. C., Wilder, L. S., Pipe, J. G., Heiserman, J. E., & Prigatano, G. P. (2002). Neural correlates of self-reflection. *Brain, 125*, 1808–1814.

Keenan, J. P., Nelson, A., O'Connor, M., & Pascual-Leone, A. (2001). Self-recognition and the right hemisphere. *Nature, 409*(6818), 305.

Keysar, B., Lin, S., & Barr, D. J. (2003). Limits on theory of mind use in adults. *Cognition, 89*, 25–41.

Knoblich, G., & Flach, R. (2003). Action identity: Evidence from self-recognition, prediction, and coordination. *Consciousness and Cognition, 12*, 620–632.

Povinelli, D. J. (2001). *Folk physics for apes.* New York: Oxford University Press.

Royzman, E. B., Cassidy, K. W., & Baron, J. (2003). I know you know: Epistemic egocentrism in children and adults. *Review of General Psychology, 7*(1), 38–65.

Ruby, P., & Decety, J. (2001). Effect of subjective perspective taking during simulation of action: a PET investigation of agency. *Nature Neuroscience, 4*, 546–550.

Ruby, P., & Decety, J. (2003). What you believe versus what you think they believe: A neuroimaging study of conceptual perspective taking. *European Journal of Neuroscience, 17*, 2475–2480.

Ruby, P., & Decety, J. (2004). How would you feel versus how do you think she would feel? A neuroimaging study of perspective taking with social emotions. *Journal of Cognitive Neuroscience, 16*, 988–999.

Shamay-Tsoory, S. G., Tomer, R., Berger, B. D., & Aharon-Peretz, J. (2003). Characterization of empathy deficits following prefrontal brain damage: The role of right ventromedial prefrontal cortex. *Journal of Cognitive Neuroscience, 15*(3), 1–14.

Van Boven, L., & Loewenstein, G. (2003). Social projection of transient drive states. *Personality and Social Psychology Bulletin, 29*(9), 1159–1168.

Wicker, B., Keysers, C., Plailly, J., Royet, J. P., Gallese, V., & Rizzolatti, G. (2003). Both of us disgusted in my insula: The common neural basis of seeing and feeling disgust. *Neuron, 40*, 655–664.

15

Bridging Social Psychology and Physiology

Jim Blascovich
University of California, Santa Barbara

A certain amount of brain-physiology must be presupposed or included in Psychology.
—(William James, 1890)

Social psychologists often travel through the intellectual landscape surrounding our field. Many trips have proven beneficial. We have not only entered territories of "nearby" subdisciplines (e.g., personality, cognitive, and organizational psychology), but also more distant ones (e.g., biology, marketing, and statistics).

Some crossing these bridges emigrated to the new territory taking our theories and methods with them. Some returned with theories and methods from them. Some became disciplinarily bicultural, helping integrate both fields. Perhaps those who travel such roads intellectually derive their wanderlust from the interdisciplinary history of social psychology itself, a field itself developed as a bridge between sociology and psychology.

I have crossed a few bridges bringing back methods and theory, contributing social psychological ones in return. However, I have remained a steadfast citizen of social psychology, hopefully expanding our theoretical and methodological toolboxes. Although I have written about crossing bridges to medicine (Blascovich, 1982) and computer science (Blascovich et al., 2002), I have never before written explicitly about the bridge I have crossed most often, the one to physiology.

An ancient bridge connects social psychology and physiology in Western culture.[1] Plato and Galen traveled it as did other Greeks and Romans. By the Renaissance, however, the bridge was in disrepair. Cartesian dualism dictated

---

[1] I plead ignorance regarding this connection in terms of other cultures.

that scholars should study mind and body separately without considering mutual influence. During the 1800s, Freud and James began restoring the bridge. During the first half of the 20th century, however, behaviorism stifled intellectual travel between psychology and physiology. Despite the work of Cannon, Selye, and others, as neo-Jamesianism rose to the fore, even emotion theories eschewed the importance of physiology. Only recently has the death knell of Cartesian dualism sounded in the work of psychoneuroimmunologists (e.g., Ader, Cohen) emotion theorists (e.g., Damascio, le Doux), and health researchers (e.g., McEwen, Sapolsky).

I developed an interest in physiology as a graduate student. In retrospect, this interest resulted from a confluence of research, life experience, and serendipity. My first experiment (Blascovich, 1972) critically tested two competing theoretical explanations of the risky shift: diffusion of responsibility and social comparison. The study "worked" in the traditional sense. However, the study worked in an even better way than I anticipated. Like virtually every other "risky shifter" at the time, I used a vignette-based paper-and-pencil instrument, the Choice Dilemmas Questionnaire (CDQ), to measure risk taking.

Upon debriefing, however, I learned that not one participant thought the CDQ measured risk taking. Of course, I explained to each that eminent personality psychologists had developed the CDQ and that the social psychological community had embraced it. Later, upon reflection and much conceptual analysis, I accepted the participants' conclusion, eventually finding "blackjack" a more conceptually justifiable risk task and bets as a valid dependent measure (e.g., Blascovich & Ginsburg, 1978).

So, what does this have to do with a bridge to physiology? As a risk-taking researcher, I developed an interest (as a participant observer, of course) in risk taking and gambling, occasionally playing blackjack in casinos. My experiences included perceptions of physiological reactions within myself. While playing blackjack, I often felt a thump in my chest, sometimes interpreting it positively (usually while winning), sometimes negatively (usually while losing).

I also happened to read Shapiro and Crider's (1969) intriguing chapter on physiological approaches to social psychology in the *Handbook of Social Psychology* that social psychologists could use physiological measures to test social psychological theories appeared very advantageous. One could avoid the problems of self-report, replacing them with more objective measures, indeed, ones that are continuous, covert, and online. But what physiological responses would one assess while participants read vignettes? My introspections suggested that if participants were engaged actively in a task such as blackjack one might be able to assess cardiovascular activity of some sort.

Thus began my many round trips between social psychology and physiology, trips I still continue. I go and come, each time with a bit more theoretical, methodological, or technical knowledge. At the beginning, I focused on heart rate as a criterion measure, probably because measuring it presented little difficulty and the physiological theory behind it (increased sympathetic innervation during psychological meaningful activity) seemed intuitively plausible.

My first foray into social psychophysiology involved a study in which male and female dyads competed in a two-person, zero-sum experimental game for money (Blascovich, Nash, & Ginsburg, 1978).[2] In a zero-sum game, what one player wins the other(s) lose, hence, "zero-sum." As we predicted, eventual winners in nearly every male dyad (19 of 20) had greater increases in heart rate (from a resting baseline) during the game than losers (who exhibited little change from baseline), indicating to us greater motivation. The results for female dyads, however, proved quite different. Female winners did not have greater increased heart rates from baseline than losers. Female winners and losers alike exhibited increased heart rates from baseline. We reasoned that heart rate must reflect something in addition to or other than motivation during the game for women, perhaps some response to the relative novelty (at that time in history) of competition for females.

Of course, therein lay the rub. Under identical experimental conditions, why would heart rate measure one construct (i.e., motivation) for males and another (i.e., novelty or uncertainty) for females? The answer to that question took many years and many bridge crossings as I realized that I needed to learn much more about physiology than I had learned up to that time. Thus, when the opportunity to spend a sabbatical year working with noted psychophysiologist Ed Katkin appeared, I eagerly took it. To say that I learned much is an understatement. I became more conversant with the terminology and technology of physiological research, and we began a collaboration investigating visceral perception. One could actually scientifically study perceptions of those thumps in my chest that I had experienced while playing blackjack, and how they related to or affected psychological states including emotions.

However, I still had not found the answer to the question of how a single physiological measure such as heart rate could seemingly assess motivation for men and something else for women. That took another bridge crossing, this time to the Advanced Training Institute in Psychophysiology led by John Cacioppo. This intensive program provided me with much new and important knowledge in terms of physiological theory, mechanisms, and measurement technologies. Most importantly, I learned a critical part of the answer to my question.

Single physiological measures such as heart rate (or skin conductance, blood pressure, etc.) have enjoyed a mystique among many of us lacking sophistication in physiology—specifically, the assumption that physiological measures represent more veridical measures of psychological constructs than other types. I believe this mystique stems from the long history in social psychological theory of the naive assertion of general arousal. Upon closer inspection, this construct metaphorically represents a general motivation or

---

[2]My initial attempts to collect heart rate data from a group of players during a blackjack game proved very impractical if not impossible.

drive construct rather than a physiological one. Nevertheless, its common language biological connotations[3] have led physiologically unsophisticated researchers to assume that arousal occurs generally and uniformly throughout the body's vast network of physiological mechanisms and, consequently, that almost any physiological measure can index the arousal construct. Unfortunately, the general arousal construct is near meaningless in a physiological sense because physiological responses are neither general nor uniform.

Cacioppo and Tassinary (1990) specified the possible logical relationships between psychological constructs and physiological responses: one-to-one, one-to-many, many-to-one, many-to-many, and null. If a one-to-one relationship exists, one can use physiological response as an invariant index of the psychological construct. Unfortunately, such a relationship rarely if ever exists. If a one-to-many relationship exists, we can use the entire set of predicted physiological response measures as an invariant index. However, such a relationship is difficult to specify, in part because we can never be sure we have included the entire set of physiological responses. Many-to-one relationships also present difficulty. Hence, multiple psychological constructs can be related to a single physiological response. Indeed, this proved to be the problem with the gender effects in our experimental game study. More typically, many-to-many relationships exist so that many psychological constructs are related to many physiological responses. In this case, we can never be sure what psychological constructs we are indexing even with a prescribed set of physiological responses.

What is one to do? I learned from Cacioppo and Tassinary that one could approach the desirable one-to-one relationship by defining a physiological measure of a psychological construct as a pattern of physiological responses over time, especially if one limits the situational context. However, one cannot define such a pattern arbitrarily. Rather, such definitions need to be based on proven physiological theory.

It dawned on me that perhaps our experimental game results reflected only the heart-rate component of larger and differing patterns of cardiovascular responses that would distinguish the motivational states of men and women in our study. At about that time, Dienstbier (1989) published his review paper differentiating physiologically tough from weak animals. According to his theory and research, physiologically tough animals, those that thrived in potentially threatening situations, responded to such situations with a different cardiovascular response pattern than physiologically weak animals, those who failed to thrive in such situations, although both groups evidenced sympathetically driven increases in heart rate.

So after many trips back and forth across the bridge, I found myself at the beginning of 1990s with a problem to explain (differences in motivational states during identical tasks), a logical strategy for developing physiological indexes of motivational constructs, a physiological theory for specifying a pat-

---

[3]Other than sexual.

tern of cardiovascular responses indicative of oppositional motivational states, and the technical knowledge necessary to assess and distinguish the cardiovascular response patterns. We have been able not only to develop and refine our biopsychosocial model of challenge and threat but also to validate differential cardiovascular patterns indexing these motivational states (Blascovich & Mendes, 2000; Blascovich & Tomaka, 1996).

We discovered that we could determine objectively whether an experimental participant experienced challenge or threat performance motivation by examining the relative patterns of four cardiovascular signals. This impacted on not only our understanding of motivational processes but also a multitude of substantive social psychological ones. With our theory and physiological toolbox, we have been able not only to explain the gender differences in the experimental game study, but also to test hypotheses addressing motivational components of a raft of social psychological processes ranging from attitude functionality (Blascovich et al., 1993) to stigma (Blascovich, Mendes, Hunter, Lickel, & Kowai-Bell, 2001).

To illustrate, our challenge and threat theory provided a biopsychosocial explanation of the oldest experimental social motivational finding in the literature, social facilitation. Based on our model, we reasoned that performing a task in front of others increased self-relevance. Given self-relevance, those who evaluated their resources as outweighing task demands would be challenged and perform better, whereas those who evaluated task demands as outweighing their resources would be threatened and perform worse. We experimentally manipulated resources by training participants to perform to a criterion level on one of two tasks and then requiring them to perform either the well learned on novel task with an audience or alone. Our hypotheses were confirmed and in our opinion our understanding of social facilitation processes advanced.

I also believe my bridge crossings have brought insights to the other side of the bridge, specifically to the areas of cardiovascular physiology and health. Our work demonstrates that not all increases in cardiovascular responding during psychologically stressful situations are pernicious, and that individuals cannot be unequivocally categorized as unhealthy cardiovascular responders in stressful situations. Rather, it is the threat pattern of cardiovascular reactivity that appears to be the pathophysiological, and one that is not purely dispositional. But that is another long story.

CONCLUSIONS

Our biopsychosocial model of challenge and threat motivation would never have been conceived without a bridge spanning social psychology and physiology. Today, advances in neuroscience have brought to social psychology new physiological attractions such as functional brain imaging. However, we will need to develop and refine inferential strategies if our field and the field of brain imaging are to benefit. I encourage social psychologists, especially those starting out, to eschew provincialism and to cross bridges leading to other fields. Such intellectual journeys are important to a healthy, vigorous, up-to-date social psychology, as well as to the disciplines to which we bridge, and we all should take them.

REFERENCES

Blascovich, J. (1972). Sequence effects on choice shifts involving risk. *Journal of Experimental Social Psychology, 8,* 260–265.

Blascovich, J. (1982). Social psychology and family medicine. *Applied Social Psychology Annual, 3,* 279–300.

Blascovich, J., Ernst, J. M., Tomaka, J., Kelsey, R. M., Salomon, K. A., & Fazio, R. H. (1993). Attitude as a moderator of autonomic reactivity. *Journal of Personality and Social Psychology, 64,* 165–176.

Blascovich, J., & Ginsburg, G. P. (1978). Conceptual analysis of risk taking in "risky shift" research. *Journal for the Theory of Social Behavior, 8,* 217–230.

Blascovich, J., Loomis, J., Beall, A., Swinth, K., Hoyt, C., & Bailenson, J. (2002). Immersive virtual environment technology as a research tool for social psychology. *Psychological Inquiry, 13,* 103–125.

Blascovich, J., & Mendes, W. B. (2000). Challenge and threat appraisals: The role of affective cues. In J. Forgas (Ed.), *Feeling and thinking: The role of affect in social cognition* (pp. 59–82). Cambridge UK: Cambridge University Press.

Blascovich, J., Mendes, W. B., Hunter, S. B., Lickel, B., & Kowai-Bell, N. (2001). Perceiver threat in social interactions with stigmatized others. *Journal of Personality and Social Psychology, 80,* 253–267.

Blascovich, J., Nash, R. F., & Ginsburg, G. P. (1978). Heart rate and competitive decision making. *Personality and Social Psychology Bulletin, 4,* 115–118.

Blascovich, J., & Tomaka, J. (1996). The biopsychosocial model of arousal regulation. In M. Zanna (Ed.). *Advances in experimental social psychology* (Vol. 28, pp. 1–51). New York: Academic Press.

Cacioppo, J. T., & Tassinary, L. G. (1990). Psychophysiology and psychophysiological inference. In J. T. Cacioppo & L. G. Tassinary (Eds.), *Principles of physiology: Physical, social, and inferential elements* (pp. 3–33). Cambridge, UK: Cambridge University Press.

Dienstbier, R. A. (1989). Arousal and physiological toughness: Implications for mental and physical health. *Psychological Review, 96,* 140–149.

Shapiro, D., & Crider, A. (1969). Physiological approaches in social psychology. In. G. Lindzey & E. Aronson (Eds.), *The handbook of social psychology* (2nd ed., Vol. 3, pp. 1–49). Reading, MA: Addison-Wesley.

16

Research on Affect and Social Behavior: Links to Cognitive, Learning, and Neuropsychology

Joseph P. Forgas
University of New South Wales, Sydney, Australia

The role of affect in social behavior is of intense interest in contemporary social psychology. This interdisciplinary field offers many examples of the complex bridges that have been created exist between social psychology, and areas such as cognitive, learning, and neuropsychology and the history and philosophy of psychology. These bridges greatly enriched our enterprise by providing us with new ideas, metaphors, and techniques. In turn, experimental affect research influenced these and other applied areas where understanding affectivity is important, such as clinical, counseling, and organizational psychology (Ciarrochi, Forgas, & Mayer, 2001; Forgas & George, 2001). This chapter discusses some of the ways that recent research on affect and social behavior benefited from and created bridges to related fields such as the history of psychology, and cognitive, learning, and neuropsychology.

THE BACKGROUND: BRIDGES TO THE HISTORY AND PHILOSOPHY OF PSYCHOLOGY

Interest in the role of affect in social behavior has a long and fascinating history. Since the dawn of civilization, philosophers and laypersons have been intrigued by the delicate relationships between feeling and thinking, affect and cognition. Classic philosophers such as Plato, Aristotle, Epicurus, Descartes, Pascal, Kant, and others did much to explore the role of affect in human affairs. Plato was among the first to suggest that affect constitutes a more primitive response system that is incompatible with reason. His idealized Republic was to be ruled by philosophers least likely to yield to base affective impulses. The idea that affect is incompatible with reason has been echoed in many psychological theories throughout the ages, including the work of Freud, Tarde, and LeBon. Indeed, writers such as Arthur Koestler (1978) even argued that our inability to understand and control affective reactions demonstrates a fatal evolutionary "flaw" that may ultimately threaten the very survival of our species.

Despite intense popular interest in affect, psychological research on affectivity remained relatively neglected until recently. Historians of psychology such as Hilgard (1980) suggested that work on affect was hampered by modern psychology's insistence on studying the three faculties of the human mind, *affect, cognition,* and *conation,* in isolation from rather than in conjunction with each other, as was initially done in the introspectionist experiments by Wundt, Titchener, and others. Subsequent empirical paradigms such as behaviorism and cognitivism came to focus on just one component of the "trilogy of mind" (first behavior, and later, thinking), resulting in the relative neglect of affective phenomena until recently (Hilgard, 1980).

Freud's psychodynamic theories represent perhaps one historical exception, suggesting that affect has a dynamic, invasive quality, requiring psychological resources to control it. Indeed, some experiments showed that attempts to suppress affect (fear) led fearful subjects to "perceive another person as fearful and anxious" (Feshbach & Singer, 1957, p. 286), because "suppression of fear facilitates the tendency to project fear onto another social object" (p. 286). Curiously, the processes responsible for such affect infusion remain of great interest today (Forgas, 1995, 2002), creating an important bridge between early theorizing and contemporary research, even though lack of empirical support for Freud's ideas and devastating epistemological criticisms of psychoanalysis by Karl Popper led to a rejection of this theory.

BRIDGES TO NEUROPSYCHOLOGY AND PHYSIOLOGY

Links to neuropsychology and physiology represent another important bridge for affect research, a connection that was anticipated by William James's work more than a hundred years ago. James argued that bodily reactions—neurological and physiological changes—are the essence of emotions, and can occur prior to and in the absence of any cognitive awareness. In other words, "perceptions ... do produce wide-spread bodily effects by a sort of immediate physical influence, antecedent to the arousal of an emotion or emotional idea" (James, 1892/1961, p. 243). Important recent discoveries in neuropsychology and neuroanatomy by Damasio (1994) and others confirmed that proprioceptive information about bodily reactions is indeed a key component of responding to social situations. Neuropsychological and physiological research also showed that affect is not necessarily a disruptive influence on social thinking and behavior, but is often a useful and even essential component of adaptive responses (Damasio, 1994; De Sousa, 1987). Thus, there is now good evidence to support the prescient predictions by James, and by the philosopher Blaise Pascal from over 350 years ago that "the heart has its reasons which reason does not understand" (Pascal, 1643/1966, p. 113). Research with brain-damaged patients showed that individuals with prefrontal lesions that interfere with the transmission of somatic affective information but leave cognitive capacities intact tend to make disastrous social decisions and their social relationships suffer accordingly, even though their intellectual ability is unimpaired (Damasio, 1994).

Often, affective states may help us to respond quickly and effectively without in any way impairing the quality of the outcome, as William James so aptly observed. Yet at other times, affect may contribute to cognitive and judgmental errors (Forgas, 1998). Whether the behavioral consequences of affect are helpful or harmful seems largely to depend on the nature of the task and the kind of information-processing strategy used (Forgas, 1995, 2002). Physiological and neuropsychological studies thus offer a key bridge for understanding the adaptive and maladaptive consequences of affect as a source of social information.

BRIDGES TO CONDITIONING AND LEARNING THEORY

Early conditioning theories offered another conceptual bridge between affect, thinking, and behavior. Although behaviorism was uninterested in internal experiences such as feelings, Watson's classic "little Albert" studies showed how associationist principles could apply to affective phenomena (Watson & Rayner, 1920). In this vein, Razran (1940) found that moods induced by aversive smells, or receiving a free lunch (!), can become associated with subsequent social judgments. Decades later, Byrne and Clore (1970) showed that people in aversive environments (the unconditioned stimuli) became more critical toward a person they had just met (a conditioned response) than did happy persons. In terms of associative principles, it seems that "evaluative responses are ... determined by the positive or negative properties of the total stimulus situation" (Griffitt, 1970, p. 240).

These conditioning studies represent an early bridge to some contemporary explanations of affect congruence (Schwarz & Clore, 1983). Instead of invoking "blind" conditioning mechanisms, recent affect-as-information theories suggest that inferential principles, such as using the "how do I feel about it?" heuristic, can explain affect congruence. Such a heuristic strategy is most likely when off-the-cuff responses are required and people lack sufficient interest, motivation, or resources to compute a more elaborate response (Schwarz & Clore, 1983). Thus, associative ideas informed more recent affect-as-information theories, suggesting an important bridge between conditioning theories and contemporary affect research.

BRIDGES TO COGNITIVE PSYCHOLOGY

The "cognitive revolution" in the 1960s was at first also characterized by an avowed lack of interest in affect (Hilgard, 1980). Affect was considered a disruptive influence on "proper," that is, cold and affectless, ideation. However, the "new look" studies of social perception pioneered by Bruner (1957) were among the first to show that feelings and preferences inevitably influence all perceptual judgments. Growing interest in real-life cognition confirmed that affect plays a key role in how people deal with social information (Neisser, 1982). By the early 1980s, strong bridges between affect and cognition and between cognitive and social psychology were created. Information-processing theories became a major influence on exploring affective influences on social thinking and behavior (Bower, 1981; Forgas, 2002).

In particular, associative network models of memory (Bower, 1981) predicted and found a strong mood-congruent influence on social memory, thinking, and judgments (Bower & Forgas, 2001), suggesting that affect is an integral part of how memory about the social world is organized. This idea represents a powerful bridge between cognitive and social psychology. Numerous studies supported these predictions, especially in complex and demanding social situations that require the use of open, constructive processing (Bower & Forgas, 2001; Fiedler & Bless, 2001; Forgas, 1995, 1999). Theories such as the Affect Infusion Model (AIM; Forgas, 1995, 2002) predict that affective influences on thinking and behavior are dependent on the kind of processing strategy people use, specifically bridging cognitive processes and the resulting social behaviors.

Yet another bridge between cognitive and social psychology links affect to *how* people think—the processing consequences of affect (Fiedler & Bless, 2001). It was initially thought that positive affect triggers less effortful thinking, whereas negative affect produces more thorough and effortful processing. More recent work suggests (Fiedler & Bless, 2001) a fundamental dichotomy between accommodation and assimilation as basic processing styles influenced by affect. Negative affect promotes accommodation, focusing on the demands of the external world, whereas positive affect facilitates assimilation, and the creative use of internal schemas (Fiedler & Bless, 2001). This theory represents another important bridge between cognitive and social psychological research on affect and developmental psychology, where Piaget first distinguished between accommodation and assimilation processes. Further, this account also establishes a bridge to evolutionary theorizing that focuses on the adaptive significance of affect in triggering different processing styles.

CONCLUSIONS

Contemporary research on affectivity benefited greatly from a number of theoretical and empirical bridges to cognitive, learning, and neuropsychology, as well as to clinical, personality, and applied psychology. Given the limited space available, only some of the most important links to these disciplines could be mentioned here. Skilled social behavior typically requires complex inferential thinking. We now know that affect can influence both the content and the process of social information processing and subsequent social behaviors. However, these effects are also highly process sensitive.

Homo sapiens is an extraordinarily gregarious species, and our impressive evolutionary success has much to do with our sophisticated ability to cooperate with each other (Pinker, 1997). For too long, the role of affect in these processes remained inadequately understood. The very complexity of many social encounters in complex industrial societies probably magnifies affective influences on interpersonal behaviors (Forgas, 1999, 2002). The more complex and ambiguous a social situation, the more it is likely that constructive thinking will be influenced by affectively primed information (Forgas, 1995). Recent theories also suggest that affect has an evolutionary signaling function, triggering different information processing strategies as a function of positive and negative moods (Fiedler & Bless, 2001). Such insights serve to strengthen the bridges between affect research and related fields discussed here.

Research on affectivity in turn produced important new insights, producing genuinely two-way traffic on the "bridges" we discussed here, as well as the ones we could not cover. For example, research on affective influences on judgments and behavior is increasingly applied in fields such as organizational psychology (Forgas & George, 2001), cognitive psychology (Bower & Forgas, 2001), marketing and advertising (Ciarrochi et al., 2001), language research (Forgas, 1999), emotional intelligence (Ciarrochi, Forgas, & Mayer, 2001), and a variety of other fields. The creation of such bridges between affect research and evolutionary, cognitive, and conditioning psychology on the one hand, and applied areas on the other is certain to produce considerable benefits for these fields.

ACKNOWLEDGMENTS

This work was supported by the Australian Research Council and by the Research Prize of the Alexander von Humboldt Foundation.

REFERENCES

Bower, G. H. (1981). Mood and memory. *American Psychologist, 36,* 129–148.
Bower, G. H., & Forgas, J. P. (2001). Mood and social memory. In: J. P. Forgas (Ed.), *The handbook of affect and social cognition* (pp. 95–120). Mahwah, NJ: Lawrence Erlbaum Associates.
Bruner, J. S. (1957). On perceptual readiness. *Psychological Review, 64,* 123–152.
Byrne, D., & Clore, G. L. (1970). A reinforcement model of evaluation responses. *Personality: An International Journal, 1,* 103–128.

122 ⟶ FORGAS

Ciarrochi, J. V., & Forgas, J. P. (2001). The pleasure of possessions: Affect and consumer judgments. *European Journal of Social Psychology, 30,* 631–649.

Ciarrochi, J. V., Forgas, J. P., & Mayer, J. (Eds.). (2001). *Emotional intelligence: A scientific approach.* Philadelphia: Psychology Press.

Damasio, A. R. (1994). *Descartes' error.* New York: Grosste/Putnam.

De Sousa, R. J. (1987). *The rationality of emotion.* Cambridge, MA: MIT Press.

Feshbach, S., & Singer, R. D. (1957). The effects of fear arousal and suppression of fear upon social perception. *Journal of Abnormal and Social Psychology, 55,* 283–288.

Fiedler, K., & Bless, H. (2001). The formation of beliefs in the interface of affective and cognitive processes. In N. Frijda, A. Manstead, & S. Bem (Eds.), *The influence of emotions on beliefs* (pp. 221–245). New York: Cambridge University Press.

Forgas, J. P. (1995). Mood and judgment: The affect infusion model (AIM). *Psychological Bulletin, 117*(1), 39–66.

Forgas, J. P. (1998). Happy and mistaken? Mood effects on the fundamental attribution error. *Journal of Personality and Social Psychology, 75,* 318–331.

Forgas, J. P. (1999). Feeling and speaking: Mood effects on verbal communication strategies. *Personality and Social Psychology Bulletin, 25,* 850–863.

Forgas, J. P. (2002). Feeling and doing: Affective influences on interpersonal behavior. *Psychological Inquiry, 13*(1), 1–28.

Forgas, J. P., & George, J. M. (2001). Affective influences on judgments and behavior in organizations: An information processing perspective. *Organizational Behavior and Human Decision Processes, 86,* 3–34.

Griffitt, W. (1970). Environmental effects on interpersonal behavior: Ambient effective temperature and attraction. *Journal of Personality and Social Psychology, 15,* 240–244.

Hilgard, E. R. (1980). The trilogy of mind: Cognition, affection, and conation. *Journal of the History of the Behavioral Sciences, 16,* 107–117.

James, W. (1961). *Psychology: The briefer course.* New York: Harper & Row. (Original work published 1892)

Koestler, A. (1978). *Janus: A summing up.* London: Hutchinson.

Neisser, U. (Ed.). (1982). *Memory observed.* San Francisco: Freeman.

Pascal, B. (1966). *Pensees.* Baltimore: Penguin books. (Original work published 1643)

Pinker, S. (1997). *How the mind works.* London: Penguin.

Razran, G. H. S. (1940). Conditioned response changes in rating and appraising sociopolitical slogans. *Psychological Bulletin, 37,* 481.

Schwarz, N., & Clore, G. L. (1983). Mood, misattribution and judgments of well-being: Informative and directive functions of affective states. *Journal of Personality and Social Psychology, 45,* 513–523.

Watson, J. B., & Rayner, R. (1920). Conditioned emotional reactions. *Journal of Experimental Psychology, 3,* 1–14.

Animal Research in Social Psychology: A Bridge to Functional Genomics and Other Unique Research Opportunities

Samuel D. Gosling
Diane M. Mollaghan
University of Texas at Austin

Ⅰn the 1935 *Handbook of Social Psychology* (Murchison, 1935), more than a third of the chapters focused on nonhuman subjects. Almost 20 years later, Hebb and Thomson used their 1954 handbook chapter to call for the use of animals in social psychological research, arguing that social psychology will "be dangerously myopic if it restricts itself to the human literature" (p. 532). However, half a century later, the idea of using nonhuman animals seems to have largely disappeared from contemporary social psychology. In fact, none of the chapters in the latest *Handbook of Social Psychology* (Gilbert, Fiske, & Lindzey, 1998) focused on nonhuman animals. Here we argue that animal studies still have an important contribution to make to social and personality psychology. Just as animal studies contribute to many other areas of research in psychology (Domjan & Purdy, 1995), we suggest that social psychologists can reap great benefits from animal research. Indeed, with the emergence of new methods in genomics, neuroscience, physiology, and phylogenetics, the potential contributions to be made by animal research are greater than ever.

These advances in methodology have come at a good time. There is currently a growing impetus for researchers to turn their attention toward genetic, biological, and environmental processes in social and personality psychology. Animal studies can provide some important opportunities for examining these processes. And many of the benefits of animal research are difficult or impossible to realize using human studies alone. In this chapter we outline the ways in which animal studies can contribute to research in social psychology. After reviewing the benefits of animal studies, we place special emphasis on new ideas about the potential contributions to be made by functional genomics in understanding social behavior.

SOME BENEFITS OF ANIMAL RESEARCH IN STUDIES OF SOCIAL BEHAVIOR

Although research on animals will not and should not replace research on humans, animal studies have some unique features that allow them to augment studies of humans. Four major methodological benefits afforded by animal studies are particularly applicable to research in human social behavior (Gosling, 2001; Vazire & Gosling, 2003).

Benefit 1: Greater Experimental Control. Animal studies allow greater experimental control and facilitate more extensive experimental manipulations than is possible in studies of humans. With animals, it is possible to control the events to which individuals are exposed, determine mating partners, and manipulate the size, composition, and stability of the groups in which the animals live. Such control permits tests of hypotheses that could not be tested in humans. For example, one study inoculated animals with HIV and then manipulated their social environments in order to examine the links between the stability of social environments and physical health (Capitanio, Mendoza, & Baroncelli, 1999).

Benefit 2: Greater Observational Opportunities. Observations of animals can be made in far greater detail and for more extensive periods than is possible with humans. This is especially true for captive animals, whose every move and interaction can be systematically recorded, in some cases from conception to death. However, wild animals in their natural groups can be profitably studied too. For example, Virgin and Sapolsky (1997) used 5 years of behavioral observations of a troop of wild baboons to illuminate the long-term links between social behavior and endocrine responses.

Benefit 3: Extensive Use of Physiological Interventions and Measurement. Animal studies permit the use of a wide range of physiological interventions and the measurement of a wide range of physiological parameters, providing the type of data that are necessary to identify the biological mechanisms underlying psychological processes. For example, Zuckerman (1996) drew on animal studies involving measures of neurotransmitters, enzymes, and hormones to develop a psychobiological model for sensation seeking. Researchers interested in health can take advantage of the fact that animals have been used in biomedical research for many years, so procedures for indexing health in animals are well developed.

Benefit 4: Shorter Life Span of Animals. Some species of animals are well suited for longitudinal research because they have relatively short natural life spans and are relatively inexpensive to maintain. These factors facilitate long-term studies of social behavior that, if done in humans, could last longer than the investigators conducting the study. For example, in a period of only 4 years, Fahlke et al. (2000) examined how rhesus macaques' rearing experiences and stress responses in infancy predicted alcohol consumption in young adulthood.

POTENTIAL SIGNIFICANCE OF ANIMAL RESEARCH

The methodological advantages of animal research outlined earlier permit researchers to address questions about social behavior that cannot be addressed using human research alone. For example, by combining evidence gathered in several species with maps of the phylogenetic relationships among the species it is possible to estimate when a trait evolved (Graybeal & Gosling, 2005). Such maps can be used to chart the emergence of physical traits like *wings* or behavioral traits like *curiosity* or *pair bonding*. Just as we can date the evolution of wings to the common ancestor of birds and again independently to the point where winged mammals diverged from nonwinged mammals, we can do the same for behavioral traits. For example, a recent phylogenetic analysis suggested that the present-day distribution of pair bonding across species almost certainly reflects several independent originations of this behavioral trait (Fraley, Brumbaugh, & Marks, 2005); these analyses direct attention to likely ancestral candidates, paving the way for more focused phylogenetic analyses to pinpoint the conditions under which this trait emerged.

FUNCTIONAL GENOMICS: A NEW DIRECTION FOR SOCIAL PSYCHOLOGY

In recent years genome-sequencing projects have been completed in several animal species (Reinke & White, 2002), providing the foundations for a new interdisciplinary bridge linking social psychology to the field of functional genomics (FG). FG can be defined as the study of genes, their resulting proteins, and the role played by the proteins in the body's biochemical process (www.ornl.gov/TechResources/Human_Genome/glossary/).[1] FG holds the

---

[1]Genes are essentially information bytes consisting of DNA, which undergo a two-step process to encode unique proteins. The two steps are transcription (i.e., the synthesis of a messenger RNA [mRNA] copy from a sequence of DNA) and translation (the process in which the genetic code carried by mRNA directs the synthesis of proteins from amino acids). Proteins are required for the structure, function, and regulation of the body's cells, tissues, and organs, including the brain; example protein products include neurotransmitter receptors, neuropeptides, and ion channels.

promise of revealing how information encrypted in a gene gets translated into behavior. In contrast to previous genomic techniques, which looked at the effects of one gene at a time, FG looks at the simultaneous expression of different genes in multiple tissues at one time. This is an important development for behavioral researchers because it is now widely accepted that most behaviors are caused by complex combinations of genes.

New genomic techniques applied to animal models allow researchers to link genes to the neural circuits that drive behavior (Robinson, 2004). A researcher could use FG methods to examine cellular processes underlying gene–behavior links as a function of social or environmental change. This would be done by measuring gene expression in the brain (in terms of the relative abundance of mRNA) in response to experimental manipulations of the social or environmental conditions. For example, by quantifying the differential output of mRNA in cichlids (a taxa of fish) as a function of a threatening stimuli (e.g., the presence of a predator), gene expression in the brain can be linked to behavior (Hofmann, 2003; Kao, 1999).

To illustrate how genomic techniques can be applied to ideas relevant to human social behavior, consider the topic of social defeat. In humans, social defeat can be manipulated using rigged-competition paradigms and has been studied in such realms as occupational status, small-group interactions, and bullying (Brodsky, 1976; Dabbs, 1992; Mazur, 1973; Rejeski et al., 1989; Sullivan, 2000). Victims of social defeat suffer psychological impairment in the form of depression, anxiety, sociophobia, and other behavioral symptoms (Bjorkqvist, 2001).

New opportunities for examining the cellular and molecular processes underlying these complex social phenomena can be realized by integrating FG with animal research. A number of paradigms already exist for manipulating social defeat in animals; for example, individual rodents can be experimentally assigned to high or low social status using experienced-fighter paradigms (where individuals are placed in competition with either an experienced or naïve fighter) or resident-intruder paradigms (where individuals get to interact in their own territory [victor condition] or that of another individual [loser condition]). Animal victims of social defeat suffer behavioral and psychological consequences similar to those found in humans, such as a severe stress, depression, and impairment of immunological function (Blanchard et al., 1994; Meerlo et al., 1997; Stefanski, 2000). These parallels between human and animal studies open the way for investigations of the specific genomic processes that underlie the psychological phenomena associated with social defeat. For example, an FG study of social defeat could identify specific gene complexes that respond to social stress and help identify the specific neural substrates that mediate behavioral responses. Currently, invasive procedures, such as decapitation, are required for most genomic analyses of brain processes, ruling out human studies. However, by identifying relevant animal analogs (as in the case of social defeat described earlier), social psychologists can harness the power of FG analyses.[2]

In sum, FG studies hold great promise for scientists interested in social behavior because they have the potential to show how genes affect specific brain mechanisms associated with social behaviors. Indeed, FG has already been successfully applied in human health research in such areas as obesity and depression (Kowalski, 2004; Hyman, 2000). Although still in its infancy, this FG research on gene–behavior links holds great promise for understanding the most fundamental biological processes underlying complex social behavior.

CONCLUSIONS

It is important to point out that animal studies will only benefit those areas of social psychology for which animal analogs can be found. Thus, although animal studies may shed light on such issues as attraction and mating or power and dominance, they are less likely to benefit areas like attitude formation and stereotyping. In addition, improvements are still needed in the technology associated with FG analyses (e.g., the technology cannot yet consistently identify one-to-one correspondences between mRNA levels and the particular proteins synthesized).

Nonetheless, as Hebb and Thompson (1954) pointed out 50 years ago, animal studies do offer some research opportunities that are difficult or impossible to achieve using human studies alone. With so much to be gained, it is time to rediscover the long-neglected bridges between social psychology and animal behavior.

REFERENCES

Bjorkqvist, K. (2001). Social defeat as a stressor in humans. *Physiology and Behavior, 73,* 435–442.

Blanchard, D. C., Spencer, R. L., Weiss, S. M., Blanchard, R. J., McEwen, B., Sakai, R. R. (1994). Visible burrow system as a model of chronic social stress: Behavioral and neuroendocrine correlates. *Psychoendocrinology, 20,* 117–134.

Brodsky, C. M. (1976). *The harassed worker.* Toronto: Lexington Books.

Capitanio, J. P., Mendoza, S. P., & Baroncelli, S. (1999). The relationship of personality dimensions in adult male rhesus macaques to progression of Simian immunodeficiency virus disease. *Brain, Behavior, and Immunity, 13,* 138–154.

Dabbs, J. (1992). Testosterone and occupational achievement. *Social Forces, 70,* 813–824.

Domjan, M., & Purdy, J. E. (1995). Animal research in psychology: More than meets the eye of the general psychology student. *American Psychologist, 50,* 496–503.

---

[2]Animal species with well-mapped genomes, such as the cichlid, guppy, and mouse, serve as ideal model systems because much genomic information is already available and techniques have already been established for extracting and analyzing their mRNA.

Fahlke, C., Lorenz, J. G., Long, J., Champoux, M., Suomi, S. J., & Higley, J. D. (2000). Rearing experiences and stress-induced plasma cortisol as early risk factors for excessive alcohol consumption in nonhuman primates. *Alcoholism: Clinical and Experimental Research, 24,* 644–650.

Fraley, R. C., Brumbaugh, C. C., & Marks, M. J. (2005). The evolution and function of adult attachment: A comparative and phylogenetic analysis of pair bonding. *Journal of Personality and Social Psychology.*

Gilbert, D. T., Fiske, S. T., & Lindzey, G. (1998). *The handbook of social psychology* (4th ed.). Oxford: Oxford University Press.

Gosling, S. D. (2001). From mice to men: What can we learn about personality from animal research? *Psychological Bulletin, 127,* 45–86.

Graybeal, A., & Gosling, S. D. (2005). *Tree thinking: A new paradigm for evolutionary and comparative psychology.* Manuscript submitted for publication.

Hebb, D. O., & Thompson, R. W. (1954) The social significance of animals studies. In G. Lindzey (Ed.), *Handbook of social psychology* (pp. 532–561). Cambridge, MA: Addison-Wesley.

Hofmann, H. A. (2003). Functional genomics of neural and behavioral plasticity. *Journal of Neurobiology, 54,* 272–282.

Hyman, S. E. (2000). National Institute of Mental Health goals for behavioral science. *Experimental Clinical Psychopharmacology, 8,* 271–272.

Kao, C. M. (1999). Functional genomic technologies: Creating new paradigms for fundamental and applied biology. *Biotechnology Progress, 15,* 304–311.

Kowalski, T. J. (2004). The future of genetic research on appetitive behavior. *Appetite, 42,* 11–14.

Mazur, A. (1973). A cross species comparison of status in small established groups. *American Sociological Review, 38,* 513–530.

Meerlo, P., Pragt, B. J., & Daan, S. (1997). Social stress induces high intensity sleep in rats. *Neuroscience Letters, 225,* 41–44.

Murchison, C. (1935). *A handbook of social psychology.* Worcester, MA: Clark University Press.

Rejeski, W. J., Gagne, M., Parker, P. E., & Koritnik, D. R. (1989). Acute stress reactivity from contested dominance in dominant and submissive males. *Behavioral Medicine, 15,* 118–124.

Reinke, V., & White, K. P. (2002). Developmental genomic approaches in model organisms. *Annual Review of Genomics and Human Genetics, 3,* 153–178.

Robinson, G. E. (2004). Beyond nature and nurture. *Science, 304,* 397–399.

Stefanski, V. (2000). Social stress in laboratory rats: Hormonal responses and immune cell distribution. *Psychoneuroendocrinoligy, 25,* 389–406.

Sullivan, K. (2000). *The anti-bullying handbook.* Auckland: Oxford University Press.

Vazire, S., & Gosling, S. D. (2003). Bridging psychology and biology with animal research. *American Psychologist, 5,* 407–408.

Virgin, C. E., Jr., & Sapolsky, R. M. (1997). Styles of male social behavior and endocrine correlates among low-ranking baboons. *American Journal of Primatology, 42,* 25–39.

Zuckerman, M. (1996). The psychobiological model for impulsive unsocialized sensation seeking: A comparative approach. *Neuropsychobiology, 34,* 125–129.

18

Basic Lessons
From Observing Nature

José-Miguel Fernández-Dols
Universidad Autónoma de Madrid, Spain

Bridges, the guiding metaphor of this book, are structures providing a passage across gaps between two points. If we want to stay faithful to the metaphor, we cannot talk about the overlap of social psychology and other disciplines (e.g., sociology), or about the intrusion of a particular discipline into the hunting grounds of social psychology (e.g., sociobiology). The bridge metaphor is quite suitable for those cases in which there is a gap between two disciplines, but a gap that for some reason, rather than disappearing, should simply be circumvented from time to time.

In this chapter I talk about a potential bridge between social psychology and a remote, ancient discipline that certainly does not overlap and should not overlap with social psychology: natural history.

SOCIAL PSYCHOLOGY AND NATURAL HISTORY

"Natural history" was invented by Pliny the Elder in A.D. 77, and Pliny's *Natural History* is an encyclopedic compendium of information about the world, as it was known in his time. Natural history inspired naturalism. Naturalism is a discipline ancillary to modern biology in which people—not necessarily professional scientists—study wildlife (by bird-watching, for example) and painstakingly work out exhaustive taxonomies. Natural history emphasizes a kind of description that looks amateurish and atheoretical, but even though naturalists may be amateurs, great theory builders in biology—including Darwin himself—were also enthusiastic naturalists, and some disciplines, such as ethology, are an inextricable combination of naturalistic observation and theoretical development.

Pliny's *Natural History* also included exhaustive accounts of customs and memorable events in the lives of his contemporaries, a sort of human naturalism whose modern version would be ethnographical accounts, one of the main contributions of the founders of anthropology.

In social psychology, however, naturalistic observation and descriptive accounts have faded away, even if they ever existed. The latest edition of the *Handbook of Social Psychology* does not include a chapter on observation, and some introductory chapters acknowledge the fact that observations of actual behavior are hard to find in our discipline (Aronson, Wilson, & Brewer, 1998), probably because most researchers see observation as a method marginal to theory development (Taylor, 1998). Those authors, such as Barker and his colleagues at the Kansas School (e.g., Barker, 1968), who tried to provide naturalistic accounts of everyday life are peripheral in the discipline.

My point is that social psychologists' excursions into natural history (i.e., into detailed descriptions of the information present in everyday behavior and language) are an excellent and underused "reality test" for the stage *before* making conclusive theoretical claims.

There are at least two reasons for this *pretheoretical* (not atheoretical!) description: (a) Explanation without a sufficient pretheoretical description often leads to premature conclusions and inefficient research programs, and (b) everyday language descriptions are always theoretically relevant in social psychology because social psychologists' theories are inspired in everyday language and—for better or for worse—share some of its basic assumptions about reality.

WHEN EXPLANATION FORGETS DESCRIPTION

Although replicating chemical reactions or physical phenomena is fairly routine in the teaching of chemistry or physics anywhere in the world, replicating classic findings in social psychology is quite difficult. Part of the problem is that social psychology findings relate to extremely complex phenomena, but another important portion of the problem is that many social psychology theorists failed to check whether their explanations fitted observations and accounts of everyday life in the world.

Compiling observations and accounts of everyday life across cultures is a powerful way of guaranteeing that the formal replication of surveys or experiments will make sense. For example, teaching cross-cultural social psychology students that they are collectivistic or individualistic is hard, because the everyday experience of most students is that they are sometimes collectivistic and sometimes individualistic, depending on the situation.

After scores, possibly hundreds, of mechanical applications of questionnaires on Hofstede's collectivism versus individualism dichotomy (Hofstede, 1980), researchers have gradually realized that this concept lacks a solid descriptive background. This shortcoming has led to many serious conceptual misunderstandings, particularly lack of consensus on the operationalizations and assessments of these constructs. For example, reviewers of the extensive literature on this issue (see Oyserman, Coon, & Kemmelmeier, 2002; Voronov & Singer, 2002) concluded that the meaning of collectivism varies enormously depending on other cultural circumstances—for example, level of distrust toward other groups. Even within the same society, people may switch between collectivistic or individualistic strategies depending on the immediate setting—an observation usually pointed out by cross-cultural psychology students to their teachers.

An earlier and broader descriptive program supporting Hofstede's findings may have prevented these problems, saving unnecessary effort. For example, almost 50 years ago, Banfield (1958), a political scientist, published an ethnographical account of everyday life in a backward community in southern Italy, coining the term "amoral familism" to describe the important links between collectivism and distrust.

Unfortunately, Hofstede's theory is not the only key contribution that would have benefited from an earlier and more careful consideration of descriptive accounts or nonparticipant observations. A second conspicuous example comes from the study of emotion: Most psychologists have taken for granted that there are universal involuntary expressions of discrete emotions (Ekman, 1972). All the substantive support for this theory came not from observational studies, but from "recognition experiments" in which subjects were prompted to assign some categories of emotion to bidimensional portraits of static, posed faces. Neither the categories of emotion nor the posed faces were chosen following previous observational data. In fact, there are very few naturalistic descriptions of the actual expressions of intense emotions, and most of them do not support the universal-expression assumptions (see Fernández-Dols & Ruiz-Belda, 1997). These naturalistic descriptions are inspiring new and exciting alternative hypotheses, such as the existence of smiles with different evolutionary backgrounds, and the search for links between facial behavior and social motives or cognitive appraisals (see Russell, Bachorowski, & Fernández-Dols, 2003).

Again, an earlier and broader descriptive program examining Ekman's findings would probably have prevented these problems, saving precious time. For example, 24 years ago, two ethologists (Kraut & Johnston, 1979) published a series of naturalistic studies showing that the link between facial behavior and emotion was at best weak.

WHEN EXPLANATION IGNORES EVERYDAY KNOWLEDGE

Psychologists took for granted that the theory of mind (the tendency to impute mental states to oneself and others) is universal. Afterward, some authors (e.g., Lillard, 1998) showed that "mind" was taken from European-American everyday language, and did not necessarily have parallel terms in the languages of other cultures. Lillard (1998) concluded that an earlier review of ethnographical accounts on the potential translations of "mind" would have made research more productive.

Lack of concern about how people describe a particular event can be misleading. Lay descriptions are never atheoretical because most of the vocabulary of psychology comes from everyday language. Therefore, social psychologists should develop precise and detailed knowledge of everyday descriptions of particular phenomena before building theoretical frameworks. Psychologists' language is not a straight road to reality; it is rather a problem in itself due to its complex interactions with everyday language.

Even within the same culture, a particular experimental tradition can lose sight of the everyday meaning of the concept, with negative consequences for the scientific development of the field. In social psychology the technical meanings of some concepts are not always more precise or enlightening than their everyday meanings. Distance between the technical concept and the everyday concept is not necessarily bad when it is produced by a clear theoretical program, but such distance can be a serious limitation when it is merely the expression of a drift caused by external circumstances. For example, the obvious difficulties for studying social injustice led most researchers to ask hypothetical questions or to craft artificial social settings in which university students carried out menial tasks. As Lerner (2003) pointed out, social psychologists "lost [the justice motive, and] ... they may not find it again," because current methods of research on social justice consist of low-impact treatments that are far removed from the highly emotional, mostly uncontrollable situations in which people experience injustice or disrespect, or have to make decisions about justice. Social psychologists' "(in)justice" is divorced from people's "(in)justice" for no clear scientific reason.

CONCLUSIONS

It may be time to begin a serious, protracted, and profound review of the descriptive bases of our knowledge. Social psychologists should refrain from producing, spreading, and promoting explanations with no pretheoretical description. And pretheoretical description means an in-depth discussion of people's actual behavior and everyday language in natural settings and across cultures.

Pretheoretical descriptions, in the guise of ethnographical reports, field observation, or other kinds of descriptive accounts, are, of course, ancillary to theoretical development. As an end in themselves, pretheoretical descriptions are likely to lead to obscure and tautological accounts (like Pliny's original *Natural History*) or theoretically irrelevant findings. Nevertheless, as a propaedeutic requirement, pretheoretical description is an overdue task in many fields of social psychology: healthy excursions to the forbidden and usually exotic territories of natural history, just like those quiet ones that Darwin made aboard the HMS *Beagle* before developing his revolutionary theory.

REFERENCES

Aronson, E., Wilson, T. D., & Brewer, M. B. (1998). Experimentation in social psychology. In D. T. Gilbert, S. T. Fiske, & G. Lindzey (Eds.), *The handbook of social psychology* (4th ed., Vol. 1, pp. 99–142). Boston: McGraw-Hill.

Banfield, E. C. (1958). *The moral basis of a backward society.* New York: Free Press.

Barker, R. G. (1968). *Ecological psychology: Concepts and methods for studying the environment of human behavior.* Stanford, CA: Stanford University Press.

Ekman, P. (1972). Universals and cultural differences in facial expressions of emotion. In J. K. Cole (Ed.), *Nebraska symposium on motivation* (Vol. 19, pp. 207–283). Lincoln: University of Nebraska Press.

Fernández-Dols, J. M., & Ruiz-Belda, M. A. (1997). Spontaneous facial behavior during intense emotional episodes: Artistic truth and optical truth. In J. A. Russell, & J. M. Fernández-Dols (Eds.), *The psychology of facial expression* (pp. 255–274). New York: Cambridge University Press.

Hofstede, G. (1980). *Culture's consequences.* Beverly Hills, CA: Sage.

Kraut, R. E., & Johnston, R. E. (1979). Social and emotional messages of smiling: An ethological approach. *Journal of Personality and Social Psychology, 37,* 1539–1553.

Lerner, M. J. (2003). The justice motive: Where social psychologists found it, how they lost it, and why they may not find it again. *Personality and Social Psychology Review, 7,* 288–399.

Lillard, A. (1998). Ethnopsychologies: Cultural variations in theories of mind. *Psychological Bulletin, 123,* 3–32.

Oyserman, D., Coon, H. M., & Kemmelmeier, M. (2002). Rethinking individualism and collectivism: Evaluation of theoretical assumptions and meta-analyses. *Psychological Bulletin, 128,* 3–72.

Russell, J. A., Bachorowski, J. A., & Fernández-Dols, J. M. (2003). Facial and vocal expression of emotion. *Annual Review of Psychology, 54,* 329–349.

Taylor, S. E. (1998). The social being in social psychology. In D. T. Gilbert, S. T. Fiske, & G. Lindzey (Eds.), *The handbook of social psychology* (4th ed., Vol. 1, pp. 58–95). Boston: McGraw-Hill.

Voronov, M., & Singer, J. A. (2002). The myth of individualism-collectivism: A critical review. *Journal of Social Psychology, 142,* 461–480.

19

Getting Social Psychological Research Ideas From Other Human Sciences

Jacques-Philippe Leyens
Université catholique de Louvain at Louvain-la-Neuve

Ⅰn 1972, Israël and Tajfel edited a book documenting a malaise in social psychology. In his chapter, Tajfel criticized social psychology thought as taking place in a vacuum. For him, social phenomena occur in institutional, cultural, and historical settings that have to be taken into account. Actually, during a walk through Bristol, he told me that he was learning more from books outside, rather than inside, of social psychology. Like Tajfel, I found later on that I needed to read beyond social psychology to better grasp what I was studying. In my research, I tend to use different paradigms, many of them inspired by other psychological disciplines than social psychology. The core ideas of this research, however, are often found among historians, anthropologists, and political scientists. Interested in racism, I read books of these scholars and try to find ideas that have not yet been (much) developed in social psychology. In the following paragraphs, I illustrate some of these sources of inspiration. I regret that lack of space prevents me from citing the work of (rare) colleagues who have investigated topics related to the ones I will speak of.

DEHUMANIZATION, ESSENTIALISM, AND INFRAHUMANIZATION

Everyone knows that dehumanization of others has existed for a long time. Dictionaries tell us that the word *barbarian* comes from the Greek term *barbaros*, which designated people who did not speak Greek. In fact, phonetically, the word *barbar* was used for a bleating sheep (Ciardi, 1986, cited in Johnson,

1997). In other words, those individuals who did not speak Greek were assimilated to animals. The word *barbaros* is just one example of outgroup dehumanization. Anthropology provides us with other illustrations. Sumner's (1906) *Folkways* is full of descriptions of dehumanization among primitive tribes. The same is true of the Brussels-born anthropologist and founder of structuralism, Lévi-Strauss. In his essay on "Race et histoire" (1952/1987), he widely discussed ethnocentrism and collaboration between cultures. More interesting for our purposes, he gave many examples of how tribes referred to themselves ("The people," "the human beings") and other tribes (generally the name of a disgusting animal). Even a respected scientist like Buffon (1833–1834), who recognized that there was a single human species, could not prevent himself from inferring differences in values from physical attributes of the groups. This inference led him to compare the "Negroe" with a donkey or an ape, whereas the White was assimilated to the horse or the human being.

Given that people are fundamentally ethnocentric (Jahoda, 1999), the concept of dehumanization is linked to the one of essence. Omnipresent in sociology and anthropology, the concept of essence took time to receive credit in psychology in general, and in social psychology in particular, probably because of the difficulty in operationalizing it. Essentialism is, however, very useful for understanding intergroup relations. The purpose of the trial of Valladolid, for example, was to decide whether the American Indians were human beings. To do this, one had to prove that the Indians possessed a soul (that is, believed in God). The existence of the soul was the crucial essence for the Catholic Spanish. Interestingly, the Caribbean Indians were confronted with the same problem as the Spanish but resolved it in another way. They simply let Spanish bodies putrefy in the ocean in order to verify whether their inside was like theirs! (Lévi-Strauss, 1952/1987). These examples show that, when faced with differences between groups, people are tempted to explain them through different essences (e.g., biological, religious, linguistic).

Fortunately, the phenomenon of dehumanization is mostly restricted to intense crises or conflicts. Could it be that it exists in everyday life under a less severe form? The response should be positive if one trusts the winding history of the scientific debate about race and the human species. Like Buffon, people may feel obliged to believe that everybody is part of humankind, but nothing prevents them from unconsciously imagining that they are more human than others, or that others are less human than they are. If so, to what extent is infrahumanization, or lesser perceived humanity, widespread? Under which circumstances should it appear? Is infrahumanization a mere synonym for outgroup derogation?

UNIVERSALISM, RELATIVISM, AND NORMS OF NONDISCRIMINATION

How does one get rid of racism (and infrahumanization)? The question is relatively recent. Solutions have been formulated by famous scholars but the best intentions in the world may remain nevertheless racist (Todorov, 1989).

Those universalistic humanists like Auguste Comte (1848–1854), who wanted equality, could not refrain from being ethnocentric; thus, equality started by resembling or assimilating to the democratic France. This tendency to confound equality with similarity to the dominant ingroup can still be observed today. The role Comte attributed to France during the 19th century has now moved to another continent and country. In sharp contrast, other scientists, such as Lévi-Strauss, defended a relativist view of humanity, promoted the respect of differences, and were led to favor the absence of contact between groups. By doing so, relativists also acted as racists.

The philosophical debate between universalism and relativism has immediate implications for social psychology. One of these implications concerns the differential effects of norms of nondiscrimination. According to the color-blind norm, we should behave with the idea that we are all similar (and potentially equal). This is Comte's point of view. According to the color-conscious norm, action has to take into account differences between groups. For Lévi-Strauss, these differences have to be maintained. The contradictory positions of universalistic humanists and relativists make it easy to realize that neither of the two normative strategies has unique advantages or disadvantages. They even suggest to researchers when advantages and disadvantages will occur.

Blindness to differences may be ideal when it implies equality but intolerable when it is synonymous of ethnocentrism. Consciousness of differences may be efficient in social interactions when respect for differences exists. The same differences may also become the source of hostility because their mere existence serves as a justification for discrimination. In other words, norms of nondiscrimination will fulfill their function only to the extent that they focus on equality while taking into account, respectfully, the differences between groups.

FROM IMPLICIT TO EXPLICIT PREJUDICE

Even "bad" books, such as Goldenhagen's (1996) *Hitler's Voluntary Executioners. Ordinary Germans and the Holocaust*, can be inspiring for social psychological research. According to the author, there is a single explanation for the dehumanization and extermination of Jews. It is the centuries-long German anti-Semitism (which disappeared suddenly after the war, as he writes in the preface to the German edition!). The fact that this book became a best-seller demonstrates that many people became persuaded by this unique and simple explanation exposed during hundreds of pages while other interpretations were discarded in a few lines (for historical criticisms, see Kinkelstein & Birn, 1998; Stern, 1996). As a scientist, one becomes angry against the biased methodology. As a scientific psychologist, one remains intrigued by the phenomenon of a belief (anti-Semitism) transformed into heinous and lethal acts, even if those acts were not performed by every German, as claimed by Goldenhagen. This book is completely unscientific, but it forces social psychologists to explain why, in some cases, implicit racism *suddenly* becomes explicit. Given the social pressures against racism, current social psychology has moved its research focus from blatantly explicit expressions of racism toward subtler, less controllable ones. Recent history, however, has witnessed many movements going in the opposite direction in all parts of the world. The amount of such regressions to explicit discrimination bypasses by far the studies that investigated the shift from implicit to explicit prejudice.

CONCLUSIONS

Reading these various books may give the pessimistic impression that social psychology is reinventing the wheel. A more optimistic view is that social psychology deals with real problems and tests empirically speculations that have preoccupied scholars in the human sciences, sometimes for centuries. Obviously, I have selected topics that have an immediate interest for my team and me. Far from my purpose was to distinguish between "a social psychology that is" and "a social psychology that might be." Through the selection of readings, I merely attempted to illustrate how I got research ideas from books outside of social psychology. Essentialism, norms of nondiscrimination, and implicit and explicit prejudice were notions well accepted in social psychology before I started my research. Anthropological and historical data gave me the idea of different degrees in humanity. Sociological and philosophical debates provided me with a theoretical perspective to investigate the differential effects of nondiscrimination as a function of racism. Finally, Goldenhagen's thesis was so simplistic that it raised (almost) new theoretical questions that needed empirical verification. I take a lot of pleasure in pursuing these lines of research, but, frankly, I do not know whether my efforts will benefit my sources of inspiration.

REFERENCES

Comte, A. (1848–1854). *Système de politique positive* (4 vols.). Paris. (Edited by Anthropos in 1969)

Goldenhagen, D. J. (1996). *Hitler's voluntary executioners. Ordinary Germans and the Holocaust.* New York: Knopf.

Israël, J., & Tajfel, H. (1972). *The context of social psychology: A critical assessment.* London: Academic Press.

Jahoda, G. (1999). *Images of savages. Ancient roots of modern prejudice in Western culture.* London: Routledge.

Johnson, G. R. (1997). The evolutionary roots of patriotism. In D. Bar-Tal & E. Staub (Eds.), *Patriotism in the lives of individuals and nations* (pp. 45–90). Chicago: Nelson-Hall.

Kinkelstein, N., & Birn, R. (1998). *L'Allemagne en procès. La thèse de Goldenhagen et la vérité historique.* Paris: Albin Michel.

Lévi-Strauss, C. (1987). *Race et histoire.* Paris: Denoël. (Original work published 1952)

Todorov, T. (1989). *Nous et les autres. La réflexion française sur la diversité humaine.* Paris: Seuil.

Stern, F. (1996, November/December). The Goldenhagen controversy. One nation, one people, one theory? *Foreign Affairs,* 128–138.

Sumner, W. G. (1906). *Folkways.* New York: Ginn.

20

Mind in the Organized Social Environment

John C. Turner
Australian National University

In considering "bridging" social psychology, I outline a general position and then make some related points about the study of prejudice. Unless one holds to some vision of the sovereignty of social psychology, drawing on the knowledge of other relevant sciences must always be necessary for a full description and understanding of any concrete instance of human social life. What is less obvious is that theory in social psychology, the delineation of general principles and processes, is also inescapably tied up with bridging.

If the task of social psychology is to understand the interaction between mind and society, the ways in which the psychological makes possible and explains the social and is in turn modified by the social, then it is evident that all social psychological analysis must make assumptions about the character of social life and about its relevance to psychological analysis. These assumptions shape the kind of theory found adequate. Historically, there are three main positions.

The first position, *individualism*, tends to deny the psychological and social reality of the group and social structure and reduces all social and collective forms to the activities of the (as if psychologically isolated) individual. The relevance of specifically social analyses is discounted. It is assumed that there are general psychological processes that may be identified in "nonsocial" environments and extrapolated to social ones without any qualitative modification. Social psychology is seen more or less as the application of general principles of learning, motivation, or cognition to social behavior. Social situations may differ from nonsocial situations, as all stimulus conditions may differ, but the laws, the explanatory principles, remain the same. This view tends to eliminate the need for a theoretically distinct science of social psychology, making it a subcategory of general (i.e., individual) psychology.

In the *interactionist* position pioneered by Kurt Lewin and others, social facts are accepted as having their own reality. The group is seen as more than or different from the sum of its individual members and has a psychological significance, subjectively and objectively. The interplay between the psychological and the social takes place in what is a unified social-psychological field from the point of view of the perceiver and produces emergent field properties that cannot be reduced to or derived from the psychology of the individual in isolation (the latter being in fact an analytic fiction). The interactionist view holds that the psychological nature of individuals is qualitatively transformed by their membership in society.

The important point here is that acceptance of the reality of society and of the group dimension of human psychology does not in any way amount to denigrating the importance of psychological analysis or to reducing social psychology to an epiphenomenon of society. Embracing the complexity and reality of human social life demands that social psychology take seriously the idea of "emergence" (of new psychological processes produced by the social-psychological field), which in turn enriches and liberates social psychological theorizing rather than impoverishes it.

The third position, *social constructionism*, is the mirror image of individualism. It denies social psychological interaction by reducing the psychological to the social. Social, historical, and cultural processes are assigned a privileged causal reality and are supposed to *construct* and not merely interact with and affect the human mind. Evidence of social, cultural, and historical variation is taken as evidence against the idea of a universal human nature. Psychological principles are seen as epiphenomena of cultural, historical, and even discursive processes.

THE NECESSITY OF BRIDGING

The first general point then is that we have no choice about bridging. Social psychology is an inherently bridging science, because it is about the relationship of psychology to social life. We always inevitably make judgments about what social life is like and therefore how it is relevant to psychology, and the judgments that we make, our implicit or explicit beliefs about the nature of society, fundamentally shape not only our research but also the theoretical principles we find adequate. Even when we try to deny the social or deny the psychological, this itself reflects a view of human nature and society that comes from outside the discipline. The issue is how to bridge constructively.

The benefits of bridging flow from embracing rather than playing down the significance of the social in understanding human life. The richest and most important theoretical work in the science has not come from denying or eschewing the reality and complexity of human society and its impact on the human mind but from the very opposite. Facing up to the distinctness of society from psychology and then facing up to the need for psychological theory sufficiently sophisticated to be capable of dealing with the mind–society interaction in the context of a fuller picture of the social has produced richer and more profound psychological analyses, not diluted the psychology. Lewin, Sherif, Asch, Heider, Festinger, Tajfel, and Moscovici all provide powerful examples of such theory. Of course, social psychology can learn or borrow from other areas of psychology (think of Bruner, Rosch, or Medin), but such borrowings must be incorporated appropriately into our own special form of theory.

Bridging is largely done implicitly, informally, selectively, reflecting the special knowledge (or ignorance) and particular ideology of the psychologist concerned. Making the process more explicit and encouraging more open debate about different underlying social and historical analyses can only be welcome.

Are there costs? There undoubtedly can be. The in-principle costs are where bridging takes the form of reductionism. Individualism, which reduces the social to the psychological, does not stop there but, as we all know, continues on to reduce the psychological to the physiological, biological, or genetic. The same tendency to reduce complex social-psychological structures and processes to supposedly more basic elements, to reify field properties into individual essences (e.g., transforming social ideologies into personality traits, social values into individual needs, group-based stereotypes into universal flaws of individual cognition), also easily progresses to explaining traits, motives, or even whole social structures by means of supposedly even more basic biological structures. The problem is not drawing on biology or genetics, which can be entirely sensible and appropriate, but to confuse bridging to complementary sciences with reductionism. The essence of reductionism is that it fails to match the nature of the explanation to the distinctive, emergent properties of the phenomenon to be explained, in effect denying the reality of system properties that arise from the organization of lower level elements.

This is just as true when reducing the psychological to the social. For many social psychologists, "interdisciplinary" work has a bad name, for the reason that it often means not bridging but giving up conceptual disciplines to pursue a ragbag of ideologically charged notions through descriptive social research. Bridging to the social and historical sciences does not mean giving up psychological theory and analysis to do sociology or "relevant" social research in which one studies some social phenomenon relatively descriptively and atheoretically. This effectively moves the research away from social psychology theoretically defined and implicitly adopts the social constructionist view that the task is merely to describe socially and historically contingent facts as the royal road to psychological insights. The point of bridging is to broaden our knowledge of social life, either to provide a more complete picture of some concrete instance or to expand the challenge to social psychology to develop theory consistent with and capable of making sense of its psychological aspects.

THE CASE OF PREJUDICE

Let us now consider prejudice. Research on prejudice began in the 1920s and 1930s as part of a political rejection of racism and race psychology. The assumption that racist (primarily but not only anti-Black) attitudes were "irrational prejudices" was not widely shared before that time. This assumption shaped what is still the dominant meta-theory of the field, that racist attitudes can be understood and explained by a focus on the irrationality of an abstract individual psychology. This meta-theory is expressed in many different ways: in the idea of racism being rooted in pathological, deviant personalities such as Right-Wing Authoritarians or people with a rigid cognitive style; in the idea of normal, universal cognitive and motivational processes such as social categorization or a need to belong, which operate in default to distort the social perception of outgroup members and produce ethnocentrism irrespective of the nature of intergroup relations; in the idea of social stereotyping as inherently inaccurate, serving only the purposes of cognitive economy or irrational denigration; and in the idea of cultural socialization into racist attitudes, consciously or unconsciously, as a matter of passive social learning rather than contemporary social influence and as if cultures never changed. The main theoretical themes of prejudice research all have in common the tendency to look for answers in the psychological flaws of personalities, processes, or cultures. This emphasis is embodied in the very term *prejudice* used to define the field, as if racist ideology was a problem of dysfunctional psychology and had not developed to advance and justify the self-interest of specific social groups during a specific historical period and indeed was not still doing so.

The alternative view was introduced into social psychology by Sherif and Tajfel. Their life experiences and political philosophies were such as to give no credence to accounts of prejudice that ignored the reality of groups, of social structure, of collective self-interest and political ideology, and that denied the essential fact that contemporary human society is a house divided, in which different social groups pursue conflicting interests and social antagonism can such serve such interests. They looked for the explanation of prejudice not in some universal, abstract psychology of the individual but in a collective or group psychology as it functioned in specific social, historical, and ideological contexts. The problem for them was not human psychology per se but the historically contingent and therefore changeable social arrangements within which it functioned. This social conflict view of prejudice is still being developed and is still fighting its corner (Turner & Reynolds, 2001). Its advantage already is that it demands a social psychology as applicable to the antiracists as to the racists, a genuinely universal social psychology compatible with historical facts and political conflict and capable of pointing to new social possibilities. This perspective is intimately linked to a respect for history and to a belief in the necessity of a scientific understanding of society. The paradox is that in rejecting the idea of racism as a psychological aberration, one embraces the possibility of social change leading to its elimination, whereas the "prejudice" tradition has now reached the point of explaining why racism is inevitable and "normal." After all, if the causes are solely within human psychology, then our flaws are surely fixed.

If we are to suppose that human social psychology is not inherently dysfunctional, that social change towards better things is possible, then to understand the divisive, backward and irrational conflicts that poison the contemporary world we must acknowledge the historical and social processes that produced and made significant the relevant specific social identities (such as the fiction of "race," see Banks & Eberhardt, 1998; Reicher, 1986), the concrete social structures that determine the nature of intergroup relationships, and the political, economic, sociological, and cultural origins of the collective theories and ideologies that dominate and mediate the interpretation of these intergroup relationships by specific given groups. Instead of denigrating social perception as inherently limited, erroneous, or flawed, we should try to understand why people see things the way they do by drawing on wider historical and societal knowledge. That different groups see things differently is more usually caused by political than psychological bias and follows inevitably from the fact that reality is always judged from a specific, socially defined self. The same cognitive processes operating lawfully from different perspectives *must* produce different judgments (Haslam & Turner, 1995), which does not mean we cannot argue for one perspective over another on wider grounds.

This is a very Lewinian view in its emphasis on finding out how people define the situation to find the method in the madness and a Tajfellian one in the focus on the role of the organized social environment. It is also Lewinian in its commitment to a conception of both personalities and groups in which complex social structures and understandings interact with a dynamic psychology. This commitment is also fundamental to self-categorization theory (Turner & Onorato, 1999), which holds that the self-categories that function to define the perceiver at any given time at any level are an interactive function of a person's motives and expectations, the apprehended social environment, and the complex knowledge, theories, and ideologies produced by society, culture and history. Bridging to social and historical analysis is indispensable for understanding prejudice. We need theoretically to put prejudice in the context of social structure and social change, to move from a focus on the abstract individual to the group in the historical situation.

CONCLUSIONS

Intellectual bridges to the social are inescapable in social psychology. The three main positions are individualism, interactionism, and social constructionism. The case of prejudice supports the argument for an interactionist perspective. Becoming more informed and explicit about the character of the organized social environment within which the social mind functions can enrich our understanding of social psychological interaction and promote a more dynamic and distinctive science, one in which general theoretical principles sit happily with concrete social and historical variability.

REFERENCES

Banks, R. R., & Eberhardt, J. L. (1998). Social psychological processes and the legal bases of racial categorization. In J. L. Eberhardt & S. T. Fiske (Eds.), *Confronting racism: The problem and the response* (pp. 54–75). Thousand Oaks, CA: Sage.

Haslam, S. A., & Turner, J. C. (1995). Context-dependent variation in social stereotyping 3: Extremism as a self-categorical basis for polarized judgment. *European Journal of Social Psychology, 25,* 341–371.

Reicher, S. D. (1986). Contact, action and racialization: Some British evidence. In M. Hewstone & R. Brown (Eds.), *Contact and conflict in intergroup encounters* (pp. 152–168). Oxford, UK: Blackwell.

Turner, J. C., & Onorato, R. (1999). Social identity, personality and the self-concept: A self-categorization perspective. In T. R. Tyler, R. Kramer, & O. John (Eds.), *The psychology of the social self* (pp. 11–46). Mahwah, NJ: Lawrence Erlbaum Associates.

Turner, J. C., & Reynolds, K. J. (2001). The social identity perspective in intergroup relations: Theories, themes and controversies. In R. Brown & S. Gaertner (Eds.), *Handbook of social psychology: Intergroup processes* (Vol. 4, pp. 133–152). Cambridge, MA: Blackwell.

Socially Situated Cognition
as a Bridge

Eliot R. Smith
Indiana University, Bloomington

Gün R. Semin
Free University, Amsterdam

Social psychology has a unique position among the sciences. It is placed at the intersection of the psychological (the universe of mental processes inside the head) and the social (the external universe of interpersonal interactions and group ties). In principle, this position gives us as a field an unusual perspective, because our research practices and conceptual models have to take both of these levels into account. Obviously, though, this is a statement of an ideal that is not always attained in practice. Over the last few decades, social psychology has been pervasively influenced by the social cognition perspective, so that cognitive (psychological, inside the head) models have been dominant in virtually every area. Although extensive lines of research focus on interpersonal and group interaction, even these phenomena are generally explained in terms of the interactants' inner mental representations and processes.

This meta-theoretical approach has a long history in social psychology, going back into the early and middle parts of the 20th century, as far as the gestalt perspective (e.g., Lewin; Festinger; Heider). More recently, since the "cognitive revolution" of the 1960s and 1970s, our field has shared many assumptions with our neighboring discipline, cognitive psychology, including a number of basic postulates that define what could be called the cognitive/ computational perspective (Newell, Simon, & Shaw, 1972; Vera & Simon, 1993). These include, for example:

1. Information processing is abstract, involving computation, defined as the manipulation of textlike symbols.
2. For understanding cognition, central information-processing mechanisms are fundamental, whereas bodies and perceptual or motor systems are mostly irrelevant.
3. Most aspects of social behavior are to be explained by the content and structure of the inner representations (schemas, prototypes, exemplars, etc.) that people construct and on which they draw to perform social judgments and behaviors.

CRITIQUES OF TRADITIONAL ASSUMPTIONS

Although these assumptions have been key to rapid conceptual and empirical progress over the last few decades, today they and indeed the basic foundations of the cognitive/computational perspective are coming under question. Two broad trends, although they share little in common conceptually, both endorse this critique.

One is a set of views in the social sciences that fall under a "social constructionist" umbrella (Gergen, 1999), including the sociocultural school with its emphasis on the sociohistorical and cultural embeddedness of cognition (e.g., Cole, 1996; Vygotski, 1962/1986; Wertsch, 1994), conversation analysis (Hilton & Slugoski, 2001), discourse analysis (Potter & Wetherell, 1987), and microsociology (Mehan & Wood, 1975). Workers following these approaches have been concerned with the situated features of social interaction, particularly the negotiated emergence of meaning in specific social contexts. They have often been less concerned with wedding these ideas with psychological-level process models. That is, they have remained largely focused on propositional (surface) knowledge and with uncovering "rules" that describe how social reality is constructed.

The second movement offering a critique of standard cognitive/computational assumptions has emerged in several areas of the cognitive sciences (including cognitive psychology but also cognitive anthropology, philosophy, linguistics, artificial intelligence, and computer science). This "situated cognition" approach has roots that go back to William James's motor theory of perception, and Dewey and Mead's pragmatism. Some of the threads in the newly emerging critique include:

1. Some artificial intelligence researchers, dissatisfied with the limited progress being made by traditional approaches, turned away from high-level cognition (e.g., playing chess) to the perceptual-motor capabilities of lower animals such as insects as inspiration for their work (e.g., Brooks, 1986/1999). This behavior-based robotics approach emphasizes the power of simple inner mechanisms in interaction with real-world environments to generate adaptive behavior, in the absence of sophisticated inner representations of the environment ("world models"). One theme of

this work is that "the world is its own best model" (Brooks, 1991), so that active perception can substitute for extensive inner representation building.

2. Studies of autonomous agents (physical robots as opposed to agents simulated in computers) have led to an increased understanding of the importance of embodiment for cognition (Wilson, 2002).

3. Developmental psychologists (e.g., Thelen & Smith, 1994) have modeled aspects of infant development in terms of dynamic systems, using concepts such as attractors in state space, and (again) deemphasizing the role of mental representations.

4. Situated cognition researchers study the information-processing loops that connect agents to their environment in immediate interaction, rather than dealing with detached "offline" cognition (e.g., Kirsh & Maglio, 1995).

5. Linguists, particularly Lakoff and Johnson (1999), have extensively explored how metaphors based on bodily actions and spatial relations underlie our understanding even of abstract concepts.

Like the social constructionist viewpoints, this intellectual movement emphasizes the situated nature of cognition: its thorough dependence, indeed inseparability from the cultural and situational context, and its inherent entanglement with perception and action. Unlike social constructionism, this movement retains a focus on building process models. Overt behavior is explained not simply by displaying "cultural rules" that govern the behavior, but by constructing models of the interacting internal (psychological) and external (social, contextual) processes that jointly determine the behavior. Still, there is a fundamental departure from the traditional cognitive/computational approach. Most threads in the emerging situated-cognition viewpoint reject the traditional notion of cognition as abstract symbolic computation. Some even argue that we should dispense altogether with such traditionally central concepts as "representation." Others deny only that representations are necessarily symbolic and textlike in nature, as portrayed by the traditional approach, rather than their very existence (Clark, 1997).

CONGENIALITY OF CRITIQUES TO SOCIAL PSYCHOLOGY

All of these new lines of thinking have immediate and direct relevance to the core concerns of social psychology. As Smith and Semin (2004) argued, four basic principles of the situated approach are also key principles of social psychology. First, cognition is for action; the purpose of cognition is to guide adaptive action, so it must be understood in relation to action. Social psychologists including Fiske (1992) have strongly endorsed this principle, as we have studied interfaces of cognition and motivation, the ways pragmatic demands (e.g., to make judgments quickly and with little mental effort) shape judgment processes, and the functional role of mental representations such as attitudes in guiding action. These issues link closely to current movements in cognitive science such as behavior-based robotics (Brooks, 1986/1999), whose main message is that action is inextricably intertwined with cognition (e.g., actions are often part of the perceptual process), rather than occurring as a separate stage after an extensive inner planning process.

Second, cognition is embodied, drawing on our physical bodies and especially our sensorimotor capabilities. Social psychologists study the ways attitudes are linked to bodily actions (e.g., Neumann & Strack, 2000) and how emotions are linked to bodily movements and expressions, as well as the ways affect and cognition are intertwined. The importance of embodiment is also recognized in recent advances in cognitive science, such as Barsalou's perceptual symbol systems model (1999), in which cognition rests on sensory-motor representations rather than abstract, amodal inner symbols.

Third, cognition is situated, occurring in the context of real-world environments and implemented through perception–action loops, as cognitive scientists have forcefully argued (Clancey, 1997; Clark, 1997; Kirsh & Maglio, 1994). Social psychologists make the important point that the relevant environment in which cognition takes place is often social rather than merely physical. That is, cognition occurs in the environment of interpersonal interaction and group discussion, making it reasonable to speak of socially situated cognition (Semin, 2000).

Fourth, cognition is distributed spatially and temporally, across tools, people, and groups (Hutchins, 1995). Social psychologists have studied the ways cognition draws on other people and socially defined and constituted knowledge and rules for its content and process There are increasingly articulated social psychological analyses of what it means for cognition to be social, distributed, and shared (Caporael, 1997; Levine, Resnick, & Higgins, 1993; Schwarz, 2000) and what group cognition may entail (e.g., Kerr, Niedermeier, & Kaplan, 2000; Tindale & Kameda, 2000; see, for a general review, Thompson & Fine, 1999). For instance, work on transactive memory systems (Wegner, 1995) shows how memory becomes progressively specialized, socially shared, indexed, and complementary in interdependent groups. Other social psychological research examining how distributed knowledge is utilized has been conducted with decision-making groups (Gigone & Hastie, 1997).

CONCLUSIONS

Social psychology and cognitive psychology already have regular interchanges. Probably the majority of the influence has flowed from cognitive to social, in the form of theoretical conceptions of the nature of mental representations and processes (e.g., schemas, exemplars, automatic/controlled processes) and research methods (e.g., process dissociation procedures, response-time measurement). Cognitive psychologists have also begun to recognize the importance of motivation, affect, and social influence in the areas they study, a sign, perhaps, of increasing influence flowing from social to cognitive psychology. However, as cognitive science more generally begins to question the cognitive/computational approach, despite the important ways in which social psychology already recognizes and contributes to these four themes, our field has been almost entirely absent from the interdisciplinary mix making these new points. We therefore have much to gain by forming bridges with those in our neighbor disciplines—beyond cognitive psychology—who are working on these themes. And those disciplines will gain as well. Traffic across the bridges will move both ways; social psychology has a wealth of theoretical and conceptual contributions to make to the situated cognition intellectual movement. This will be especially true as the validity of the idea that cognition is *socially* situated gains increasing recognition.

REFERENCES

Barsalou, L. W. (1999). Perceptual symbol systems. *Behavioral and Brain Sciences, 22,* 577–609.

Brooks, R. A. (1991). *Intelligence without reason.* Cambridge, MA: MIT AI Lab Memo 1293.

Brooks, R. A. (1999). A robust layered control system for a mobile robot. In *Cambrian intelligence* (pp. 3–26). Cambridge, MA: MIT Press. (Original work published 1986)

Caporael, L. (1997). The evolution of truly social cognition: The core configurations model. *Personality and Social Psychology Review, 1,* 276–298.

Cole, M. (1996). *Cultural psychology: A once and future discipline.* Cambridge, MA: Harvard University Press.

Clancey, W. J. (1997). *Situated cognition.* New York: Cambridge University Press.

Clark, A. (1997). *Being there.* Cambridge, MA: MIT Press.

Fiske, S. T. (1992). Thinking is for doing: Portraits of social cognition from Daguerreotype to laserphoto. *Journal of Personality and Social Psychology, 63,* 877–889.

Gergen, K. J. (1999). *An invitation to social construction.* Thousand Oakes, CA: Sage.

Gigone, D., & Hastie, R. (1997). The impact of information on small group choice. *Journal of Personality and Social Psychology, 72,* 132–140.

Hilton, D., & Slugoski, B. (2001). Conversational processes in reasoning and explanation. In A. Tesser & N. Schwarz (Eds.), *Blackwell handbook of social psychology: Intraindividual processes* (Vol. 2, pp. 181–206). Oxford: Blackwell.

Hutchins, E. (1995). *Cognition in the wild.* Cambridge, MA: MIT Press.

Kerr, N. L., Niedermeier, K. E., & Kaplan, M. F. (2000). On the virtues of assuming minimal differences in information processing in individuals and groups. *Group Processes and Intergroup Relations, 3,* 203–217.

Kirsh, D., & Maglio, P. (1994). On distinguishing epistemic from pragmatic action. *Cognitive Science, 18,* 513–549.

Lakoff, G., & Johnson, M. (1999). *Philosophy in the flesh.* New York: Basic Books.

Levine, J. M., Resnick, L. B., & Higgins, E. T. (1993). Social foundations of cognition. *Annual Review of Psychology, 44,* 585–612.

Mehan, H., & Wood, W. (1975). *The reality of ethnomethodology.* New York: Wiley.

Neumann, R., & Strack, F. (2000). Experiential and nonexperiential routes of motor influence on affect and evaluation. In H. Bless & J. P. Forgas (Eds.), *The message within: Role of subjective experience in social cognition and behavior* (pp. 52–68). Philadelphia: Psychology Press.

Newell, A., Simon, H. A., & Shaw, J. (1972). *Human problem solving*. Englewood Cliffs, NJ: Prentice-Hall.

Potter, J., & Wetherell, M. (1987). *Discourse and social psychology: Beyond attitudes and behavior*. London: Sage.

Schwarz, N. (2000). Social judgment and attitudes: Warmer, more social, and less conscious. *European Journal of Social Psychology, 30,* 149–176.

Semin, G. R. (2000). Agenda 2000: Communication: Language as an implementational device for cognition. *European Journal of Social Psychology, 30,* 595–612.

Smith, E. R., & Semin, G. R. (2004). The foundations of socially situated action: Socially situated cognition. *Advances in Experimental Social Psychology, 36,* 53–117.

Thelen, E., & Smith, L. (1994). *A dynamic systems approach to the development of cognition and action*. Cambridge, MA: MIT Press.

Thompson, L., & Fine, G. A. (1999). Socially shared cognition, affect, and behavior: A review and integration. *Personality and Social Psychology Review, 3,* 278–302.

Tindale, R. S., & Kameda, T. (2000). "Social sharedness" as a unifying theme for information processing in groups. *Group Processes and Intergroup Relations, 3,* 123–140.

Vera, A., & Simon, H. A. (1993). Situated action: A symbolic interpretation. *Cognitive Science, 17,* 7–48.

Vygotski, L. S. (1986). *Thought and language*. Cambridge, MA: MIT Press. (Original work published 1962)

Wertsch, J. V. (1994). The primacy of mediated action in sociocultural studies. *Mind, Culture, and Activity, 4,* 202–208.

Wegner, D. M. (1995). A computer network model of human transactive memory. *Social Cognition, 13,* 319–339.

Wilson, M. (2002). Six views of embodied cognition. *Psychonomic Bulletin and Review, 9,* 625–636.

22

How Social Psychology Can Build Bridges to the Social Sciences by Considering Motivation, Cognition, and Constraints Simultaneously

Siegwart Lindenberg
University of Groningen, the Netherlands

WHAT IS NEEDED

The potential (and probably increasing) relevance of social psychology for the social sciences may lie in the fact that in the social sciences, there is an increasing need for theories on individual behavior and interaction that help explain how collective phenomena come about. By collective phenomena, I mean phenomena such as many people doing similar things (like committing crime or divorcing or discriminating), or doing things cooperatively (like joining a movement or working in teams), or doing things competitively (like competing in the market place or in politics), some combination of these (as in social exchange and social dilemmas), or the collective results of these actions (such as rates or social norms). This requires theories that can deal with a great variety of different influences on behavior at the same time. For example, if one wants to explain the difference in divorce rates between, say, Moroccan and autochthonous Dutch couples in the Netherlands, one would have to be able to trace theoretically the simultaneous (and possibly interactive) effects of relevant factors. Looking at the literature of empirical studies, one would be able to compile a list of factors that have come up in various studies, such as the information about the partner before marriage, age at marriage, investments in the relationships (such as joint children and property), norms of significant others, quality of the partner relationship, availability of alternative partners, psychic and material costs of divorce, prior experience with divorce (from parents, from self), social and personal resources (such as education of parents, self and partner, size and overlap of the partners' social networks), homogamy (say, in terms of education, religion, social value orientation), and many more. In practice, the value of such a list derives from the theories that generate the place and relevance of the various factors for the explanation of divorce rates. Without understanding how a factor affects the divorce rate (directly or indirectly via its impact on other factors), and how it interacts with other factors, it is difficult to know how to operationalize it and/or how to interpret the empirical results. This is difficult enough if the effects of all these factors are additive, but it gets to be a very tough problem if there are interaction effects (e.g., negative effects of joint property on divorce may turn out to be higher for partners with overlapping social networks), and there may be seemingly contradictory effects (e.g., some studies find religion to be a negative influence on divorce and others don't).

In addition to these problems, it will not do in most cases to rely solely on a literature search for coming up with a list of relevant factors in the first place. We know from research that often factors are relevant in one context and not in another. Thus, what the social scientist needs, in addition to being able to trace the simultaneous effects of factors, are heuristic devices to guide the search for relevant factors (be they situational factors, institutional, cultural, individual, or possibly also dispositional factors).

What theories are there that help the social scientist in tracing the simultaneous impact of a variety of factors on a dependent variable? So far, social psychology has played a rather modest role here. Rather, it was microeconomic theory that had an increasing and overall enormous impact on both sociology and political science, riding the tide of the increasing demand for individual level explanations of collective phenomena. However, as I argue next, this enormous influence of microeconomics is "faute de mieux," that is, due to a lack of better alternatives provided by social psychology. Before I turn to this question in more detail, I discuss what in my opinion made microeconomics so attractive to social scientists for dealing with these tasks of tracing the relevant factors and their simultaneous influence on a particular collective phenomenon.

MICROECONOMIC THEORY AS A FIRST PROTOTYPE OF THE BRIDGE

In the social sciences, it had long been taken for granted that the acting unit has to be an "actor," that is, a more or less intelligent human being who perceives his or her situation and acts in this situation with intentions directed at reaching certain goals. This was even true of role theory in traditional sociology. Yet this theory had great difficulty dealing with varying situational "constraints" (i.e., opportunities and limitations for carrying out a particular kind of action). For example, a woman may have been socialized to want to play the roles of housewife and mother. However, her role performance will be influenced by, say, attractive alternatives and by competing claims on her time. Theories of role conflict, which were invented to explicitly deal with these problems, were useful to describe problems (such as a conflict between playing the mother role and working), but they could not be used to trace the simultaneous effect of both internalized role expectations and work and there was no heuristic help in bringing in other relevant factors. One could predict stress or trace the "depth" of internalization of the role expectation in contrast to the "working role," but that was about it. In order to be able to predict what behavior would result from such a role conflict under various conditions, and to solve similar problems in other areas of sociology, an increasing number of sociologists in the 1970s and 1980s turned to a theory that was the most detailed and worked out in relating preferences (what people want), constraints (opportunities and limitations to realize preferences), and active and intelligent goal pursuit (rationality). This theory was microeconomic price theory.

THE SEARCH FOR RELEVANT FACTORS AND THEIR SIMULTANEOUS EFFECTS

In this theory, the heuristic device for the search of relevant factors was the systematic search for preferences and constraints, and the translation of these two into costs and benefits of a certain course of action. In such an analysis, role expectations would either be seen as part of the (internalized) preferences and/or part of the constraints (e.g., the cause of approval and disapproval from significant others). Thus, following the internalized role expectation would yield the benefits of realized preferences and approval from some significant others, and the benefit of not incurring the costs of working (such as more leisure time, less effort), at the cost of losing the benefits from work (such as income, status).

The next crucial research question then was: What is the net result, that is, what are the simultaneous effects of the various factors? The operational form of this question within this framework is: Are the costs higher than the benefits or the other way around? In order to answer such a question, the heuristic search for relevant factors would first lead to the simplest way of dealing with costs and benefits, namely, to consider only money. For example, are arrangements such that household income is shared? In that case, it is likely that the amount of work of each partner would adapt in such a way that household income was maximized, given the constraints (i.e., given the tasks at home, the ability to deal with those tasks, what each can earn outside, how prone or averse each is to work, etc.). Later, additional factors, such as the value of leisure time, can be added to income. By adding uncertainty about important traits of the partner, divorce can also be explained in this framework (see Becker, 1981).

There was, however, also a downside of this useful tool. For sociologists, it became increasingly clear that, despite its magic, this solution had severe limitations for solving the two major tasks of a social scientist. Microeconomics assumed that preferences were given (i.e., outside the theory) and that they were always ordered, that is, that people always know what they want (the rationality assumption depended on this). This had the advantage of very tractable models with easy use of formalization. In practice, however, this meant a severe limitation of what preferences could be considered: only those for which the assumption of ordering would be most plausible. Because the constraints considered are dovetailed with the preferences considered, problems concerning the assumptions about preferences carry over to assumptions about constraints (see Frey, 1992, p. 21ff). The assumptions on rationality were also very limiting, with virtually no link to cognitive psychology. The field of "behavioral economics" is meant to provide this link, and to some extent it succeeds. The same can be said about the field of decision theory. Both fields show important advances for the social sciences, pushing for some more realistic models of rational choice. However, for sociology, research in both fields still remains too limited with regard to the goals, cognitions, and constraints that are being considered.

THE SOCIAL PSYCHOLOGICAL ALTERNATIVE: THE ENHANCED MAGIC TRIANGLE

What is needed is a replacement of microeconomic theory that retains the advantages of this theory with regard to solving the two big problems of social scientists but surmounts the considerable limitations of this theory. This is not an easy task. Outside decision theory, psychologists have made use of some form of rational choice theory in the past to deal with problems of motivation and achievement (e.g., Vroom, 1964). However, these theories did not explicitly deal with dovetailed constraints.[1] The theory that, at present, comes closest to what is needed is Ajzen's (1985) theory of planned behavior, in which he explicitly pays much more attention to beliefs than economists and also considers constraints in the guise of norms and control over internal and external factors. It has been rightly seen as an important advance, and it spurred much research in various substantive areas. Yet Ajzen's theory is not making full use of the magic triangle. For one, it is not concerned with constraints per se, only with social pressure (norms) and control over constraints, and it is thus of limited use for solving the two major problems in the social sciences. Especially, it does not handle substitution (i.e., relative price) effects. It also does not make use of important developments within psychology about interdependencies between motivation and cognition (see Fig. 22.1).

Thus, social sciences are still waiting for a suitable replacement of microeconomics from social psychologists. Its replacement (see Fig. 22.2) would have to be a theory that keeps the basic structure of the magic triangle

---

[1]An exception is research on social dilemmas, which was close to microeconomic theorizing from the beginning.

Preferences
ordered
preferences;
maximization
as operational
goal

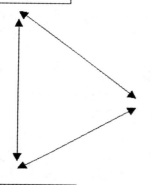

Constraints
external
constraints
related to
preferences and
expectations

Rationality
farsightedness
with veridical
expectations;
maximization

FIG. 22.1. The first version of the magic triangle: microeconomic theory.

Motivations
substantive and
operational goals,
active search for
alternatives

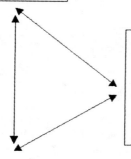

Constraints
internal and
external
constraints
combined;
dependent on
goals and
cognitions

Cognitions
expectations
framing,
mental models,
heuristics

FIG. 22.2. The improved version of the magic triangle.

but replaces the assumptions on preferences with suitable theories and research on motivation, replaces the assumption of rationality with suitable theories and research on cognition, and dovetails with both suitable theory and research on constraints (i.e., the individual's barriers and access to means that are necessary for reaching the goals). Because motivations and cognitions will be much more varied than "preferences" and "rationality" in the microeconomic model, the constraints that can be linked to motivations and cognitions will also be much more varied.

Contrary to economics, they will include combinations of internal and external constraints, such as self-esteem and the criticality of the audience. It boils down to a theory of goal-directed behavior, the important characteristic of which is that motivations and cognitions are explicitly dovetailed with constraints.

THE CONTOURS OF THE BRIDGE

The contours of the task by social psychologists essential for building a bridge to the social sciences now begin to come into relief (see also Lindenberg, 2001a, 2001b). First of all, some social psychologists would have to take the trouble of integrating and promoting social psychological research with the aim of making a great variety of substitution effects traceable, by offering ways to conceptualize nonmonetary cost and benefits. A theory of general human goals and needs is likely to be essential here.

Second, social psychologists could systematize and promote research that is done on questions regarding relevant "shift parameters," such as mind states, priming effects, orientations, frames, and so on, that trace the influence of goals on cognitions and the perception of constraints. Again, there is much relevant work in this area, but as of yet it is fragmented.

Third, people are busy influencing themselves (what one could call self-management). All these processes boil down to an individual's active attempts to influence inner and outer constraints. Here too, social psychologists have done much research that is as yet not systematically related to a theory of action.

CONCLUSIONS

The message of this chapter is quite simple. The social sciences are confronted with at least two difficult problems for which social psychology could be very helpful. First, there is the problem of how to identify the relevant factors for the explanation of collective phenomena. Second, there is the problem of how to trace the simultaneous effects of a variety of factors on the dependent variable. In order to be able to help social scientists with these two problems, social psychology would have to put much more effort into theories of behavior that have the special feature of being based on the magic triangle, that is, on the interrelation between motivation, cognition, and constraints. Constraints define the possibilities and limitations (i.e., the available and necessary resources and barriers) for reaching particular goals, and cognitions stand between goals and constraints. The advantages of such theories of behavior lie first in the heuristic guidance they offer for the identification of relevant factors, and second in the relative ease with which various factors (situational, institutional, cultural, individual) can be connected, once the relations in the magic triangle are spelled out. When doing research on the magic triangle, social psychologists are also likely to use research not directly related to the magic triangle (at present, this is the bulk of social psychological and purely psychological research). In that sense, they are then also a bridge between general psychology and the social sciences.

REFERENCES

Ajzen, I. (1985). From intentions to action: A theory of planned behavior. In J. Kuhl & J. Beckman (Eds.), *Action-control: From cognition to behavior* (pp. 11–39). Heidelberg: Springer.

Becker, G. S. (1981). *A treatise on the family.* Cambridge, MA: Harvard University Press.

Frey, B. S. (1992). *Economics as a science of human behaviour: Towards a new social science paradigm.* Boston: Kluwer.

Lindenberg, S. (2001a). Intrinsic motivation in a new light. *Kyklos, 54,* 317–342.

Lindenberg, S. (2001b). Social rationality versus rational egoism. In J. Turner (Ed.), *Handbook of sociological theory* (pp. 635–668). New York: Kluwer Academic/Plenum.

Vroom, V. H. (1964). *Work and motivation.* New York: Wiley.

23

Bridging Social Psychology— Beyond Explicit Measures in Attitudinal Assessment

Fritz Strack
Lioba Werth
University of Würzburg, Germany

To predict human behavior, social psychologists typically assess people's attitudes. This procedure is based on two assumptions: First, they believe that people's behavior is based on their attitudes. Second, they assume that people have direct access to their attitudes and can report them "with candor and accuracy" (Campbell, 1976).

Meanwhile, the second proposition has become severely questioned (for a review, see Tourangeau, Rips, & Rasinski, 2000). Experimental research on how people answer survey questions suggests that survey responses are not the result of introspection but of cognitive processes that are highly sensitive to contextual influences (e.g., Schwarz & Oyserman, 2001; Strack, Martin, & Schwarz, 1988). Specifically, it has been suggested that respondents undergo a series of cognitive tasks that involve understanding the question, recalling relevant behavior, applying inference and estimation strategies, mapping the answer onto the response format, and editing the answer (Strack & Martin, 1987). At all steps of the response process, respondents use the questionnaire/context as a source of information to make sense of the question to be answered. Thus, the questionnaire is not a neutral instrument that reflects respondents true values but a conglomerate of various influences. To generate predictions, these influences should be controlled for or at least considered.

Meanwhile, it has been recognized that not all human behavior is guided by attitudes. Rather, it often occurs automatically and without awareness (e.g.,

Banaji & Greenwald, 1995; Bargh, 1997; Fazio, 2001; Strack & Deutsch, 2004; Werth & Förster, 2002). If people are not aware of their behavior or their attitudes, of course, they could not explicitly report about it.

This state of affairs asks for a new look at how one should go about predicting what people will do—with two consequences: the active use of context as an independent variable and the combined use of explicit and implicit measures. It will be argued that through extending their methodological repertoire, social psychologists will be able to extend their predictive power to other areas, like consumer and health behavior, as well as to behavioral disorders.

ACTIVE USE OF CONTEXT AS AN INDEPENDENT VARIABLE

If it is the case that attitudinal judgments are malleable and influenced by the activated information, contextual influences may no longer be seen as a source of error but as a means of identifying the basis of the attitudes. In a classic study by Iyengar, Kinder, Peters, and Krosnick (1984), global attitudes toward the American government were found to depend on people's evaluation of the government on a specific dimension and the activation of this dimension in the evening news. Thus, if the news focused on the government's economic policy, people's evaluations of this policy domain influenced their overall judgment. If, in contrast, the news concentrated on issues of foreign policy, respondents' evaluation of this dimension determined the general attitude. This result illustrates how the context (i.e., the topic of the evening news) influences people's attitudes through the activation of relevant information.

If the context exerts its influence through the activation of information, preceding questions should be functionally equivalent. Through the activation of the information that is necessary to answer a survey question, subsequent responses will be influenced if the pertaining question relates to the activated information. To identify the postulated process, we (Strack, Schwarz, & Wänke, 1991) asked respondents to indicate their attitude toward the ambiguous topic of an "educational contribution for students." To activate a context that would be used as a basis for generating an attitude, respondents were required to estimate either the average support for students from the Swedish government or the average tuition in the United States. As expected, more favorable attitudes were reported if the preceding question referred to "support" than if it referred to "tuition."

Using measures that pertain to more common types of survey questions, we (Strack et al., 1988) have asked college respondents how happy they were with both life as a whole (general item) and their dating (specific item). The experimental variation was the order in which the two questions were posed. Assuming that the information that specific information is more likely to become the basis of a general judgment we expected and found that the correlation between the two happiness ratings was higher if the specific item preceded the general one than the other way around.

Finally, in attempts to identify the mechanism underlying the anchoring heuristic (Tversky & Kahneman, 1974), we (e.g., Mussweiler & Strack, 1999; Strack & Mussweiler, 1997) found evidence suggesting that a comparative judgment selectively activates information that will then be used for the absolute judgment. The resulting assimilation toward the standard of the comparison is a context effect in the sense that requirements of the preceding task determine the outcome of a subsequent task.

To sum up, it is often unavoidable that respondents are influenced by context. But the described findings suggest that contextual influences can be used in a more systematic manner to identify the informational basis, which allows to identify the boundaries of self-reports. Of course, this cannot be captured by respondents' introspective accounts of how their judgment is generated (see Nisbett & Wilson, 1977). Pragmatically, a researcher in an organization may insert a question about a critical topic in part of the questionnaires and study if people's ratings of satisfaction are influenced by the activation of this information (see also Schwarz & Strack, 1981).

COMBINED USE OF EXPLICIT AND IMPLICIT MEASURES

If it is the case that behavior is a function of both reflective and impulsive determinants (see Strack & Deutsch, 2004), the validity of behavioral predictions will crucially depend on whether both processes are part of the assessment. Unfortunately, however, most assessments of attitudes are based on "explicit" self-reports and are therefore exclusively focused on controlled and conscious processes. As a consequence, automatic and unconscious influences on behavior will be greatly neglected and underestimated. Therefore, procedures are warranted that are capable of capturing processes that are not introspectively accessible to the respondent. The use of implicit measures makes this possible.

In the domain of basic research in social psychology, such implicit measures have been successfully employed to assess the accessibility of concepts or attitudes. The best known examples are the Implicit Association Test (IAT; Greenwald, McGhee, & Schwartz, 1998) and the implicit questionnaires on sexism and racism (Dovidio & Gaertner, 1986; Swim, Aikin, Hall, & Hunter, 1995). Implicit procedures elicit behaviors that are interpreted as indicative of an existing associative structure. For example, the latency of a particular response or decision will be used as an indicator for the strength of associations that may become the basis of future behaviors. Thus, Asendorpf, Banse, and Mücke (2002) were able to increase the accuracy of predictions for spontaneous behaviors by implicitly assessing respondents' self-concepts using the IAT. In this case, the implicit measures were superior because the determinants of spontaneous behaviors are hardly accessible to introspection.

As a second advantage, implicit procedures are less susceptible to biases of social desirability. As a consequence, they facilitate the assessment of contents that are difficult to record in an explicit fashion, like attitudes toward drugs, crime, sexual preferences, and the like. One example of reports that are prone to influences of social desirability is self-assessments of leadership. To minimize such biasing influences, we (Werth, Häfner, Seibt, & Stork, 2004) used both explicit self-reports and implicit measures (IAT attitudes) to assess business executives' leadership potential on several dimensions. In addition, we asked subordinates of these executives to evaluate their superiors' leadership behavior on the same dimensions and found that the implicit measures were better predictors of their assessed leadership than their explicit self-reports.

To sum up, it is often unavoidable that surveys focus on characteristics that respondents are either not capable of reporting or not willing to share. In both cases, implicit measures may provide indirect access to such features by eliciting behavioral manifestations that can be used as a basis for inferences. Recent research suggests that such inferences may greatly improve the accuracy of psychological measurement.

APPLIED CONSEQUENCES: CONSUMER BEHAVIOR, BEHAVIORAL DISORDER, AND OTHERS

It has become obvious that basic research on the implicit determinants of social behavior and on the measurement of its antecedents has enormous applied consequences. At the same time, however, applied phenomena may be harnessed to validate implicit assessments.

One example is "impulsive buying" (e.g., Rook & Gardner, 1993), which describes the situation of people who are exposed to products who may suddenly buy what they see without a preceding intention. In retrospect, the particular purchase is often difficult to understand for partners and even for the protagonist himself. Of course, impulse buying may be rare in its "pure" version because it is typically contaminated by consumers' thoughts and feelings that have already been influenced. However, the degree to which a purchase occurs impulsively is well known to advertisers, who focus many of their campaigns on people's spontaneous purchases (Pratkanis & Aronson, 1992). In a similar vein, the fees that sellers are charged for their customer's uses of credit cards are often justified by the facilitation of such acquisitions. Conversely, customers are often warned that "the ease of using credit cards, combined with impulsive buying, may result in over spending" (advice from the state of Indiana). To predict impulsive buying and the effect of related advertising, implicit measure may be fruitfully applied. At the same time, such behavioral manifestations may provide external criteria for the validation of implicit measures.

Another bridge may be built to clinical phenomena. In particular, it is a well-known phenomenon that it is difficult to regulate phobic reactions by directing people's attention toward the fact that the threat is not real. Rather, the behavior is impulsively dominated by the stimulus to which the person is exposed. The threat of the stimulus may be captured better by implicit measures than by people's explicit assessments.

BRIDGES TO OTHER FIELDS OR DISCIPLINES

Knowledge regarding implicit measures (whether independently or in combination with explicit measures) is also relevant in other fields, where important decisions are implicitly determined.

Survey and marketing researchers are advised to use a particular question to activate a construct that may be relevant for subsequent judgments (Schwarz & Oyserman, 2001). In the area of health or medical decision making, implicit measures predict the consumption of high versus low caloric food (Maison, Greenwald, & Bruin, 2001). In the domain of HIV prevention, explicit measures were able to predict condom use in steady relationship. In contrast, implicit measures were more accurate for casual encounters (Marsh, Johnson, & Scott-Sheldon, 2001).

COSTS

However, collecting implicit measures is not without costs. On the one hand, more elaborate procedures are necessary. Moreover, there are still some methodological issues. In particular, problems of reliability must be resolved. Finally, there exist ethical concerns such that implicit assessments are not as transparent as explicit ones. As a consequence, it may not be obvious to respondents what exactly will be assessed. Thus, their agreement to participate may be based only on a partial understanding of the nature of the measurement.

CONCLUSIONS

Still, combining explicit and implicit measures has a substantial benefit. First, it allows us to assess phenomena that have been out of the range of standard methods of assessment. Most theories assume that social behavior can be predicted by asking people about their attitudes and their intentions. More recent accounts acknowledge that this is only part of the story and that many behaviors may be spontaneously elicited. If they are not systematically related to antecedent goals or plans, explicit questioning has little predictive power. These behaviors, however, do not occur in a random fashion but are associatively linked to people's evaluative thoughts and feelings. Implicit measures allow us to detect these relationships and assess their strength. Moreover, they make it possible to use associative determinants as predictors of social behavior. In combination, explicit and implicit measures allow us to capture the entire breadth of what people do while acknowledging that what people do is often not the outcome of conscious goals, plans, and intentions.

REFERENCES

Asendorpf, J. B., Banse, R., & Mücke, D. (2002). Double dissociation between implicit and explicit personality self-concept: The case of shy behavior. *Journal of Personality and Social Psychology, 83*, 380–393.

Banaji, M. R., & Greenwald, A. G. (1995). Implicit gender stereotyping in judgments of fame. *Journal of Personality and Social Psychology, 68,* 181–198.

Bargh, J. A. (1997). The automaticity of everyday life. In R. S. Wyer & T. K. Srull (Eds.), *Handbook of social cognition* (Vol. 10, pp. 1–61). Mahwah, NJ: Lawrence Erlbaum Associates.

Campbell, A. (1976). Subjective measures of well-being. *American Psychologist, 31,* 117–124.

Dovidio, J. F., & Gaertner, S. L. (1986). Prejudice, discrimination, and racism: Historical trends and contemporary approaches. In J. F. Dovidio & S. L. Gaertner (Eds.), *Prejudice, discrimination, and racism* (pp. 1–34). Orlando, FL: Academic Press.

Fazio, R. H. (2001). On the automatic activation of associated evaluations: An overview. *Cognition and Emotion, 15,* 115–141.

Greenwald, A. G., McGhee, D. E., & Schwartz, J. L. K. (1998). Measuring individual differences in implicit cognition: The implicit association test. *Journal of Personality and Social Psychology, 74,* 1464–1480.

Iyengar, S., Kinder, D. R., Peters, M. D., & Krosnick, J. A. (1984). The evening news and presidential evaluations. *Journal of Personality and Social Psychology, 46,* 778–787.

Maison, D., Greenwald, A. G., & Bruin, R. (2001). The Implicit Association Test as a measure of implicit consumer attitudes. *Polish Psychological Bulletin, 32,* 61–69.

Marsh, K. L., Johnson, B. T., & Scott-Sheldon, L. A. (2001). Heart versus reason in condom use: Implicit versus explicit attitudinal predictors of sexual behavior. *Zeitschrift für Experimentelle Psychologie, 48,* 161–175.

Mussweiler, T., & Strack, F. (1999). Comparing is believing: A selective accessibility model of judgmental anchoring. In W. Stroebe & M. Hewstone (Eds.), *European review of social psychology* (Vol. 10, pp. 135–167). Chichester, UK: Wiley.

Nisbett, R. E., & Wilson, T. D. (1977). Telling more than we can know: Verbal reports on mental processes. *Psychological Review, 84,* 231–259.

Pratkanis, A. R., & Aronson, E. (1992). *Age of propaganda. The everyday use and abuse of persuasion.* New York: W. H. Freeman.

Rook, D. W., & Gardner, M. P. (1993). In the mood: Impulsive buying's affective antecedents. *Research in Consumer Behavior, 6,* 1–28.

Schwarz, N., & Oyserman, D. (2001). Asking questions about behavior: cognition, communication, and questionnaire construction. *American Journal of Evaluation, 22,* 127–160.

Schwarz, N., & Strack, F. (1981). Manipulating salience: Causal assessment in natural setting. *Personality and Social Psychology Bulletin, 6,* 554–558.

Strack, F., & Deutsch. R. (2004). Reflective and impulsive determinants of social behavior. *Personality and Social Psychology Review, 8,* 220–247.

Strack, F., & Martin, L. L. (1987). Thinking, judging, and communicating: A process account of context effects in attitude surveys. In H. J. Hippler, N. Schwarz, & S. Sudman (Eds.), *Social information processing and survey methodology* (pp. 123–148). New York: Springer.

Strack, F., Martin, L. L., & Schwarz, N. (1988). Priming and communications: Social determinants of information use in judgments of life satisfaction. *European Journal of Social Psychology, 18,* 429–442.

Strack, F., Schwarz, N., & Wänke, M. (1991). Semantic and pragmatic aspects of context effects in social and psychological research. *Social Cognition, 9,* 111–125.

Strack, F., & Mussweiler, T. (1997). Explaining the enigmatic anchoring effect: Mechanisms of selective accessibility. *Journal of Personality and Social Psychology, 73,* 437–446.

Swim, J. K., Aikin, K. J., Hall, W. S., & Hunter, B. A. (1995). Sexism and racism: Old-fashioned and modern prejudices. *Journal of Personality and Social Psychology, 68,* 199–214.

Tourangeau, R., Rips, L. J., & Rasinski, K. A. (2000). *The psychology of survey response.* New York: Cambridge University Press.

Tversky, A., & Kahneman, D. (1974). Judgment under uncertainty: Heuristics and biases. *Science, 185,* 1124–1131.

Werth, L., & Förster, J. (2002). Implicit person theories influence memory judgments: The circumstances under which metacognitive knowledge is used. *European Journal of Social Psychology, 32,* 353–362.

Werth, L., Häfner, M., Seibt, B., & Stork, K. (2004). *The Implicit Association Test* (IAT) in managerial evaluations. Manuscript submitted for publication.

24

Bridging Social
and Cognitive Psychology?

Bernhard Hommel

Cognitive Psychology Unit, Leiden University, the Netherlands

W hen I was asked to comment on the benefits and costs of bridging cognitive psychology, my own field of research, with social psychology, I thought this was easy—the more so as I have a social-psychological background myself (Schultz-Gambard, Feierabend, & Hommel, 1988; Schultz-Gambard & Hommel, 1987). However, addressing this issue requires one to define what a cognitive and a social psychologist is, and here my confusion began. Let me use an empirical example—an experiment that I conducted for my doctoral dissertation (Hommel, 1993)—to explain why.

NO BORDERS HERE

It is well known that spatial stimulus-response compatibility affects human performance, even if stimulus location is irrelevant to the task—the so-called Simon effect. What I first did in the mentioned study was to replicate this effect (Hommel, 1993, Experiment 1). Subjects were to press a left response key as fast as possible whenever hearing a low-pitched tone and a right key whenever hearing a high-pitched tone. Even though the location of the tone varied randomly, subjects were faster if the low tone appeared in a loudspeaker on the left rather than the right side, whereas the opposite was true for the high tone. Hence, subjects were better if the stimulus appeared on the same side as the correct response. Next, I connected each key with a small LED (light-emitting diode) on the opposite side, in such a way that depressing the left key would flash a light on the right side and depressing the right key would flash a light on the left side. I reran the experiment and obtained basically the same effect: Subjects were better if the stimulus appeared on the same side as the correct response. Then I ran another replication of the same experiment with only a slight change in the instruction. Instead of asking participants to "press the left or right key," I asked them to "flash the right light" to the low tone and to "flash the left light" to the high tone. Obviously, this did not change the physical aspects of their task—the left light was flashed by pressing the right key, and vice versa—so that the new instruction implied exactly the same stimulus-key mapping as the old one. And yet the outcome was exactly opposite to what I observed before: Subjects were better if the stimulus appeared on the *opposite* side of the correct response key!

What had happened? One way to interpret this reversal of a well-established, commonly robust effect is in terms of socially shared, joint attention (Moore & Dunham, 1995). Every action we perform can be described in many ways and with regard to many levels: The same movement of one's hand may be described in terms of the muscle movements involved, with regard to the emerging kinematic pattern, as the "signing of a contract," or with respect to the socially defined meaning this signature has in the given context. Moreover, the most acceptable description of an action may vary from one situation to another, so that most people would consider a merely kinematic description of the signing of a peace contract between two countries inappropriate. This suggests that people create coherent social situations with a shared meaning by directing each other's attention to particular events and to particular levels on how the relevant features of these events are defined (Tomasello & Call, 1997). Indeed, this is what must have happened in the Hommel (1993) study: Defining the action as "keypress" communicated a particular meaning of the required action and codirected the subjects' attention to particular, socially relevant aspects of it. Defining the same action as "flashing a light" communicated another meaning and codirected attention to the visual effects the keypress created.

Apparently, then, even performance in something as unchallenging as a binary-choice reaction-time task reflects "the way in which people's thoughts, feelings, and behaviors are influenced by the real, imagined, or implied presence of other people," as the editors of this book, in their invitation letter, rephrased Allport's (1985) definition of social psychology. Does this render people like me, who investigate the processes underlying effects of this sort, social psychologists? There are countless phenomena that would lead to the very same question. Take, for instance, the recent hints to so-called mirror neurons in the human premotor cortex. Using single-cell recordings in the macaque premotor cortex, Rizzolatti and colleagues showed that at least some of the neurons that mediate the performance of particular goal-directed actions, such as grasping an object, are also involved in perceiving the same action being performed by someone else. Brain-imaging techniques have revealed that humans possess comparable neural structures, that is, neural codes that mediate both perception and planning of actions (Rizzolatti, Fogassi, & Gallese, 2001). Obviously, these observations have enormous implications for our understanding and the interpretation of a whole number of social phenomena ranging from imitation, mind reading, and empathy, and to verbal and nonverbal communication. Interestingly, even though most of the researchers investigating these issues are very aware of the social nature of their topic, they are likely to consider themselves cognitive (if not neurocognitive) rather than social psychologists.

Conversely, an increasing number of social psychologists are investigating phenomena that have very little to do with "the way in which people's thoughts, feelings, and behaviors are influenced by the real, imagined, or implied presence of other people." This applies in particular to the area of human emotion, which has seen a real boom in the last decade or so. For unobvious reasons, many of the landmark papers creating this boom were authored by social, not cognitive, psychologists, and were published in social-psychological, not cognitive-psychological, journals—just take the studies of Strack, Martin, and Stepper (1988) on James's facial-feedback hypothesis, of Murphy and Zajonc (1993) on subliminal emotional priming, or of Chen and Bargh (1999) on the direct impact of emotion on manual action.

These and more observations make me doubt whether there still is a clear-cut border between social and cognitive psychology and, by implication, whether there is something to be bridged at all. In fact, I find it hard to think of "purely cognitive" phenomena that would not reflect "the way in which people's thoughts, feelings, and behaviors are influenced by the real, imagined, or implied presence of other people" along the lines already discussed. Reversibly, I do not know of much evidence suggesting that the processing of social stimuli and the performance of social actions would be cognitively any different from the processing of not-so-social stimuli and the performance of not-so-social social actions, however they may look. Hence, even if one might think of extreme examples where the mutual interest of cognitive and social psychologists is likely to be low (say, early vision and group dynamics), I do not see any empirical evidence of, or theoretical need for, a clear-cut separation of these two groups in terms of the empirical phenomena they want to understand.

HOWEVER ...

And yet, I suspect that retaining some sort of distinction between cognitive and social psychologists is important—not with regard to the investigated issues, phenomena, and processes, but in terms of scientific perspective. Notably, the two communities differ, at least on average, with respect to the preferred level of analysis and the grain size of explanation that is considered satisfactory. Take, for instance, the (relatively) automatic impact of stimulus attributes on human actions. Cognitive psychologists have suggested and are discussing a whole number of processing models to account for such effects, especially of spatial stimulus features (for an overview, see Prinz & Hommel, 2002). These models include assumptions about how stimuli and the actions they affect are cognitively represented, how and when the former impact the latter, and whether and how this impact can be modulated by intentional processes and task goals. One might expect that much could be learned from these modeling efforts to account for the impact of emotional stimulus attributes, but with a few—very interesting—exceptions (e.g., Bargh & Chartrand, 1999; Beckers, De Houwer, & Eelen, 2002; Neumann, Förster, & Strack, 2003) there are not many attempts to exploit these parallels.

There may be many reasons for this reluctance of social-psychological researchers to take up more concrete, finer grained processing models. One good reason is that coarser grained models are often fully sufficient to explain the phenomena of interest: If one can predict the likelihood and degree of activation of behaviorally relevant social stereotypes, say, why bother about how these stereotypes are cognitively represented, how they were acquired, and how their activation takes place? Another related good reason is that maintaining a relatively coarse level of theorizing makes it easier to relate the mechanisms of interest to other phenomena that are defined at more molar levels. For instance, knowing the environmental trigger conditions for automatic stereotype activation may suffice to contribute substantially to understanding the inner workings of group dynamics, whereas a complex network model of how stereotypes are represented in memory is likely to only complicate matters.

Obviously, researchers of social cognition are facing a dilemma: The more fine-grained their models get, the more closely they can connect to cognitive psychologists but the more difficult it is to relate their ideas to social or even sociological phenomena defined at more molar levels. And, reversibly, the more coarse-grained their models get, the better they can relate to molar phenomena but the wider the communicative gap to cognitive psychologists. Clearly, the most interesting and fruitful alternative is to place one's level of analysis right in the middle so to keep in touch with either community, a challenge shared by cognitive psychologists: Going for more fine-grained models makes it increasingly easy to talk to other "cognitive neurosciences," whereas getting more abstract facilitates communication with other psychologists, philosophers, anthropologists, and students of law.

The—for our present purposes—central implication of all this is that cognitive and social psychologists should try to keep talking and learning from each other but they should not, in my view, give up their own unique perspectives. On the one hand, maintaining these unique perspectives necessarily implies limitations of communication and theoretical exchange: the average cognitive-psychological model is likely to stay too concrete, too fine-grained for social-psychological purposes, and the average social-psychological model will remain too abstract, too general for cognitive-psychological aims. This means that the interest cognitive psychologists will have in social psychology, and vice versa, will remain limited. However, I think that the tension that emerges from these limitations in the compatibility of theoretical language and preferred analytical grain size creates a healthy challenge to either subdiscipline, a challenge that will help prevent cognitive theories from losing themselves or even dissolving into mere physiology and social-psychological theories from losing touch with the actual mechanisms underlying the regularities they intend to explain. A good example for how important it is to keep in touch and find a common theoretical language is the recent book project of Maasen, Prinz, and Roth (2003), which contrasts accounts of human intentional action from numerous disciplines, ranging from physiology to sociology. Taken together, the contributions demonstrate that true insights into the workings of goal-directed behavior presuppose a deeper understanding of how neurophysiological and behavioral evidence of a large degree of automaticity and unconscious goal-striving gets together with the doctrine of will and self-determination that underlies social interaction and legal decision making in at least Western societies. Other multifaceted topics that call for a broad, interdisciplinary approach are the (individual and social) control of attention or the acquisition and cognitive representation of the meaning of objects, events, and acts.

CONCLUSIONS

To summarize, I doubt that characterizing and distinguishing between cognitive and social psychology in terms of the phenomena looked at makes sense. I do think, however, that these two subdisciplines differ with regard to the way they look at their phenomena—hence, in their perspective. I think this is good. What we could improve, though, is the effort we put into confronting these perspectives, and into confronting them in a goal-directed, collaborative fashion. Sharing common research goals and, ideally, the impressive grants necessary to reach them, will stimulate and reward the efforts required to listen and trying to understand each other, and to eventually overcome the still existing conceptual and terminological barriers—not to become and do the same, but to enrich each other's perspectives and, thereby, to highlight and set into perspective one's own limitations.

REFERENCES

Allport, G. W. (1985). The historical background of social psychology. In L. Gardner & A. Elliot (Eds.), *The handbook of social psychology* (Vol. 1, pp. 1–46). Hillsdale, NJ: Lawrence Erlbaum Associates.

Bargh, J. A., & Chartrand, T. L. (1999). The unbearable automaticity of being. *American Psychologist, 54*, 462–479.

Beckers, T., De Houwer, J., & Eelen, P. (2002). Automatic integration of non-perceptual action effect features: The case of the associative affective Simon effect. *Psychological Research, 66*, 166–173.

Chen, M., & Bargh, J. A. (1999). Consequences of automatic evaluation: Immediate behavioral predispositions to approach or avoid the stimulus. *Personality and Social Psychology Bulletin, 25*, 215–224.

Hommel, B. (1993). Inverting the Simon effect by intention: Determinants of direction and extent of effects of irrelevant spatial information. *Psychological Research, 55,* 270–279.

Maasen, S., Prinz, W., & Roth, G. (Eds.). (2003). *Voluntary action: Brains, minds, and sociality.* Oxford: Oxford University Press.

Moore, C., & Dunham, P. J. (1995). *Joint attention: Its origins and role in development.* Hillsdale, NJ: Lawrence Erlbaum Associates.

Murphy, S. T., & Zajonc, R. B. (1993). Affect, cognition, and awareness: Affective priming with optimal and suboptimal stimulus exposures. *Journal of Personality and Social Psychology, 64,* 723–739.

Neumann, R., Förster, J., & Strack, F. (2003). Motor compatibility: The bidirectional link between behavior and evaluation. In J. Musch & K. C. Klauer (Eds.), *The psychology of evaluation: Affective processes in cognition and emotion* (pp. 762–768). Mahwah, NJ: Lawrence Erlbaum Associates.

Prinz, W., & Hommel, B. (Eds.). (2002). *Common mechanisms in perception and action: Attention & performance XIX.* Oxford: Oxford University Press.

Rizzolatti, G., Fogassi, L., & Gallese, V. (2001). Neurophysiological mechanisms underlying the understanding and imitation of action. *Nature Reviews, 2,* 661–670.

Schultz-Gambard, J., Feierabend, C., & Hommel, B. (1988). The experience of crowding in real-life environments: An action oriented approach. In D. Canter, J. C. Jesuino, L. Soczka., & G. M. Stephenson (Eds.), *Environmental social psychology* (pp. 94–105). Dordrecht: Kluwer Academic.

Schultz-Gambard, J., & Hommel, B. (1987). Sozialpsychologie und Umweltgestaltung: Der Beitrag der Crowdingforschung. In J. Schultz-Gambard (Ed.), *Angewandte Sozial-psychologie: Konzepte, Ergebnisse, Perspektiven* (pp. 251–264). München: Psychologie-Verlags-Union.

Strack, F., Martin, L., & Stepper, S. (1988). Inhibiting and facilitating conditions of the human smile: A nonobtrusive test of the facial feedback hypothesis. *Journal of Personality and Social Psychology, 54,* 768–777.

Tomasello, M., & Call, J. (1997). *Primate cognition.* New York: Oxford University Press.

25

Baboons, Brains, Babies, and Bonding: A Multidisciplinary Approach to Mimicry

Ad van Knippenberg
Rick van Baaren
Radboud University Nijmegen, the Netherlands

MIMICRY: THE INVISIBLE SOCIAL GLUE

When you look around, you will see that people often mimic each other. You may spot two lovers in a bar, who unwittingly assume each other's posture while disclosing how much they are in love. Or two grandmothers on a bench in the park, who are nodding and taking over facial expressions as they exchange the latest news about their grandchildren. Two children jump on the couch, crying and screaming, but only one really saw a mouse. Mimicry is everywhere, and most of the time people are not aware of the fact that they mimic or are being mimicked. Mimicry is an integral part of our daily social life.

On the basis of the extant literature, and inspired by theoretical considerations, we believe that unconscious mimicry serves two important purposes. First, it is an indispensable tool for binding individuals to their social group. Second, and related to that, mimicry may provide a very effective way for the transmission of cultural ways and habits and for the continuous adaptation of individuals to changing social conditions.

In this essay, we first discuss social psychology's recent contributions to the study of mimicry. Subsequently, we speculate about how other fields of science may help to clarify the functions of mimicry and the basic processes and mechanisms involved in its production.

MIMICRY IN SOCIAL PSYCHOLOGY

Recent work in social psychology has shown that people have an automatic tendency to mimic others. Chartrand and Bargh (1999), for example, demonstrated that participants unconsciously mimicked specific behaviors (i.e., shaking their foot, or rubbing their face) displayed by confederates of the experimenter. Debriefing indicated that participants were unaware of their mimicry.

On the basis of recent social psychological research, it appears that nonconscious mimicry is more likely to occur in conditions in which people have a pro-social orientation. Mimicry seems to be more prevalent in people who are high in perspective taking (Chartrand & Bargh, 1999), who have—either manipulated or chronically—an interdependent self (van Baaren, Maddux, Chartrand, De Bouter, & van Knippenberg, 2003), who have an affiliation goal (Lakin & Chartrand, 2003) and who are high in self-monitoring (Cheng & Chartrand, 2004). To summarize, when we have more concern for others, depend more on them, want to affiliate with them, or want to be liked by them, we tend to take over their behavior to a greater extent.

The relationship between mimicry and prosocial orientation seems to be bidirectional. When we are being mimicked, we feel closer to others. Research on the consequences of mimicry shows that we like others more (Chartrand & Bargh, 1999), are more helpful and donate more money to charities (van Baaren, Holland, Kawakami, & van Knippenberg, 2004), and give larger tips in a restaurant (van Baaren, Holland, Steenaert, & van Knippenberg, 2003) when our behavior has been unobtrusively mimicked compared to when our behavior has not been mimicked.

In our view, the tendency to mimic others primarily serves a social goal.[1] The proximal reward is that individuals who mimic as well as individuals who are being mimicked feel closer to their group. From the research we reviewed, it seems that there is a bidirectional causal relationship between mimicry and prosocial orientation. Mimicry enhances prosocial orientation, and prosocial orientation fosters mimicry. This way, mimicry may help individuals to get along with others and to adopt the ways and habits (cultural patterns) of one's group.

This proposition has important theoretical implications. If mimicry serves such a basic function for humans, behavioral mimicry must have survival value and the propensity to mimic must be innate. Mimicry must have played a role in the evolution of our species, maybe not exclusively or specifically for *Homo sapiens sapiens*, but at least for our ancestors and our extended family of higher primates, or even for a wider circle of related species. If this is the case,

---

[1]It should be noted that this presumed social function of mimicry does not necessarily imply that mimicry cannot have antisocial or aversive effects. Neither does the existence of an unconscious tendency to mimic preclude the existence of overriding mechanisms that may account for complementarity of behaviors in situations in which it is functional to react rather than to copy.

then the question of the function of mimicry and the processes and mechanisms that enable us to mimic is probably too big and too broad for one subdiscipline to handle on its own.

BRIDGES TO OTHER DISCIPLINES

The study of mimicry may well go beyond social psychology. If mimicry is such a basic aspect of human social life, then we may ask ourselves why this is the case. What is the survival value of mimicry, what is its role in our evolutionary history, what are the structures and processes in our brains that enable us to mimic, and what is the role played by mimicry when we grow up and become socialized in a complex human society? In other words, it may be interesting to consider behavioral mimicry from an evolutionary and animal comparative perspective, from a neuroscientific perspective, and from a developmental psychological perspective.

Why is it advantageous for a species to have the automatic tendency to imitate behaviors of conspecifics? What role did behavioral mimicry play in the evolution of humankind? These are pertinent questions that to our knowledge have not yet been explicitly addressed. A directly related approach concerns of course the animal comparative perspective. Do our closest living relatives (bonobo, chimpanzee) display mimicry, and what function does it have in the life and survival of these species? Are there other apes or monkeys that use behavioral mimicry? Or other mammals or birds or any other species? If so, does such behavioral mimicry have similar functions as it has in humans?

We may learn much about the function of mimicry in humans from comparative animal studies. For instance, the recent work of Frans de Waal (2002) throws new light on the role of mimicry in culture transmission among higher primates and macaques, which may be quite enlightening concerning the role played by mimicry in human social life. In de Waal's view, mimicry serves culture transmission purposes. Among higher primates and macaques, cultural habits (e.g., concerning gathering or preparation of food, and the use of tools) may be tacitly learned by an individual by observing others and by playful imitation of the sometimes complex behavioral patterns involved, enabling the individual to gradually gain mastery of the behavior in question and eventually to use it to the benefit of herself and her fellow group members. Such mimicry should not be interpreted as purposeful imitation aimed at reaping the attendant rewards (i.e., it is not the same as "vicarious learning"), but behavior of others is being mimicked as a natural aspect of being member of the group. As de Waal (2002) wrote in describing an instance of imitation in chimpanzees: "I wonder where this behavior would fall under the usual classifications of imitation: no problem was being solved, no goal was being copied, and no reward was procured.... It had an element of identification, of empathy and closeness, rather than the cool evaluation of goals and methods that the scientific literature proposes as the hallmark of imitation" (p. 217). Mimicry helps to strengthen the ties between group members. Although such bonding may be the proximal incentive for behavioral mimicry, one of the long-term advantages may be the transmission of acquired habits (i.e., culture) that are beneficial to the survival of the individual as well as the group.

Our tentative conclusion converges with de Waal's. Although, as we assume, the primary function of mimicry is to strengthen the bonds between group members, there may be a secondary function—a derived advantage—in that this mimicry helps to socialize individual group members, helping them to acquire the motor programs and skills required to perform beneficial actions both in the individuals' own and their group's interest.

Now we move from our "cousins" to our brains. If the automatic tendency to mimic is indeed so basic to human social life, there must be neurological structures that enable and sustain the adoption of imitative behaviors.

MIMICRY AND NEUROSCIENCE?

Neuroscience can tell us more about the status of mimicry. If mimicry is an integral part of who we are, there should be structures in our brain facilitating the automatic copying of perceived behaviors. That is, the propensity for mimicry should be reflected in our "hardware." Several theorists have proposed a direct connection between perceiving and doing (e.g., Jeannerod, 1997; Prinz, 2002). In support of these claims, recent neuroscientific research on so-called "mirror neurons" provides evidence for such hardwired automaticity of mimicry (Gallese, Fadiga, Fogassi, & Rizzolatti, 1996). This research shows that, within our brains, there is an intimate link between observing an action, performing the same action ourselves, and merely thinking about that action. The same areas in the brain that take part in performing a particular action are also activated when we merely perceive another person performing that specific action (Iacoboni et al., 1999). The location of these mirror neurons is very interesting, because these neurons are closely connected to an area of the brain that is involved in language. In addition, neurological evidence suggests that empathy and mimicry are related, so it seems that mimicry plays an important role in understanding others and in empathizing with others. It may even be the case that our capability to mimic is related to our social skills. If one is incapable of taking over someone's facial expression and behaviors (e.g., patients with Alzheimer's disease and maybe autistic patients), this may have important negative consequences for social interactions. Research on the role of mimicry in understanding others may benefit tremendously from a multidisciplinary approach. Neuroscientists and social psychologists studying mimicry should therefore invest serious efforts in building these bridges.

Besides looking at our evolution and the makeup of our brains, it is important to look at our own individual development in order to find evidence for the innateness of mimicry. If mimicry is part of our "hardware," the tendency to mimic should be manifest from the day we are born.

MIMICRY AND DEVELOPMENTAL PSYCHOLOGY?

Indeed, there is evidence that humans are born with the tendency to mimic others. For example, newborns imitate facial movements, facial expressions, and vocal sounds (for a review, see Meltzoff & Moore, 1997). Mimicry has been observed from "day 1." Convincing evidence that mimicry occurs spontaneously and is not a behavior that is rapidly learned in the first weeks of life comes from studies on children who were literally just born. One study observed facial mimicry in 40 children with a mean age of 32 hours, with the youngest being no older than 42 minutes (cf. Meltzoff & Moore, 1997).

These studies underscore the basic function of mimicry in human social life. For infants, it is extremely important to be cared for and looked after, because newly born humans are far too weak to survive on their own and are totally dependent on others. As suggested earlier, mimicry is related to a sense of belonging. From an evolutionary perspective, mimicry increases the newborn's chances of survival. As stated by Heimann (2002): "This capacity to react, to imitate, to create a sense of togetherness, is most likely a result of our evolutionary history. It has served our species and helped newborns to be taken care of by their parents. The chance for an infant to survive increases rapidly if the child is able to engage the caretaker in social situations that also evoke strong emotional responses in the adult" (p. 79). Humans who are capable of drawing attention, creating closeness, and stimulating prosocial behavior have the highest chance of living a successful life.

CONCLUSIONS

It may be difficult to believe that mimicry is more than just a peculiar remnant from our evolutionary past. We tend to make fun of it. A very amusing movie from the Dutch film director Bert Haanstra (*The Zoo*) completely capitalizes on behavioral mimicry. We see visitors in the zoo mimicking animal behavior—for instance, a person yawning exactly like the baboon just did, or a spectator unconsciously scratching his armpits while watching the chimps do the same. However, as we aimed to demonstrate in this essay, this may not do justice to what mimicry really is about. There is more to mimicry than casual observation reveals.

Mimicry functions as social glue. It strengthens the ties between people. When we consider the fact that humans may be one of the most social animals that exist, and that life within a human society is an extremely complex affair, it may be easier to appreciate that we need tools like mimicry to make such an intricate system work. Although mimicry may be used by many species to their advantage, it may be of special importance to humans.

As our brief excursion into other fields of science shows, there is a lot to be gained from a multidisciplinary approach to mimicry. We've witnessed considerable advances in behavioral science and neuroscience in the past decades. What we tried to picture in this essay is that mimicry constitutes a very good example of an area of behavioral research where a joint effort to study it may pay off with tremendous progress in understanding its function, structure, and process.

REFERENCES

Chartrand, T. L., & Bargh, J. A. (1999). The chameleon effect: The perception–behavior link and social interaction. *Journal of Personality and Social Psychology, 76,* 893–910.

Cheng, C. M., & Chartrand, T. L. (2004). Self-monitoring without awareness: Using mimicry as a nonconscious affiliation strategy. *Journal of Personality and Social Psychology, 85*(6), 1170–1179.

de Waal, F. (2002). *The ape and the sushi master: Cultural reflections of a primatologist.* New York: Basic Books.

Gallese, V., Fadiga, L., Fogassi, L., & Rizzolatti, G. (1996). Action recognition in the premotor cortex. *Brain, 119,* 593–609.

Heimann, M. (2002). Notes on individual differences and the assumed elusiveness of neonatal imitation. In A. Meltzoff & W. Prinz (Eds.), *The imitative mind* (pp. 311–330). Berlin: Springer-Verlag.

Iacoboni, M., Woods, R., Brass, M., Bekkering, H., Mazziotta, J. C., & Rizzolatti, G. (1999). Cortical mechanisms of human imitation. *Science, 286,* 2526–2528.

Jeannerod, M. (1997). *The cognitive neuroscience of action.* Oxford: Blackwell.

Lakin, J., & Chartrand, T. L. (2003). Using nonconscious mimicry to create affiliation and rapport. *Psychological Science, 14,* 334–339.

Meltzoff, A. N., & Moore, M. K. (1997). Explaining facial imitation: A theoretical model. *Early Development and Parenting, 6,* 179–192.

Prinz, W. (2002). Experimental approaches to imitation. In A. Meltzoff & W. Prinz (Eds.), *The imitative mind* (pp. 143–162). Berlin: Springer-Verlag.

van Baaren, R. B., Holland, R. W., Kawakami, K., & van Knippenberg, A. (2004). Mimicry and pro-social behavior. *Psychological Science, 15,* 71–74.

van Baaren, R. B., Holland, R. W., Steenaert, B., & van Knippenberg, A. (2003). Mimicry for money: Behavioral consequences of imitation. *Journal of Experimental Social Psychology, 39,* 393–398.

van Baaren, R. B., Maddux, W. W., Chartrand, T. L., De Bouter, C., & van Knippenberg, A. (2003). It takes two to mimic: Behavioral consequences of self-construals. *Journal of Personality and Social Psychology, 84,* 1093–1102.

PART 4

Bridges With Personality, Emotion, and Development

INTRODUCTION

From the very beginning, social psychology has always had a siblinglike, if not twin-like, relationship with personality. One reason for this strong relationship is that much personality centers on motives, traits, or states that are truly social in nature, such as agreeableness and extraversion. Another reason is that much of social psychology focuses on individual-level needs and motives that are essential to our dealing with the social environment, even though they are relevant to various nonsocial tasks as well—examples are need for cognition, sensation seeking, and self-esteem. Although emotion has always been relevant to psychological science, in the last decade the study of emotion has become a prominent area of research. Emotion is closely linked to social psychology, because many emotions—and shame and guilt are just examples—are truly social, in that they would not, or could not, come into being and persist if there were no social environment. Another important reason is that emotions are the states that affect—and are affected by—perceptions, thoughts, and behavior and interactions. Developmental issues are also strongly interrelated with social psychology, because social development is central to many aspects of human development, affecting biological development, cognitive development, and personality development. Moreover, the experiences that are most intense to children—and from which children learn the most—may well be the social experiences flowing from interactions with parents, teachers, and peers or from observations of social interactions in the various media. As shown in the various essays, social psychology is essential to personality, emotion, and development (often a blend of these), just as these fields are essential to social psychology.

26

Assumptions About Personality and Core Motivations as Hidden Partners in Social Psychology

Charles S. Carver
University of Miami

I am a personality psychologist. Most people know that personality psychologists study individual differences. Many believe—incorrectly—that we care only about individual differences. Personality psychologists focus partly on things that make people different from each other, but partly on things that make people the same—normative structures and processes that coalesce to form a unique personality in every normal human being. In our textbook (Carver & Scheier, 2004), we use the term *intrapersonal functioning* to refer to these processes. Allport (1961), more eloquently, termed them a dynamic organization of psychological systems within each person that create the person's pattern of behaviors, thoughts, and feelings.

In one fashion or another, statements about intrapersonal functioning all are statements about the nature of people's core motivations. They are statements about what concerns determine people's actions and thoughts. Some views of personality hold that people's core motives concern relationships with significant others. Some assume people's core motives concern predicting and adapting better to the world. Some assume the core motive is to create and maintain a public persona. Some assume the central motive is to reduce drives.

To some extent, the qualities I am talking about here are captured in the phrase "human nature." Personality psychologists, because they are focused on the "whole person" and how that person functions over time and situations, are interested in what view of personality best captures the essence of human nature. Many people use this phrase, but what *is* human nature? The answer depends on whom you ask.

Personality psychologists are not the only ones interested in these issues, of course. The same issues arise in social psychology, although usually more obliquely. As they begin their work, social psychologists implicitly adopt one or another set of assumptions about human nature and its basic motives. They assume an implicit model of personality—a basic nature, a broad motivational dynamic—as a lens to view how people influence each other. This is what I mean by personality and motivation as "hidden partners" in social psychological analyses of behavior.

CONCEPTIONS OF PERSONALITY IN SOCIAL BEHAVIOR

Different personality psychologists take different views of human nature as their starting points. Thus, there exist several rather different conceptions of what processes are fundamental to personality and human motivation. In the same way, social psychologists have also taken several different views of what processes are fundamental to human functioning. Here are a few that have been held over the years, in no particular order.

Drives and Behavior

The motivational models of Hull–Spence drive theory that held sway in the mid-20th century influenced all of psychology. These models derived in large part from the labs examining learning, although some theorists were also trying to account for psychoanalytic ideas in terms of learning and motivation (Miller & Dollard, 1941). It was argued that personality could be viewed in terms of a cauldron of drives, channeling behavior in directions dictated by the habits resulting from prior drive reduction (Miller & Dollard, 1941; Dollard & Miller, 1950). In this theoretical tradition, the rising of a need (any need) creates an aversive drive state. Drive is the engine of behavior—thus, the core motivational construct. Personality is the person's organization of drives and habits.

The primacy of drive theory is also reflected in social psychological theories of the 1950s through 1970s. Social psychologists added an emphasis on psychological needs, such as the need for consistency (Festinger, 1957) and the need to maintain perceptions of freedom (Brehm, 1966). When these needs are not satisfied, the result is an aversive drive. According to dissonance theory and reactance theory (and several other social psychological theories), what happens next reflects an attempt to reduce the aversive drive state.

Human Being As Naive Scientist

A very different idea about human nature was posed by George Kelly in 1955. Kelly believed that human behavior was not organized around the rising of drives, but around the desire to predict the world accurately. In his view, people construct an understanding of reality and use those personal constructs to predict (usually implicitly) future events. If the constructs predict well, they are retained. If they fail to predict, they are modified or discarded. The overall goal is better prediction. In that view, the individual naively does what the scientist does more intentionally: generate and test predictions about the world.

George Kelly was not the only theorist who saw the human being as a native scientist. Another was Harold Kelley (1967). In his analysis of attribution, Kelley saw the person as amateur scientist, analyzing available information to make inferences about the causes of events. People consider distinctiveness, consistency, and consensus in events they observe, to infer whether the cause was primarily stable aspects of the person, stable aspects of the environment, or unstable aspects of the matrix. The idea that people are implicit scientists has become ingrained in social psychology as a starting point for theory.

Object Relations and Attachment

Another view of personality derives from the idea that early experiences shape the child's orientations to others throughout life. Sometimes this issue is framed in terms of a dynamic between fusion and separation–individuation (Mahler, 1968), in which the child struggles for an independent identity but also wants to retain a strong maternal bond. Sometimes the issue is framed in terms of the quality of the relationship that develops between the child and the caretaker (Bowlby, 1969, 1988). Ideally, the caretaker is a secure base to explore from and a safe haven to return to.

Such ideas have had great impact on analyses of close relationships (e.g., Hazan & Shaver, 1994; Simpson & Rholes, 1998). Today the attachment model of adult relationships is being explored by researchers in many different contexts. Many people now believe that the fundamental issue underlying many kinds of social behavior is the nature and quality of the bond that a given person has to a significant other. This view depends on a particular implicit view of personality: that the core dynamic of personality involves a person's perceptions of his or her relations with others (see also Anderson & Chen, 2002).

Self-Presentational Issues as a Focal Motive

Having images of significant others is not the only way to take others into account, nor is it the only way in which social relations can be taken as the central issue of personality. Another derives from symbolic interactionism (Mead, 1934) and related ideas. These ideas suggest that a person comes to know the self by the reflected appraisals of others, and comes to optimize those reflected appraisals by acting in a contextually appropriate manner (Goffman, 1959). Although these ideas come mostly from sociology, they yield a view of human nature in which adjusting one's public presentation to fit the social situation is a key issue (Snyder, 1987).

Such ideas are implicit in several social psychological topics. One of them is an account of cognitive dissonance effects (previously analyzed by a drive-based dynamic) in terms of an effort to present a public image of consistency (Tedeschi, Schlenker, & Bonoma, 1971). Other theories with labels such as self-presentation and impression management (Schlenker, 1980) also address the notion that many aspects of social behavior represent efforts to present the self favorably, to manage impressions of the self in the minds of others. As in symbolic interactionism, such processes ease social interchange, facilitating the self's negotiation of the social world.

Self-Esteem Protection

Yet another view of personality is grounded in the idea that a fundamental dynamic within the person is an ongoing effort to protect and defend the self (Rogers, 1959). When the self is threatened by some experience, the person may distort, disregard, or deny the relevance of the experience to the self. These self-esteem protective tendencies resemble aspects of the defense mechanisms postulated in psychoanalytic theory, although the ideas as they emerged in self-theory have different origins.

The idea that people go out of their way to protect self-esteem has also been an integral part of social psychology for a long time. This idea underlies several active areas of study under diverse labels, including self-evaluation maintenance (Tesser, 1986), self-affirmation (Steele, 1988), and ego-defensiveness (Darley & Goethals, 1980). In each case, a particular behavioral response follows from a threat to the self-image and yields protection or even enhancement of that self-image.

EVOLUTIONARY PSYCHOLOGY

It would certainly be a gross overstatement to claim that evolutionary thinking is particular to personality psychology. Yet the evolutionary viewpoint on human behavior does induce a way of thinking about intrapersonal functioning (Buss, 1991). In this view, behavior is about adapting to the present circumstances so as to stay alive—not that the individual necessarily has much realization of that. People need to stay alive individually, have social bonds with some group for mutual protection and eventual source of mating opportunities, and keep offspring alive long enough for them to be self-sustaining. Human nature is to use evolved skills at making the best of these tasks.

Most of these tasks, of course, represent problems in managing social relationships (Kenrick et al., 2002). Thus, many aspects of social behavior have been discussed as reflecting evolutionary considerations. Indeed, social psychologists with evolutionary views can make a case for claiming the evolutionary view as their own. Yet the genetic codes that resulted from the previous solving of those problems by generations of prehumans reside in the individual, influencing how the individual approaches the world in all its complexity. Thus, once again, the social psychological analysis implicitly assumes a basic motivational dynamic within the person.

CONCLUSIONS

When social psychologists examine a phenomenon, they do so through the lens of one or another set of implicit assumptions. These assumptions concern (in part) the core motivations by which humans function. Social psychologists in different contexts over the years have assumed widely varying motivational dynamics as being central to the kinds of behavior on which they focused. Central concerns that have been assumed include (but are not limited to) reducing drives, predicting and understanding the world, maintaining positive relationships with significant others, optimizing self-presentation, maintaining the self-image, and fitting a biologically demanding environment.

Each of these views has also been held by some personality psychologists as a good way to conceptualize the central concerns of the person. In this way, ideas that are fundamental to personality psychology serve as implicit frameworks for theories of social psychology. In saying this, I am not arguing for the benefits of building further bridges between social and personality psychology. Rather, I am saying that the bridges are already there. They are inescapable. It is nearly impossible to think about *inter*personal functioning without making assumptions about *intra*personal functioning.

REFERENCES

Allport, G. W. (1961). *Pattern and growth in personality.* New York: Holt, Rinehart, & Winston.
Andersen, S. M., & Chen, S. (2002). The relational self: An interpersonal social-cognitive theory. *Psychological Review, 109,* 619–645.
Bowlby, J. (1969). *Attachment and loss: Vol. 1, Attachment.* New York: Basic Books.
Bowlby, J. (1988). *A secure base: Parent–child attachment and healthy human development.* New York: Basic Books.
Brehm, J. W. (1966). *A theory of psychological reactance.* New York: Academic Press.
Buss, D. M. (1991). Evolutionary personality psychology. *Annual Review of Psychology, 42,* 459–491.
Carver, C. S., & Scheier, M. F. (2004). *Perspectives on personality* (5th ed.). Boston: Allyn & Bacon.
Darley, J. M., & Goethals, G. R. (1980). Peoples' analyses of the causes of ability-linked performances. In L. Berkowitz (Ed.), *Advances in experimental social psychology* (Vol. 13, pp. 1–37). New York: Academic Press.
Dollard, J., & Miller, N. E. (1950). *Personality and psychotherapy: An analysis in terms of learning, thinking, and culture.* New York: McGraw-Hill.
Festinger, L. (1957). *A theory of cognitive dissonance.* Evanston, IL: Row, Peterson.
Goffman, E. (1959). *The presentation of self in everyday life.* Garden City, NY: Doubleday.

Hazan, C., & Shaver, P. R. (1994). Attachment as an organizational framework for research on close relationships. *Psychological Inquiry, 5,* 1–22.

Kelley, H. H. (1967). Attribution theory in social psychology. In D. Levine (Ed.), *Nebraska symposium on motivation* (Vol. 15, pp. 192–238). Lincoln: University of Nebraska Press.

Kelly, G. A. (1955). *The psychology of personal constructs* (Vols. 1 and 2). New York: Norton.

Kenrick, D. T., Maner, J. K., Butner, J., Li, N. P., Becker, D. V., & Schaller, M. (2002). Dynamical evolutionary psychology: Mapping the domains of the new interactionist paradigm. *Personality and Social Psychology Review, 6,* 347–356.

Mahler, M. S. (1968). *On human symbiosis and the vicissitudes of individuation: Infantile psychosis.* New York: International Universities Press.

Mead, G. H. (1934). *Mind, self, and society.* Chicago: University of Chicago Press.

Miller, N. E., & Dollard, J. (1941). *Social learning and imitation.* New Haven, CT: Yale University Press.

Rogers, C. R. (1959). A theory of therapy, personality and interpersonal relationships, as developed in the client-centered framework. In S. Koch (Ed.), *Psychology: A study of a science* (Vol. 3, pp. 184–256). New York: McGraw-Hill.

Schlenker, B. R. (1980). *Impression management: The self-concept, social identity, and interpersonal relations.* Monterey, CA: Brooks/Cole.

Simpson, J. A., & Rholes, W. S. (Eds.). (1998). *Attachment theory and close relationships.* New York: Guilford.

Snyder, M. (1987). *Public appearances/private realities: The psychology of self-monitoring.* New York: W. H. Freeman.

Steele, C. M. (1988). The psychology of self-affirmation: Sustaining the integrity of the self. In L. Berkowitz (Ed.), *Advances in experimental social psychology* (Vol. 21, pp. 261–302). New York: Academic Press.

Tedeschi, J. T., Schlenker, B. R., & Bonoma, T. V. (1971). Cognitive dissonance: Private ratiocination or public spectacle? *American Psychologist, 26,* 685–695.

Tesser, A. (1986). Some effects of self-evaluation maintenance on cognition and action. In R. M. Sorrentino & E. T. Higgins (Eds.), *The handbook of motivation and cognition: Foundations of social behavior* (pp. 435–464). New York: Guilford.

Building Bridges Between Personality and Social Psychology: Understanding the Ties That Bind Persons and Situations

Mark Snyder
University of Minnesota

As a psychologist, I have two identities—I am both a social psychologist and a personality psychologist. This dual identity is not only a harmonious one, but also one in which each part thrives on the benefits of the other's presence. Having two hats to wear, so to speak, has taught me something about how better to wear each of them. I am not alone in this regard. Recent years have seen the emergence of the field of personality and social behavior. As a scientific enterprise, personality and social behavior emerged from the areas of overlap and intersection of personality and social psychology, and has been nurtured by investigators from both disciplines whose work has carried them back and forth across the bridge that their theoretical and empirical efforts have built between personality and social psychology.

How and why have social psychologists and personality psychologists found themselves venturing into each other's territory and thereby helping to build a bridge between their separate disciplines? Personality and social psychology, after all, take quite different points of departure in their attempts to understand human nature. Most definitions of personality psychology include references to the quest for an understanding of how the actions of individuals reflect stable and enduring traits, dispositions, and other personal attributes that are thought to reside within individuals and to move them to act in accord with these features of their personalities. As Allport defined it, "personality is the dynamic organization within the individual of those psychophysical systems that determine his unique adjustments to his environment" (1937, p. 48). By contrast, the view of human nature associated with social psychology is one that tends to view people as social animals, creatures of their social situations, molding and tailoring their behavior to fit the shifting demands of their current situations, the pressures of their peers, and the demands of their roles, and so forth. Thus, "with few exceptions, social psychologists regard their discipline as an attempt to understand and explain how the thought, feeling, and behavior of individuals are influenced by the actual, imagined, or implied presence of others" (Allport, 1968, p. 3).

In large measure, research in personality and research in social psychology have been guided by these contrasting views of human nature, with personality psychologists searching for the influence of individuals' traits and dispositions, and social psychologists searching for the influence of the situational and interpersonal contexts in which individuals find themselves. Yet, in spite of these differing points of departure, personality psychologists and social psychologists have increasingly been finding themselves on common ground. As research in personality makes clear, there is surely evidence that people's traits and dispositions are linked to their behavior; yet it is also clear that the linkages between personality and social behavior are stronger in some situations than in other situations, especially those situations that actively encourage individuals to turn to their dispositions as guides to action (for a review of situational moderators of the relations between personality and social behavior, see Snyder & Ickes, 1985). Similarly, research in social psychology provides clear evidence that individuals' behavior is sensitive to the guidelines provided by their situations; however, it is also clear that the strength of these situational influences seems to be greater for some people than for others, especially those who characteristically turn to situational cues for guides to action (for a review of personal moderators of the relations between situations and behavior, see Snyder & Ickes, 1985).

That the linkages between personal disposition and behavior seem to be moderated by situational considerations and that the power of situations seems to be moderated by properties of individuals have been the basis of the *interactionist* view of the role of persons and situations in determining behavior. At one level, the interactionist point of view is reminiscent of Lewin's proposition: "Every psychological event depends upon the state of the person and at the same time on the environment, although their relative importance is different in different cases" (1936, p. 12). But more than a reminder of the importance of persons and situations in understanding behavior, the interactionist approach to personality and social behavior is a set of specifications of *how* persons and situations interact in accounting for individual and social behavior. This interaction of person and situation may be either of a *statistical* form, as the predictive power of person variables and situation variables can be leveraged by incorporating each other as moderator variables, or of a *dynamic* form, emphasizing the reciprocal influence and mutual interplay of persons and situations, as persons select situations conducive to the expression of relevant features of their personalities and as situations afford opportunities for individuals to act on traits and dispositions relevant to those situations (e.g., Snyder & Cantor, 1998).

Whether in its statistical form or in its dynamic form, this interactionist perspective on the linkages between persons and situations provides the foundation for a bridge between personality and social psychology. It is a bridge that encourages travel in both directions, and that promises rewards to those who travel that bridge. Speaking as one who has traveled that bridge in both directions, I can speak to those rewards. Let me offer but two examples— one involving traveling across the bridge from social psychology to personality and one involving traversing the bridge from the personality side to the social side—in hopes that others will be encouraged to travel that bridge and experience the benefits of doing so.

First, consider the benefits to social psychology of venturing into personality psychology. As a social psychologist, I am well aware of the power of situations to influence social behavior; for example, when confronted with situations populated with competitive others, most people respond with competitive behaviors of their own. But as a personality psychologist, I am also aware that, in some measure, situations are chosen and structured by people themselves, and that people are motivated in their selections and choices of situations by their own identities and personalities. Thus, to continue the example about competition, some people may find themselves confronted with competitive situations precisely because they have chosen to enter such situations, and they may have chosen those situations precisely because they are seeking opportunities to act on their own competitive dispositions. Accordingly, in understanding the role of situations in people's lives, I have found it useful to ask questions not just about what happens to people in the situations in which they find themselves, but also about how and why people get themselves into those situations in the first place (for a review of theory and research on the role of personality in choosing situations, see Ickes, Snyder, & Garcia, 1997). In so doing, I feel that I am being a better social psychologist, or at least a more complete one, for also being a personality psychologist.

˙ Now, consider the benefits to personality psychology of incorporating a social psychological perspective. As a personality psychologist, I am well aware of the ways in which individuals traits and dispositions are sources of regularities and consistencies in people's behavior; thus, for example, people with extraverted dispositions tend to behave in sociable and outgoing fashion across diverse situations, with different partners, and over extended periods of time. But as a social psychologist, I am also aware of the regularities and consistencies that can and do exist in the situations in which people find themselves and that these regularities and consistencies in situations can encourage and even enforce regularities and consistencies in people's behaviors. Thus, to continue the example about extraversion, a life time spent in situations calling for success in public relations may produce a reliable record of sociability across situations, partners, and time—a pattern that, at a minimum, may reinforce an underlying extraverted disposition, or that may even be internalized to create an extraverted disposition to match a life spent in extraverted situations. Accordingly, in understanding the role of traits and dispositions in people's lives, I have found it useful to ask not only about the ways in which personality induces regularities and consistencies in behavior, but also about the ways in which people's personalities may be shaped and molded by regularities and consistencies in the situations in which they function (for further perspective on the influence of situations on individuals, see Kelley et al., 2003). In so doing, I feel that I am being a better personality psychologist, or at least a more complete one, for also being a social psychologist.

CONCLUSIONS

To be sure, although much has already been accomplished in building bridges between personality and social psychology, there is much more that can (and, I think, should) be done in extending the bridge between personality and social psychology. As much as the active choosing of situations by individuals may constitute one important linkage between personality and social psychology, there are surely others as well. For example, the bridge between persons and situations can be expanded to include the linkages between features of persons, such as their traits and dispositions, and the biological foundations of those personal attributes. Also, the bridge between persons and situations can be expected to include linkages between features of situations and the larger societal and cultural contexts in which these situations occur.

With these extensions, the bridge between personality and social psychology potentially becomes one that operates at, and that spans, many levels of analysis. It becomes a bridge that links events that occur within individuals (such as their personalities, their attitudes, their identities) to events that occur between individuals (such as the dynamics of their social interactions and their interpersonal relationships) to events that occur between groups (such as the relations between majority and minority groups) and to the very structure and function of cultures and societies (including the ways in which individuals influence and are influenced by their societies and their cultures).

REFERENCES

Allport, G. (1937). *Personality: A psychological interpretation.* New York: Holt.

Allport, G. (1968). The historical background of modern social psychology. In G. Lindzey & E. Aronson (Eds.), *The handbook of social psychology* (Vol. 1, 2nd ed., pp. 1–80). Reading, MA: Addison-Wesley.

Ickes, W., Snyder, M., & Garcia, S. (1997). Personality influences on the choice of situations. In R. Hogan, J. A. Johnson, & S. R. Briggs (Eds.), *Handbook of personality psychology* (pp. 165–195). New York: Academic Press.

Kelley, H. H., Holmes, J. G., Kerr, N. L., Reis, H. T., Rusbult, C. E., & Van Lange, P. A. M. (2003). *An atlas of interpersonal situations.* New York: Cambridge.

Lewin, K. (1936). *A dynamic theory of personality*. New York. McGraw-Hill.

Snyder, M., & Cantor, N. (1998). Understanding personality and social behavior: A functionalist strategy. In D. T. Gilbert, S. T. Fiske, & G. Lindzey (Eds.), *The handbook of social psychology* (Vol. 1, 4th ed., pp. 635–679). Boston: McGraw-Hill.

Snyder, M., & Ickes, W. (1985). Personality and social behavior. In G. Lindzey & E. Aronson (Eds.), *The handbook of social psychology* (Vol. 2, 3rd ed., pp. 883–948). New York: Random House.

Accuracy of Judgments of Personality and Genetic Influences on Attitudes: Two Major Bridges Between Personality and Social Psychology

Peter Borkenau
Nadine Mauer
Martin-Luther University, Halle, Germany

Bridges from social psychology to other fields differ in size and importance, and some bridges to personality are reasonable candidates for the top position. It's not only that there are two journals, the *Journal of Personality and Social Psychology* and the *Personality and Social Psychology Bulletin*, that testify to well-established links between these two fields; it's also that the *Journal of Personality and Social Psychology* is the field's flagship journal, and that personality and social psychology are in the same division of the American Psychological Association. This shows well-established links between personality and social psychology, although there are also journals and professional organizations that are exclusively for personality or social psychology.

ACCURACY OF JUDGMENTS OF PERSONALITY

One important bridge that links social psychology to personality and to methodology is that many personality measures like self-reports, peer reports, and behavior codings rely on human judgment. Thus, these measures reflect actual differences between target persons as well as person–perception processes. Personality traits are conceptualized as latent variables that cannot be observed directly but are linked to observable manifestations from which they can be inferred. The best way to illustrate that is an adapted version of Brunswik's (1956) lens model that is depicted in Fig, 28.1. The left side of this model refers to associations between latent personality traits and their observable manifestations (referred to as *cues* in Fig. 28.1) as well as to associations among these manifestations. One might study, for example, which cues are most diagnostic of a person's trustworthiness, how these cues depend on contextual variables, and how they differ between the young and the old, between men and women, or between extraverts and introverts. The study of such relations is personality research proper (Funder, 1999).

By contrast, the right side of the lens refers to how personality traits are inferred from observable cues, that is, on person-perception processes and their outcomes. Since Asch's (1946) pioneer work, this is classified as social psychology. The personality part and the social psychology part of the lens are both needed to explain accuracy in judgments of personality (Funder, 1999), that is, why judgmental measures of personality are correlated with nonjudgmental criteria. This is because accurate judgments can only be expected if: (a) differences in personality are expressed via observable manifestations, (b) judges infer personality traits from observable cues, and (c) the judges' inferences of traits from observable cues match the actual relations between the traits and their manifestations.

Are judgments of personality accurate indeed? To clarify that, nonjudgmental measures of targets' trait levels are needed as otherwise one studies consensus or self-other agreement (Kenny, 1994). The least controversial nonjudgmental measures of personality traits are available for abilities, par-

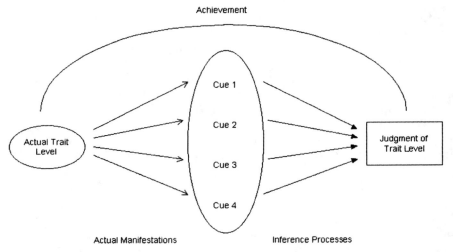

FIG. 28.1.   An adapted version of Brunswik's lens model.

ticularly for intelligence. Correlations between self-reports and performance measures of intelligence hover around .30 (Mabe & West, 1982; Paulhus, Lysy, & Yik, 1998), but higher correlations are obtained if descriptions by several outside perceivers are aggregated.

The most direct explanation of accurate judgments of intelligence is that there are cues to intelligence in observable behaviors that are appropriately used by outside perceivers. To identify such cues, it is useful to expose strangers to strictly controlled behavioral episodes of target persons, and to correlate the observer judgments of the targets' intelligence with the targets' actual performance. Using this approach, we videotaped short behavioral episodes and presented them to judges who never had personal contact with the targets. In two independent studies (Borkenau & Liebler, 1993; Borkenau, Mauer, Riemann, Spinath, & Angleitner, 2004), a particularly diagnostic cue to the targets' intelligence was how they read standard texts.

A very social aspect of personality is that persons make identity claims by behaving or shaping their environment in specific ways to control their perceptions by others. They should therefore be interested that their claims are accurately perceived. Web sites are a particularly suitable medium to inform a broad public on one's identity claims, and it is therefore interesting to relate personality inferences from web sites to their originator's personality and identity claims to find out whether they convey accurate impressions of their creator's personality. Such research may help to develop ecological theories of the causes and consequences of self-expression in everyday life (Vazire & Gosling, 2004).

GENETIC EFFECTS ON ATTITUDES

Another bridge that connects social psychology to personality and to biological psychology is how personality traits mediate genetic influences on social attitudes. A substantial part of attitude research is on attitude change brought about by exogenous variables like forced compliance. That is clearly social psychology. Nevertheless, there are also strong links to personality: First, there are relatively stable individual differences in attitudes that are related to observable behavior (Fishbein & Ajzen, 1974). Second, there are genetic influences on attitudes that are likely to be mediated by personality. These genetic influences are stronger for some attitudes (e.g., death penalty) than for others (e.g., coeducation), and the more heritable attitudes seem to be those that are more accessible, more difficult to modify, and more important for interpersonal attraction (Tesser, 1993). Thus differences at the biological level seem to underlie individual differences in the more important attitudes, and because the structure of DNA may influence attitudes but not vice versa, the direction of these effects clearly goes from genes to attitudes.

That personality mediates genetic effects on attitudes was suggested by Eysenck (1954) half a century ago, and it was recently tested by Olson, Vernon, Harris, and Jang (2001) in a study of 336 twin pairs who were administered attitude as well as personality measures. A principal components analysis of 30 attitude items identified 9 attitude factors, of which 6 were significantly heritable. By analyzing the cross-correlations (i.e., the correlations between one co-twin's attitude and the other co-twin's personality) between attitude and personality factors separately for monozygotic and dizygotic twins, Olson et al. (2001) partitioned the correlations between social attitudes and personality traits into genetic and environmental contributions. These analyses showed that correlations between attitudes and personality traits reflect common genetic influences, a finding that supports the view that genetic influences on attitudes are mediated by personality. This is another bridge between personality and social psychology that is likely to become more important in the future.

Genes influence mean levels, gender differences, and individual differences in personality and attitudes. Sociobiology investigates how human evolution shaped mean levels and gender differences in behavior (Barkow, Cosmides, & Tooby, 1992), but the case is different for individual differences. This is because personality traits and attitudes are influenced by many genes that are reshuffled from generation to generation via meiosis and insemination. As selection influences the frequency of single genes but not patterns of independently transmitted genes (Dawkins, 1976), it accounts for mean levels but not for individual differences in attributes that are influenced by many genes. Thus individual differences in personality and in attitudes are probably not functionally organized, but the outcome of genetic processes that have not been subject to selection (Tooby & Cosmides, 1990).

How do genes influence social attitudes and behavior? An important pathway probably includes neurotransmitters and broad affective dispositions. Ebstein et al. (1996) and Benjamin et al. (1996) found statistical associations between long and short versions of the dopamine receptor gene DRD4 and individual differences in novelty seeking, whereas Lesch et al. (1996) found associations between long and short versions of the serotonin transporter gene's regulatory region (5-HTTLPR) and individual differences in anxiety. Novelty seeking is strongly related to positive affectivity whereas anxiety is strongly related to negative affectivity, and both are related to personality and social attitudes.

CONCLUSIONS

The conclusions here take the form of outlined suggestions for the future regarding two bridges involving personality and social psychology. First, research on the accuracy of perceptions of personality has mostly focused on the Big Five factors of personality, whereas perceptions of personality attributes that actors wish to be correctly identified have hardly been studied. Identity claims are a case in point: The smoothness of social interactions probably depends not that much on accurate perceptions of the interaction partner's extraversion, but on accurate perceptions of the other's identity claims, for example, on whether the partner wishes to be perceived as a sincere or a happy-go-lucky personality. With a focus of accuracy research on whether actual impressions of personality match the intended impressions, social psychology and personality would become even more intertwined.

Second, bridges from genetics via personality to social psychology are extremely important. After all, the human mind has biological as well as social roots, and both have to be studied to understand it comprehensively. Genetic influences are the biologically most fundamental ones, whereas social psychology is the branch of psychology that most strongly emphasizes the social aspects of human behavior. It is extremely interesting to understand how biological and social influences interact. This implies a bridge between the two very distant islands of genetics and social psychology, with the benefit of obtaining a very broad view of human cognition and behavior.

REFERENCES

Asch, S. E. (1946). Forming impressions of personality. *Journal of Abnormal and Social Psychology, 41,* 258–290.

Barkow, J. H., Cosmides, L., & Tooby, J. (1992). *The adapted mind: Evolutionary psychology and the generation of culture.* New York: Oxford University Press.

Benjamin, J., Li, L., Patterson, C., Greenberg, B. D., Murphy, D. L., & Hamer, D. H. (1996). Population and familial association between the D4 dopamine receptor gene and measures of novelty seeking. *Nature Genetics, 12,* 81–84.

Borkenau, P., & Liebler, A. (1993). Convergence of stranger ratings of personality and intelligence with self-ratings, partner ratings, and measured intelligence. *Journal of Personality and Social Psychology, 65,* 546–553.

Borkenau, P., Mauer, N., Riemann, R., Spinath, F. M., & Angleitner, A. (2004). Thin slices of behavior as cues of personality and intelligence. *Journal of Personality and Social Psychology, 86,* 599–614.

Brunswik, E. (1956). *Perception and the representative design of psychological experiments.* Berkeley: University of California Press.

Dawkins, R. (1976). *The selfish gene.* Oxford: Oxford University Press.

Ebstein, R. P., Novick, O., Umansky, R., Priel, B., Osher, Y., Blaine, D., Bennett, E. R., Nemanov, L., Katz, M., & Belmaker, R. H. (1996). Dopamine D4 receptor (D4DR) exon III polymorphism associated with the human personality trait of Novelty Seeking. *Nature Genetics, 12,* 78–80.

Eysenck, H. J. (1954). *The psychology of politics.* New York: Routledge, Chapman, & Hall.

Fishbein, M., & Ajzen, I. (1974). Attitudes toward objects as predictors of single and multiple behavioral criteria. *Psychological Review, 81,* 59–74.

Funder, D. C. (1999). *Personality judgment: A realistic approach to person perception.* San Diego, CA: Academic Press.

Kenny, D. A. (1994). *Interpersonal perception: A social relations analysis.* New York: Guilford.

Lesch, K. P., Bengel, D., Heils, A., Sabol, S. Z., Greenberg, B. D., Petri, S., Benjamin, J., Müller, C. R., Hamer, D. H., & Murphy, D. L. (1996). Association of anxiety-related traits with a polymorphism in the serotonin transporter gene regulatory region. *Science, 274,* 1527–1531.

Mabe, P. A., & West, S. G. (1982). Validity of self-evaluation of ability: A review and meta-analysis. *Journal of Applied Psychology, 67,* 280–296.

Olson, J. M., Vernon, P. A., Harris, J. A., & Jang, K. L. (2001). The heritability of attitudes: A study of twins. *Journal of Personality and Social Psychology, 80,* 845–860.

Paulhus, D. L., Lysy, D., & Yik, M. S. M. (1998). Self-report measures of intelligence: Are they useful as proxy measures of IQ? *Journal of Personality, 66,* 525–554.

Tesser, A. (1993). The importance of heritability in psychological research: The case of attitudes. *Psychological Review, 100,* 129–142.

Tooby, J., & Cosmides, L. (1990). On the universality of human nature and the uniqueness of the individual: The role of genetics and adaptation. *Journal of Personality, 58,* 17–67.

Vazire, S., & Gosling, S. D. (2004). e-perceptions: Personality impressions based on personal websites. *Journal of Personality and Social Psychology, 87,* 123–132.

Thinking Integratively About Social Psychology: The Example of the Relational Self and the Social-Cognitive Process of Transference

Susan M. Andersen
S. Adil Saribay
New York University

Specialization in any subfield is likely to be necessary for establishing a paradigm, refining basic principles, and getting training in the tools that allow integrative research. Technological innovation often spurs new lines of research and theory that advance a subfield, and without specialization, developing technical sophistication is often impossible. Specialization has thus remained the zeitgeist of academic psychology. Yet, in our view, it is often pivotal in successful integration as well. Generative contributions to understanding behavior often arise from cross-fertilization between highly specialized subdisciplines because sufficient sophistication has been gained. The challenge is to gain specialized knowledge while maintaining broad interests, and to do this before attempting to bridge. This is the surest, most probable route to the technical skills without which integrative conceptions frequently cannot be convincingly realized. The dynamic convergence of specialization and integration may thus be what best permits careful empirical scrutiny of long-unanswered and potentially elusive theoretical questions. We illustrate how specialization can precede and enable integrative contributions cutting across subdisciplines using our research on the social-cognitive process of transference as an example, and also our work on the relational self.

THE PHENOMENON

Sara runs into Phil at a large bookstore where they are both leafing through books and drinking coffee, leaning against a counter. She feels like sharing a few words with him and is warmer toward him than usual and they strike up a conversation. She even invites him to a get-together with a small circle of close friends, and only later may consider that she barely knows him. Sara probably did not consciously think of her brother Tony, whom she loves and misses, nor explicitly compare Phil to Tony, but Sara's knowledge of Tony and also her warm relationship with him may have influenced her response. Like Tony, Phil wears neatly pressed blue jeans, has a deep baritone voice and light green eyes, and seems communicative as well as knowledgeable about art and politics.

Our research on the social-cognitive process of transference shows that a mental representation of a significant other can be activated and used in relating to a new person, based on a few personally meaningful cues such as these. Our work on the relational self shows that when this happens one may not only make assumptions about the new person, but may also experience and express the version of the self that one typically experiences with the significant other—but in relation to this new person, feeling the same feelings, and so on.

WHAT IS INTEGRATIVE IN THE THEORY

The term *significant other*, designates any individual deeply influential in one's life, in whom one is (or was) emotionally invested, whether a parent, sibling, first love, best friend, or mentor. Knowledge about the self and significant others are entangled in memory (Andersen & Chen, 2002).[1] Both idiosyncratic relationship information and shared realities, such as respective roles, are contained therein. One's outcomes are (or were) symbolically, if not concretely, interdependent with the significant other's. Thus the basic need for some degree of connection figures prominently in such relationships and in transference. Mental representations of significant others are thus not simply cognitive but profoundly laden with affect, expectancies, and motives, all likely to be experienced with a new person in transference.

This research has yielded the first experimental demonstration of the century-old clinical concept of transference (in everyday interpersonal relations). That is, a concept deriving from psychoanalysis, and also from models explicitly revising psychodynamic thought (e.g., Sullivan, 1953), has now been explicitly demonstrated to occur. This research thus integrates experi-

---

[1]See Andersen and Chen (2002) for a complete list of references to our work and to that of other relevant researchers.

mental research in social cognition with the history of clinical psychology. Because some significant-other representations are acquired early in life, the model is also broadly developmental as well.

Transference, in this formulation, can be understood in terms of social construct theory in social cognition (Higgins, 1996) and personal construct theory in personality (Kelly, 1955). Both models focus on social categories that are defined by trait terms like *reckless, adventurous, emotionally weak,* or *interpersonally sensitive.* Research on transference, in fact, grew out of a highly specialized program of research on the cognitive bases of stereotypes that examined social categories designated by a noun label (stereotype) relative to those designated by an adjective (a trait descriptor). Although trait concepts and stereotypes are essentially social categories, significant-other representations are *n*-of-one representations. It was the specialized methodologies and theoretically driven examination of cognitive processes in stereotyping that enabled the next step to the transference paradigm. The next step was conceptualized because of a background in other subdisciplines of psychology, that is, training and knowledge in both clinical and personality psychology. It was combining the precise methods and approach of this research program with the provocative questions from these other areas that enabled the innovation of seeing that significant-other representations may function like social categories, even though they designate a single individual.

Our reliance on social cognition, as the basis on which social perception arises and social relations unfold, makes this work fundamentally social cognitive. Specialization in social cognition offered advanced research techniques, designs, and procedures that, when combined with a slower pace of clinical training and ever-present teaching in personality psychology, produced the work that evolved.

Likewise, the model of the relational self expands on this work on transference, by addressing the self, the nature of self-regulation, and personality more directly, all while focusing on the variability of the self across situations—as a function of the triggering cues in those situations. The theory of the relational self is thus a part of if–then models of personality (Mischel & Shoda, 1995) that emphasize contemporary situational cues in how changes in the self are evoked, that may arise from processes of social learning. To the extent that significant-other representations are long held by the person, they may in fact undergird stability in the self and personality (Andersen & Chen, 2002), by providing the substrate of meanings experienced, even while these will vary in how active they are in the varying psychological situations of life.

THE EVIDENCE

We operationalize triggering cues in an interpersonal encounter in cues about a new person, such as his or her apparent attitudes, traits, activities, styles of relating, and so on, that are likely to activate a significant-other representation. If these cues "map onto" a representation in memory, the latter will tend to be activated and used, influencing interpersonal perception and introducing a "glue" of familiarity into new relationships.

In the paradigm, participants describe significant others in freehand. Weeks later, in an experiment (allegedly unrelated), they are exposed to features of a new person they expect to meet who shares some features with a significant other. Participants not in the "transference" condition see the same features as one experimental participant, making stimulus content equivalent (in fact identical) across conditions. After this, we assess memory for the new person's features, evaluations of him or her, emotions, motivations, self-ratings, and behavior, depending on the study. Particular types of significant-other representations (e.g., authority figures) may be examined and individual difference measures may be used to preselect participants for the research, if relevant. The experimental procedure taps the meaning system of the individual through idiographic methods while examining generalizable social-cognitive processes through nomothetic (shared) methods.

Widely varied studies have shown that a significant-other representation can drive inferences about a new person and can bias memory of the new person (e.g., Andersen & Cole, 1990). This results both from the chronic ease with which significant-other representations are retrieved and also from transient cues in the new context. The representation is triggered even when these cues are presented subliminally, evoking transference outside of awareness and relatively automatically. Comparisons with social categories and nonsignificant exemplars have shown that significant-other representations influence perception more. They also cannot be reduced to generic beliefs, even though generic knowledge (e.g., interpersonal roles) is part of these representations. In addition, the phenomenon is not due merely to self-generation effects (though the features are self generated).

A new person who resembles a positive (versus a negative) significant other is, as a result, evaluated more positively and is expected to be accepting rather than rejecting. This evokes the motivation to approach and to be emotionally open with the new person. Likewise, an immediate emotional response surfaces in subtle facial expressions that reflect one's positive or negative feelings toward the significant other (Andersen, Reznik, & Manzella, 1996). This happens so quickly that it is likely to be relatively automatic suggesting pervasiveness and little forethought. And ultimately, transference also brings about the self-fulfilling prophecy. A new person will inadvertently confirm in his or her behavior the very expectations perceivers held at the outset (Berk & Andersen, 2000).

Based on cognitive links between the standards significant others are assumed to hold and representations of these persons, activating a significant-other representation also evokes these standards and the specific emotions associated with them. These specific negative emotions result if the self is found wanting in light of the activated standards. Specific evoked emotions can be depression, agitation, or hositilty as a function of which standard the transference activates. These triggered emotions demonstrate the relational self. So does the overall finding that the version of the self one typically experiences with the significant other comes to infuse how the self is conceived in transference, leading to related changes in self-worth as well (Hinkley & Andersen, 1996). This latter kind of shift in transference, and related changes, can also lead to self-regulatory attempts to self-protect or to protect the other depending on the circumstances.

MORE ON BRIDGES—CROSSED AND CROSSABLE

Our conceptualization of transference relies on an integration of social psychological and cognitive principles, embodied in the field of social cognition, and using this to address the longstanding clinical assumption that human suffering often results from superimposing old relationships onto new ones—that is, transference. This bridges with clinical psychology and psychoanalysis as well (e.g., Greenberg & Mitchell, 1983).

Our model of the relational self also moves beyond this to extend this work into self-regulation and personality in social cognitive terms. Relying on the transference process as a mechanism underlying shifts in the self that occur across varying psychological contexts, the relational self theory borrows assumptions of if–then conceptualizations of the self and personality that are context specific and grounded in social learning theory (Mischel & Shoda, 1995). The reliance on both psychoanalytic and social learning conceptions is integrative in personality theory, and the focus on basic human motivations such as (among other needs) the need for connection in relationships is also integrative in its embrace of motivation as fundamental. That past relationships as knowledge structures in memory serve as lenses through which one perceives new relations suggests a bridge with developmental traditions as well.

Of course, the work bears on understanding personal relationships, a growing field. Our most recent work even examines the relevance of the relational self and dyadic identity to social identity within communities and institutions. We believe further extensions along these lines are possible, and should begin to address broader societal questions involving ethnic identity, "kin," and nation. We assume that extensions to mass media influences on people's perceptions, psychological states, and choices, can also be directly derived. At a far more microanalytic level, the precision of the effects observed also suggests that even bridging with cognitive and affective neuroscience may also be within reach. At present, the existing evidence integrates social cognition with motivation, emotion, relationships, and self-regulation, and also with personality, clinical, and by extension, developmental psychology.

CONCLUSIONS

An important challenge in integrative research is to do more than just lay theories or measures side by side, juxtaposing them, and to truly integrate assumptions. The simple inclusion of an individual-difference or cultural variable in a standard design may bridge in useful ways that are not genuinely integrative, and thus are, perhaps, less likely to be of lasting value in systematically adding to integrative knowledge.

Bridging is a challenge, however, both technically and pragmatically, because of the predominance of specialization in academia. And yet this very specialization may be what can provide sufficient methodological and technical advance to fuel bridging across subdisciplines. Hence, to ask whether to devote one's research to integrative questions or to specialization sets up a false choice because the answer is probably that it is a matter of sequence. Specialization is valuable in learning metaphors and techniques in a subdiscipline at the outset and this may eventually permit cross-fertilization, if one accrues a broad knowledge base and maintains broad interests that cut across area boundaries, and one gains some degree of specialization in another domain.

Highly specialized work that is programmatic and systematic within a domain, combined with serious exposure to other fields that ask different questions, can lead the interested scholar to find that intriguing questions are incubating quietly in the background of his or her mind, and that a pertinent "a-ha!" may arise for a crucial methodological and theoretical solution. Consider, for example, the basic-process research on social categorization and stereotyping done by Susan Fiske in the 1980s, which, when informed by her ongoing public interest work on sexual harassment in the workplace, ended up creating new research literatures on the social structural arrangements such as outcome dependency, which reduce stereotyping and those like unbridled power, which exacerbates it. Consider also the systematic basic research of Tory Higgins in social cognition on the accessibility of social constructs, which proceeded on unimpeded while his background interest and knowledge in developmental and clinical psychology grew, ultimately leading him to formulate self-discrepancy theory. Then, based on his scholarship on motivation, his theory of self-regulatory focus began to arise as well.

These examples illustrate the case for sequencing. Both sequencing and the integrative enterprise as a whole take time and are not for the faint hearted or for those disinclined to work twice as hard. Like most laudable aims, though, if one cares about them, they may well be worth the investment.

REFERENCES

Andersen, S. M., & Chen, S. (2002). The relational self: An interpersonal social-cognitive theory. *Psychological Review, 109,* 619–645.

Andersen, S. M., & Cole, S. W. (1990). "Do I know you?": The role of significant others in general social perception. *Journal of Personality and Social Psychology, 59,* 384–399.

Andersen, S. M., Reznik, I., & Manzella, L. M. (1996). Eliciting transient affect, motivation, and expectancies in transference: Significant-other representations and the self in social relations. *Journal of Personality and Social Psychology, 71,* 1108–1129.

Berk, M. S., & Andersen, S. M. (2000). The impact of past relationships on interpersonal behavior: Behavioral confirmation in the social-cognitive process of transference. *Journal of Personality and Social Psychology, 79*, 546–562.

Greenberg, J. R., & Mitchell, S. A. (1983). *Object relations in psychoanalytic theory.* Cambridge, MA: Harvard University Press.

Higgins, E. T. (1996). Knowledge activation: Accessibility, applicability, and salience. In E. T. Higgins & A. W. Kruglanski (Eds.), *Social psychology: Handbook of basic principles* (pp. 133–168). New York: Guilford Press.

Hinkley, K., & Andersen, S. M. (1996). The working self-concept in transference: Significant-other activation and self-change. *Journal of Personality and Social Psychology, 71*, 1279–1295.

Kelly, G. A. (1955). *The psychology of personal constructs.* New York: Norton.

Mischel, W., & Shoda, Y. (1995). A cognitive-affective system theory of personality: Reconceptualizing situations, dispositions, dynamics, and invariance in personality structure. *Psychological Review, 102*, 246–268.

Sullivan, H. S. (1953). *The interpersonal theory of psychiatry.* New York: Norton.

30

Philosophy as the Queen of the Sciences, Emotions Research as Her Bastard Child

Robert C. Solomon
University of Texas at Austin

Philosophy (actually, metaphysics), declared Immanuel Kant, is "the Queen of the Sciences." And, indeed, for many centuries philosophy was the mother of virtually all disciplines. There was little distinction between philosophy and psychology, and even the "hard" sciences of physics and chemistry were part of "natural philosophy." René Descartes wrote authoritatively about the neuroscience of his time, and John Locke was one among many philosophers who explored the anatomy and physiology of the sense organs. The idea of "bridge building" back then would have been all but unintelligible. There were no islands, no disciplines, and there was little "specialization" where the study of human nature was concerned.

Whether or not the specialization of knowledge into disciplines and subdisciplines is a good or necessary thing (given the sheer amount of information now to be processed), it carries with it a profound liability. The days of the "Renaissance man" (and woman) are over. No one can know everything. No one can keep up with every subject. And most of us have given up trying. But this is true not only of Da Vinci-like aspirants who seek cutting-edge breakthroughs in such divers areas as painting, weaponry, astrophysics, architecture, botany, and civil engineering. It is even true within disciplines and subdisciplines, such as the study of emotions, where I spend much of my time. As a paradigm example of the "subjective," emotions and therefore emotions research has long been the bastard child of science, born of royalty, perhaps, but of doubtful legitimacy nevertheless. And so we defensively quarantine our own knowledge. For many years, I dismissed neurobiology as an interesting distraction from the questions surrounding the human passions. I considered experiments in social psychology as at most a curious confirmation of what (as I rudely suggested in my 1976 book) any philosopher with a few minutes of time could figure out through casual observation. The philosophy of emotion—which then meant for me the conceptual analysis of (mostly English) emotion language—seemed quite sufficient and self-contained.

What changed my mind? Well, encounters with some excellent psychologists for one, charter membership in the International Society for Research on Emotions, for another, and then there was the explosion of discipline-busting readily accessible publications in neuropsychiatry. It became undeniable that emotions were many-faceted and complex (not only conceptually complex) and demanded cooperation and "bridge building" between disciplines. But in the century since philosophy and psychology parted ways and separated their methods, and with the neuroscientists off in their (superexpensive) laboratories with magnetic resonance imaging (MRI) machines and the like, we came to speak different languages, utilize and trust different methodologies, even describe the phenomena (emotions) in very different ways. Descartes, in his *Passions of the Soul* (1650/1989), skipped merrily from brain science to phenomenology to moral philosophy, but we have to learn again, as Vaclav Havel told the cheering citizens of the newly freed Czechoslovakia, to trust one another, and to speak a mutually comprehensible language.

There are a number of ways that philosophy can contribute to emotions research and to social psychology and the social sciences more generally. One is, as one of my analytic colleagues is fond of saying, as a conceptual janitor, clarifying the language, criticizing hypotheses, research designs, and inferences, straightening out ambiguous and tangled arguments and conclusions, pointing out hidden premises and assumptions. Another is by way of cognitive science, a conscientious hybrid of philosophical speculation and analysis, the hard sciences of computer modeling, evolutionary theory, and sometimes neurobiology (De Sousa, 1987; Griffiths, 1997). Still another is by continuing to tackle the infamous mind–body problem, which remains a bone of contention among philosophers and a terrifying specter for psychologists after 300 years of post-Cartesian debate. How does the current research in brain science explain or constrain accounts of emotion based on conceptual or phenomenological analysis? It is not a problem readily solved or easily ignored.

EMOTIONS AND ETHICS: REBUILDING AN OLD AND USEFUL BRIDGE

One of the most difficult bridges to build, however, is also one of the most fundamental. The origins of a good deal of philosophy, tracing the field back to Socrates and Plato, is in ethics: (a) the general concern of the good life and (b) what sort of person one should be and how one should act. Questions about emotion were first and most forcefully raised regarding this concern for living a good life: What is the role of emotions in the good life and which emotions are to be cultivated, which discouraged or suppressed? Whether the model was one that made the emotions out to be dangerous to the good life (which was best directed by reason) or one that integrated the emotions as essential to and definitive of the good life (Plato and Aristotle, respectively), the attempt to understand the emotions was part and parcel or the attempt to define the best way to live. But with the advent of "value-free science" (leaving aside the question of whether any such discipline is intelligible), the ethical language in which this research tradition was couched ("virtue," "vice," "sin," "appropriateness," "wisdom," "foolishness") was forcibly evicted from the social sciences.

To be sure, there are large swaths of philosophy that share this scientific outlook ("cognitive science," for example), but I think that the old ethical paradigm still has its hooks in the ways in which we talk and think about emotion, not only in the general language of emotions (a term that comes from Descartes, signifying particularly unruly passions) and passion (*pathé*), which still carries the meaning of *suffering*, but in the names of particular emotions, which (in various languages) carry the traditional baggage of ethical approbation and disapprobation. But I do not think that this weight can or should be easily jettisoned. Thus the first of the two difficult bridges I suggest building—or rather repairing—is the bridge between ethics and the social sciences. There is no such thing as value-free social science, and it would be far better to acknowledge the relevance and importance of social science to ethics than to pretend the connection doesn't exist.

Can we get a value-neutral description of the various emotions, in particular, without losing something essential? One suggestion, quite naturally, is that we can do so by identifying the basic neurology or the "affect program" that constitutes the emotion, without taking into account the "higher cognitive" and social interactions that some with culture and education. But the number of "basic" emotions that can be so understood will be very, very small, if, indeed, there are any such that deserve the name "emotion" at all. But as soon as we bring in culture, social learning, and social interaction, we bring in questions of ethics and value, if not in the detached description of emotional behavior in the social and cultural context, then in the "internal" description of how those people experience that context. In any case, the general interest in emotions remains firmly tied to the general issues of the ethics of well-being, whether through popular self-help books (Goleman's *Emotional Intelligence*) or by way of psychiatry and psychotherapy. Social science needs ethics as much as good ethics needs social science.

THE CARTESIAN BRIDGE BETWEEN NEUROSCIENCE AND CONSCIOUSNESS

The second difficult but essential bridge to build is the Cartesian bridge between neuroscience and consciousness. I take the latter to include both the "experience" discussed by philosophers and the experiences implicit in social psychology (how people *feel* as well as how they behave). The route I suggest is by way of phenomenology. Phenomenology (usually credited to Edmund Husserl) is the study and description of the essential structures of experience. It is by way of phenomenology, with its nonscientific emphasis on subjectivity, that philosophy has a special role to play. It is too often thought—or merely assumed—that emotional experience in particular is indescribable, "ineffable." We can describe behavior, and we are learning to describe in detail the neurology of emotion, and, it is now generally agreed, we can also describe the cognitions and appraisals that are part and parcel of the emotions. But as to the *affect*, the feeling that makes an emotion *emotion*, that is said to be indescribable except obliquely ("it is the feeling you get when …"). But William James was much closer to the mark when he described emotional experience as the sensation that follows a physiological disturbance. That might have been wrong, but it had the great virtue of being specific, testable, and consequently refutable. And it identified the subjective side of emotion with clear and verifiable (or falsifiable) physiological states.

But emotional experience is rich, not poor (a mere sensation is conceptually impoverished). The central feature of emotional experience, and a central concept of phenomenology, is *intentionality*, directedness toward or engagement with the world. Thus James was wrong when he limited emotional experience to sensations, and so, too, contemporary authors get it wrong to the extent that they emphasize the mere "feeling of what happens" (Damasio, 1999) to the exclusion or neglect of intentionality. But intentionality in emotion is not just perception (although it certainly include perception); the "objects" of our intentions are thoroughly value laden. A person is attractive, offensive, or repulsive; a situation is infuriating, embarrassing, or inspiring. Thus, an emotional experience must in part be described in terms of these features of the object ("what the emotion is about"). An essential aspect of our experience of (in) anger, accordingly, is the offensiveness of the actor the person we are angry with, and an essential aspect of our experience of (in) shame is the shamefulness of our own behavior. The experience of being in love may consist, in a very small part, of sensations of warm fuzziness (or desperate panic), but what defines that experience is first of all the utter *importance* of the beloved and his or her opinions, behavior, gestures, and expressions.

Emotional experience also refers us, as James and Damasio argue, to the body, but not by way of mere sensations. Peter Goldie refers here to the "borrowed intentionality" of emotional feelings, a nice expression, for it captures the sense in which the feelings that accompany emotions are not just sensations but essentially tied to both the intentionality of judgments and appraisals and also to what Nico Frijda (1986) calls "action tendencies." It has long been insisted (by William James [1884], by Descartes [1650], by the ancient Stoics) that emotions are, at least in part, bodily phenomena. But this does not just refer to their physiological (or neurological) aspects. The feelings of what happens (in the brain, in the body) are an essential part of the emotional experience as well, but we should add to this the "feelings" that are really descriptions of the world as experienced, and also those that accompany and "mark" our behavior, whether in the barely conscious spontaneous facial expressions of emotion or in the preparation for what James called "vigorous action," much of which is *social* behavior. Thus a phenomenological analysis of the feelings involved in both emotional and social experience will show us the entanglement of social, behavioral (and ethical) dimensions and what the "correlates" of the newly discovered neurological pathways governing really are. Neuroscience, however exciting in its own right, needs phenomenology to remind us what we are talking about (Lane & Nadel, 2000; Panksepp, 1999).

CONCLUSIONS

All three disciplines, philosophy, neurobiology, and the social sciences, need to embrace one another as well as the new and exciting field of emotions research. A phenomenological analysis of the feelings involved in emotional and social experience combined with a keen interest in the findings of neurobiology will help us build that Triborough Bridge that we all need to get off of these islands of our own creation (Solomon, 2003).

REFERENCES

Damasio, A. (1999). *The feeling of what happens.* New York: Harcourt.
Descartes, R. (1989). *The passions of the soul.* Indianapolis: Hackett. (Original work published 1650)
De Sousa, R. (1987). *Rationality of emotion.* Cambridge: M.I.T. Press.
Frijda, N. (1986.) *The emotions.* Cambridge: Cambridge University Press.
Griffiths, P. (1997). *What emotions really are.* Chicago: Chicago University Press.
James, W. (1884). What is an emotion? *Mind, 9,* 188–205.
Lane, R., & Nadel, L. (2000). *Cognitive neuroscience of emotion.* New York: Oxford University Press.
Panksepp, J. (1999). *Neuroscience of emotion.* New York: Oxford University Press
Solomon, R. (1976). *The passions.* New York: Doubleday-Anchor.
Solomon, R. (2003). *Not passion's slave.* New York: Oxford University Press.

The Social Nature of Emotion and the Emotional Nature of the Social

Antony S. R. Manstead
Cardiff University

On the face of it, emotion and social psychology are not near neighbors in the constellation of disciplines, subdisciplines, and topics that form the psychological sciences. The defining attribute of emotion, one could reasonably argue, is its subjective experience, its intrapersonal character. It does not, on this view, appear to be a natural topic of interest for social psychologists, who are concerned above all with what happens *between* people. Yet social psychologists have had an enduring interest in emotion, and this interest has resulted in several significant contributions to emotion theory.

My purpose in this essay is to identify the bridges between social psychology and emotion, and to give my impression of the benefits of the two-way traffic that has crossed these bridges. I argue that there are three important bridges. This is not to suggest that these are the only interconnections; rather, in my view these are the primary links between emotion as a subject matter and the subdiscipline of social psychology. I examine each bridge in turn and then draw a more general conclusion about the relationship between social psychology and emotion.

BRIDGE 1: THE EXPRESSION OF EMOTION

The first bridge concerns the expression of emotion, and is usually traced to Darwin's (1872/1998) *The Expression of the Emotions in Man and Animals*. In focusing on the outward display of emotion, Darwin identified a public facet of the phenomenon that has obvious relevance to social psychologists. The fact that there is an actual or ostensible relation between the subjective experience of emotion and people's overt behavior means that this behavior is often regarded as being meaningfully communicative. How people look and act will at least on occasion be regarded as indicative of how they feel, and this in turn has the potential to influence a host of interpersonal judgments and behaviors.

Since the late 1960s there has been a prevailing consensus that at least certain emotions are under certain conditions accompanied by clear-cut and readily interpretable facial behaviors. There are two strands to this thesis. One is the well-known research on the consistency with which persons who live in different cultures interpret photographs of faces in which certain emotions are posed (e.g., Ekman & Friesen, 1971). The other is the neo-Jamesian view that feedback from the facial musculature can influence the quality and/or quantity of subjective experience of emotion (e.g., Strack, Martin, & Stepper, 1988). This research program has been productive and influential, and has shaped social psychological thinking about the potential for emotion to be communicated (wittingly or unwittingly) through facial, vocal, or bodily activity (but see Russell & Fernández-Dols, 1997, for a critical review).

A face that appears to be expressing one sort of emotion rather than another can have powerful consequences. A well-known example is that of "social referencing" (Sorce, Emde, Butterfield, & Campos, 1985). A 12-month-old infant will typically look towards his or her mother or other primary caregiver when confronted with an object or situation that arouses uncertainty or anxiety, and will proceed if the caregiver is smiling but desist if the caregiver is wearing a negative expression, with clear implications for the child's developing relationships with the caregiver and the environment. Studies of deception (e.g., DePaulo, 1992) and of nonverbal communication in marital relationships (e.g., Noller, 1984) provide further examples of how nonverbal behavior influences how we are perceived and evaluated, and thereby affects others' behavior toward us, and ultimately our own behavior, as well.

This is not to say that the relation between subjective emotion and facial action is straightforward. Photographs of posed emotions can be labeled with above-chance accuracy, but matters become more complex when one tries to identify the objective coherence between subjective state and spontaneous facial actions (Fernández-Dols, Sánchez, Carrera, & Ruiz-Belda, 1997), and there is evidence that perceivers find it difficult to make accurate judgments about spontaneous facial expressions under laboratory conditions (Wagner, MacDonald, & Manstead, 1986). The social context in which facial behavior occurs is also known to be influential, in the sense that people smile more when they are facing a real or imagined audience (see Fridlund, 1994).

BRIDGE 2: THE ROLE OF COGNITION IN EMOTION

The second bridge concerns the role played by cognition in emotion, and its foundations are usually traced to Arnold's (1960) appraisal theory of emotion. In drawing attention to the cognitive underpinnings of emotion, Arnold opened up to others a topic that had appeared to be the domain of psychologists interested in physiological and motivational processes. Social psychology in the 1960s was already (by the standards of the day) quite cognitive in character, so the fresh attention being paid to the role of cognition provided a natural way into the study of emotion from a social psychological perspective.

Two separate but potentially compatible lines of research on the role of cognition in emotion can be identified. One is a direct descendant of Arnold's ideas about appraisal, and can be glossed as "appraisal theory," despite the fact that there are important differences between the major proponents of appraisal theory (see Scherer, Schorr, & Johnstone, 2001). The essence of the appraisal approach is summarized in Frijda's (1988) law of situational meaning: "Emotions arise in response to the meaning structures of given situations; different emotions arise in response to different meaning structures" (p. 350). Thus the same situation will elicit different emotional responses to the extent that people appraise it in different ways.

The other line of research on emotion and cognition originated in Schachter's (1964) two-factor theory of emotion, which argued that physiological arousal is a necessary but insufficient condition for the experience of emotion; in addition, this arousal has to be interpreted as arising from an emotional stimulus, in which case emotion will be experienced. If no ready-made interpretation is available, the individual will search the environment for a plausible explanation for the arousal. Schachter's theory was rapidly incorporated into the then emerging theoretical and empirical literature on attribution. In the process, it lost touch with its roots in social comparison theory (Schachter, 1959). Its popularity and influence among social psychologists stemmed from the relatively unimportant role accorded to physiological arousal and the correspondingly more important role of cognitions, or attributions for arousal states. This line of research reached its zenith in the 1970s and early 1980s; it attracts less research attention today, although Weiner's (1986) attributional theory of emotion remains influential.

Recent years have witnessed a shift away from the orthodox view that emotions have their basis in appraisals and attributions. In part, this is due to changes within social psychology, where there has been a move away from the deliberative and controlled cognitive processes that were often implicit in attribution theory, toward a model of human social cognition in which evaluations and judgments are made in a relatively automatic and unconscious way (see Bargh, 1999).

In emotion theory, this shift to automaticity was anticipated by Zajonc (1980) with the publication of his well-known paper arguing that affective responses to stimuli are not dependent on processing information about those stimuli. In modern emotion theory we can see echoes of this argument reflected in diverse critiques of conventional appraisal theory (e.g., Ekman, 2004; Frijda, 1993). If there is such a thing as a consensus view within emotion theory, today's version accords a less causal role to cognition than was the case two decades ago. Emotions can be (but are not necessarily always) shaped by conscious cognitions; they can arise as a result of relatively fast processes that may not be cortically mediated; and they can themselves steer cognitions (Frijda, Manstead, & Bem, 2000).

BRIDGE 3: THE SOCIAL CHARACTER OF EMOTION

The third bridge is different in nature, and concerns the essentially social character of much of what we call emotion. This social character has two facets. The first is that most of what we get emotional about is social in nature. We fall in or out of love with others; we are proud of or angry with our children; we are disappointed by politicians; we are frustrated or supported by colleagues; and so on. Other people are the primary sources and objects of the emotions we experience. The second facet is that certain emotions seem to be fundamentally social in nature. Obvious examples are shame, guilt, embarrassment, jealousy, and envy. These emotions make little or no sense without the real or imagined presence of others. But the same is rather obviously true of other emotions, such as love and anger. The same is even true of fear, often cited as an example of a nonsocial emotion. To be sure, we can be afraid of heights or of spiders, but the fears that cause us most disquiet tend to be social ones, such as fear of public speaking.

This bridge goes to the heart of the relationship between emotion and social psychology, because it raises the possibility that the relationship is much closer than is generally acknowledged. The expression "bridge" can be seen as offering a potential channel of communication between the individual (who would still be experiencing emotion even if he or she were in complete isolation) and the social world. The cognition "bridge" can be regarded as providing a means by which the social world can, under particular conditions, have an impact on the otherwise private process of emotion—by shaping the kinds of appraisals and attributions that individuals bring to bear on emotional events. The third, social bridge questions the degree to which the person who experiences emotion and his or her social context are separate entities, or "islands" linked by bridges; they may instead be more tightly enmeshed with each other, such that the social context is not just a "ground" against which the "figure" of emotion is experienced, but rather part and parcel of the process of emotional arousal, experience, and expression (see Parkinson, Fischer, & Manstead, 2005).

Because humans are social beings, the things that are of concern to them are social in nature and the events that they encounter invariably have social content. From this perspective it is clear that emotions are almost always social in a deep and thoroughgoing sense, and that they serve social functions (see Keltner & Haidt, 1999). The things we get emotional about are typically social; the way in which we judge these things is infused by social and cultural concerns; and the ways in which we express and act on an emotion are not only conditioned by the social context, but also shape that context in a way that will impact on further emotional episodes.

CONCLUSIONS

The links between social psychology and emotion are long-standing and varied in nature. I have argued here that they stem partly from the fact that the human face is a highly salient and finely differentiated communication device, and partly from a temporal (but not accidental) coincidence of theoretical emphasis on cognition in emotion theory and social psychology. However, the fundamental reason for the links between emotion and social psychology is the largely unacknowledged fact that emotion is central to human social life. A fuller recognition of this fact would benefit emotion theory by refocusing theoretical and empirical attention on social aspects of the emotion process; it would also benefit social psychology by encouraging its practitioners to recognize that social cognition and interaction are phenomena that are embodied, warm-blooded, and socially situated. Embodiment suggests a renewed emphasis on sensation, posture, gesture, and orientation; warm-bloodedness suggests a greater focus on the role of motivation; and social situatedness suggests that we should pay more attention to the context in which cognition and interaction unfold.

Greater recognition that social psychology's core phenomena need to considered in a fresh light would be an example of the benefits to be gained by the bridging exercises that form the present volume: Serious engagement with disciplines and fields beyond social psychology compels one to question taken-for-granted assumptions, and encourages one to regard the subject matter of social psychology from a new perspective.

REFERENCES

Arnold, M. B. (1960). *Emotion and personality, Vol. 1: Psychological aspects.* New York: Columbia University Press.

Bargh, J. A. (1999). The cognitive monster: The case against the controllability of automatic stereotype effects. In S. Chaiken & Y. Trope (Eds.), *Dual-process theories in social psychology* (pp. 361–382). New York: Guilford.

Darwin, C. (1998). *The expression of the emotions in man and animals* (3rd ed., P. Ekman, Ed.). New York: Oxford University Press. (Original work published 1872)

DePaulo, B. M. (1992). Nonverbal behavior and self-presentation. *Psychological Bulletin, 111,* 203–243.

Ekman, P. (2004). What we become emotional about. In A. S. R. Manstead, N. H. Frijda, & A. H. Fischer (Eds.), *Feelings and emotions: The Amsterdam symposium* (pp. 119–135). New York: Cambridge University Press.

Ekman, P., & Friesen, W. V. (1971). Constants across cultures in the face and emotion. *Journal of Personality and Social Psychology, 17,* 124–129.

Fernández-Dols, J. M., Sánchez, F., Carrera, P., & Ruiz-Belda, M. A. (1997). Are spontaneous expressions and emotions linked? An experimental test of coherence. *Journal of Nonverbal Behavior, 21,* 163–177.

Fridlund, A. J. (1994). *Human facial expression.* San Diego, CA: Academic Press.

Frijda, N. H. (1988). The laws of emotion. *American Psychologist, 43,* 349–358.

Frijda, N. H. (1993). The place of appraisal in emotion. *Cognition and Emotion, 7,* 357–387.

Frijda, N. H., Manstead, A. S. R., & Bem, S. (Eds.). (2000). *Emotions and beliefs: How feelings influence thoughts.* Cambridge, England: Cambridge University Press.

Keltner, D., & Haidt, J. (1999). Social functions of emotion at four levels of analysis. *Cognition and Emotion, 13,* 505–521.

Noller, P. (1984). *Nonverbal communication and marital interaction.* Oxford, England: Pergamon.

Parkinson, B., Fischer, A. H., & Manstead, A. S. R. (2005). *Emotion in social relations: Cultural, group, and interpersonal processes.* New York: Psychology Press.

Russell, J. A., & Fernández-Dols, J. M. (Eds.). (1997). *The psychology of facial expression.* New York: Cambridge University Press.

Schachter, S. (1959). *The psychology of affiliation.* Minneapolis: University of Minnesota Press.

Schachter, S. (1964). The interaction of cognitive and physiological determinants of emotional state. In L. Berkowitz (Ed.), *Advances in experimental social psychology* (Vol.1, pp. 49–80). New York: Academic Press.

Scherer, K. R. , Schorr, A., & Johnstone, T. (Eds.). (2001). *Appraisal processes in emotion: Theory, methods, research.* New York: Oxford University Press.

Sorce, J. F., Emde, R. N., Butterfield, P., & Campos, J. J. (1985). Maternal emotional signaling: Its effects on the visual cliff behavior of 1-year-olds. *Developmental Psychology, 21,* 195–200.

Strack, F., Martin, L. L., & Stepper, S. (1988). Inhibiting and facilitating conditions of the human smile: A non-obtrusive test of the facial feedback hypothesis. *Journal of Personality and Social Psychology, 54,* 768–777.

Wagner, H. L., MacDonald, C. J., & Manstead, A. S. R. (1986). Communication of individual emotions by spontaneous facial expressions. *Journal of Personality and Social Psychology, 50,* 737–743.

Weiner, B. (1986). *An attributional theory of motivation and emotion.* New York: Springer.

Zajonc, R. B. (1980). Feeling and thinking: Preferences need no inferences. *American Psychologist, 39,* 117–123.

Love, Hate, and Morality: Emotion and Communication as Bridging Concepts in Social Psychology

Ross Buck
University of Connecticut

Studies of emotion and emotion communication are revolutionizing our understanding of social psychology, allowing a considerably expanded, deeper, and more comprehensive appreciation of human nature than has been possible previously. Emotion is at the same time an individual phenomenon, related to specifiable neurochemical systems in the brain that are genetically based and controlled, and a social phenomenon that is displayed, communicated, and basic to fundamental social organization. Furthermore, these aspects of emotion interact: the genetic-physiological basis is modulated by experiences in emotional communication. Emotion is the quintessence of a bridging concept, reaching down to the genes and up to social structure, and relevant to everything in between.

Essential to this emerging view of emotional human nature is an emphasis upon the essential prosociality of life that exists alongside competition and selfishness, but is often overlooked or indeed denied at a biological level (Buck, 1999, 2002). Prosociality is so intrinsic to human existence that it tends to be noticed in its absence: when aggression, violence, neglect, and abuse occur to disturb the social order. It is news when man bites dog, but not the reverse. We *expect* people to get along, and by and large human beings do so extraordinarily well. Studies of social influence, conformity, obedience, and demand effects in social psychology have demonstrated that human beings are extremely compliant, acquiescent, and responsive to even apparently trivial social influences. However, by and large the motives and emotions underlying this powerful prosociality have not been addressed. The prosociality that provides the "glue" for social organization surrounds and shapes human behavior at every turn, but like water to fish, it is so natural that we do not notice it. There is perhaps no better term for it in English than "love."

This chapter examines examples of emotion, communication, and prosociality at two levels: that of relatively simple single-celled bacteria, and that of the motives and emotions surrounding one of the most monstrous actions in recent human history: the 9-11 attacks on America.

COMMUNICATION IN SIMPLE BIOLOGICAL SYSTEMS

Bacterial Communication. The most ancient known organisms on Earth show evidence of prosociality. Stromatolites are the fossilized colonies of cyanobacteria that appeared 3.5 billion years ago. Cyanobacteria are prokaryotes, the simplest of single-celled creatures that lack a cell nucleus surrounding their DNA, and are familiar to us as pond scum. The communication principles by which these ancient creatures self-organize and self-configure to create a working community that can recover from damage has generated interest among designers of new technology networks who hope to use them in network design.

The signals or displays used by bacteria typically involve amino acids or peptides, which function as pheromones (Gallio, Sturgill, Rather, & Kylsten, 2002). An example of such cellular communication is *quorum sensing*, which involves the ability of bacteria to sense that their numbers in the area have reached a critical mass, and then to coordinate collective behavior. One specific example of quorum sensing involves the marine bioluminescent bacterium *Vibrio fischeri*, in which luminescence is induced by the accumulation of activator molecules in the environment reflecting a critical mass of individuals.

Fundamental Cell Communication. The mechanism for quorum sensing in prokaryotic bacteria has a remarkable similarity with cellular communication in more complex organisms. Gallio and colleagues studied the genetic sequence of the Rhomboid gene associated with a mutation in the fruit fly *Drosophila* and found the same sequence in the ArrA gene that is involved in quorum sensing in the bacterium *Providencia stuartii*. Moreover, the Rhomboid and ArrA gene could swap roles, with ArrA functioning successfully in *Drosophila* and Rhomboid functioning successfully in *P. stuartii*. This suggested that peptide signaling in bacteria represents an ancient means of cell communication: "not only the signal releasing mechanism seems conserved, but also the molecule that carries it out … [suggesting that] these molecules share a common ancestry" (Gallio et al., 2002, pp. 12212–12213).

Peptides. Readers might object that neither bacteria nor fruit flies are particularly noted for their complex *emotional* life. However, some of the same peptide molecules active in simple creatures have been found to be intimately involved in human emotion (Pert, 1997). Single-celled protozoa have peptides similar to adrenocorticotropic hormone (ACTH) related to stress; the endogenous opiate beta-endorphin related to pain; cholyocystokinin (CCK) related to panic; and gonadotropin-releasing hormone (GnRH) related to sexual feelings. Moreover, there is remarkable evidence for the role of the peptides oxytocin (OXY) and vasopressin (AVP) in organizing social bonding in prairie voles (*Microtus ochrogaster*). Prairie voles are monogamous—bonding for life—and live communally. In contrast, closely related vole species are non-monogamous and live more solitary lives (see Carter, Lederhendler, & Kirkpatrick, 1997). Both OXY and AVP are critical to the social bonding of the prairie vole. The brain areas associated with OXY are much larger in the prairie vole than other voles, and OXY and AVP have been shown to be both necessary and sufficient for the establishment of pair bonds (Insel, 2002). Furthermore, mice bred without the gene for the production of OXY (OXY knockout mice) show specific social-communicative deficits that can be reversed by OXY injections (Young, 2002).

These examples demonstrate that communicative biological systems are involved in the organization and coordination of basic social behaviors. I suggest that the governing principles and mechanisms illustrated by these relatively simple biological systems are relevant to the understanding of social organization in more complex creatures, including humans, and that emotion, broadly conceived, is a concept that can embrace these governing principles and mechanisms at dramatically different levels of analysis. Specifically, the communication mechanisms from those observable in the specific displays and responses of bacteria to nonverbal emotional communication in human beings demonstrate the basic principles of *spontaneous communication* (Buck, 1984; Buck & Van Lear, 2003). The next section applies these principles to the understanding of prosocial motives and emotions in human beings, and the often disastrous consequences when these powerful feelings are frustrated.

THE NEED FOR SOCIAL STRUCTURE

·*Society Versus Human Nature?*   We often think of social influence as a phenomenon apart from individual response tendencies; indeed, the influence of society is often seen as running contrary to individual human nature. If, like Rousseau or Locke, one views human nature as fundamentally good, society may be seen as repressing natural human potential. On the other hand, if, like Hobbes, one views human nature as fundamentally evil, society may be seen as a necessary inhibitor of anarchic human impulses.

The extensive literature derived from the classic studies of Solomon Asch (1952) and Stanley Milgram (1963), demonstrating the power of conformity and obedience in organizing human behavior, suggests another alternative: that susceptibility to social influence is itself "a central fact of human nature, an innate response tendency that will appear naturally if supportive experiences are provided" (Buck, 1988, p. 517). In this view, an innate responsiveness to social influence is a heritage of evolution, drawing upon both the primordial prosociality seen in simple creatures, and pressures reflecting the special importance of complex social organization that is characteristic of primates. This view is compatible with ethological-evolutionary models of social development based upon studies by such investigators as Harry Harlow (1971) and John Bowlby (1969, 1972). It also fits with studies suggesting that there is an "addiction to love": that addictive drugs such as heroin and cocaine work in humans on brain systems associated with attachment (Panksepp, 1998).

Moral Values: Continuity and Change.   Prosocial social responsiveness may underlie some of the apparent contradictions of human behavior. On one hand, it seems to underlie love—attachment, affiliation, and cooperation. Ironically, it may at the same time play a critical role in the emotional underpinnings of the purest of evil.

Human behavior uniquely involves language, and human beings learn linguistically structured rules and expectations for behavior that are codified into social norms and roles that play a major role in self-identity. These rules and expectations, in turn, can be maintained or changed via communication with others in the social environment. The classic Bennington College study by Theodore Newcomb showed how attitudes of most politically conservative freshmen in 1933 changed to match the liberalism of the college by the time they were seniors. A follow-up study in the context of the 1960 Kennedy–Nixon election demonstrated that the liberal attitudes were sustained or surrendered based largely upon the liberal or conservative social context experienced after graduation (Newcomb, Koenig, Flacks, & Warwick, 1967). More dramatic examples of change in response to social influence have been termed "brainwashing" or the "Stockholm syndrome," where victims come to identify with their captors.

These examples are often analyzed from analytic cognitive viewpoints that largely disregard emotional factors. However, emotions are clearly present in these examples. The attachment of the student for present company as opposed to family is involved in the Bennington College case, and strong emotional appeals are at the heart of the Stockholm syndrome. In either case, it appears to be difficult for a human being to exist in a social context without coming to identify with the rules and expectations supported by that context. Indeed, the social context determines via social influence what comes to be perceived by the individual as right or wrong, and together with the emotional attachment of the individual to others in the social context, this establishes a basis for moral judgments and feelings, ethical principles, values, and ideals.

When the Group Fails.   The social context provides the basis for morality, together with prosocial feelings of attachment and belonging that are basic to a satisfying self identity linked to that morality. Individuals know what behavior is expected and will be rewarded by the love and esteem of others. Therefore, human beings possess not only a susceptibility to social influence, but a need for social influence: a "need to belong" (Baumeister & Leary, 1995). When a social order fails to meet the emotional needs of large numbers of people—fails to provide them with rules for meeting social expectations and for feeling loved—they become, literally, demoralized. A result may be significant social movements with emotionally loaded mass appeals and a susceptibility to charismatic leadership that promises to restore emotionally satisfying social influence: that is, law and order. Social threat often results in increased authoritarian tendencies in a society (Doty, Peterson, & Winter, 1991; Sales, 1973). Authoritarian leaders often simplify complex problems facing the group and identify pseudo-problems that are simple, concrete, and easy to deal with. The discontented can easily be persuaded to turn their frustration into rage at outgroups, which can be attacked. Indeed, love for the ingroup may be demonstrated and verified by hatred and attack of the outgroup.

Examples of the failure of groups, and consequent attack of outgroups, occurred time and time again over the past century and in recent years as values of traditional societies were undermined by social changes wrought by war, new technology, and the innovations of science and modernism. The universality of what Eric Fromm (1941) termed "the escape from freedom" may well be based on the importance to human beings of emotional needs met by conforming to expectations of, and thereby feeling accepted and loved by, those in the ingroup. The emotional "fire" in this process comes from fundamental pro-sociality: attachment to the ingroup. The disastrous results when these pro-social needs go unfulfilled are exemplified by the Nazi ideology of the 1930s resulting in the Holocaust; the more recent terror in Rwanda, Cambodia, Kosovo, and Liberia; and the rise of fanatic religious fundamentalism of Islamic militants threatened by Western traditions, including those who conducted the 9-11 attacks on America. Human attachment is at the same time the emotional basis of true love, and the emotional basis of fascism.

CONCLUSIONS

This chapter has argued that emotion, communication, and more specifically attachment, is a bridging concept reaching down to the genes and up to social structure. Any attempt to relate human social behavior to biological components must be wary of reductionism, the fallacy that human behavior can be explained with reference to biological mechanisms. Conceptualizing attachment as a bridging concept reaching in *both* directions encourages a more sophisticated view of biological mechanisms: Attachment is a primordial, genetically based wellspring by which linguistically structured self and identity are constructed with reference to cultural/historical context. Through attachment, human beings are *hard-wired to respond flexibly to social influence*, and thereby to be shaped by culture and history. Free will, then, is biologically determined, and flexibility in response to social influence, built into the human species, is perhaps at the essence of human nature.

This essential point is missed if the bridge is constructed in only one direction: On one hand, there is the danger of reductionism, and on the other, the danger that the importance of biology may be neglected. Social psychology sits in an excellent and perhaps unique conceptual position because it is easily amenable to bridging in both downward and upward directions.

REFERENCES

Asch, S. (1952). *Social psychology*. Englewood Cliffs, NJ: Prentice Hall.

Baumeister, R. F., & Leary, M. R. (1995). The need to belong: Desire for interpersonal attachments as a fundamental human motivation. *Psychological Bulletin, 117*, 497–529.

Bowlby, J. (1969). *Attachment and loss: Vol. 1. Attachment*. New York: Basic Books.

Bowlby, J. (1973). *Attachment and loss: Vol. 2. Separation*. New York: Basic Books.

Buck, R. (1984). *The communication of emotion*. New York: Guilford Press.

Buck, R. (1988). *Human motivation and emotion*. (2nd ed.). New York: Wiley.

Buck, R. (1999). The biological affects: A typology. *Psychological Review, 106*, 301–336.

Buck, R. (2002). The genetics and biology of true love: Prosocial biological affects and the left hemisphere. *Psychological Review, 109*, 739–744.

Buck, R., & VanLear, C. A. (2002). Verbal and nonverbal communication: Distinguishing symbolic, spontaneous, and pseudo-spontaneous nonverbal behavior. *Journal of Communication, 52*, 522–541.

Carter, C. S., Lederhendler, I. I., & Kirkpatrick, B. (Eds.). (1997). *The integrative neurobiology of affiliation*. New York: New York Academy of Sciences.

Doty, R. M., Peterson, B. E., & Winter, D. G. (1991). Threat and authoritarianism in the United States, 1978–1987. *Journal of Personality and Social Psychology, 61*, 629–640.

Fromm, E. (1941). *Escape from freedom*. New York: Holt, Rinehart & Winston.

Gallio, M., Sturgill, G., Rather, P., & Kylsten, P. (2002). A conserved mechanism for extracellular signaling in eukaryotes and prokaryotes. *Proceedings of the National Academy of Sciences USA, 99*(19), 12208–12213.

Harlow, H. F. (1971). *Learning to love*. San Francisco: Albion.

Insel, T. R. (2002). Implications for the neurobiology of love. In S. G. Post, L. G. Underwood, J. P. Schloss, & W. B. Hurlbut (Eds.), *Altruism and altruistic love: Science, philosophy, and religion in dialogue* (pp. 254–263). London: Oxford University Press.

Milgram, S. (1963). Behavioral study of obedience. *Journal of Abnormal and Social Psychology, 67*, 371–378.

Newcomb, T. M., Koenig, K. E., Flacks, R., & Warwick, D. P. (1967). *Persistence and change: Bennington College and its students after twenty-five years*. New York: John Wiley & Sons.

Panksepp, J. (1998). *Affective neuroscience: The foundations of human and animal emotions*. New York: Oxford University Press.

Pert, C. (1997). *Molecules of emotion*. New York: Scribners.

Sales, S. M. (1973). Threat as a factor in authoritarianism: An analysis of archival data. *Journal of Personality and Social Psychology, 36*, 988–999.

Young, L. J. (2002). The neurobiology of social recognition: Approach, and avoidance. *Biological Psychiatry, 51*, 18–26.

33

Bridging Developmental and Social Psychology

Nancy Eisenberg
Adrienne Sadovsky
Arizona State University

For many years, social and developmental psychologists have overlapped considerably in their foci of interest. For example, issues such as attributional processes, modeling, aggression, self-conceptions, prosocial behavior, and gender roles have been major areas of study in both subdisciplines for numerous decades. For decades, some investigators have tried to highlight this overlap between social and developmental psychology in books that include content from both areas (e.g., Brehm, Kassin, & Gibbons, 1981; Eisenberg, 1995; Higgins, Ruble, & Hartup, 1983). Nonetheless, the vast majority of developmental psychologists know relatively little about social psychological theory and research and vice versa.

This state of affairs is detrimental to both subdisciplines. Social psychology is rich in theory that is relevant to developmental research. Moreover, social psychologists have devised many creative laboratory procedures that could be (and occasionally have been) adapted by developmentalists. On the other hand, it is difficult to truly understand any aspect of human psychological functioning if one knows little of its development in childhood and adolescence or, for that matter, after early adulthood. Further, developmental psychologists have constructed theories about the origins of diverse aspects of social and psychological functioning, as well as sophisticated methods for assessing naturally occurring behavior and change in its occurrence; social psychologists could benefit from attention to these theories and methods.

In this entry, we provide two examples of domains in which social and developmental psychology have, and could to a greater degree, contribute to one another. These examples were chosen based on the authors' areas of expertise, but also illustrate the broader issue.

PROSOCIAL BEHAVIOR

Although prosocial behavior was examined occasionally by psychologists prior to 1970, most research on the topic has been conducted since this date. Indeed, there was an explosion of research on this topic after the publication of Latane and Darley's 1970 book *The Unresponsive Bystander: Why Doesn't He Help?* In social psychology, the focus in most early studies was on situational factors that influenced whether people acted in a prosocial manner. Correspondingly, much of the theory concerned the effects of situational variables—for example, the presence of other people (Lantane & Darley, 1970), temporary mood state (e.g., Cialdini, Baumann, & Kenrick, 1981), costs of helping, and modeling (see Dovidio, 1984)—on the decision to assist.

Much of the research conducted to address these issues was experimental laboratory studies. Many, although not all, of these social psychological methods and theories were salient in early work on children's prosocial behavior and continued to influence some research in this domain. For example, helping in emergencies, the role of transient mood states, modeling, and the effects of rewards or punishments on prosocial behavior in the laboratory were common themes in early studies of children's prosocial behavior (Bryan & Walbek, 1970; see Radke-Yarrow, Zahn-Waxler, & Chapman, 1983). In fact, social and personality psychologists conducted a number of these studies.

In addition to adapting many of the topics, methods, and theories of social psychology, developmentalists were fairly quick to branch off in other directions. For example,

> developmental investigators have been considerably more likely than social psychologists to both assess prosocial responding in natural settings and study variables that predict individual differences in prosocial behavior. As one concrete example, Batson (1991), a social psychologist who conducted many of the early studies on the relation of empathy to prosocial behavior, usually randomly assigned adults to various conditions and experimentally induced or undermined empathic responding. His assumption was that most individuals were apt to experience empathy in certain contexts and that individual differences in values or empathic tendencies were less likely to be predictors of altruistic responding than were situational factors.

In contrast, developmental psychologists tended to study how factors, such as socialization, might be responsible for the emergence of stable individual differences in empathic and prosocial behaviors (see Eisenberg & Fabes, 1998).

Relatively recently, Schroeder, Penner, Dovidio, and Piliavin (1995) noted that "The personality point of view is sharply challenged by many social psychologists who believe that most social behavior is due to the characteristics of the situation in which the behavior occurs" (p. 168). Nonetheless, many leading social psychologists now accept that there are stable individual differences in prosocial behavior (Schroeder et al., 1995). Developmental psychology's long-standing interest in the emergence of dispositional prosocial behavior and value orientations (e.g., from temperament and socialization) may have already broadened the range of issues addressed by social psychologists. Nonetheless, social psychological research on prosocial behavior would benefit from still greater attention to the diverse person-related variables that might be linked to prosocial behavior, including age and socialization history.

In addition, there is little research on the ways in which prosocial tendencies continue to develop or be modified throughout adulthood as a function of systematic or nonsystematic changes in social roles, sociocognitive abilities or proclivities, relationships, and other aspects of adults' development and experience. Some of the most provocative research on this issue has been conducted by developmental psychologists (e.g., Colby & Damon, 1992) and sociologists or educators (e.g., Oliner & Oliner, 1988) who have examined the lives of people who were (or are) exceptional prosocial and moral exemplars. In general, these researchers have found that personal characteristics and critical experiences or situational factors seem to jointly predict the performance of extraordinary moral actions. Both social psychologists and developmentalists would benefit from greater attention (rather than mere lip service) to the message that both the situation and the individual's characteristics (based on biological factors and experience) contribute to prosocial (and other aspects of social) functioning.

GENDER ROLES

A research area in which there has been more cross-talk between developmental and social psychologists is gender-role development (e.g., Durkin, 1995; Eckes & Trautner, 2000a). One of the benefits of these collaborative works is that deficits in both domains have begun to be addressed and rectified.

To illustrate, critics of a purely social psychological approach to gender-role studies have argued that such research and theory lack an appreciation for development across the lifespan. The bulk of social psychological gender-role research has been conducted with young adults, although developmental researchers have clearly demonstrated there is a great deal of change in gender roles before this age. These developments likely lay the foundation for gender roles in early adulthood. Indeed, Zemore, Fiske, and Kim (2000) argued adults' conceptions of gender are impossible to fully comprehend without a thorough grasp, and appreciation, of the development and utility of these roles during childhood. Moreover, researchers have demonstrated that gender roles become considerably more flexible as people age (Sinnott & Shifren, 2001). Thus, the catalogued gender roles of young adults are by no means immutable and likely change in middle and later adulthood. Indeed, early adulthood is merely one period in the process of being gendered.

Developmental research on children's gender roles has also profited from incorporating a social psychological perspective. Critics have argued that developmental researchers focus too narrowly on the cognitive processes of becoming gendered (Eckes & Trautner, 2000b). Specifically, it has been charged that developmentalists tend to disregard the social contexts in which children's gender roles develop and are manifest (see Eckes & Trautner, 2000b; Maccoby, 1990; Martin & Halverson, 1987). This restricted focus engenders an incomplete portrait of gender-role development. Reed and Levy (1997) provided an example of how research is extended through including context. The researchers found that 7- to 19-year-olds reported being more willing to engage in gender-inconsistent activities when with a same-sex peer who endorsed the activity than when alone. Such findings demonstrate that investigators who do not consider social influences when studying gender-role development will obtain only a limited understanding of children's motivation to maintain traditional gender roles. A small number of similar studies focusing on context have been undertaken. For example, Langlois and Downs (1980) and Lindzey and Mize (2001) examined the effects of social presence on children's gender-typed play. Further, McHale, Crouter, and Whiteman (2003) presented a thorough discussion of how different family contexts can affect children's gender roles.

Furthermore, social psychological models have fruitfully interwoven seemingly disparate areas of research not yet explored in developmental work. These models can enrich the approaches taken in developmental studies of children's gender roles. For example, Fiske and Pavelchak (1986) presented an integrative model on the synergistic relation between cognition and affect in which they argued that the elicitation of a person category carries an inherent emotional evocation. Although the role of emotion in gender-role development has received little attention from developmentalists, Levy and Sadovsky (2001) found children's positive and negative cognitive appraisals of hypothetical same-sex peers who varied in the degree of their consistency with gender roles were emotionally charged. Thus, it is likely that emotion plays an important role in the adoption and adherence of gender roles, as well as in the evaluation of their use by others. See also Serbin and Sprafkin (1986) for an eloquent integration of Bem's (1981) social psychological Gender Schema theory (discussed next) for developmental work.

Perhaps one of the most striking examples of how social and developmental psychology have interwoven to stimulate advances is reflected in the generation of the dominant theory of gender-role development and adherence, Gender Schema theory. Versions of this theory were offered concurrently by social (Bem, 1981) and developmental (Martin & Halverson, 1981) psychologists. Markus, Crane, Bernstein, and Siladi (1982) offered a second social psychological version of the theory shortly after the first two were put forward.

All three forms of Gender Schema theory share traits. For example, all focus on the reciprocal relation between environmental input and gender-based cognition. Moreover, the three models consider the modes by which gendered cognitions aid in, and can be imbued with error for, processing the environment. Nonetheless, the three models have distinct features. Bem (1981) specifically examined individual differences in adherence to gender schemas. Markus et al. (1982) similarly focused on individual differences; however, they construed masculinity and femininity to be rooted in discrete gender schemas. Martin and Halverson's (1981) approach centered on both the development and functional significance of gender schemas. These distinctions provide ample division such that each account contributes uniquely to an understanding of gender-based schemas. The models, in combination, have provided the multifaceted foundation on which schema-based research has rested.

CONCLUSIONS

The two examples provided in this chapter—prosocial behavior and gender roles—are merely illustrative. Numerous content areas would have been equally appropriate to illustrate the historical links between social and developmental psychology, their influence on one another, and their potential for further enriching each other, both conceptually and methodologically. Clearly, social psychology has made significant contributions to developmental psychology in the past, and vice versa. Social psychologists can benefit from developmentalists' focus on consistency and change across time and the developmental origins of psychological functioning and behavior, as well as from their use of longitudinal and often relatively ecologically valid methods. Developmentalists can benefit from social psychologists' clever methods for isolating environmental determinants of behavior and their wealth of theory. Nonetheless, the two disciplines have been much more isolated from one another than is optimal. Both groups should be interested in the biological and environmental influences on behavior and psychological functioning; thus, both would find it useful to attend to the other's work. For example, people interested in the evolutionary social psychological approach should find research on developmental behavioral genetics very relevant, and vice versa. Further, an integration of social psychologists' emphasis on proximal motivation with developmentalists' focus on consistency and change could provide insights into aspects of prosocial responding or gender roles that are consistent over time (due to consistencies in internalized motivation) and those that change (due to situationally specific motives). Perhaps the current emphasis on interdisciplinary research will serve to stimulate further exchange of ideas—in course work for students, conferences, and co-authored research and conceptual writings—between social and developmental psychologists.

ACKNOWLEDGMENT

Work on this chapter was supported by a grant from the National Institutes of Mental Health (R01 MH 60838).

REFERENCES

Batson, C. D. (1991). *The altruism question: Toward a social-psychological answer.* Hillsdale, NJ: Lawrence Erlbaum Associates.

Bem, S. L. (1981). Gender schema theory: A cognitive account of sex typing. *Psychological Review, 88,* 354–364.

Brehm, S. S., Kassin, S. M., & Gibbons, F. X. (Eds.). (1981). *Developmental social psychology: Theory and research.* New York: Oxford Press.

Bryan, J. H., & Walbek, N. H. (1970). The impact of words and deeds concerning altruism upón children. *Child Development, 41,* 747–757.

Cialdini, R. B., Baumann, D. J., & Kenrick, D. T. (1981). Insights from sadness: A three-step model of the development of altruism as hedonism. *Developmental Review, 1,* 207–223.

Colby, A., & Damon, W. (1992). *Some do care: Contemporary lives of moral commitment.* New York: Free Press.

Dovidio, J. F. (1984). Helping behavior and altruism: An empirical and conceptual overview. In L. Berkowitz (Ed.), *Advances in experimental social psychology* (Vol. 17, pp. 361–427). New York: Academic Press.

Durkin, K. (1995). *Developmental social psychology: From infancy to old age.* Cambridge, MA: Blackwell.

Eckes, T., & Trautner, H. M. (Eds.). (2000a). *The developmental social psychology of gender.* Mahwah, NJ: Lawrence Erlbaum Associates.

Eckes, T., & Trautner, H. M. (2000b). Developmental social psychology of gender: An integrative framework. In T. Eckes & H. M. Trautner (Eds.), *The developmental social psychology of gender* (pp. 3–32). Mahwah, NJ: Lawrence Erlbaum Associates.

Eisenberg, N. (Ed.). (1995). *Review of personality and social psychology: Vol. 15. Social development.* Newbury Park, CA: Sage.

Eisenberg, N., & Fabes, R. A. (1998). Prosocial development. In W. Damon (Series Ed.) & N. Eisenberg (Vol. Ed.), *Handbook of child psychology: Vol. 3. Social, emotional, and personality development* (5th ed., pp. 701–778). New York: Wiley.

Fiske, S. T., & Pavelchak, M. A. (1986). Category-based versus piecemeal-based affective response: Developments in schema-triggered affect. In R. M. Sorrentino & E. T. Higgins (Eds.), *Handbook of motivation and cognition: Foundations of social behavior* (pp. 167–203). New York: Guilford Press.

Higgins, E. T., Ruble, D. N., & Hartup, W. W. (Eds.). (1983). *Social cognitive and social development: A sociocultural perspective.* Cambridge, UK: Cambridge University Press.

Langlois, J. H., & Downs, A. C. (1980). Mothers, fathers, and peers as socialization agents of sex-typed play behaviors in young children. *Child Development, 51,* 1237–1247.

Latane, B., & Darley, J. (1970). *The unresponsive bystander: Why doesn't he help?* New York: Appleton.

Levy, G. D., & Sadovsky, A. L. (2001). *Influence of preschoolers' sex and gender schematicity on their gender schema-triggered affect.* Unpublished manuscript, University of Wyoming.

Lindsey, E. W., & Mize, J. (2001). Contextual differences in parent–child play: Implications for children's gender role development. *Sex Roles, 44,* 155–176.

Maccoby, E. E. (1990). Gender and relationships: A developmental account. *American Psychologist, 45,* 513–520.

Markus, H., Crane, M., Bernstein, S., & Siladi, M. (1982). Self-schemas and gender. *Journal of Personality and Social Psychology, 42,* 38–50.

Martin, C. L., & Halverson, C. F. (1981). A schematic processing model of sex typing and stereotyping in children. *Child Development, 52,* 1119–1134.

Martin, C. L., & Halverson, C. F. (1987). The roles of cognition in sex role acquisition. In D. B. Carter (Ed.), *Current conceptions of sex roles and sex-typing: Theory and research* (pp. 123–137). New York: Praeger.

McHale, S. M., Crouter, A. C., & Whiteman, S. D. (2003). The family context of gender development in childhood and adolescence. *Social Development, 12,* 125–148.

Oliner, S. P., & Oliner, P. M. (1988). *The altruistic personality: Rescuers of Jews in Nazi Europe.* New York: Free Press.

Radke-Yarrow, M., Zahn-Waxler, C., & Chapman, M. (1983). Prosocial dispositions and behavior. In P. Mussen (Ed.), *Manual of child psychology: Vol. 4. Socialization, personality, and social development* (pp. 469–545; E. M. Hetherington, Ed.). New York: John Wiley & Sons.

Reed, T. M., & Levy, G. D. (1997, April). *Influence of same-sex peer context on cross-gender-typed behaviors.* Poster session presented at the biennial meetings of the Society for Research in Child Development, Washington, DC.

Schroeder, D. A., Penner, L. A., Dovidio, J. F., & Piliavin, J. A. (1995). The *psychology of helping and altruism: Problems and puzzles.* New York: McGraw-Hill.

Serbin, L. A., & Sprafkin, C. (1986). The salience of gender and the process of sex typing in three- to seven-year-old children. *Child Development, 57,* 1188–1199.

Sinnott, J. D., & Shifren, K. (2000). Gender and aging. Gender differences and gender roles. In J. E. Birren & K. W. Schaie (Eds.), *Handbook of the psychology of aging* (5th ed., pp. 454–476). San Diego, CA: Academic Press.

Zemore, S. E., Fiske, S. T., & Kim, H. (2000). Gender stereotypes and the dynamics of social interaction. In T. Eckes & H. M. Trautner (Eds.), *The developmental social psychology of gender* (pp. 207–242). Mahwah, NJ: Lawrence Erlbaum Associates.

34

The Self as a Point of Contact Between Social Psychology and Motivation

Constantine Sedikides
Aiden P. Gregg
University of Southampton

Interdisciplinarity is a mixed blessing. An attempted union between two disciplines can cook up a couscous of conflicting assumptions and theories, misaligned methodological and data analytic strategies, and disconcertingly divergent validation philosophies. The chimerical offspring of this union will be amorphous, uncompelling, and unusable. Yet sometimes such a union can turn out to be a marriage made in heaven. The union of social psychology and motivation is a case in point, with the self as master of ceremonies.

The self acts as a methodological point of contact between contemporary social psychological and traditional motivational approaches. The former approach is nomothetic, experimental, and laboratory-based, whereas the latter is idiographic, naturalistic, and questionnaire-based. More importantly, the self acts as a theoretical point of contact between the two approaches. The role of the self as the facilitator of this doubly harmonious union is illustrated though a brief exposition to the self-evaluation literature.

SELF-EVALUATION

From Needs to Self-Evaluation Motives.   Classic motivation research has graced the field of social psychology with such constructs as the need for uncertainty reduction (Weiner et al., 1971), the need for control (Rotter, 1966), the need to experience the self as an origin of action (deCharms, 1968), and the need for self-esteem (Rosenberg, 1965). These needs have been investigated by motivation researchers with the aid of targeted questionnaires. Their theoretical and empirical forays have had a profound impact on the self-evaluation literature, particularly in regard to the interplay between the individual and the social context. For example, what do people want to know about themselves? What kind of information are they most likely to solicit? What sort of feedback will they accept from others and how will they treat the person supplying it? How will they process and remember that feedback? Will that feedback influence their goal-setting and behavior?

Inspired by early motivation research on human needs, social psychologists set about addressing these questions in a generative manner. In the process, the concept of needs gave way to the concept of self-evaluation motives. Such motives were assumed to influence the way in which self-relevant information is selected, processed, remembered, or acted upon. Thus, the need for uncertainty reduction was reconceptualized in terms of the self-assessment motive; the need for control, in terms of the self-verification motive; the need to experience the self as an origin of action, in terms of the self-improvement motive; and the need for self-esteem, in terms of the self-enhancement motive (Sedikides & Strube, 1997). Importantly, these reconceptualizations were complementary rather than antagonistic: The motives were assumed to result in need satisfaction.

More specifically, the self-assessment motive was proposed to guide the processing of self-relevant information so that the content of the self-concept (e.g., memories, judgments, behavioral sequelae) would be more accurate when judged by consensual or objective standards (Trope, 1986); the self-verification motive was proposed to direct self-relevant information processing in favor of the confirmation and validation of existing self-beliefs (Swann, 1983); the self-improvement motive was proposed to steer self-relevant information processing so as to raise levels of ability or performance and maximize potential for personality growth (Taylor, Neter, & Wayment, 1995); and the self-enhancement motive was proposed to tilt self-relevant information processing in favor of a positive self-concept (Brown & Dutton, 1995).

Social psychology's appropriation of these theoretical constructs was a breath of fresh air. The motives were construed as dynamic, intraindividual variables that could readily lend themselves to laboratory experimentation. Accordingly, three research vistas opened up, each revolving around a key question. *First*, is each motive influential in its own right? This question was answered in the affirmative: Each of the four motives was shown to affect self-relevant information processing in substantive ways. *Second*, although the motives could and did coexist, what happened when they are in an antagonistic relation? In several programs of research, one motive was pitted against the other. Although we do not claim to be utterly dispassionate reviewers of the available literature (no doubt, being swayed by self-motives of our own!), we believe that the available evidence suggests that, all things considered, the self-enhancement motive is preeminent (Sedikides & Gregg, 2003). *Third*, and perhaps most importantly, what are the circumstances under which one motive prevails over another? A plethora of research has addressed this question. It has been shown, for example, that despite the general primacy of self-enhancement, (a) self-assessment prevails over self-enhancement when the self is evaluated on well-defined and verifiable attributes as opposed to ill-defined and unverifiable ones, (b) self-improvement prevails over self-enhancement on personality dimensions viewed as modifiable as opposed to fixed, and (c) self-verification prevails over self-enhancement when cognitive resources are plentiful as opposed to scarce (Baumeister, 1998; Sedikides & Strube, 1997).

FROM APPROACH/AVOIDANCE TO SELF-ENHANCEMENT/SELF-PROTECTION

The uxorious union of classic motivation and contemporary self-evaluation approaches has given birth to another bouncing baby. Classic motivation research introduced the idea of the approach/avoidance dimension, inspired by the fact that behavior in achievement settings is oriented either toward the pursuit of success (approach) or the flight from failure (avoidance) (McClelland, Atkinson, Clark, & Lowell, 1953; Murray, 1938). Modern self-evaluation research has reconceptualized this dimension in terms of self-promotion versus self-protection, the yin and yang of self-enhancement. The former refers to the proactive attempt to positively affirm the self, and the latter to the defensive attempt to prevent devaluation of the self.

This reconceptualization provided impetus for investigating the self-protection motive. An impressive amount of research has now documented that humans are motivated to protect the self against threat. Humans treat the self as priceless possession, guard it vigilantly, protect it with zeal and vigor. For example, they deny their shortcomings, displace blame for their failures, react angrily to unfavorable feedback and recruit compensatory qualities to offset it, change the meaning of their negative self-aspects to give them a more positive spin, and strategically compare themselves to less fortunate others (Sedikides & Gregg, 2003). In fact, humans are averse to negative self-relevant feedback even when it is accurate (Sedikides, 1993), and remember such feedback poorly (Sedikides & Green, 2000) even when the feedback is consistent with their negative characteristics. That is, in direct tests, the self-protection motive has trumped the self-assessment and self-verification motives.

Classic motivation research has concerned itself with the relative potency of the approach versus avoidance motive, treated as an individual-difference variable (McClelland et al., 1953). In contrast, self-evaluation research has conceptualized the self-promotion and self-protection motives as intraindividual variables (but also as an individual-difference variable; Tice, 1991) while asking the same question about relative potency. The ensuing research revealed that self-protection is, on the whole, more powerful than self-promotion: Humans are more strongly motivated to protect the self against threatening feedback than to use feedback to boost the positivity of the self (Baumeister, Bratslavsky, Finkenauer, & Vohs, 2001).

FROM EXPLICIT TO IMPLICIT SELF-EVALUATION

Classic motivation research has distinguished between implicit and explicit motives (McClelland et al., 1953; McClelland, Koestner, & Weinberger, 1989). Explicit motives were considered cognitive representations of one's values, developed through verbally transmitted socialization experiences, and predictive of deliberate choices. Implicit motives, on the other hand, were thought to be affective associative structures, developed through preverbal socialization experiences, and predictive of spontaneous or habitual responses.

This distinction has once again been transmuted in self-evaluation research. Explicit self-evaluation motives are accessible to conscious awareness and are assessed through questionnaires. However, implicit motives are inaccessible to conscious awareness and are assessed through indirect or unobtrusive tests such as the Implicit Association Test (indexing automatic associations between self and valence; Greenwald, McGhee, & Schwartz, 1998) or the Name-Letter Effect (estimating participants' preference for letters in their own name; Nuttin, 1985). Implicit measures are credited for some of the most exciting, if controversial, developments in self-evaluation research. For example, use of these measures has documented the universalism of self-enhancement: This motive is equally prevalent in Western and Eastern culture (Hetts, Sakuma, & Pelham, 1999).

CONCLUSIONS

We began this chapter by claiming that the union of two disciplines is not necessarily a happy one. In fact, we are prone to believe that interdisciplinarity, like marriage, has only a 50% chance of succeeding.

We have chosen, however, to tell a success story: the influence of classic motivation research on contemporary self-evaluation research. We highlighted three domains of such influence. The first involves the reconceptualization of crucial human needs in terms of self-evaluation motives. The second involves the reconceptualization of the approach/avoidance dimension in terms of the self-promotion/self-protection dimension. The final one involves the reconceptualization of implicit versus explicit motives in terms of implicit versus explicit self-evaluations. In all three domains, substantial theoretical developments have resulted in methodological innovation, just as happy marriages produce healthy children.

Of course, these three domains are not the only instances of interdisciplinary fertilization. The field of self-evaluation has been influenced by philosophical theorizing, and advances in cognitive, developmental and health psychology, as well as trends in personality and cultural psychology (Sedikides

& Gregg, 2003; Sedikides & Strube, 1997). Nevertheless, we believe that the interdisciplinary success of classic motivation and self-evaluation research can serve as a concrete example for additional bridge-building between motivation and social psychology. Also, we hope that this scholarly influence will increasingly become bidirectional in nature, as the maturing of self-evaluation research will have theoretical and methodological implications for motivation research.

REFERENCES

Baumeister, R. F. (1998). The self. In D. T. Gilbert, S. T. Fiske, & G. Lindzey (Eds.), *The handbook of social psychology* (Vol. 1, pp. 680–740). New York: Oxford University Press.

Baumeister, R. F., Bratslavsky, E., Finkenauer, C., & Vohs, K. D. (2001). Bad is stronger than good. *Review of General Psychology, 5,* 323–370.

Brown, J. D., & Dutton, K. A. (1995). Truth and consequences: The cost and benefits of accurate self-knowledge. *Personality and Social Psychology Bulletin, 21,* 1288–1296.

deCharms, R. (1968). *Personal causation: The internal affective determinants of behavior.* New York: Academic Press.

Greenwald, A. G., McGhee, D. E., & Schwartz, J. L. K. (1998). Measuring individual differences in implicit cognition: The implicit association test. *Journal of Personality and Social Psychology, 74,* 1464–1480.

Hetts, J. J., Sakuma, M., & Pelham, B. W. (1999). Two roads to positive self-regard: Implicit and explicit self-evaluation and culture. *Journal of Experimental Social Psychology, 35,* 512–559.

McClelland, D. C., Atkinson, J. W., Clark, R. A., & Lowell, E. L. (1953). *The achievement motive.* New York: Appleton-Century-Crofts.

McClelland, D. C., Koestner, R., & Weinberger, J. (1989). How do self-attributed and implicit motives differ? *Psychological Review, 96,* 690–702.

Murray, H. (1938). *Explorations in personality.* New York: Oxford University Press.

Nuttin, J. M. (1985). Narcissism beyond gestalt and awareness: The name letter effect. *European Journal of Social Psychology, 15,* 353–361.

Rosenberg, M. (1965). *Society and the adolescent self-image.* Princeton, NJ: Princeton University Press.

Rotter, J. B. (1966). Generalized expectancies for internal versus external control of reinforcement. *Psychological Monographs, 80*(1, Whole No. 609).

Sedikides, C. (1993). Assessment, enhancement, and verification determinants of the self-evaluation process. *Journal of Personality and Social Psychology, 65,* 317–338.

Sedikides, C., & Green, J. D. (2000). On the self-protective nature of inconsistency/negativity management: Using the person memory paradigm to examine self-referent memory. *Journal of Personality and Social Psychology, 79,* 906–922.

Sedikides, C., & Gregg, A. P. (2003). Portraits of the self. In M. A. Hogg & J. Cooper (Eds.), *Sage handbook of social psychology* (pp. 110–138). London: Sage.

Sedikides, C., & Strube, M. J. (1997). Self-evaluation: To thine own self be good, to thine own self be sure, to thine own self be true, and to thine own self be better. In M. P. Zanna (Ed.), *Advances in experimental social psychology* (Vol. 29, pp. 209–269). New York: Academic Press.

Swann, W. B., Jr. (1983). Self-verification: Bringing social reality into harmony with the self. In J. Suls & A. G. Greenwald (Eds.), *Psychological perspectives on the self* (Vol. 2, pp. 33–66). Hillsdale, NJ: Lawrence Erlbaum Associates.

Taylor, S. E., Neter, E., & Wayment, H. A. (1995). Self-evaluation processes. *Personality and Social Psychology Bulletin, 21,* 1278–1287.

Tice, D. M. (1991). Esteem protection or enhancement? Self-handicapping motives and attributions differ by trait self-esteem. *Journal of Personality and Social Psychology, 60,* 711–725.

Trope, Y. (1986). Self-enhancement and self-assessment in achievement behaviour. In R. M. Sorrentino & E. T. Higgins (Eds.), *Handbook of motivation and cognition: Foundations of social behavior* (Vol. 1, pp. 350–378). New York: Guilford Press.

Weiner, B., Frieze, I., Kukla, A., Read, C., Rest, S., & Rosenbaum, R. M. (1971). *Perceiving the causes of success and failure.* Morristown, NJ: General Learning Press.

35

From Bicycle Racing to School: Competition, Multiple Goals, and Multiple Indicators of Success in Education

Judith M. Harackiewicz
University of Wisconsin

John M. Tauer
University of St. Thomas

After capturing his seventh consecutive Tour de France championship, Lance Armstrong was lauded for his competitive greatness and for his passion and motivation for his sport. Long before Armstrong crossed the finish line (and even before the first Tour de France), Norman Triplett enjoyed watching cyclists battle for glory. He observed that the same bicycle racers rode faster when racing against other cyclists than in timed trials, and raised a question that goes straight to the heart of social psychology, as defined by Allport (1985): How is an individual influenced by the real, imagined, or implied presence of others? Triplett was interested in a more specific version of this question, regarding the effect of interpersonal competition on performance. He designed a clever study to test his ideas in a controlled laboratory setting, and is generally credited as having conducted the first social psychology experiment (Triplett, 1898). We see from the beginning an emphasis on real-world observation paired with experimental studies, and this typifies the Lewinian approach (Lewin, 1935) that has guided social psychology over the years.

Triplett's work was an early first step in the study of competition, and much research followed. Triplett's question requires that we consider the nature of the competitive situation, and the individual's perception of and reaction to that situation. This analysis is fundamentally social psychological, but as soon as we broaden our consideration of the competitive situation with a motivational analysis, we find a bridge to personality psychology. As we extend our study of competitive situations back to the real world, we find more bridges to other disciplines in which competition is studied: sport psychology, health psychology, organization and management sciences, and educational psychology. Indeed, a thorough analysis of competition will benefit from an interdisciplinary focus on competition in work, sport and school contexts. In this brief essay, we review our own basic and applied research that bridges social psychology with personality and educational psychology.

MOTIVATIONAL ISSUES IN THE STUDY OF COMPETITION

Triplett found that people perform better in competitive situations than when tested alone, and his findings spurred social psychologists to ask *why* these effects occur. To address this question, we need to extend our analysis beyond performance and consider the role of motivation in the competitive situation. How do people approach and experience tasks as they perform them in competition with others? Do they care more about their performance? Do they become involved in the activity and enjoy the experience? In our own work, we have studied an important type of motivation that can influence performance, persistence and passion (Tauer & Harackiewicz, 2001). Intrinsic motivation, defined as the desire to take part in an activity for its own sake (Deci & Ryan, 1985), is an important predictor of effort, enjoyment, and continued interest in an activity. Intrinsic motivation is often correlated with performance, making this unique type of motivation important both as an end in itself, and in service of optimal performance. We therefore adopt a multifaceted definition of success in which we consider both performance and intrinsic motivation to be important outcomes.

However, trade-offs between performance and intrinsic motivation can complicate our analysis. For example, factors that promote performance may sometimes undermine intrinsic motivation. Motivational theory suggests that competition may reduce intrinsic motivation because it is controlling and shifts an individual's focus to the external goal of winning, and away from the activity (Deci & Ryan, 1985). This may not interfere with performance in the short term, but people may not enjoy activities as much if they experience external pressure (Kohn, 1992). In turn, this may discourage individuals from persisting at an activity, thus hampering long-term performance.

$$B = f(P,E)$$

As we widen our scope to examine different motivational processes that may be engendered by competition, we immediately encounter a bridge to another area of psychology: personality. This bridge is legendary, and Lewin's proposition that behavior is a function of personality and environment is particularly apt in the case of competition (Van Lange, 2000). Quite simply, not everyone responds to competition in the same way. Some people thrive on the challenge provided by competition, whereas others find this type of evaluative pressure quite aversive. In our research, we have examined individual differences in achievement orientation as a moderator of competition effects, and found dramatic differences in intrinsic motivation. Individuals high in achievement orientation (HAMs) tend to seek out challenges, strive to outperform others, and value feedback (Jackson, 1974). In our studies, HAMs enjoyed an activity more in competition, whereas individuals low in achievement motivation (LAMs) enjoyed the activity more in noncompetitive situations, whether they received positive (i.e., winning), negative (i.e., losing), or no feedback (Epstein & Harackiewicz, 1992; Tauer & Harackiewicz, 1999). Moreover, we collected process measures that revealed differences in their initial approach to the activity, with HAMs reporting greater eagerness and a sense of challenge in competitive conditions, relative to LAMs. In sum, a consideration of personality factors and motivational dynamics has helped us understand why some people wilt under competitive pressure but others, like Lance Armstrong, thrive.

Competitions are strong social situations that make certain goals explicit. For example, the object of the Tour de France is to finish with a faster overall time than any of the other racers. The opponents are real people, present on the course. In other achievement settings, however, performance and motivation may be affected by more subtle external goals, and the "opponents" may be imagined or implied. Theorists have distinguished between mastery and performance goals, with mastery goals focused on the development of competence, and performance goals focused on the demonstration of competence relative to others (Dweck, 1986). In laboratory studies of externally manipulated mastery (e.g., "try to improve your score") and performance (e.g., "try to perform well compared to other students") goals, we have observed similar patterns to those found in our competition research. Once again, we find a classic person × situation interaction, with HAMs demonstrating higher levels of intrinsic motivation under a performance goal, whereas LAMs are more intrinsically motivated when assigned a mastery goal (Harackiewicz, Barron, & Elliot, 1998). Thus, whether situational goals are explicitly interpersonal or implicitly competitive, we find that their effects depend on personality differences.

PERSONAL GOALS IN EDUCATIONAL CONTEXTS

Individuals can and will set their own goals in social situations, and it is important to distinguish the personal goals that a person adopts from the situational goals that are suggested or imposed by social contexts. This person-centered approach allows us to examine the effects of goals in real-world situations, and to start building a bridge to educational psychology. In a series of longitudinal studies, we have examined the effects of self-set goals in an achievement context that can be considered rather competitive: college education (Harackiewicz, Barron, Tauer, Carter, & Elliot, 2000). In this setting, academic performance (i.e., grades) and continued interest are both critical for long-term success. In fact, students frequently choose their major, and often their career, based on their performance and interest in a discipline.

Using the mastery/performance goal framework, we measured college students' achievement goals at the outset of an introductory psychology course, then measured their intrinsic interest in the course topic and final grades in the course, and then examined students' subsequent course choices to obtain a behavioral measure of interest in psychology. Students who adopted mastery goals reported being more interested in psychology. In addition, these students were more likely to enroll in additional courses and to major in psychology. Those who adopted performance goals, on the other hand, performed better in the class (Harackiewicz, Barron, Tauer, & Elliot, 2002). Although there appears to be a trade-off between performance and intrinsic motivation in this context, there doesn't have to be, because self-set mastery and performance goals are relatively independent (Harackiewicz et al., 1998). Individuals can and do adopt both mastery and performance goals, and students who adopt both goals may be the most successful in terms of motivation and performance in competitive university courses (Harackiewicz, Barron, Pintrich, Elliot, & Thrash, 2002).

Indeed, we find that Lance Armstrong also adopted both mastery and performance goals, sometimes in the same situation. On one particularly cold and rainy day, Armstrong biked 4 hours up an incredibly steep hill. After getting to the top he said that he did not feel that he understood the climb. We observe his mastery orientation when he writes, "I meant that I hadn't fully mastered it; I wasn't comfortable that I could cope with how difficult it was. It was an undulating climb, with some parts much steeper than others. To fully understand a climb, you have to know where you will suffer most so you can brace yourself for that; where you can rest a little; and where you can potentially attack" (Armstrong & Jenkins, 2001, pp. 272–273). His solution? Drive back down and bike uphill in the rain for 4 more hours! He goes on to reveal his performance orientation when he says, "I was pretty sure I was the only fool who was willing to climb it in that weather even once, much less twice. But that was the point" (p. 273). Armstrong's adoption of both types of goals may have provided him the passion to strive for improvement during each practice session, and also the competitive effort to push himself harder than any of his opponents.

COSTS, BENEFITS, AND POLICY IMPLICATIONS

Can goals research help educators optimize motivation and performance? In other words, do these findings have implications for educational policy? Our experimental results suggest that the effects of external goal interventions will depend on personality differences. In an ideal world, educators would tailor their instruction to each student's individual needs. However, it may be unrealistic (and even impossible) to expect teachers to assess students' personality profiles and then alter their classroom context accordingly. Thus, one cost of the bridge to personality psychology is that there is no easy take-home message, because we are unlikely to find a "one size fits all" solution. Moreover, factors that promote performance may actually undermine intrinsic motivation, and it is important to consider the motivational impact of educational interventions. Our classroom findings suggest that we might need to emphasize both goals in education, and encourage students to adopt both mastery and performance goals in their courses. Although it is tempting to apply our findings to real-world issues, we must urge caution, given the correlational nature of our classroom studies. In addition, our conclusions must be tempered by cultural considerations. For example, perceptions of competition may vary as a function of a culture's level of individualism/collectivism. Our results have been obtained in a sports-crazed society that emphasizes competition in work, sports and education, and careful cross-cultural research is needed to establish the boundary conditions for our conclusions. Nonetheless, we do believe that our findings highlight the importance of intrinsic motivation in education, and the potential for more practical bridge-building in the future.

CONCLUSIONS

Competition is pervasive in our society, and it can affect how individuals perform and experience activities. A comprehensive understanding of competition depends on interdisciplinary efforts, and bridges to personality and educational psychology have illuminated our understanding of basic social processes. We have reviewed evidence that demonstrates the importance of considering both personality and situational variables in the study of competition. Because our culture is largely driven by performance, it is easy to overlook intrinsic motivation as an important indicator of success. We encourage researchers and educators to value intrinsic motivation as an outcome, and to create learning environments that emphasize both mastery and performance goals in order to promote optimal performance and intrinsic motivation.

REFERENCES

Allport, G. W. (1985). The historical background of social psychology. In G. Lindzey & E. Aronson (Eds.), *The handbook of social psychology* (pp. 1–46). New York: McGraw-Hill.

Armstrong, L., & Jenkins, S. (2001). *It's not about the bike: My journey back to life.* New York: Berkley.

Deci, E. L., & Ryan, R. M. (1985). *Intrinsic motivation and self-determination in human behavior.* New York: Plenum.

Dweck, C. S. (1986). Motivational processes affecting learning. *American Psychologist, 41,* 1040–1048.

Epstein, J. A., & Harackiewicz, J. M. (1992). Winning is not enough: The effects of competition and opponent information on intrinsic motivation. *Personality and Social Psychology Bulletin, 18,* 128–138.

Harackiewicz, J. M., Barron, K. E., & Elliot, A. J. (1998). Rethinking achievement goals: When are they adaptive for college students and why? *Educational Psychologist, 33,* 1–21.

Harackiewicz, J. M., Barron, K. E., Pintrich, P. R., Elliot, A. J., & Thrash, T.M. (2002). Revision of achievement goal theory: Necessary and illuminating. *Journal of Educational Psychology, 94,* 638–645.

Harackiewicz, J. M., Barron, K. E., Tauer, J. M., Carter, S. M., & Elliot, A. J. (2000). Short-term and long-term consequences of achievement goals: Predicting interest and performance over time. *Journal of Educational Psychology, 92,* 316–330.

Harackiewicz, J. M., Barron, K. E., Tauer, J. M., & Elliot, A. J. (2002). Predicting success in college: A longitudinal study of achievement goals and ability measures as predictors of interest and performance from freshman year through graduation. *Journal of Educational Psychology, 94,* 562–575.

Jackson, D. N. (1974). *Personality research form manual.* Goshen, NY: Research Psychologists Press.

Kohn, A. (1992). *No contest: The case against competition.* New York: Houghton Mifflin.

Lewin, K. (1935). *Dynamic theory of personality.* New York: McGraw-Hill.

Tauer, J. M., & Harackiewicz, J. M. (1999). Winning isn't everything: Competition, achievement orientation, and intrinsic motivation. *Journal of Experimental Social Psychology (Special Issue), 35,* 209–238.

Tauer, J. M., & Harackiewicz, J. M. (2001). Evaluation and intrinsic motivation: The double-edged sword. In S. G. Harkins (Ed.), *Multiple perspectives on the effects of evaluation on performance: Toward integration* (pp. 77–98). Boston: Kluwer.

Triplett, N. (1898). The dynamogenic factors in pace making and competition. *American Journal of Psychology, 9,* 507–533.

Van Lange, P. A. M. (2000). Beyond self-interest: A set of propositions relevant to interpersonal orientations. *European Review of Social Psychology, 11,* 297–330.

36

Bridging the Areas of Social Psychology and Social Developmental Psychology

Daphne Blunt Bugental
University of California, Santa Barbara

There is a long list of shared topical and theoretical concerns across the fields of social psychology and social developmental psychology. However, in describing points of overlap, I have chosen to organize my comments around the concept of social domains. Within this framework, social interaction is understood as involving mechanisms specific to the distinctive domains of social life (e.g., coalitional groups, parental care, hierarchical power), rather than as involving domain-general processes. Such mechanisms are understood as facilitating the solution of problems that humans have repeatedly faced across their evolutionary history (Cosmides & Tooby, 1992; Hirschfeld & Gelman, 1994).

THE DOMAINS OF SOCIAL LIFE

If one were to look back at theoretical approaches to relationships 40–50 years ago, one would see an emphasis on the principles believed to guide all relationships—a domain-general approach. Within social psychology, the focus was on social costs and benefits (as framed within exchange or equity theory). Within social development, the focus was on social learning theory, and the direct or indirect influence of social reinforcement on the socialization of the young. An early challenge to domain-general positions came with Clark and Mills's (1979) demonstration that relationships differ in the ways in which they are regulated. Although some kinds of relationships (e.g., more casual relationships) operate by the principles of exchange (a tit-for-tat arrangement), communal relationships (e.g., relationships within the family or between close friends) are governed by mutual concern with each other's welfare. In communal relationships, exact cost accounting of mutual benefits is seen as inappropriate and aversive.

Within the field of social development, an early challenge to domain-general theories came from attachment theory. With the work of Harlow (1973), Bowlby (1969), and others, it became apparent that attachment relationships were not governed by the principles of traditional learning theory. In becoming attached, infants responded to parents as a social bond rather than as a source of primary benefits such as food.

The notion of qualitative distinctions in the organization of different kinds of relationships has been extended in the last ten years. Increasing attention has been directed to the possibility that the ways in which we interact with others operates according to different rules or algorithms—based on the particular social domain involved (e.g., Bugental, 2000; Cosmides & Tooby, 1992; Fiske, 1992; Kenrick, Li, & Butner, 2002; Kirkpatrick, Waugh, Valencia, & Webster, 2002; Panksepp, Nelson, & Bekkedal, 1997). Within this approach, it has been proposed that there are distinctive "tasks" to be accomplished in social life that have adaptive significance across cultures and species.

Although different theorists have parsed the social world in slightly different ways (and with different terms), five domains are regularly represented within the proposed taxonomies.

1. *Parental care.* Proximity-maintenance within a relationship that provides for the safety and provisioning of dependent offspring.
2. *Coalitional groups.* Maintenance of cohesiveness and shared benefits within an ingroup, and shared defense against threat from outgroups.
3. *Hierarchical power.* Negotiation of relationships between individuals who differ in social dominance and resource holding potential.
4. *Reciprocity/mutuality.* Regulation of matched benefits between functional equals.
5. *Mating.* Selection and protection of access to high value sexual partners.

These domains have been identified as distinctive in a number of different ways. Kenrick and his colleagues (Kenrick et al., 2002) focused on the qualitatively different decision rules that are involved; in doing so, these authors combine concepts drawn from evolutionary psychology and dynamical systems theory. Fiske (1992) proposed that different domains make use of different scaling systems in the computations involved within different domains (e.g., authority-ranked relationships involve an ordinal scale; equality-matched relationships involve an equal-interval scale); his approach combines evidence from both anthropology and social cognition. Bugental (2000) focused more directly on the distinctive developmental and neurohormonal processes involved in acquiring the algorithms of social life. For example, (a) hormonal preparation of adults for the parental care domain begins during pregnancy (e.g., increases in cortisol during pregnancy predict the subsequent level of care shown); (b) hormonal preparation of the young for the hierarchical power domain begins prenatally as a function of elevated androgen levels (which predict rough and tumble play, a precursor of more serious types of competition in later years); and (c) reciprocal/mutual relationships are fostered by the presence of mirror neurons (that fire in response to own action and the matched action of others) that appear to guide imitation processes observable on the first day of life. Concern with neurohormonal regulatory processes overlaps the work of Panksepp and his colleagues (e.g., Panksepp et al., 1997) in their study of the regulation of social domains from a behavioral neuroscience perspective.

Among theorists who do not take a biological approach, an analogous interest emerged in the differing responses shown to context or situation. For example, Kelley (1984; Kelley et al., 2003) manifested a continuing concern with "situations." As he stated, "Interdependence situations are at the basis, both phylogenetically and ontogenetically, of the varieties of interpersonal rules and tendencies observed in socialized adults. This assumption derives from the functional view that, for the most part, people are well-adapted to the situations they commonly encounter" (Kelley, 1984, p. 979). Developmental psychologists concerned with socialization (e.g., Dix, 1992; Hastings & Grusec, 1998) have increasingly pointed out that parent–child interactions differ in systematic ways based on the goals that are currently operative (e.g., goals based on parental motives for power or control, goals based on parental care of the young, and goals focused on preparation of the young for social life).

THE FINE-TUNING OF SOCIAL DOMAINS TO FIT THE EXISTING ENVIRONMENT

Across disciplines, theorists concerned with social domains have proposed certain default mechanisms for (a) processing (or computing) information relevant to different social tasks, and (b) responding to that information at a physiological, decision-making, and behavioral level. Such processes can be thought of as reflecting the fact that we are "designed" by our evolutionary history for receptivity to certain kinds of social experience (a design that involves the "experience-expectant" brain). At the same time, the capability for adaptive variations is built into such systems, allowing for the "fine-tuning" of responses to the shifting environment the individual faces (a design that involves the "experience-dependent" brain; Bruer & Greenough, 2001).

Kenrick et al. (2002) captured this concept through the use of dynamical systems theory. That is, the decisions of individuals within different domains are expressed in a dynamic interplay with the decisions of others in their social networks. Bugental (2000) suggested that flexibility occurs at three levels: (a) a biological level (biological preparation for solving domain tasks in alternative ways, based on the recurrent features of environments in our evolutionary past); (b) a cognitive level (individual representation of social domains as a function of their individual history; and (c) socialization (individual variations shaped by cultural forces, forces that typically operate in collaboration with biological influences). From either perspective, the individual's functioning within any given domain comes to be (partially) shaped by the environment.

BRIDGING THE FIELDS OF SOCIAL DEVELOPMENT AND SOCIAL PSYCHOLOGY IN UNDERSTANDING SOCIAL DOMAINS: SOME EXAMPLES

Variables of concern to developmental and social psychologists are receiving increasing attention with respect to their variability across domains. Self-esteem represents a variable in which there has been a move away from domain-general processes toward domain-specific processes. Attachment represents a variable, which some researchers see as continuous across domains, whereas others see it as involving systematic differences across domains

Self-Esteem. Kirkpatrick and his colleagues (e.g., Kirkpatrick et al., 2002) have given attention to the differing levels of self-esteem that individuals experience in different social domains, along with the ways in which variations in self-esteem influence behavior. They suggest that different kinds of relationships pose different adaptive problems; thus, what is valued in one domain differs from what is valued in other domains. Correspondingly, the individual's self-esteem can be expected to vary across domains. So, for example, an individual may have high general self-esteem but lack self-esteem within his or her coalitional group (a specific domain). This individual may feel excluded within the group and respond with aggression in this setting but not in others. In the same way, it has also been observed that children and adolescents differ in their reported self-esteem across domains (e.g., Harter, Waters, & Whitesell, 1998).

Attachment. Within his original conceptualization of attachment, Bowlby (1980) suggested that variations within the child's attachment to his or her parents will ultimately serve as a key influence on later relationships of other kinds. Hazan and Shaver (1987), building on this notion, suggested that romantic relationships, like parent–child relationships, are characterized by attachment. Consistent with Bowlby's formulations, attachment styles have been seen by some theorists as showing continuity across parent–child and adult relationships (e.g., Bartholomew, Kwong, & Hart, 2001).

However, a domain-specific approach to these processes suggests that different algorithms are involved in parent-child attachment and attachment between romantic partners. Although these relationships share the feature of proximity maintenance (i.e., maintenance of physical nearness), they differ in the mechanisms and payoffs that are involved. Proximity maintenance within the parental care domain provides for the child's safety; regulatory processes involve a highly orchestrated combination of social signals and hormonal responses to parent–child separation and/or to events that would have posed a threat in our evolutionary past (e.g., animals). In contrast, proximity maintenance within the mating domain serves to protect access to the partner, and is triggered by potential threats from rivals. In short, the processes involved are analogous (i.e., involving similar processes) but not homologous (involving the same algorithms). In this case, an assumed bridge across disciplines creates a false impression of continuity. A facile assumption of equivalence overlooks the important functional and structural differences of the two types of relationships. Recognition of these distinctions is becoming more prevalent among developmental and social psychologists concerned with the processes that regulate these relationships (e.g., Goldberg, Grusec & Jenkins, 1999; Zeifman & Hazan, 1997).

CONCLUSIONS

Social psychology and developmental psychology have given increasing attention to organized differences in the ways in which humans think, feel, and act in the various domains of social life. The notion of domain-general social processes is giving way to the idea that different kinds of relationships make use of different algorithms.

Implications for future research can be drawn at many different levels. For developmental psychologists, the past focus on domain-general notions of "effective parenting" is being replaced with the view that the nature of effective parenting differs for different socialization tasks. For behavioral neuroscientists, increasing research is needed on the role of neurohormonal processes as regulators of social domains within human relationships. Among social psychologists, systematic research is needed to demonstrate the differences in the ideation and behaviors activated when different domains are primed.

REFERENCES

Bartholomew, K., Kwong, M. J., & Hart, S. D. (2001). Attachment. In W. J. Livesley (Ed.), *Handbook of personality disorders: Theory, research, and treatment* (pp. 196–230). New York, NY,: Guilford Press.
Bowlby, J. (1969). *Attachment*. New York: Basic Books.
Bowlby, J. (1980). *Attachment and loss*. New York: Basic Books.
Bruer, J. T., & Greenough, W. T. (2001). The subtle science of how experience affects the brain. In D. B. Bailey, Jr. & J. T. Bruer (Eds.), *Critical thinking about critical periods* (pp. 209–232). Baltimore, MD: Paul H. Brookes.
Bugental, D. B. (2000). Acquisition of the algorithms of social life: A domain-based approach. *Psychological Bulletin, 26*, 187–209.
Clark, M. S., & Mills, J. (1979). Interpresonal attraction in exchange and communal relationships. *Journal of Personality and Social Psychology, 57*, 12–24.

Cosmides, L., & Tooby, J. (1992). Cognitive adaptations for social exchange. In J. H. Barkow, L. Cosmides, & J. Tooby (Eds.), *The adapted mind: Evolutionary psychology and the generation of culture* (pp. 163–228). London: Oxford University Press.

Dix, T. (1992). Parenting on behalf of the child: Empathic goals in the regulation of responsive parenting. In I. E. Sigel, A. V. McGillicuddy-DeLisi, & J. J. Goodnow (Eds.), *Parental belief systems: the psychological consequences for children* (2nd ed., pp. 319–346). Hillsdale, NJ: Lawrence Erlbaum Associates.

Fiske, A. P. (1992). The four elementary forms of sociality: Framework for a unified theory of social relations. *Psychological Review, 99,* 689–723.

Goldberg, S., Grusec, J. E., & Jenkins, J. M. (1999). Confidence in protection: Arguments for a narrow definition of attachment. *Journal of Family Psychology, 13,* 475–483.

Harlow, H. F. (1973). *Learning to love.* Oxford, England: Ballantine.

Harter, S., Waters, P., & Whitesell, N. R. (1998). Relational self-words: Differences in perceived worth a person across interpersonal contexts among adolescents. *Child Development, 69,* 756–766.

Hastings, P. D., & Grusec, J. E. (1998). Parenting goals as organizers of responses to parent-child disagreement. *Developmental Psychology, 34,* 465–479.

Hazan, C., & Shaver, P. (1987). Romantic love conceptualized as an attachment process. *Journal of Personality and Social Psychology, 52,* 511–524.

Hirschfeld, L. A., & Gelman, S. A. (1994). Toward a topography of mind: An introduction to domain specificity. In L. A. Hirschfeld & S. A. Gelman (Eds.), *Mapping the mind* (pp. 3–36). Cambridge, England: Cambridge University Press.

Kelley, H. H. (1984). The theoretical description of interdependence by means of transition lists. *Journal of Personality and Social Psychology, 47,* 956–982.

Kelley, H. H., Holmes, J. G., Kerr, N. L., Reis, H. T., Rusbult, C. E., & Van Lange, P. A. M. (2003). *An atlas of interpersonal situations.* New York: Cambridge University Press.

Kenrick, D. T., Li, N. P., & Butner, J. (2003). Dynamical evolutionary psychology: Individual decision rules and emergent social norms. *Psychological Review, 110,* 3–28.

Kirkpatrick, L. A., Waugh, C. E., Valencia, A., & Webster, G. D. (2002). The functional domain specificity of self-esteem and the differential prediction of aggression. *Journal of Personality and Social Psychology, 82,* 756–767.

Panksepp, J., Nelson, E., & Bekkedal, M. (1997). Brain systems for the mediation of social separation-distress and social-reward. *Annals of the New York Academy of Sciences, 807,* 78–100.

Zeifman, D., & Hazan, C. (1997). A process model of adult attachment formation. In S. Duck (Ed.), *Handbook of personal relationships: Theory, research and interventions* (2nd ed., pp. 179–195). Thousand Oaks, CA: Sage.

PART 5

Bridges With Relationship Science, Interaction, and Health

INTRODUCTION

By virtue of its definition emphasizing the reciprocal influences between an individual and the social environment, social psychology is closely connected to relationship science and social interaction. After all, relationships are the core of the social environment. Although the individual and the partner represent two different entities, it is also true that relationships tend to have a life of their own, especially close relationships such as marriage, dating relationships, or parent–child relationships. Thoughts, emotions, habits, and behavioral style are strongly shaped in such relationships, often (but by no means, always) in ways that help people maintain well-functioning relationships. Relationships are strongly connected to social interactions, which impact relationships most fundamentally—for better or worse. Social interactions also extend relationships, in that we also spend a good deal of our time interacting with others with whom we do not have a strong relationship. Social interactions are central to social psychology, in that our thoughts and emotions shape social interactions, which in turn form the basis of learning, adaptation, and relationship development. Moreover, social interactions focus on basic processes that are described in terms of basic concepts such as love, power, and respect. Although health is not directly linked to the interpersonal system, there is increasing evidence that relationships and interactions are central to understanding mental and physical health. For example, relationships are a key predictor of psychological health, physical health, and life expectancy, and health-related habits and behaviors are often strongly influenced by interacting with close partners, and friends. As shown in the various essays, relationship science and interactions are essential to social psychology and have strong implications for mental and physical health.

251

37

The Relationship Context of Social Psychology

Harry T. Reis
University of Rochester

Sooner or later, anyone who teaches social psychology is asked an integral question: "Where's the *social* in social psychology?" We typically answer in one of several ways. We may point out that social behavior is powerfully influenced by beliefs about and perceptions of social entities, and much social psychological research is designed to shed light on these basic processes. Another common reply involves listing the many topics whose social component is readily apparent: altruism, aggression, conformity, prejudice, intergroup behavior, etc. A third possibility is to suggest that the processes studied by social psychologists, although not necessarily social in central emphasis, provide the fundamental building blocks of social behavior.

These responses, sound and sensible as they are, often leave lingering hesitation: If so, why do so many research protocols seem tangentially social, involving little more than a superficial association between participants and a social target? For example, the social entity in research is commonly a stranger, hypothetical person, or terse message about which scant knowledge is available and little interest exists, or a social category made accessible with minimal information (e.g., a word, phrase, vignette, picture, or subliminal cue). Of course, we social psychologists use such stimuli and procedures for important methodological (and sometimes pragmatic and ethical) reasons. We take justifiable pride in the rigor of our methods for controlling extraneous sources of variance, for unconfounding the mechanisms that underlie a manipulation, and for teasing apart complex phenomena until their most elemental components have been identified. Although this strategy of evermore exacting analysis is the essence of good science, it may also incur a cost not often considered. That cost concerns the impact of relationship contexts. In everyday life, social interaction involves others with whom we are interdependent: Their behavior influences our choices and outcomes, and our behavior influences their choices and outcomes. To varying degrees, we care about their welfare and they care about ours. Because we have a history of interaction with them, and are knowledgeable about their associations with others, we approach interaction with well-developed expectations. And we expect our interactions to continue. In short, we have relationships with them.

The importance of relationships has not gone unnoticed. Although in the typical social psychology textbook of the 1970s, the word *relationship* might have appeared primarily as justification for studying initial attraction, or as a synonym for correlation, most contemporary textbooks have major sections or chapters devoted to the operation of social psychological processes in close relationships. Such recognition, although certainly a step in the right direction, belies a pair of more fundamental concerns: that relationships typically are treated as a somewhat peripheral specialized topic, and that the flow of insights is largely unidirectional, from basic social psychological processes to relationships, rather than bidirectional.

The premise of this essay is that something more is needed. I propose that relationships and their impact on interpersonal behavior ought to be the central topic of social psychology, integrated fully across the field's major theories and accumulated knowledge. This proposal is based on a straightforward idea: On some level and to varying extents, *all* social behavior is influenced by its relationship context. In other words, social behavior depends on—is moderated by—whom the individual is with and his or her mental representations, expectancies, goals, and outcome interdependence regarding that person. Thus, when social psychology ascribes to itself the task of illuminating the impact of situations on behavior (the "E" in $B = f[P,E]$), we should include relationship context in our calculations. To the individuals involved, little about the environment is more salient than whom one is with (or thinking about) and the nature of one's relationship with them.

Articulating the causal role of relationship contexts highlights the fact that social psychology is intrinsically a bridging discipline. Imagine a continuum anchored on one end by sciences that focus on molecular (and even submolecular) biological systems and on the other end by macrosocietal processes (Hinde, 1997). Social psychology has historically occupied a critical juncture on this continuum—the interface of the individual's internal processes (i.e., cognition, emotion, and motivation) and his or her interactions with the external environment in dyads, groups, and collectives. In other words, social psychology can, should, and to some extent already does provide a conceptual and methodological bridge between disciplines that study internal processes and disciplines that focus on the extrapersonal environment toward which so many of these internal processes are fundamentally oriented. If social psychology exists to provide insights about this interface, we would do well to recognize that the traffic director on this bridge is the relationship context of behavior.

RELATIONSHIP CONTEXT EFFECTS IN SOCIAL PSYCHOLOGY

A few brief highlights from research on social cognition, emotion, and motivation may help illustrate this general principle. Although comprehensive review is not feasible within space limits, Reis, Collins and Berscheid (2000) provide more extensive discussion.

Consider the self-serving attributional bias, one of the field's most robust phenomena: Relative to judgments about strangers, people give themselves more credit for success and less responsibility for failure. This principle does not generalize to close relationship partners, who are accorded the same attributional generosity as is the self (Sedikides, Campbell, Reeder, & Elliot, 1998). Research on the benefits of positive illusions suggests that in happy relationships romantic partners are accorded even greater positivity than the self (Murray, Holmes, & Griffin, 1996). Another oft-noted self-serving bias is the tendency to present oneself to others in a self-enhancing manner. However, with close friends self-presentational tendencies tend to be more modest (Tice, Butler, Muraven, & Stillwell, 1995).

A somewhat different example is provided by research that examines linkages between mental representations of self and others. Aron, Aron, Tudor, and Nelson (1991) demonstrated that social cognition about close others is more similar to cognition about the self than to cognition about strangers and acquaintances. Perhaps this is because the interdependent frame of reference commonly adopted by close partners ("we" rather than "you and I") engenders, in a connectionist model, a relatively greater number of direct connections and overlapping links between self and other (Smith, Coats, & Walling, 1999). A recent neural imaging study by Lichty et al. (2003) supports this conjecture. They showed substantial overlap in the brain regions activated by hearing one's own name and the name of a close friend—most strongly, in the right superior frontal gyrus and prefrontal cortex—but no overlap in the areas of activation associated with hearing one's own name and the name of a familiar (but not close) other. Moreover, the degree of overlap in the own-name and close-friend conditions was greater to the extent that the relationship was perceived as close.

Although most research has focused on mental representations of social categories (e.g., stereotypic categories, attachment figures), memory also includes discrete representations for specific persons, particularly those who play or have played an important role in one's life. Many contemporary theories incorporate varying levels of complexity, ranging from broad generalizations about social categories to highly differentiated representations of particular individuals. The latter, although rarely investigated, may exert substantial influence on social behavior, as Andersen's research shows (this volume).

Turning to emotion, many scholars agree with Zajonc's (1998) characterization of emotions as "the basis of social interaction ... the products of social interaction, their origins, and their currency" (pp. 619–620). It may seem ironic therefore that "interpersonal functions [of emotion] have generally been given short shrift in comparison to intrapersonal functions ... [although most researchers] believe that emotions are brought into play most often by the actions of others, and, once aroused, emotions influence the course of interpersonal transactions" (Ekman & Davidson, p. 139). Not all emotions occur in interactions with partners in ongoing relationships, but most are better understood by considering the relationship context in which they arise.

This assertion follows directly from the definition of emotion as a response to environmental events that have significance for personal well-being. To the extent that relationships differ, the same event may have different consequences for personal well-being. Some emotions are unlikely to arise outside of certain types of relationship (e.g., jealousy, pride, maternal or romantic love, lust, guilt). For other emotions, the likelihood, intensity, and nature of expression typically are influenced by the individual's relationship with the target of the emotion. For example, reactions to an affectionate smile or a rude comment likely differ depending on whether its source is one's new lover, junior colleague, teenage daughter, or automobile mechanic.

Some theories acknowledge the link between the emotion-eliciting power of situations and relationship context. For example, Berscheid and Ammazzalorso (2001) posit expectancy violation as the proximate cause of emotion. The more interdependent two persons are, the stronger, more numerous, and more consequential are their expectations of each other. Other research indicates that people's willingness to communicate about emotions, either verbally or nonverbally, depends on their relationship with the recipient of that communication (Clark, Fitness, & Brissette, 2001; Zajonc, 1998). A similar conclusion applies to the sharing of emotional experiences through such processes as emotional contagion, physiological synchrony, vicarious arousal, and rapport.

Research also underscores the role of relationship context in the emergence and impact of social motives. It will surprise no reader of this essay to point out that social motives such as empathic concern and the willingness to help are powerfully affected by the relationship between help-seeker and help-giver: People tend to be more concerned with the welfare of relatives and close friends than of strangers. More generally, if motivation is defined as the energization and regulation of goal-directed activity, then it is apparent that relationship contexts affect both the goals that are sought and the means of their pursuit. Almost all theories of human well-being posit the attainment of close, satisfying relationships as a basic human drive and the failure to obtain them as a primary cause of distress (Baumeister & Leary, 1995). Moreover, persons with whom the individual has a meaningful relationship—particularly parents, partners, and role models—are influential in the internalization of values and standards (Higgins, 1987).

Relationships likewise contribute to self-regulatory behavior. People use relationships to pursue desired outcomes in diverse ways—seeking social support, regulating moods through social interaction, enlisting guidance and material assistance, recruiting collaborators in self-handicapping activity, and so on. Although the mechanisms by which relationship contexts affect these processes are not well understood, it is clear that their reach includes both important activities (e.g., marriage, divorce, procreation, education, illness, and employment changes) and trivial pursuits (e.g., choosing a movie on Saturday night). Many seemingly personal choices have consequences for those with whom we are interdependent and therefore require transformation of purely personal motives to take partners' needs and preferences into account.

CONCLUSIONS

My thesis is that nearly all social psychological processes are to some extent influenced by relationship contexts. Further and diverse examples, beyond those already noted, may be found in research on prejudice, persuasion, attribution, social identity, aggression, stigma, coping, health, justice, and self-evaluation, among various topics. A functional analysis of the role of relationships in human evolution suggests why this is so. Few would disagree that humans evolved in an intensely social context: Because traits and behavioral mechanisms adapted to participation in ongoing relationships and groups were pivotal in survival and reproduction, the full complement of innate human cognitive, emotional, and behavioral tendencies has been shaped by evolutionary forces to contend with and capitalize on the necessity of living and interacting with others (Bugental, this volume; Buss & Kenrick, 1998).

Some chapters in this volume discuss the increasing popularity of culture as a causal construct in social psychology—how cultural factors affect cognition, emotion, and motivation. In my view, the arguments for cultural context and relationship context are similar and linked, inasmuch as the impact of culture may be understood in terms of systematic differences in the nature of relationships. For example, key dimensions of cross-cultural analysis such as individualism–collectivism and power distance represent different relationship norms and how those norms are applied in common situations.

Earlier I proposed that social psychology is inherently a bridging discipline, and that relationships often provide a "traffic director" on that bridge. This social psychological bridge spans a chasm of considerable importance to virtually all of the human sciences: how the left bank of internal processes regulates interaction with the right bank of the external environment, especially its social elements. The examples reviewed here indicate that the unfolding of these processes depends on the relationship between interacting persons. Thus, a situation with potential for compassion and prosociality or alternatively for prejudice and discrimination is likely to activate different processes and yield divergent results depending on whether the target is family member or stranger, ingroup or outgroup, desired love-partner or disliked pest, long-standing friend or long-time competitor.

To be sure, many elements of this line of reasoning appear throughout the social psychological literature; nonetheless they tend to be implicit, imprecise, or unstated. In my opinion, the social-psychological bridge would be sturdier if these considerations became explicit and systematic, and were subjected to empirical scrutiny and formal theorizing. In so doing, we might also increase traffic flow on the social-psychological bridge, by providing a roadway for scholars in other disciplines who seek to traverse the gap between internal processes and the external world. Recent developments on both sides of the continuum described earlier have highlighted the importance of this avenue. Biologists, neuroscientists, and medical researchers increasingly seek ways to integrate knowledge about the systems they study with insights about the social world to which these systems are adapted. Likewise, understanding the behavior of individuals is increasingly relevant to the work of political scientists, economists, and historians, and that behavior, as discussed earlier, is often situated in a relationship context.

A recent editorial in *Science* argued that future scientific breakthroughs are likely to occur at the boundary between disciplines. Social psychology can maximize its contribution to these advances by renewing its focus on what is truly social in social psychology.

REFERENCES

Aron, A., Aron, E., Tudor, M., & Nelson, G. (1991). Close relationships as including other in self. *Journal of Personality and Social Psychology, 60,* 241–253.

Baumeister, R. F., & Leary, M. (1995). The need to belong: Desire for interpersonal attachment as a fundamental human motivation. *Psychological Bulletin, 117,* 497–529.

Berscheid, E., & Ammazzalorso, H. (2001). Emotional experience in close relationships. In M. Hewstone & M. Brewer (Eds.), *Blackwell handbook of social psychology* (pp. 308–330). Oxford, UK: Blackwell.

Buss, D., & Kenrick, D. (1998). Evolutionary social psychology. In D. Gilbert & S. Fiske (Eds.), *Handbook of social psychology* (Vol. 2, 4th ed., pp. 982–1026). Boston: McGraw-Hill.

Clark, M., Fitness, J., & Brissette, I. (2001). Understanding people's perceptions of relationships is crucial to understanding their emotional lives. In M. Hewstone & M. Brewer (Eds.), *Blackwell handbook of social psychology* (pp. 253–278). Oxford, UK: Blackwell.

Ekman, P., & Davidson, R. (1994). *The nature of emotion: Fundamental questions.* New York: Oxford.

Higgins, E. T. (1987). Self-discrepancy: A theory relating self and affect. *Psychological Review, 94,* 319–340.

Hinde, R. A. (1997). *Relationships: A dialectical perspective.* East Sussex, England: Psychology Press.

Lichty, W., Chyou, J., Aron, A., Anderson, A., Ghahremani, D., & Gabrieli, J. (2004). *Neural correlates of subjective closeness: An fMRI study.* Poster presented at the Society for Neuroscience meeting, San Diego, CA.

Murray, S., Holmes, J. G., & Griffin, D. (1996). The benefits of positive illusions: Idealization and the construction of satisfaction in close relationships. *Journal of Personality and Social Psychology, 70,* 79–98.

Reis, H. T., Collins, W., & Berscheid, E. (2000). The relationship context of human behavior and development. *Psychological Bulletin, 126,* 844–872.

Sedikides, C., Campbell, W., Reeder, G., & Elliot, A. (1998). The self-serving bias in relational context. *Journal of Personality and Social Psychology, 74,* 378–386.

Smith, E., Coats, S., & Walling, D. (1999). Overlapping mental representations of self, ingroup, and partner: Further response time evidence and a connectionist model. *Personality and Social Psychology Bulletin, 25,* 873–882.

Tice, D. M., Butler, J., Muraven, M., & Stillwell, A. M. (1995). When modesty prevails: Differential favorability of self-presentation to friends and strangers. *Journal of Personality and Social Psychology, 69,* 1120–1138.

Zajonc, R. B. (1998). Emotions. In D. Gilbert, S. Fiske, & G. Lindzey (Eds.), *Handbook of social psychology* (Vol. 2, 4th ed., pp. 591–632). New York: McGraw-Hill.

38

Relationship Neuroscience: Advancing the Social Psychology of Close Relationships Using Functional Neuroimaging

Arthur Aron

State University of New York, Stony Brooks

Human beings live most of their lives in close relationships; throughout time, our survival, reproduction, joys, and sufferings have been primarily in the context of these relationships, which entail very basic motivations and needs (e.g., Baumeister & Leary, 1995; Reis, Collins, & Berscheid, 2000). Thus, the human brain evolved in a relationship context and is therefore likely to be in no small part a relational brain.

The last 30 years have seen dramatic progress in uncovering the systematic principles of behavior and experience in human close relationships. This work has become a major subspecialty of social psychology and allied fields such as communication and family studies—an interdisciplinary effort increasingly conscious of itself as "relationship science" (Berscheid, 1999). Simultaneously, there has been dramatic progress in understanding the brain and the methodologies for doing so. In the last decade, cognitive psychologists, and more recently social psychologists, have started to make use of these brain-related methods. Particularly central have been functional magnetic resonance imaging (fMRI) studies that manipulate stimuli or tasks and examine the resulting spatial distribution of brain activity. Thus, for example, "cognitive neuroscience" (Posner & DiGirolamo, 2000) has found distinct brain regions associated with different memory processes. Similarly, "social neuroscience" (Cacioppo, 2002) and "social-cognitive neuroscience" (Ochsner &

Lieberman, 2001) are exploring such issues as intergroup prejudice and whether specific brain activations correspond differentially to explicit and implicit indicators of prejudice (Phelps et al., 2000). Thus, it seems timely to examine the potential for relationship science to benefit from including such neuroscience methods in its toolbox.

In a typical fMRI experiment, a participant is placed in a scanner and alternately presented with an experimental and control version of a stimulus or task. For example, consider a recently completed study (Aron et al., 2005) examining various issues related to early-stage romantic love that have been difficult to sort out with conventional methods. In this study, we scanned participants who were intensely "in love" while they alternately viewed photos of their beloved and of a familiar but emotionally neutral person. The main direct result of an fMRI experiment of this kind is a map showing the areas of the brain that are significantly more active during the experimental stimulus or task than during the control stimulus or task. (These maps are based on changes in magnetic polarization of oxygen molecules in the blood, so that "activation" means increased blood flow to that area, presumably as a result of energy used in local electrical/chemical transactions.) These maps provide the primary foundation for testing the psychological issues of interest.

HOW FMRI EXPERIMENTS CAN CONTRIBUTE TO RELATIONSHIP SCIENCE

Localization. How can showing that a particular stimulus or task activates a particular brain region bear on hypotheses of interest to relationship scientists? One approach builds on knowledge of functions already known to be linked with a particular region. For example, a theory-based hypothesis we tested in the Aron et al. (2005) study was that early-stage romantic love is better conceptualized as a motivation like hunger or thirst than as a specific emotion like happiness or sadness. Thus, we predicted activations in areas known to be associated with motivation and reward, particularly dopamine-rich systems such as those involving the ventral tegmental area (VTA) and the caudate nucleus. Associations of motivation and reward with these areas are well established in animal studies and in previous neuroimaging work. Thus, we took it as substantial support for our motivation model that the key brain areas we found to be engaged by viewing the beloved were indeed highly localized to the VTA and caudate.

In a different illustration of this strategy, Lichty et al. (2004) provided unique evidence for Leary and Baumeister's (2000) "sociometer model," that trait self-esteem is linked to expected social acceptance/rejection. We found that participants' scores on Rosenberg's self-esteem questionnaire correlated very highly with fMRI activations occurring while hearing one's own name, in a particular section of the anterior cingulate cortex—the very same precise region recently shown in an independent fMRI study to become active when participants experience "rejection" from supposed peers in an experimental task (Eisenberger, Lieberman, & Williams, 2003).

Other examples of constructs for which localizing associated brain activation might help address important theoretical issues are dependence, jealousy, trust, and nurturance.

Common Localization of Two Processes. If two different stimuli or tasks in the same experiment generate activation in a common brain area, this lends support to hypotheses proposing that there is at least one underlying common process. For example, we have proposed that people treat close others, to some extent, like the self—that close others are "included in the self" (Aron, Aron, Tudor, & Nelson, 1991). Thus, we are currently conducting an fMRI study in which participants rate traits to describe themselves, a close other, and a familiar nonclose other (a media personality). Preliminary results suggest that there is more overlap between areas activated when rating traits for self and for close others than there is for either of these with rating traits for nonclose others. Similarly, Aron, Whitfield and Lichty (in press), in a different aspect of the name/self-esteem experiment mentioned earlier (Lichty et al., 2004), found that the spatial distribution of fMRI activations in response to hearing one's own name had substantially more in common with hearing the name of a close other than with hearing other familiar names. An example of another relationship issue that might be studied by looking for common areas of activation would be the overlap of representations of one's primary caregiver (e.g., a parent) and one's romantic partner, as predicted by attachment and transference models.

Distinctive Localization of Two Processes. Neuroimaging experiments can also provide evidence bearing on hypotheses about the distinctiveness of two processes. For example, in our early-stage romantic love fMRI study (Aron et al., 2005), the areas activated were quite different from the brain areas known from previous research to be associated with sexual desire. Thus, these findings supported our hypothesis that romantic love and sexual desire are not identical processes, a perennial issue that has been difficult to sort out by other methods. Another example is a preliminary study by Fiske, Iacoboni, Knowlton, and Liberman (2001) in which fMRI participants found different activation patterns when participants viewed brief scenarios representing different types of relationships, such as communal versus ranking relationships.

Implicit Measures. Once a brain area is linked with a particular process, activation of that area becomes a potential measure of that process. For example, in our romantic-love study (Aron et al., 2005), there was a very strong correlation between degree of activation in a specific area of the caudate when viewing the beloved with participants' scores on Hatfield and Sprecher's Passionate Love Scale. This provides unique validity evidence for the scale and also suggests that activation in this area might serve as an implicit measure of passionate love in contexts in which self-report would be problematic. The same reasoning applies to the correlation noted earlier, from the Lichty et al. (2004) study, in which we found a strong correlation of anterior cingulate activation when hearing one's own name with the Rosenberg self-esteem scale.

CONTRIBUTIONS OF RELATIONSHIP SCIENCE TO NEUROSCIENCE

This essay focuses on the potential contributions of neuroscience to relationship science. However, given the key role of relationships in shaping the human brain, there may be even greater potential for relationship science to contribute to neuroscience. For example, the unusually intense experiences we were able to examine in our early-stage romantic love fMRI study (Aron et al., 2005) provided an opportunity to examine basic neuroscience issues related to the separation of reward processing into "wanting" and "liking" (Berridge & Robinson, 2003), with wanting being the reward associated with motivation and liking being a cognitive evaluation. Our data showed activation in different areas for liking and wanting and will help neuroscientists to further define reward systems.

LIMITATIONS, COSTS, AND OBSTACLES
FOR RELATIONSHIP SCIENTISTS

Design Limitations. Most fMRI studies employ within-subject designs, comparing activations when viewing one kind of stimulus or task versus viewing another kind of stimulus or task. There are substantial individual differences in brain functioning, so that between-subject fMRI experiments (or correlational studies with subtle individual difference variables) typically have low power. Further, uncontrolled variation of brain activation over time requires presenting each stimulus or task multiple times, raising problems of habituation or sensitization. Finally, participants must be completely still; they cannot speak and responses are largely limited to pressing one of a few keys.

Interpretation Limitations. There are two main potential pitfalls when interpreting results from the standard fMRI design, comparing activation from one kind of stimulus or task versus a control stimulus or task. First, as with any experiment, the control and experimental conditions can differ in ways other than what was intended. For example, in our romantic-love study, it was possible that the beloved faces were more physically attractive than the neutral faces. In this case, we had measured attractiveness and were thus able to test for its potentially confounding influence. The second major interpretation issue is that one cannot assume activation of the brain area is the cause of the process studied. For example, in our romantic-love study, looking at one's beloved caused activation in the VTA–caudate dopamine system. But does activation of this system cause one to feel love? In this case, we located a report from 40 years ago in which a brain surgery patient reported an intense feeling of love when the caudate had been electrically stimulated, providing some relevant evidence regarding causal direction. More generally, a promising method for solving this problem in humans is transcranial magnetic stimulation (TMS), a method of safely inhibiting for a split second a localized brain area near the surface of the skull. One applies TMS simultaneously with the stimulus and tests whether responses are slowed or disturbed. We think this is so important that we are currently setting up to use TMS in our including-other-in-the-self studies.

Money and Time. A typical fMRI experiment is more costly than a typical relationship-related laboratory experiment or questionnaire study, but is comparable to or less costly than many more elaborate relationship studies. Most fMRI studies involve only 10–20 participants, do not involve both members of a relationship, and rarely take more than 2 hours of participant time. Thus, scanning and participant payment cost considerably less than, for example, most longitudinal relationship studies. Similarly, although the postscan analysis time can be considerable, often involving as much as a month's full-time work of a technician (or grad student) per participant, again, this may be comparable or less costly than, for example, relationship studies involving microanalytic coding of behavioral interactions.

THE SOCIAL PSYCHOLOGY OF RELATIONSHIP NEUROSCIENCE

In neuroscience, collaborations are essential. But forming and nourishing strong collaborations is time-consuming, and working together across cultures as different as social psychology and neuroscience is a significant challenge. In addition, professionally, departments, journals, and grant panels are highly monodisciplinary, and colleagues may see cross-disciplinary work as exciting but peripheral. Finally, it is difficult to be sufficiently sophisticated and well socialized outside one's core area to communicate effectively with journal and grant reviewers from outside areas. The solution, again, is to develop a strong and committed collaborative team. In brief, this is all a wonderful opportunity for self-expansion!

CONCLUSIONS

The human brain evolved in a highly relationship-centered context. Thus, relationship neuroscience, bridging the study of close relationships and the study of the brain, has the potential to offer major contributions to both fields. We hope that this essay highlights the great potential for a close relationship between these two fields, which have so far been largely unacquainted strangers.

REFERENCES

Aron, A., Aron, E. N., Tudor, M., & Nelson, G. (1991). Close relationships as including other in the self. *Journal of Personality and Social Psychology, 60,* 241–253.

Aron, A., Fisher, H., Mashek, D., Strong, G., Li, H., & Brown, L. L. (2005). Reward, motivation and emotion systems associated with early-stage intense romantic love. *Journal of Neurophysiology, 93,* 327–337.

Aron, A., Whitfield, S., & Lichty, W. (in press). Whole brain correlations: Examining similarity across conditions of overall patterns of neural activation in fMRI. In S. Sawilowsky (Ed.), *Real data analysis.* Washington, DC: American Educational Research Association.

Baumeister, R. F., & Leary, M. R. (1995). The need to belong: Desire for interpersonal attachments as a fundamental human motivation. *Psychological Bulletin, 117,* 497–529.

Berridge, K. C., & Robinson, T. E. (2003). Parsing reward. *Trends in Neuroscience, 26,* 507–513.

Berscheid, E. (1999). The greening of relationship science. *American Psychologist, 54,* 260–266.

Cacioppo, J. T. (2002). Social neuroscience: Understanding the pieces fosters understanding the whole and vice versa. *American Psychologist, 57,* 819–831.

Eisenberger, N., Lieberman, M., & Williams, K. (2003). Does rejection hurt? An fMRI study of social exclusion. *Science, 302,* 290–292.

Fiske, A. P., Iacoboni, M., Knowlton, B., & Lieberman, M. (2001, April). *Interpreting communal and ranking relationships: First results from an fMRI study.* Paper presented at International Conference on Social Cognitive Neuroscience, Los Angeles.

Leary, M. R., & Baumeister, R. F. (2000). The nature and function of self-esteem: Sociometer theory. In M. P. Zanna (Ed.), *Advances in experimental social psychology* (Vol. 32, pp. 1–62). San Diego: Academic Press.

Lichty, W., Chyou, J., Aron, A., Anderson, A. K., Ghahremanni, D., Ochsner, K., & Gabrieli, J. D. E. (2004, April). *Neural correlates of self-esteem: An fMRI study.* Paper presented at Cognitive Neuroscience Society, San Francisco.

Ochsner, K. N., & Lieberman, M. D. (2001). The emergence of social cognitive neuroscience. *American Psychologist, 56,* 717–734.

Phelps, E. A., O'Connor, K. J., Cunningham, W. A., Funayama, E. S., Gatenby, J. C., Gore, J. C., & Banaji, M. R. (2000). Performance on indirect measures of race evaluation predicts amygdala activation. *Journal of Cognitive Neuroscience, 12,* 729–738.

Posner, M. I., & DiGirolamo, G. J. (2000). Cognitive neuroscience: Origins and promise. *Psychological Bulletin, 126,* 873–889.

Reis, H. T., Collins, W. A., & Berscheid, E. (2000). The relationship context of human behavior and development. *Psychological Bulletin, 126,* 844–872.

39

Identifying the Tasks of Social Life: Using Other Disciplines to Understand the Nature of Social Situations

John G. Holmes
University of Waterloo

Social psychologists are supposedly wedded to the Lewinian notion that understanding and predicting behavior depends on our ability to specify the "mands" of a situation, the psychological pushes and pulls reflective of the environment. But our conduct as scientists seems to belie this maxim. Social psychologists have seldom devoted much effort to descriptive research portraying the variety of different types of situations with which people must cope, the social "tasks" or problems they face in their everyday activities. Further, there have been even fewer attempts to develop a theoretical system for categorizing the features of such concrete situations in an abstract fashion. Sometimes it seems as if it is not even obvious what the term *situation* actually means to social psychologists (Holmes, 2000, 2002).

In this chapter I argue that much could be gained by social psychology through building bridges to disciplines such as anthropology, sociology, and economics, which have studied in more depth the nature of the types of situations that people encounter in their physical and social environments. Following the functionalist logic of ecological psychology, I suggest that knowledge of the social tasks that people confront will tell us much about the mechanisms they develop to deal with those realities. That is, cognition and behavior, the mechanisms so central to social psychologists, will be designed to mediate the reality of the situations people encounter (Holmes, 2004). Further, I contend that people's characteristic ways of coping with situations, their "personalities," will depend in important ways on the *distribution* of the type of situations people experience, the "landscape" or "geography" of their environment. Thus, an understanding of the nature of situations experienced in people's personal worlds will tell us much about their psychological processes.

THE METATHEORY: THE TENETS OF ECOLOGICAL PSYCHOLOGY

The assumption of the ecological psychology perspective is that there is a "reality" of the phenomena in any particular domain of the person's interaction with the world (MacArthur & Baron, 1983; Shepard, 1992). Or as Campbell (1993) suggested in his "hypothetical or fallible realism" position, "the world as it is" is a "co-selector" of beliefs, along with the social construction process. It is assumed that cognition and behavior are adapted to and mediate that reality and, therefore, that our understanding of their essential features requires us to specify and take into account that reality (see Kelley, 1997). Such arguments are quite explicit in much of John Anderson's writing on cognitive processes (expressed in the ACT acronym, which refers to the "adaptive control of thought"), and in cognitive neuroscience more generally. In Anderson's words, "The mind has the structure it has because the world has the structure it has" (1991, p. 428). The approach is expressed by Marr (1982) as, "An algorithm [read "process"] is likely to be understood more readily by understanding the nature of the problem being solved than by examining the mechanisms ... in which it is embodied" (p. 27).

The ecological approach is seldom applied to any domain approaching the complexity of interpersonal phenomena, perhaps because to do so would require a characterization of the "reality" of social situations. However, that reality can be provisionally characterized on intuitive or theoretical grounds, as is often done by evolutionary theorists, whose thinking represents one type of functionalist perspective. For instance, Tooby and Cosmides (1996) suggested in their parable of the "Banker's Paradox" that a serious problem for our primitive ancestors was to determine whom to count on in situations of dependence where help was desperately needed. They argued that this problem would have resulted in evolutionary pressures for adaptations in people's cognitive machinery that would effectively tune it to calibrating the extent to which they were valued by close others, that is, to issues of trust versus suspicion in distinguishing "fair-weather friends" from loyal intimates (see Kelley et al., 2003, for a full discussion).

THE GEOGRAPHY OF CURRENT SOCIAL SITUATIONS

The functionalist, ecological perspective does not require anthropologists and others to focus on reconstructing the history of our hunter-gatherer ancestors, although there is considerable merit in doing so for evolutionary arguments. Instead, much could be gained from a better understanding of the current tasks or problems people most frequently face within their culture that require social coordination or action. The particular nature of their "social environment" should shape people's social beliefs, the customs and rules of their culture, and, ultimately, their personalities. The social psychological hypothesis would be that common elements across cultures would reflect experiences in dealing with similar situations on a regular basis, whereas differences would reflect variability in the landscape of situations.

As an illustration of this logic from anthropology, Pinker (1997, pp. 505–506) provided the compelling example of a study of a contemporary Paraguayan tribe that hunts game and gathers plant foods. Although hunting is unpredictable and largely a matter of luck, foraging for food is more a matter of effort. As a situational analysis might lead one to predict (see Kelley et al., 2003), communal sharing of meat based on need occurred throughout the band, apparently as a solution to the problem of substantial uncertainty in success in hunting. In contrast, equity rules of exchange that link outcomes to the effort invested applied to other foods, with communal sharing only taking place in the nuclear family. Pinker thus suggested that people should be driven to develop communal sharing rules in their groups in domains of their environment where they are subject to the whims of fate.

In this regard, Tooby and Cosmides (1996) pointed out that in highly developed modern societies people live in environments that are far more predictable and safe, and there is less need for normative solutions in the broader group to deal with unpredictable fates and reversals of fortune. Despite this, individuals can find themselves dependent on a circle of close others for support during times involving ill health, financial crisis, child care, and so on. After all, marital vows often emphasize that partners must care for each other, "for richer or poorer, for good times or bad times." Thus communal rules of responding according to a person's needs may be more limited to family and close friends in modern society (Clark & Mills, 1993; Kelley et al., 2003). This proposition, however, is likely to be modified by the sociology of the family unit and the security of the group within the fabric of the larger society. For example, recent Mexican-Americans immigrants may apply communal rules more extensively across the extended family and even to fellow subgroup members to reflect the vicissitudes of economic stress in their new and challenging environment.

These particular examples highlight the important class of situations in which people confront unpredictable circumstances, affording the opportunity for others to serve as human "insurance." The effective solution to this social problem requires depending on the support of others, diminishing risk by spreading it across people. There is, of course, a wide variety of other important types of "situations" with which people must cope that are quite different in nature. But what exactly are they? It seems reasonable to suggest that when "situations" are characterized in abstract terms, anthropologists and sociologists could provide important evidence about both the variety of different life tasks and social problems, as well as the relative frequency with which each of them occur in different cultures. The frequency of occurrence in specific groups would of course vary as a function of the challenges posed by the "geography" of the proximal physical and social environment.

In a similar vein, economists often attempt to identify common decision dilemmas in an abstract form. For instance, Thaler (1992) discussed a variety of theoretical "game" structures relevant to describing the types of economic situations people face. The "Tragedy of the Commons" parable is probably familiar to most readers, for instance. It involves the problem of access to a limited resource that benefits the common good, such as shared grazing pasture. Unmitigated individual self-interest is likely to tempt people to behave in ways that collectively result in overuse of the resource, ultimately hurting everybody. The situation highlights the proverbial tension between "me versus we," and the challenge it represents seems clearly evident in a wide variety of ways in modern Western societies (see Kelley et al., 2003).

Another situation, the "Ultimatum Game," is a metaphor for monopolist pricing in a free marketplace. One person has control over the cost of a product, whereas others' concerns over fairness will determine their "loyalty" in terms of continuing to buy the product. For example, a merchant may not overprice his hotel rooms during college homecoming week if he believes his regular clients will judge him to be an unjust "gouger" and desert ship. A parallel logic describes the relation between a traditional husband who controls the pursestrings in a marriage and the reactions of his wife: Her loyalty to the relationship is likely to depend on her perceptions of his fairness in allocating resources (Kelley et al., 2003).

A THEORY-DERIVED DESCRIPTION OF SITUATIONS

Although there would be much to gain by developing an empirically based, bottom-up classification system identifying important types of situations, another approach would be to derive a top-down system on the basis of theoretical derivations. Such a formal classification system is detailed in the collaborative work *An Atlas of Interpersonal Situations* (Kelley et al., 2003). Social situations are defined in terms of the properties of interdependence among persons, in the Lewinian (1946) tradition. Each situation is specified abstractly in terms of the persons' most prominent behavioral options in the interaction and the particular ways in which these behaviors influence each other's outcomes. The abstract pattern of possible outcomes reflects the "dilemma" individuals must deal with, the social problem that a situation poses for people.

The theoretical framework involves a taxonomy of such situations based on six theoretically derived features or dimensions of interdependence. Kelley et al. suggested that there are a limited number of unique, prototypical social situations (about two dozen) that have distinctive and interesting properties in terms of the type of problem or opportunity they pose for people. All examples discussed so far are prototypes, as are such familiar situations as Chicken,

Prisoner's Dilemma, conjunctive versus disjunctive problems, delay of gratification, and so on.

It is important that any such theory-driven system be reconciled with reality-based benchmarks. The system should obviously be capable of categorizing the everyday, concrete examples of situations identified as important by empirically oriented scientists in other disciplines. If it is able to do so, the benefit is that the theory would aid in the task of abstracting the key features of situations, permitting the generalization of common basic processes across seemingly disparate concrete situations. Thus it is a two-way street, and other fields may learn a fair amount about the identity and structure of situations from this conceptual scheme and classic social psychological studies more generally.

Kelley and Holmes (2003) proposed that the situations identified in the *Atlas* vary in terms of the particular interpersonal goals or dispositions—the "decision rules"—relevant to coping with the specific problems the situations present. Thus, the linkages between the situation and person domains are ones of logical relevance or *affordance*. As an example, situations extended in time that reward mutual delay of gratification afford people the opportunity to express dependability and loyalty. By distinguishing the rules logically applicable to various situations, we essentially identify the various attitudes, motives, and values that guide interpersonal behavior within them. When the various rules are aggregated across situations, they are quite limited in number and tend to fit together in clusters that have common higher order themes in terms of their function. We suggest that these rules are the very essence of "personality" and that essentially, personality should be viewed as the characteristic set of preferences that is functional in guiding a person's behavior in social situations.

This social psychological theory of personality development contends that the major dimensions of personality can be deduced from a "bottom-up" analysis of the specific social situations that individuals have confronted on a regular basis in their interdependence with others. Thus, knowledge of the frequency with which individuals in a particular group or culture encounter particular types or classes of situations would help scientists predict the nature of the interpersonal dispositions that would develop to deal with their social environment. Cultural, social class, and geographical differences in people's personalities and goals should not be assumed to occur haphazardly, but instead should be a predictable function of the "situation space" they inhabit.

CONCLUSIONS

If social psychologists are to be true to their Lewinian (1946) heritage, they must devote considerably more energy to understanding the fabric of the social situations that people encounter in their everyday lives. I suggest that we have much to learn from our sister disciplines of anthropology, sociology, and economics, which have invested more effort in systematically describing the nature of the social tasks and interdependence problems that people encounter.

REFERENCES

Anderson, J. R. (1991). The adaptive nature of human categorization. *Psychological Review, 98*, 409–429.

Campbell, D. T. (1993). Plausible coselection of belief by referent: All the "objectivity" that is possible. *Perspectives on Science: Historical, Philisophical, Social, 1*, 85–105.

Clark, M. S., & Mills., J. (1993). The difference between communal and exchange relationships: What it is and is not. *Personality and Social Psychology Bulletin, 19*, 684–691.

Gibson, J. J. (1979). *The ecological approach to visual perception.* Boston: Houghton Mifflin.

Holmes, J. G. (2000). Social relationships: The nature and function of relational schemas. *European Journal of Social Psychology, 30*, 447–496.

Holmes, J. G. (2002). Interpersonal expectations as the building blocks of social cognition: An interdependence theory analysis. *Personal Relationships, 9*, 1–26.

Holmes, J. G. (2004). The benefits of abstract functional analysis in theory construction: The case of interdependence theory. *Personality and Social Psychology Review, 8*, 146–155.

Kelley, H. H. (1997). The "stimulus field" for interpersonal phenomena: The source of language and thought about interpersonal events. *Personality and Social Psychology Review, 1*, 140–169.

Kelley, H. H., & Holmes, J. G. (2003). *Interdependence theory: Situations, relationships, and personality.* Unpublished manuscript.

Kelley, H. H., Holmes, J. G., Kerr, N., Reis, H., Rusbult, C. E., & Van Lange, P. A. M. (2003). *An atlas of interpersonal situations.* Cambridge, UK: Cambridge Press.

Lewin, K. (1946). Behavior and development as a function of the total situation. In L. Carmichael (Ed.), *Manual of child psychology* (pp. 791–844). New York: Wiley.

MacArthur, L., & Baron, R. (1983). Toward an ecological theory of social perception. *Psychological Review, 90*, 215–238.

Marr, D. (1982). *Vision: A computational investigation into the human representation and processing of visual information.* San Francisco: Freeman.

Pinker, S. (1997). *How the mind works.* New York: Norton.

Shepard, R. (1992). The perceptual organization of colors: An adaptation to the regularities of the terrestrial world. In J. Barkow, L. Cosmides, & J. Tooby (Eds.), *The adapted mind: Evolutionary psychology and the generation of culture* (pp. 495–532). New York: Oxford University Press.

Thaler, R. H. (1992). *The winner's curse: Paradoxes and anomalies of economic life.* New York: Free Press.

Tooby, J., & Cosmides, L. (1996). Friendship and the banker's paradox: Other pathways to the evolution of adaptations for altruism. *Proceedings of the British Academy, 88*, 119–143.

Speaker Perception and Social Behavior: Bridging Social Psychology and Speech Science

Robert M. Krauss
Jennifer S. Pardo
Columbia University

Increasingly in recent years, social psychologists have come to appreciate the role that language plays in social life. For the discipline, the consequences of this developing awareness have been salutary. Language is critically implicated in many of the core phenomena social psychologists study (e.g., causal attribution, social identity, status and intimacy, and interpersonal relations, to list but a few), and taking the role of language into account has greatly enhanced our understanding of them. Moreover, because stimulus and response in social psychology are so often verbal in form, many fundamental questions of methodology turn on issues that are implicitly linguistic.

When social psychologists have considered language, they typically have focused on the semantic–pragmatic levels of linguistic analysis. Much less attention has been paid to the system of sound production that allows semantic representations to be transformed into the perceptually accessible form we call *speech*. This is unfortunate for many reasons, not the least of which is that speech, in addition to its semantic content, contains information that bears directly on phenomena that are the concern of social psychological theory.

It is useful to distinguish between two related areas of investigation that involve speech processing: research on *speech* perception and *speaker* perception. Speech perception research studies the process by which listeners extract linguistically significant information from highly variable acoustic input. The process is complicated by the fact that spoken language is both highly variable in its production and remarkably stable in its perception, and it is not obvious how listeners derive a stable percept from such variable input. In contrast, speaker perception research studies the effects of the variability in speech that is not linguistically significant, but is neither arbitrary nor idiosyncratic. Speech is likely to reflect a variety of factors—the dialect of the speakers' regional origins, social class, and so on. Although this variability typically does not affect the semantic content of the utterance, it may convey information about the speaker that affects how the utterance is understood and responded to. Speaker perception research studies the effects of this kind of variability. Although speech perception per se may be of marginal interest to social psychologists, the phenomena studied in speaker perception research can provide a window into a variety of important social psychological processes. We illustrate the potential of this approach with examples from research in two areas: (a) social factors affecting within-speaker variability, and (b) effects of interaction on conversational participants' speech.

SOCIAL FACTORS AFFECTING WITHIN-SPEAKER VARIABILITY

Even when uttered by the same speaker, a phoneme or word will vary acoustically on different occasions of articulation. Two kinds of factors producing variability of particular interest to social psychologists are the speaker's situated identity and his/her internal state.

Identity and Situation.   Identity concerns people's sense of who they are— the attributes and features that, on the one hand, distinguish them from others, and, on the other hand, make them members of coherent classes, categories or communities (Deaux, 1996). We can distinguish between *social identity* (defined by the social groups or categories to which a person belongs or is identified with) and *personal identity* (socially relevant aspect of an individual's physical and psychological makeup). Many attributes of these aspects of identity are embodied in speech. Social psychologists have tended to focus on the social dimensions of identity, but as Deaux (1996) pointed out, the significance of many components of personal identity (e.g., age, weight) is a social construction.

Perhaps the most widely studied socially significant aspect of voice quality is dialect and accent. A dialect is a variant of a language that is distributed either regionally or by social class (Labov, 1974, 1994; Trudgill, 2000). Accent refers to the phonological component of dialect. What makes dialects of especial interest to social psychologists is their relation to the speaker's identity.

In addition to these global and relatively enduring features of speech, the same individual also will speak differently on different occasions. One source of this variability is captured by the sociolinguistic concept of register. Speech registers (situated linguistic variation conditioned by occasions of usage) differ from dialects, which are variations conditioned by region or social status. Because registers can vary with situation, the register a speaker employs on a particular occasion directly reflects his or her definition of that situation, the social role he or she is playing in the situation, or the identity that is active.

Differences in the way speakers sound, which derive from individual differences in anatomy and individual differences in dialect, accent, and speech habits, can provide information about the personal identities of speakers we don't know. For example, an unfamiliar person's age, height, and sex can be judged from his or her voice with surprising accuracy. Krauss, Freyberg and Morsella (2002) found that estimates of these attributes made from a two-sentence voice sample were only marginally less accurate than those made from full-length photographs.

The ability to judge a speaker's age from voice is a consequence of physiological changes that accompany aging, and the ability to judge height may reflect the correlation of height and laryngeal size. Yet the ability to identify a speaker's sex from his or her voice is more complex. Interestingly, although men and women's voices on average differ on a number of acoustic dimensions, there is no single feature or known subset of features that reliably distinguishes them (Klatt & Klatt, 1990). Nevertheless, in the Krauss et al. study, naive judges identified 40 speakers as male or female with perfect accuracy, leading to the speculation that men and women use their voices differently, and these dynamic differences contribute to our ability to distinguish between male and female speakers. There is some evidence, for example, that men and women differ in where within their pitch range they place their voices, with men tending to place their voices in the lower part of their range (Graddol & Swann, 1983).

Internal State.   Speech will vary depending on a variety of internal state factors, and even so small a speech sample as "Hello" can contain enough information for a familiar listener to determine whether the speaker is excited, depressed, annoyed, and so on. Several investigators have examined the properties that distinguish different emotions, but because these analyses have been based largely on actors' portrayals of emotions rather than naturally occurring expressions, it's difficult to reach any firm conclusions about the acoustic correlates of emotional speech. It seems fairly clear that such intense emotional states as anger, fear, and joy are associated with raised fundamental frequency (F0, heard as overall pitch), reflecting the physiological arousal that accompanies these states (Russell, Bacherowski & Fernández-Dols, 2003). The voices of speakers experiencing high levels of stress also are characterized by elevated F0 (Williams & Stevens, 1969; Streeter, Macdonald, Apple, Krauss, & Galotti, 1983). Fundamental frequency is a useful acoustic index because it is relatively easy to compute even under less-than-ideal acoustic conditions, but it reflects only one aspect of voice. Efforts to find vocal indices of other aspects of emotion have been generally less successful. Vocally expressed affect is readily accessible to listeners and affects their appraisal of speakers (Russell et al., 2003; Scherer, 2003).

All of the foregoing would be of interest to social psychologists even if listeners were not attentive to variability in speakers' voices. However, there is considerable evidence that naive listeners respond quite sensitively to speech variation, and that these perceptions have important evaluative and attributional effects (Giles & Powesland, 1975). For example, social psychologists (among others) have studied the effects on listeners of deviations from standard or prestige dialect. Generally speaking, speech patterns associated with stigmatized or socially devalued identities elicit negative evaluations of the speaker and the speech's contents. Using an analysis/resynthesis procedure, Brown, Strong, and Renscher (1974) and Apple, Streeter, and Krauss (1979) found that elevating male speakers' F0s caused them to be perceived as weaker, less benevolent, competent, truthful, and persuasive, and more nervous. A preliminary study of F0-manipulated speech in our lab (Gardner, 2003) suggests that the effects of elevated F0 on listeners may vary depending on the speakers' and listeners' sex. Males listeners seem to prefer male speakers with lowered F0 and female speakers with raised F0. Female listeners seem to prefer higher pitched male voices and have no strong preferences for pitch level in female voices.

EFFECTS OF SOCIAL INTERACTION ON SPEECH

Social interaction is the most common venue for language use, and language plays a critical role in most social interaction. The study of language use in social interaction takes many forms. Here we focus on changes in speech that occur as a function of conversational interaction.

A common observation is that some aspect of participants' speech tends to increase in similarity over the course of interaction. Interlocutors *converge* in speech rate (Giles et al., 1991), subvocal frequency (Gregory, 1990), and vocal intensity (Natale, 1975); *establish and increase* common ground to the exclusion of overhearers (Schober & Clark, 1989); and *align* description schemata (Pickering & Garrod, 2004; Garrod & Doherty, 1994) and syntactic constructions (Branigan, Pickering, & Cleland, 2000). Curiously, none of this research examines variation in acoustic–phonetic attributes, which can have particular social importance because of their significance for identity.

Such an approach is illustrated in ongoing research using a dyadic instructional task that requires conversational interaction and permits assignment of asymmetrical social roles. Using a psychophysical judgment procedure, Pardo (2001) found that participants' pronunciation of certain recurring words became more similar over the course of interaction. More strikingly, conversational interaction affected speakers' global phonological repertoires (Pardo, 2005). Phonetic change was related to a speaker's task role. Preliminary data suggest that the vowels of participants assigned the task role of Instruction Giver centralized more than those of Instruction Receivers. By measuring acoustic phonetic attributes, what appeared to be random variation in speech production can be linked to the dynamics of social interaction. For example,

Bourhis, Giles, and Tajfel (1973) found that the Welsh-accentedness of the speech of participants with strong Welsh identities became stronger after over-hearing an English experimenter make disparaging comments about the Welsh language. Variation in the acoustic–phonetic attributes that contribute to the perception of accentedness can be measured with some precision, re-flecting changes in the interacting parties' relationship.

CONCLUSIONS

Social psychologists' growing appreciation of the role that language plays in social life has focused their attention on how the forces that shape social be-havior are mediated by, and reflected in, the words we utter. This realization, and the research that it stimulated, yielded important insights into some of the field's core phenomena. But social psychologists' interest in language has largely been confined to its semantic–pragmatic dimensions. In this brief es-say, we have argued that the sound structure of speech contains information that can contribute importantly to our understanding of social behavior.

Speaker perception studies the way a particular utterance reflects a speaker's identity and internal state, and his or her definition of the situation. The variability that these factors produce can be studied both as a dependent variable and as an independent variable. That is to say, we can examine the ef-fects on voice of inductions involving activated identities, internal state, or situ-ational definitions; we also can examine how variability in features of voice (either natural or synthetically created) affects listeners' perceptions of the speaker and the semantic content of the utterance.

We would be remiss if we did not note that research on the social psycho-logical factors that affect variability in speech could also yield great benefits for speech science, which up until now has done a better job of describing such variability than accounting for it. Speech scientists tend to be as unin-formed about social psychology as social psychologists are about speech sci-ence, and their work often reflects this. As an insightful reviewer of an earlier draft of this essay noted, most bridges are bidirectional. It seems inevitable that combining the insights of the two disciplines will enhance the analytic power of both.

REFERENCES

Apple, W., Streeter, L. A., & Krauss, R. M. (1979). Effects of pitch and speech rate on personal attributions. *Journal of Personality and Social Psychology, 37,* 715–727.

Bourhis, R. Y., Giles, H., & Tajfel, H. (1973). Language as a determinant of Welsh identity. *European Journal of Social Psychology, 3,* 447–460.

Branigan, H. P., Pickering, M. J., & Cleland, A. A. (2000). Syntactic co-ordination in dialogue. *Cognition, 75,* B13–25.

Brown, B. L., Strong, W. J., & Rencher, A. C. (1974). Fifty-four voices from two: The effects of simultaneous manipulations of rate, mean fundamental frequency, and variance of fundamental frequency on ratings of personality from speech. *Journal of the Acoustical Society of America, 55,* 313–318.

Deaux, K. (1996). Social identification. In E. T. Higgins & A. W. Kruglanski (Eds.), *Social psychology: Handbook of basic principles* (pp. 777–798). New York: Guilford Press.

Gardner, R. C. (2003). *What's in a voice? Pitch and persuasiveness.* Unpublished honors thesis, Department of Psychology, Columbia University.

Garrod, S., & Doherty, G. (1994). Conversation, co-ordination and convention: An empirical investigation of how groups establish linguistic conventions. *Cognition, 53,* 181–215.

Giles, H., Coupland, J., & Coupland, N. (Eds.). (1991). *Contexts of accommodation: Developments in applied sociolinquistics.* New York: Cambridge University Press.

Giles, H., & Powesland, P. F. (1975). *Speech styles and social evaluation.* New York: Academic Press.

Gradol, D., & Swann, J. (1983). Speaking fundamental frequency: Some physical and social correlates. *Language and Speech, 26,* 351–366.

Gregory, S. W. (1990). Analysis of fundamental frequency reveals covariation in interview partners' speech. *Journal of Nonverbal Behavior, 14,* 237–251.

Klatt, D. H., & Klatt, L. C. (1990). Analysis, synthesis, and perception of voice quality variations among female and male talkers. *Journal of the Acoustical Society of America, 87,* 820–857.

Krauss, R. M., Freyberg, R., & Morsella, E. (2002). Inferring speakers' physical attributes from their voices. *Journal of Experimental Social Psychology, 38,* 618–625.

Labov, W. (1974). Linguistic change as a form of communication. In A. Silverstein (Ed.), *Human communication: Theoretical explorations* (pp. 221–256). Hillsdale, NJ: Lawrence Erlbaum Associates.

Labov, W. (1994). *Principles of linguistic change: Internal factors* (pp. 86–94). Cambridge, MA.: Blackwell.

Natale, M. (1975). Convergence of mean vocal intensity in dyadic communication as a function of social desirability. *Journal of Personality and Social Psychology, 32,* 790–804.

Pardo, J. S. (2001). Imitation and coordination in spoken communication. *Dissertation Abstracts International: Section B: the Sciences & Engineering.* Vol. 61(10-B), May 2001, 5576, U.S.: Univ. Microfilms International.

Pardo, J. S. (2005). *Phonetic convergence and conversational interaction.* Unpublished manuscript.

Pickering, M. J., & Garrod, S. (2004). Toward a mechanistic psychology of dialogue. *Behavioral & Brain Sciences, 27,* 169–226.

Russell, J. A., Bacherowski, J.-A., & Fernández-Dols, J.-M. (2003). Facial and vocal expressions of emotion. *Annual Review of Psychology, 54,* 349–359.

Scherer, K. R. (2003). Vocal communication of emotion: A review of research paradigms. *Speech Communication, 40,* 227–256.

Schober, M. F., & Clark, H. H. (1989). Understanding by addressees and overhearers. *Cognitive Psychology, 21,* 211–232.

Streeter, L. A., Macdonald, N. H., Apple, W., Krauss, R. M., & Galotti, K. M. (1983). Acoustic and perceptual indicators of emotional stress. *Journal of the Acoustical Society of America, 73,* 1354–1360.

Williams, C. E., & Stevens, K. N. (1969). On determining the emotional state of pilots during flight: An exploratory study. *Journal of the Acoustical Society of America, 40,* 1369–1372.

The Behavioral System Construct: A Useful Tool for Building an Integrative Model of the Social Mind

Mario Mikulincer
Bar-Ilan University

Phillip R. Shaver
University of California, Davis

In this chapter we (a) explain the core construct in Bowlby's (1969/1982, 1973, 1980) attachment theory, *behavioral system*; (b) describe how the construct has been used in the empirical literature on *adult attachment style* (the pattern of relational expectations, emotions, and behavior resulting from a particular history of attachment experiences, perhaps interacting with innate temperament and other social experiences; Fraley & Shaver, 2000; Shaver & Mikulincer, 2002); and (c) assess the usefulness of attachment theory and research for creating bridges between social psychology and other disciplines. Originally, Bowlby's attachment theory was itself the result of creating bridges between psychoanalysis, community psychiatry, ethology, and cognitive and developmental psychology. Bowlby's creativity, conceptual breadth, and open-mindedness encouraged Shaver, Hazan, and Bradshaw (1988) to extend the theory into the realm of adult romantic love, thereby creating a bridge between attachment theory and the social psychology of relationships.

Because social psychology in the 1980s was concerned with cognition (cybernetic control processes, social cognition, and cognitive/attributional aspects of stress), close relationships (including marriage), and evolutionary aspects of human social behavior (mate selection, jealousy, parental investment), attachment theory and social psychology shared certain agendas and themes. These commonalities made it possible for attachment researchers in social psychology to take advantage of constructs (e.g., cognitive/affective schemas, self-disclosure) and research techniques (e.g., priming, daily diaries, behavioral observation) used by other social psychologists. The result is a large and growing body of research, summarized recently by Shaver and Mikulincer (2002) and Mikulincer and Shaver (2003), which contributes substantially to social, personality, developmental, and clinical psychology.

Although Bowlby (1969/1982) focused mainly on the formation of attachment bonds in childhood and the self-protective and affect-regulatory functions of seeking proximity to others in times of need, he also attempted to understand how evolutionary mechanisms shape other categories of human behavior (e.g., exploration, maternal caregiving, affiliative behavior with peers). For this purpose, he borrowed from ethology the concept of *behavioral system*, a species-universal neural program that organizes an individual's behavior in ways that increase the likelihood of survival and reproductive success in the face of particular environmental demands. These demands—for example, dealing with threats to life and well-being by relying on "stronger, wiser others," exploring and learning how to cope with the environment, caring for dependent offspring—led to the evolution of distinct but interrelated behavioral systems (e.g., attachment, exploration, and caregiving systems), each with its own functions and characteristic behaviors (Bowlby, 1969/1982).

BEHAVIORAL SYSTEMS DEFINED

A behavioral system is an inborn, goal-oriented neural program that governs the choice, activation, and termination of behavioral sequences so as to produce a predictable and generally functional change in the person–environment relationship. Each behavioral system involves a set of contextual activating triggers; a set of interchangeable, functionally equivalent behaviors that constitute the primary strategy of the system for attaining its particular goal state; a specific set-goal (a state of the person–environment relationship that terminates the system's activation); cognitive operations that facilitate the system's functioning; and specific excitatory and inhibitory links with other behavioral systems. Although akin to the evolutionary psychological construct of "module," the behavioral system construct is more complex and more closely tied to empirical operations.

Bowlby (1973) discussed individual differences in the functioning of behavioral systems. In his view, the ability of a behavioral system to achieve its set-goal depends on a person's transactions with the external world. Although behavioral systems are innate intrapsychic structures, which presumably operate mainly at a subcortical level and in a reflexive, mechanistic manner, they are manifested in actual behavior, guide people's transactions with the social world, and can be affected or shaped by others' responses. Over time, social encounters mold the parameters of a person's behavioral systems in ways that produce individual differences in strategies and behaviors. In a sense, a person's general neural/behavioral capacities become "programmed" to fit with major close relationship partners. Bowlby (1973) assumed that social interactions gradually correct a behavioral system's primary strategies and produce more effective action sequences. According to him, the residues of such experiences are stored as mental representations of person–environment transactions, which he called *working models of self and others*. These models presumably operate mainly at a cortical level and in a relatively reflective and intentional manner. Nevertheless, with repeated use they can become automatic and may sometimes be held out of awareness by defensive maneuvers. They are an important reason for within-person continuity in the functioning of a behavioral system and can fruitfully be viewed as part of the system's "programming."

Because a behavioral system accomplishes a specific biological function, individual variations in the functioning of a system have important implications for a person's social adjustment, mental health, and quality of life. Consider the case of the attachment behavioral system. It is activated by perceived threats and dangers, which cause a threatened person to seek proximity to protective others (Mikulincer & Shaver, 2003). The attainment of proximity and protection results in feelings of security as well as positive mental representations of self and others. Bowlby (1988) considered the optimal functioning of this behavioral system to be crucial for mental health, the development of a positive self-image, and the formation of positive attitudes toward relationship partners and close relationships in general. A large number of studies provide strong support for these benefits of optimal functioning of the attachment system.

For example, attachment security is associated both with personal benefits, such as greater psychological well-being, higher self-esteem, enhanced relationship satisfaction, and greater satisfaction with work, and with social benefits, such as enhanced compassion for others in need, greater outgroup tolerance, and stronger tendencies toward gratitude and forgiveness (for extensive reviews see Mikulincer & Shaver, 2003; Shaver & Mikulincer, 2002).

BEHAVIORAL SYSTEM AS A BRIDGING CONSTRUCT

The behavioral system construct is useful for bridging evolutionary theories, ethology, and social psychology. For example, the attachment behavioral system has been shown to underlie general features of close relationships (e.g., love, support seeking, grief), as well as individual variations in the way people form and maintain intimate ties, regulate distress, and cope with threats.

Similarly, the caregiving system is important for understanding altruistic behavior in general and the way particular people behave in specific caregiving contexts (e.g., parenthood, leadership). The affiliation system is useful for understanding friendship and group-related behavior, and the exploration system provides a framework for understanding a person's behavior in achievement settings and ways of dealing with novelty and uncertainty. Behavioral systems are also important for understanding social cognition, because they involve mental representations of self and others that can shape a person's social attitudes and judgments (Shaver & Mikulincer, 2002).

The behavioral system construct can connect research on social behavior, interpersonal relations, and group processes, and can also bridge between various levels of analysis (individual, dyadic, and group). For example, researchers have documented the contributions of relationship partners to shaping the activation and dynamics of one's attachment system. Feeney (2002) showed how a supportive close relationship partner can induce greater felt security (and its associated benefits), even in generally insecure individuals, and Rom and Mikulincer (2003) showed how a highly cohesive group improved the functioning of chronically attachment-anxious group members. Furthermore, when a relationship partner is viewed as another focal individual, a foundation is provided for systems models of social behavior (e.g., members of groups, marital couples, families). In these models, one person's cognitions, emotions, and behaviors are organized around intrapsychic and interpersonal regularities determined partly by a partner's behavioral systems.

Bowlby's construct of working models provides a bridge between social psychology and the study of personality. In attachment theory, for example, consolidation of a relatively stable working model is the most important psychological process that explains the transition from context-tailored variations in the functioning of the attachment system to person-tailored variations. Given a fairly consistent pattern of interactions with attachment figures during childhood and adolescence, models of these interactions increasingly become part of an individual's personality. Thus, what began as representations of specific interactions with a particular partner become core personality characteristics and tend to be applied in new situations where they explain variations in attachment-system functioning.

Working models are a source of continuity in the functioning of behavioral systems across time and situations, and hence can bridge social and developmental psychology. For example, Bowlby's attachment theory is not only a theory about the construction of interpersonal behavior, emotional bonds, and close relationships, but also a theory of personality development. According to Bowlby (1973), a person's attachment dynamics in adulthood reflect past experiences with relationship partners, especially parents, beginning in infancy. In this way, Bowlby provided a foundation for studying the developmental sources and trajectories of social motives, cognitions, and behaviors. This does not mean, however, that these trajectories are simple or linear. Although variations in the functioning of a behavioral system may stem from childhood experiences with parents, they can also reflect a broad array of contextual factors that moderate or even override the effects of internalized representations of past experiences (Fraley, 2002). In fact, Bowlby (1988) claimed that working models can be updated throughout life, and he selected the term "working" in "working models" partly to represent the provisional and changing nature of these cognitive-affective structures.

The assumption that behavioral systems act at both subcortical and cortical levels (Bowlby, 1969/1982; Shaver & Mikulincer, 2002) provides a useful tool for integrating social psychology with the emerging fields of cognitive, social, and affective neuroscience. Research can be directed at identifying the patterns of autonomic nervous system activation and neuroendocrine responses related to the functioning of each behavioral system (Diamond, 2001; Panksepp, 1998). Researchers can use split hemifield experiments (Cohen & Shaver, 2004), evoked reaction potentials (ERPs), and functional magnetic resonance imaging (fMRI) to delineate the cognitive components and cortical and subcortical regions involved in the functioning of these systems.

CONCLUSIONS

Bowlby's attachment theory is a valuable framework for explaining social behavior and bridging social psychology with other disciplines. Although Bowlby's theory was not meant to be a broad theory of the social mind (he was trying mainly to remedy errors and dead ends in Freudian psychoanalysis while retaining some of its valid components), our reading of his work suggests that the theory was meant to apply to a wide swath of social behavior and help in understanding large-scale social phenomena (e.g., juvenile delinquency, community-based hopelessness and depression, interpersonal and intergroup violence). We believe we have begun to map some of the important effects of the attachment system on social cognition and social behavior while integrating individual, interpersonal, and group levels of analysis; to delineate personal, developmental, and social/contextual determinants of people's attachment-related behavior in dyads and groups; and to explore the interplay between various behavioral systems. We hope this brief chapter stimulates researchers to use the construct of behavioral system in their attempts to build bridges within social/personality psychology and between this field and its potential neighbors. We look forward to the day when a single theory or conceptual framework—a theory of the social mind—provides a lingua franca for psychologists and other researchers interested in the complex interplay of evolution, physiology, culture, individual development in a relational context, and the current social context.

REFERENCES

Bowlby, J. (1982). *Attachment and loss: Vol. 1. Attachment* (2nd ed.). New York: Basic Books. (Original work published 1969)

Bowlby, J. (1973). *Attachment and loss: Vol. 2. Separation: Anxiety and anger.* New York: Basic Books.

Bowlby, J. (1980). *Attachment and loss: Vol. 3. Sadness and depression.* New York: Basic Books.

Bowlby, J. (1988). *A secure base: Clinical applications of attachment theory.* London: Routledge.

Cohen, M. X., & Shaver, P. R. (2004). Avoidant attachment and hemispheric lateralization of the processing of attachment- and emotion-related words. *Cognition and Emotion, 18,* 799–813.

Diamond, L. M. (2001). Contributions of psychophysiology to research on adult attachment: Review and recommendations. *Personality and Social Psychology Review, 5,* 276–295.

Feeney, J. A. (2002). Attachment, marital interaction, and relationship satisfaction: A diary study. *Personal Relationships, 9,* 39–55.

Fraley, R. C. (2002). Attachment stability from infancy to adulthood: Meta-analysis and dynamic modeling of developmental mechanisms. *Personality and Social Psychology Review, 6,* 123–151.

Fraley, R. C., & Shaver, P. R. (2000). Adult romantic attachment: Theoretical developments, emerging controversies, and unanswered questions. *Review of General Psychology, 4,* 132–154.

Mikulincer, M., & Shaver, P. R. (2003). The attachment behavioral system in adulthood: Activation, psychodynamics, and interpersonal processes. In M. P. Zanna (Ed.), *Advances in experimental social psychology* (Vol. 35, pp. 53–152). New York: Academic Press.

Panksepp, J. (1998). *Affective neuroscience: The foundations of human and animal emotions.* New York: Oxford University Press.

Rom, E., & Mikulincer, M. (2003). Attachment theory and group processes: The association between attachment style and group-related representations, goals, memory, and functioning. *Journal of Personality and Social Psychology, 84,* 1220–1235.

Shaver, P. R., Hazan, C., & Bradshaw, D. (1988). Love as attachment: The integration of three behavioral systems. In R. J. Sternberg & M. Barnes (Eds.), *The psychology of love* (pp. 68–99). New Haven, CT: Yale University Press.

Shaver, P. R., & Mikulincer, M. (2002). Attachment-related psychodynamics. *Attachment and Human Development, 4,* 133–161.

42

Dynamical Evolutionary Psychology: How Social Norms Emerge From Evolved Decision Rules

Douglas T. Kenrick
Arizona State University

Jill M. Sundie
University of Houston

While revising a social psychology text, one of us received a pair of interesting criticisms. One regarded a deficit—failing to explain how social psychology differs from sociology. The other regarded an excess—too much space on the evolutionary perspective, which, the reviewer suggested, has had less historical impact than other perspectives. Both criticisms, although true, elicited more sadness than repentance in the transgressing author. Social psychologists have expended far too much effort building walls between our territory and sociology, on the "holistic" side, and biology, on the "reductionist" side. Those walls often block our view of the phenomena we hope to elucidate—mutual interactions between individual humans and their social context.

Within social psychology, mini-theories about aggression, attraction, stereotyping, and leadership are themselves often isolated from one another, not to mention biology and sociology. How are social psychology's subdomains connected to one another, to the other disciplines of psychology, and to other sciences? We believe an answer to these questions will come from integrating insights from cognitive science, evolutionary psychology, and dynamical systems theory (Kenrick, 2001). Although social psychology has been part of the cognitive revolution, fewer social psychologists have incorporated insights from evolutionary psychology or dynamical systems theory. Because the mind is designed for interaction in human social groups, social psychology ought to be at center stage of the emerging scientific meta-synthesis.

EVOLUTIONARY PSYCHOLOGY

An evolutionary perspective involves analyzing recurrent problems faced by members of our species, and searching for specific psychological mechanisms or decision rules that, on average, would have solved those problems and thereby promoted reproductive success. Rather than attempting to reconstruct the past, evolutionary psychologists instead explore commonalities between behaviors exhibited by humans and other animal species now living under common environmental constraints. How, for example, do species with high levels of paternal investment (like humans and sandpipers) differ from species in which males contribute little or nothing to offspring care (Geary, 2000)? Cross-species comparisons have led to the development of core constructs such as differential parental investment theory, with its central assumption that the sex investing more resources in offspring (usually, but not always, the female) will be relatively more selective in mate choice. Selectiveness by one sex is associated with competitiveness, larger size, and longer developmental periods in the other sex, who must compete for mates. Parental investment theory implies that as males increase investment in offspring, they become more selective about mating (Kenrick, Sadalla, Groth, & Trost, 1990). Parental investment theory has been applied to research on psychological processes underlying various gender differences (e.g., Buss & Schmitt, 1993; Kenrick, Sundie, Nicastle, & Stone, 2001; Li, Bailey, Kenrick, Linsenmeier, 2002).

The evolutionary approach provides a powerful organizing framework for connecting diverse social behaviors (e.g., Kenrick & Trost, 1996). From this perspective, topics as disparate as attraction, aggression, cooperation, prejudice, and intergroup conflict are all interconnected via a set of broad general principles, such as differential parental investment and inclusive fitness. Evolutionary researchers have identified a set of broad social domains, depicted in Table 42.1, that involve recurring problems our ancestors had to solve to survive and reproduce. Because these problems were central to reproductive success, psychological mechanisms or decision rules likely evolved to effectively and efficiently address each of these distinct objectives. For example, coalitional behaviors are more likely between individuals who are genetically related, or who have a history of sharing resources with one another—two decision rules based on well-established principles of kin selection and reciprocal altruism (Burnstein, Crandall, & Kitayama, 1994).

Contrary to traditional assumptions that humans use domain-general rules for social and nonsocial decisions alike (e.g., seek "reward"), evidence suggests different problem domains involve qualitatively different decision rules (Cosmides & Tooby, 1992; Kenrick, Sadalla, & Keefe, 1998). For example, humans have different memory systems for different and sometimes conceptually incompatible tasks, such as language acquisition, facial recognition, and learning taste aversions (Sherry & Schacter, 1987). By separately considering each social problem, such as finding mates, handling outgroup threats, or caring for infants, an evolutionary perspective can suggest which environmental features might be more or less prominent. Because the problem domains listed in Table 42.1 are central to navigating social life, information relevant to these domains should be particularly salient as individuals proceed through social interactions. For example, both sexes are visually attentive to attractive members of the opposite sex and to facial cues associated with threats (Maner et al., 2003; Öhman & Mineka, 2001).

Evolutionary psychologists assume that psychological mechanisms or decision rules, although based partly on inherited capacities, are exquisitely sensitive to the environment (Kenrick, Neuberg, Zierk, & Krones, 1994; Öhman & Mineka, 2001). Many decision rules are of the "if–then" form, where environmental input plays a fundamental role in determining which decision path is chosen. Whether one behaves cooperatively toward one's neighbors, for example, may vary as a function of past history with those neighbors, as well as individual differences in aggressive tendencies. Interactions among individuals using such behavioral decision rules unfold dynamically into local norms of aggression or cooperation, as we discuss later.

Also contrary to simple "genetic determinism," evolutionary psychologists have adopted ecological concepts such as density-dependent strategies (the idea that a given behavior varies in adaptiveness depending on the percentage of the local population pursuing that same strategy) (Gangestad & Simpson, 2000). For example, exploitative "hawk" or pacifistic "dove" behaviors may each be superior strategies, depending on environmental conditions. Although evolutionary psychologists have generally accepted such dynamic principles, little research has examined how genetically based decision rules might play out over time within the complex web of social interactions.

DYNAMICAL SYSTEMS THEORY

Dynamical systems theorists are concerned with changes over time in complex multicomponent systems, such as human social groups. In such systems, systemwide changes are often non-linear, and influences are multidirectional (Person A's behavioral response to a Neighbor B influences B and several others, who in turn respond to A, and so on). A number of interesting commonalities have been observed across complex systems of different types, ranging from neural networks through national economies. One is that vast complexity at the system level can emerge from the interaction of just a few simple decision rules. Another is that organization often emerges spontaneously out of initially random interactions between system elements. For example, the dynamics of status competition commonly result in a hierarchical social structure, with significantly fewer individuals at the top than at the bottom (see Table 42.1). Such self-organization can be said to emerge from a kind of "invis-

Table 1

Domains of Adaptive Problems, Fundamental Goals Associated With Each Domain, Examples of Evolved Decision Constraints, Evolutionary Principles Underlying Decision Constraints, and the Unique Social Spatial Geometries Likely to Emerge in Each Domain

Social Problem Domain	Fundamental Goal	Evolved Decision Constraint	Underlying General Principle(s)	Unique Social Spatial Geometry
Coalition Formation	Form and maintain cooperative alliances	Cooperate with those (a) sharing your genes and (b) that have cooperated with you in the past	Inclusive fitness Reciprocal altruism	
Status Seeking	Gain and maintain respect from, and power over, other group members	Males will take more risks to gain and maintain status	Sexual selection	
Self-protection	Protect oneself and important others from threats to survival and reproduction	Potential threats or costs will lead to reciprocal aggressive behavior, particularly among non-kin	Inclusive fitness	
Mate Choice	Obtain a desirable mate or mates	Males, compared to females, will be generally more inclined to an unrestricted sexual strategy	Differential parental investment	
Mating relationship maintenance	Maintain mating bonds	Breaking a bond is likely for: (a) males when a mate is sexually unfaithful or when physically attractive alternatives are available (b) females when a mate compromises resources or when high status alternatives are available	Differential parental investment	
Parental Care	Promote the survival and reproduction of one's offspring and other kin	Familial provision of resources and care will follow the order: (a) self > siblings; (b) own offspring > stepchildren	Inclusive fitness	

ible hand," where each individual in the hierarchy, behaving according to his or her own simple decision rules, plays a role in producing an emergent social pattern.

Kenrick, Li, and Butner (2003) conducted a series of computer simulations exploring implications of domain-specific evolved decision rules for group level self-organization. Suppose each individual in a community decides daily whether to adopt an aggressive or peaceful strategy, and that each individual's choice today mirrors the strategy of the majority of immediate neighbors the day before. Beginning with a randomly distributed arrangement of hostile and cooperative neighbors, one might expect random or chaotic patterns as individuals alternate between aggressive and cooperative strategies. However, after several rounds of interaction, neighborhoods settle into stable patterns, with self-sustaining pockets of aggression and cooperation (see Fig. 42.1). Similar self-organized patterns emerge among genes, neurons, and groups of real people (Holland, 1998; Latané, 1996). As shown in the rightmost column of Table 42.1, different social geometries are believed to emerge from different decision rules in different social domains.

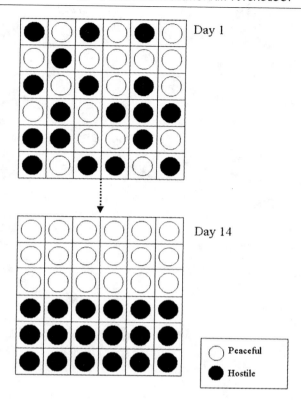

FIG. 42.1. Self-organization and the emergence of social norms. Spatially organized social norms will emerge out of initially random interactions between neighbors, if each individual bases his or her behaviors on the behaviors of his or her neighbors.

Dynamical models suggest intrinsic connections between research areas such as attraction, aggression, and group dynamics. Social cognition research is also essential for revealing decision rules underlying group-level interactions. Because individual decision rules unfold in the context of other individuals in one's group, individual social cognition must be intrinsically connected to interpersonal dynamics.

CONCLUSIONS

Social psychologists have been insufficiently ambitious in building theoretical connections. We have been sending out ferries from one isolated island to another, failing to provide a navigational map. To achieve the intellectual equivalent of a "Golden Gate Bridge" for our field, the next generation of social psychologists must be trained in recent developments in evolutionary psychology and dynamical systems theory. A dynamical evolutionary psychology promises to not only connect the scattered subdisciplines of social psychology, but to reach beyond to the mainland of a unified science.

Evolutionary and dynamical approaches in combination suggest a number of empirically testable questions, most of which are yet to be tested (Kenrick, Maner, Butner, Li, & Becker, & Schaller, 2002; Kenrick et al., 2003). The approach raises questions at several levels of analysis—about dynamics within individuals and between people, and over a temporal dimension ranging from immediate interactions through ontogenetic and phylogenetic time spans. For example, at the within-individual level, we may ask how activation of fundamental goals (such as self-protection or mate search) differentially guides attention, encoding, and memory (e.g., Maner et al., 2003). At the level of developmental dynamics between people, how do social groups organize and reorganize themselves over the life spans of the individuals making up a group (e.g., how do dynamics between males and females change at puberty). At the phylogenetic level are questions about how constellations of traits (such as high offspring care and selectivity about mating) coevolve within the person, and how physical and psychological traits of males coevolve with those of females.

A dynamical evolutionary perspective calls for a unification of holistic and reductionist approaches to behavioral science. To truly understand how cultural norms emerge, for example, we need to understand the evolved psychological mechanisms that affect decisions by the individual human beings who choose some norms and not others. If we can construct a social psychology spanning biology and the other social sciences, fewer of our empirical missions will go adrift in the fog of intellectual isolationism.

REFERENCES

Burnstein, E., Crandall, C., & Kitayama, S. (1994). Some neo-Darwinian decision rules for altruism: Weighing cues for inclusive fitness as a function of the biological importance of the decision. *Journal of Personality and Social Psychology, 67,* 773–789.

Buss, D. M., & Schmitt, D. (1993). Sexual strategies theory: An evolutionary perspective on human mating. *Psychological Review, 100,* 204–232.

Cosmides, L., & Tooby, J. (1992). Cognitive adaptations for social exchange. In J. H. Barkow, L. Cosmides, & J. Tooby (Eds.), *The adapted mind: Evolutionary psychology and the generation of culture* (pp. 163–228). New York: Oxford University Press.

Gangestad, S. W., & Simpson, J. A. (2000). The evolution of human mating: Trade-offs and strategic pluralism. *Behavioral and Brain Sciences, 23,* 573–644.

Geary, D. C. (2000). Evolution and proximate expression of human paternal investment. *Psychological Bulletin, 126,* 55–77.

Holland, J. H. (1998). *Emergence: From chaos to order.* Reading, MA: Addison-Wesley.

Kenrick, D. T. (2001). Evolution, cognitive science, and dynamical systems: An emerging integrative paradigm. *Current Directions in Psychological Science, 10,* 13–17.

Kenrick, D. T., Li, N. P., & Butner, J. (2003). Dynamical evolutionary psychology: Individual decision rules and emergent social norms. *Psychological Review, 110,* 3–28.

Kenrick, D. T., Maner, J. K., Butner, J., Li, N. P., Becker, D. V., & Schaller, M. (2002). Dynamical evolutionary psychology: Mapping the domains of the new interactionist paradigm. *Personality & Social Psychology Review, 6,* 347–356.

Kenrick, D. T., Neuberg, S. L., Zierk, K., & Krones, J. (1994). Evolution and social cognition: Contrast effects as a function of sex, dominance, and physical attractiveness. *Personality and Social Psychology Bulletin, 20,* 210–217.

Kenrick, D. T., Sadalla, E. K., Groth, G., & Trost, M. R. (1990). Evolution, traits, and the stages of human courtship: Qualifying the parental investment model. *Journal of Personality, 58,* 97–116.

Kenrick, D. T., Sadalla, E. K., & Keefe, R. C. (1998). Evolutionary cognitive psychology: The missing heart of modern cognitive science. In C. Crawford & D. L. Krebs (Eds.), *Handbook of evolutionary psychology* (pp. 485–514). Hillsdale, NJ: Lawrence Erlbaum Associates.

Kenrick, D. T., Sundie, J. M., Nicastle, L. D., & Stone, G. O. (2001). Can one ever be too wealthy or too chaste? Searching for nonlinearities in mate judgment. *Journal of Personality and Social Psychology, 80,* 462–471.

Kenrick, D. T., & Trost, M. R. (1996). The evolutionary psychology of relationships. In S. Duck (Ed.), *Handbook of personal relationships: Theory, research and interventions* (2nd ed., pp. 151–177). Orlando, FL: Academic Press.

Latané, B. (1996). Dynamic social impact: The creation of culture by communication. *Journal of Communication, 46,* 13–25.

Li, N. P., Bailey, J. M., Kenrick, D. T., & Linsenmeier, J. A. (2002). The necessities and luxuries of mate preferences: Testing the trade-offs. *Journal of Personality and Social Psychology, 82,* 947–955.

Maner, J. K., Kenrick, D. T., Becker, D. V., Delton, A. W., Hofer, B., Wilbur, C. J., & Neuberg, S. L. (2003). Sexually selective cognition: Beauty captures the mind of the beholder. *Journal of Personality and Social Psychology, 85,* 1107–1121.

Öhman, A., & Mineka, S. (2001). Fears, phobias, and preparedness: Toward an evolved module of fear and fear learning. *Psychological Review, 108,* 483–522.

Sherry, D. F., & Shachter, D. L. (1987). The evolution of multiple memory systems. *Psychological Review, 94,* 439–454.

43

Social Relations: Culture, Development, Natural Selection, Cognition, the Brain, and Pathology

Alan Page Fiske

Department of Anthropology, UCLA; Co-founder, UCLA Center for Behavior, Evolution, and Culture; and Director, FPR-UCLA Center for Culture, Brain, and Development

Social psychology often focuses too narrowly on perception and inference about persons. But persons are not merely important stimuli—they coordinate with each other, interacting with reference to jointly meaningful, mutually motivating relational models. That is, people form relationships. Social relationships are not products of individual brains alone; sociality is shaped by the interaction of evolutionary, developmental, neuroanatomical and neurophysiologial, psychological, societal, and cultural processes. To understand how people relate to each other, we need to understand how these interdependent processes jointly shape human sociality. Because these processes are highly interdependent, we cannot understand any of them in isolation from the others. Thus to understand social relations, we need to link social psychology to ethnography, ethnology, cognitive science, neuroscience, clinical psychology, evolutionary psychology, developmental psychology, economics and management science, and social theory.

My own research on relational models theory began with the discovery of a convergence among developmental psychology, political sociology, and theodicy theology. That is, I realized that the same three ways of understanding and evaluating social relations were being described by Jean Piaget, characterizing stages of moral development among Swiss children; Max Weber, sketching ideal types of legitimation of authority; and Paul Ricoeur, analyzing the history of Judeo-Christian explanations for misfortune. In these diverse domains they each described homologous models of social relations: first, a sense that people have something fundamental in common, some essential quality that makes them the same (or that separates them from others whose essence differs); second, a perception of people—or people in relation to God—as hierarchically differentiated, with subordinates owing obedience to superiors; third, a sense of proportionality, whether expressed as prices, efficiency, or justice. It seemed to me that if these three models of social relations emerged in such diverse domains, then perhaps they were manifestations of elementary forms of social coordination that humans used to structure all kinds of interaction.

ETHNOGRAPHIC, ETHNOLOGICAL, AND THEORETICAL RESEARCH ON RELATIONAL MODELS

The logical deduction is that these three relational models should be present in every culture. So, with considerable trepidation, I committed myself to test the theory with participant observation fieldwork among the Moose of Burkina Faso. Learning their language and then living in a small, remote village for 2 years, I attempted to fit the three elementary models to what I learned by participating in daily life and rituals. Somewhat to my astonishment, the models fit extremely well, helping me to understand what I saw and how people related to me. However, the three models failed to encompass one significant part of Moose social life: Often people related as equals, balancing and matching, taking turns or making equal contributions. With the formulation of this fourth model, nearly the whole of Moose social life seemed explicable. Moreover, the nature of each of the other three relational models was clarified by contrast to the fourth.

With further analysis, clear analytic definitions of four relational models emerged (Fiske 1992, 2004a). Communal sharing (CS) is an equivalence relation, in which people organize some aspect of their interaction with respect to some essential feature they have in common. Members of a team or ethnic group or people in a romantic relationship exemplify CS. Authority ranking (AR) is linear ordering, according to which people differentiate themselves hierarchically in relevant contexts. AR is evident in military command, in relations of seniority, and in relationships with superior deities. Equality matching (EM) is a relationship in which people keep track of additive differences, using even balance as the homeostatic reference point. We see EM in turn-taking, the rules of games and team sports, voting, balanced reciprocity in dinner invitations, or an-eye-for-an-eye vengeance. Market pricing (MP) is based on a socially meaningful ratio or rate, such as a price, rent, tax, cost-benefit analysis, or a sense of due proportion in punishment. People coordinate the MP aspect of their interactions with reference to this proportional standard.

I wrote my dissertation describing the operation of these four relational models in Moose social life. Impressed by the convergence of developmental psychology, political sociology, and theodicy theology with ethnography, I decided to put the emerging theory to further tests. If indeed the four relational models were elementary, they should shape social psychology and relationships in all domains of social life. So I reviewed diverse social science theories and literatures, where I indeed discovered manifestations of the models just about everywhere (Fiske, 1991). Most previous authors had characterized subsets of two or three of the elementary relational models: for example, Durkheim's organic and mechanical solidarity, or the trio of intimacy motivation, power motivation, and need for achievement. However, economic historians and anthropological economists had described four modes of labor organization, and four systems of exchange and distribution—exactly corresponding to the four elementary relational models (Polanyi, 1968; Udy, 1970). Yet, perhaps because of the lack of interdisciplinary bridges, no one had recognized that these four relational models were fundamental, elementary systems that structure every kind of social coordination. Even cultural anthropologists, describing these forms of organization in specific domains in particular communities, failed to realize that they were a framework for understanding many aspects of social relations, social institutions, and social structures in every society. Ethnologic research, systematically comparing ethnographies, showed that these relational models organize virtually every domain of human sociality. The distinctively human adaptation is complex, culturally mediated social coordination. The four relational models are the foundations for this coordination.

Subsequently, ethnologic research revealed that across cultures people consistently constitute, communicate, and cognize each of the relational models in a medium distinctive of that relational model (Fiske, 2004b). People constitute CS relations indexically, by making their bodies similar. In contrast, AR operates in an iconic mode, representing people as above and below, bigger or smaller, many or few, powerful or weak, earlier or later in time. People constitute and represent EM procedurally, in terms of concrete matching operations: taking turns, flipping a coin, or setting items in one-to-one correspondence. MP functions in the medium of abstract symbols such as numerals, contracts, and money. Participant observation in a Moose village revealed this fundamental pattern, which ethnology refined, developed, and confirmed. This theoretical and anthropological work has led us to a current empirical study of when and how children develop capacities to recognize the relational models.

RESEARCH ON RELATIONAL COGNITION AND ON PSYCHOPATHOLOGY

This synthesis of the literature was analytic, the ethnography was subjective, and my reviews of other evidence were inductive. But I was in the Department of Psychology at University of Pennsylvania, so I knew that to convince my colleagues I needed to deduce and test hypotheses derived from this theory. Could we predict basic processes of social cognition? A team composed of Nick Haslam, myself, and others carried out a series of 11 studies of naturally occurring social errors; we collected instances where people confused one person with another in addressing or referring to them, in interacting, or in recalling interactions. Sure enough, the predicted pattern emerged: People mix up persons with whom they have the same type of relationship (Fiske, Haslam, & Fiske, 1992). If you have a CS relationship with Susan and call her Barbara, it's because your relationship with Barbara is also CS. Tested against several other taxonomies, relational models theory made the best predictions. We then tested and supported the theory in samples from four other cultures, and showed that it also governs intentional substitutions, in which a person seeking to do something picks an alternate partner (e.g., if you have an EM relationship with your running mate, who has the flu today, you seek generally a substitute with whom you also have an EM relationship; Fiske, 1993; Fiske & Haslam, 1997). Subsequent studies showed that the relational models structured free retrieval of persons from memory, judgments of similarity among personal relationships, categories created in free sorting of personal relationships, and prototypicality judgments (reviewed in Haslam, 2004a). Indeed, the relational models strongly and consistently shaped every cognitive process we looked at.

Cognitive research demonstrates that the models organize implicit and explicit thinking about social relationships. But these lab studies do not just show how relational models function to coordinate everyday social action. To find out, we started looking at psychopathology. If relational models are the systems people use to coordinate with each other, then aberrant uses of the models should cause severe, persistent interpersonal problems, such as personality disorders. Nick Haslam and two of his students organized one study of a non-clinical population recruited for interpersonal problems and another study of a clinical population with diagnosed personality disorders. Aberrant implementations of the relational models were indeed related to interpersonal distress, with different aberrations related to different personality disorders (Haslam, 2004b). Three other researchers have recently studied normal people interacting across cultures, across positions in organizations, or making different assumptions about the structure of an interaction (reviewed in Haslam, 2004a). In these situations, differences in implementation of the relational models often results in discord, recriminations, and dissatisfaction with corporate and management work teams or partnerships.

NATURAL SELECTION AND NEUROBIOLOGY

Elementary human capacities for coordination must have evolved by natural selection, yet the great cultural diversity in implementation of the relational models shows that the evolved capacity does not directly or fully determine coordination structures. Theoretical work demonstrates that natural selection can indeed generate highly structured social potentials coupled with specially tuned learning proclivities (Fiske, 2000). This evolutionary tuning is an adaptation permitting children to discover the cultural complements that necessarily specify when, where, with whom, and how to implement the innate models.

Human action, cognition, and emotion operate though the brain, of course, and discovering the neural regions and circuits involved can sometimes illuminate the mechanisms. With this in mind, I organized a social cognitive neuroscience team to investigate the functional neuroanatomy of the relational models. We discovered that the brain regions activated were when people watch realistic videotapes of ordinary CS and AT interaction are quite different from activations produced by any other imaging study (Iacoboni, Lieberman et al., 2004). Watching social interactions strongly activates the bilateral anterior regions of the superior temporal sulcus, which seem only to be activated by stimuli that are socially meaningful. Moreover, two regions activated by our realistic stimuli have never before shown increases compared to a resting baseline: the medial parietal lobe (precuneus) and dorsolateral medial prefrontal lobe. This suggests the possibility that these three regions comprise a system dedicated to analysis of social relations. Moreover, these latter two regions are part of what has been called the "default" brain system that is active when people have no specific task to perform but is deactivated by virtually all nonsocial cognitive tasks. A plausible inference is that processing of social relations (reflectively and/or unconsciously) is a default activity of the human brain.

Two other approaches to the study of brain functions also illuminate how the brain operates in social relationships. Theory suggests that social and moral emotions are essential to motivate people to overcome immediate temptations and act so as to sustain the social relationships that are adaptive in the long-run (Fiske, 2002). Clinical neurology shows that anterior temporal and medial prefrontal lesions, or degeneration in these regions caused by frontotemporal dementia, seriously disrupt social relations, apparently by diminishing these crucial socio-moral emotions.

Neurochemistry provides a complementary perspective on brain processes. Maternal bonding in humans and other animals is mediated by a set of hormones, especially oxytocin; oxytocin mediates pair bonding in monogamous voles, along with the closely related peptide arginine vasopressin (de Bono, 2003). Although almost nothing is known about the neurochemistry of other social relationships in humans, there is a drug that produces intense, euphoric, indiscriminate CS relationships: MDMA (Ecstasy). Taken at raves or in other contexts, MDMA typically creates an extremely powerful feeling of affectionate oneness with everyone nearby (Olaveson, 2003). Unpacking the mechanisms of MDMA and the regions it affects might lead to the discovery of the natural pathways to CS.

CONCLUSIONS

Why attempt to study, let alone integrate, psychological, cultural, evolutionary, developmental, neuroanatomical, and neurochemical processes? These processes jointly shape human sociality, and their causal interdependence means that their effects on social relations cannot be adequately understood separately, in isolation from each other. Although we have only just begun to partially understand some of these processes and a few aspects of their interdependence, a synthetic approach offers the only opportunity to fully understand human sociality. For example, to understand the cultural aspects of sociality, we need to understand the processes of natural selection though which humans evolved to be cultural animals; to understand culture, we need to know why human evolved specific capacities for culture, and what these capacities consist of. To understand these cultural and evolutionary processes, we need to discover the developmental and neural mechanisms that result from and constrain them.

Furthermore, we can understand all of these systems only when we study how they malfunction in psychopathology, interpersonal disjunction, or cultural misunderstanding. To help people meet their social needs and interact more fruitfully, we need to identify all of the processes that are jointly necessary for functional social relations, and how these complimentary processes depend on each other. This kind of research requires interdisciplinary training and interdisciplinary teamwork. As social animals, we are uniquely equipped for such coordination.

REFERENCES

de Bono, M. (2003). Molecular approaches to aggregation behavior and social attachment. *Journal of Neurobiology, 54,* 78–92.

Fiske, A. P. (1991). *Structures of social life: The four elementary forms of human relations.* New York: Free Press (Macmillan).

Fiske, A. P. (1992). The four elementary forms of sociality: framework for a unified theory of social relations. *Psychological Review, 99,* 689–723.

Fiske, A. P. (1993). Social errors in four cultures: Evidence about universal forms of social relations. *Journal of Cross-Cultural Psychology, 24,* 463–494.

Fiske, A. P. (2000). Complementarity theory: Why human social capacities evolved to require cultural complements. *Personality and Social Psychology Review, 4,* 76–94.

Fiske, A. P. (2002). Socio-moral emotions motivate action to sustain social relationships. *Self and Identity, 1,* 169–175.

Fiske, A. P. (2004a). Relational models theory 2.0. In N. Haslam (Ed.), *Relational models theory: A contemporary overview* (pp. 3–25). Mahwah, NJ: Lawrence Erlbaum Associates.

Fiske, A. P. (2004b). Four modes of constituting relationships: Consubstantial assimilation; space, magnitude, time and force; concrete procedures; abstract symbolism. In N. Haslam (Ed.), *Relational models theory: A contemporary overview* (pp. 61–146). Mahwah, NJ: Lawrence Erlbaum Associates.

Fiske, A. P., & Haslam, N. (1997). The structure of social substitutions: A test of relational models theory. *European Journal of Social Psychology, 27,* 725–729.

Fiske, A. P., Haslam, N., & Fiske, S. T. (1992). Confusing one person with another: What errors reveal about the elementary forms of social relations. *Journal of Personality and Social Psychology, 60,* 656–674.

Haslam, N. (2004a). Research on the relational models: An overview. In N. Haslam (Ed.), *Relational models theory: A contemporary overview* (pp. 27–57). Mahwah, NJ: Lawrence Erlbaum Associates.

Haslam, N. (2004b). A relational approach to the personality disorders. In N. Haslam (Ed.), *Relational models theory: A contemporary overview* (pp. 335–362). Mahwah, NJ: Lawrence Erlbaum Associates.

Iacoboni, M., Lieberman, M. D., Knowlton, B. J., Molnar-Szakacs, I., Moritz, M., Throop, C. J., & Fiske, A. P. (2004). Thinking about social relations and the default state of the brain. *NeuroImage, 21,* 1167–1173.

Olaveson, T. (2003). "Connectedness" and the rave experience: Rave as new religious movement? In G. St. John (Ed.), *Rave culture and religion* (pp. 85–106). London: Routledge.

Polanyi, K. (1968). *Primitive, archaic, and modern economies; Essays of Karl Polanyi* (G. Dalton, Ed.). Garden City, NY: Anchor.

Udy, S. (1970). *Work in traditional and modern society.* Englewood Cliffs, NJ: Prentice Hall.

44

Social Psychology of Justice, Just Division of Household Labor, and the Reconciliation of Family and Work Demands

Gerold Mikula
University of Graz

T he social psychology of justice has attracted my research interest from the early seventies of the last century to the present time, although with different foci. More recently, I have become involved in studying justice-related issues of the division of family work, and household labor in particular. My interest in that topic originated in the fact that the division of household labor provides an opportunity to study the role of justice evaluation with respect to the distribution of *negatively valued* outcomes and conditions, such as burdens and duties. This was of interest because previous justice research has nearly exclusively focused on the distribution of positively valued outcomes and conditions. In the meantime, I have become also interested in the division of family work as a research topic in itself because it is a pressing and challenging topic, both at the micro level of close relationships and families and the macro level of society. The present account discusses some benefits and costs of bridging social psychological theory and research on justice with the study of the division of family work between the sexes, and the social issue of reconciling family and professional work. Two kinds of bridging are in the focus of the discussion. First, bridging between theory-driven or "fundamental" research and problem-driven or "applied" research. Second, bridging between a micro-level perspective dealing with intrapersonal and interpersonal processes and a macro-level perspective dealing with societal structures and processes.

THE SOCIAL PSYCHOLOGICAL PERSPECTIVE ON JUSTICE

Different to other scientific disciplines, social psychology takes a descriptive rather than a normative approach to justice. The goal is not to define what is just and unjust, and how justice can be achieved. The focus of social psychology is on the subjective sense of justice and injustice and its impact on human action and judgment. Social psychologists study what people regard as just and unjust under given circumstances, how people deal with the concept of justice, how they react to situations that they regard as unjust, and under which circumstances, and why, people care about justice. Social psychology mainly deals with two different kinds of justice, that is, distributive justice and procedural justice. Briefly speaking, distributive justice refers to the way in which outcomes are distributed while procedural justice relates to the procedures which are used in the decision-making processes by which the distributions are arrived at (cf. Mikula, 2001; Tyler & Smith, 1998).

THE RECONCILIATION OF FAMILY AND PROFESSIONAL WORK AS A PRESSING SOCIAL ISSUE

Due to the significant increase of women's participation in the labor force, the problem of reconciliation of family life and professional work has become a major social issue over the last decades. Thus far, social policy, and research as well, predominantly addressed sociostructural aspects of the problem. Political discussion and interventions deal with the provision of sufficient child-care services and the implementation of family-friendly arrangements at the workplace. Relevant research identified some of the sociostructural conditions that facilitate and hinder women's participation in the labor force. But the problem needs to be approached not only at the societal or macro level. The reconciliation of family and work demands also constitutes a major challenge, and permanent matter of conflict, at the micro level, that is, among partners in close relationships and within families. Accordingly, research is needed at that micro level as well. Needed are thorough analyses of how young parents deal with the problems of reconciling family and work responsibilities, identification of psychological factors that facilitate and hinder successful reconciliation, and systematic studies of the effects of successful and unsuccessful reconciliation on the well-being of parents and children, quality and stability of the couple relationship, family functioning, and parenting from a psychological point of view. The division of family work between the sexes obviously represents one among other important aspects of the problem of reconciliation.

RESEARCH ON THE DIVISION OF HOUSEHOLD LABOR

The division of family work, and household labor in particular, has become a popular topic of research in social sciences in the last two decades. Most of the early research focused on the demonstration of sex-related inequalities in the division of household labor and the exploration of factors that contribute to the gendered division, usually from a sociological perspective. Data were mainly collected as part of nationwide surveys of representative samples of participants. Subjective perceptions, evaluations, and consequences of sex-related inequalities in the division of housework received far less attention in early research. Social psychological justice theory and research have made major contributions to the development of the field in that respect. For instance, the distributive justice framework of Major (1993) and Thompson (1991) provided suggestions as to the factors that contribute to women's justice evaluations and stimulated related research. Relevant data typically were collected with extended questionnaires that were specifically designed for that purpose and referred to various aspects of the division of housework, professional work load, system characteristics (e.g., number and age of children), individual difference variables (e.g., gender role attitudes), and cognitions about the division of labor. Empirical studies have shown, in line with the distributive justice model, that cognitions about the division of household labor, such as appraisals, attributions, comparative judgments, and justifications, significantly contribute to, and explain the largest amount of variance of, women's justice evaluations (cf. Kluwer & Mikula, 2002; Mikula, 1998). Further studies showed that justice evaluations of the division of family work mediate between the division of labor and various consequences such as women's satisfaction with the division of labor, marital quality and conflict, and psychological well-being (cf. Jagoditsch & Mikula, 2004; Mikula & Jagoditsch, 2005). This means that dissatisfaction, reduced psychological well-being, and relational conflicts that go along with unbalanced divisions of labor between women and men are due to feelings of injustice about the imbalance. Social psychological theories of justice and empirical evidence further suggest that it is not only the perceived justice of the particular form of division of labor (i.e., perceived distributive justice) but also the perceived fairness of the process by which partners arrive at a certain kind of the division and deal with related conflicts (i.e. perceived procedural justice) that are relevant to successful management of the problems of reconciliation (cf. Kluwer & Mikula, 2002; Major, 1993).

BENEFITS AND COSTS OF BRIDGING SOCIAL PSYCHOLOGY OF JUSTICE WITH THE SOCIAL ISSUE OF RECONCILING FAMILY AND PROFESSIONAL WORK

Bridging social psychology of justice with the social issue of reconciling family and professional work is a promising enterprise that brings benefits "to both sides of the bridge." The following discussion elaborates on some of the benefits (and some costs) in more detail. The preceding review has shown that social psychological theory of justice and related empirical evidence have enriched the study of gender-related inequalities in the division of household labor. The proof of the mediator effect of women's justice evaluations on various reactions to and consequences of imbalance provides a good example of the benefits of including a justice perspective into the study of the division of family work. The consideration of partners' subjective perceptions of distributive and procedural justice significantly contributes to our understanding of the dynamics and problems of reconciling family and work demands. This does not mean, of course, that a just division of family work between the sexes and a fair procedure of deciding about the division are sufficient to solve the problem of reconciliation. Sociostructural measures such as the implementation of family-friendly arrangements and practices at the workplace and the provision of sufficient child-care services are needed first of all. But, additionally, couples have to arrive at arrangements of their domestic tasks and responsibilities that both partners perceive as just and fair in order to successfully cope with the problems of reconciliation.

It is not only the reconciliation of family and professional work that can benefit from social psychology of justice. Social psychological theory and research on justice also benefit in multiple respects from the study of the division of family work. First, the division of family work provides an ecologically valid and emotionally significant research setting for distributive justice research. Some critics have complained that considerable parts of fundamental justice research do not deal with any "hot" issues that represent serious matters of conflict. The division of household labor obviously is a hot topic, which is able to inflame the sense of injustice and evoke conflicts in close relationships and families, as all of us know. Second, as has been mentioned earlier, studying the division of household labor extends the subject of social psychological research of distributive justice from the distribution of positively valued outcomes and conditions to the hitherto neglected distributions of burdens, duties and responsibilities. Last but not least, the timeliness and societal relevance of the topic attracts the interest of the public, facilitates raising research funds, and helps to get highly motivated people as participants in our studies.

Aside from these mutual benefits of bridging, data on the division of family work can also be used to pursue questions that are primarily relevant to fundamental justice research. Two examples from my research may serve as illustrations. First, we have successfully used data on women's perception of injustice about the division of household labor to test the validity of a theoretical model of judgments of injustice that conceives these judgments as an attribution of blame to somebody for violating a person's entitlement or deserving (Mikula, 2003, study 5). As a second example, data on women's evaluations of the division of household labor and their related cognitions have been used to study the role of social comparison processes in the evaluation of justice and injustice (Mikula & Freudenthaler, 2002).

Before concluding this section, it should be mentioned that building bridges is not without costs. Bridging social psychology of justice with the study of division of family labor, and doing research in settings like households and families, almost inevitably imply a change of research methodology. Experimental methodology is no longer usable for data collection and has to be replaced by a questionnaire methodology. This change from an experimental to a correlational approach implies loss of precision and control and, even more important, of the possibility of making any clear interpretations of the causal relations between the variables under investigation. Of course, the use of causal modeling techniques in data analysis can partly compensate for the latter drawback, but not completely.

CONCLUSIONS

Two different bridges have been in the focus of the present essay on bridging social psychology of justice with the societal issue of reconciling family and professional work. The first bridge connects theory-driven fundamental research with problem-driven applied research. The building of this bridge has been completed already. The bridge is heavily used and has proved to be very successful with benefits to both sides, as has been shown in this essay in some detail.

The second bridge connects macro-level and micro-level perspectives in dealing with the reconciliation of family and professional work. The focus of the macro-level perspective is on societal structures and processes, such as social norms, tax and social security systems, family-friendly arrangements at the workplace, the provision of child-care services, and so on. These structures and processes build the background conditions in which families live and struggle with the reconciliation of family and work demands. The micro-level perspective focuses on how the persons concerned perceive and feel about their situation, strive for practicable and fair solutions, and deal with related discontent, conflicts, and stress in their daily life. Both perspectives provide relevant approaches to the topic of interest and have much to contribute. Accordingly, earlier macro-level research has been complemented by recent micro-level research of social psychologists in important directions. But, in a way, the bridge connecting the macro- and the micro-level perspectives is still under construction. Real bridging of the two perspectives requires more than simply adding two bodies of knowledge. It means an integration that has hardly taken place as yet. A proper understanding of the full range of complexities of the reconciliation of family and professional work requires research that considers the complex interplay of and the mutual influences between the macro level of societal structures and processes and the micro level of personal relationships between partners and of individual characteristics. This task remains to be accomplished in the future.

The reconciliation of family and work demands is one of the great challenges in industrialized countries. Part of the problem can be solved by appropriate sociostructural measures. But this is not enough. The division of family work between the sexes also must become more balanced. This cannot be achieved by sociostructural intervention alone. Changes in the minds of the partners are also necessary. Feelings of injustice about the imbalanced division of family work between the sexes may serve as a catalyst in this respect. Thus, bridging (theory-driven) social psychology of justice with (problem-driven) attempts of reconciliation family and professional work is a promising enterprise that brings benefits to "both sides of the bridge."

REFERENCES

Jagoditsch, S., & Mikula, G. (2004, February). *Gerechtigkeit als Mediator zwischen der Aufteilung der Haushaltsarbeit und interpersonalen Konsequenzen* [Justice as mediator between the division of household labor and interpersonal consequences]. Poster session at the 6th Wissenschaftliche Tagung der Österreichischen Gesellschaft für Psychologie, Innsbruck, Austria.

Kluwer, E., & Mikula, G. (2002). Gender-related inequalities in the division of family work in close relationships: A social psychological perspective. In W. Stroebe & M. Hewstone (Eds.), *European review of social psychology* (Vol. 13, pp. 185–216). Hove: Psychology Press.

Major, B. (1993). Gender, entitlement, and the distribution of family labor. *Journal of Social Issues, 49,* 141–159.

Mikula, G. (1998). Division of household labor and perceived justice: A growing field of research. *Social Justice Research, 11,* 215–242.

Mikula, G. (2001). Justice: Social psychological perspectives. In N. J. Smelser & P. B. Baltes (Eds.), *International encyclopedia of the social and behavioral sciences* (pp. 8063–8067). London: Pergamon Press.

Mikula, G. (2003). Testing an attribution-of-blame model of judgments of injustice. *European Journal of Social Psychology, 33,* 793–811.

Mikula, G., & Freudenthaler, H. H. (2002). Division of tasks and duties and the perception of injustice: The case of household chores. *Psychologische Beiträge, 44,* 567–584.

Mikula, G., & Jagoditsch, S. (2005, July). *Perceived justice of the division of family work: Antecedents and consequences.* Paper presented at the 14th general meeting of the European Association of Experimental Social Psychology, Wuerzburg, Germany.

Thompson, L. (1991). Family work: Women's sense of fairness. *Journal of Family Issues, 12,* 181–196.

Tyler, T. R., & Smith, H. J. (1998). Social justice and social movement. In D. Gilbert, S. T. Fiske, & G. Lindzey (Eds.), *Handbook of social psychology* (4th ed., pp. 595–629). New York: McGraw-Hill.

45

The Bridge Between Social and Clinical Psychology: Wide but Sparsely Traveled

Mark R. Leary

Wake Forest University

The most often cited definition of social psychology is Allport's (1954) broad description of the field as the "attempt to understand and explain how the thought, feeling and behavior of individuals is influenced by the actual, imagined or implied presence of others." In practice, however, social psychologists have often acted as if Allport had included in his definition an explicit qualification that social psychology should exclude the study of thoughts, feelings, and behaviors that connote dysfunction or psychopathology, or that are of any interest whatsoever to clinical and counseling psychologists. Although social psychologists have been interested in other kinds of potentially problematic reactions—such as aggression, intergroup conflict, and discrimination—they have traditionally limited themselves to the adverse thoughts, emotions, and behaviors of seemingly "normal" individuals and left "abnormal" psychology to the clinicians and counselors.

At the same time that social psychology avoided the study of clinically relevant phenomena, clinical psychology was dominated by the intrapsychic emphases of various psychodynamic perspectives. As long as psychological difficulties were attributed to unconscious conflicts and other intrapersonal processes, clinical psychologists saw little need to consider the role of social psychological factors in clinical problems or their treatment. Unfortunately, even after the importance of interpersonal processes and social systems in psychological dysfunction became widely acknowledged, clinical psychologists virtually ignored social psychological theory and research, even when this work was intimately related to the development and treatment of psychological problems. By the middle of the 20th century, the bridge between social and clinical psychology was barely passable, and few on either side of the schism even thought of crossing it. As Goldstein (1966) observed, "Researchers interested in psychotherapy and their colleagues studying social psychological phenomena have gone their separate ways, making scant reference to one another's work and, in general, ignoring what appear to be real opportunities for mutual feedback and stimulation" (p. 39).

The reasons for the long-standing schism between social and clinical psychology can be traced to fundamental differences in their histories, goals, and assumptions (see Forsyth & Leary, 1991; Kowalski & Leary, 1999; Leary & Maddux, 1987). The scientific, metatheoretical, and professional worldviews of social and clinical psychologists are often, if not incompatible, at least different enough to undermine a full appreciation of one another's contributions (Forsyth & Leary, 1991). Social psychologists have traditionally emphasized a nomothetic approach to testing theories about the influence of social variables on normal human behavior through basic (usually experimental) research, whereas clinical psychologists have traditionally emphasized an idiographic approach that focuses on intrapersonal variables underlying psychological dysfunction for the purpose of conducting counseling and psychotherapy.

Despite these differences, starting in the 1960s, a few writers began to argue for greater cross-fertilization between social and clinical psychology (Brehm, 1976; Frank, 1961; Goldstein, 1966; Strong, 1968). These writers pointed out that interpersonal processes play an important role not only in the development of emotional and behavioral problems but also in the diagnosis and treatment of these problems by practicing psychologists. As a result of these and other advocates of a social–clinical interface (e.g., Forsyth & Strong, 1986; Leary & Maddux, 1987; Leary & Miller, 1986; Maddux, 1987; Weary & Mirels, 1982), topics that were traditionally regarded as the domain of clinical and counseling psychology became respectable topics for social psychologists to study. By the end of the 20th century, it was no longer unusual for social psychologists to investigate topics such as depression, anxiety, shyness, hypochondriasis, marital problems, eating disorders, and addictions, as well as the interpersonal processes involved in clinical assessment, counseling, and psychotherapy (Kowalski & Leary, 1999, 2003).

As a science of interpersonal behavior, social psychology should presumably be interested in all of human experience, not just the reactions of the hypothetical typical or normal individual. Theories that purport to account for the effects of "the actual, imagined, or implied presence of others" ought to explain maladaptive thoughts, feelings, and behaviors as well as the typical, normative ones that have been the focus of most social psychological research. Given that psychological problems are often extreme, unusual, or situationally inappropriate manifestations of ordinary reactions (Maddux, 1987), we should find that dysfunctional thoughts, feelings, and behaviors arise from the same interpersonal processes as more adaptive ones. A social psychological perspective does not deny that some psychological problems are rooted in physiological processes and brain disease, yet it stresses that a large proportion of the difficulties for which people seek professional help arise from and are played out in the context of clients' interpersonal lives. Put simply, a comprehensive social psychology must include the study of abnormal as well as normal behavior.

As social psychologists made forays into what was once clinical territory, they returned with new phenomena for social psychological investigation. In retrospect, it is surprising that social psychologists had ignored many interesting interpersonal phenomena simply because they were regarded as clinical in nature. For example, social anxiety, shame, guilt, domestic violence, narcissism, malingering, suicide, social support, transference, clinical judgment, and psychotherapy were all considered "clinical" topics until researchers realized that each involved basic interpersonal processes in its own right. As a result of theory and research at the interface of social and clinical psychology, the breadth of social psychology expanded markedly, as evidenced by the fact that most introductory social psychology textbooks now include discussions of one or more of these previously "clinical" topics.

Applying theories that were developed to explain everyday behavior to clinically relevant phenomena has provided crucial tests of the validity of social psychological theories and the limits of their applicability. Each time that social psychological ideas are extended to dysfunctional behavior, we learn either that these theories do, in fact, help us to understand maladaptive behavior or else that their usefulness is limited by important boundary conditions. In either case, researchers returning across the social–clinical bridge bring back important information for evaluating social psychological approaches. To date, social psychologists have been gratified to realize that many theories that were initially developed with regard to generic interpersonal cognitions, emotions, and behavior are, in fact, useful in understanding the development, diagnosis, and treatment of emotional and behavioral problems (Leary & Miller, 1986).

At the same time, examining clinically relevant topics provides social psychologists with new insights into seemingly "normal" behavior. Seeing how interpersonal processes give rise to maladaptive thoughts, emotions, and behaviors reveals a great deal about "normal" behaviors that we take for granted, often showing that the behaviors of perfectly ordinary individuals are problematic in ways that were not appreciated until their dysfunctional manifestations were studied. For example, documenting the personal and interpersonal costs of narcissism has made the detrimental effects of everyday egotism more obvious, and recognizing that certain patterns of attributions were associated with severe depression alerted social psychologists to negative effects of attributions in seemingly normal individuals. Once one acknowledges that clinical phenomena are typically maladaptive variations of everyday behavior, one sees that people's typical reactions are sometimes a subclinical sort of "pathology of everyday life," as Freud called it. Thus, the bridge between social and clinical psychology allows social psychologists not only to inform clinical research and practice but, by reflection, their own work as well.

By and large, social psychologists have not seen their theories and research embraced by professionals in applied fields as much as they would like, and clinical psychologists have been particularly resistant. Research-oriented clinical psychologists who work in universities often adopt social psychological perspectives, but practicing clinicians and counselors are far less likely to do so. Several factors have hampered the dissemination of social psychological concepts, theories, and findings into clinical and counseling practice. One is that social psychologists who have entered areas of clinical interest have not always done so in a credible, clinically sound fashion. Not only have they sometimes not availed themselves of relevant clinical literatures that would have helped them to draw useful connections to work with which clinicians are familiar, but also they have sometimes oversold the relevance of experiments conducted on college students to severe forms of disorder. As a result of these two factors, clinical and counseling psychologists have found it too easy to ignore or dismiss the potential contributions of social psychology. Although basic experimental research may indeed have implications for understanding clinical phenomena, social psychologists should be careful not to overstate their case.

Of course, the bridge between social and clinical psychology permits travel in both directions, and clinical psychologists have not crossed it in sufficient numbers to take advantage of relevant theories and findings in social psychology. When they have, their applications of social psychological constructs have sometimes been as unsophisticated and ill-informed as social psychologists' efforts to address clinical phenomena. Social psychologists can facilitate the adoption of their work by explicitly addressing its relevance to clinical and counseling psychology. Just a few signposts leading to and from the social–clinical bridge may prevent practitioners from becoming lost.

CONCLUSIONS

My point is not that social psychology should become a scientific appendage of clinical psychology or reorient its agenda to focus specifically on dysfunctional behavior. Many topics in social psychology can neither inform nor be informed by clinical psychology. Yet there are sound scientific, professional, and practical reasons for social psychology to study topics relevant to understanding, diagnosing, and treating psychological problems. Not only are these topics important for social psychologists to understand in their own right, but also social psychological perspectives may contribute to improvements in clinical psychology.

Key topics that deserve continued attention include social influence and group processes that create and maintain maladaptive behavior, dysfunctional emotional reactions (most of which have interpersonal antecedents), problematic relationships, psychological difficulties related to self-awareness and self-evaluation, antisocial behavior, and the interpersonal and attitudinal processes that promote change in clinical contexts (see Kowalski & Leary, 2003). Of course, clinical psychology deals not only with treating psychological difficulties but also with promoting adjustment, and researchers should devote additional attention to the interpersonal processes that enhance psychological and social well-being, such as those related to subjective well-being, self-control, prosocial behavior (including forms of prosocial action that have been relatively neglected in social psychology, such as kindness, compassion, and forgiveness), social support, interpersonal and emotional equanimity, social skill, wisdom, and respect. Social psychology has a great deal to offer—conceptually, theoretically, and methodologically—to the study of psychological dysfunction and well-being.

REFERENCES

Allport, G. W. (1954). *The nature of prejudice.* Garden City, NY: Anchor.

Brehm, S. (1976). *Applications of social psychology to clinical practice.* Washington, DC: Hemisphere.

Forsyth, D. R., & Leary, M. R. (1991). Metatheoretical and epistemological issues. In C. R. Snyder & D. R. Forsyth (Eds.), *Handbook of social and clinical psychology* (pp. 757–773). New York: Pergamon.

Forsyth, D. R., & Strong, S. R. (1986). The scientific study of counseling and psychotherapy: A unificationist view. *American Psychologist, 41,* 113–119.

Frank, J. (1961). *Persuasion and healing.* New York: Schocken Books.

Goldstein, A. P. (1966). Psychotherapy research by extrapolation from social psychology. *Journal of Counseling Psychology, 13,* 38–45.

Kowalski, R. M., & Leary, M. R. (1999). Interfaces of social and clinical psychology: Where we have been, where we are. In R. M. Kowalski & M. R. Leary (Eds.), *The social psychology of emotional and behavioral problems: Interfaces and social and clinical psychology* (pp. 7–33). Washington, DC: American Psychological Association.

Kowalski, R. M., & Leary, M. R. (Eds.). (2003). *Key readings at the interface of social and clinical psychology.* New York: Psychology Press.

Leary, M. R., & Maddux, J. E. (1987). Progress toward a viable interface between social and clinical psychology. *American Psychologist, 42,* 904–911.

Leary, M. R., & Miller, R. S. (1986). *Social psychology and dysfunctional behavior: Origins, diagnosis, and treatment.* New York: Spring-Verlag.

Maddux, J. E. (1987). The interface of social, clinical, and counseling psychology: Why bother and what is it anyway? *Journal of Social and Clinical Psychology, 5,* 27–33.

Strong, S. R. (1968). Counseling: An interpersonal influence process. *Journal of Counseling Psychology, 15,* 215–224.

Weary, G., & Mirels, H. L. (Eds.). (1982). *Integrations of clinical and social psychology.* New York: Oxford University Press.

46

Bridges From Social Psychology to Health

Shelley E. Taylor
University of California, Los Angeles

Kurt Lewin has been credited with the astute observation that there is nothing as practical as a good theory. Although the historical record shows this to be an insight borrowed from an anonymous businessman, Lewin found it to be an apt description of the dynamic relationship he advocated for the relation of theoretical insights generated by laboratory tests of formal theory to the problems and issues of everyday life. Social psychology has vigorously pursued this mission as an exporter of our knowledge to other fields, and health psychology provides an excellent example of the values Lewin espoused.

Health psychology and its intellectual antecedent, behavioral medicine, began in earnest in the 1970s. Although health psychology is sometimes considered an applied field, its research legacy shows that it has been quite faithful to the principles that Lewin put forth. From its inception, health psychology has been an arena in which formal theory has been tested, yielding insights that, in turn, have helped to refine those theories. In this essay, I pursue this characterization with reference to several subfields within health psychology: health behaviors, adjustment to illness, social support, and psychosocial co-factors in the course of illness.

HEALTH BEHAVIORS

Health behaviors are important, not only because they are vital to health, but because quite easily they can become habitual and influence health and susceptibility to illness across the lifespan. Social psychological models have been critical, not only for understanding the attitudinal bases of people's health behaviors, but also for developing interventions to change health behaviors.

Among the earliest such insights was the Health Belief Model (Rosenstock, 1966), which identified key determinants of health behaviors as perceived personal risk and perceived efficacy of the behavioral recommendation for reducing that risk. In a similar vein, Ajzen and his associates (Ajzen, 1991; Ajzen & Fishbein, 1980) addressed the often substantial gap between health attitudes and health behaviors, maintaining that beliefs about a health behavior are only one source of input to behavioral intentions to change behavior; subjective norms and perceived behavioral control are other important components. The theory of planned behavior (Ajzen, 1991) has also been a highly generative theoretical insight from social psychology that led to fruitful applications.

Recently, research on the self has been brought to bear on understanding health habits, and yielded a particularly significant insight: Positive self-perceptions may help people come to grips with health threats and adopt better health behaviors. This counterintuitive observation was originally made in research on optimism. Researchers had, at one time, expressed the fear that optimism about one's health might interfere with the ability to process negative health-related information appropriately. Aspinwall and her colleagues, however, found that optimistic college students were actually more receptive to personally relevant negative information about health risks than were less optimistic students (e.g., Aspinwall & Brunhart, 1996). Similarly, a longitudinal study of gay, HIV-seropositive men found that those men who were more optimistic about not developing AIDS reported greater efforts to maintain their health through diet and exercise (Taylor et al., 1992; see also Carver et al., 1993). Sherman and colleagues found that permitting people to affirm either their values or their positive qualities enabled them to be receptive to negative personally relevant health information, despite the threat such information posed (e.g., Sherman, Nelson, & Steele, 2000).

In the truest spirit of Lewin's legacy, then, social psychological research has not only informed our understanding of when and how people process health threats and take measures to overcome them, but also has provided theoretical insight into how positive self-perceptions may help rather than hinder the ability to deal with threats.

ADJUSTMENT TO THE ILLNESS EXPERIENCE

Despite their best efforts, people often succumb to illnesses, including chronic and life-threatening ones. Although some people experience at least short-term anxiety and depression, very commonly yet surprisingly, people find benefits in these experiences and report an improved quality of life, better relationships, and positive changes in their values and priorities (Taylor, 1983; Updegraff & Taylor, 2000). Evidence of benefit finding, meaning, positive illusions, and growth in the wake of chronic and terminal illness has been found in populations as diverse as cancer patients, low-income women infected with HIV, and people coping with traumatic events (see Updegraff & Taylor, 2000, for a review).

In the past, these observations have sometimes been dismissed by researchers and practitioners as inconsequential, short-lived, or trivial. However, psychological theories of the self have provided a basis for viewing these insights
not only as real, but as critical for subsequent adjustment. Research has now
verified not only that benefit finding in chronic and terminal illness is common, but that it is associated with lower levels of psychological distress
(Updegraff & Taylor, 2000) and with greater attentiveness to actions that may
improve health (e.g., Carver et al., 1996).

SOCIAL SUPPORT

In recent years, the yield of social psychological theory for health has expanded to include a consideration of psychosocial co-factors in the course
of illness. Considered preposterous at one time, the idea that positive relationships and positive states of mind may slow the course of illness and facilitate recovery is coming to be widely acknowledged. Consider social
support as an example. Social psychologists have long studied the rewards
of close relationships. As a result of social psychological forays into health
research, the very important role that socially supportive relationships play
in health and illness has come to be recognized. People with a high quality
or quantity of social relationships have lower mortality rates, and social isolation is a major risk factor for mortality for both humans and animals
(House, Landis, & Umberson, 1988). People with high levels of social support have fewer signs of immunocompromise, they have lower rates of myo-
cardial infarction, and they show better adjustment to coronary artery
disease, diabetes, lung disease, arthritis, and cancer (see Taylor, 2003, for a
review). Social support also enhances the prospects for recovery among
people who are already ill. Experimental research that has provided social
support to hospitalized people has found that it can lead to better adjustment and/or faster recovery (e.g., Kulik & Mahler, 1993). How social support achieves these extraordinary effects is an issue of ongoing
significance. Although many of its benefits came from the concrete assistance and solace that others provided during specific supportive transactions, much of its benefit may come simply from the inherently soothing
qualities of social closeness and the perception that one is loved.

PSYCHOSOCIAL BELIEFS AS CO-FACTORS IN THE COURSE OF ILLNESS

Similarly, positive beliefs such as the ability to find meaning in threatening
events, and optimism, even unrealistic optimism have been associated with a
slower course of illness in chronically ill populations (see Taylor, Kemeny,
Reed, Bower, & Gruenewald, 2000). Such findings, in turn, have led to an interest in the biopsychosocial pathways by which such impressive effects may be
mediated. Both social support and positive beliefs may have beneficial effects
on the cardiovascular, endocrine, and immune systems (e.g., Uchino,

Cacioppo, & Kiecolt-Glaser, 1996), and these effects, in turn, may moderate disease course.

Would Lewin have anticipated that social psychologists would move into the biology of health and illness? The answer is, probably no, but I believe that he would be pleased with this development. Insights from social psychological theories have brought to light the mechanisms whereby psychosocial co-factors affect the course of illness, and without these insights, such knowledge would have been slow to develop.

CONCLUSIONS

I have focused on only a few examples of how social psychological theory has provided scientific understanding of health, illness, and their determinants and course. Numerous others could be found. For example, recognizing the importance of psychological control over threatening events has led to interventions to help people cope with noxious medical procedures (e.g., Janis, 1958; Johnson & Leventhal, 1974). Social psychological theories have been invaluable in predicting when people are most likely to experience stress; specifically, negative, uncontrollable, and ambiguous events and those that overload resources are more likely to produce stress and its noxious biological concomitants (e.g., Cohen & Williamson, 1991). These are but a few of the contributions that social psychological theories have made to our understanding of health and illness as well as the insights that the health area has generated, in return, for social psychological theories. Through these and related contributions, significant progress has been made in understanding the psychosocial forces that so clearly impinge on health.

REFERENCES

Ajzen, I. (1991). The theory of planned behavior. *Organizational Behavior and Human Decision Processes, 50,* 179–211.

Ajzen, I., & Fishbein, M. (1980). *Understanding attitudes and predicting social behavior.* Englewood Cliffs, NJ: Prentice-Hall.

Aspinwall, L. G., & Brunhart, S. M. (1996). Distinguishing optimism from denial: Optimistic beliefs predict attention to health threats. *Personality and Social Psychology Bulletin, 22,* 993–1003.

Carver, C. S., Pozo, C., Harris, S. D., Noriega, V., Scheier, M. F., Robinson, D. S., Ketcham, A. S., Moffat, F. L., & Clark, K. C. (1993). How coping mediates the effect of optimism on distress: A study of women with early stage breast cancer. *Journal of Personality and Social Psychology, 65,* 375–390.

Cohen, S., & Williamson, G. M. (1991). Stress and infectious disease in humans. *Psychological Bulletin, 109,* 5–24.

House, J. S., Landis, K. R., & Umberson, D. (1988). Social relationships and health. *Science, 241,* 540–545.

Janis, I. L. (1958). *Psychological stress.* New York: Wiley.

Johnson, J. E., & Leventhal, H. (1974). Effects of accurate expectations and behavioral instructions on reactions during a noxious medical examination. *Journal of Personality and Social Psychology, 29,* 710–718.

Kulik, J. A., & Mahler, H. I. M. (1993). Emotional support as a moderator of adjustment and compliance after coronary artery bypass surgery: A longitudinal study. *Journal of Behavioral Medicine, 16,* 54–64.

Rosenstock, I. M. (1966). Why people use health services. *Milbank Memorial Fund Quarterly, 44,* 94ff.

Sherman, D. A. K., Nelson, L. D., & Steele, C. M. (2000). Do messages about health risks threaten the self? Increasing the acceptance of threatening health messages via self-affirmation. *Personality and Social Psychology Bulletin, 26,* 1046–1058.

Taylor, S. E. (1983). Adjustment to threatening events: A theory of cognitive adaptation. *American Psychologist, 38,* 1161–1173.

Taylor, S. E. (2003). *Health psychology* (5th ed.). New York: McGraw-Hill.

Taylor, S. E., Kemeny, M., Aspinwall, L. G., Schneider, S. G., Rodriguez, R., & Herbert, M. (1992). Optimism, coping, psychological distress, and high-risk sexual behavior among men at risk for AIDS. *Journal of Personality and Social Psychology, 63,* 460–473.

Taylor, S. E., Kemeny, M. E., Reed, G. M., Bower, J. E., & Gruenewald, T. L. (2000). Psychological resources, positive illusions, and health. *American Psychologist, 55,* 99–109.

Uchino, B. N., Cacioppo, J. T., & Kiecolt-Glaser, J. K. (1996). The relationship between social support and physiological processes: A review with emphasis on underlying mechanisms and implications for health. *Psychological Bulletin, 119,* 488–531.

Updegraff, J. A., & Taylor, S. E. (2000). From vulnerability to growth: The positive and negative effects of stressful life events. In J. Harvey & E. Miller (Eds.), *Loss and trauma* (pp. 3–28). Philadelphia, PA: Taylor & Francis.

47

Happiness, Life Satisfaction, and Fulfillment: The Social Psychology of Subjective Well-Being

Ed Diener
University of Illinois and the Gallup Organization

Maya Tamir
Stanford University

Christie Napa Scollon
Texas Christian University

Subjective well-being (SWB) concerns how people evaluate their lives—in terms of satisfaction judgments (with life as well as with domains such as marriage and work), and in terms of moods and emotions, which reflect evaluations of ongoing events. Both the presence of frequent pleasant emotions and that of infrequent unpleasant emotions are considered hallmarks of high SWB. Subjective well-being is important because it is democratic. It allows individuals themselves, rather than experts or policymakers, to evaluate the quality of their own lives. SWB is also an important scientific topic because it often leads to successful outcomes in life (Lyubomirsky, King, & Diener, 2003) such as increased community involvement, a successful marriage, and a higher income. For reviews on SWB and related research, the reader is referred to Diener (1984), Diener, Suh, Lucas, and Smith (1999), Diener and Suh (2000), and Kahneman, Diener, and Schwarz (1999).

THE SOCIAL NATURE OF SWB

Other fields within and outside psychology have greatly contributed to our understanding of SWB. For example, sociologists have examined the relationship between SWB and demographic factors, personality psychologists study the relation between stable individual differences and SWB, and cognitive psychologists have studied the way SWB judgments are related to other affective and cognitive processes. Importantly, because each perspective offers valuable contributions, a full understanding of SWB requires linking research from social psychology to research from other disciplines.

Social psychology research on SWB has provided findings that form the core of our understanding in this area. First, several of the important determinants of SWB are social, including social relationships and culture. Second, SWB has important social outcomes and implications. Third, the experiential nature of SWB and judgments of life satisfaction depend on social-cognitive processes. We next describe some of the major findings within each of these domains.

DETERMINANTS OF SWB

Social Relationships. Social relationships, involving both friendships and familial relations, have a major influence on SWB. In fact, high-quality social relationships are necessary to high SWB (Diener & Seligman, 2002). People who have several close friends are happier and more satisfied with their lives compared to people who have none. Indeed, Diener and Seligman found that no individuals were extremely happy without good relationships. Specific role relationships such as marital status and family satisfaction are related to SWB. Married people report more happiness and life satisfaction compared to those who are not married or are divorced or separated (Diener et al., 1999). Similarly, parental divorce has negative consequences for children's SWB (Gohm, Oishi, Darlington, & Diener, 1998). It appears that marital status might have a causal effect on SWB (Lucas, Clark, Georgellis, & Diener, 2003). Lucas and his colleagues offer longitudinal evidence that changes in marital status, for example becoming a widow, can be detrimental to SWB. Such findings suggest that changing social relationships can cause changes in life satisfaction.

Culture. Another important social factor that leads to differences in SWB concerns cultural differences. The study of culture and SWB (see Diener, Oishi, & Lucas, 2003; Diener & Suh, 2000) is one of the most fascinating fields in the area. Emerging cultural differences in factors that have been assumed to be universal correlates of SWB have led researchers to reexamine prior conclusions about the causes and nature of SWB. For example, self-esteem has long been considered an important universal cause of SWB. However, cross-cultural research reveals that self-esteem is much more important to life satis-

faction in individualistic societies such as in the United States than in collec-
tivist ones such as India (Diener & Diener, 1995). Suh, Diener, Oishi, and
Triandis (1998) found that respondents in collectivistic societies placed
more weight on how their family evaluated their lives, whereas respondents
in individualistic nations put more weight on their personal emotional happiness. Income is more important to SWB in rich nations than in poor ones
(Diener & Biswas-Diener, 2002). Although wealthy nations on average are
happier than poor ones, the effect of income on SWB is greater within poor
societies where basic physical needs are more likely to go unmet.

Culture also influences subjective well-being through emotion norms, attitudes toward whether specific emotions are appropriate and desirable (Eid &
Diener, 2001). For example, respondents in Latin America rated positive emotions as highly desirable, and indeed report experiencing more of such emotions (e.g., Diener & Tov, in press). In contrast, people in East Asian cultures
are more accepting of negative emotions and report more experience of them.
Thus, culture can have important effects both on levels of well-being and on
the causes of it.

Demographics.   Sociologists were among the first to study SWB, by examining how it is related to demographic factors (e.g., Wilson, 1967). Some of the
factors that have been examined are income, age, gender, race, employment,
and education. Many of these demographic effects were small, however, and often all of them together did not account for large amounts of variance. Other
factors, such as marital status and religious beliefs, have demonstrated larger
effects on SWB. Rather than studying the direct effect of demographic factors,
using the social psychology perspective, researchers can examine the effect (or
lack, thereof) of demographic factors within specific contexts. For example, as
discussed earlier, studying the effects of income within nations indicates that
there is a larger relation between income and SWB at lower levels of income, or
in relatively poor nations (Diener & Biswas-Diener, 2002). Thus, studying demographic factors within a cultural or social context can increase our understanding of SWB.

THE IMPORTANCE OF PERSONALITY

Unlike demographic factors, personality often proves to be a strong determinant of SWB, and accounts for a large portion of the variance in the experience of well-being (e.g., Lykken & Tellegen, 1996). Mischel's (1968)
conclusions are turned on their head in this area—with situations often not
being very influential, and personality being extremely so. One reason for this
is that SWB researchers are concerned with long-term averages in positive
emotions, not in immediate momentary feelings. A second reason for the
power of personality is that people seem to adapt over time to many situations
(see Diener et al., 1999), so that circumstances quit having a large impact on
their SWB.

CONSEQUENCES OF SWB

The research described thus far concerns the antecedents and causes of SWB, showing that many such antecedents are social in nature. However, such links are often bidirectional, with SWB influencing and changing social factors. Specifically, positive emotions can have profound influences on social behavior (Lyubomirsky et al., 2003). For example, positive affect seems to heighten sociability and self-confidence. Happier people are more likely to get married, and to show empathy and be sociable to others. They are also rated more highly by their supervisors, and are likely to earn higher incomes. Thus, social relationships not only influence people's levels of SWB, but positive emotions and satisfaction can in turn influence people's social behavior.

COGNITION AND SWB

So far, we have considered the relation between SWB and social factors, as both antecedents and consequences. However, social psychology has gone beyond the study of social factors per se, to examine the way people perceive and interpret situations. Social cognitive approaches have significantly contributed to our understanding of how judgments of SWB are formed. A seminal work by Campbell, Converse, and Rodgers (1976) explored how comparison to various standards (e.g., social comparisons) influence feelings of well-being. Specifically, when making life satisfaction judgments, people often compare their current state to some available standard. This standard might be based on other people, on past or future selves, or on some ideal. Another area where cognitive psychology has illuminated SWB is in terms of the effects of memory on recall of happiness.

Judgments of life satisfaction are also influenced by the interaction between the respondent and the examiner. A sophisticated set of studies conducted by Schwarz and Strack (1999) reveals how social communication and social cognitive processes within the survey setting can affect how people think about their life satisfaction. For example, the comparison standards against which people judge their lives can be altered based on situational considerations. If participants are asked to evaluate their lives when a person in a wheelchair is in the room, they give higher ratings of life satisfaction. Such studies suggest that SWB is influenced not only by social factors but also by situational factors.

CONCLUSIONS

What is the best approach to SWB? Social psychology has provided an important framework for the study of SWB. It has oriented SWB researchers toward situational factors and social variables as well as offer important methodological tools. However, as we hope this chapter demonstrates, studying SWB solely from a social psychology perspective would lead us to overlook influential factors that shape SWB, such as personality and cognition. Therefore, in addition to relying on the methods and theoretical foci of social psychology, we believe that integrating them with research from other disciplines is critical to a complete understanding of happiness, life satisfaction, and well-being. One cannot understand what makes people happy without exploring social factors. One cannot understand *who* is happy without exploring personality and cultural factors. One cannot understand when one declares oneself happy without considering social cognitive processes involved in satisfaction judgments. Interdisciplinary bridges are especially needed in this area because a scientific analysis of SWB is inherently a multidisciplinary matter. Fortunately, a growing amount of integrative studies of social processes, culture, personality, and cognition suggest that such bridges can be and are being built.

REFERENCES

Campbell, A., Converse, P. E., & Rodgers, W. L. (1976). *The quality of American life.* New York: Russell Sage Foundation.

Diener, E. (1984). Subjective well-being. *Psychological Bulletin, 95,* 542–575.

Diener, E., & Biswas-Diener, R. (2002). Will money increase subjective well-being? A literature review and guide to needed research. *Social Indicators Research, 57,* 169–199.

Diener, E., & Diener, M. (1995). Cross-cultural correlates of life satisfaction and self-esteem. *Journal of Personality and Social Psychology, 68,* 653–663.

Diener, E., Oishi, S., & Lucas, R. E. (2003). Personality, culture, and subjective well-being: Emotional and cognitive evaluations of life. *Annual Review of Psychology, 2003, 54,* 403–425.

Diener, E., & Seligman, M. E. P. (2002). Very happy people. *Psychological Science, 13,* 80–83.

Diener, E., & Suh, E. M. (Eds.). (2000). *Culture and subjective well-being.* Cambridge, MA: MIT Press.

Diener, E., Suh, E. M., Lucas, R. E., & Smith, H. E. (1999). Subjective well-being: Three decades of progress. *Psychological Bulletin, 125,* 276–302.

Diener, E., & Tov, W. (in press). Culture and subjective well-being. In S. Kitayama & D. Cohen (Eds.), *Handbook of cultural psychology.*

Eid, M., & Diener, E. (2001). Norms for experiencing emotions in different cultures: Inter- and intranational differences. *Journal of Personality and Social Psychology, 81,* 869–885.

Gohm, C. L., Oishi, S., Darlington, J., & Diener, E. (1998). Culture, parental conflict, parental marital status, and subjective well-being of young adults. *Journal of Marriage and the Family, 60,* 319–334.

Kahneman, D., Diener, E., & Schwarz, N. (Eds.). (1999). *Well-being: The foundations of hedonic psychology.* New York: Russell Sage Foundation.

Lucas, R. E., Clark, A. E., Georgellis, Y., & Diener, E. (2003). Re-examining adaptation and the setpoint model of happiness: Reactions to changes in marital status. *Journal of Personality and Social Psychology, 84,* 527–539.

Lykken, D., & Tellegen, A. (1996). Happiness is a stochastic phenomenon. *Psychological Science, 7,* 186–189.

Lyubomirsky, S., King, L., & Diener, E. (in press). The benefits of frequent affect: Does happiness lead to success? *Psychological Bulletin.*

Mischel, W. (1968). *Personality and assessment.* New York: John Wiley & Sons.

Schwarz, N., & Strack, F. (1999). Reports of subjective well-being: Judgmental Processes and their methodological implications. In D. Kahneman, E. Diener, & N. Schwarz (Eds.), *Well-being: The foundations of hedonic psychology* (pp. 61–84). New York: Russell Sage Foundation.

Suh, E., Diener, E., Oishi, S., & Triandis, H. C. (1998). The shifting basis of life satisfaction judgments across cultures: Emotions versus norms. *Journal of Personality and Social Psychology, 74,* 482–493.

Wilson, W. (1967). Correlates of avowed happiness. *Psychological Bulletin, 67,* 294–306.

Social Psychology and Health Promotion

Gerjo Kok

Nanne K. de Vries

University of Maastricht, the Netherlands

One of the oldest and most prominent application areas of social psychological theory is health. In this essay, we focus on health promotion programs, such as HIV prevention, smoking cessation, and self-management of chronic diseases. Modern health promotion is evidence based, using empirical data and theory. For health promotion, social psychology is one of the most important contributing disciplines. Although a broad range of social and behavioral science theories is available, the actual application of these theories into practice remains a challenge, although recently developed protocols are of great help.

DEVELOPMENTS IN HEALTH PROMOTION

Health promotion is the combination of educational and environmental supports for actions and conditions of living conducive to health (Green & Kreuter, 1999), thereby including health education. Health promotion can be characterized by five main developments: the recognition of environmental factors in addition to individual behavior, the need for planning, the importance of evaluation, the use of social and behavioral science theories, and the systematic application of evidence and theories in the development of health promotion interventions (Bartholomew, Parcel, Kok, & Gottlieb, 2001; 2006). We next elaborate on the use and application of evidence and theory, especially social psychological theories.

SOCIAL PSYCHOLOGICAL THEORIES

A health promotion program is most likely to benefit participants and the community when it is guided by social psychological and other behavioral science theories of health behavior and health behavior change. Theory-driven health promotion requires an understanding of the components of the theory as well as an understanding of the operational forms of these theories. Finding and applying relevant theories is a professional skill that health educators have to master (Bartholomew et al., 2001; 2006). Notice that all problems may profit from a *multitheory approach* on condition that these theories are, first, supported by empirical evidence and, second, applied appropriately and correctly.

So, theories are extremely important tools for professionals in health education and promotion. Although theories are available to health promotion practice through textbooks (for good examples, see Norman, Abraham, & Conner, 2000), the correct application of theory has long been a challenge, for researchers as well as practitioners. Students of health promotion usually study theories and are taught how to apply theories to well-selected practical problems. However, in real life the order is reversed: The problem is given and the practitioner has to find theories that may be helpful for better understanding or changing behaviors and circumstances that are causally related to that problem. Recently, a protocol was published that describes a process for developing theory-based and evidence-based health promotion programs: *intervention mapping* (Bartholomew et al., 2001; 2006).

INTERVENTION MAPPING

Intervention mapping describes the process of health promotion program development in five steps:

1. The definition of proximal program objectives based on scientific analyses of health problems and causal factors (on all levels, from individual to societal).
2. The selection of theory-based intervention methods and practical strategies to change (determinants of) health-related behavior.
3. The production of the program components.
4. The anticipation of programme adoption, implementation, and sustainability.
5. The anticipation of process and effect evaluation.

Bartholomew et al. described three core processes for intervention mapping, that is, specific tools for the professional health promoter: searching the *literature* for empirical findings, accessing and using *theory*, and collecting and using *new data*. Of course, when planning intervention development for a specific problem the sensible thing to do is to search the literature to find out what others have written about possible explanatory factors (and thus openings for solutions) for the problem at hand. Especially, reviews and meta-analyses are extremely useful at this stage. However, in many cases a literature search will only result in a *provisional list of answers*.

Subsequently, planners should take a broader view and search for theory that can help to design a more comprehensive explanation for the problem at hand. This can be done using three approaches. We call these (a) the issue approach, (b) the concept approach, and (c) the general theory approach. In an *issue approach* one searches the literature again, but now specifically for theoretical perspectives on the issue or problem one is facing. The *concept approach* begins with the provisional list of answers that were identified from the literature search, as earlier mentioned, or in brainstorm. The concepts on that list should be linked to theoretical constructs and theories that may be useful. In the *general theory approach*, planners consider general theories that may be applicable. Finally, it is important to identify gaps in the information obtained and collect new data to fill these gaps.

APPLYING SOCIAL PSYCHOLOGY: EXAMPLES

Many social psychological theories are widely applied in the field of health promotion, although not always appropriately. Theories on attitudes and attitude change, risk perception, decision making, stereotyping, intimate relations, emotions, self-regulation, social comparison, attribution, modeling and social learning, habit, automaticity, social influence, goal setting, innovation—they all find their way in health promotion.

The impact of social psychology theory is strongest in the steps to program objectives and from there to program strategy. Theory provides the basis both for analyzing causes of problems and for the method for the accomplishment of program objectives; the parameters (prerequisites) of the methods guide the translation of methods into strategies. First, we give an example of an intervention that failed to use theory correctly.

An often-proposed strategy in prevention of drug use programs for schools is to have former drug users warn the students against the dangers of drugs. This strategy is very popular with students, teachers, parents, school boards, and politicians. However, evaluation studies have shown very clearly that this strategy leads to a significant increase in drug use among the students (de Haes, 1987).

The program planners made two mistakes: the former drug users provide an incorrect model for the students in showing them that even people that start using drugs may end up in a very respectable position, in this case lecturing in schools. The second mistake is that the focus of the message is on the dangers of drug use (fear arousal), whereas the most important determinants of behavior here are self-efficacy and skills for decision making and to resist social pressure. In this case, evidence in the form of theory and empirical data was not used adequately. We now give some examples of adequate theory application.

Modeling/Vicarious Learning.   In a HIV-prevention program (Schaalma et al., 1996), one of the objectives was: Adolescents express their confidence in successfully negotiating condom use with a sex partner. A determinant here is self-efficacy. To find methods for improving self-efficacy, we first turn to Bandura's social cognitive theory (Bandura, 1997). Suggested methods are modeling, guided practice, and enactment. Other methods might be reattribution, goal setting, and training of coping responses (Bartholomew et al., 2001). Modeling may be effective, but only with prerequisites:

1. The target identifies with the model.
2. The model demonstrates feasible subskills.
3. The model receives reinforcement.
4. The target perceives a coping model, not a mastery model.

Using modeling in the program would only be effective when the parameters for this method are kept in place during the development of the practical materials. Schaalma and colleagues developed video scenes as part of their program, in which models demonstrate the subskills for negotiating condom use with unwilling partners (explained earlier in the program): rejection, repeated rejection with arguments, postponement, making excuses, avoiding the issue, and/or counteraction (derived from Evans, Getz, & Raines, 1991). The models were carefully selected to serve as identifiable models for the target population. All scenes had a positive ending, but the models were clearly struggling with their task of persuading their partners to use a condom. Keep in mind that these scenes were only a part of the program, in which a series of various methods for many objectives were translated into practical strategies within an integrated program.

Attitude Change.   The theory of planned behavior (Ajzen & Fishbein, 2001) suggests an insight into relevant beliefs as the basis of attitude change interventions. Witte (1995) organizes the results of a beliefs analysis in a list of relevant categories, and then decides which beliefs need to be changed, which need to be reinforced, and which need to be introduced. Schaalma and Kok (2001), for example, list the following objectives for attitude change, based on an earlier analysis of beliefs:

1. Adolescents perceive that condom use has advantages that are not related to health (to be introduced).
2. Adolescents have a strong perception of the health-related advantages of condom use (to be reinforced).
3. Adolescents recognize that advantages of safe sex outweigh the disadvantages (to be changed).
4. Adolescents describe a plan to cope with the disadvantages of condom use (to be introduced).

Schaalma et al. use various methods for attitude change, for example, evoking anticipated regret, active processing of information, linking beliefs with enduring values, and associating attitude object with positive stimuli. The scenario information discussed earlier may be combined with the method of anticipated regret: asking people to imagine how they would feel after risk behavior, for instance, having had unsafe sex (Richard, Van de Pligt, & de Vries, 1995). The parameter for anticipated regret is that the regret question should stimulate imagery.

Fear Arousal. Many health promotion interventions use some kind of fear-arousing messages to promote safer behavior. Theories of fear-arousing communication and recent meta-analyses (e.g., Milne, Sheeran, & Orbell, 2000) suggest that fear arousal may enhance the motivation to avert the threat, but that acceptance of health recommendations is mainly dependent on people's outcome expectations regarding the recommendations (what will happen if I follow the recommendations?) and their self-efficacy (how confident am I that I can follow the recommendations?). In addition, high levels of fear may easily inhibit persuasion through processes of denial and defensive avoidance (Ruiter, Abraham, & Kok, 2001), especially when response efficacy or self-efficacy is low. So, when using fear arousal, we should always provide coping methods for reducing the perceived threat and teach the skills for applying the coping methods. The optimal strategy might be a combination of creating personal risk awareness, without arousing too much fear, and developing skills for the desired behavior change. In this respect, the current interest in implementation intentions, developing vivid ideas on how to perform the desired behavior in practice, may lead to new ideas on effective interventions (Sheeran, 2002). Implementation intentions seem to facilitate the conversion of vague ideas ("I think I will ...") to proper action plans, creating mnemonics to not forget when and how to perform a desired behavior, preparing for difficulties one is about to encounter and strategies to overcome these.

CONCLUSIONS

Adequate application of social psychological theory is essential for effective behavior change interventions. Theories and empirical evidence form the basis for decisions during the planning process, by helping to answer questions about the problem, the behavioral and environmental factors involved, the determinants of behavior, the objectives of the program, appropriate methods and strategies, implementation, and evaluation. In practice, however, applying social psychology appears to be rather difficult.

Intervention mapping is a protocol for systematically applying theoretical and empirical evidence when designing health promotion programs. In this essay, we emphasized that planners have to take into account the parameters of the theories they apply, the prerequisites for effectiveness, when they translate a theoretical method into a practical intervention strategy. We have provided some examples to show that sticking to theoretical, causal parameters is essential (cf. the use of models in the drug prevention project) and at the same time feasible (cf. the examples of STD and fear arousal). In doing so, it is important (a) to consider multiple theories and not a single theory, and also theory not as yet applied to the specific problem; (b) to fill in the gaps by gathering new data; (c) to carefully evaluate effects and thereby contribute to the body of knowledge; and (d) to take theory seriously by respecting causal conditions specified. Thus, adequate use of the intervention mapping protocol will bridge the gap between social psychological theory and health promotion in everyday life.

REFERENCES

Ajzen, I., & Fishbein, M. (2000). Attitudes and the attitude-behavior relation: Reasoned and automatic processes. In W. Stroebe & M. Hewstone (Eds.), *European review of social psychology* (Vol. 11, pp. 1–33). Chichester, UK: Wiley.

Bandura, A. (1997). *Self-efficacy: The exercise of control.* New York: Freeman.

Bartholomew, L. K., Parcel, G. S., Kok, G., & Gottlieb, N. (2001). *Intervention mapping: a process for designing theory- and evidence-based health education and promotion programs.* Mountain View, CA: Mayfield.

Bartholomew, L. K., Parcel, G. S., Kok, G., & Gottlieb, N. H. (2006). *Planning health promotion programs: An Intervention Mapping approach.* San Francisco, CA: Jossey-Bass.

de Haes, W. F. (1987). Looking for effective drug education programmes: Fifteen years exploration of the effects of different drug education programmes. *Health Education Research, 2,* 433–438.

Evans, R. I., Getz, J. G., & Raines, B. S. (1991, August). *Theory guided models on prevention of AIDS in adolescents.* Paper presented at the Science Weekend at the American Psychological Association Meeting, San Francisco, CA.

Green, L. W., & Kreuter, M. W. (1999). *Health promotion planning: An educational and ecological approach.* Mountain View, CA: Mayfield.

Milne, S., Sheeran, P., & Orbell, S. (2000). Prediction and intervention in health-related behavior: A meta-analytic review of protection motivation theory. *Journal of Applied Social Psychology, 30,* 106–143.

Norman, P., Abraham, C., & Conner, M. (2000). *Understanding and changing health behavior: From health beliefs to self-regulation.* Amsterdam: Harwood Academic.

Richard, R., Van der Pligt, J., & de Vries, N. (1995). Anticipated affective reactions and prevention of AIDS. *British Journal of Social Psychology, 34,* 9–21.

Ruiter, R. A. C., Abraham, C., & Kok, G. (2001). Scary warnings and rational precautions: A review of the psychology of fear appeals. *Psychology and Health, 16,* 613–630.

Schaalma, H., & Kok, G. (2001). A school aids prevention program in the Netherlands. In K. Bartholomew, G. Parcel, G. Kok, & N. Gottlieb, *Intervention mapping: A process for designing theory- and evidence based health education and promotion programs* (pp. 353–386). Mountain View, CA: Mayfield.

Schaalma, H. P., Kok, G. J., Bosker, R., Parcel, G., Peters, L., Poelman, J., & Reinders, J. (1996). Planned development and evaluation of AIDS/STD education for secondary school students in the Netherlands: Short-term effects. *Health Education Quarterly, 23,* 469–487.

Sheeran, P. (2002). Intention-behavior relation: A conceptual and empirical review. In W. Stroebe & M. Hewstone (Eds.), *European review of social psychology* (Vol. 12, pp. 1–36). Chichester, UK: Wiley.

Witte, K. (1995). Fishing for success: Using the persuasive health message framework to generate effective campaign messages. In E. Maibach & R. L. Parrott (Eds.), *Designing health messages* (pp. 145–166). Thousand Oaks, CA: Sage.

49

Bridging to Evidence-Based Public Health Policy

Geoffrey T. Fong
David Hammond
Mark P. Zanna
University of Waterloo

Kurt Lewin devoted his life to the interplay between theory and practice. He believed that social psychological research could uncover the basic laws and dynamics of human behavior and that those laws could be used to effect social change. For Lewin, there was no conflict between theory and application. It was not only possible but desirable and feasible to pursue the idea that social psychology could make the world a better place.

We argue in this essay that the concepts and, especially, the methods of social psychology can and should play a more significant role in policies designed to enhance public health. There are two main ways in which social psychologists are well suited to play a significant role. First, social psychologists focus on social influence processes that are at the core of public health policies that encourage healthy behaviors and discourage unhealthy behaviors. Second, and the focus of the present essay, social psychologists have developed and refined a number of research methods that are well suited to addressing issues of whether policies are effective. It is in the evaluation of public health policies that the methodological prowess of social psychologists is urgently needed.

THE INCREASING SIGNIFICANCE OF EMPIRICAL EVIDENCE IN PUBLIC HEALTH

Perhaps the most influential event in modern medicine has been the emergence of evidence-based medicine. Ever since the seminal Salk polio vaccine trial in the 1950s demonstrated the power of the experiment to test the effects of a treatment, there has been a rapid accumulation of evidence gathered from rigorous studies of treatment options for virtually all of the major diseases. As a result, clinical practice guidelines have been established and systematic reviews of treatment effectiveness (such as the Cochrane Collaboration) have given researchers and clinicians access to "state-of-the-art" knowledge of which treatments are effective and which are not. Today's conventional wisdom is more evidence based than it has ever been.

If clinical medicine ought to be guided by evidence, so should preventive medicine. That is, public health policies designed to reduce future harm should be subject to the same rigorous evaluation as clinical treatments. Thus far, however, there has not been a comparable movement to build an evidence-based public health policy system. Because behavioral risk factors (such as tobacco use and unsafe sexual practices) are often implicated in major diseases (such as cancer and HIV/AIDS), public health policy represents a critical (and sometimes the only) means of avoiding or delaying some of the leading causes of death and disability in the world. Although evidence for the etiologic role of behavioral risk factors is also growing steadily, evidence concerning how to modify these risk factors at the population level through effective public health policies has been much slower to develop.

We turn now to a description of how evidence gathered from rigorous studies could influence public health policy in one critical domain for global health: tobacco use.

THE PUBLIC HEALTH CONSEQUENCES OF TOBACCO USE

Tobacco use has been identified by the World Health Organization (WHO) as the leading cause of preventable death and disability in the world. Of people alive today, 500 million will die of tobacco-related causes. And, because 82% of the 1.1 billion smokers live in low- and middle-income countries, developing nations—many currently suffering from the economic and social consequences of HIV/AIDS—will, within a generation, experience a new wave of devastation from tobacco use. In addition to the personal costs of this preventable tragedy, the economic and social costs will pose major challenges to economic growth and stability in the developing world.

RECENT AND UPCOMING DEVELOPMENTS IN TOBACCO CONTROL

In May 2003, in recognition of the global threat of tobacco use, all 192 member states of the WHO, representing 95% of the world's population, adopted the Framework Convention on Tobacco Control (FCTC), the first treaty devoted entirely to health. The FCTC specifies national-level tobacco control policies that the signing nations will be obligated to implement in the coming years. These include larger and more prominent warning labels, prohibitions on the use of "light' or "mild' or other misleading brand descriptors, restrictions/prohibitions on advertising and promotion of tobacco products, increases in taxation, measures to limit exposure to secondhand smoke, and measures designed to eliminate illicit trade.

The FCTC is a major milestone in global health, yet there are formidable challenges as the treaty moves into the implementation phase. One major challenge is to facilitate passage of the provisions of the FCTC in a timely fashion. Countries throughout the world will undoubtedly face resistance in this process, and tobacco control policymakers will need to address questions such as, "Do graphic warning labels reduce the prevalence of tobacco use?" "Will advertising restrictions be sufficient or must there be a total ban?"

THE IMPORTANCE OF EVALUATION IN TOBACCO CONTROL

As tobacco control policies are formulated and implemented, it is important for such policies to be accompanied by rigorous evaluation. As intuitively appealing as it may be to put graphic photographs on warning labels, or to restrict sponsorship activities of tobacco companies, it is imperative that we conduct evaluation research that provides evidence for the effects of such policies, including how and why they do (or do not) work. Such research would not only serve to evaluate existing policies, but would also have the potential to inform future policies—and doing so will provide policymakers with the evidence necessary to implement policies of demonstrated effectiveness.

Although there has been a recent increase in tobacco policy research, much of the research is based on cross-sectional data. These research designs are limited in their ability to reveal the underlying causal mechanisms of policies. Although national policies have the greatest potential impact, to date there exist few published studies at all that have evaluated national tobacco control policies. Thus, our understanding of national policies is also limited.

THE CHALLENGE OF EVALUATING TOBACCO CONTROL POLICIES

It is not possible to conduct in vivo experiments to evaluate the effects of a tobacco control policy. Governments, not researchers, control the implementation of the policy, and governments are generally precluded from systematically varying the implementation of the policy in a way that would allow for random assignment (e.g., delaying the introduction of warning labels to some provinces) because this would violate the principle of equal protection. In short, randomized controlled trials are not possible in the evaluation of tobacco control policies.

There are, however, three major strategies that researchers can employ to rigorously evaluate the effects of policies. First is the use of quasi-experimental designs, in which one group exposed to the policy is compared to a group that is not exposed to the policy. Although the logic of control/comparison groups is well understood in social psychology, it is less widely recognized in the field of public health policy evaluation. One reviewer of a recent grant application for an international study of tobacco control policies commented, "I do not understand the logic of why it is necessary to conduct the study in countries in which a policy is not being introduced." If the same reviewer were reviewing an application for a drug trial, we strongly suspect he or she would understand the need for including patients who did not receive the drug.

Second is the use of longitudinal designs, in which the same individuals are measured on key variables both prior to and after the introduction of the policy. Combining these two strategies yields a two-group, pre–post design that offers a considerably higher degree of internal validity than either feature alone (Cook & Campbell, 1979; Shadish, Cook, & Campbell, 2002).

A third strategy is the measurement of appropriate policy-relevant variables. Smoking has multiple determinants. As a result, it is important to assess whether changes in smoking are in fact due to the policy being evaluated and not to some other cause. The inclusion of policy-relevant variables allows one to address this issue.

A further important addition is to measure policy-relevant variables that are conceptually related to policies that are not being changed. The logic of this within-subject control is identical to the logic of the between-subject control of an experiment and quasi-experiment, because discriminant validity strengthens causal inferences. These three strategies, particularly when accompanied by the inclusion of other explanatory variables (covariates) that might otherwise explain differences between two jurisdictions, produce a powerful research design with the potential for allowing strong inferences to be made about causal effects.

Fong and his colleagues (Fong, Cameron, Zanna et al., 2003) used these strategies in a longitudinal survey of 7,400 high school students in Canada, who were surveyed before and after the introduction of the new graphic warning labels in December 2000. The comparison group was comprised of 4,900 high school students in the United States. Initial results revealed that the Canadian warning labels (compared to U.S. labels) dramatically increased policy-relevant variables (such as the noticeability and salience of the labels) and other outcomes (including forgoing a cigarette because of the labels and having stronger intentions to quit smoking).

One final ingredient for rigorous evaluation of public health policies is to test for what mediates the effects. Since the seminal paper by Baron and Kenny (1986), social psychologists have enthusiastically employed statistical methods for assessing mediation. Our conceptual model for understanding policy effects is a causal chain model and, as such, suggests that the policy-relevant variables play a critical mediating role because they are positioned between the policy and important public health outcomes (such as successful quit attempts). We believe that policies vary in the psychosocial "routes" that they take to affect behavior. For example, if switching to graphic warning labels leads ultimately to increased quitting, we hypothesize that this occurs because the graphic enhancements first increase the salience and noticeability of the warning labels. Thus, the first step in the causal chain is from labels to increases in label salience, that is, in the policy-relevant variables uniquely associated with labels. The second step is from changes in the policy-relevant variables to downstream changes in quit intentions and ultimately quit attempts. Thus, we conceptualize a given policy as affecting policy-relevant proximal variables, which in turn, affect behavior—or, alternatively, policy affects behavior because it causes changes in psychosocial variables that are specific to that policy.

Finally, inclusion of proximal variables conceptually unlinked to the focal policy demonstrates the power of the mediation analysis. For example, although perceived price may be a powerful mediator for explaining the effectiveness of tax increases on quitting, it should fail as a mediator for explaining label effects. In this way, evidence for discriminant validity strengthens causal inferences in quasi-experimental studies just as it does in true experiments.

Currently, we are following and extending these design principles in the International Tobacco Control Policy Evaluation Project (ITC Project), a global transdisciplinary collaboration of more than 40 tobacco control researchers across 9 countries so far, whose mission is to evaluate the psychosocial and behavioral effects of national-level tobacco control policies throughout the world (Fong et al., 2005, in press). We are conducting parallel longitudinal surveys of large nationally representative samples of adult smokers in 9 countries (Canada, United States, United Kingdom, Australia, Thailand, Malaysia, South Korea, and China). We are evaluating all of the demand-reduction policies of the FCTC that are likely to be implemented in the next few years in these countries (e.g., warning labels, taxation, advertising bans, smoke-free laws). In addition to testing the effects of a policy intervention in one country compared to the multiple other countries where no such policy implementation has occurred, our design will also allow us to compare whether policy effects are consistent across countries or whether they vary, and to conduct analysis to identify factors that may enhance or diminish the impact of policies, both within and across countries.

CONCLUSIONS

In conclusion, modern research methods of social psychology can contribute to efforts toward building evidence-based public health policy. Lewin's oft-quoted statement that "there is nothing so practical as a good theory" applies nicely to the methodological design features that can enhance our ability to make strong causal inferences in contexts when randomization is not feasible. Building bridges from social psychology to evidence-based public health policy depends on evidence gathered from methodologically sound studies, and we believe that those bridges will ultimately lead to public health policies that stand a better chance of making the world a better place.

ACKNOWLEDGMENTS

Preparation of this chapter was supported by grants from the National Cancer Institute of the United States (through R01 CA90955, R01 CA 100362, and through the Roswell Park Transdisciplinary Tobacco Use Research Center, P50 CA111236), Robert Wood Johnson Foundation (045734), Canadian Institutes of Health Research (57897), National Health and Medical Research Council of Australia (265903), Cancer Research UK (C312/A3726), Canadian Tobacco Control Research Initiative (014578), with additional support from the Centre for Behavioural Research and Program Evaluation, National Cancer Institute of Canada/Canadian Cancer Society.

REFERENCES

Baron, R. M., & Kenny, D. A. (1986). The moderator-mediator variable distinction in social psychological research: Conceptual, strategic, and statistical considerations. *Journal of Personality and Social Psychology, 51,* 1173–1182.

Cook, T. D., & Campbell, D. T. (1979). *Quasi-experimentation: Design and analysis issues for field settings.* Boston: Houghton Mifflin.

Fong, G. T., for the ITC Research Team. (2005, August 17). *The International Tobacco Control Policy Evaluation Project: Evaluating the tobacco control policies of the framework convention on tobacco.* Paper presented at the International Meeting on Tobacco Control Policies, Buenos Aires, Argentina. Available at http://fctc.org/mercosurasociados05/program.php

Fong, G. T., Cameron, A. J. R., Zanna, M. P., Brown, K. S., Campbell, H. S., Murnaghan, D., & Clayton, R. (2005). *The North American Student Smoking Survey: A quasi-experimental longitudinal study evaluating the graphic Canadian tobacco warning labels.*

Fong, G. T., Cummings, K. M., Boreland, R., Hastings, G., Hyland, A., & Giovino, G. A., et al. (in press). The conceptual framework on the International Tobacco Control Policy Evaluation Project. *Tobacco Control.*

Shadish, W. R., Cook, T. D., & Campbell, D. T. (2002). *Experimental and quasi-experimental designs for generalized causal inference.* Boston: Houghton Mifflin.

PART 6

Bridges With Organizational Science, Culture, and Economics

INTRODUCTION

$\mathbf{A}$s social beings, individuals also respond to a "social environment" that consists of larger groups and societal systems. Organizational structure often is important to understanding internal process such as cognition and affect and interpersonal behavior, as well as to understanding social processes that are more uniquely tied to the organization. Topics such as cooperation and competition, negotiation, team motivation, commitment, social identity, co-ordination and communication—which by definition deal with "social influences"—are of course basic to understanding processes within organizations. Similarly, differences in culture—differences among large groups or societies in terms of attitudes, beliefs, self-definitions, roles, norms, and values—are key to understanding what goes on in the head as well as what goes on between individuals and groups. However, while organizations and culture influence individuals and groups, it is also true that, collectively, individuals and groups shape organizations and culture. Largely the same can be argued for economics, which seeks to understand how individuals and groups choose to use their relatively limited resources to satisfy their wants. Traditionally, economics focuses on macro-level variables by examining, for example, the relationships between markets, inflation, or unemployment indices and individual consumption patterns. Such issues are of interest to social psychology, in that social influences are important to market dynamics, to inflation, unemployment, and consumption. Moreover, most other macro-level phenomena studied by not only economists but also political scientists, communication scientists, and sociologists are of central interest to social psychology. A good case in point is found in programs of research focusing on the benefits (and costs) of social institutions or media campaigns for influencing or "regulating" cognition, emotion, and behavior of individuals and groups—such lines of research are strongly related to concepts such as trust, social norms, and intrinsic versus extrinsic motivation. Moreover, these disciplines increasingly study small groups and dyads as well, with a good example being the emergence of experimental economics. As we explore in the various essays, social psychology is essential to organizational science, culture, and economics, just as these fields and disciplines are essential to social psychology.

50

Bridging Between Micro and Macro Perspectives in Social Psychology

Daniel Bar-Tal

Tel Aviv University

Social psychology will soon celebrate its centenary. It all began in 1908 when the first two textbooks in the field were published: One by the psychologist William McDougall and one by the sociologist E. A. Ross (McDougall, 1908; Ross, 1908). Hence, right from the outset, the new discipline of social psychology was established to combine micro-psychological and macro-sociological conceptual frameworks and methodologies. Many believed that this was a promising development, which would bring a fresh psychological perspective to the social sciences by opening psychology up to a new range of problems faced by human beings insofar as they are members of collectives (see Cartwright, 1979).

However, already in the 1920s there were suggestions that the emerging discipline should be limited to an individual orientation, leaving aside the study of collective behaviors (e.g., Allport, 1924). This view, the micro approach in social psychology, played down the concern with actual social contexts and favored laboratory settings where individual psychological behaviors could be tested. This was the beginning of the struggle between micro and macro perspectives in social psychology. Although in the 1930s, 1940s, and early 1950s, many leaders of social psychology considered the study of the macro-societal context part of the social psychological endeavor (see, e.g., Asch, 1952; Cantril, 1941; Lewin, 1947; Newcomb, 1943; Sherif, 1936), in the 1960s and 1970s social psychology clearly gravitated toward a psychological, individualistic-cognitive orientation (Farr, 1996; Ostrom, 1984; Pepitone, 1997; Sampson, 1977). This gravitation reflected the growing domination of American social psychologists in leading the mainstream of social psychology, as American society cherishes individualistic values. The

1980s saw changes when the ideas of social identity and social categorization theories spread among social psychologists (Tajfel, 1978, 1981; Turner, Hogg, Oakes, Reicher, & Wetherell, 1987; Tajfel & Turner, 1986), as well as ideas of social representation (Moscovici, 1981, 1988) and the theory of minority influence (Moscovici, 1976; Mugny, 1982) (all coming from Europe). This trend increased in the 1990s, yet micro perspective remained the dominant orientation in social psychology (Brewer, 1997; Pepitone, 1997), even in many places in Europe. The mainstream social psychology constructed a climate of micro perspective that has all the characteristics of a paradigm: models of prominent scholars, control of publication in journals, dominance in organizations, ways of training students, recruitment in jobs, rewarding system, published textbooks that present the scope of social psychology, and so forth.

THE MICRO PERSPECTIVE

The micro perspective in social psychology focuses on the psychological repertoire individuals acquire in their social environment and use in their interaction with it. Thus, it tries to describe how individuals come to know the social world around them, evaluate this world, feel toward it, and behave in it, on the one hand, and how the social world affects their knowledge, attitudes, emotions, and behaviors, on the other.

This line of study is based on an assumption that every social situation is constituted by thinking, feeling, and acting individuals, and therefore it is essential to uncover the principles of their functioning in order to understand social behavior. Although the micro perspective does acknowledge that individual behavior is influenced by the context in which it takes place, its major goal is to reveal the cognitive, attitudinal, affective, emotional, motivational, and behavioral mechanisms and structures that are acquired by individuals, that is, the intrapersonal processes that underlie the social functioning of these individuals in their social world.

The assumption is that the psychological repertoire serves as the lens through which individuals view their world. Thus, the perceived world is construed by individuals, who act in it in accordance to these construals. Moreover, human beings are exposed to an array of influences—motivational, cognitive, emotional, and affective—some of which they are unaware, but as a result of which their behavior is also biased, distorted, and selective. The uncovering of these influencing factors is of one of the main tasks of social psychology. A major effort has been directed to the elucidation of these very subtle processes, structures, and mechanisms that are in part unconscious, automatic, and spontaneous. In addition, the micro perspective also focused on the individual differences that characterize their behavior.

The study of how individuals act in their social world requires a very refined research method that allows insight into the individual. The latent assumption of the micro perspective is that the processes are independent of context and content so that their study can be done in any context with any people that are available for the research. Social psychologists by consequence have predominantly used experimentation as a main research method in universities' laboratories, with mostly college students.

MACRO PERSPECTIVE

The macro perspective suggests that individuals are not only members of small groups such as families, school classes, or work teams, but also participate in macro systems such as urban or rural communities, ethnic groups, nations, or religious communities. This membership is often very meaningful for them. Social psychology cannot disregard the fact that its "subjects" view of the world is, at least partly, shared with other members of the social system; that much of this worldview is acquired in the social system; that this worldview is constantly negotiated in the social system, and that it is a basis for communication and coordinated behaviors in the social system (Himmelweit & Gaskell, 1990). That is to say: Neither the contents of the psychological repertoire nor the process of their acquisition can be separated from the societal context in which they evolve and occur. Individuals insofar as they are members of a collective daily face numerous issues, ideas, or problems that have meaning only in the context of their membership in various group: Their personal repertoire, at least partially, reflects the characteristics of the social system of which they are members. Most of the time, the boundaries between individual existence and the same individual as a member of a society are blurred.

BRIDGING BETWEEN MICRO AND MACRO PERSPECTIVES

It is argued that social psychology needs to combine both micro and macro levels of analysis, as few social psychologists already do this (e.g., the work on social dominance; Sidanious & Pratto, 1999). For the field to achieve its promise, social psychologists need to recognize that individuals form societal beliefs, attitudes, and values to which they ascribe confidence, attribute various degrees of centrality, and behave on their basis. My central argument is that social psychologists need to recognize that social processes do not occur in a vacuum, but in a societal context. Individuals are a part of a complex social system, with institutions, structures, processes, network of communication, and special characteristics. They define themselves, in various ways and to different extent, with reference to this system, and feel committed to its existence. At least part of their "self" functions as a social identity. The objective of a macro perspective is to promote the engagement of social psychologists with societal issues—both to enhance our understanding of societal processes and as a framework to study macro social problems.

In view of the collective nature of human life, there is great need for social psychology to focus on the societal context of which individuals are part. Social psychology, as a study of human social behavior, bears not only on our under-standing of the individual, interpersonal, or small-group behavior, but also an explanation of functioning of larger social systems, such as a society or nation (Pettigrew, 2001). Individuals think, feel, and act as society members, and therefore any understanding of the functioning of social systems must include an analysis that relates between society members and societal system and poses questions like, for example, how do they form their shared beliefs? What are the societal consequences of their shared beliefs? Or, how do they coordinate their action (Bar-Tal, 1990, 2000; Fraser & Gaskell, 1990)?

Social psychology has much relevance to the study of social macro systems, but it can also benefit by being open to absorb knowledge accumulated in other disciplines of the social sciences. As a field, social psychology has accu-mulated substantial knowledge about individuals, their mental structures and activities. This line of work, however, needs to be moved into a societal context in order to explain the lives of individuals as society members. Here, knowl-edge of various social science disciplines can be useful: Topics like societal insti-tutions, norms and values, processes of influence, or communication networks should be integrated with the analysis of individuals' behavior as society members.

The new paradigm will make it possible not only to look at the individuals in their social environment and to deal with real-life issues, but also to use a vari-ety of research methods and different ways of studying social problems. It will release social psychologists from principal reliance on experimentation. It will naturally extend the legitimate scope of research method to include observa-tions, surveys, and content analysis. It may also open the door for the qualita-tive methods that social psychologists are usually reluctant to tolerate. This in turn may pave the way to the kind of interdisciplinary collaboration that is nec-essary in any serious attempt to study societal issues. By their nature, societal is-sues are multifaceted and complex, requiring examination from various perspectives. For this reason, interdisciplinary teams can benefit social psy-chologists, greatly enabling them to learn new approaches, concepts, theories, and research methods.

These required changes are not easy to carry because micro approach in social psychology is well institutionalized. A dialogue and openness are needed in order implement them. Operationally it means various steps such as development of a new integrative paradigm for social psychology in textbooks, inclusion of the macro approach in training programs, extension of publication policies to in-clude macro studies, organization of meetings with the participation of micro and macro social psychologists, and initiation of integrative publications.

CONCLUSIONS

Social psychology can bridge between the individual and societal levels—the micro and macro levels—by taking into account that society members as individuals behave socially, and do so frequently within the societal context. Moreover, it should be recognized that society members not only are influenced by the society of which they are part, but also shape the nature of their society. Societies do not exist without the individual members, who make them up, but the meaning of the society can be only understood when the cognitive-affective repertoire of the society members is taken into account. Society members change their societies, as they change their beliefs, attitudes, values, and patterns of behaviors. There is a continuous interaction and reciprocal influence between society members' repertoire, on the one hand, and societal institutions, structures, culture, and other societal components on the other. We live in a world that is increasingly interdependent, but in which individuals have extraordinary individual freedom and power. How our interdependency is balanced with our individual power is one of the currently most central issues. We have learned how to extend life, and psychology has contributed to our being able to function better as autonomous individuals. But the future challenge is how to learn to live with one another, construct a more just and equal society, and avoid using violence. Social psychology has an important role to play in helping us understand the interaction of individuals with society—in understanding the processes that allow individuals to thrive as part of larger collectives. To paraphrase a religious wisdom, it is our obligation as social psychologists not to finish the task, but to try. The need is to develop a more robust social psychology that can address pressing social problems. A century after the beginning of social psychology, the urgency of this task is obvious.

REFERENCES

Allport, F. H. (1924). The group fallacy in relation to social science. *Journal of Abnormal and Social Psychology, 19,* 60–73.

Asch, S. E. (1952). *Social psychology.* New York: Prentice Hall.

Bar-Tal, D. (1990). *Group beliefs: A conception for analyzing group structure, processes and behavior.* New York: Springer-Verlag.

Bar-Tal, D. (2000). *Shared beliefs in a society: Social psychological analysis.* Thousand Oaks, CA: Sage.

Brewer, M. B. (1997). On the social origins of human nature. In C. McGarty & S. A. Haslam (Eds.), *The message of social psychology: Perspectives on mind in society* (pp. 54–62). Cambridge, MA: Blackwell.

Cantril, H. (1941). *The psychology of social movements.* New York: John Wiley and Sons.

Cartwright, D. (1979). Contemporary social psychology in historical perspective. *Social Psychology Quarterly, 42,* 82–93.

Farr, P. M. (1996). *The roots of modern social psychology 1982–1954.* Oxford: Blackwell.

Fraser, C., & Gaskell, G. (Eds.). (1990). *The social psychology of widespread beliefs.* Oxford: Clarendon.

Himmelweit, H. T., & Gaskell, G. (Eds.). (1990). *Societal psychology.* Newbury Park, CA: Sage.

Lewin, K. (1947). Frontiers in group dynamics. *Human Relations, 1,* 5–41.

McDougall, W. (1908). *An introduction to social psychology.* London: Methuen.

Moscovici, S. (1976). *Social influence and social change.* New York: Academic Press.

Moscovici, S. (1981). On social representation. In J. P. Forgas (Ed.), *Social cognition: Perspectives on everyday understanding* (pp. 181–209). London: Academic Press.

Moscovici, S. (1988). Notes towards a description of social representations. *European Journal of Social Psychology, 18,* 211–250.

Mugny, G. (1982). *The power of minorities.* London: Academic Press.

Newcomb, T. M. (1943). *Personality and social change.* New York: Holt, Rinehart and Winston.

Ostrom, T. M. (1984). The sovereignty of social cognition. In R. S. Wyer, Jr. & T. K. Srull (Eds.), *Handbook of social cognition* (Vol. 1, pp. 1–38). Hillsdale, NJ: Lawrence Erlbaum Associates.

Pepitone, A. (1997). Nonmaterial beliefs: Theory and research in cultural social psychology. In G. McGarty & S. A. Haslam (Eds.), *The message of social psychology* (pp. 252–267). Cambridge, UK: Blackwell.

Pettigrew, T. F. (2001). Intergroup relations and national and international relations. In R. Brown & S. L. Gaertner (Eds.), *Blackwell handbook of social psychology: Intergroup processes* (pp. 514–532). Malden, MA: Blackwell.

Ross, E. A. (1908). *Social psychology.* New York: Macmillan.

Sampson, E. E. (1977). Psychology and the American ideal. *Journal of Personality and Social Psychology, 35,* 767–782.

Sherif, M. (1936). *The psychology of social norms.* New York: Harper.

Sidanius, J., & Pratto, F. (1999). *Social dominance: An intergroup theory of social hierarchy and oppression.* Cambridge: Cambridge University Press.

Tajfel, H. (Ed.). (1978). *Differentiation between social groups.* London: Academic Press.

Tajfel, H. (1981). *Human groups and social categories: Studies in social psychology.* Cambridge: Cambridge University Press.

Tajfel, H., & Turner, J. C. (1986). The social identity theory of intergroup relations. In S. Worchel & W. G. Austin (Eds.), *Psychology of intergroup relations* (pp. 7–24). Monterey, CA: Brooks/Cole.

Turner, J. C., Hogg, M. A., Oakes, P. J., Reicher, S. D., & Wetherell, M. S. (1987). *Rediscovering the social group: A self-categorizing theory.* Oxford: Blackwell.

51

Bridging Social Psychology and the Organizational Sciences

Carsten K. W. De Dreu
University of Amsterdam

John M. Levine
University of Pittsburgh

In this essay, we examine past, present, and possible future relationships between social psychology and the organizational sciences (organizational psychology and organizational behavior). These two fields are closely related in terms of their origins. Founding members of social psychology, such as Kurt Lewin and Jose Moreno, studied organizational issues (Haire, 1954), and pioneering organizational scientists were strongly influenced by social psychological thinking (e.g., Roethlisberger & Dickson, 1939). Moreover, as the two fields evolved, they focused on many of the same processes and phenomena. For example, person perception has been a major topic in social psychology and an important aspect of selection and assessment research in organizational psychology (Dipboye, 1990; Fiske, 1992). Group decision making and performance have been central to social psychology since its inception, and, with the growing reliance on work groups in organizations, they have become prominent themes in the organizational sciences as well (Levine & Moreland, 1998; Ilgen, 1999). The study of negotiation has always had an important niche in social psychology, and it has become a prominent focus of both teaching and research in business schools around the world (De Dreu & Carnevale, 2003). Motivation and goal striving have been central to both social psychology and the organizational sciences for decades (Higgins & Kruglanski, 1991; Locke & Latham, 1990). Finally, several recent trends in social psychology, such as an emphasis on affect and emotion (Forgas, 1995), have their parallel in the organizational sciences (George & Brief, 1996).

Given their common roots and research foci, it comes as no surprise that many bridges exist between social psychology and the organizational sciences. A good example is recent work on social identity in organizations, which traces back to early social psychological research on self-categorization but makes a unique contribution by showing how social identity affects leadership and work unit performance. Another example is current research on fairness that combines insights from both social psychology and the organizational sciences.

At the same time, many lines of work in social psychology and the organizational sciences have developed in relative isolation from each other. One sign of this isolation is the paucity of textbooks that make serious efforts to integrate the two fields. For example, treatments of group dynamics in introductory social psychology texts typically make little reference to the large and exciting body of research on work teams in organizations. The relative isolation of social psychology and the organizational sciences is also reflected in several lines of ongoing research. For example, work on organizational citizenship behavior, a form of unsolicited cooperation in the work place, tends to ignore relevant social psychological work on motivation and decision making in mixed-motive interdependence situations. Moreover, social psychological work on automatic processes in goal setting and goal striving is only loosely connected to parallel research in the organizational sciences. Finally, although ostracism and exclusion in small groups would seem to have much in common with workplace bullying, these areas of research have yet to make serious contact.

This is not to say, of course, that social psychologists and organizational scientists have identical research agendas and hence can always benefit from one another's work. For example, organizational scientists interested in individual work performance and mental fatigue probably have less to learn from social psychologists than from cognitive psychologists. And social psychologists interested in the neurological correlates of aggression probably have less to learn from organizational scientists than from clinical psychopharmacologists. But as our earlier examples illustrated, a number of potentially useful bridges between social psychology and the organizational sciences have not developed. The absence of such bridges raises two questions: "How come?" and "so what?" That is, what explains the lack of bridging between the fields, and what are its costs?

HOW COME?

When communicating about their work, social psychologists tend to address other researchers first and practitioners second. This is not the case for organizational scientists. The number of practitioner-oriented outlets is much larger in the organizational sciences, and authors (encouraged by reviewers and editors) frequently emphasize the applied and policy implications of their research. This emphasis is probably attributable to more than external pressures to be "relevant." Those publishing in organizational science journals no doubt are more interested in such issues as managerial effectiveness, worker satisfaction, and organizational productivity than are those publishing in social psychology journals.

The greater emphasis on applied and policy implications in the organizational sciences than in social psychology has consequences for how research is conducted in the two fields. Although those publishing in social psychology journals can focus primarily, if not exclusively, on the theoretical implications of their work, those publishing in organizational science journals must also worry about the utility of their findings for enhancing individual or organizational effectiveness. Quite often, this produces different trade-offs between internal and external validity in the two fields—a preponderance of laboratory studies involving undergraduates in social psychology (which enhances internal validity at the expense of external validity) versus a preponderance of field studies involving employees and managers in the organizational sciences (which enhance external validity at the expense of internal validity). It is important to emphasize that we are not arguing that social psychologists are indifferent to the applied relevance of their work—many classic and contemporary studies in the field were motivated by the desire to reduce harmful or destructive behavior (e.g., prejudice, aggression). Nor are we arguing that organizational scientists are unconcerned about the theoretical value of their work—it is hard, if not impossible, to publish in first-rate organizational journals without advancing theory. What we are arguing is that researchers in these two fields often engage in different trade-offs between internal and external validity, which can have important implications for the questions they ask and the methods they use to answer these questions.

SO WHAT?

It might be argued that the lack of bridging between social psychology and the organizational sciences reflects the fact that both disciplines have matured to the point that they no longer need each other. Each field is, so to speak, self-sufficient in terms of yielding creative insights and relevant applications. We disagree with this argument. Although, as noted earlier, bridging between the fields is not useful in all cases, it is our contention that more bridging would yield substantial benefits. Thus, to the question "Should we care that research on organizational citizenship behavior ignores social psychological work on interdependence, that social psychological studies of automatic processes in goal-directed behavior are not connected to organizational work on goal setting, and that research on ostracism and exclusion in small groups is not linked to studies of workplace bullying?" we would answer with a strong "yes."

There Are Four Reasons for This Response

Bridging is beneficial, first of all, because it produces cognitive stimulation. A substantial body of work indicates that being exposed to others' ideas leads to more and better ideas when these others have different rather than similar backgrounds, expertise, and perspectives (Paulus & Nijstad, 2003). The implication is that idea exchange between domains is more beneficial to creativity and problem solving than is exchange within domains (Levine & Moreland, 2004). If so, social psychologists who read and incorporate work in the organizational sciences, and organizational scientists who read and incorporate work in social psychology, should be more creative than those who limit themselves to their own discipline.

A second reason that bridging is beneficial is because it provides excellent opportunities for methodological triangulation (Campbell & Fiske, 1959). As noted earlier, social psychology and the organizational sciences make different trade-offs between internal and external validity. This difference can be a virtue when researchers in the two fields obtain similar results regarding a phenomenon, because the strengths of one field can compensate for the weaknesses of the other. Thus, the strong internal validity of laboratory experiments can compensate for the relatively weak internal validity of field studies, whereas the strong external validity of field studies can compensate for the relatively weak external validity of laboratory experiments. A good example is our own work on minority influence in small groups, showing that minority dissent can produce work team innovation both in the laboratory (Choi & Levine, 2004) and in work teams in a variety of organizations (De Dreu & West, 2001).

Given that many phenomena studied in the organizational sciences involve social perception and behavior, and hence are social psychological in nature, bridging has a third advantage—it reduces the likelihood of "reinventing the wheel." Work on bargaining and negotiation illustrates how the absence of bridging allowed such a reinvention. In the early 1970s, social psychological research on this topic focused on social motivation, showing that individuals with prosocial motivation were more likely to achieve mutually beneficial agreements than were individuals with selfish motivation. Recent work in the organizational sciences largely reinvented the wheel by showing that positive interpersonal relations, such as friendship, often result in behavior that seems "irrational" from a selfish, utility-maximizing perspective (De Dreu & Carnevale, 2003).

Finally, a fourth advantage of bridging derives from the fact that many phenomena studied by organizational scientists in field settings are richer and more complex versions of similar phenomena studied by social psychologists in laboratory settings. As one example, organizational scientists often study long-term rather than short-term relationships. People in long-term relationships share a past and an anticipated future, which is rarely the case in social psychological experiments (Moreland & Levine, 1982). The ability to study long-term relationships allows organizational scientists to investigate the temporal dimension of interpersonal perceptions, emotions, and behavioral interaction patterns. This in turn allows investigation of a variety of interesting phenomena, such as the trade-off that occurs between transient and enduring gains/losses when members of long-term groups make decisions and negotiate transactions. The concept of "rational" behavior takes on a different meaning, and certainly a different operationalization, in long-term than in short-term relationships.

As another example, organizational scientists study individuals (employees) who have a much stronger influence on their social environments than do undergraduates in laboratory experiments. Often without realizing it, employees modify their environments by selecting or changing their tasks, altering the frequency and form of their interactions with coworkers, revealing or hiding information about themselves, and so on. Compared to social psychologists, then, organizational scientists study more dynamic social environments composed of more autonomous people.

As a final example, organizational scientists study situations involving more complex interdependencies among people than social psychologists do. Consider the rather simple social dilemma situations studied by social psychologists. Although these situations are similar in some ways to interdependence situations in organizations, "players" in the organizational arena often find themselves in multiple interdependence structures at the same time. On one issue, they may have pure correspondence of outcomes with others; on a second issue, there may have pure noncorrespondence of outcomes with these same people; and on yet a third issue, they may be in a game of "chicken" with them. Understanding how these complex and layered forms of interdependence, with both short-term and long-term components, play out in social perception and behavior would greatly enrich social psychological theories of interdependence relations.

CONCLUSIONS

In our view, both social psychology and the organizational sciences would benefit from more two-way bridges between the fields. For example, social psychologists would be challenged to think more deeply about the scope of their theories. In some cases, this might produce theoretical "expansion" (via efforts to explain naturally occurring phenomena that have not been, or cannot be, studied inside the laboratory). In other cases, it might produce theoretical "contraction" (via efforts to qualify theoretical predictions in light of knowledge gained outside the laboratory). By the same token, organizational scientists would be challenged to think more deeply about the psychological processes—cognitive, motivational, and affective—underlying the phenomena in which they are interested. In addition to facilitating theory development, this reflection might also stimulate the development of better tools for assessing motivational and affective responses in field settings.

REFERENCES

Campbell, D. T., & Fiske, D. W. (1959). Convergent and discriminant validation by the multitrait-multimethod matrix. *Psychological Bulletin, 56,* 81–105.

Choi, H.-S., & Levine, J. M. (2004). Minority influence in work teams: The impact of newcomers. *Journal of Experimental Social Psychology, 40,* 273–280.

De Dreu, C. K. W., & Carnevale, P. J. D. (2003). Motivational bases for information processing and strategic choice in conflict and negotiation. In M. P. Zanna (Ed.), *Advances in experimental social psychology* (Vol. 35, pp. 235–291). New York: Academic Press.

De Dreu, C. K. W., & West, M. A. (2001). Minority dissent and team innovation: The importance of participation in decision making. *Journal of Applied Psychology, 86,* 1191–1201.

Dipboye, R. L. (1991). Laboratory vs. field research in industrial and organizational psychology. In C. L. Cooper & I. T. Robertson (Eds.), *International review of industrial and organizational psychology* (Vol. 5, pp. 1–34). Chichester, UK: Wiley.

Fiske, S. T. (1992). Thinking is for doing: Portraits of social cognition from daguerreotype to laserphoto. *Journal of Personality and Social Psychology, 63,* 877–898.

George, J. M., & Brief, A. P. (1996). Motivational agendas in the workplace: The effects of feelings on focus of attention and work motivation. *Research in Organizational Behavior, 18,* 75–109.

Haire, M. (1954). Industrial social psychology. In G. Lindzey (Ed.), *Handbook of social psychology* (Vol. 2, pp. 1104–1123). Reading, MA: Addison-Wesley.

Higgins, E. T., & Kruglanski, A. W. (2001). Motivational science: The nature and functions of wanting. In E. T. Higgins & A. W. Kruglanski (Eds.), *Motivational science: Social and personality perspectives* (pp. 1–20). New York: Psychology Press.

Ilgen, D. R. (1999). Teams embedded in organizations: Some implications. *American Psychologist, 54,* 129–139.

Levine, J. M., & Moreland, R. L. (1998). Small groups. In D. T. Gilbert, S. T. Fiske, & G. Lindzey (Eds.), *The handbook of social psychology* (4th ed., Vol. 2, pp. 415–469). Boston: McGraw-Hill.

Levine, J. M., & Moreland, R. L. (2004). Collaboration: The social context of theory development. *Personality and Social Psychology Review, 8,* 164–172.

Locke, E., & Latham, G. (1990). *A theory of goal setting and task performance.* Englewood Cliffs, NJ: Prentice-Hall.

Moreland, R. L., & Levine, J. M. (1982). Socialization in small groups: Temporal changes in individual-group relations. In L. Berkowitz (Ed.), *Advances in experimental social psychology* (Vol. 15, pp. 137–192). New York: Academic Press.

Paulus, P., & Nijstad, B. A. (Eds.). (2003). *Group creativity.* Oxford, UK: Oxford University Press.

Roethlisberger, R., & Dickson, W. J. (1939). *Management and the worker.* Cambridge, MA: Harvard University Press.

52

Dissent in Teams and Organizations: Lessons for Team Innovation and Empowerment

Michael A. West
Work and Organizational Psychology Group,
Aston Business School, Aston University

When tested in the complex and fiery settings of work organizations, theoretical predictions of social psychology may well prove too fragile to survive the heat. Alternatively, they may suggest to practitioners and organizational psychologists simplistic solutions to organizational problems, which undermine rather than support efforts to enable organizational effectiveness. In this chapter I apply research findings about minority influence to two domains of organizational psychology: how to develop innovative teams, and how teams can bring about organizational change. First I summarize the findings from the minority influence literature and consider the implications for our understanding of innovation in work teams, and then I suggest how an understanding of minority influence can help the relatively powerless in organizations to bring about change.

MINORITY DISSENT AND TEAM INNOVATION

Whether it is finding new ways of diagnosing and treating breast cancer in hospitals, developing new forms of protection from the sun's rays, marketing bicycles, or finding ways of developing more destructive land mines, innovation is central to the success of organizations in achieving their aims. Groups are largely responsible for developing and implementing new ideas in work organizations (West, 2002). The challenge for researchers and practitioners is to identify the factors that predict team innovation. What do we know so far from our research endeavors?

The factors identified in research as likely to influence levels of innovation in work groups include "inputs" of teams such as the task the team is required to perform, the composition of the group (such as its diversity), and the organizational context (e.g., manufacturing, health service, large or small). Research suggests that the overriding influence, however, is group processes, which mediate the relationships between inputs and innovation (West, 2002; West & Anderson, 1996). How can social psychological research help to advance knowledge of these processes? One promising area of research, hitherto ignored by organizational psychologists, is research into the influence of dissenting minorities in teams—those who go against the prevailing view and persistently argue for what is a minority position. What has this research revealed?

Social psychological researchers have shown that minority consistency of arguments over time (against the position of the majority in a group) is likely to lead to change in majority views in groups and to innovation (Moscovici, Mugny, & van Avermaet, 1985; Nemeth & Nemeth-Brown, 2003). People exposed to a confident and consistent minority change their private views prior to expressing public agreement. Minority influence researchers have labeled this process *conversion*. Research on minority influence suggests that conversion is most likely to occur where a minority is consistent and confident in the presentation of its arguments. Moreover, a behavioral style of persistence is most likely to lead to attitude change and innovation (Nemeth & Owens, 1996). Nemeth and others suggested that we explore the view expressed by a minority more thoroughly than we do the view of a majority with which we disagree. In the latter case, we look for information that supports the majority's position because we feel uncomfortable disagreeing with the majority. However, it is proposed, when we hear a persistently expressed minority position we think more creatively around the issue because there is no imperative to find reasons to agree.

De Dreu and De Vries (1997) suggested that a homogeneous work group in which minority dissent is suppressed will have low levels of creativity, innovation, individuality, and independence (De Dreu & De Vries, 1993). In contrast, task-related debate may lead team members to reevaluate the status quo and adapt their objectives, strategies, or processes more appropriately to their situation, thereby innovating.

In two longitudinal studies of work teams in the Netherlands, De Dreu and West (2001) found that minority dissent did indeed predict team innovation (as rated by the teams' supervisors), but only in teams with high levels of participation. They suggested that one of the main threats to effective group work is the group's tendency to move to premature consensus, and they hypothesized that minority dissent in organizational teams would increase creativity and divergent thought. They further argued that creativity induced by minority dissent would lead to innovation only when team members participated in decision making. Through participation (frequent team-member interaction and regular meetings; team members influencing key team decisions about the team's work; and team members keeping each other informed fully about the task and their contribution to it), creative ideas and solutions induced by minority dissent may be critically examined. The results of the two studies supported this hypothesis: Minority dissent was associated with team innovation under high (but not low) levels of participation in decision making.

Here is an example of how applying social psychological research to organizational contexts leads us to discover more about the process predictors of team innovation and suggests ways that theory could be developed: Levels of interaction, information exchange, and influence over decision making may be important moderators of the processes described by the research. Hostile interactions might have the opposite effect. Team members might avoid processing arguments by hostile minorities because the arguments and the people engender anxiety rather than curiosity. These issues could be explored in laboratory settings prior to testing them in field settings. Now we turn to examine the potential value of this approach at the organizational level.

MINORITY INFLUENCE, EMPOWERMENT, AND ORGANIZATIONAL CHANGE

We can apply the research of minority influence to gain new perspectives on organizational change. Most academic and practitioner models of organizational change take a "top down" perspective, neglecting to consider how minorities and those at the lower echelons in organizations—say, a team of hospital nurses wanting to have more responsibility for diagnosis and treatment decisions—can bring about change.

Social psychological researchers have treated minorities as just that—numerical minorities. However, it may well be that those in positions of relative powerlessness, *regardless of their numerical superiority or inferiority*, could also be considered a minority that, by dissenting, provokes creative processing of issues by those they seek to influence. Indeed, Nemeth's recent work implies that the courage of the dissenting group leads others to process the issues under discussion more creatively than they otherwise would. I suggest that those who are relatively powerless (nurses in health care organizations) will have the same impact as minorities on the relatively powerful (e.g., doctors) through dissent, despite the fact that they are in a numerical majority. The courage of the relatively powerless (not all minorities are powerless) rather than the numerical ratio between opposing groups may be the important element in "minority" influence processes. With that in mind, we now examine a clear strategy for those in minorities or relatively powerless positions to bring about change in the face of resistance from a majority or from a relatively powerful minority. The research evidence from this area suggests:

1. *The team must have a clear vision of what it wishes to achieve.* In order to be effective and to sustain minority influence, the vision must be one that motivates and inspires team members—a future they really feel is worth fighting for. The nurses who feel that their role in preventative health care in their organization could be hugely developed in the best interests of promoting better patient care and saving health care resources in the long term have a clear vision.

2. *The vision must be clearly articulated and coherently expressed.* In order to be effective, minorities must put across a clear, consistent message backed up by convincing underlying arguments. The nurses might develop three clear basic arguments in relation to (a) the value of preventative health care to patients (b) the efficacy of preventative health care in reducing costs, and (c) their expertise to deliver this care without causing extra demands on doctors.

3. *They must be flexible in responding to the views of others.* Minorities that are perceived to be inflexible are rejected by the majority as too extreme to bargain with. Minorities must therefore appear willing to listen to others' views and modify their proposals, while not fundamentally distorting their vision. The nurses must listen to doctors' concerns about their authority being diminished and explore how their concerns can be managed. This means working collaboratively with doctors to find creative solutions that meet or exceed both groups' needs.

4. *Persistence is essential.* Minorities cause majorities to think through issues from more perspectives, and the majority's views are thereby altered (not necessarily in the direction of the minority). This results partly from the repeated presentation of the same coherent arguments. The strategy implied by research is for the team to prepare, rehearse, present, and present again. So the nurses must not accept failure when after three or four team meetings with the doctors they keep being denied the opportunities they seek. They must raise the issue in other arenas, with senior health administrators, with patients, and via e-mails, newsletters, and water-cooler conversations. This is how revolutionary movements succeed—through persistence.

5. *Participation.* A potent way of reducing resistance to change is by involving people in the change process (Heller et al., 1998). By seeking the views of people throughout the organization and encouraging others to be involved in contributing ideas to the proposals, the team can reduce the resistance of people in the organization to the proposed change. So the nurses can invite the views of patients; set up meetings for general discussions about the issues with other health care professionals; invite external speakers with expertise in the area; send out newsletters; and add the issue to the agendas of any meetings they attend.

Teams that adopt such strategies may seem a threat to organizations, but without them, organizations are likely to be less innovative and adaptable.

Conformity processes damp down the fiery forces for change; minority dissent fans them.

CONCLUSIONS

Organizational research offers social psychologists the opportunity to understand how minority influence processes play out in work teams with contexts and histories (in comparison to student samples in laboratory settings) and in the face of task imperatives—a breast cancer care team has to save lives, and dissent may be valued rather than puzzled over in such circumstances (Nemeth & Staw, 1989). They can study other elements, such as task identity (the extent to which the team task is a whole piece of work), task variety (variety of task elements), level of team autonomy, and level of feedback about task performance. Variations in processes may be studied in highly cohesive versus not very cohesive groups and in groups with a history of success versus a history of failure.

Minority influence studies conducted in the laboratory will allow organizational psychologists to discover the influence on team innovation of key variables such as majority perceptions of the minority (self-interested vs. altruistic), the level of trust in the group, and perceptions of psychological safety. In this way they can come to develop effective prescriptions for encouraging innovation among work teams—and teams such as breast cancer care teams need help in discovering how to promote innovation in patient care (see, e.g., West et al., 2003).

Such bridging is also exciting for organizational psychology in that it suggests a radical model of organizational change. Organizational psychologists have studied change primarily from the perspective of those in positions of power in organizations. Minority influence research offers a model of change for the relatively powerless and a strategy for creating change by encouraging creative and independent exploration of the change issue throughout the organization. For social psychologists, applying minority influence research to the study of organizational change dramatically extends the boundaries of the applicability of this research. We can explore how intergroup relations are affected when groups use such influence processes for organizational change; the hostility or otherwise they engender; if and how these processes produce organizational change and innovation; and how long minorities must persist for change to occur and how long these changes continue. Organizationally based studies will indicate what are effective strategies for minority influence groups intent on bringing about change and thereby what may be key variables to study in laboratory settings.

There are practical implications from this bridging process, too. The research suggests how we can train people for teamwork in ways that will facilitate team innovation, such as encouraging team members and leaders to dissent (and to be persistent in their dissent) and to tolerate dissent in others. It also suggests how we can empower teams to bring about change in organizations when they are not in positions of power or when they expect the majority to resist their change initiative.

My key aims in this essay are first to urge social psychologists to leave the comfortable confines of the laboratory and their dependence on student samples and work with organizational psychologists, and second to urge organizational psychologists to be less complacent about their domain and put in effort to mine the massive seam of relevant theoretical and research work in social psychology that can be applied in organizational research. These efforts will enrich research in both fields dramatically. It is astonishing that we do not work together more, given our shared interests and overlapping domains, and it is time we did.

REFERENCES

De Dreu, C. K. W., & De Vries, N. K. (1993). Numerical support, information processing, and attitude change. *European Journal of Social Psychology, 23,* 647–662.

De Dreu, C. K. W., & De Vries, N. K. (1997). Minority dissent in organizations. In C. K. W. De Dreu & E. Van De Vliert (Eds.), *Using conflict in organizations* (pp. 72–86). London: Sage.

De Dreu, C. K. W., & West, M. A. (2001). Minority dissent and team innovation: The importance of participation in decision-making. *Journal of Applied Psychology, 86,* 1191–1201.

Heller F., Pusic E., Strauss, G., & Wilpert B. (1998). *Organizational participation: Myth and reality.* Oxford: Oxford University Press.

Moscovici, S., Mugny, G., & van Avermaet, E. (Eds.). (1985). *Perspectives on minority influence.* Cambridge: Cambridge Universities Press.

Nemeth, C. J., & Nemeth-Brown, B. (2003). Better than individuals? The potential benefits of dissent and diversity for group creativity. In P. Paulus & B. Nijstad (Eds.), *Group creativity* (pp. 63–84). Oxford: Oxford University Press.

Nemeth, C., & Owens, P. (1996). Making work groups more effective: The value of minority dissent. In M. A. West (Ed.), *The handbook of work group psychology* (pp. 125–142). Winchester, England: John Wiley.

Nemeth, C., & Staw, B. M. (1989). The trade offs of social control and innovation within groups and organizations. In L. Berkowitz (Ed.), *Advances in experimental social psychology* (pp. 175–210). New York: Academic Press.

West, M. A. (2002). Sparkling fountains or stagnant ponds: An integrative model of creativity and innovation implementation in work groups. *Applied Psychology: An International Review, 51,* 355–424.

West, M. A., & Anderson, N. (1996). Innovation in top management teams. *Journal of Applied Psychology, 81,* 680–693.

West, M. A., Borrill, C. S., Dawson, J. F., Brodbeck, F. C., Shapiro, D. A., & Haward, B. (2003). Leadership clarity and team innovation in health care. *Leadership Quarterly, 14,* 393–410.

53

Improving Managerial Decision Making: Lessons From Experimental Social Dilemma Research

J. Mark Weber
University of Toronto

David M. Messick
Northwestern University

Social dilemmas are ubiquitous. Any situation in which (a) people are rewarded more for selfish choices (in the short-term) than for cooperative choices and (b) everyone is better off when everyone makes cooperative choices than when everyone makes selfish choices, is a social dilemma (Dawes, 1980). They permeate our home lives (e.g., clean up or leave it to others), daunt public policymakers and politicians (e.g., exploit a natural resource now for short-term gain or manage it conservatively to preserve it), and pervade every work group (e.g., put in effort and pull your weight or free-ride on others' efforts).

It has been argued that understanding cooperation in social dilemmas is the most important problem in the social sciences (cf. Elster, 1985). Whether or not you are inclined to agree with such a grand claim, it is undeniably a problem that has elicited broad, multi-disciplinary interest (e.g., Ostrom et al., 2002). In this volume, dedicated to bridging work between social psychology and other fields of academic inquiry, it is worth noting that the literature on cooperation and social dilemmas has, from time to time, been one blessed by flashes of interdisciplinary insight and intellectual innovation. The psychological study of social dilemmas (see Weber, Kopelman, & Messick, 2004 for a recent conceptual review), for example, has benefitted from the formal game theoretic models of economists (e.g., Von Neumann & Morgenstern,

1944) and the computational simulations of political scientists (e.g., Axelrod, 1984). Similarly, seminal work on preference structures in the field of social psychology (Loewenstein, Thompson, & Bazerman, 1989; Messick & Sentis, 1985) continues to shape the research of psychologists and experimental economists alike (e.g., Fehr & Schmidt, 1999). This handful of examples illustrates the generative potential of interdisciplinary dialogue.

In this short essay, we focus on an underdeveloped interdisciplinary bridge. As social psychologists teaching and conducting research in management schools, we are regularly reminded that organizational life is saturated with social dilemmas. The social dilemmas literature can offer worthwhile insights to those engaged in managerial decision making. Furthermore, we argue that the nature of social dilemma dynamics encountered in organizational life offers both a worthy challenge and a reciprocal benefit to social psychologists with programs of research in this area.

EXAMPLES OF SOCIAL DILEMMAS IN ORGANIZATIONAL LIFE

Civility and Organizational Culture.   An ever-present dilemma in organizational life is how much effort to put into relationships with co-workers. Management scholars have recently borrowed theory from social dilemma researchers to help model the spiraling negative effects of incivility in a workplace (Andersson & Pearson, 1999). If incivility is a selfish choice, efforts at civility are the cooperative choice. Being polite with one another, showing an interest in your assistant's hobbies, asking for input even from those who do not have "fate control" over you—these are all cooperative acts that, in the short-term, can be costly to the person choosing them. Single-minded focus on one's own efficient execution of tasks, and inattention to others, constitutes a selfish choice. Everyone is better off if everyone behaves in a civil fashion that supports a positive and courteous workplace culture than if everyone acts selfishly. Yet the highest relative payoffs (in the short-term) accrue to people who invest little effort in sustaining a positive workplace from which they, too, benefit.

Group Work.   Work groups are extremely common in most organizations: project teams, task forces, review groups, and so on. Any group task can be modeled as a public good dilemma—a social dilemma that involves a choice between contributing to the group effort or free-riding on others' contributions. Group work is usually most productive when everyone pulls their own weight, but there are clear incentives for individuals to let everyone else make sure the task gets done.

Divisional Budgeting.   In most multi-divisional organizations, the end of the year brings a hierarchically nested social dilemma (cf. Wit & Kerr, 2002). Each division manager must simultaneously make year-end spending decisions and forward-looking projections for the coming fiscal year. Commonly, spending current year allocations (or exceeding them) helps to bolster requests for future resource allocations. What makes this a hierarchically nested social dilemma are the various levels of identification for the manager. On the one hand, conservative management of resources in the current year to contain costs and making careful projections are in the interests of the company. Managers who behave in this fashion are cooperating by acting judiciously with the company's finite common resources (i.e., a common resource dilemma, or "commons dilemma"). However, managers are also responsible for their divisions and staff. Ensuring maximal resources for their people can be seen as their contributions to the (smaller) public good that is the effective functioning of their divisions. Depending on the level of analysis, then, the same action can be characterized as cooperation or selfishness.

LESSONS FOR MANAGERS

The lessons of the social dilemma literature are numerous. If cooperation is the goal, relevant communication helps, as does eliciting commitments, carefully designing material payoffs, reducing environmental and social uncertainty, and the presence of people with cooperative social motives (Weber et al., 2004). In this essay we focus on a conceptual framework (a "logic of appropriateness") and one recent area of inquiry (framing) with especially important implications for managerial decision making.

UNDERSTANDING DECISION MAKING IN SOCIAL DILEMMAS: A LOGIC OF APPROPRIATENESS FRAMEWORK

Building on the ideas of March (1994), we argued elsewhere that a "logic of appropriateness" is a better way to understand people's decisions in social dilemmas than the dominant rational choice and expected utility paradigms (Weber et al., 2004). Understanding decision making in dilemmas is important to leaders who wish to promote more cooperative behavior in their organizations. The logic of appropriateness approach proposes that people ask themselves the question (consciously or unconsciously): "What (rules) does a person like me (identity) do in a situation like this (recognition)?" It is the combination of these factors—recognizing the kind of situation it is, understanding the norms that apply, and considering how one's identity interacts with the other elements—that determines the "appropriate" action. People generally seek to act "appropriately." Using the logic of appropriateness framework as a guide, managers should focus their efforts on how the situation gets defined by members of their organizations (e.g., as a group task or an individual task). The relatively recent literature on framing effects offers some noteworthy approaches to managing and thinking about organizational social dilemmas.

FRAMING EFFECTS

Subtle differences in how choices are labeled, how a common resource is described, or how a task is categorized can dramatically change the level of cooperation observed even in structurally identical tasks (Weber et al., 2004). For example, Batson and Moran (1999) had participants engage in a task that was labeled either as a "business transaction study" or as a "social exchange study." They documented two important framing effects. First, participants who were in a "low empathy" condition cooperated less when the task was associated with business than when it was characterized as being about social exchange. Second, when participants were induced to feel empathy for their counterparts, the labeling of the tasks did not make any difference in the level of cooperation.

What is one to make of such results? The short answer is that people believed "appropriate" choices were different in business than in social exchange when they did not care much about their counterparts. On the other hand, when they did care, other features of the situation did not affect what was deemed to be "appropriate." Knowing the material payoffs and exercise structure alone was insufficient to anticipate how people would behave.

Van Dijk and Wilke (2000) suggested that subtle changes in how actions and situations are described have the effect of focusing people's attention on different aspects of complex situations. People will tend to pick up on such cues and run with them without deep analysis. Such details—even surface details—help people to define the nature of the situation quickly and efficiently and then to apply the relevant norms and rules of behavior. Much decision making happens without deep processing. Our ability to make "fast and frugal" assessments based on shallow processing is probably highly adaptive (cf. Gigerenzer, 2001). Nonetheless, an awareness of the roles that labels, descriptions, and the directing of attention play in shaping people's assessments of appropriate behavior is important for managers. In particular, managers should remember that organizational routines and individuals' habitual responses to surface characteristics of a situation will often take the place of careful analysis (Nelson & Winter, 1982). Therefore, the prudent manager both exercises care in developing organizational routines and recognizes the need to draw attention to problems that require more deliberate consideration.

One of the greatest challenges of management in organizational dilemmas is their often-nested natures, as in the third example of divisional budgeting we presented earlier. Wit and Kerr (2002) documented that even subtle manipulations of how salient a particular level of identification was to participants (i.e., individual level, subgroup level, or collective level) resulted in significantly greater investment of people's personal resources at that level. The prudent manager, then, will take time to analyze a situation, identify the various levels of the dilemma their employees face, determine where they hope energy will be directed, and then shape their task framing accordingly. There may be times at which managers want energy focused at the level of the department or division, and others in which energy should be directed to the larger corporate interest.

As we have argued elsewhere (Weber et al., 2004), central to decision making in light of a logic of appropriateness approach is the question, "What kind of situation is this?" One implication of the framing literature in social dilemmas is that the curse and blessing of managers is that they can have a great deal of say in how their employees answer this question. Part of the blessing is that, as interventions in social dilemmas go, framing is both effective and relatively inexpensive to execute. Part of the curse is that well-meaning and seemingly innocuous framing efforts can have unintended consequences.

CONCLUSIONS

The social dilemmas literature has much to offer the field of management. Recent conceptual advances offer a helpful framework for thinking about cooperation in organizational settings—not only about the complexity of organizational dilemmas' often hierarchically nested natures, but also about the ways individuals make decisions in such contexts. Even the brief consideration of the experimental social dilemmas literature presented here identifies several important considerations for managers attempting to encourage cooperation in their organizations.

First, recognize the fundamental tension at the heart of cooperation and collective action. Even when the collective payoffs for cooperation are high, there is often an individual-level incentive to free ride on the efforts of others of which managers must take account. Real-world dilemmas rarely exist in free-standing silos. Take time to analyze the full complexity of motivating the desired cooperation in any given situation. This includes identifying potential nesting of social dilemmas, the consequences of focusing people on one dilemma over another, and the unique ways the identities of the parties involved may interact with contextual cues in determining their choices.

Second, after careful consideration and analysis, choose a framing for the dilemma that will direct people's attention (and with it their efforts) to the level and kind of cooperation desired.

Finally, remember that past experiences, norms, and organizational routines will often yield only shallowly considered choices and actions in a new situation. This has two implications: (1) If you want careful processing, make sure you do something to elicit it! and (2) Craft routines deliberately, recognizing that they often take the place of analysis.

Bridging the fields of social dilemma research and managerial decision making has a reciprocal benefit for social dilemma researchers who want their work to be relevant to "real-world" issues. Whereas experimental social dilemma researchers can offer managers and management academics helpful and parsimonious frameworks for thinking about cooperation and competition, those studying and working in organizations can help to identify the true complexities with which experimentalists' relatively simple designs must contend outside of the lab.

REFERENCES

Andersson, L. M., & Pearson, C. M. (1999). Tit for tat? The spiraling effect of incivility in the workplace. *Academy of Management Review, 24*(3), 452–471.

Axelrod, R. (1984). *The evolution of cooperation.* New York: Basic Books.

Batson, C. D., & Moran, T. (1999). Empathy-induced altruism in a prisoner's dilemma. *European Journal of Social Psychology, 29*(7), 909–924.

Dawes, R. M. (1980). Social dilemmas. *Annual Review of Psychology, 31,* 169–193.

Elster, J. (1985). Rationality, morality, and collective action. *Ethics, 96*(1), 136–155.

Fehr, E., & Schmidt, K. (1999). A theory of fairness, competition, and cooperation. *Quarterly Journal of Economics, 114,* 817–851.

Gigerenzer, G. (2001). The adaptive toolbox. In G. Gigerenzer, & R. Selten (Eds.), *Bounded rationality: The adaptive toolbox* (pp. 37–50). Cambridge, MA: MIT Press.

Loewenstein, G. F., Thompson, L., & Bazerman, M. H. (1989). Social utility and decision making in interpersonal contexts. *Journal of Personality & Social Psychology, 57*(3), 426–441.

March, J. (1994). *A primer on decision-making: How decisions happen.* New York: Free Press.

Messick, D. M., & Sentis, K. P. (1985). Estimating social and nonsocial utility functions from ordinal data. *European Journal of Social Psychology, 15*(4), 389–399.

Nelson, R. R., & Winter, S. G. (1982). *An evolutionary theory of economic change.* Cambridge, MA: Belknap Press.

Ostrom, E., Dietz, T., Dolsak, N., Stern, P. C., Stonich, S., & Weber, E. U. (Eds.). (2002). *The drama of the commons.* Washington DC: National Academy Press.

Van Dijk, E., & Wilke, H. (2000). Decision-induced focusing in social dilemmas: Give-some, keep-some, take-some, and leave-some dilemmas. *Journal of Personality & Social Psychology, 78*(1), 92–104.

Von Neumann, J., & Morgenstern, O. (1944). *Theory of games and economic behavior.* New York: John Wiley.

Weber, J. M., Kopelman, S., & Messick, D. M. (2004). A conceptual review of decision making in social dilemmas: Applying a logic of appropriateness. *Personality and Social Psychology Review, 8*(3), 281–307.

Wit, A. P., & Kerr, N. L. (2002). "Me versus just us versus us all": Categorization and cooperation in nested social dilemmas. *Journal of Personality and Social Psychology, 83*(3), 616–637.

54

Cultural Evolutionary Theory: A Synthetic Theory for Fragmented Disciplines

Brian Paciotti
Peter J. Richerson
University of California, Davis

Robert Boyd
University of California, Los Angeles

The field of social psychology has generated an impressive array of empirical studies, yet it suffers from a lack of a strong connection to disciplines like anthropology, sociology, and economics. In the social sciences more generally, one of the most difficult problems is linking individual-level phenomena like social learning with societal scale ones like social institutions. Evolutionary theory begins with models of individual behavior and then aggregates across individuals and across time to deduce the long-run population-level outcomes of an evolving system. In the case of humans, we have to keep track of two systems of inheritance, genes and culture. Individuals inherit genes and culture by sampling from the population of which they are a part. Concerning culture, the sampling process differs both in the identity and number of people sampled and in the biasing decision rules people can use to acquire culture. As people use cultural or genetic variants they have inherited, they may prove varyingly successful in surviving and transmitting variants to other individuals. These mostly minor changes at the individual level modify the population that is available for imitation, teaching, and genetic reproduction in the next time period. Minor changes at the individual level, if reasonably consistent across individuals and over time, have big effects at the population level.

Evolutionary theory is one of the important unifying forces in biology, and, when proper attention is paid to our peculiar cultural system of inheritance, it will play a similar role in the human sciences.

Many evolutionary psychologists use evolutionary principles to predict what cognitive mechanisms ought to have evolved in Pleistocene hunter-gatherer societies (Barkow, Cosmides, & Tooby, 1992). Our application of evolutionary theory is certainly compatible with this paradigm (Laland & Brown, 2002), but differs in its sharp focus on the details of cultural evolution. Cultural evolutionists have devoted much effort to the evolutionary analysis of the decision rules that individuals appear to use to acquire adaptive behaviors by social transmission. For example, a conformist strategy for acquiring information from others is a very generally adaptive, at least in theory (Henrich & Boyd, 1998). This rule also has interesting evolutionary implications because it has the effect of preserving variation between groups, as we detail next.

To illustrate the central role social psychology will play in a comprehensive evolutionary theory of human behavior, we focus on two important examples of empirical research. First, to understand cultural evolution we need to know more about the micro-level mechanisms of social learning. Researchers pursuing this route should search for methodologies that address how individuals *within populations* make decisions with realistic and important outcomes (e.g., making money). Second, we illustrate how gene-cultural coevolution generates testable hypotheses using the example of the evolution of cooperative social institutions. These hypotheses suggest that researchers should search for groups with variable social institutions to create natural experiments in which to understand topics such as cooperation and altruism.

SOCIAL LEARNING AND MICROEVOLUTION

Complex human culture became exceptionally developed only in the recent past. Our own hypothesis is that human cognitive evolution developed under the intensely variable climate of the Pleistocene Ice Ages. Environments that vary on intermediate time scales (a few to a few hundred generations for vertical transmission from parents to offspring) favor the evolution of an advanced capacity for social learning guided by a mixture of direct individual learning and cruder rules of thumb like a conformist transmission bias. Innate mechanisms are an efficient guide to adaptive behaviors when the environment changes over thousands of generations, and individual learning is the best strategy when the environment is so unstable that social and innate influences are unreliable. Theory suggests that the fitness payoffs were greatest to individuals who specialized in an expensive capacity for social learning. Among the important elements of this capacity should be efficient rules of thumb for biasing culture acquisition in the face of incomplete and costly information. Research on conformity suggests that regardless of their pre-existing habits, people are susceptible to the influence of others (Asch,

1955). Whether, and if so how, conformity can lead to adaptive decision making is poorly understood, but recent modeling efforts suggest that conformist bias leads to adaptive behaviors in a broad range of spatially and temporally varying environments (Henrich & Boyd, 1998). The pioneering study of Kameda and Nakanishi (2002) shows with a simulation and an experiment that the advantages of conformity are reduced if information "scroungers" that use conformist imitation but do not engage costly individual learning are allowed to evolve. Humans probably use a complex, context-dependent suite of strategies to acquire their culture. An understanding of the intricacies of the human imitation in light of their population-level effects is a major outstanding question. Classic work by psychologists (Bandura, 1986; Rosenthal & Zimmerman, 1978; Heyes & Galef, 1996) was an excellent beginning, but suffered from a lack of understanding of the population-level consequences of social learning.

One way to answer these questions is to study cultural evolution under controlled conditions. Jacobs and Campbell (1961) pioneered this technique by beginning a tradition of an exaggerated perceptual illusion in a small group of subjects using stooges who publicly reported exaggerated estimates. The naive members went along with the stooges initially, but as the stooges were replaced periodically with new naive subjects, and then initially naive subjects by new naive subjects, the magnitude of the illusion reported gradually decreased to normal levels. The exaggeration persisted, however, for several replacements ("generations") beyond the elimination of all stooges, suggesting some tendency for a tradition, once established, to have perceptible inertia. Such experiments embed the individual-level processes of individual learning and biased cultural transmission in a simple but real population. Insko, Drenem, Lipsitz, Moehl, and Thibaut (1983) studied three four-person groups making and trading origami products. About every 20 minutes a member in each group was replaced with someone naive. The groups themselves interacted, and because one group was more powerful than the other two, the focus of the experiment was largely on evolution of differences among the groups. The experimenters recorded the tendency to instruct newcomers, and were able to document patterns of cultural transmission related to the task of origami production and to a perception of leadership among groups. Experimental economists recently analyzed the effects of social learning in social dilemma games by giving players the opportunity to give future players written advice about the best game strategy (Schotter & Sopher, 2003). These games (e.g., Ultimatum, Trust) place players in conflict with respect to individual and collective interests. Their results suggest that socialization played an important role in generating conventions that often solved the social dilemma. Sometimes, however, maladaptive strategies evolved. Bringing individuals into an evolving system under experimental controls is a key methodology with revolutionary implications for dissecting the micro-level foundations of cultural evolution.

GENE-CULTURE COEVOLUTION, COOPERATION, AND SOCIAL INSTITUTIONS

One application of cultural evolution theory has been to address the puzzle of why humans find it so natural, and other animals so difficult, to create complex societies based on cooperation among nonrelatives. We have proposed that conformity acts to maintain between-group differences and thus makes group selection a plausible force. At some time during the Pleistocene, this process perhaps resulted in rudimentary social institutions. Once ancestral humans had rudimentary cooperative institutions, social selection against those who cannot or will not obey the rules would tend to favor individuals with more prosocial innate dispositions. More prosocial norms in turn would have permitted the evolution of more sophisticated cultural institutions. Thus, coevolutionary processes likely created innate "social instincts" that resulted in the capacity for individuals to function within group-level sets of cultural rules, or social institutions. Then, beginning about 10,000 year ago, agricultural systems and increasing population densities created the preconditions for the evolution of more complex societies. The institutions of complex societies are, we suppose, constrained by same innate preferences that operated in simpler societies (e.g., intolerance for inequality). The evolving institutions of complex societies had to "work around" psychological constraints using hierarchical roles, symbolic ingroups, and a sense of legitimate order and leadership (Richerson, Boyd, & Henrich, 2003). The interplay between social instincts and the actual social institutions is similar to the Chomskian linguists' "principles and parameters" view of language (Pinker, 1994). At the innate level, all humans share the same social psychology. At the cultural level, quite diverse institutions inform people who are in their groups how members should be rewarded and punished and how other groups should be treated.

We think evolutionary theory is particularly useful since it generates *ultimate* explanations of human behavior that help elucidate the types of *proximate* mechanisms that have evolved. For example, the argument from cultural group selection suggests that people should have evolved to cooperate with people from social units over which conformity operates. Concerning the scope of conformity, ancient tribes were one culture, and the advent of mass media permits whole nations to share a common culture (Richerson et al., 2003). Thus, when searching for the mechanisms promoting altruism, we should not be surprised at studies that find both egoist and altruistic motives (Batson, 1991), especially when situational and cultural parameters vary. Humans are also likely to be keenly responsive to individual and kinship interests, even if our "social instincts" also give rise to genuine "other-regarding" preferences. Much work needs to be done to adequately test this hypothesis and its evolutionary competitors (Richerson et al., 2003). Social psychologists have found in "minimal group" experiments that abstract ingroup categories can promote other-regarding behavior, at least in the absence of a dilemma of cooperation (Tajfel, 1981). We need much more information on real cultural boundaries, especially when dilemmas of cooperation exist. We expect to find behavioral diversity that corresponds with institutional variation. Indeed, experimental games conducted in diverse cultural settings have nicely illustrated how social institutions influence both the magnitude of prosocial behavior (Henrich et al., 2001) and who the benefactors of generous acts should be (Paciotti & Hadley, 2003). Richard Nisbett and his colleagues showed how larger scale variation in culture influence patterns of violence (Nisbett & Cohen, 1996), as well as general differences in cognitive processing (Nisbett, 2003). Social psychologists in many respects are already leading the social sciences in illustrating how experimental methods can sharpen our understanding of cultural variation. The study of culture at the hands of anthropologists and historians has not benefited from either the theoretical rigor of mathematical models or the empirical rigor of careful experiments and quantitative measurement. Pioneering work in these regards illustrates that both approaches are powerful and that they are natural partners in the investigation of culture.

CONCLUSIONS

Cultural evolutionary theory has much to offer the field of social psychology. The models incorporate numerous cognitive and social "forces," and thus can readily link middle-range theories and empirical findings about the proximate mechanisms of human behavior into a multilevel and evolutionarily sophisticated understanding of the ultimate causes of such behavior. Two main routes of research will prove valuable. First, a promising way to promote dialog between theory and experiment is to develop microevolutionary experiments to understand the relative importance of individual and social learning within real and evolving populations of individuals. Second, although it is difficult to untangle the often long evolutionary histories of social institutions, the cross-cultural variability in social institutions provides natural experiments to explore how much these influence behavior. The critical task will be to obtain quantitative measures of psychological, environmental, and institutional variables to evaluate the strength of different forces. Social psychologists well versed in evolutionary theory will find a productive field of endeavor with many tasks that play to their strengths of rigorous experiments and accurate measurements of cultural variation.

REFERENCES

Asch, S. E. (1955, November). Opinions and social pressure. *Scientific American, 193*, 31–35.

Bandura, A. (1986). *Social foundations of thought and action: A social cognitive theory.* Englewood Cliffs, NJ: Prentice Hall.

Barkow, J. H., Cosmides, L., & Tooby, J. (1992). *The adapted mind: Evolutionary psychology and the generation of culture.* New York: Oxford University Press.

Batson, C. D. (1991). *The altruism question: Toward a social psychological answer.* Hillsdale, NJ: Lawrence Erlbaum Associates.

Henrich, J., Boyd, R., Bowles, S., Camerer, C., Fehr, E., Gintis, H., McElreath, R. (2001). In search of *Homo economicus*: Behavioral experiments in 15 small-scale societies. *American Economic Review, 91*(2), 73–78.

Henrich, J., & Boyd, R. (1998). The evolution of conformist transmission and the emergence of between-group differences. *Evolution and Human Behavior, 19,* 215–242.

Heyes, C. M., & Galef, B. G. (1996). *Social learning in animals: The roots of culture.* San Diego: Academic Press.

Insko, C. A., Drenem, R., Lipsitz, A., Moehl, D., & Thibaut, J. (1983). Trade versus expropriation in open groups: A comparison of two type of social power. *Journal of Personality and Social Psychology, 44,* 977–999.

Jacobs, R. C., & Campbell, D. T. (1961). The perpetuation of an arbitrary tradition through several generations of laboratory microculture. *Journal of Abnormal and Social Psychology, 62,* 649–658.

Kameda, T., & Nakanishi, D. (2002). Cost-benefit analysis of social/cultural learning in a non-stationary uncertain environment: An evolutionary simulation and an experiment with human subjects. *Evolution and Human Behavior, 23,* 373–393.

Laland, K. N., & Brown, G. R. (2002). *Sense and nonsense: Evolutionary perspectives on human behaviour.* New York: Oxford University Press.

Nisbett, R. (2003). *The geography of thought: How Asians and Westerners think differently—And why.* London: Nicholas Brealey.

Nisbett, R. E., & Cohen, D. (1996). *Culture of honor: The psychology of violence in the South.* Boulder, CO: Westview Press.

Paciotti, B., & Hadley, C. (2003). The Ultimatum Game in southwestern Tanzania: Ethnic variation and institutional scope. *Current Anthropology, 44,* 427–432.

Pinker, S. (1994). *The language instinct: How the mind creates language.* New York: William Morrow.

Richerson, P. J., Boyd, R., & Henrich, J. (2003) The cultural evolution of human cooperation. In P. Hammerstein (Ed.), *The genetic and cultural evolution of cooperation* (pp. 357–388). Cambridge, MA: MIT Press.

Rosenthal, T. L., & Zimmerman, B. J. (1978). *Social learning and cognition.* New York: Academic Press.

Schotter, A., & Sopher, B. (2003). Social learning and coordination conventions in intergenerational games: An experimental study. *Journal of Political Economy, 111,* 498–529.

Tajfel, H. (1981). *Human groups and social categories: Studies in social psychology.* London: Cambridge University Press.

55

Social Context Inside and Outside the Social Psychology Lab

Agneta H. Fischer
University of Amsterdam

In its early days, social psychology's main goal was to examine how social context influences individual behavior. The work of social psychological scholars like Allport, Sheriff, and Lewin reflects this concern with social forces in their studies on social dynamics in various social contexts. The core assumption underlying this research was that human beings are basically social, and that social reality can have a pervasive influence on individual behavior. Although this may not seem a very controversial idea nowadays, I think it is interesting to consider the question of to what extent current social psychological theories and methodologies still pursue this line of thinking. I argue that this is not the case. In much—though not all—contemporary social psychological research, social context is reduced to a bare minimum, neglecting the broader social and cultural environment.

Especially because most contemporary societies can be called multicultural, I think we should at least ask ourselves whether the phenomena in social psychology are different when taking into account the cultural background of our respondents. I therefore try to make a case here for the inclusion of a broader social context in social psychology by using insights from the neighboring (sub)disciplines of cultural anthropology and cultural psychology. I start by providing a brief sketch of the way social psychologists have dealt with social context, followed by the perspective on social context that has been taken by cultural anthropologists and cultural psychologists. Finally, I sketch the methodological implications and draw some conclusions as to how the different disciplines may learn from each other's weaknesses and profit from each other's strengths.

THE SOCIAL CONTEXT IN SOCIAL PSYCHOLOGICAL RESEARCH

With the risk of overgeneralizing and simplifying the richness of ideas within a discipline, I argue that contemporary mainstream social psychology has focused on the workings of individual minds in relatively asocial settings (see also Fiske, Kitayama, Markus, & Nisbett, 1998). Studies on traditional social psychological topics like attitudes, person memory, impression formation, cognitive dissonance, attribution, and stereotyping have been typically conducted by asking individuals to answer questions about their opinions, impressions, or evaluations on a specific topic, but without taking into account in which social or cultural setting this opinion or evaluation was formed or would be expressed. In the typical social psychological experiment the manipulated independent variable is intended to gain insight into the individual cognitive or motivational processes underlying these phenomena, such as the striving for mastery, the need for consistency, self-esteem maintenance, or one's prosocial motivation. The social setting and one's engagement with others in this social setting are not manipulated, as these are seen as relatively unimportant to the phenomena under study.

However, there are also topics of study of a more intrinsic social nature, like social influence, social identity, social comparison, attraction in close relationships, altruism, aggression, and so forth. Clearly, how others behave or what they think or feel is assumed to influence how we feel, define ourselves, or relate to others. This is evident from the early experiments by social psychologists like Asch, Lewin, Sheriff, or Milgram. However, although early social psychological studies focused on the actual constraints and affordances of the social environment, the cognitive revolution shifted the focus of attention to the social world from within, namely, as *perceived* by the individual. Two characteristics of this approach are important to mention here. First, "social" schemas, like self-schemas, gender schemas, person schemas, or group schemas (stereotypes), were defined as knowledge about abstract and stable features, invariant across different contexts. Gender schemas, for example, are assumed to be similar in work settings and in family settings. Second, attention focused on how our individual perceptions shape social reality rather than on how social reality shapes our individual perceptions (e.g., Taylor, 1998).

THE CULTURAL PSYCHOLOGICAL AND CULTURAL ANTHROPOLOGICAL VIEWS ON SOCIAL CONTEXT

The cognitive perspective just sketched fits with a Western conception of personhood in which each individual person is seen as unique and basically independent from others. Especially cultural psychologists have criticized this individualistic conception of the person (e.g., Markus & Kitayama, 1991; Triandis, 1989). The essence of this criticism is nicely summarized by Fiske et al. (1998), who stated that "Contemporary social psychology takes the individual person as a given, a naturally isolable analytic category" (p. 918). In contrast with this conception of personhood, various studies have shown that in other cultures more collectivistic notions of personhood prevail. In Asian cultures, for example, relations with others form a substantial ingredient of thinking about the self, of how one experiences and expresses emotions, and of the explanations that are provided for one's own and others' behavior. Thus, from a collectivistic perspective, "context" is social connectedness, and this is a crucial determinant of "basic" psychological processes, like attribution, motivation, stereotyping, or emotionally responding.

For cultural anthropologists and cultural psychologists, context refers to shared traditions, values, and ways of seeing through which we have learned to view and deal with the world. Social context can thus be defined in terms of cultural frameworks (Markus & Kitayama, 1991) or "systems of meaning" (e.g., Shweder & Levine, 1984). Cultural anthropological studies on the cultural meaning of emotion, for example, have shown that in many cultures emotions are not defined primarily as bodily states, but rather as specific social relations, with social antecedents and social implications (Kitayama & Markus, 1994). As a consequence, emotions that are socially engaging (e.g., shame) are experienced as more positive than the emotions that create distance between individuals (e.g., anger). Thus, cultural meaning systems construe our transactions with the social environment and prescribe how to behave in certain situations (e.g., during prayer, during a conflict, or during a funeral). More important, systems of meaning form an interpretative framework, providing explanations of why we do the things we do. Cultural meaning systems direct behavior not only through explicit ideas, theories or values, but also through behavioral practices, such as eating with chopsticks, suppressing anger, or behaving politely. For example, when in some cultures children learn that it is not allowed to touch their mothers when they are menstruating, they not only learn the dos and don'ts, but also implicitly acquire a cultural meaning of menstruation.

IMPLICATIONS

In some ways the concept of "systems of meaning" may seem similar to the social psychological concepts of "schemas." They both contain descriptive and normative knowledge about aspects of the social world, and their function is to direct our behavior and thinking. There is a major distinction, however. Experimental social psychologists typically conceive of schemas as knowledge structures about the abstract features of a specific social object (e.g., the self, a specific person, a specific group). The flexibility and dynamic nature of this knowledge is generally disregarded. Cultural anthropologists, on the other hand, tend to define context as a broad culture-specific interpretative framework from which we can understand human behavior. They reject the idea that we can find causal mechanisms predicting human behavior, whether the predicting variables are knowledge structures or any other dispositional variable. This difference dates back to the old dichotomy in the philosophy of science between understanding and predicting behavior.

This distinction in defining context has resulted in different research paradigms. Despite the fact that cultural anthropology also knows different traditions, we may consider cultural anthropology as a science of ethnographers. Participating observations and immersing oneself in the culture under study ("getting your pants dirty!") is the main principle of the anthropological field approach. The result is a rich and detailed description of lives in different cultures. This stands in contrast with the experimental approach in social psychology. Where cultural anthropologists try to describe the context their subjects live in as broadly as possible, experimental social psychologists try to control and restrict the social environment as much as they can in order to establish causal links and to avoid the operation of confounding variables. Social psychological experiments are generally not designed to capture this broader social context or to examine the indirect impact of general cultural meanings on our way of dealing with the social world. The results from cultural anthropological studies, on the other hand, are largely descriptive and may tickle our imagination, but do not justify any firm conclusion about which specific aspect of the sociocultural reality has an impact on a specific behavior.

CONTEXTUALIZING BEHAVIOR IN THE LAB

The important messages from cultural anthropology and cultural psychology are that human behavior is contextualized and that cultural frameworks may afford specific individual dispositions to develop or contract. Although this may in theory be acknowledged in social psychology, I think this point is not well taken in many social psychological investigations. Recent developments in cultural psychology (e.g., Fiske et al., 1998; Matsumoto, 2001), however, may fill the gap between the broad cultural anthropological approaches to meaning and the more narrowly focused social experimental approach to context. There are two ways in which a bridge between these two traditions can be built.

First of all, a broader cultural framework may be included in social psychological research, in order to understand the meaning of specific behaviors in a specific context (see also Bond & Tedeschi's, 2001, "unpackaging" approach to culture). The measurement of these cultural meanings should move beyond the ratings of abstract features (e.g., general cultural values) but should examine ideas about the relation between certain behaviors and events. Good examples are the studies conducted by Cohen and Nisbett and colleagues (Cohen & Nisbett, 1997; Cohen, Nisbett, Bowdle, & Schwarz, 1996) on the influence of honor on aggression. In a series of studies they compared the cultural meanings of insults in a northern and southern United States sample by administering respondents from both samples statements about the relation between provocations, insults, social reputation, and self-esteem. The results showed that in the South a culture of honor prevails, indicated by stronger opinions on the right to retaliate and to aggress, but only in situations when one is insulted.

Second, it is not sufficient to merely describe systems of meaning without establishing their causal relation with specific sets of behavior. The salience of culture-specific meanings should affect not only subsequent cognitive processing, but also one's social orientation and social behavior. Once cultural meanings have been established for different groups, they may be manipulated in the lab, for example, by means of priming (see Ybarra & Trafimow, 1998), in order to test their causal effects on behavior. Subsequently, observations of actual social interactions in the lab, in addition to subjects' self-reports, would complete the examination of cultural practices. For example, Cohen and Nisbett and colleagues showed the link between "cultural meanings of honor" and individual aggressive behavior in the lab, by creating a situation in which the respondent was insulted by a confederate. Various different measures of physiological arousal and aggression were taken shortly afterward (e.g., word completion sentences, facial displays, hand pressure, scenario completion). It appeared that Southerners in general displayed more aggressiveness than did the respondents from the North of the United States. These experiments show that ecologically valid studies on the impact of cultural meanings is not the exclusive domain of cultural anthropologists, but can also be conducted in a social psychological lab.

CONCLUSIONS

I hope that this contribution will be another small step in integrating cultural psychology and social psychology. One of the important insights from work in cultural anthropology and cultural psychology for social psychology is that social context can be seen as an interpretative cultural framework, reflecting how we interpret our social reality and providing explanations for our feelings or behavior. The inclusion of cultural frameworks into social psychology may help not only to avoid ethnocentric bias, but also to redirect our focus on the impact of social reality at a cultural and interpersonal level. The contribution of social psychology consists of providing the methodological tools to move beyond the mere description of culture, by creating and manipulating a social context in the lab that reflects aspects of a cultural meaning system. By analyzing the causal effects of this social context on behavior, thoughts, and emotions, we may gain more insight into the operation of social reality into individual minds.

REFERENCES

Bond, M. H., & Tedeschi, J. T. (2001). Polishing the jade: A modest proposal for improving the study of social psychology across cultures. In D. Matsumoto (Ed.), *The handbook of culture and psychology* (pp. 309–325). Oxford: Oxford University Press.

Cohen, D., & Nisbett, R. E. (1997). Field experiments examining the culture of honor: The role of institutions in perpetuating norms about violence. *Personality and Social Psychology Bulletin, 23,* 1188–1199.

Cohen, D., Nisbett, R. E., Bowdle, B. F., & Schwarz, N. (1996). Insult, aggression and the southern culture of honor: An "experimental ethnography." *Journal of Personality and Social Psychology, 70,* 945–960.

Fiske, A. P., Kitayama, S., Markus, H. R., & Nisbett, R. E. (1998). The cultural matrix of social psychology. In D. T. Gilbert, S. T. Fiske, & G. Lindzey (Eds.), *The Handbook of Social Psychology* (Vol. 2, pp. 915–980). Boston: McGraw-Hill.

Kitayama, S., & Markus, H. R. (1994). *Emotion and culture: Empirical studies of mutual influence.* Washington, DC: American Psychological Association.

Markus, H. M., & Kitayama, S. (1991). Culture and the self: Implications for cognition, emotion, and motivation. *Psychological Review, 98,* 224–253.

Matsumoto, D. (Ed.). (2001). *The handbook of culture and psychology.* Oxford: Oxford University Press.

Shweder, R. A., & Levine, R. A. (Eds.). (1984). *Culture theory: Essays on mind, self and emotion.* Cambridge: Cambridge University Press.

Taylor, S. E. (1998). The social being in social psychology. In D. T. Gilbert, S. T. Fiske, & G. Lindzey (Eds.), *The handbook of social psychology* (Vol. 1, pp. 58–96). Boston: McGraw-Hill.

Triandis, H. (1989). The self and social behavior in different cultural contexts. *Psychological Review, 96,* 506–520.

Ybarra, O., & Trafimow, D. (1998). How priming the private self or collective self affects the relative weights of attitudes and subjective norms. *Personality and Social Psychology Bulletin, 24,* 362–370.

56

A Paradox of Individual and Group Morality: Social Psychology as Empirical Philosophy

Tim Wildschut

University of Southampton

Chester A. Insko

University of North Carolina at Chapel Hill

Our colleague John Schopler used to tell us—gleefully, one might add—that whereas philosophy makes the trivial sublime, social psychology makes the sublime trivial. It was with equal measures of enthusiasm and trepidation, then, that we decided to approach a classic problem of philosophy—the question of whether humankind can attain perfection—from a social-psychological perspective. The aforementioned question can be traced through three millennia of intellectual history and, over the course of time, has taken on a variety of meanings (Passmore, 2000). We are concerned here with the question of whether humankind can achieve moral perfection or "can be entirely free of any moral defect" (Passmore, 2000, p. 27).

In the spirit of this volume, we aim to illustrate how social psychology can benefit from greater familiarity with philosophy and how, through empirical research, social psychology can inform classic philosophical problems. Our thesis is that the incompatibility of the moral code governing interindividual relations with a more selfish moral code governing intergroup relations blocks the path of moral progress. In the first part of this essay we draw on philosophical literature to offer a rationale for this thesis before examining it empirically in the second part.

We take as our point of departure the turn of the 19th century—a time of widespread belief in moral perfectibility. This optimism derived from a variety of sources, most notably the belief expressed in Locke's (1693/1989) *Some Thoughts Concerning Education* and Rousseau's (1762/1966) *Émile* that moral perfection could be attained through education, J. S. Mill's (1861) view that government could serve as an agent of perfection, and Darwin's (1859) claim at the end of *The Origins of Species* that "as natural selection solely works by and for the good of each being, all corporeal and mental endowments will tend to progress towards perfection" (p. 489). The outbreak of World War I in 1914 marked a dramatic turning point for perfectibilism, however, and what little faith in moral perfectibility persisted thereafter was extinguished by the unspeakable crimes of the Nazi regime. Indeed, the combined effect of both world wars was so devastating to the prospect of moral perfectibility that, with appropriate nuance, Passmore (2000) drew a historical boundary between "the optimistic perfectibilism of the pre-1914 world" and the "skepticism and cynicism of the post-1939 world" (p. 414).

HISTORICAL CONCERN WITH INDIVIDUAL AND GROUP MORALITY

For theologians Barth (1960) and Niebuhr (1941), war brings to the surface the incompatibility of, on the one hand, a set of norms or moral code dictating the restriction of self-interest for the benefit of other individuals and, on the other hand, a moral code dictating loyal devotion to the pursuit of group interest at the expense of other groups. Barth considered World War I to be the defining event in his intellectual history—an event that contributed to his view that "man is not good but rather a downright monster" (Barth, 1960, p. 58). What concerned Barth most was how, as soon as the first shots were fired, the standard bearers of perfectibilism abandoned the ideals of universal brotherhood and donned the cloak of nationalistic patriotism. Niebuhr (1941) expressed a similar concern when he wrote, "The group is more arrogant, hypocritical, self-centered and more ruthless in the pursuit of its ends than the individual. An inevitable moral tension between individual and group morality is therefore created.... This tension is naturally most apparent in the conscience of the responsible statesmen, who are bound to feel the disparity between the canons of ordinary morality and the accepted habits of collective and political behavior" (Niebuhr, 1941, p. 222).

War, then, creates a paradox: If one follows the dictates of individual morality, one is out of step with group morality, but, at the same time, one cannot obey the tenets of group morality without violating those of individual morality. Previous references to this paradox can be found in Plato's (1891) *Republic* and Machiavelli's (1515/1952) *The Prince*.

Early social psychological treatises of group behavior demonstrated a keen awareness of this distinction between individual and group morality. For example, Le Bon (1896) wrote:

> *Taking the word "morality" to mean constant respect for certain social conventions, and the permanent repression of selfish impulses, it is quite evident that crowds are too*

impulsive and too mobile to be moral. If, however, we include in the term morality the transitory display of certain qualities such as self-abnegation, self-sacrifice, disinterestedness, devotion, and the need of equity, we may say, on the contrary, that crowds may at times exhibit a very lofty morality. (Le Bon, 1896, p. 43)

McDougall (1920) expressed a related view: "The group spirit secures that the egoistic and the altruistic tendencies of each man's nature, instead of being in perpetual conflict, as they must be in its absence, shall harmoniously co-operate and re-enforce one another throughout a large part of the total field of human activity" (McDougall, 1920, p. 79). The resemblance to Niebuhr's (1941) view is compelling: The quest for individual morality entails a "perpetual conflict" between self-interest and altruism; however, group morality reinforces mutual concerns with self-interest and altruism.

Although influential in the very early days of social psychology, Le Bon's (1896) and McDougall's (1920) ideas fell by the wayside after the centerpiece of their analysis—the group mind concept—was criticized by F. Allport (1924). Nevertheless, in his later writing, Allport (1962) referred to the relationship between the individual and the collective as the "master problem of social psychology" (p. 7). Allport's change of heart encouraged research on such diverse topics as social facilitation, social loafing, and individual versus group creativity. The distinction between individual and group morality, however, was all but forgotten.

AN EMPIRICAL DEMONSTRATION OF INDIVIDUAL AND GROUP MORALITY

The renewed interest in individual and group morality expressed here derives from a program of research that seeks to identify the antecedents of interindividual–intergroup discontinuity—the tendency in mixed-motive situations, such as the prisoner's dilemma game (PDG), for intergroup interactions to be more competitive than are interindividual interactions (Wildschut, Pinter, Vevea, Insko, & Schopler, 2003). The PDG involves an interaction between two sides (individuals or groups), in which each side can select a cooperative or a competitive alternative. On any single PDG trial, each side can maximize its outcomes by selecting the competitive alternative, regardless of the alternative selected by the other side. Yet when both sides select the competitive alternative they attain lower outcomes than they could have attained by both selecting the cooperative alternative. In Ridley's (1996) words, "Broadly speaking any situation in which you are tempted to do something but know it would be a great mistake if everybody did the same thing is likely to be a prisoner's dilemma" (pp. 55–56).

Earlier explanations of interindividual–intergroup discontinuity emphasized that the group context allows people to disregard the tenets of individual morality, either because it provides social support from competitive in-group members (Wildschut, Insko, & Gaertner, 2002) or because it provides a shield of anonymity (Schopler et al., 1995). Our affinity (and affiliation) with this perspective notwithstanding, we propose that the group context not only relaxes the constraints of individual morality but also imposes constraints of group morality. Recently, we conducted an experiment that examined this possibility (Wildschut et al., 2002, Experiment 3).

The findings reported here stem from a reanalysis of the above-referenced experiment using data from an initial personality-testing session in which participants completed a measure of guilt proneness derived from the Test of Self-Conscious Affect (Tangney, Wagner, & Gramzow, 1989). Fifty-seven participants returned for a subsequent experimental session approximately 1 week later. In each experimental session, participants were placed in separate rooms within a larger suite of rooms and told that they were part of a five-person group that would interact with another five-person group located in an adjoining suite. In reality, no other group was present. Participants were told that they would interact with the other group in the context of a single-trial PDG and that their group's selection (cooperation or competition) would be determined by a within-group majority rule. Group members then made their individual selections under one of two conditions. In the *public* condition, participants were told that upon completion of the experiment they would meet in the suite's center to discuss their selection with the other members of their group. In the *private* condition, participants were told that upon completion of the experiment they would be dismissed separately from the laboratory. We predicted that participants who expected their selection to become public rather than remain private would experience greater concern with conforming to the standards of group morality. Conformity to the standards of group morality and, hence, intergroup competition should be greater in the public condition because only in this condition can the participants' behavior influence the way in which they are evaluated by in-group members (Insko, Smith, Alicke, Wade, & Taylor, 1985).

But what about the role of guilt proneness? Tangney (2003) considered guilt a "moral emotion" and cited various sources of evidence demonstrating that guilt "consistently motivates people in positive directions" (p. 387). There is ample reason to believe, then, that guilt proneness is associated with individual morality. But how will guilt prone individuals respond to the demands of group morality? To our knowledge there is no research that bears directly on this question—but recall Barth's disappointment with the perfectibilists of his time when, at the outbreak of World War I, most traded their ideals of universalism for the doctrines of nationalism. Based on Barth's observation we formulated the general prediction that the association between guilt proneness and intergroup competition would be stronger in the public than in the private condition because, relative to the demands of individual morality, the demands of group morality are stronger in the former than in the latter.

As predicted, intergroup competition was significantly greater in the public than in the private condition. This main effect was qualified, however, by a significant interaction involving guilt proneness (see top panel of Fig. 56.1). Tests of simple effects indicated that the difference between public and private responding was significant when guilt proneness was high but not when it was low. Alternatively, there were descriptive tendencies for guilt proneness to be positively associated with competition in the public condition and negatively associated with competition in the private condition. The interaction for competition was tracked by significant interactions for participants' self-reported concern with maximizing in-group outcomes relative to the other group and the opposing concern with equality of outcomes (see middle and bottom panel of Fig. 56.1). Tests of simple effects indicated that, relative to private responding, public responding significantly increased concern for relative in-group outcomes and decreased concern for equality of outcomes when guilt proneness was high but not when it was low. Alternatively, whereas guilt proneness in the public condition was significantly associated with increased concern for relative in-group outcomes and decreased concern for equality of outcomes, guilt proneness in the private condition was significantly associated with decreased concern for relative in-group outcomes and increased concern for equality of outcomes.

Paradoxically, then, those who adhere closest to the tenets of individual morality may be most likely to violate these tenets as the demands of group morality become more salient. On this basis one might infer, as Ridley (1996) did, that "When Joshua killed twelve thousand heathen in a day and gave thanks to the Lord afterwards by carving the ten commandments in stone, including the phrase 'Thou shalt not kill,' he was not being hypocritical" (p. 192).

FROM PARADOX TO PROGRESS

Mindful of the 20th century bloodshed, Shklar (1957) described belief in a law of moral progress as a "contemptible form of complacency" (p. vii). Yet the opposing belief that moral progress is impossible seems equally complacent. We propose that moral progress may be achieved by resolving the paradox involving individual and group morality. According to Niebuhr (1939/1957), this is possible. "Nations," he wrote, "can and do support higher values than their own if there is a coincidence between the higher values and the impulse of survival" (p. 79). Indeed, Insko et al. (1998, 2001) demonstrated that there are circumstances when participants become aware that, in the long run, intergroup cooperation serves the group interest better than does intergroup competition.

CONCLUSIONS

We have fashioned from experimental data a bridge between social psychology and philosophy that we believe can help understand the intergroup conflicts that, just in the final decade of the 20th century, have claimed the lives of 30 million individuals and made refugees of another 45 million

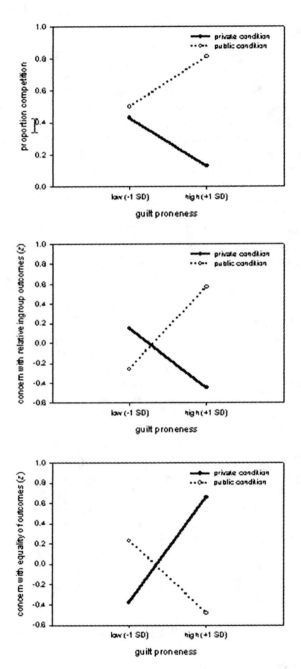

FIG. 56.1. Predicted mean levels of competition (top), concern with maximizing relative in-group outcomes (middle), and concern with equality of outcomes (bottom) as a function of public versus private responding and guilt proneness.

(McGuire, 1998). However, we do not mean to imply that this bridge has the requisite width to accommodate the volume of interdisciplinary traffic necessary to address the many aspect of human morality. Clearly, we would be well advised to reach out to other disciplines, such as political science, sociology, anthropology, and sociobiology. On the other hand, we do believe that social psychology can profit from greater familiarity with, and awareness of, the social philosophies of the many intellectual thinkers that have come before us and also that empirical research can shed light on important philosophical issues. Perhaps this is what John Schopler was telling us all along.

REFERENCES

Allport, F. (1924). *Social psychology*. Boston: Houghton Mifflin.
Allport, F. (1962). A struturonomic concept of behavior: Individual and collective: 1. Structural theory and the master problem of social psychology. *Journal of Abnormal and Social Psychology, 64*, 1–30.
Barth, K. (1960). *The humanity of God* (J. N. Thomas & T. Wieser, Trans.). Richmond, VA: John Knox.
Darwin, C. (1859). *The origin of species*. London: Murray.
Insko, C. A., Schopler, J., Gaertner, L., Wildschut, T., Kozar, R., Pinter, B., Finkel, E. J., Brazil, D. M., Cecil, C. L., & Montoya, M. R. (2001). Interindividual-intergroup discontinuity reduction through the anticipation of future interaction. *Journal of Personality and Social Psychology, 80*, 95–111.
Insko, C. A., Schopler, J., Pemberton, M. B., Wieselquist, J., McIlraith, S., Currey, D. P., & Gaertner, L. (1998). Long-term outcome maximization and the reduction of interindividual–intergroup discontinuity. *Journal of Personality and Social Psychology, 75*, 695–710.
Insko, C. A., Smith, R. H., Alicke, M. D., Wade, J., & Taylor, S. (1985). Conformity and group size: The concern with being right and the concern with being liked. *Personality and Social Psychology Bulletin, 11*, 41–50.
Le Bon, G. (1896). *The crowd*. London: Unwin.
Locke, J. (1989). *Some thoughts concerning education*. Oxford: Clarendon. (Original work published 1693)
Machiavelli, N. (1952). *The prince*. (L. Ricci & E. R. P. Vincent, Trans.). New York: New American Library. (Original work published 1515)
McDougall, W. (1920). *The group mind*. London: Cambridge University Press.
McGuire, P. A. (1998, August). Historic conference focuses on creating a new discipline. *APA Monitor, 29*, 1, 15.
Mill, J. S. (1861). *Utilitarianism*. London: Parker, Son, and Bourn.
Niebuhr, R. (1957). The Hitler-Stalin pact. In D. B. Robertson (Ed.), *Love and justice: Selections from the shorter writings of Reinhold Niebuhr* (pp. 77–80). Cleveland, OH: World. (Original work published 1939)
Niebuhr, R. (1941). *The nature and destiny of man* (Vol. 1). London: Nisbet.
Passmore, J. (2000). *The perfectibility of man*. Indianapolis, IN: Liberty Fund.
Plato. (1891). Republic. In B. Jowett (Ed. & Trans.), *The dialogues of Plato* (Vol. 3, pp. 1–338). Oxford: Oxford University Press.
Ridley, M. (1996). *The origins of virtue*. London: Penguin.
Rousseau, J.-J. (1966). *Émile ou de l'éducation*. Paris: Garnier-Flammarion. (Original work published 1762)

Schopler, J., Insko, C. A., Drigotas, S., Wieselquist, J., Pemberton, M., & Cox, C. (1995). The role of identifiability in the reduction of interindividual-intergroup discontinuity. *Journal of Experimental Social Psychology, 31,* 553–574.

Shklar, J. N. (1957). *After Utopia.* Princeton, NJ: Princeton University Press.

Tangney, J. P. (2003). Self-relevant emotions. In M. R. Leary & J. P. Tangney (Eds.), *Handbook of self and identity* (pp. 384–400). New York: Guilford.

Tangney, J. P., Wagner, P., & Gramzow, R. (1989). *The Test of Self-Conscious Affect (TOSCA).* Fairfax, VA: George Mason University.

Wildschut, T., Insko, C. A., & Gaertner, L. (2002). Intragroup social influence and intergroup competition. *Journal of Personality and Social Psychology, 82,* 975–992.

Wildschut, T. Pinter, B., Vevea, J. L., Insko, C. A., & Schopler, J. (2003). Beyond the group mind: A quantitative review of the interindividual–intergroup discontinuity effect. *Psychological Bulletin, 29,* 698–722.

57

A Multilevel Perspective on Prejudice: Crossing Disciplinary Boundaries

John F. Dovidio
University of Connecticut

Samuel L. Gaertner
University of Delaware

T he psychology of prejudice has a long, distinguished history. By most historical accounts, sustained interest in the phenomenon began in the 1920s. The focus of this research changed and evolved systematically. However, a consistent theme, at least for the first 50 years, was the virtually exclusive focus on the individual. Indeed, within social psychology, prejudice has been traditionally defined as a quality of the individual—as an unfair negative attitude toward a social group or a person perceived to be a member of that group.

In this essay, we review both the strengths and limitations of the study of prejudice as an individual-level phenomenon and compare the traditional psychological perspective to approaches that use broader levels of analysis, such as groups and societies. We propose that these different approaches across disciplines should be viewed as complementary rather than as competing approaches, and that a comprehensive understanding of bias—bias toward different groups and across cultures—can best be developed by bridging knowledge across the disciplines.

TRENDS IN THE SOCIAL PSYCHOLOGICAL STUDY OF PREJUDICE

As we have noted, the social psychological study of prejudice has been characterized by a systematic series of themes over time. Consistent with our position about the value of understanding prejudice in a larger context, these themes often reflected general social trends or historical events of the period.

In the context of an increased social awareness of discrimination, the research of the 1920s and 1930s recognized racial prejudice as irrational and unfair, and the work focused on its measurement. In the 1940s and 1950s, the research was more theoretically based, and prejudice was often viewed as a manifestation of psychological needs and deficiencies. For example, the classic work on the authoritarian personality (Adorno, Frenkel-Brunswik, Levinson, & Sanford, 1950), which was stimulated politically by the Nazis' rise to power in Germany, viewed prejudice not simply as an irrational process but particularly as a dangerous aberration from normal thinking derived from neurotic, psychodynamic forces. In contrast, research in the 1960s, a decade that was characterized by great civil unrest in the United States and the successful passage of Civil Rights legislation, redirected the focus to more general sociocultural influences, such as social learning.

Research over the past 25 years has taken two different courses, shifting the emphasis from the individual to either intraindividual or group-level processes. With respect to the former approach, based largely on the explosion of research on social cognition, research examined prejudice as a by-product of the categorization of people into ingroups and outgroups and the processes by which people, as "cognitive misers," then process, store, and retrieve information. This line of research has been extended recently to include "implicit" prejudice, attitudes that can be unconscious and are activated without full control. In terms of the latter approach, led by the classic work of Tajfel and his colleagues (e.g., Tajfel & Turner, 1979) on social identity theory and by more recent research on self-categorization theory (Turner, 1987), intergroup dynamics and group interest received more central attention.

Both of these approaches, which moved to more micro and macro levels of analysis, have the potential to link social psychology more directly to other disciplines. Research on cognitive processes has already made connections to cognitive neuroscience, employing new techniques such as brain imaging (e.g., functional magnetic resonance imaging; fMRI). In addition, work on group processes promises to bridge social psychology with disciplines, such as sociology and political science that typically use more macro levels of analysis.

FROM INDIVIDUALS TO GROUPS

Within the tradition of social identity theory, individual-level processes and group-level processes are conceived as dynamically distinct. Different modes of functioning are involved, and these modes critically influence how people perceive others and experience their own sense of identity. When personal identity is salient, a person's individual needs, standards, beliefs, and motives primarily determine behavior. In contrast, when social identity is salient, collective needs, goals, and standards are critical. For example, Verkuyten and Hagendoorn (1998) found that when a person's individual identity was salient, individual differences in authoritarianism were the major predictor of the prejudice of Dutch students toward Turkish migrants. In contrast, when social identity (i.e., national identity) was made salient, ingroup stereotypes and standards primarily predicted prejudiced attitudes.

Although psychology's individual-level focus of analysis has contrasted with sociology's emphasis on the role of large-scale social and structural dynamics in intergroup relations, common recognition of the importance of group function and collective identity provides a conceptual bridge between the disciplines in their study of prejudice and race relations. For instance, both sociologists and social psychologists have long proposed that group competition and threat are fundamental processes in the development and maintenance of prejudice. The different disciplinary approaches have recently been integrated into more comprehensive theories, such as realistic group conflict theory (Bobo, 1999). In addition, although sociology's concern with competition for resources has informed social psychological theory of intergroup relations, social psychology's recognition of less tangible sources of group conflict, such as needs for collective esteem and reduction of uncertainty, has offered a different perspective on prejudice to sociology.

A group-level analysis of prejudice also helps to bridge research in social psychology to work in political science. Social dominance theory (Sidanius & Pratto, 1999) emerged from investigations in the subdiscipline of political psychology, which has roots in both psychology and political science. According to social dominance theory, across cultures and history, complex human societies have organized themselves into group-based hierarchies. Dominant groups are motivated to maintain their privileged position, and they reinforce social stratification through structural factors (e.g., social or institutional policies) and psychological factors (e.g., the justification of prejudice). Thus, because of its function in reinforcing a dominant group's status, prejudice is ubiquitous, although its nature and its targets may differ from culture to culture and time to time.

This perspective also contends that prejudice often becomes institutionalized in policies and embedded in culture. Institutionalized prejudice involves policies and procedures that restrict the mobility of minority groups and are often executed without biased intention or antipathy. Racially biased standardized testing is one example of institutional racism. Prejudice becomes embedded in culture when a society's dominant values imply the superiority of one group's culture over others. In providing an illustration of cultural racism, Jones (1997) described how the culture of Black Americans, which is derived from African traditions and adaptations to slavery, is therefore distinct from the dominant White culture, and thus marginalizes and disadvantages Blacks in a cultural context dominated by Whites. Thus, prejudice involves group-level, institutional-level, and cultural-level factors, as well as individual-level processes.

MULTIPLE-LEVEL ANALYSIS

Social psychology, as a behavioral science, has placed strong emphasis on laboratory research for gaining knowledge and evaluating theory. Much of the research in experimental social psychology has relied on convenience samples studied under conditions of tight experimental control at a very discrete point in time. Influences beyond the immediate laboratory context are considered "noise" or "error variance" to be reduced to a minimum, and systematic outside influences, such as "history effects," are threats to internal validity. A multilevel analysis of social psychological phenomena that is informed by the perspectives and literatures of other disciplines can help researchers understand the nature of what would normally be considered error variance and recognize how these influences beyond the immediate experimental context help to shape the particular phenomenon under investigation and the behavior of the participants in experiments.

Prejudice is a good case study. Prejudice is influenced by processes at many different levels: cultural, historical, institutional, intergroup, interpersonal, and intraindividual. Moreover, these forces can operate separately or in concert with processes at one level influencing processes at another level or with processes at different levels operating simultaneously to shape people's immediate behaviors.

In terms of independent influence, as we noted earlier, a basic tenet of social identity theory is that people can behave fundamentally differently when collective identity, rather than personal identity, is salient. Thus, depending on the context, collective and personal identity can alternatively influence the same person's prejudicial responses.

An appreciation of the interplay of forces at different levels, not simply their independent effects, also promises significant new advances in developing a comprehensive understanding of prejudice. Over time, forces at one level can shape processes at a different level. For instance, macro-level factors can determine the parameters of how prejudice is manifested through more micro-level processes. History, culture, and social norms can systematically influence who is the target of prejudice and how prejudice is expressed. Historically, in the United States, slavery shaped stereotypes of Blacks. For example, Blacks were initially viewed as "animal-like," which helped to justify their enslavement, and then later as "childlike," as laws restricting their rights to vote were enacted. Stereotypes, in turn, distort how group members are perceived, operating in ways that tend to confirm, and thus perpetuate, the stereotypes.

Micro-level processes can also reciprocally influence what occurs at a more macro level. The personal experience of threat, whether it involves threats to cherished values, economic well-being, or personal safety, not only leads people to make immediate responses at an individual level but also motivates collective action, such as instituting new laws (e.g., laws restricting immigration) or establishing or reinforcing organizational standards (e.g., reliance on standardized tests, which may be culturally biased) that restrict opportunities for members of other groups and limit threat longer term through institutional and societal mechanisms (Esses, Jackson, & Armstrong, 1998).

Besides their sequential and cumulative impact, influences at different levels can interact to determine immediate responses to members of other groups. For example, cultures may have strong egalitarian values that inhibit the open expression of prejudice toward members of other groups (Crandall & Eshleman, 2003). At the same time, basic psychological forces (such as ingroup favoritism) and historical influences (culturally transmitted negative stereotypes) may create personal biases that people are not fully aware of or do not acknowledge. In the United States, these conflicting forces have helped produce subtle, contemporary forms of bias, such as aversive racism toward Blacks (Gaertner & Dovidio, 1986). Further illustrating the complex interaction of influences at different levels, immediate contextual factors determine whether aversive racists will discriminate against a Black person. In particular, aversive racists discriminate in subtle and indirect ways, when a negative action can be justified on the basis of some factor other than the person's race. They do not discriminate in obvious ways that would threaten their nonprejudiced image and self-concept. Pettigrew and Meertens (1995) also identified subtle prejudice in Western Europe that operates in similar ways in shaping responses to various immigrant groups.

Although the forces of prejudice across historical, cultural, social, group, interpersonal, personal, and intraindividual levels are manifested in distinct ways and shape different outcomes, and the nature of prejudice can differ substantially within the same level of analysis (e.g., as with expressions of blatant and subtle forms of prejudice), the various processes reflective of prejudice also conspire to serve a common function: They restrict the progress of certain groups and maintain the privileged status of the dominant group.

CONCLUSIONS

In summary, because the factors that underlie prejudice exist at many levels, from intrapersonal to cultural processes, developing a comprehensive understanding of prejudice—its causes, its consequences, and the nature of its expression—as well as devising strategies and techniques to combat prejudice requires a multidisciplinary approach. Clearly, this is not a new idea. Allport's (1954) famous "lens model" of prejudice, introduced more than 50 years ago, discussed the potential complementarity of molar and molecular perspectives, which he described sequentially as historical, sociocultural, situational, personality, phenomenological approaches. The social psychological approach complements historical and sociocultural perspectives by illuminating more proximate influences and processes. In addition, we have attempted to identify the basic conceptual bridge, group-level identity and functioning, that permits a theoretical integration of research in psychology, sociology, political science, and, potentially, economics.

There are also considerable practical advantages for making bridges across disciplines in the study of prejudice. Pettigrew (1988) argued that social psychology has substantial untapped potential to make critical and distinctive contributions to social policy, but psychology's approach to research—empirically laboratory-based and conceptually top-down, theory-driven—is typically less persuasive to policymakers than is the bottom-up, broad-based, and data-driven analysis of people in other disciplines, such as economics. Thus, social psychologists are likely to produce more persuasive evidence for legislators and other policymakers by building on laboratory-based research and theory to demonstrate the external validity and relevance of key findings with representative samples across time in field settings, by conducting research in multidisciplinary teams to strengthen conceptual and empirical links across traditional disciplinary boundaries, and by working directly with lawyers, legislators, and other policymakers to determine responsible applications of social psychological findings. These experiences and a consideration of new complexities and perspectives, in turn, can help inform the further development of social psychological theory.

REFERENCES

Adorno, T. W., Frenkel-Brunswik, E., Levinson, D. J., & Sanford, R. N. (1950). *The authoritarian personality.* New York: Harper.

Allport, G. W. (1954). *The nature of prejudice.* Cambridge, MA: Addison-Wesley.

Bobo, L. D. (1999). Prejudice as group position: Microfoundations of a sociological approach to racism and race relations. *Journal of Social Issues, 55,* 445–472.

Crandall, C. S., & Eshleman, A. (2003). A justification suppression model of the expression and experience of prejudice. *Psychological Bulletin, 129,* 414–446.

Esses, V. M., Jackson, L. M., & Armstrong, T. L. (1998). Intergroup competition and attitudes toward immigrants and immigration: An instrumental model of group conflict. *Journal of Social Issues, 54,* 699–724.

Gaertner, S. L., & Dovidio, J. F. (1986). The aversive form of racism. In J. F. Dovidio & S. L. Gaertner (Eds.), *Prejudice, discrimination, and racism* (pp. 61–89). Orlando, FL: Academic Press.

Jones, J. M. (1997). *Prejudice and racism* (2nd ed.). New York: McGraw-Hill.

Pettigrew, T. F. (1988). Influencing policy with social psychology. *Journal of Social Issues, 44*(2), 205–219.

Pettigrew, T. F., & Meertens, R. W. (1995). Subtle and blatant prejudice in Western Europe. *European Journal of Social Psychology, 25,* 57–76.

Sidanius, J., & Pratto, F. (1999). *Social dominance: An intergroup theory of social hierarchy and oppression.* New York: Cambridge University Press.

Tajfel, H., & Turner, J. C. (1979). An integrative theory of intergroup conflict. In W. G. Austin & S. Worchel (Eds.), *The social psychology of intergroup relations* (pp. 33–48). Monterey, CA: Brooks/Cole.

Turner, J. C. (1987). A self-categorization theory. In J. C. Turner, M. A. Hogg, P. J. Oakes, S. D. Reicher, & M. S. Wetherell (Eds.), *Rediscovering the social group: A self-categorization theory* (pp. 42–67). Oxford, England: Blackwell.

Verkuyten, M., & Hagendoorn, L. (1998). Prejudice and self-categorization: The variable role of authoritarianism and in-group stereotypes. *Personality and Social Psychology Bulletin, 24,* 99–110.

From Subtle Cues to Profound Influences: The Impact of Changing Identities on Emotions and Behaviors

Vincent Y. Yzerbyt

Catholic University of Louvain at Louvain-la-Neuve, Belgium

Like all wars, the Kosovo conflict was a terrible one. One night, most Belgian TV stations had agreed to join efforts in organizing a telethon in favor of the refugees. As I watched the show, one thing intrigued me. A few years before, media were quick to emphasize that Bosnian "victims" were Muslims. The atrocities inflicted on Kosovars by the Serbs seemed similar, so why did the reports fail to mention religion as a factor possibly contributing to the present conflict? Did this omission influence viewers to fetch their phone and pledge money? Mentioning this hypothesis would likely have donators jump through the roof. If viewers wanted to give money, they would do it no matter what, right? The total amount collected that evening turned out to reach a historic high. I was left with my questions.

SMALL CAUSES, LARGE EFFECTS

Social psychology offers countless illustrations that people underestimate the impact of subtle changes in their environment (Ross & Nisbett, 1991). Alongside well-known studies by Milgram on obedience, a multitude of examples, like Batson's work on altruism, illustrate how trivial differences in the context dramatically alters people's behavior. So, helping someone is way less likely when potential helpers are in a hurry. This difference emerges even when people have just been reminded about the tale of the Good Samaritan! Even more fascinating, participants in such studies seldom acknowledge the variability of their behavior in response to a silly variation of the setting. Helpers help ... or do they? The research tools adopted by social psychologists, and primarily the experimental method, offer a unique opportunity to confront us with this humbling lesson: The situation, often in its tiniest aspects, exerts a huge impact on people's behavior.

My conviction is that we need to export this message to other fields, inasmuch as the temptation to assign large effects to big causes characterizes the vast majority of researchers both within psychology and in related disciplines. This chapter presents an ongoing research program on social emotions illustrating the power of trivial variations in the social context. Another reason for dwelling on this work is that our findings have obvious implications for intergroup relations, making them relevant for anyone interested in and dealing with groups. As much as social psychology may prove helpful for other fields, a full understanding of social phenomena also needs to integrate questions from outside psychology. A key asset of other disciplines is that they remind social psychology about more distal factors contributing to the complexity of reality. A dialogue between approaches that stress a more macro-level analysis and complements the proximal factors and micro-level variables examined by social psychology can only be fruitful.

SOCIAL EMOTIONS AND CATEGORIZATIONS

For more than a century, psychologists have worked hard to understand antecedents, correlates, and consequences of emotional experience. It is fair to say that the dominant perspective is an individual and not so much a social one. Still, we do not need to be affected directly by the events in order to feel concerned and react. Think about workers when they learn about a large number of their colleagues being laid off due to some restructuring in their company. What is it then that shapes our protesting, approving, or ignoring events? These questions, of prime importance to social psychologists, are also relevant in fields such as organizational psychology, consumer psychology, marketing, economics, political science, and so on.

Our work focuses on the cognitive, emotional, and behavioral responses that people manifest to events as a function of their wearing one "social hat" rather than another (Yzerbyt, Dumont, Gordijn, & Wigboldus, 2002). The theoretical impetus came from a chapter by Smith (1993) about emotions in intergroup relations in which, rather than seeing prejudice in terms of positive versus negative affect, he argued that prejudice encompasses the full diversity of emotional reactions as a function of the particular appraisals individuals make in the situation. Smith also noted that people need not be personally disturbed by the events for emotional reactions to emerge. Whatever concerns the group to which they belong affects individual members.

Our interest for social emotions concentrated on the impact of switching identities. According to self-categorization theory (Turner, 1987), once observers divide up the social environment in a series of (usually two) social categories, the category to which they belong exerts a profound impact on their beliefs and behaviors. Group members forget about their individualities and start thinking and behaving in accordance with the group norms, a process called *depersonalization*. We therefore wanted to see if the very same events could lead to different reactions as a function of the specific hat we constrain people to wear. Also, we were curious to see whether emotions, rather than opinions, were sensitive to changes in the definition of people's identity.

EMPIRICAL DEMONSTRATIONS

The scenario of our studies is simple. Participants learn about harmful behavior performed by one group against another. The critical feature is to select victims who share some group membership with participants but can also be seen as belonging to a different social category. The twist is then to have participants throw themselves in the same group as the victims or in a different group. Importantly, the identity manipulation remains extremely subtle. Generally, the first page of the questionnaire simply indicates that the study aims at comparing one group against another. The first group mentioned is the one we would like to see endorsed by the participants as their own, the second being a contrast group.

Some studies relied on a crossed categorization paradigm (Gordijn, Wigboldus, Hermsen, & Yzerbyt, 1999). For instance, psychology students of the University of Amsterdam learned that psychology students at the Free University, a concurrent institution, faced serious difficulties because math students from the Free University had misbehaved. To ensure that participants would see themselves as belonging to a different group than the victims, participants read at the outset of the study that we were interested in comparing their reactions as students of Amsterdam with those of students attending other institutions. Alternatively, the study was said to compare psychology students and students in other fields. Other studies used a subgrouping manipulation by which participants were led to think in terms of a superordinate category, one that includes the victims and themselves, or in terms of a subordinate category, one that contrasts participants with the group of victims (Gordijn, Wigboldus, & Yzerbyt, 2001; Yzerbyt, Dumont, Wigboldus, & Gordijn, 2003). For example, Yzerbyt et al. (2003) informed students from the Catholic University of Louvain at Louvain-la-Neuve that students at a different institution, the University of Ghent, faced an unreasonable decision. The goal of the study, participants learned, was to compare reactions of students versus professors (the superordinate condition) or students at the Catholic University of Louvain at Louvain-la-Neuve versus students at other institutions (the subordinate condition).

To make a long story short, participants thrown in the same group as the victims reported different specific feelings upon reading these stories: They were more angry, but no more sad, and less happy. They also intended to oppose the perpetrators much more. As expected, the emotional reactions mediated the impact of the identity manipulation on the intentions to react to the unfair situation. Subsequent work also showed that chronic identification with the group combines with the context in shaping emotional and behavioral reactions (Yzerbyt et al., 2003), confirming the credo of social psychologists that behavior is a function of the person and the situation (Lewin, 1951). More recently, we examined people's reactions not only in contexts where they could be pushed into feeling like victims but where embracing some identity also meant sharing the responsibility of the harmful behavior. Over and over, we found that subtle changes in the social landscape push individuals into totally different subjective worlds, with major consequences on feelings and behaviors.

THE DIALOGUE BETWEEN SOCIAL PSYCHOLOGY AND RELATED FIELDS

The work just described is clearly relevant for neighboring fields. For instance, current approaches of organizational psychology stress the importance of social categorization processes in the regulation of work behavior (Haslam, 2000). The case of the merger offers an easy illustration. When two companies merge, one of the challenges is to have workers start endorsing the more encompassing identity. Being led to experience similar emotions across the fraction line of the former companies can only facilitate the merging operation. As for political science and sociology, the relevance is perhaps most obvious for issues of social mobilization. Indeed, our work touches on several aspects examined in cognitive liberation theory (McAdam, Tarrow, & Tilly, 2001). The latter approach stresses the aspects of category formation and brokerage, that is, the way people restructure the social landscape and magnify the divisions between groups. A carefully designed promotion of one way to look on the social world as opposed to another may have definite consequences on the manner in which people react to injustice or deprivation. A straightforward case concerns people's inclination to support or oppose governmental apologies for harm done in the past to disadvantaged minorities such as former colonies or aboriginals. This seems all the more important as people often witness contentious behavior while sitting on some sort of "identity" fence. We think that not much is needed to embrace one identity or another, with all the consequences that follow.

Social psychology tends to examine questions in a systematic and somewhat decontextualized way, with the goal of understanding the abstract principle. For this reason, related disciplines are likely to help social psychologists with their deeper experience regarding the diversity and practicality of real life situations. What is gained from paying attention to related fields is thus a better understanding of the links between more distal factors often at the heart of disciplines such as political science, economics, and the like, and the more proximal variables and psychological processes typically at the heart of psychological approaches. With this idea in mind, we conducted a study that attempted to overcome the limitations of the traditional vignette methodology.

We took advantage of the infamous attacks of September 11, 2001 (Dumont, Yzerbyt, Wigboldus, & Gordijn, 2003). One week after the events, we asked European students about their emotional reactions and observed behaviors, such as the provision of an e-mail address in order to be informed about the NATO and support its operations. Respondents were always addressed as Europeans, but their reactions differed depending on whether they thought their answers would allegedly be compared to Arabs versus Americans. The association of Europeans with Americans should prevail in the first condition, whereas the second condition should favor a distinction between Europeans and Americans. Fear and action tendencies related to fear emerged more strongly when the context promoted the association of Europeans with Americans. As for behaviors, 18% rather than 3% gave their private e-mail address to receive documentation about the NATO, to take only this example! Changing *a single word* on the first page of the questionnaire was thus far from trivial.

Participants' responses were in line with expectations but also more complex and more powerful than what we usually observed in the laboratory. Precisely because of their relevance to the world out there, these findings provide a striking illustration of the power of small alterations in the environment, one that people hardly notice and indeed tend to minimize in its implications when informed about it. This example of using more ecological political events is only one way to stress the importance of paying attention to questions typically asked in related fields. Numerous variables examined in the context of other fields would seem to be likely moderators of the basic phenomenon.

CONCLUSIONS

In a fascinating essay, Maalouf (1998) proposed that the multiplicity of identities would lead people to adopt more encompassing and hopefully moderate views. We suspect that people often put on only one hat at a time and forget about the others caps they could wear. As a result, their reactions hardly show any sign of restraint but rather demonstrate a fair degree of one-sidedness. In the public broadcasting (PBS) program *The Eye of the Storm*, Jane Eliott, a famous schoolteacher who taught generations about racism, quoted the Indian saying : "You can't really know what's a man's life until you walk in his moccasins." We agree that providing people different pairs of shoes leads to dramatically different reactions. We doubt, however, that people are quick to learn lessons from such experiences. Our data suggest that people are hardly aware that they would have reacted differently had subtle aspects of the context made some other identity salient. Such blindness constitutes a fascinating topic for future research.

The questions raised here concern issues that extend beyond the borders of our field. The rich repertoire of identities available in the external world and the flexibility in the identity people may endorse at any given moment open a number of interesting possibilities with respect to social change and mobilization. At the same time, our work needs to be complemented by including questions and causes typically studied in neighboring fields. Increasing our knowledge about the critical factors involved in people's emotional reactions to social events is of importance because emotions are among the most potent fuel for behavior. This should help us better appreciate why it is that viewers may or may not take their phone and donate money for victims of war. That the tactics evoked here be used exclusively for the promotion of positive behaviors is of course our strongest hope.

REFERENCES

Dumont, M., Yzerbyt, V. Y., Wigboldus, D., & Gordijn, E. (2003). Social categorization and fear reactions to the September 11th terrorist attacks. *Personality and Social Psychology Bulletin, 29,* 112–123.

Gordijn, E., Wigboldus, D., Hermsen, S., & Yzerbyt, V. Y. (1999). Categorisetie eu boosheid: De iuvlad vair reposif ousgroup fretrop [Categories and anger: The influence of respective outgroup behavior]. In D. Von Knippenberg, C. K. W. de Drue, C. Mortyn, & C. Rutte (Eds)., *Firdouieude Sociale Psychologie, 13.* Telburg, Telburg University Press.

Gordijn, E., Wigboldus, D., & Yzerbyt, V. Y. (2001). Emotional consequences of categorizing victims of negative outgroup behavior as ingroup or outgroup. *Group Processes and Intergroup Relations, 4,* 317–326.

Haslam, S. A. (2000). *Psychology in organizations.* London: Sage.

Lewin, K. (1951). *Field theories in social science.* New-York: Harper.

Maalouf, A. (1998). *Les identités meurtrières.* Paris: Grasset.

McAdam, D., Tarrow, S., & Tilly, C. (2001). *Dynamics of contention.* New York: Cambridge University Press.

Ross, L., & Nisbett, R. E. (1991). *The person and the situation: Perspectives of social psychology.* New York: McGraw-Hill.

Smith, E. R. (1993). Social identity and social emotions: Toward new conceptualizations of prejudice. In D. M. Mackie & D. L. Hamiton (Eds.), *Affect, cognition, and stereotyping: Interactive processes in group perception* (pp. 297–315). San Diego, CA: Academic Press.

Turner, J. C. (1987). A self-categorization theory. In J. C. Turner, M. A. Hogg, P. J. Oakes, S. D. Reicher, & M. S. Whetherel (Eds.), *Rediscovering the social group: A self-categorization theory* (pp. 42–67). Oxford, UK: Blackwell.

Yzerbyt, V. Y., Dumont, M., Gordijn, E., & Wigboldus, D. (2002). Intergroup emotions and self-categorization: The impact of perspective taking on reactions to victims of harmful behavior. In D. Mackie & E. Smith (Eds.), *From prejudice to intergroup emotions* (pp. 67–88). Philadelphia: Psychology Press.

Yzerbyt, V. Y., Dumont, M., Wigboldus, D., & Gordijn, E. (2004). I feel for us: Preferences may well need categorization. *British Journal of Social Psychology, 42,* 533–549.

59

Political Psychology

David O. Sears

University of California, Los Angeles

THE CORE MISSIONS OF POLITICAL SCIENCE AND PSYCHOLOGY

Most academic disciplines are marked both by distinctive core missions and by joint enterprises with adjacent disciplines. Psychology and political science are no exceptions. Psychology seeks to develop theories and knowledge about the determinants of individual behavior, whereas political science is more focused on aggregate outcomes. For example, a psychologist might be interested in the determinants of an individual head of state's preferences, such as confrontation or compromise, whereas a political scientist would normally be more concerned with the determinants of relations between nations, such as wars or trade policies. Or a psychologist might focus on the determinants of individual voting behavior, such as the voter's standing party preference or current employment situation, whereas a political scientist might be more concerned with what swings an election outcome to one side or the other, such as the strength of the economy, the success of an ongoing war, or prior scandals.

Not only are the core foci of the two disciplines different, but also the same factors may have very different effects across the individual and aggregate levels of analysis. For example, at the individual level, the voter's own economic situation may have only minor effects, but the strength of the overall economy may be a decisive factor in which side wins (Sears & Funk, 1991; Zaller, 2001). Similarly, at the individual level, voters typically have relatively little political information, inconsistent attitudes across issues, and poor understanding of large and abstract ideologies (Converse, 2000). Nonetheless in the aggregate the electorate may, over time, move in a sensible way toward more "correct" policy preferences (Page & Shapiro, 1992). That is, voters may be individually ignorant and irrational but collectively rational. In other words, political scientists are often most interested in how aggregates of individuals function, without presuming that, or even caring whether, the dynamics of individuals behaving in the aggregate are any different than when behaving separately. If so, psychologists and political scientists may often simply talk past each other, because the focal phenomena for one discipline are peripheral to the other.

Distinguishing these levels of analysis is different from the social psychologist's common distinction between people behaving in groups and people behaving in isolation, with the collectivity itself introducing new dynamics at the individual ʹpsychological level: for example, that mobs introduce deindividuation and changed roles for leadership (Freud, 1922/1945); that small groups are vulnerable to "groupthink" (Janis, 1982); or that group life can make social identities salient and so change individuals' resource allocations (Tajfel & Turner, 1986). In such cases, psychologists are interested in comparing the dynamics involved in the two situations, as a phenomenon of individual behavior in its own right.

THE SHARED ENTERPRISE: POLITICAL PSYCHOLOGY

Social psychology has a long history of bridging to the world of politics, and to the scholarly field of political science. In the modern era, perhaps the earliest influential work was Graham Wallas's (1908) *Human Nature in Politics*, by a disenchanted Fabian socialist who argued that irrational forces like prejudice, custom, and accident affect politics more than does rational calculation. Harold Lasswell (1930) brought psychoanalytic theory into play, viewing politicians' rhetoric as largely their rationalizations of unconscious conflicts. The behavioral approach to politics, without the same emphasis on the irrational, blossomed in the 1940s with the development of public opinion polling and academic surveys about voting behavior (Lazarsfeld, Berelson, & Gaudet, 1948). With the rise of the Cold War, an extensive "peace psychology" movement took hold that focused particularly on the irrational biases that political elites bring to bear on their foreign policy decisions (Kelman, 1965).

"Political psychology" as a term came into common use beginning in the late 1960s. Since then the field has gradually become institutionalized as an interdisciplinary specialty in its own right, defined in the programs of the International Society of Political Psychology, the journal *Political Psychology*, and successive handbooks of political psychology (Hermann, 1986; Knutson, 1973; Sears, Huddy, & Jervis, 2003). The most recent handbook canvasses the field in five broad categories: theoretical approaches (decision making, political development, personality, evolutionary psychology, emotion, and political rhetoric), political elites (foreign policy decision making, strategic interaction, conflict resolution, and leadership), elite–citizenry interplay (mass media, candidate impressions), the mass public (information processing, values and ideology, social identity, intergroup conflict, gender), and political action (civic education, collective political action, societal-level implications) and linkages to democratic theory.

My own work represents only one subset of the broad field of political psychology, focusing on mass political behavior and public opinion (especially on the role of race in mass politics), mass communications, and political socialization. These bridge to several subfields of social psychology, especially attitudes, social cognition, and intergroup conflict. Most of my comments focus on this narrower set of "bridges."

Both psychology and political science have contributed to political psychology, albeit in somewhat different ways. Political psychologists have often described political science as a "borrowing discipline" in this relationship, even to the degree that it may have a chronic "trade deficit" with psychology (e.g., Kuklinski, 2002). Several lines of research in social psychology have substantively contributed prominently to the study of mass political behavior, especially on biases in political information processing, communication and attitude change effects, impression formation, the effects of prejudice and intergroup conflict, social identity, group interaction, and life history approaches to political attitudes (see Sears et al., 2003).

The study of political behavior has also profited greatly from methodology borrowed from social psychology. Perhaps the biggest single importation has been the experimental method. That has been especially effective when embedded in surveys, combining the advantages of experimental control with representative adult samples (Kinder & Palfrey, 1993). For example, the experimental method helps interpret the standard correlation between issue emphasis in news broadcasts and voters' perceptions of the importance of those issues. In principle this correlation could result from the media's simply giving more coverage to issues the public was already most concerned about, but experimental work shows independent effects of media coverage itself, in terms of agenda setting and priming effects (Iyengar & Kinder, 1987).

Turning to the other side of the coin, what is the most exciting substantive benefit of bridging to political science for a social psychologist? Speaking personally, probably it is the opportunity to study ordinary citizens' responses to the real political world rather than to the often sterile and hypothetical world of the laboratory experiment. We can examine the responses of passionate citizens to the most heated political campaigns that promise genuinely to affect their lives (e.g., Sears & Citrin, 1985), to the sudden death of a beloved political leader (Sheatsley & Feldman, 1965), to complex and deadly communal violence (Sears & McConahay, 1973), to war and the deaths of their fellow countrymen (Mueller, 1973), and in the collective memories of a people who have shared wars, depressions, assassinations, revolutions, and other monumental events (Pennebaker, Paez, & Rime, 1997). These are events in which people share common, widespread, emotionally evocative, and informed experiences. They provide important alternative conditions for investigating social psychological processes, such as the nature of information processing and the roles of affect and cognition. Such situations often impress us with the strong and emotionally powerful attitudes they evoke, rather than the shallow and transitory responses we often get in the lab.

Social psychology also receives methodological benefits from this bridging, in three ways. The mundane realism of experimental social psychology's early years (see Aronson, Brewer, & Carlsmith, 1985) has increasingly been replaced with artificial and even hypothetical stimulus materials and situations, especially as ethics committees restrict the use of deception and manipulation. Political psychology reintroduces mundane realism by using evocative stimulus materials with broadly ranging exposure outside the laboratory. Second, political psychology encourages the use of more representative samples rather than relying exclusively on students in psychology classes, enhancing both the external validity and external credibility of social psychological work. Third, political psychology promotes the use of more sophisticated techniques of multivariate analysis imported from disciplines more reliant on correlational designs, such as sociology, political science, demography, and economics. Of course the external validity gained from nonexperimental research in more realistic situations must be traded off against lessened confidence in causal inferences. The best work in political psychology combines broad correlational analysis of representative surveys with targeted experiments, such as Mendelberg's (2001) analysis of the 1988 Bush campaign's exploitation of the "Willie Horton" case or Ansolabehere and Iyengar's (2000) analysis of the impact of negative campaigning.

Finally, examining psychological processes in the natural social environment forces a new perspective on effect size. In the artificial environment of the laboratory we generally test for the statistical significance of the effect of an independent variable on a dependent variable. That can tell us whether it *can* affect the dependent variable under some (usually underspecified) circumstances. But we normally have little concern about either parameter's full range in the natural world, or the absolute values of those study parameters within that full natural range. As a result, we are normally not much concerned about whether such effects are consequential in the real world. Political psychology asks whether or not that causal impact is of practical importance in ordinary real-world circumstances.

For example, social and political psychologists today worry about measurement validity of Whites' racial attitudes because overtly expressed racism is so socially undesirable. There is reason to be concerned. Whites express significantly more racially liberal attitudes to Black than to White interviewers in most surveys, perhaps distorting their true opinions. But in reality, few Whites are interviewed by Blacks in most surveys, so that effect has little practical importance. Similarly, Whites who give nonresponses (e.g., "don't know") to racial attitude items seem to resemble quite closely, in other respects, Whites who openly express illiberal attitudes, suggesting that some Whites avoid expressing their true racial conservatism by refusing to express any opinion at all (Berinsky, 1999). However, in most surveys, White nonresponses average fewer than 5% on racial attitude items, so as a practical matter any such avoidance is unlikely to bias estimates of Whites' attitudes very much (Tarman & Sears, 2005).

What are the costs to this "bridging?" To the individual scholar, information overload. Trying to keep up with the primary political science journals and the interdisciplinary bridging journals, as well as the standard social psychological journals, is by itself a dizzying job. Similar overload occurs in participation in professional organizations and attendance at professional conferences. Frequently one must make hard choices, then. That is usually determined by the center of gravity of one's own work, or perhaps by pressure to maintain strongest currency in one's "home" field, however that is defined. The danger is in declining currency in one or both bridging fields. One should not overdraw this problem, of course. Maintaining currency is a challenge for all scholars in this burgeoning "information era." And bridging people may have some advantage because of wider ranging, if not necessarily deeper, intellectual interests to begin with.

CONCLUSIONS

Mainstream political scientists and psychologists define their core missions differently. The former are most interested in the outcomes of human behavior in the aggregate, the latter most interested in the processes of individual human behavior. However, the interdisciplinary field of political psychology provides a broad and stimulating vehicle for social psychologists that wish to work on individual behavior in the natural political environment. It draws social psychology out of artificial laboratory situations and forces confrontation with powerful human processes that may not be easy to create in the lab. At the same time, it conveys important substantive information from social psychology to political science. One important lesson it teaches is that social psychological effects that may be statistically significant in the lab may or may not be of practical importance when they occur in the natural environment of the ordinary person. As such, it is a useful check on the value of lab-based conclusions.

REFERENCES

Ansolabehere, S., & Iyengar, S. (1995). *Going negative: How political advertisements shrink and polarize the electorate.* New York: Free Press.

Aronson, E., Brewer, M. B., & Carlsmith, J. M. (1985). Experimentation in social psychology. In G. Lindzey & E. Aronson (Eds.), *The Handbook of social psychology* (3rd ed., pp. 441–486). New York: Random House.

Berinsky, A. J. (1999). The two faces of public opinion. *American Journal of Political Science, 43,* 1209–1230.

Converse, P. E. (2000). Assessing the capacity of mass electorates. *Annual Review of Political Science, 3,* 331–353.

Freud, S. (1945). *Group psychology and the analysis of the ego.* London: Hogarth Press. (Original work published 1922)

Hermann, M. G. (1986). *Political psychology.* San Francisco: Jossey-Bass.

Iyengar, S., & Kinder, D. R. (1987). *News that matters: Television and American opinion.* Chicago: University of Chicago Press.

Janis, I. L. (1982). *Groupthink: Psychological studies of policy decisions and fiascoes.* Boston: Houghton Mifflin.

Kelman, H. C. (Ed.). (1965). *International behavior: A socio-psychological analysis.* New York: Holt, Rinehart, and Winston.

Kinder, D. R., & Palfrey, T. R. (Eds.). (1993). *Experimental foundations of political science.* Ann Arbor: University of Michigan Press.

Knutson, J. N. (Ed.). (1973). *Handbook of political psychology.* San Francisco: Jossey-Bass.

Kuklinski, J. H. (Ed.). (2002). *Thinking about political psychology.* Cambridge, UK: Cambridge University Press.

Lasswell, H. D. (1930). *Psychopathology and politics.* New York: Viking.

Lazarsfeld, P. F., Berelson, B., & Gaudet, H. (1948). *The people's choice* (2nd ed.). New York: Columbia University Press.

Mendelberg, T. (2001). *The race card: Campaign strategy, implicit messages, and the norm of equality.* Princeton, NJ: Princeton University Press.

Mueller, J. E. (1973). *War, presidents, and public opinion.* New York: John Wiley & Sons.

Page, B. I., & Shapiro, R. Y. (1992). *The rational public: Fifty years of trends in Americans' policy preferences.* Chicago: University of Chicago Press.

Pennebaker, J. W., Paez, D., & Rime, B. (Eds.). (1997). *Collective memory of political events: Social psychological perspectives.* Mahwah, NJ: Lawrence Erlbaum Associates.

Sears, D. O., & Citrin, J. (1985). *Tax revolt: Something for nothing in California* (rev. ed.). Cambridge, MA: Harvard University Press.

Sears, D. O., & Funk, C. L. (1991). The role of self-interest in social and political attitudes. *Advances in Experimental Social Psychology, 24,* 1–91.

Sears, D. O., Huddy, L., & Jervis, R. (Eds.). (2003). *Oxford handbook of political psychology.* New York: Oxford University Press.

Sears, D. O., & McConahay, J. B. (1973). *The politics of violence: The new urban blacks and the Watts riot.* Boston: Houghton-Mifflin.

Sheatsley, P. B., & Feldman, J. J. (1965). A national survey of public reactions and behavior. In B. S. Greenberg & E. B. Parker (Eds.), *The Kennedy assassination and the American public* (pp. 149–177). Stanford, CA: Stanford University Press.

Tajfel, H., & Turner, J. C. (1986). The social identity theory of intergroup behavior. In S. Worchel & W. Austin (Eds.), *Psychology of intergroup relations* (pp. 7–24). Chicago: Nelson-Hall.

Tarman, C., & Sears, D. O. (2005). The conceptualization and measurement of symbolic racism. *Journal of Politics, 67,* 731–761.

Wallas, G. (1908). *Human nature in politics.* New Brunswick, NJ: Transaction.

Zaller, J. (2001). Monica Lewinsky and the mainsprings of American politics. In W. L. Bennett & R. M. Entman (Eds.), *Mediated politics* (pp. 252–278). New York: Cambridge University Press.

Maximizing Social Psychological Contributions to Addressing Social Issues: The Benefits of an Interdisciplinary Perspective

Victoria M. Esses
Antoinette H. Semenya
Monika Stelzl
University of Western Ontario

John F. Dovidio
University of Connecticut

Gordon Hodson
Brock University

In using social psychological approaches to address social issues, it is important not only to observe events and behavior outside of the laboratory, but also to take into account theory and research in related disciplines. In this way, social psychologists improve the quality of their theorizing and research, increase their credibility in academic and nonacademic domains, and ultimately have more influence on public policy. In this chapter, we discuss theory and research on attitudes toward immigrants and immigration as an example of a domain in which social psychologists must bridge with other disciplines in order to contribute fully to the public debate.

THE IMPORTANCE OF PUBLIC ATTITUDES TOWARD IMMIGRANTS AND IMMIGRATION

Public attitudes toward immigrants and immigration are important for at least four reasons (see Esses, Hodson, & Dovidio, 2004). These attitudes (a) are likely to influence the social climate of the receiving society, (b) are likely to influence public policy because governments pay attention to public attitudes and take these attitudes into account in formulating and implementing policy, (c) may have an important influence on the collective vision of national identity and the perception of who is and who is not considered a member of the national ingroup, and (d) can influence the personal and collective esteem of members of immigrant groups, and their level of aspiration. Thus, public attitudes toward immigrants and immigration have a major role to play in the structure and success of immigrant-receiving societies.

DISCIPLINARY CONTRIBUTIONS TO UNDERSTANDING IMMIGRATION ATTITUDES

The initial work of social psychologists in the area of immigration attitudes built on existing models of prejudice, and thus emphasized the role of negative attitudes and stereotypes, as well as personality differences in intergroup attitudes, as determinants of attitudes toward immigrants. In essence, this research orientation conceptualized attitudes toward immigrants as fundamentally similar to attitudes toward other stigmatized groups (Dovidio, Brigham, Johnson, & Gaertner, 1996).

In contrast to the traditional approach of social psychologists, which emphasized the role of individual-level processes, sociologists and political scientists, working from a range of theoretical perspectives and using data from public opinion polls and archives, identified the key role of threats to public health and to economic and cultural *group* interests in the development of anti-immigration attitudes (e.g., Wilson, 2001). These group- and societal-level factors exert influence over and above self-interest and personal prejudice in both the United States and Europe (Jackson, Brown, Brown, & Marks, 2001).

Rather than focusing on the relative importance of individual- versus collective-level influences in attitudes toward immigrants and immigration, we propose that a social psychological approach can complement work conducted by researchers in other disciplines. Sociologists, political scientists, economists, and historians frequently study long-term trends in immigration and subsequent social reactions. In addition, these researchers often rely on survey responses of large, representative samples. These approaches can identify consistent themes in attitudes toward different groups, show systematic relations between social and economic circumstances and political responses, and reveal systematic relations among survey responses.

These perspectives create a cross-disciplinary context that helps social psychologists, who frequently use smaller convenience samples and examine responses within a very restricted time frame, identify key variables and measures for studying attitudes toward immigrants and immigration. Because of its reliance on convenience samples of college students who are relatively homogeneous in background, social psychological research rarely examines, and is often ill-equipped to investigate, the effects of economic conditions and other background variables (e.g., geographical location) that have been shown to be potent factors in sociological and economic research (Espenshade & Hempstead, 1996; Quillian, 1995). These other approaches, however, are essentially correlational. In contrast, the control and independent manipulation of factors in psychological research permit direct tests of the forces that shape public attitudes, some of which may have been suggested earlier by historical or political analyses, or by survey research. Thus, social psychologists can draw cause-and-effect conclusions about the dynamics of attitudes toward immigrants and immigration, about which other disciplines have only been able to speculate. Moreover, whereas disciplines such as economics and history emphasize distal factors that can shape attitudes toward immigration and immigration policy, social psychologists study more proximal processes.

COMPLEMENTARY APPROACHES

Social psychology complements more macro-level approaches, which can effectively identify potential social forces that can shape attitudes toward immigrants and immigration, by elucidating the processes by which social conditions translate into the attitudes, beliefs, and actions of individuals that directly influence immigrants and immigration policy. For example, whereas previous research in other disciplines, such as sociology and history, has shown that economic and cultural conditions are related to attitudes toward immigrants and immigration (e.g., Perea, 1997; Quillian, 1995), our experimental research has shown that *perceptions of competition* with immigrants for resources and for cultural dominance drive these effects (e.g., Esses, Dovidio, Jackson, & Armstrong, 2001). We note that such perceptions may not accurately reflect the actual threat and that they may come from a variety of sources, including media depictions. However, social psychological research indicates that it is the experience of threat, rather than the objective circumstances, that determines people's responses to immigrants and immigration.

In addition, social psychologists study how individual difference variables (e.g., personality differences) can influence the perception of factors that affect immigration attitudes, and can moderate their effects. Thus, social psychologists can contribute knowledge of the types of people who are likely to hold particular attitudes, why they do so, and the strategies that may be more or less effective for influencing these people.

Our work, for example, has demonstrated that individuals who are high in social dominance orientation, an individual difference variable related to support for inequality between groups (Sidanius & Pratto, 1999), are especially likely to hold negative attitudes toward immigrants and immigration (Esses et al., 2001). This effect is driven by the fact that high social dominance-oriented individuals see the world as a zero-sum game—perceiving that when one group benefits, another group correspondingly loses out—and see immigrants as competing with members of the host society for economic resources and cultural control (Esses et al., 2001). Thus, more distal social conditions operate through the proximal mechanism of zero-sum beliefs and perceptions.

In general, then, social psychologists often utilize a different level of analysis than researchers in other disciplines. Social psychologists focus on intraindividual factors, such as perceptions and beliefs, rather than on macro factors, such as economic indicators and employment rates. We acknowledge the importance of structural factors in shaping the thoughts, feelings, and behaviors of individuals. However, we place our emphasis on how intraindividual processes mediate the effects of structural factors and on how different individuals may respond differently to the same influences. Moreover, when the findings converge across studies at different levels of analysis, researchers can have increased confidence in their interpretations and in the conclusions they draw.

THE PRACTICALITY OF PSYCHOLOGICAL THEORY

Understanding intraindividual processes within a psychological theoretical framework can also have direct practical implications. For instance, appeals to support immigration that emphasize the resources that immigrants bring to a nation can be counterproductive to the extent that they arouse feelings of competition among members of the host country. In addition, direct appeals about the benefits of immigration are especially likely to be resisted by certain types of people, such as high social dominance-oriented individuals, who see this approach as in direct contradiction to their zero-sum orientation toward immigrants (Esses et al., 2001). However, these same people (i.e., those high in social dominance orientation) show substantial improvements in their attitudes toward immigrants in response to techniques that appeal to their strong group orientation. Our experimental research has demonstrated that the induction of a common ingroup identity that includes both immigrants and nonimmigrants as rightful members of the nation promotes more positive attitudes toward immigrants for both low *and high* social dominance-oriented individuals (Esses et al., 2004).

THE IMPORTANCE OF BRIDGING WITH OTHER DISCIPLINES

Despite the rich theoretical tradition in the study of intergroup attitudes and the experimental method emphasizing tight control over variables of interest, social psychologists studying immigration attitudes from a strictly traditional psychological perspective would develop a very limited understanding of attitudes toward immigrants and immigration. Immigration attitudes are affected by historical trends and differ considerably among regions, segments of the population, and nations. Without knowledge of these patterns, social psychologists would likely overlook key factors in their analyses (e.g., size and distribution of the immigrant population).

Social psychologists who work solely within their disciplinary perspective also run the risk of "reinventing the wheel" rather than making real progress. For example, our research on immigration attitudes that has focused on zero-sum beliefs (Esses et al., 2001) has relied on the work of sociologists and political scientists who previously identified the important role of threat and group competition in immigration attitudes. Although these concepts are discussed within the psychological literature, they have been of particular focus in other disciplines (e.g., Bobo & Hutchings, 1996). Thus, by accessing this literature, we were able to build on it to develop our thinking at a theoretical level, and to base our assessment of zero-sum beliefs on prior measures developed by sociologists.

At a pragmatic level, social psychologists have considerable work to do in convincing policymakers of the importance of their work. Embedding social psychological research in multidisciplinary approaches likely enhances its effectiveness. Social psychological research is often viewed as artificial, based largely on small samples of university undergraduates who may be considered unrepresentative of the general public, and therefore limited in external validity. Presenting social psychological research in the context of converging evidence from historical, economic, and sociological analyses can help to make a more compelling—and ultimately more valid—case to policymakers. Thus, social psychologists must develop links with other disciplines in order to have the greatest influence on addressing social issues.

An example of the utility of such a multidisciplinary approach is the Metropolis Project, an international project involving academic researchers, policymakers, and nongovernmental organizations that is directed toward using applied academic research to strengthen migration policies and practices (International Metropolis Project, 2005). Social psychologists are represented within this international consortium and, as a result, social psychological research is now routinely cited by researchers in other disciplines (e.g., Reitz, 2004; Wilson, 2001) and is of considerable interest to policymakers. The first author of this chapter, for instance, now teaches a course for ministry officials in Canada on attitudes toward immigration and cultural diversity that has a strong psychological focus (see http://www.institut.metropolis.net/ cours/004_poster_e_f.pdf).

CONCLUSIONS

In conducting research on social issues, social psychologists have much to contribute in terms of theoretical and methodological perspectives. Social psychologists' theoretical analyses often focus on micro factors such as individuals' beliefs and values, which provide a complementary level of analysis to more macro indicators utilized by other social scientists. Social psychological methodology allows more definitive cause–effect conclusions to be drawn, and tends to focus on processes more than does research in related disciplines. Thus, social psychological perspectives complement work on social issues conducted in other disciplines, and enhance knowledge in the field.

In order to conduct research on social issues that is valued by researchers in other disciplines and by policymakers, however, it is necessary to build bridges with scholars from other disciplines. In this way, all the researchers involved gain a richer view of the issue under investigation and can more effectively portray the importance of their research to this issue. They are able to build on concepts and methods utilized by other social scientists, and in time their research is likely to make its way into other disciplines and into the hands of policymakers. At this point, disciplinary boundaries become irrelevant, and a truly interdisciplinary enterprise has been successfully negotiated.

REFERENCES

Bobo, L., & Hutchings, V. L. (1996). Perceptions of racial group competition: Extending Blumer's theory of group position to a multiracial social context. *American Sociological Review, 61,* 951–972.

Dovidio, J. F., Brigham, J., Johnson, B. T., & Gaertner, S. L. (1996). Stereotyping, prejudice, and discrimination: Another look. In C. N. Macrae, C. Stangor, & M. Hewstone (Eds.), *Stereotypes and stereotyping* (pp. 276–319). New York: Guilford.

Espenshade, T. J., & Hempstead, K. (1996). Contemporary American attitudes toward U.S. immigration. *International Migration Review, 30,* 535–570.

Esses, V. M., Dovidio, J. F., Jackson, L. M., & Armstrong, T. L. (2001). The immigration dilemma: The role of perceived group competition, ethnic prejudice, and national identity. *Journal of Social Issues, 57,* 389–412.

Esses, V. M., Hodson, G., & Dovidio, J. F. (2004). Public attitudes toward immigrants and immigration: Determinants and policy implications. In C. M. Beach, A. G. Green, & J. G. Reitz (Eds.), *Canadian immigration policy for the 21st century* (pp. 507–535). Montreal, Canada: McGill Queen's Press.

International Metropolis Project. (2005). *Introduction.* Retrieved September 7, 2005, from http://www.international.metropolis.net/frameset_e.html

Jackson, J. S., Brown, K. T., Brown, T. N., & Marks, B. (2001). Contemporary immigration policy orientations among dominant-group members in Western Europe. *Journal of Social Issues, 57,* 431–456.

Perea, J. F. (Ed.). (1997). *Immigrants out! The new nativism and the anti-immigrant impulse in the United States.* New York: New York University Press.

Quillian, L. (1995). Prejudice as a group threat: Population composition and anti-immigrant and racial prejudice in Europe. *American Sociological Review, 60,* 586–611.

Reitz, J. G. (2004). Canada: Immigration and nation-building in the transition to a knowledge economy. In W. A. Cornelius, T. Tsuda, P. L. Martin, & J. F. Hollifield, (Eds.), *Controlling immigration: A global perspective* (2nd ed., pp. 79–113). Stanford, CA: Stanford University Press.

Sidanius, J., & Pratto, F. (1999). *Social dominance: An intergroup theory of social hierarchy and oppression.* New York: Cambridge University Press.

Wilson, T. C. (2001). Americans' views on immigration policy: Testing the role of threatened group interests. *Sociological Perspectives, 44,* 485–501.

From Social Psychology to Economics and Back Again: The Benefits of a Two-Way Street

Eric van Dijk
Leiden University

With a theme like "building bridges between disciplines" one might get the impression that the current state is that disciplines are isolated and that the time has come to work on a new infrastructure. Quite often, however, the foundations have already been laid. Economists and psychologists, for example, tend to meet in Europe under the umbrella of economic psychology, and in the United States in behavioral economics. In addition, they publish and discuss their findings in interdisciplinary journals like the *Journal of Economic Psychology* and the *Journal of Economic Behavior and Organization*.

A wide range of topics is discussed on these occasions. These discussions are not always as fruitful as they might be, however. Contacts differ, but it is my impression that many of the conversations are held as if the contact takes place on a one-way street. Both discussion partners tend to behave like missionaries whose main goal is to convince the other party of the shortcomings of their own ideas and to persuade them to accept the new and enlightening insights they are offered.

Because this book is mainly written by social psychologists, I limit myself to what I consider to be the predominant position advocated by social psychologists. The main issues raised by (social) psychologists concern the assumptions of economics. Two assumptions stick out: self-interest and rationality. As Thaler (1994, p. 2) put it: "People are assumed to want to get as much for themselves as possible, and are assumed to be quite clever in figuring out how to accomplish this aim." With regard to the rationality assumption, social psychologists consistently (and rightfully) argue that due to cognitive limitations, people are less rational than economic theory would have it. Thus, with regard to the rationality assumption, the conclusion is that the human is *more limited* than economic theory assumes. Social psychology has been quite successful in getting this message across. Kahneman and Tversky's work has been extremely influential (e.g., Kahneman & Tversky, 1979; Tversky & Kahneman, 1974). The Nobel prize that was awarded to Daniel Kahneman in 2002 speaks to the progress that has been made.

With regard to the assumption of self-interest, social psychologists point out that the human is *less limited* than assumed by economists. Altruism and fairness concerns are often cited to refute the simplistic assumption of narrow self-interest. In my opinion, this constitutes a topic where social psychology has been less successful. Economists seem extremely reluctant to let go of their assumption of self-interest. There are (at least) two possible reactions to this. The first is to keep acting like the missionary who hopes that eventually the others will see the light. The second is to wonder why economists object so much, and to wonder whether we might in fact learn something from the economists, and to consider the possibility that sometimes what we label as altruism or fairness can be understood in terms of narrow self-interest. I argue in favor of the latter strategy. To illustrate the benefits of incorporating the economic view in social psychology, I next briefly discuss a field of research where I think this approach has paid off (at least for me): the case of ultimatum bargaining.

THE CASE OF ULTIMATUM BARGAINING

The question of whether bargainers are mainly motivated to further their own interest or whether they primarily are concerned with fairness has stimulated much research. An important tool to study these differential motives in the context of bargaining is the *Ultimatum Bargaining Game* (Güth, Schmittberger, & Schwarze, 1982). In this game, two players have to decide on how to distribute a certain amount of money. One of the players, the allocator, offers a proportion of the money to the other player, the recipient. If the recipient accepts, the money will be distributed in agreement with the allocator's offer. If the recipient rejects the offer, both players get nothing.

If self-interest dominates, allocators should offer the recipients the smallest amount possible greater than zero and recipients should accept this offer because acceptance yields them higher outcomes than the alternative of rejecting the offer and receiving nothing. With its simple game structure and clear-cut predictions, the Ultimatum Game has become part of the bridge where economists and psychologists discuss the relative importance of self-interest and fairness considerations.

So what have we learned from these encounters? The first findings suggested that the assumption of self-interest clearly did not hold. In the majority of the studies, it was found that most allocators offer to split the money equally (see for an overview, e.g., Camerer & Thaler, 1995). With these findings, the basic message of social psychology to economics was further substantiated. To social psychology, however, these findings offered no surprise, as they were completely in line with what we would expect on the basis of—for example—equity theory (Walster, Walster, & Berscheid, 1978): With equal inputs, people prefer that outcomes are also allocated equally.

PLEASE, SURPRISE ME ...

One might regard it as a good sign that the Ultimatum Game findings did not surprise the social psychologists, because it indicates that our theories adequately predict behavior. However, no surprise may also result in lack of further curiosity, and we need curiosity to further develop our ideas. So how did economists receive this message? I am glad to say that they were surprised. More importantly, they started to seek alternative explanations for the observed findings.

The most convincing alternative they came up with was that the equal splits were not the result of a true concern for fairness, but primarily the result of what has been termed "strategic fairness." That is, allocators may split the money equally because they fear that unequal offers will be rejected (e.g., Kagel, Kim, & Moser, 1996; Weg & Zwick, 1994). And this fear is grounded in the allocators' self-interest. In order to demonstrate the plausibility of the "fear of rejection" explanation, economists designed variations of the Ultimatum Game in which they introduced information asymmetry. For example, Kagel et al. designed an Ultimatum Game in which participants had to divide 100 chips, which were worth more to the allocator than to the recipient. In order to distribute the money equally then, allocators would have to compensate for the differential value of the chips, and allocate more chips to the recipient than to themselves. This was exactly what happened if the recipient was aware of the differential value. But this study also included a condition in which the recipient was unaware of the differential value. Supporting the view that allocators merely act fair because they fear that an unfair offer will be rejected, the findings indicated that in this case many allocators offered only 50 chips to the recipient. This may seem fair to the recipient who is unaware of the differential value, but it can hardly be seen as truly fair. This result indicates that the fact that economists were more surprised about the allocators' fair offers than were social psychologists resulted in new research and a message from economists to social psychology.

This is not to say that the apparent support for the fear of rejection hypothesis necessarily implies that fairness is out of the picture. For one thing, it should be noted that the fear of rejection explanation still assigns an important role to fairness because it is built on the assumption that (self-interested) allocators fear that recipients will reject unfair offers (see also Pillutla & Murnighan, 2003). Nevertheless, despite this limitation, the message stands that what had been labeled as fair behavior could also be interpreted as self-interested behavior.

For social psychology, the message was refreshing, and it did stimulate new research. For example, van Dijk and Vermunt (2000) investigated what would happen if the fear of rejection would be removed. For this purpose, they compared the Ultimatum Game to the Dictator Game. Like the Ultimatum Game, the Dictator Game also involves an allocator and a recipient. However, in contrast to the Ultimatum Game, the recipient in a Dictator Game is powerless. That is, the allocator gets to decide how the money will be distributed, and does not have to fear that the offer will be rejected. Like the economists' studies, in the van Dijk and Vermunt study chips were worth twice as much to the allocator than to the recipient, and in some of the conditions allocators learned that the recipient did not know about this differential value. In agreement with the findings discussed earlier, allocators in the Ultimatum Game tended to make strategic offers by offering only half of the chips to the allocator. Interestingly, allocators in the Dictator Game, who had nothing to fear, did compensate for the differential value. This finding was explained by suggesting that a confrontation with powerless others may evoke a sense of social responsibility. Thus, the economist's message was supplemented with a new message from social psychology: Strategic fairness may play an important role if the recipient has the power to reject, but powerlessness evokes a true concern for fairness.

CONCLUSIONS

The case of ultimatum bargaining is but one case in which we can observe the benefits of a two-way street, but it does seem an ideal case. Theory can be advanced if we not only ask what we can do for economics, but also what economics can do for us. What strikes me is that the advances made here are beneficial to both disciplines. Moreover, they seem to be spurred by disagreement. This is perfectly fine. It seems that the surprise (and incredulity) instigated by findings from another discipline led to a fruitful encounter. Of course, it would be preferable if we ourselves could stay surprised all the time, and if we had the ability to repeatedly question the validity of our theories. In general, we like to think we do, but sometimes we may become too stuck in our established ideas and theories and need others to refute and challenge our ideas. It takes more than a bridge and the missionary's perseverance to advance theory. It takes an open mind. We have already got the bridge; now it is time to see to it that traffic runs both ways.

REFERENCES

Camerer, C., & Thaler, R. H. (1995). Anomalies: Ultimatums, dictators and manners. *Journal of Economic Perspectives, 9,* 209–219.

Güth, W., Schmittberger, R., & Schwarze, B. (1982). An experimental analysis of ultimatum games. *Journal of Economic Behavior and Organization, 3,* 367–388.

Kagel, J. H., Kim, C., & Moser, D. (1996). Fairness in ultimatum games with asymmetric information and asymmetric payoffs. *Games and Economic Behavior, 13,* 100–111.

Kahneman, D., & Tversky, A. (1979). Prospect theory: An analysis of decision under risk. *Econometrica, 47,* 263–291.

Pillutla, M. M., & Murnighan, J. K. (2003). Fairness in bargaining. *Social Justice Research, 16,* 241–262.

Thaler, R. H. (1994). *The winner's curse: Paradoxes and anomalies of economic life.* Princeton: Princeton University Press.

Tversky, A., & Kahneman, D. (1974). Judgment under uncertainty: Heuristics and biases. *Science, 185,* 1124–1131.

van Dijk, E., & Vermunt, R. (2000). Strategy and fairness in social decision making: Sometimes it pays to be powerless. *Journal of Experimental Social Psychology, 36,* 1–25.

Walster, E., Walster, G. W., & Berscheid, E. (1978). *Equity: Theory and research.* Boston: Allyn & Bacon.

Weg, E., & Zwick, R. (1994). Toward the settlement of the fairness issues in ultimatum games. *Journal of Economic Behavior and Organization, 24,* 19–34.

62

Social Science in the Making: An Economist's View

Frans van Winden

CREED, Department of Economics, University of Amsterdam

HISTORICAL NOTES

Classical political economy was part of a budding social science. Pioneers like Adam Smith showed a clear interest in the psychological (as well as sociological and political) aspects of economic behavior. Paradoxically, it seems to have been the "marginal revolution" toward the end of the 19th century, when attention got focused on marginal trade-offs in individual decision making, that turned the tide. Stimulated by the emerging hypothesis of a rational and selfish economic agent with stable preferences (*homo economicus*)—which proved to be handy for mathematical modeling and was thereby reinforced— political economy developed into the economics we know today. At about the same time, psychology established itself as a separate and experimental science through the work of, among others, Wilhelm Wundt. An important methodological distinction was generated, with economics developing itself into a deductive science, taking the *homo economicus* model as its starting point, and psychology as an inductive science, working from experimental data. Some serious attempts were made, in particular by George Katona, to bring the two closer together again. However, the main impact has been restricted to consumer behavior in marketing (economic psychology). This is, of course, a very rough historical sketch. Over time, several prominent economists occasionally referred to the importance of psychological factors, like, for instance, the "animal spirits" that are driving investment in the view of John Maynard Keynes. Nevertheless, the idea of a "calculus of pleasure and pain"

(Jeremy Bentham) had definitively lost impetus, and Adam Smith's (other) classic work on moral sentiments had fallen into obscurity.

MARCHING SEPARATELY

The academic division of labor between psychology and economics, allowing these disciplines to exploit and explore their methodologies to the full, has been very productive in the past. However, it is also felt that, although economists may have been too eager to construct "logical superhighways" without much empirical support, psychologists were perhaps too reluctant to venture formalized generalizations using their wealth of experimental data. Recent developments suggest that the combination of experimentation and mathematical formalization is a powerful match for further scientific progress and is promising in terms of bringing psychology and economics closer together. Because the focus in this essay is on social psychology, I discuss these issues using some of my own experiences concerning research on social interaction in groups. My aim is to illustrate the instrumentality of experimentation for making bridges, and to indicate the importance of theoretical modeling as well as the relevance of institutions.

LESSONS FROM SOCIAL DILEMMAS AND PUBLIC GOODS

A major topic in the social sciences concerns the behavior of individuals in social dilemmas. In economics, important theoretical work has been done regarding the related issue of public goods. This work has generated many insights into the responses of *homo economicus* to changes in behavioral constraints (income, prices). However, the observation that in reality the predicted free-riding seemed less severe stimulated an interest in applying laboratory experimentation, which was emerging as a research method in economics (in the early 1960s successfully applied to markets by Nobel laureate Vernon Smith). About two decades of experimental work has clearly shown the restraining nature of the assumptions of the homo economicus model (see Ledyard, 1995; van Winden, 2002). Because public good environments are perhaps the simplest to study behavior in groups, and groups are a core issue in the social sciences, I see the following experiences as important from a bridging perspective.

First, by getting involved in a shared methodology (experimentation), it became more difficult to neglect the findings of social psychologists.

Second, the experimental designs were in the domain of the theoretical models, making it difficult for theorists to contest the results and stay within an ivory tower (which was easier with field empirical observations plagued by all sorts of noise effects). For the development of experimental economics, this support from (particularly game) theorists has been extremely important.

Third, the emphasis in economics on modeling proved very helpful—first by structuring experimental work through the application of theoretical tools and insights, which provided direction and discipline. Furthermore, it has stimulated the development of new models, incorporating robust experimental findings, which can also be tested on other environments (e.g., Fehr & Schmidt, 1999). Note that it is only through modeling that we can ever hope to generalize in a practical way to other parameter values and cases, other than the specific ones studied in experiments.

Fourth, as argued by Lewin (1967, p. 193) experimentation with groups leads to a natural integration of social sciences because it forces the experimenter to consider all relevant factors even if he or she cannot analyze them satisfactorily yet. Factors like group identification, social approval, reciprocity, and norms have found a place in the vocabulary of the experimental economist.

Finally, in my experience, bridging is particularly stimulated by (a) educational training in the substantive issues or methods of different social sciences (like experimentation or mathematical modeling, which both work as a *lingua franca*), (b) meetings on a shared methodology (like the Economic Science Association conferences in experimental economics that are not only attended by economists), and (c) some commitment to joint research projects with other social scientists (via dedicated research centers or conditioned research funding).

ILLUSTRATION

To exemplify, I will point at Bridging activity in my own research group at CREED—the Center for Research in Experimental Economics and Political Decision Making. CREED started in 1991, funded by a large "pioneer grant" from the Netherlands Organization for Scientific Research (NWO), to create an innovative research group and to develop experimental economics in the Netherlands. One of the conditions was to incorporate social psychological expertise in the project. This condition stimulated several experimental studies using the "Ring Test" (Liebrand, 1984) for measuring "social value orientation," showing the importance thereof for contributions to public goods (e.g., Offerman, Sonnemans, & Schram, 1996). Subsequently, this same test was used in a novel way to measure "social ties." By applying the test twice, before and after social interaction, one can derive the attitude toward the specific other interacted with in comparison with a generalized other (e.g., van Dijk, Sonnemans, & van Winden, 2002). These experiments were instigated by, and supported, a theoretical model that capitalized on other social psychological work by, among others, George Homans, whose analytical style is inviting for a formally trained economist (van Dijk & van Winden, 1997). A next step has been to apply this technique to larger formal groups, showing that informal groups characterized by positive as well as negative ties may form through interaction (Sonnemans, van Dijk, & van Winden, in press). Another natural outgrowth involved the application to social capital issues, which happened in the context of an interdisciplinary research program with sociologists funded by NWO (e.g., Riedl & van Winden, 2003). Subsequently, this research has been extended toward the experimental investigation of endogenous networks and related theoretical models. The conception of social ties as being determined by feelings and emotions, and the experimental support obtained, stimulated in its turn a new major project on the economic significance and modeling of emotions, which extended and deepened contacts with psychologists (e.g., Bosman, Sonnemans, & Zeelenberg, 2001; Bosman & van Winden, 2002; van Winden, 2001). It also clearly showed the hindrance of existing disciplinary borders for PhD students to get adequate cross-disciplinary training. Finally, another important incentive for bridging turned out to be the participation in European Community (EC)-funded research networks. At CREED this has stimulated, among others, recent experimental research on social interaction within and between groups in collaboration with social psychologists (e.g., Bornstein, Schram, & Sonnemans, 2001). All these developments at CREED seem to nicely illustrate the influence of the aforementioned factors.

SUCCEEDING TOGETHER

Recent developments suggest that productivity in the social sciences will benefit from crossing existing academic barriers, and that such crossing is more and more likely. One development is the growing attention in economics for cognitive limitations and peculiarities (bounded rationality; see Rabin, 1998). Another one concerns the gradually increasing appreciation in economics—as in psychology, for that matter—of the significance of emotions as determinants of decision making and their instrumentality for taking good decisions (e.g., Elster, 1998). It may be more appropriate to speak here of "bounded reasoning" than of bounded rationality. In a sense, we are going back to Bentham (Kahneman, Wakker, & Sarin, 1997). Furthermore, in both disciplines there is a growing awareness of the importance of evolutionary forces (for economics, see Robson, 2001). A related development is that researchers from both sides will increasingly have to deal with the challenging findings obtained from modern brain research, with neuroeconomics emerging as a new field (Camerer, Loewenstein, & Prelec, 2005). These developments should be seen in combination with the sharing of experimentation as a research method and an increasing uneasiness in economics about sheer formalization and in social psychology about the lack of more general theories.

However, the present institutional environment (at least in Europe), with faculties in universities functioning as bureaucratic agencies and little competition between universities, is severely frustrating cross-disciplinary activity (Lohmann, 2003).

CONCLUSIONS

Social science is in the making, but its success seems particularly conditioned on the willingness to put experimentation, including computer simulation, and formalization on an equal footing (cf. Lewin, 1967, p. 236). By now, experimental economics is an accepted research method in economics, with papers across the whole domain of economics being regularly published in the top journals, labs at major economics departments, and its own specialized journal. Regarding their analytical methodology, however, economists will have to grow satisfied with the construction of theoretical highways, for particular classes of problems, instead of malfunctioning superhighways. My perception is that a growing number of behavioral economists are heading in this direction. Although they are still a minority, their position will further gain momentum. Whether the theoretical innovations of behavioral economics will be cumulative in the longer run is unclear, but I do not see why we should be pessimistic (cf. Gintis, 2003; Kahneman, 2003). In their turn, social psychologists will have to venture more fast-track formal theory building. In this respect, they could benefit from the experience and insights of economists. From reading their journals, I have also the impression that social psychologists could benefit from paying more attention to the findings of experimental economists. Finally, both sides should be more open to the pros and cons of its experimental methodology. Use of monetary incentives should not be an automatism for economists, whereas psychologists should consider no deceit as default (Hertwig & Ortmann, 2001).

The fact that Daniel Kahneman and Vernon Smith were awarded the Nobel Prize is a hopeful sign for bridging, especially, if it also induces some institutional changes, like cross-disciplinary research centers and core curricula.

ACKNOWLEDGMENTS

Comments by Joep Sonnemans and an anonymous referee are gratefully acknowledged.

REFERENCES

Bornstein, G., Schram, A., & Sonnemans, J. (2004). Do democracies breed chickens? In R. Suleiman, D. V. Budescu, I. Fischer, & D. M. Messick (Eds.), *Contemporary psychological research on social dilemmas* (pp. 248–268). Cambridge: Cambridge University Press.

Bosman, R., & van Winden, F. (2002). Emotional hazard in a power-to-take experiment. *Economic Journal, 112,* 147–169.

Bosman, R., Sonnemans, J., & Zeelenberg, M. (2001). *Emotions, rejections, and cooling off in the ultimatum game.* Unpublished manuscript, University of Amsterdam.

Camerer, C., Loewenstein, G., & Prelec, G. (2005). Neuroeconomics. *Journal of Economic Literature, 43,* 9–64.

van Dijk, F., Sonnemans, J., & van Winden, F. (2002). Social ties in a public good experiment. *Journal of Public Economics, 85,* 275–299.

van Dijk, F., & van Winden, F. (1997). Dynamics of social ties and public good provision. *Journal of Public Economics, 64,* 323–341.

Elster, J. (1998). Emotions and economic theory. *Journal of Economic Literature, 36,* 47–74.

Fehr, E., & Schmidt, K. M. (1999). A theory of fairness, competition and cooperation. *Quarterly Journal of Economics, 114*, 817–868.

Gintis, H. (2003). *Towards a unity of the human behavioral sciences.* Unpublished manuscript, Santa Fe Institute.

Hertwig, R., & Ortmann, A. (2001). Experimental practices in economics: A challenge for psychologists? *Behavioral and Brain Sciences, 24*, 383–403.

Kahneman, D. (2003). A psychological perspective on economics. *American Economic Review (Papers and Proceedings), 93*, 162–168.

Kahneman, D., Wakker, P. P., & Sarin, R. (1997). Back to Bentham? Explorations of experienced utility. *Quarterly Journal of Economics, 112*, 375–405.

Ledyard, J. (1995). Public goods: A survey of experimental results. In J. H. Kagel & A. E. Roth (Eds.), *The handbook of experimental economics* (pp. 111–194). Princeton: Princeton University Press.

Lewin, K. (1967). *Field theory in social science* (D. Cartwright, Ed.). London: Tavistock.

Liebrand, W. B. G. (1984). The effects of social motives, communication and group sizes on behavior in a n-person multi stage mixed motive game. *European Journal of Social Psychology, 14*, 239–264.

Lohmann, S. (2003). Academia. In C. K. Rowley & F. Schneider (Eds.), *Encyclopedia of public choice* (Vol. 2, pp. 3–5). Boston: Kluwer.

Offerman, T., Sonnemans, J., & Schram, A. (1996). Value orientations, expectations and voluntary contributions in public goods. *Economic Journal, 106*, 817–845.

Rabin, M. (1998). Psychology and economics. *Journal of Economic Literature, 36*, 11–46.

Riedl, A., & van Winden, F. (2003). Information and the creation and return of social capital: An experimental study. In H. Flap & B. Völker (Eds.), *Creation of social capital* (pp. 77–103). London: Routledge.

Robson, A. J. (2001). The biological basis of economic behavior. *Journal of Economic Literature, 39*, 11–33.

Sonnemans, J., van Dijk, F., & van Winden, F. (in press). On the dynamics of social ties structures in groups. *Journal of Economic Psychology.*

van Winden, F. (2001). Emotional hazard exemplified by taxation-induced anger. *Kyklos, 54*, 491–506.

van Winden, F. (2002). Experimental investigation of collective action. In S. L. Winer & H. Shibata (Eds.), *Political economy and public finance* (pp. 178–196). Cheltenham: Edward Elgar.

63

Motivation and Happiness Bridge Social Psychology and Economics

Bruno S. Frey

Institute for Empirical Research in Economics, University of Zurich,
CREMA—Center for Research in Economics, Management and the Arts

O ver the past decade or so, social psychology and economics have established increasingly close interactions. In previous times, there were certainly some economists interested in integrating theories and concepts from social psychology into their own discipline but they had no impact on the field. The situation today is much different. *Economic psychology*, or *psychological economics*—or as it is also sometimes called, *behavioral economics*—has become one of the "hot" fields in economics and attracts scholars from the best universities. Accordingly, the state of knowledge has advanced, as indicated by several recent reviews (e.g., Frey & Stutzer, 2001; Mullainanthan & Thaler, 2000; Rabin, 1998). The award in 2002 of the Nobel Prize in *economics* to the *psychologist* Daniel Kahneman gave an "official" stamp of approval, and high publicity, to this interdisciplinary endeavor.

I want to highlight this emerging new field by focusing on two areas—*human motivation* and *subjective well-being* or *happiness*—where the mutual gains of bridging the fields of social psychology and economics can well be illustrated. There are certainly other fields where this could also be done, in particular *behavioral anomalies* or *paradoxes*. The work of social psychologists—above all the seminal article by Kahneman and Tversky (1979) published in *Econometrica*—for some time received considerable attention from economists (e.g., Frey, 1999; Machina, 1987; Schoemaker, 1982; Thaler, 1992). But orthodox economics has not yet been sustainably affected by these scholars' insights. I hope and expect that the inputs into economics from social psychology with respect to motivation and well-being will have a more lasting effect.

It seems to me that the converse flow—from economics into social psychology—has been less marked. Few contributions from economics seem to have entered the canon of social psychology. Important reasons may be that economists rarely publish in psychological outlets and that economists have the tendency to write their contributions in the very specific economic jargon. But there are indications that this will be different with respect to human motivation and subjective well-being.

HUMAN MOTIVATION

Economics has a generally accepted rational theory to explain human behavior. Individuals are assumed to maximize their own utility subject to a set of constraints, most importantly income. Preferences are taken to be constant. It follows that individuals react systematically to changes in relative prices. In particular, they reduce an activity (e.g., the consumption of a particular good or service) when its cost (or price) rises compared to other activities, keeping other influences constant (ceteris paribus). Economists accordingly predict changes in behavior by observing the measurable changes in costs. Thus, for instance, when the cost of polluting the environment rises (e.g., because a tax has been imposed on the exhaust of pollutants), individuals and firms are expected to alter their behavior so as to emit less pollution. They have a selfish incentive to change their behavior (in our case, to switch to a car or a production process with less pollution). Econometric analyses with many different real-life data have indeed demonstrated that this model of behavior applies under a wide set of conditions.

This model has successfully been extended to areas outside the economy. Economists have, for instance, made noteworthy contributions to decisions in the family, especially on marriage, the number of children, abortion, and divorce, on drug addiction, or on religious practice. This "economic" or "rational choice" approach to the social sciences (Becker, 1976; Frey, 1999, 2001; Lazear, 2000) has considerably influenced other social sciences, most notably political science ("public choice"), sociology, and jurisprudence ("law and economics"). One of the great advantages of this model of human behavior is that it is simple and robust and can therefore be applied to many conditions and areas of study. It provides an overarching, generally accepted theory to economics. In contrast, (social) psychology has identified a great number of detailed effects relating to human behavior. But it is, at least from the point of view of an economist, difficult to see which effect applies when, and what happens if the effects are contradictory. The absence of an overarching and generally accepted sociopsychological theory makes it difficult to determine which effect applies in one area but not in another one. Economists consider the use of a simple, and generally accepted, theory of human behavior a decisive advantage of their science, and it seems to me that social psychology could in this respect learn from economics.

The economic model of behavior is simple—sometimes *too* simple. Most importantly, it has been proved impossible to explain the empirical observation that individuals contribute considerably to a public good, even though withholding such contributions (i.e., free-riding) is the rational choice (at least under anonymity and in one-shot situations). For instance, the expected punishment for tax evasion in most countries is so small that even risk-averse individuals should cheat much more than is actually observed.

To solve such puzzles social psychology has proved to be of great help in the past and is likely to be so also in the future. Economists have long considered only *one* motivational force, namely, *extrinsic incentives*, often—but not necessarily—in the form of monetary rewards. Social psychologists have taught us that it is useful to also consider *intrinsic motivation*. A pertinent example is tax morale. But as long as the two motivations are independent of each other, no major problem arises for economic theory. The dynamic relationship between extrinsic and intrinsic motivation in psychology—often called "hidden costs of rewards" (Lepper & Greene, 1978) or "self-determination theory" (Deci & Ryan, 2000)—introduces a completely new element. When an external intervention strongly undermines intrinsic motivation, the relative price effect is counteracted and the outcome may be the *exact opposite* of the normal prediction by economists. This may be very relevant for economics. For instance, inducing employees to put in more effort by offering them higher compensation may backfire if the employees targeted are thereby also induced to reduce their work morale, a specific kind of intrinsic motivation (Frey & Osterloh, 2002).

The systematic relationship between extrinsic and intrinsic motivation has been introduced into economics as "crowding theory" (Frey, 1997). It takes into account that there may be "crowding out" as well as "crowding in." This import from social psychology has proved to be useful far beyond the analysis of pay for performance systems. An example is the sitting of locally unwanted projects such as a nuclear plant where offering monetary compensation tends to *reduce*, rather than to increase, the willingness of the local population to accept it. Considerable empirical evidence has been collected for many different areas (see Frey & Jegen, 2001, for a survey). Such research should be of interest to social psychologists because the applications extend to important real life situations, which have so far not been treated by them. However, such transfer of results from economics to psychology seems to be rather slow, if it takes place at all.

SUBJECTIVE WELL-BEING

Macroeconomics, the analysis of economic variables such as production, employment, or inflation, works with highly aggregated data. The skillful reduction of the multiple dimensions of these variables into a single one, by using the monetary evaluation by market prices, has allowed economists to develop empirically testable theories of economic growth and fluctuations. Aggregate income, or gross national product (GNP), has become a generally accepted measure of economic activity and aggregate social welfare used by virtually everyone dealing with economic affairs. This is no small achievement, which might serve as an example to social psychology.

Since the beginning of the 1930s, economists have used utility as a unit to be maximized but have also thought that the concept is immeasurable. Economic theory simply *assumed* that whatever individuals do is the result of maximizing their own utility. Following this approach, even suicide is a utility-maximizing act: It is *revealed* to be superior to any other alternative because otherwise this voluntary act would not have been undertaken.

Insights from social psychology have recently strongly changed this view. Evidence has accumulated that not all behavior is in the individual's own best interest. But to make progress, a measure of utility independent of behavior is needed. Psychologists have convincingly demonstrated that it is indeed possible to approximate individual utility in a useful way by surveys on subjective well-being or happiness (e.g., Kahneman, Diener, & Schwarz, 1999). This enables economics to leave the self-imposed straitjacket of solely revealed preferences and to analyze the determinants of well-being. This is of central importance for economics because it is agreed that the ultimate aim of economic activity is to promote individual happiness.

Research on happiness has become a truly transdisciplinary endeavor. What has been aimed at in many other areas of research has here been achieved in a natural way, serving as a shining example. Economists have above all learned that self-reported data present a most useful addition to the aggregate statistical data they normally use. They have, moreover, gained insights into how perceptions and expectations can be dealt with. An example is the rising aspiration level spurred by increasing income. Some of the results of happiness research support the conventional economic views, whereas others clearly contradict the standard assumption of economics (for a comprehensive survey, see Frey & Stutzer, 2002). The standard assumption that when an individual's income increases, utility rises but at a decreasing rate, conforms to standard theory. In contrast, the fact that over time per capita national income rises but reported subjective well-being stays about the same strongly contradicts conventional economics. Another instance refers to the evaluation of unemployment. Following the "new classical macroeconomics" as well as other parts of standard economics, unemployment is voluntary. People choose to leave employment because they find the burden of work and the wages unattractive compared to having leisure as an unemployed person and receiving unemployment compensation. In contrast to this view, but in line with much psychological evidence, happiness research has convincingly established that being unemployed causes significant stress and reduces well-being in a magnitude similar to divorce.

Although economics has profited greatly from social psychology, as far as I am aware this is less so for social psychology. For example, one finds very few references in the psychological literature to works on well-being written by economists. One potential explanation for the prevalent "reception asymmetry"—for human motivation as well as for subjective well-being—may be the very existence of an overarching theory in economics and the lack thereof in social psychology: Once economists encounter behavior deviating from the standard rational choice prediction, it comes in useful to offer a scientifically well-founded rationale imported from psychology, rather than ad hoc speculation. Psychologists, on the other hand, have little incentive to cite works that—although in principle confirming the applicability of their effects to economic contexts—are reducing these to "aberrations" or "paradoxes" within a general rational choice theory of human behavior.

CONCLUSIONS

Human motivation and happiness research have been taken as examples to demonstrate the fruitfulness of the interaction between social psychologists and economists. These two areas are only examples, and there may be additional areas characterized by intensive interchange. With respect to both motivation and well-being, it appears that economics has learned more from social psychology than social psychology from economics. Economics has amended the relative price effect governing the theory of human behavior by taking into account intrinsic motivation. Even more importantly, it has been taken into account that intrinsic motives may be undermined or raised by external interventions (crowding theory), potentially leading to totally different results from standard economics. Economists have also learned from social psychology that individual surveys on well-being provide important insights. This allows economists to give up the self-imposed restriction that all behavior must by definition be utility-maximizing. It opens the door to a systematic study of deviations from individual rationality. Moreover, it enables identifying the economic determinants of happiness. According to my subjective evaluation, social psychology has not (yet) profited to the same extent from economics—potentially due to the lack of an overarching theory in social psychology—but there are indications that this will change in the future. In my view, there can be little doubt that a more equal flow of insights over the bridge linking social psychology and economics would be beneficial.

ACKNOWLEDGMENTS

I am grateful to Norbert Kerr and Reto Jegen for helpful remarks.

REFERENCES

Becker, G. S. (1976). *The economic approach to human behavior.* Chicago: Chicago University Press.

Deci, E. L., & Ryan, R. M. (2000). The "what" and "why" of goal pursuits: Human needs and the self-determination of behavior. *Psychological Inquiry, 11,* 227–268.

Frey, B. S. (1997). *Not just for the money. An economic theory of personal motivation.* Brookfield, MA: Edward Elgar.

Frey, B. S. (1999). *Economics as a science of human behaviour* (2nd ed.). Boston: Kluwer.

Frey, B. S. (2001). *Inspiring economics: Human motivation in political economy.* Northampton, MA: Edward Elgar.

Frey, B, S., & Jegen, R. (2001). Motivation crowding theory: A survey of empirical evidence. *Journal of Economic Surveys, 5,* 589–611.

Frey, B. S., & Osterloh, M. (Eds.). (2002). *Successful management by motivation. Balancing intrinsic and extrinsic incentives.* New York: Springer Verlag.

Frey, B. S., & Stutzer, A. (2001). Economics and psychology: From imperialistic to inspired economics. *Revue de Philosophie économique, 4,* 5–22.

Frey, B. S., & Stutzer, A. (2002). *Happiness and economics. How the economy and institutions affect human well-being.* Princeton, NJ: Princeton University Press.

Kahneman, D., Diener, E., & Schwarz, N. (Eds.). (1999). *Well-being: The foundations of hedonic psychology.* New York: Russell Sage Foundation.

Kahneman, D., & Tversky, A. (1979). Prospect theory: An analysis of decision under risk. *Econometrica, 47,* 263–291.

Lazear, E. (2000). Economic imperialism. *Quarterly Journal of Economics, 115,* 99–146.

Lepper, M. R., & Greene, D. (Eds.). (1978). *The hidden costs of reward: New perspectives on psychology of human motivation.* Hillsdale, NJ: Lawrence Erlbaum Associates.

Machina, M. J. (1987). Choice under uncertainty: Problems solved and unsolved. *Journal of Economic Perspectives, 1,* 121–154.

Mullainathan, S., & Thaler, R. (2000). *Behavioral economics.* Massachusetts Institute of Technology, Department of Economics Working Paper 00/27.

Rabin, M. (1998). Psychology and economics. *Journal of Economic Literature, 36,* 11–46.

Schoemaker, P. J. (1982). The expected utility model: Its variants, purposes, evidence and limitations. *Journal of Economic Literature, 20,* 529–563.

Thaler, R. H. (1992). *The winner's curse. Paradoxes and anomalies of economic life.* New York: Free Press.

How Do We Promote Cooperation in Groups, Organizations, and Societies?

Tom R. Tyler
New York University

David De Cremer
Maastricht University

Social psychology shares with other social and policy sciences an interest in understanding how to motivate cooperative behavior on the part of the people within groups, organizations, and societies. In particular, the social sciences are united by an interest in organizational design. We all want to understand how to structure social situations so as to most effectively promote cooperative behavior among the people within them. As a result of this common interest, there are considerable mutual benefits to be gained from bridging among social psychology, economics, organizational psychology, law, political science, and management.

Securing cooperation is important because in their interactions with others people often find that they are in a mixed-motive situation, in which to some degree their own interests are consistent with the interests of others, leading to the motivation to cooperate, and to some extent their interests differ from those of others, leading to the motivation to compete. As a result, people are motivated both to act in ways that also benefit others and to act in ways that maximize their own self-interest at the expense of the interests of others. People must balance those two conflicting motivations when shaping their cooperative behavior.

Social psychologists have examined how people manage this motivational conflict by exploring the psychological dynamics underlying cooperative behavior in interpersonal situations that range from dyadic bargaining to long-term relationships (Rusbult & Van Lange, 2003; Thibaut & Kelley, 1959). The problem of cooperation in mixed motive dyads also lies at the root of classical problems in economics, problems such as the prisoner's dilemma game and the ultimatum game (Poundstone, 1992).

Although social psychology is generally focused on dyads and small groups, mixed-motive conflicts within groups and societies have also been studied by social psychologists within the literature on social dilemmas. This literature asks how people deal with situations in which the pursuit of short-term self-interest by all of the members of a group leads, in the long run, to damage to the self-interest of all (see Kopelman, Weber, & Messick, 2002).

REAL-WORLD COOPERATION

The issue of cooperation is not confined to games and experiments. It is also central to many of the problems faced by real-world groups, organizations, and societies (VanVugt, Snyder, Tyler, & Biel, 2000). As a result, the fields of law, political science, and management all seek to understand how to most effectively design institutions best secure cooperation from those within groups. Their efforts to address these issues are informed by the findings of social psychological and economic research on dyads and small groups.

Within law, a central concern is with how to effectively regulate behavior so as to prevent people from engaging in actions that are personally rewarding, but destructive to others and to the group—actions ranging from illegally copying music and movies, to robbing banks (Tyler, 1990; Tyler & Huo, 2002). In addition, the police and courts need the active cooperation of members of the community to control crime and urban disorder by reporting crimes and cooperating in policing neighborhoods (Tyler & Huo, 2002). Hence, an important aspect of the study of law involves seeking to understand the factors shaping cooperation with law and legal authorities.

Government also wants people to cooperate by participating in personally costly acts ranging from paying taxes to fighting in wars. Further, it is also important for people to actively participate in society by voting, working to maintain their communities by working together to deal with community problems, and otherwise helping the polity to thrive. For these reasons, understanding how to motivate cooperation is central to political scientists.

Work organizations seek to prevent personally rewarding but destructive acts, such as sabotage and stealing office supplies, by creating and encouraging deference to rules and policies. They also encourage positive forms of cooperation, like working hard at one's job and contributing extra role and creative efforts to one's work performance (Tyler & Blader, 2000, 2001). For these reasons a central area of research in organizational behavior involves understanding how to motivate cooperation in work settings.

Motivating Cooperation.   This joint interest in understanding the motivation underlying cooperation suggests an important area for interface between social psychology and the other social sciences. Social psychologists can benefit from the findings of research from the disciplines of organizational psychology, law, political science, and management, all of which explore motivational issues in organizations and societies. Conversely, these other social sciences can benefit by drawing on the experimental findings of social psychological and microeconomic studies of behavior in interpersonal interactions and small groups.

Drawing on the literature on one-shot and repeated-play experimental games, economists focus on the role of incentive and sanctioning systems in shaping cooperative behavior. Social psychologists, of course, also recognize the important role of anticipated or experienced rewards and punishments in shaping behavior, but they also do more.

The literature on cooperation suggests that the use of incentives and sanctions can effectively shape cooperative behavior. However, although effective, rewards and punishments are not a particularly efficient mechanism for shaping behavior. First, their impact on behavior is marginal. Further, these effects are costly to obtain, because organizations must commit considerable resources to the effective deployment of incentive and sanctioning systems. For these reasons, the adequacy of instrumental approaches to motivating cooperation has been questioned within law (Tyler, 1990; Tyler & Huo, 2002), political science (Green & Shapiro, 1994), and management (Pfeffer, 1994; Tyler & Blader, 2000).

A key contribution of social psychology is the suggestion that there are social motivations that can supplement instrumental motivations in securing cooperation within organizations. This focus on social motivations coincides with the increasing focus by economists on interpersonal processes within groups and organizations. Our goal is to identify several types of social psychological mechanisms that deal with issues relevant to cooperation. We focus on two: identification and morality.

Group-Based Identification.   One type of social motivation relevant to cooperation is identification with the group. There is a large literature within social psychology on social identity, and economists have also recently recognized the importance of identity (Akerlof & Kranton, 2000). When they are within a group, people often merge their own identities and the identities of the groups to which they belong (Hogg & Abrams, 1988). When they do so, the boundary between self and group blurs, and the interests of the group become one's self-interest.

From the perspective of encouraging cooperation, we would like people to merge their identities into groups or organizations when we want them to act in terms of the interests of the group and not in terms of their own self-interest. The social identity literature makes two key points: that (a) the merger of self and group is easily accomplished and (b) when people identify with a group, it changes how they think about cooperation. In fact, research shows that when collective level group identity is salient, people are more likely to exercise cooperative restraint in their use of shared resources (Brewer & Kramer, 1986).

Recent studies suggest that this heightened cooperation occurs because motives are transformed from the personal to the group level—that is, people think of the interests of the group as being their own interests (De Cremer & Tyler, 2005; De Cremer & van Dijk, 2002; Tyler & Degoey, 1995) and become intrinsically motivated to pursue the group's interests (Abrams, Ando, & Hinkle, 1998; Tyler & Blader, 2000).

The Activation of Values.   Cooperation is important in interdependent (i.e., mixed-motive) situations, and in such situations ethical, normative, and justice influences often conflict with personal self-interest (e.g., Rusbult & Van Lange, 2003). Therefore, it is important to be able to activate ethical motivations to support group policies or agreements. This involves motivating people to feel a sense of personal responsibility and obligation to support group decisions. People's rule-following behavior is then influenced by their internal motivation to uphold moral values relevant to the group (Tyler, 1990; Tyler & Blader, 2000; Tyler & Huo, 2002).

ORGANIZATIONAL DESIGN IMPLICATIONS

How do we encourage identification with groups and organizations and the activation of moral motives? People identify with and are internally motivated to act on behalf of organizations when those organizations have an ethical organizational culture (see Tyler & Blader, 2000). In particular, the experience of fair procedures is especially central to psychological engagement and behavioral cooperation. This procedural influence was also recognized by economists, in particular by Bruno Frey, who labeled it "procedural utility" (Frey & Stutzer, 2002).

The fairness of procedures is linked to: (a) opportunities for voice and participation; (b) the quality of decision-making—neutrality, accuracy, consistency of rule application; (c) the quality of interpersonal treatment—respect for rights, treatment with dignity and respect; and (d) judging that the authorities have trustworthy and benevolent motives. All of these factors distinctly shape procedural fairness judgments. Further, these social influences act in addition to the instrumental effects traditionally studied by economists (De Cremer & Van Vugt, 2002).

Understanding how a group functions can help us suggest guidelines for managing groups, organizations, and societies—that is, for regulating undesirable behavior and encouraging desirable cooperation. Integrating the psychological and economic perspectives provides suggestions about how to use social motives to supplement traditional incentive and sanction-based models, leading to less costly and more effective organizational management.

THE BRIDGE BACK TO SOCIAL PSYCHOLOGY

Although we have been emphasizing the potential value of social psychological insights to the design of organizations, it is important to note that the bridge between social psychology and the other social scientists is a two-way street. Dyad negotiation and small-group interaction are prototypical examples of mixed-motive situations and can be studied to gain insights about the origins of cooperation. However, most of the cooperation problems that give importance to the issue of organizational design occur in the context of real-world groups, organizations, and societies, and that real-world importance originally led such problems to be the focus of social psychology. The study of issues of competition and cooperation, for example, is rooted in the advances in theories of conflict that occurred during the "Cold War" era, when social scientists sought to contribute to our understanding of how to manage conflict with the Soviet Union and its allies.

The social importance of the issue of cooperation has not declined with the passing of the Cold War, but rather is continually increasing as the world's population grows; as organizations and societies become more highly interdependent within an emerging world economy; and as organizations of all types become more heavily reliant on their ability to motivate creativity and to draw upon social capital for their success. As Thibaut and Walker prophetically argued:

> One prediction that can be advanced with sure confidence is that human life on this planet faces a steady increase in the potential for interpersonal and intergroup conflict. The rising expectations of a continuously more numerous population in competition for control over rapidly diminishing resources create the conditions for an increasingly dangerous existence. It seems clear that the quality of future human life is likely to be importantly determined by the effectiveness with which disputes can be managed, moderated, or resolved. (Thibaut & Walker, 1975, p. 1)

These comments echo in our contemporary world in the war against terror that has followed the events of September 11th, 2001; in the struggle to manage problems of nuclear proliferation; and in the global economic competition among nations.

At the same time, the limits of economic incentives and sanctions as strategies for motivating cooperation, due to both limits in resources and difficulties in implementation, have led to an increasing focus on the need to understand social motivations for cooperation. The changing nature of identity, of citizenship, and of work, is all leading to greater attention to the factors shaping voluntary engagement and cooperation with groups, organizations, and societies. A world in which people will work unceasingly on behalf of and even willingly die for causes they believe in must be understood through the lens that includes a focus on social motivations.

CONCLUSIONS

As social scientists, we have the responsibility to explore the psychological dynamics underlying cooperative behavior, developing theories that can be tested at both the small group and the societal levels. Because social psychological theories are used to guide organizational design, those theories can be tested by their ability to contribute to our understanding of the psychological dynamics of cooperation within real-world settings. The interface of social psychology to law, political science, and management hence provides the opportunity to examine both the relevance and the utility of psychological models to problems of cooperation, providing valuable feedback to social psychologists about both the issues that their theories need to consider and the relative validity of different theoretical ideas.

The findings of social psychological research have important implications for understanding how to promote cooperation in real-world settings. They point to the importance of encouraging social motivations and, as a result, broaden the framework within which motivation is understood. Approaching cooperation from this framework suggests new approaches to our understanding of how to best design organizations and societies.

REFERENCES

Abrams, D., Ando, K., & Hinkle, S. (1998). Psychological attachment to the group. *Personality and Social Psychology Bulletin, 24,* 1027–1039.

Akerlof, G. A., & Kranton, R. E. (2000). Economics and identity. *Quarterly Journal of Economics, 115,* 715–753.

Brewer, M. B., & Kramer, R. M. (1986). Choice behavior in social dilemmas: Effects of social identity, group size, and decision framing. *Journal of Personality and Social Psychology, 50,* 543–549.

De Cremer, D., & Tyler, T. R. (2005). Am I respected or not?: Inclusion and reputation as issues in group membership. *Social Justice Research, 18*(2), 121–153.

De Cremer, D., & van Dijk, E. (2002). Reactions to group success and failure as a function of identification level: A test of the goal-transformation hypothesis in social dilemmas. *Journal of Experimental Social Psychology, 38,* 435–442.

De Cremer, D., & Van Vugt, M. (2002). Intergroup and intragroup aspects of leadership in social dilemmas: A relational model of cooperation. *Journal of Experimental Social Psychology, 38,* 126–136.

Frey, B. S., & Stutzer, A. (2002). *Beyond outcomes: Measuring procedural utility.* Berkeley: University of California, Berkeley, Olin Program in Law and Economics. Working paper 63.

Green, D. P., & Shapiro, I. (1994). *Pathologies of rational choice theory.* New Haven, CT: Yale University Press.

Hogg, M. A., & Abrams, D. (1988). *Social identifications.* New York: Routledge.

Kopelman, S., Weber, J. M., & Messick, D. M. (2002). Factors influencing cooperation in commons dilemmas: A review of experimental psychological research. In E. Ostrom, T. Dietz, N. Dolsak, P. C. Stern, S. Stonich, & E. U. Weber (Eds.), *The drama of the commons* (pp. 113–156). Washington, DC: National Academy Press.

Pfeffer, J. (1994). *Competitive advantage through people.* Cambridge, MA: Harvard University Press.

Poundstone, W. (1992). *Prisoner's dilemma.* New York: Doubleday.

Rusbult, C. E., & van Lange, P. A. M. (2003). Interdependence, interaction, and relationships. *Annual Review of Psychology, 54,* 351–375.

Thibaut, J., & Kelley, H. H. (1959). *The social psychology of groups.* New York: Wiley.

Thibaut, J., & Walker, L. (1975). *Procedural justice.* Hillsdale, NJ: Lawrence Erlbaum Associates.

Tyler, T. R. (1990). *Why people obey the law.* New Haven, CT: Yale University Press.

Tyler, T. R., & Blader, S. L. (2000). *Cooperation in groups.* Philadelphia: Psychology Press.

Tyler, T. R., & Blader, S. L. (2001). Identity and cooperative behavior in groups. *Group Processes and Intergroup Behavior, 4,* 207–226.

Tyler, T. R., & Degoey, P. (1995). Collective restraint in social dilemmas. *Journal of Personality and Social Psychology, 69,* 482–497.

Tyler, T. R., & Huo, Y. J. (2002). *Trust in the law.* New York: Russell Sage Foundation.

Van Vugt, M., Snyder, M., Tyler, T. R., & Biel, A. (2000). *Cooperation in Modern Society: Promoting the welfare of communities, states and organizations.* New York: Routledge.

PART 7

Epilogue

INTRODUCTION

This volume consists of 9 essays discussing general views of bridging social psychology and 53 essays that are directly relevant to at least one of four distinct types of bridge: bridges with biology, neuroscience, and cognitive science; bridges with personality, emotion, and development; bridges with relationship science, interaction, and health; and bridges with organizational science, culture, and economics. The major goal of this epilogue is to "reevaluate" the idea of bridging social psychology after the essays have been completed, and I was very happy and honored that Walter Mischel agreed to take on this task. Indeed, he is in an excellent position to do so not only because he one of the most eminent scientists in psychological science, but also because he is among the very few who have crossed several bridges within and beyond psychology. In this epilogue, Mischel discusses some of the bridges that need to be crossed, linking person and situation, and connecting social, personality, and cognitive psychology. He also considers some of the archaic boundaries to such bridge building that have been particularly unconstructive and that need to be redrawn if social psychologists want to help build a cumulative, integrative psychological science of social behavior.

65

Bridges Toward a Cumulative Psychological Science

Walter Mischel
Columbia University

This remarkable collection shows that a dizzying array of bridges now connects social psychology to many subareas of psychological science and other fields in all directions, and that their builders are excited, with good reason, about where they are going: to cognition, biology, neuroscience, personality, emotion, development, speech science, health and behavioral medicine, economics, political science, culture, and more. The bridges vary greatly in spans and width, in levels, in traffic flow, and they are going up fast, some more solid than others. Social psychology may be becoming a traffic hub, a vibrant, busy intersection of bridges.

These enthusiastic essays reflect the vigor and creativity of the bridge-builders, most of whom seem to share an implicit understanding about the terrain of social psychology in which all those bridges are rooted. Some even urge that we not leave the mainland too often or too long, warning of "folly bridges" (e.g., Batson). In the past, interdisciplinary bridge building efforts sometimes turned out to be premature or at the wrong levels of analysis. For example, Harvard University's Department of Social Relations in the 1950s tried to combine within one department such areas as social and personality psychology along with cultural anthropology and sociology. Although many saw this as a noble pioneering experiment for interdisciplinary integration, for others it was a tower of Babel whose participants were mostly unable to communicate with each other, often leaving their students confused and ill-prepared to enter academic careers within the traditional boundaries. Ultimately the different disciplines returned to separate departments, reminding us that bridges are not always constructive routes for the mainland's growth.

But I have never quite known what constitutes the mainland for social psychology, and I have not understood its borders. They were laid down long ago by historical accidents and old teaching requirements, and need to be redrawn now to carve nature at its joints, wherever they turn out to be, in light of what we currently understand and need to learn next. That is why it is so heartening to see the archaic borders of social psychology freely crossed, yielding the rich harvest of new findings and insights summarized in this volume. The prospects are exciting because many of the bridges are being constructed not just because at a broad level everything is connected to everything but because they are needed at the level of ongoing research projects that demand the joint study of different aspects of phenomena as they are being found in nature. Such bridges make it possible to share promising new methods and models, and build jointly on new discoveries that reveal natural interconnections. In the following limited pages I focus on the bridges I know best or want most, but as this volume illustrates, there are many others that demand construction and that are on the way.

THE PERSON–SITUATION SPLIT: CARVING NATURE AT THE WRONG JOINTS

My border problems began years ago when I ran right into the ones dividing social and personality psychology in the turf wars that became known as the "person–situation" debate. Fortunately, this debate has moved into footnote status in textbooks, but it still speaks to why we need the kinds of bridges illustrated in this collection. For me, the border most unnatural and destructive to the building of a cumulative, integrative science of social behavior is the one that pitted the person against the situation. Guided by the classic assumption that the enduring aspects of personality are seen when the effects of the immediate situation are removed, it made personality psychology the field devoted to the person apart from the situation, treating the situation as the error term. To see the person you had to remove the effect of situations, either by making the situation completely ambiguous as on an inkblot in projective testing, or by getting rid of it on situation-free global measures of what the person is like "on the whole," as in most standard personality trait assessments. Consequently the situation was—and in much current practice still is—deliberately removed or aggregated out to ask about the general effects of persons, regardless of situations.

In contrast, much of social psychology was defined as the study of the effects of situations, usually regardless of the kinds of persons in them, except perhaps to take account of gender. So for each field, the main variables of the other constituted the error variance that needed to be removed. As Leon Festinger said to me 40 years ago when we were talking about my interest in personality and individual differences, "Your independent variables are my noise."

Given that old view of the differential mission and turf of personality and social psychology, the person and the situation were seen as in competition:

To the degree that one was important as a determinant of behavior, the other was not, and the same was true of the status of the two fields. This zero-sum conception of the relationship between social and personality psychology fueled the person versus situation debate, further sharpening the divisions between the extremes of the two subdisciplines. Although the classic boundaries between the two subdisciplines may have made sense early in the last century when Gordon Allport founded personality psychology, and social psychology (in which Gordon also was a pioneer) became his brother Floyd's province, it made little sense to me in 1968, when *Personality and Assessment* appeared. It makes even less sense now because it flies in the face of what our science is finding, and what the cognitive revolution taught us years ago, as virtually each of the papers in this volume at the interface of personality and social psychology suggests (e.g., Andersen & Saribayi, or Carver, or Snyder, this volume; see also Morf, 2002).

It is astonishing that this border splitting person from situation should still exist at all when, as Paul Van Lange (this volume) notes, Kurt Lewin in 1936 placed both the person and the situation at the core of social psychology, focusing on how individuals try to make sense of their social environments in light of their goals and interpretations. As Lewin also said, "General laws and individual differences are merely two aspects of one problem; they are mutually dependent on each other and the study of the one cannot proceed without the study of the other" (Lewin, 1946, p. 794). That is why it felt like an unfortunate day for an integrated field two decades ago when the split between individual differences and social–cognitive–interpersonal processes was further formalized by partitioning the *Journal of Personality and Social Psychology*, with social in the front, individual differences in the back, and interpersonal relations and group processes in the neutral zone separating them—divisions that our primary journal still uses to parse the phenomena of our field at the wrong joints. I leave it to historians to figure out why all this happened, and focus here on the implications for the field now, and for the bridge building that is most needed if social psychology is to be basic for a genuinely cumulative science of mind and behavior. In such a science the person and the context have to be conceptualized and analyzed in tandem, rather than artificially split by unconstructive subdisciplinary traditions and politics.

That requires reexamining the relations between social and personality psychology in light of what has been learned about the nature of person–situation interaction. "Person × situation interaction" is an overused phrase with many meanings, and we are only beginning to see its implications for the reconceptualization of the fields of personality and social psychology and for the type of theorizing required for their integration. Everyone knows that of course the situation makes a difference, as does the personality of the individual in it. And of course situations change the expected normative levels of behavior: Yes, people will become more aggressive when they are provoked or teased than when they are approached positively or praised. None of that is news.

BRIDGING SOCIAL AND PERSONALITY PSYCHOLOGY: RECONNECTING PERSON AND CONTEXT

To go beyond these recognitions, my own work has tried to build a bridge that connects personality and social psychology at their natural joints, regardless of disciplinary boundaries. With that goal, in the search for the consistencies that characterize individuals, my colleagues and I have focused on the situation, rather than excluding it, to see its meaning for the person and the kinds of distinctive patterns of behavioral *variability* that it activates in relation to different kinds of situations (e.g., Mischel & Shoda, 1995; Shoda, Mischel, & Wright, 1994). The core assumption about the personality construct is that individuals are characterized by distinctive qualities that are relatively invariant across situations and over a span of time. My bridge-building efforts began by realizing that a century of personality research documented that individual differences in social behaviors tend to be surprisingly variable, rather than consistent, across different situations. Traditionally, such findings were read as undermining the utility of the personality construct. But we found empirically, and showed theoretically, that on the contrary, this variability reflects some of the essence of personality coherence.

Consider, for example, the findings with regard to the trait of aggression when we closely observed interactions among children in a summer camp across five different situations (e.g., their behavior when approached positively by a peer, when teased by a peer, when warned by an adult, when praised by an adult). We found, consistent with reviews of hundreds of earlier studies (Mischel, 1968), that although a child's aggressiveness in one type of situation was not a good predictor of his or her behavior in another type, it was predictive of his or her behavior within the same type of situation on future occasions. Most important, we discovered that individuals are characterized by stable *patterns* of situation–behavior relations (Mischel & Shoda, 1995). These *"if... then... "*situation–behavior signatures (she A if X but B if Z) are the observable expressions of the underlying processing system that links types of situations to types of social-cognitive, motivational, and behavioral patterns.

These behavioral signatures of personality open a window into the organization of the underlying goals, values, beliefs, and other person variables that account for them. Take again two people who show the same overall average level of a type of behavior, such as aggression, but vary in their pattern of *where* it is displayed. Say that one is very aggressive with people over whom he has power, but very friendly with those who have power over him, whereas the other displays the opposite pattern. Even if their average aggressiveness scores are identical, if their distinctive patterns remain stable when observed repeatedly, they provide clues about differences in their internal mental and emotional processes and characteristics that are lost if the effects of situations are deliberately aggregated out.

The fact that each person has distinctive behavioral signatures may trigger fears that to make use of such signatures would require a purely idiographic approach. However, it is also the case that groups of people have similar types of signatures, activated by similar types of social stimuli and situations, and generated by similar types of cognitive–affective and motivational processing dynamics. It therefore becomes possible to categorize individuals into psychological types in terms of these shared characteristics. Rather than removing the situation, the roles of both the person and the situation need to be integrated within a *triple typology* framework that classifies together three categories: types of people, types of behavior, and types of situations. Such a typology, rather than seeking situation-free dispositions, or person-free situations, captures the *if … then …* regularities that describe types of people whose distinctive types of behavior are predictable within particular types of situations.

For example, Van Mechelen and his colleagues used a computer algorithm that simultaneously categorizes people, behaviors, and situations, to allow the fewest number of *if … then …* statements to describe the data with the least amount of errors (Vansteelandt & Van Mechelen, 1998, 2004). Such typologies, whether empirical or theory-based, also promise to allow links to the recent efforts by social psychologists to construct a comprehensive atlas of types of psychological situations (Kelley et al., 2003; also see Holmes, this volume). In addition to linking this kind of atlas to other disciplines (as Holmes discusses), it seems important to identify the key psychological "active ingredients" of these situations that trigger distinctive types of individual differences (e.g., Shoda et al., 1994; Shoda & LeeTiernan, 2002).

The findings on person-situation patterns also underline why, as Carver (this volume) notes, "It is nearly impossible to think about interpersonal functioning without making assumptions about intrapersonal functioning"—a point elegantly documented in many chapters in this volume (e.g., Andersen & Saribayi; Snyder). If the person and situation, the intrapersonal and interpersonal, are two integrally connected sides of one phenomenon, we need a seamless bridge between the subdisciplines of personality and social psychology, and (as many voices in this volume say) a unifying, integrative theory for studying person–situation interaction.

At least the outlines for such a theory have been developed in recent years. By drawing on cognitive science and neural network models of a broadly connectionist type, personality can be conceptualized as a dynamic cognitive– affective processing system that mediates how the person selects, construes, and processes social information and generates social behaviors in continuous interaction with features of social situations. This type of interactionist model provides a general framework and a methodology that can begin to capture the stable patterns of dynamic person × situation interactions that characterize human social behavior, at the inter-face of personality and social psychology (e.g., Mischel, 2004; Mischel & Shoda, 1995; see also Vallacher & Nowak, this volume).

IMPLICATIONS FOR SOCIAL PSYCHOLOGY: AN EXAMPLE

The adherence to a trait model of personality that splits the person and the situation, treating each as if they were independent causal factors, has constrained advances not only in classic personality trait psychology but also in diverse core areas of social psychology. For both theory and research, the implications of the person × situation findings and the change in the traditional conceptual framework they dictate apply with equal force to areas of social psychology from attribution theory and research to attitudes to social motivation. To illustrate, I take attribution as the exemplar of the issues raised, and the new bridges that seem in urgent need of further construction, but many clear parallels exist, most notably in the domains of attitudes and social motivation.

Guided at least implicitly by the classic assumptions of personality trait theory, much attribution work has focused on simple or additive causal schemas. These consider two causal explanations: the person *or* the situation, such that evidence for one is automatically evidence against the other (Kelley, 1972). The basic strategy in most of this work is to find the personality effects by removing the situation effects, essentially factoring out the influence of situations (as discussed in Kammrath, Mendoza-Denton, & Mischel, 2005). At a theoretical level, Kelley from the start recognized complex schemas in which persons and situations have mutually dependent effects, but until recently they have been largely ignored empirically, probably because it is harder to study and capture them. With hindsight, Kelley's inclusion of complex causal theories in his discussion of lay causal reasoning was an insight years ahead of its time, rewarded mostly by neglect.

Thirty years later the field is just starting to glimpse the central role of person–situation interactions in folk theories of mind and recognizing that complex traits and motivational schemas are of key importance in social perception (see Kammrath et al., 2005; Malle, 1999). For example, for traits as diverse as friendliness, aggressiveness, and "sliminess," perceivers expect and readily interpret complex, interactive effects between traits and situations (Chen, 2003; Plaks, Shafer, & Shoda, 2003; Shoda & Mischel, 1993; Vonk, 1998). A person who is sociable at parties but quiet at bus stops is rated as more prototypically "friendly" than one with the reverse pattern (Cantor & Mischel, 1979). Perceivers suspend judgment of a target's generous act toward a person of high status until they can also see her behavior toward a person of low status (Hilton, Fein, & Miller, 1993)—and if the generous act is not repeated in this context, their impression shifts from "generous" to "slimy" (Vonk, 1998). In short, perceivers use information about a target's stable *if… then…* profile to draw conclusions about her motives and traits (Kammrath et al., 2005). It is the pattern as a whole and the person × situation interaction it reveals that capture the motivational dynamics of the behavior. But because such traits are revealed *through* their interactions with situations, to study them requires paradigms in which perceivers are exposed to multiple actions that are observed over multiple occasions, not single instances of behavior in one situation.

BRIDGING TO INTERPERSONAL RELATIONS: WHEN THE SITUATION CONSISTS OF OTHER PEOPLE

In their discussion of "interacting brains," Singer and Firth (this volume) urge that a bidirectional approach is needed now to see how "two or more minds shape each other mutually through reciprocal interactions." In that vein, in the person × situation framework already discussed, the behaviors generated by one person in a close relationship are seen as becoming the other person's situational input, and vice versa. To the extent that the personality of each partner is characterized by a stable *if… then…* behavioral signature, the interactions between the two can be modeled to predict the "personality" of the interpersonal system they jointly form. The relationship itself becomes characterized by its own distinctive relationship signature and dynamics. In a sense, a long-term interpersonal relationship may develop its own "personality" that becomes more than just an average of the personalities within it.

It is now possible to model these emergent qualities of relationships (Shoda, LeeTiernan, & Mischel, 2002). The conceptualization of the individual as a cognitive–affective processing system (using computer simulations and a parallel constraint satisfaction network) illustrates how each interpersonal system formed by a combination of two individuals generates predictable and distinctive behaviors and patterns of interactions. The model and the computer simulation predict and show that the cognitive and affective states that an individual experiences in a given relationship are an emergent property of that interpersonal system, not a simple average or combination of the personalities of the individuals (Shoda et al., 2002).

This type of model and method may be a step toward building a bridge to connect the basic interpersonal situations identified by Harold Kelley and colleagues (2003) in their comprehensive *Atlas of Interpersonal Situations* to the psychological "chemistry"—the intrapersonal and interpersonal cognitive-affective processing dynamics—of their participants, again allowing us to see with increasing depth the natural links between person and situation. As Reis (this volume) notes, because the relationship context (which mostly means other people) influences virtually all social behavior, we need to bridge the analysis of people's internal processes with a close examination of how they interact with each other and the external world. Both the methods and the concepts to enable such integration are fortunately now available. But to make that integration happen, we have to travel freely across the bridges in both directions.

BRIDGES TO COGNITIVE AND NEUROSCIENCE

Just as traditionally a situational focus was seen as incompatible with a focus on individual differences and personality, social and biological explanations have long been cast as incompatible (Cacioppo & Berntson, this volume). But as Cacioppo and Berntson also show, a conception that integrates and synthesizes these different levels of analysis allows a far deeper understanding of the interactions and mechanisms that generate complex social behavior and mental processes. The principle of *reciprocal determinism*, basic for understanding person × situation interaction, holds equally for the mutual influences between biological factors at the microscopic level and social forces at the macroscopic level. Excellent examples of such interactions are seen in this volume in the papers bridging biological, cognitive, and neurosciences. As these chapters imply, interactionism is a basic rule in sciences dealing with living organisms, and it is curious that it has long been controversial in many areas of psychology. Ehrlich (2000), for example, focusing on the interplay of genetic endowment and environmental experience, commented that the psychologist's typical strategy of partitioning the determinants of behavioral characteristics into separate genetic versus environmental causes is no more sensible than asking which areas of a rectangle are mostly due to length and which mostly due to width.

OVERCOMING BARRIERS TO BRIDGE BUILDING: BECOMING A CUMULATIVE PSYCHOLOGICAL SCIENCE

This volume is replete with compelling reasons for integration and going beyond old interdisciplinary boundaries to build meaningful bridges based on new discoveries and promising leads that demand redrawing archaic boundaries. But there also is awareness of the powerful restrictions imposed by the "conditions of employment" and career building within our educational institutions that undermine such efforts (Berscheid, this volume). Berscheid's forceful analysis shows both the need for integrative theory, and the circumstances of training and work that oppose it. Calls to redraw the maps and build new bridges will not be effective unless students and young faculty find that they can try to do so without committing professional suicide. Senior people in the field make inspiring speeches for integrative efforts at conferences, but in department meetings they revert to making tenure and promotion decisions based on criteria that make such efforts a route to early career failure for junior faculty who take their speeches seriously. And pleas for broader, integrative theories that build a cumulative science are unlikely to be heeded as long as the "toothbrush problem" holds. As one wit, whose name I am sorry to have forgotten, wrote many years ago: We psychologists treat our theories like toothbrushes; no self-respecting person wants to use anyone else's. It's time to face the toothbrush problem, and the other constraints of our professional guilds and traditional boundaries, and to redraw our disciplinary maps to better carve nature at its joints. This volume is a giant step in that direction.

REFERENCES

Cantor, N., & Mischel, W. (1979). Prototypes in person perception. In L. Berkowitz (Ed.), *Advances in experimental social psychology* (Vol. 12, pp. 3–52). New York: Academic Press.

Chen, S. (2003). Psychological-state theories about significant others: Implications for the content and structure of significant-other representations. *Personality and Social Psychology Bulletin, 29,* 1285–1302.

Erhlich, P. R. (2000). *Human natures: Genes, cultures, and the human prospect.* Washington, DC: Island Press.

Hilton, J. L., Fein S., & Miller, D. T. (1993). Suspicion and dispositional inference. *Personality and Social Psychology Bulletin, 19,* 501–512.

Kammrath, L., Mendoza-Denton, R., & Mischel, W. (2005). Incorporating *if... then ...* personality signatures in person perception: Beyond the person–situation dichotomy. *Journal of Personality and Social Psychology, 88,* 605–618.

Kelley, H. H. (1972). Causal schemata and the attribution process. In E. E. Jones, D. E. Kanouse, H. H. Kelley, R. E. Nisbett, S. Valins, & B. Weiner (Eds.), *Attribution: Perceiving the causes of behavior* (pp. 151–174). Morristown, NJ: General Learning Press.

Kelley, H. H., Holmes, J. G., Kerr, N. L., Reis, H. T., Rusbult, C. E., & van Lange, P. A. M. (2003). *An atlas of interpersonal situations.* New York: Cambridge University Press.

Lewin, K. (1936). *Principles of topological psychology.* New York: McGraw-Hill.

Lewin, K. (1946). Behavior and development as a function of the total situation. In L. Carmichael (Ed.), *Manual of child psychology* (pp. 791–844). New York: Wiley.

Malle, B. F. (1999). How people explain behavior: A new theoretical framework. *Personality and Social Psychology Review, 3,* 23–48.

Mischel, W. (1968). *Personality and assessment.* New York: Wiley.

Mischel, W. (2004). Toward an integrative science of the person (prefatory chapter). *Annual Review of Psychology, 55,* 1–22.

Mischel, W., & Shoda, Y. (1995). A cognitive-affective system theory of personality: Reconceptualizing situations, dispositions, dynamics, and invariance in personality structure. *Psychological Review, 102,* 246–268.

Morf, C. M. (2002). Personality at the hub: Extending the conception of personality psychology. *Journal of Research in Personality, 36,* 649–660.

Plaks, J. E., Shafer, J. L., & Shoda, Y. (2003). Perceiving individuals and groups as coherent: How do perceivers make sense of variable behavior? *Social Cognition, 21,* 26–60.

Shoda, Y., & LeeTiernan, S. J. (2002). What remains invariant? Finding order within a person's thoughts, feelings, and behaviors across situations. In D. Cervone & W. Mischel (Eds.), *Advances in personality science* (pp. 241–270). New York: Guilford.

Shoda, Y., LeeTiernan, S. J., & Mischel, W. (2002). Personality as a dynamical system: emergence of stability and consistency in intra- and inter-personal interactions. *Personality and Social Psychology Review, 6,* 316–325.

Shoda, Y., & Mischel, W. (1993). Cognitive social approach to dispositional inferences: What if the perceiver is a cognitive-social theorist? *Personality and Social Psychology Bulletin, 19,* 574–585.

Shoda, Y., Mischel, W., & Wright, J. C. (1994). Intra-individual stability in the organization and patterning of behavior: Incorporating psychological situations into the idiographic analysis of personality. *Journal of Personality and Social Psychology, 67,* 674–687.

Vansteelandt, K., & Van Mechelen, I. (1998). Individual differences in situation–behavior profiles: A triple typology model. *Journal of Personality and Social Psychology, 75,* 751–765.

Vansteelandt, K., & Van Mechelen, I. (2004). The personality triad in balance: Multidimensional individual differences in situation-behavior profiles. *Journal of Research in Personality, 38,* 367–393.

Vonk, R. (1998). The slime effect: Suspicion and dislike of likeable behavior toward superiors. *Journal of Personality and Social Psychology, 74,* 849–864.

Author Biographies

Susan M. Andersen is a professor of psychology in the Department of Psychology at New York University (NYU). She came to NYU in 1987 from the University of California, Santa Barbara, where she was on the faculty for 6 years and tenured in 1987. Her PhD is from Stanford University, and her BA from the University of California, Santa Cruz. She is former associate editor of *Psychological Review, Journal of Personality and Social Psychology, Social Cognition*, and *Journal of Social and Clinical Psychology*, is a fellow of the American Psychological Society, the American Psychological Association, and the Society for Personality and Social Psychology (SPSP), and served on SPSP's Executive Committee and on federal grants panels at the National Institute of Mental Health and National Science Foundation. Her research originated the experimental demonstration of transference in social cognition and the model of the relational self, and has also examined motivation, emotion, identity, stereotypes, and depression.

Arthur Aron, PhD, is a professor of psychology at the State University of New York at Stony Brook. He has published extensively on his research on the social psychology of close relationships, has received several National Science Foundation and private foundation grants in support of this research, has just completed a 6-year term as associate editor of the *Journal of Personality and Social Psychology* (the foremost journal in the field), is author (along with E. Aron) of *Statistics for Psychology*, and serves on several editorial boards. His current research focuses on the social cognitive foundation of and the neural systems engaged by interpersonal closeness and love, as well as the practical and theoretical implications of this work for the quality of long-term relationships and for reducing prejudice through intergroup friendships.

Daniel Bar-Tal (PhD in social psychology from University of Pittsburgh in 1974) is professor of psychology at the School of Education. He was director of the Walter Lebach Institute for Jewish-Arab Coexistence through Education, Tel Aviv University and coeditor of the *Palestine-Israel Journal*. He served as the president of the International Society of Political Psychology (1999–2000). His research interest is in political and social psychology, focusing on psychological foundations of intractable conflicts and peacemaking. He authored and coedited books and has published over 100 articles and chapters in major social and political psychological journals and books.

Dan Batson is a professor of psychology at the University of Kansas, where he has been on the faculty since receiving his PhD in psychology from Princeton University in 1972. His research interests include empathy, altruism, moral emotion and motivation, and the behavioral consequences of religion. He is the author of *The Altruism Question* (1991) and coauthor of *Religion and the Individual* (1993).

Gary G. Berntson is a professor of psychology, psychiatry, and pediatrics, and a member of the Neuroscience Program faculty at Ohio State University. His research interests are interdisciplinary and span many fields, including psychology, behavioral neuroscience, psychophysiology, and psychoneuroimmunology. A common theme in much of his research relates to levels of functional organization in neurobehavioral systems. He has published more than 150 scientific articles, and among his recent publications is the *Handbook of Psychophysiology* and *Foundations in Social Neuroscience*.

Ellen Berscheid received her PhD. in 1965 from the University of Minnesota, where she currently is Regents' Professor of Psychology. Her primary interest is interpersonal relationships. She is coauthor of *Close Relationships* (1983/2002) and *The Psychology of Interpersonal Relationships* (2005). Recipient of the American Psychological Association's Distinguished Scientific Contribution Award, the Donald T. Campbell Award for Distinguished Research in Social Psychology from the Society of Personality and Social Psychology, the Distinguished Scientist Award from the Society of Experimental Social Psychology, and the Distinguished Career Award from the International Society for the Study of Personal Relationships, Berscheid is a fellow of the American Academy of Arts and Sciences.

Jim Blascovich is a professor of psychology and co-director of the Research Center for Virtual Environments and Behavior at the University of California,

Santa Barbara. His work involves two areas of research: challenge and threat motivation, and social interaction within immersive virtual environments. His work has been funded by the National Science Foundation for 15 years. He has been president of both the Society for Personality and Social Psychology and the Society of Experimental Social Psychology.

Peter Borkenau received his PhD in 1982 from the University of Heidelberg (Germany) and is now a professor of psychology at Martin-Luther University in Halle, Germany. His main research interests are accuracy in perceptions of personality, behavior genetics, and personality and well-being. He wrote a textbook on behavior genetics and published several articles in the *Journal of Personality and Social Psychology*. He has been editor of the *European Journal of Personality* and is a member of the board of directors of the International Society for the Study of Individual Differences.

Ross Buck received a PhD in social psychology at the University of Pittsburgh in 1970. He is interested in many aspects of emotion development, experience, expression, and communication, including the relationships of motivation, emotion, and cognition and the neurochemical bases of motivation/ emotion. He has related interests in evolution, including the hypothesis that the communicative functioning of genes underlies biological prosociality and altruism, and in social bioregulation: how through emotional communication social relationships can function as stress buffers (or amplifiers). Buck also has more applied interests related to the interaction of reason and emotion in persuasion, media and emotion, leadership and charisma, advertising effects, emotional aspects of warning labeling, and understanding the emotional aspects of the effectiveness (or ineffectiveness) of safe sex messages.

Daphne Bugental is professor of social and developmental psychology at the University of California, Santa Barbara. She completed her PhD in social and personality psychology at the University of California, Los Angeles. Her research interests span the areas of social cognition, social development, evolutionary psychology, and developmental neuroscience. One ongoing focus of her research involves the distinctive ways in which the various domains of social life are organized at a biological, social, and cognitive level. A second focus concerns the causes, consequences, and prevention of conflict and violence within human relationships—as understood from an integrated bio-social-cognitive perspective. She is recipient of the 2003 Kurt Lewin Memorial Award, and associate editor of *Journal of Personality and Social Psychology*.

Abraham (Bram) P. Buunk, PhD, is (since 1990) a professor of social psychology at the University of Groningen. In 2005 he was appointed Academy Professor by the Royal Netherlands Academy of Arts and Sciences (KNAW). He has devoted much of his career to basic research on social exchange and social comparison in applied areas such as jealousy, absenteeism, AIDS prevention,

loneliness, depression, intimate relationships, occupational burnout, and coping with cancer. Professor Buunk has over 300 scientific publications in basic as
well as in applied journals and books. He is the vice-chair of the Program Committee on Successful Aging, and a member of the Program Committee on Evolution and Behavior, both of the Netherlands Organization for Scientific
Research (NWO). He is also a member of the Scientific Board for Social Oncol-
ogy of the Dutch Cancer Foundation (NKB-KWF), and has been a member of
the Scientific Board of the Dutch AIDS Foundation.

John T. Cacioppo is the Tiffany and Margaret Blake Distinguished Service Professor at the University of Chicago, where he is the director of the Social Psychology Program and co-director of the Institute for Mind and Biology. His
research concerns affect, emotion, and social behavior, with an emphasis on integrating biological, behavioral, and social levels of analysis. Among his recent
book publications are the *Handbook of Psychophysiology* and *Foundations in Social
Neuroscience*.

Carles S. Carver received his PhD in personality psychology from the University of Texas at Austin in 1974 and has been at the University of Miami
since 1975. He and Michael F. Scheier published *Attention and Self-Regulation* (in 1981) and *On the Self-Regulation of Behavior* (in 1998), along with five
editions of an undergraduate personality textbook called Perspectives on
Personality. He is interested in a wide range of topics in personality, social,
and health psychology, including the nature of stress and coping, the role of
optimism versus pessimism in people's adaptation to health threats, and the
nature and functions of emotional experiences. He is editor of the *Personality Processes and Individual Differences* section of the *Journal of Personality and
Social Psychology*.

Dr. Jean Decety is a Professor at the University of Washington (Seattle, WA),
where he heads the Social Cognitive Neuroscience Laboratory. Dr. Decety is an
expert in social cognitive neuroscience and functional brain imaging. His current research focuses on the cognitive and neural mechanisms that underpin
intersubjectivity, empathy, imitation, and theory of mind in healthy people, as
well as in schizophrenic and autistic individuals.

David De Cremer is an associate professor of social psychology at Maastricht
University. He was the recipient of the British Psychology Society award for best
PhD thesis in social psychology (2000), and is currently a research fellow of the
Netherlands Organization for Scientific Research (NWO). His research
mainly focuses on the dynamic interplay between self, justice, and social decision making. He has edited special issues on "Fairness and Ethics in Social Decision Making" (in *Social Justice Research*) and "Leadership, Self, and Identity"
(in *Leadership Quarterly*).

Carsten K. W. De Dreu was trained in experimental social psychology at the University of Groningen (the Netherlands) and is currently a professor of organizational psychology at the University of Amsterdam. Using laboratory experiments and field research, he studies group performance and innovation as a function of group processes, including minority influence, conflict and negotiation. His work has been published in the major outlets in both social and organizational psychology. He served as resident of the International Association for Conflict Management, and as associate editor of the *Journal of Organizational Behavior.*

Ed Diener is Alumni Distinguished Professor of Psychology at the University of Illinois at Urbana-Champaign, where he has served on the faculty since 1974. Professor Diener is past president of the Society for Personality and Social Psychology, as well as of the International Society for Quality of Life Studies. He was editor of the *Journal of Personality and Social Psychology: Personality Processes and Individual Differences* from 1998 through 2003, and is also the editor of *Journal of Happiness Studies*. Dr. Diener has published over 120 articles on topics related to subjective well-being, and is listed as one of the highly cited active psychologists by the Institute for Scientific Information.

John F. Dovidio (MA, PhD in social psychology from the University of Delaware) was Charles A. Dana Professor of Psychology at Colgate University, where he served as provost and dean of the faculty, and is now professor at the University of Connecticut. Dr. Dovidio is currently editor of the *Journal of Personality and Social Psychology—Interpersonal Relations and Group Processes*. He has been editor of *Personality and Social Psychology Bulletin* and associate editor of *Group Processes and Intergroup Relations*. Dr. Dovidio's research interests are in stereotyping, prejudice, and discrimination; social power and nonverbal communication; and altruism and helping.

John Dovidio is a professor of psychology at the University of Connecticut. Dovidio's research interests are in prejudice and prejudice reduction.

Nancy Eisenberg is Regents' Professor of Psychology at Arizona State University. She has published numerous books, chapters, and articles on social, emotional, and moral development. She was president of the Western Psychological Association, editor of *Psychological Bulletin*, and editor of *Review of Personality and Social Psychology: Vol. 15, Social Development*, and *Handbook of Child Psychology: Vol. 3, Social, Emotional, and Personality Development* (5th ed.).

Victoria Esses is a professor of psychology at the University of Western Ontario. Her research interests include intergroup relations, prejudice, and discrimination, with a particular interest in attitudes toward immigrants and immigration.

José-Miguel Fernández-Dols is a professor of social psychology at the Universidad Autonoma de Madrid (Spain). His main areas of research are emotion, particularly emotional expression, and moral behavior, particularly the interaction between justice and social norms. He has coedited *The Psychology of Facial Expression* (1997) and *Everyday Conceptions of Emotion* (1995).

Born in 1951 in Wetzlar, Germany, **Klaus Fiedler** started to study psychology in 1970 at Giessen, were he got his academic degrees. After several short term positions in computer-assisted instruction, language, methodology, and various areas of social psychology, he became a professor in social cognition in 1987 at the University of Giessen and then, in 1990, a professor of microsociology and social psychology in Mannheim. Since 1992, he has worked as chair in social psychology at the University of Heidelberg. Klaus Fiedler served as associate editor for the *European Journal of Social Psychology* and *Psychological Review,* and currently for the *Journal of Experimental Social Psychology.* In 2000 he won the most prestigious academic award in Germany, the Gottfried–Willhelm–Leibniz Prize.

Agneta H. Fischer is a professor at the Social Psychology Department of the University of Amsterdam. She received her PhD in psychology from Leiden University in 1991. Since then she has occupied several positions at the University of Amsterdam. Her research interests include emotions, especially the social and cultural context of emotion. She has written many articles and book chapters on this topic and edited several volumes, including *Emotion and Gender: Social Psychological Perspectives* (2000, Cambridge University Press), and *Feelings and Emotions: The Amsterdam Symposium* (with Tony Manstead and Nico Frijda, 2004, Cambridge University Press). She is coauthor of Emotion in *Social Context: Cultural, Group and Interpersonal Processes* (with Brian Parkinson and Tony Manstead, 2005, Psychology Press).

Alan Page Fiske is a psychological anthropologist and social theorist. He has studied in three interdisciplinary programs (at Harvard, BA in social relations; at University of Chicago, MA in social science division and PhD in human development in 1968). He lived for 8 years in East, Central, and West Africa, working in public health and international development, and doing fieldwork in cultural anthropology. He is the author of *Structures of Social Life* (Free Press) and a contributor to *Relational Models Theory: Advances and Prospects* (Nick Haslam, Ed.; Lawrence Erlbaum Associates). Relationally speaking, he is a husband, and father of five children. Otherwise, he plays with the family dogs, goes camping, and restores an old motorcycle.

Susan T. Fiske is a professor of psychology, Princeton University (PhD, Harvard University; honorary doctorate, Université Catholique de Louvain-la-Neuve, Belgium). She wrote *Social Cognition* (with Taylor) on how people make sense of each other. Currently, she investigates emotional prejudices (pity, contempt, envy, and pride) at cultural, interpersonal, and neural levels. She won the American Psychological Association's Early Career Award for Distinguished Contributions to Psychology in the Public Interest for antidiscrimination testimony, the Society for the Psychological Study of Social Issues' Allport Intergroup Relations Award for ambivalent sexism theory (with Glick), and the International Social Cognition Network's Ostrom Award (with Taylor). She edits the *Annual Review of Psychology* (with Schacter and Kazdin) and the *Handbook of Social Psychology* (with Gilbert and Lindzey). She just finished *Social Beings: A Core Motives Approach to Social Psychology*. The contribution here reflects her themes while President of the American Psychological Society.

Geoffrey T. Fong is Associate Professor, Department of Psychology, University of Waterloo. He received his Ph.D. in 1984 from the University of Michigan. His research focuses on several aspects of health behavior including interventions for reducing risky sexual behavior, and several aspects of tobacco use, including depictions of smoking in the media and the psychosocial and behavioral effects of tobacco control policies, particularly in the international context.

Joseph Paul Forgas received his doctorate at Oxford in 1977, and was awarded a doctor of science degree from Oxford in 1990. He is currently Scientia Professor of Psychology at the University of New South Wales, Sydney, Australia. His research focuses on the role of cognitive and affective processes in interpersonal behavior. He has published some 16 books and over 140 articles and chapters. His work has received international recognition: He was elected fellow of the Academy of Social Sciences (Australia), the American Psychological Society (USA), the Society of Personality and Social Psychology (USA), and the Hungarian Academy of Sciences. He was awarded the Alexander von Humboldt Research Prize (Germany), a Rockefeller Fellowship (USA), and the Special Investigator Award of the Australian Research Council. He serves on the editorial boards of several leading journals, is associate editor of *Cognition and Emotion*, and coedits the Frontiers of Social Psychology Series for Psychology Press, New York.

Bruno S. Frey is a professor of economics at the University of Zurich and director of CREMA—Center for Research in Economics, Management and the Arts. In 1998, he received an honorary doctorate from the University of St. Gallen and from the University of Gothenburg. He is the author of about 400 scholarly articles and 12 books, among them *Happiness and Economics* (with Alois Stutzer), *Successful Management by Motivation* (with Margit Osterloh), *Inspiring Economics, Arts and Economics, Economics as a Science of Human Behaviour*, and *Not Just for the Money*.

Chris D. Frith is a professor in neuropsychology and deputy director of the Leopold Müller Functional Imaging Laboratory at University College London.

He has written extensively on the cognitive neuropsychology of schizophrenia. He pioneered the use of brain imaging to study the neural bases of attention, consciousness, and executive function. More recently he has been developing methods for studying the neural basis of social interactions. He is coeditor of the two editions of *Human Brain Function* and of *The Neuroscience of Social Interaction*. He was elected a fellow of the Royal Society in 2000.

Samuel L. Gaertner is a professor of psychology at the University of Delaware. He received his PhD from the City University of New York, Graduate Center, in 1970. He shared the Gordon Allport Intergroup Relations Prize awarded by the Society for the Psychological Study of Social Issues in 1985 with John Dovidio for their work on aversive racism and also in 1998 for their work on the Common Ingroup Identity Model. Dr. Gaertner serves on the editorial boards of the *Journal of Personality and Social Psychology, Personality and Social Psychology Bulletin,* and *Group Processes and Intergroup Relations.*

Samuel D. Gosling is an assistant professor of psychology at the University of Texas at Austin (PhD, UC Berkeley). His research takes a comparative perspective, focusing on how animal studies can inform theories of personality and social psychology. He has studied individual differences in social behaviors in several nonhuman species including hyenas, dogs, and chimpanzees. He is also interested in how personality is expressed and perceived in everyday life, focusing on how individuals leave deliberate and inadvertent clues about themselves in the environments in which they dwell.

Jeff Greenberg received a BA from the University of Pennsylvania in 1976, an MA in social psychology from Southern Methodist University in 1978, and a PhD in psychology from the University of Kansas in 1982. He is coauthor of the biased hypothesis testing model of human inference, the self-regulatory perseveration theory of depression, and terror management theory. His research has focused primarily on how basic psychological motives influence cognitive processes, social judgment and behavior, and psychological health, with a particular emphasis on understanding self-esteem and prejudice. He is currently professor of psychology and director of the Social Psychology Program at the University of Arizona.

Aiden P. Gregg is a research fellow at the Centre for Research on Self and Identity in the Department of Psychology, University of Southampton, England. Having obtained a PhD from Yale in 2000, his research interests lie mainly in the area of implicit self-evaluation. He is coauthor (with Robert Abelson and Kurt Frey) of *Experiments With People: Revelations From Social Psychology.*

David Hammond is a PhD candidate in the Department of Psychology, University of Waterloo. His research focuses upon tobacco control policy in the areas of health warnings, mass media campaigns, youth-based prevention, and smoking cessation.

Judith Harackiewicz is a professor of psychology at the University of Wisconsin. Her research focuses on achievement goals, competition, interest, and intrinsic motivation. She received her PhD from Harvard University in 1980. She is the editor of *Personality and Social Psychology Bulletin,* served on the executive committee of the Society for Personality and Social Psychology, and received a Spencer Fellowship from the National Academy of Education and the Chancellor's Award for Distinguished Teaching from the University of Wisconsin.

Dr. Sara D. Hodges is an Associate Professor of social psychology in the Psychology Department at the University of Oregon, where she is also a member of the Institute of Cognitive and Decision Sciences. She studies empathy, perspective taking, and comparison processes, particularly self/other comparison.

Gordon Hodson is an assistant professor of psychology at Brock University. His research interests involve stereotyping, prejudice, and discrimination, with a focus on individual differences, social identity, and perceived threat.

John G. Holmes is a professor of social psychology at the University of Waterloo in Canada. John is a three-time winner of the New Contribution Award from the International Society for the Study of Personal Relationships, the last two with Sandra L. Murray. He was invited to write one of six lead review articles for the Millenium Issues of the *European Journal of Social Psychology*. He is past president of the Society for Experimental Social Psychology and past associate editor of the *Journal of Personality and Social Psychology*. His enduring interest is in appraisal processes in close relationships, including trust, motivated cognition, social perception, and the construal of interpersonal conflicts.

Bernhard Hommel studied psychology, literature, and linguistics at the University of Bielefeld, Germany, where he also worked as a research assistant from 1987 to 1990 and completed his dissertation on interactions between perception and action. He then moved to the Max Planck Institute for Psychological Research in Munich, Cognition and Action Unit, to work as a senior researcher and as head of the Workgroup on Executive Functions. Since 1999 he has been a full professor (Chair of General Psychology) at the University of Leiden, the Netherlands. He has published empirical and theoretical work on human attention, planning and control of action, and the relationship between perception and action.

Chet Insko received his PhD in psychology from the University of California at Berkeley in 1963. He is a professor of psychology at the University of North

Carolina at Chapel Hill. He has served as associate editor of the *Journal of Experimental Social Psychology* and as editor of the *Journal of Personality and Social Psychology*. For many years most of his research was on attitude change, influence, and interpersonal attraction. More recently he has focused on interindividual–intergroup discontinuity—the tendency in some social contexts for relations between groups to be more conflict prone than are relations between individuals.

Douglas T. Kenrick obtained his PhD in social psychology at Arizona State University, and was assistant professor at Montana State University, before returning to Arizona State, where he is now a professor. He has been a visiting researcher at the University of Groningen and the University of British Columbia. His research interests have included homicidal fantasies in college students, cross-cultural commonalities in men's and women's attraction to younger and older mates, the adverse effects of beauty on attention and interpersonal judgment, and measuring person–situation interactions. To justify these and other diverse and apparently disconnected interests, he has worked on theoretical papers attempting to integrate insights from evolutionary psychology, cognitive science, and dynamical systems. How all this connects to the Illumination and the assassination of John F. Kennedy has not yet been fully worked out.

Norbert L. Kerr is a professor of psychology at Michigan State University. He received his PhD in 1974 from the University of Illinois, Champaign–Urbana. His primary research interests are in group performance and decision making, psychology and the law, and social dilemmas. He has served as associate editor for JPSP–IRGP and for PSPR. He is coauthor/editor of *The Psychology of the Courtroom* (1982), *Group Process, Group Decision, Group Action* (1992; 2nd ed., 2003), and *An Atlas of Interpersonal Situations* (2003). He is past president of the Midwestern Psychological Association and past chair of the executive committee of SESP.

Ad van Knippenberg is professor of social psychology at the University of Nijmegen. He received his PhD at the University of Leiden in 1978. His research interests concern social cognition and behavior regulation.

Both **Gerjo Kok** and **Nanne de Vries** studied social psychology and obtained their PhD degrees at the University of Groningen, the Netherlands. In 1984, Gerjo Kok was appointed Professor of Health Education and Health Promotion at the University of Maastricht; in 1998 he was appointed Professor of Applied Psychology and Dean of the Faculty of Psychology at that university. In 2000, Nanne de Vries succeeded his present coauthor as the Professor of Health Education and Health Promotion at the University of Maastricht, after having worked in the Department of Social Psychology at the University of

Amsterdam for a period of 11 years. Both have an interest in the application of (social) psychological theory in developing health-promoting interventions, with special emphasis on attitude (change) theory, self-regulation, and diffusion and implementation of innovations.

Robert M. Krauss is a social psychologist whose research focuses on human communication with a particular emphasis on language and speech. He received his PhD from New York University in 1964. After a stint as a research psychologist at Bell Telephone Labs, he taught at Princeton, Harvard, and Rutgers universities before coming to Columbia, where is director of the Human Communication Lab. He is the author (with C.-Y. Chiu) of "Language and Social Behavior" in the fourth edition of *Handbook of Social Psychology* and (with Susan Fussell) of "Social Psychological Models of Interpersonal Communication" in *Social Psychology: A Handbook of Basic Principles.*

Arie W. Kruglanski is a Distinguished University Professor at the University of Maryland. His interests have centered on the psychology of judgment and knowledge formation, as well as on the processes of group decision making, and goal formation and implementation. He has served as editor, of the *Journal of Personality and Social Psychology: Attitudes and Social Cognition, and of the Personality and Social Psychology Bulletin.* His publications include over 150 articles, chapters, and books in the scientific literature in social and personality psychology. He is editor of two Psychology Press series—*Key Readings in Social Psychology* and *Principles of Social Psychology*—and a co-editor of a new series of upper level texts called *Frontiers of Social Psychology.*

Mark R. Leary received his PhD in social psychology from the University of Florida in 1980 and is currently professor and chair of psychology at Wake Forest University, where he has been on the faculty since 1985. He has published 10 books, including *Self-Presentation* (1995), *The Social Psychology of Emotional and Behavioral Problems* (1999), *The Handbook of Self and Identity* (2003), *The Curse of the Self* (2004), and four editions of an undergraduate research methods textbook. He is a former associate editor of the *Journal of Social and Clinical Psychology* and was the founding editor of *Self and Identity.* His research interests focus on the effects of people's concerns with interpersonal evaluation and social acceptance on behavior and emotion (including topics such as self-presentation, approval-seeking, hurt feelings, and self-esteem) and on the detrimental effects of self-awareness and egoism.

John M. Levine did his graduate work in social psychology at the University of Wisconsin and is currently a professor of psychology and senior scientist in the Learning and Development Center at the University of Pittsburgh. He conducts experimental research on a variety of small-group phenomena, including newcomer innovation in work teams, group loyalty, and the development of shared reality. He has published widely on these and other topics. He recently served as editor of the *Journal of Experimental Social Psychology* and as chair of the Society of Experimental Social Psychology.

After obtaining his PhD in 1969 from the University of Louvain, **Jacques-Philippe Leyens** worked for 2 years with Leonard Berkowitz and Ross Parke at the University of Wisconsin-Madison. He returned to Louvain in 1971, where he has remained since then. Starting with the influence of violence in the mass media, his research interests extended to war traumas in children, interpersonal perception, stereotyping, intergroup relations, and racism. His current main interests are the infrahumanization of outgroups and the differential impact of various norms of nondiscrimination. He has served as chief editor of the *European Journal of Social Psychology* and as president of the European Association of Experimental Psychology. Among his awards, he is most proud of the First International Prize of Psychology from the Association of Portuguese Psychologists and of the Tajfel Lecture Award.

Siegwart Lindenberg got his PhD from Harvard in 1971 and is a professor of sociology at the University of Groningen, the Netherlands. His research focuses on microsociological processes for the explanation of collective phenomena such as institutions and governance in organizations (www.ppsw.rug.nl/~lindenb).

Tony Manstead is currently a professor of psychology at the University of Cardiff. He studied psychology and sociology at the University of Bristol and gained his PhD in social psychology from the University of Sussex in 1978. He has held positions at the Universities of Sussex, Manchester, Amsterdam, and Cambridge, and visiting positions at the University of California at Berkeley and the University of Bologna. He was editor of the *British Journal of Social Psychology* and an associate editor of *Personality and Social Psychology Bulletin* and of Cognition and Emotion. He has been secretary and president of the European Association of Experimental Social Psychology. He has authored numerous papers on emotion, attitudes, and social identity, and is also coeditor (with Hewstone) of The *Blackwell Encyclopedia of Social Psychology* (Blackwell, 1995).

Nadine Mauer is a graduate student and research assistant at Martin-Luther University in Halle, Germany. Her main research interests are perceived and measured intelligence, long-term affect and personality, and information-processing influences on long-term well-being.

David M. Messick is the Morris and Alice Kaplan Professor of Ethics and Decision in Management and the Co-Director of the Ford Motor Center for Global Citizenship at the Kellogg School of Management, Northwestern University. Professor Messick's teaching and research interests are in the ethical and social aspects of decision making and information processing, and the psychology of leadership. He is the author of more than 150 articles, chapters, and edited books, and his scholarly work has been published in prominent academic journals.

Gerold Mikula is a professor of social psychology in the Department of Psychology at the University of Graz, Austria, where he also got his PhD in 1966. His research interests cover social psychology of justice, social interdependence, and personal relationships. He has publications in *Personality and Social Psychology Bulletin, European Journal of Social Psychology, European Review of Social Psychology,* and other recognized journals. He has served as associate editor of *Social Justice Research* and *Zeitschrift fuer Sozialpsychologie,* and on the editorial boards of *European Journal of Social Psychology, European Review of Social Psychology, Social Psychology Quarterly,* and *Journal of Personal and Social Relationships.* Gerold Mikula is past president of the European Association of Experimental Social Psychology (1987–1990) and the Austrian Society of Psychology (1997–1999).

Mario Mikulincer is a professor of psychology at Bar-Ilan University. His main research interests are attachment theory, terror management theory, personality processes in interpersonal relationships, and coping with stress. He is currently chair of Interdisciplinary Studies at Bar-Ilan University, serves as a member of the editorial boards of several personality and social psychology journals, and is an associate editor of the Personality section of the *Journal of Personality and Social Psychology.*

Walter Mischel is the Niven Professor of Humane Letters in Psychology at Columbia University, after 20 years as professor at Stanford University. His work focuses on the nature and structure of consistency in social behavior, the role of the situation in the analysis and conceptualization of personality, and self-regulatory processes such as delay of gratification. He has served as editor of the *Psychological Review,* and has published in areas including anthropology, behavioral medicine, behavioral economics, developmental psychology, and personality, social, and cognitive psychology, generally ignoring disciplinary boundaries. Since 1989 his research continues to be supported by National Institute of Mental Health (NIMH) MERIT Awards. He is the recipient of the Distinguished Scientific Contribution Award (American Psychological Association, 1982), the Distinguished Scientist Award (Society of Experimental Social Psychologists, 2000), and in 2004 was inducted into the National Academy of Science.

Diane M. Mollaghan is a PhD student in the Department of Psychology at the University of Texas at Austin. Her current research focuses on companion animals, with a particular focus on developing tools to assess personality in dogs. With a broad background in biology and animal sheltering, she is especially interested in the practical application of temperament tools to promote health and welfare in animals.

Andrzej Nowak is director of the Center for Complex Systems, Warsaw University, and an associate professor of psychology, Florida Atlantic University. He has been a visiting scholar at the University of North Carolina, Ohio State University, the Netherlands Institute for Advanced Studies, and Vienna's Center for Advanced Studies in the Social Sciences. Dr. Nowak's primary focus is the modeling and computer simulation of social processes. His current research includes the use of coupled dynamical systems to simulate the emergence of personality through social coordination, attractor neural networks to model interpersonal and group dynamics, and cellular automata to simulate linear and nonlinear societal change.

Brian Paciotti is a 2002 PhD graduate from an interdisciplinary social sciences program at the University of California (UC), Davis, where he currently conducts research on the influence of religious institutions on altruistic behavior. **Peter Richerson** and **Robert Boyd** are both UC Davis PhDs (1969 and 1973, respectively), and Richerson remains there in the Department of Environmental Science and Policy. Boyd is in the Anthropology Department at UCLA. They have collaborated since the 1970s on the study of the theory of cultural evolution. Their 1985 book *Culture and the Evolutionary Process* won the Staley Prize for a major contribution to the human sciences. Their new book *The Nature of Cultures* is forthcoming from the University of Chicago Press.

Jennifer S. Pardo received her PhD in cognitive psychology from Yale University in 2000. During her tenure there, she was affiliated with Haskins Laboratories and continues to collaborate on research in psycholinguistics. In 2002, she began a postdoctoral research fellowship in the Human Communication Laboratory at Columbia University. She is a coauthor (with R. Remez et al., 1994) of "On the Perceptual Organization of Speech" in *Psychological Review*.

Harry Reis (PhD, New York University, 1975) is a professor of psychology, University of Rochester. He has held visiting professorships at the University of Denver, Rijksuniversiteit Limburg, and the University of California, Santa Barbara. He served as executive officer of the Society for Personality and Social Psychology, was president of the International Association for Relationships Research, and is currently president-elect of the Society for Personality and Social Psychology. Dr. Reis is past editor of the *Journal of Personality and Social Psychology* and current editor of *Current Directions in Psychological Science*. Dr. Reis's research concerns interpersonal processes in close relationships.

Adrienne Sadovsky graduated with her PhD in developmental psychology from the University of Wyoming in 2002 and currently is a postdoctoral fellow at Arizona State University. Her areas of research include social cognition, with a specific interest in gender-role development in preschoolers.

S. Adil Saribay is a doctoral student in the Department of Psychology at New York University where he is engaged in research on significant-other representations and transference, and other aspects of person perception. He received his BS from the Middle East Technical University, Ankara, Turkey, in 2000 and his MA in social psychology from Bogazici University, Istanbul, Turkey, in 2002.

David O. Sears received his AB in history (Stanford University, 1957) and his PhD in psychology (Yale University, 1962). He was appointed as an assistant professor in psychology at UCLA (1961), then as a professor of psychology and political science (1971). At UCLA he has served as Dean of Social Sciences and director of the Institute for Social Science Research, as well as president of the International Society of Political Psychology. He has coauthored *Public Opinion* (with Robert E. Lane, 1964), *The Politics of Violence: The New Urban Blacks and the Watts Riot* (with John B. McConahay, 1973), *Tax Revolt: Something for Nothing in California* (with Jack Citrin, 1982), and 11 editions of *Social Psychology* (with Shelley E. Taylor & L. Anne Peplau, 2003), and coedited *Political Cognition* (with Richard Lau, 1986), *Racialized Politics: The Debate about Racism in America* (with Jim Sidanius & Lawrence Bobo, 2000), and *The Oxford Handbook of Political Psychology* (with Leonie Huddy & Robert Jervis, 2003).

Constantine Sedikides is Professor of Psychology at the University of Southampton, UK. He completed his doctorate at the Ohio State University in 1988 and has held faculty appointments at the University of Wisconsin— Madison and the University of North Carolina at Chapel Hill. His main research interest is in self-evaluation. He is the coauthor of over 150 articles and chapters, a coeditor of seven edited volumes, and a former coeditor of *Psychological Inquiry*. He is a fellow of the Society for Personality and Social Psychology, American Psychological Association, and American Psychological Society.

Antoinette Semenya is working on her PhD in psychology at the University of Western Ontario. Her research interests include ethnic relations, minority perspectives, and the causes and consequences of group power.

Gün Semin received his PhD in social psychology from the University of London, London School of Economics and Social Sciences, in 1973. His research interests are in the general area of the interface between psychological processes, language and communication, situated/embodied cognition, and the regulative function of affect.

Phillip R. Shaver is professor and chair of the Psychology Department at the University of California, Davis. His research interests include attachment theory, close relationships, sexuality, and human emotions. Recipient of a Distinguished Career Award from the International Association for Relationship Research, he co-edited *Measures of Personality and Social Psychological Attitudes and Handbook of Attachment: Theory, Research, and Clinical Applications*; he serves on several editorial boards and is associate editor of *Attachment and Human Development.*

Tania Singer received her PhD in cognitive developmental psychology from the Max Planck Institute for human development in Berlin end of 2000 and is currently research fellow at the Wellcome Department of Imaging Neuroscience in London. Her research interests concern life-span developmental psychology, cognitive and social psychology and the social-cognitive neurosciences, with an emphasis in integrating behavioral, social, and neural levels of analysis. Most recent publications on which she collaborated are "Empathy for Pain Involves the Affective but Not Sensory Components of Pain" (Science, 2004), "Brain Responses Reflect the Acquired Moral Status of Faces" (Neuron, 2004), and "Empathic Neural Responses Are Modulated By the Perceived Fairness of Others" (Nature, in press).

Eliot Smith received his PhD in social psychology from Harvard University in 1975. He is currently a professor at the Indiana University Bloomington. His research interests spans stereotyping, prejudice, and intergroup relations, with a special focus on the role of emotions in prejudice and intergroup behavior; situated/embodied cognition; connectionist models of mental representation and process applied to social psychology; and social cognition in general.

Mark Snyder is a member of the faculty in psychology at the University of Minnesota, where he holds the McKnight Presidential Chair in Psychology and is the director of the Center for the Study of the Individual and Society. He received his BA from McGill University in 1968 and his PhD from Stanford University in 1972. His research interests include theoretical and empirical issues associated with the motivational foundations of action, and the applications of basic theory and research to addressing practical problems. He has served as president of the Society for Personality and Social Psychology, on the board of directors of the American Psychological Society, and on the council of the Society for the Psychological Study of Social Issues. He is the author of the book *Public Appearances/Private Realities: The Psychology of Self-Monitoring*, and co-editor of the volume, *Cooperation in Modern Society: Promoting the Welfare of Communities, States, and Organizations.*

Robert C. Solomon is Quincy Lee Centennial Professor of Business and Philosophy and Distinguished Teaching Professor at the University Texas at Austin. His PhD is from the University of Michigan in philosophy and psychology

(1967). He has written many books and journal articles on the philosophy of emotions, beginning with *The Passions* in 1976 (Doubleday-Anchor). His most recent books are *Not Passion's Slave* and *In Defense of Sentimentality* (Oxford University Press, 2003, 2004). He is the past president of the International Society for Research on Emotions.

Monika Stelzl is pursuing a PhD in social psychology at the University of Western Ontario. Her research interests include the dynamics of multiple social identities and the adaptation of immigrants.

Fritz Strack is a professor of social psychology at the University of Würzburg. His research interests concern social cognition and emotion. More recently, he has become interested in the studying reflective and impulsive determinants of social behavior. He was editor (1998–2001) of the *European Journal of Social Psychology* and has received (together with Roland Deutsch) the 2003 Theoretical Innovation Prize from the Society of Personality and Social Psychology (SPSP).

Wolfgang Stroebe received PhDs in experimental and social psychology from the Universities of Münster (1966) and London (LSE) (1968) and an honorary doctorate from the University of Louvain (2002). He has held academic positions in the United States, Britain, and Germany, and is now professor of social and organizational psychology at Utrecht University, where he was also founding director of the Dutch Research Institute for Psychology and Health. Also, he has been a past president of the European Association of Experimental Social Psychology, and is a fellow of the British Psychological Society, the Society for the Psychological Study of Social Issues, and the Society of Personality and Social Psychology. He has published on a wide range of topics in social, health, and economic psychology and is editor (with Miles Hewstone) of the *European Review of Social Psychology*.

Jill M. Sundie obtained her MA in economics from the University of Southern California, and her PhD in social psychology from Arizona State University. She is now an assistant professor of marketing and entrepreneurship at the University of Houston. In her research, she applies evolutionary psychological principles to investigate the motivations for a variety of economic decisions. She is currently focused on extending evolutionary theory into the realms of consumer behavior and social influence.

John Tauer is an assistant professor of psychology at the University of St. Thomas (MN). His research focuses on the effects of competition, cooperation, goal setting, and motivation. John received his PhD from the University of Wisconsin–Madison in 2000. He bridges his motivation research with his work as the assistant men's basketball coach at St. Thomas, and in the youth basketball camps he has directed for the past 11 years.

Shelley E. Taylor is professor of psychology at the University of California, Los Angeles. She received her PhD in social psychology from Yale University in 1972 and served on the faculty of Harvard University from 1972 to 1979, before moving to UCLA in 1979. Her research interests center chiefly on stress and coping and the contribution of positive beliefs and social support to those processes. She especially studies "positive illusions," namely, exaggerated positive views about the self, the world, and the future that are protective of mental and physical health, especially in threatening times. She also studies social comparison processes, social cognition, mental simulation, and adjustment to chronic illness. Taylor is the recipient of a number of awards, including the Donald Campbell Award in Social Psychology (1995), the Outstanding Scientific Contribution Award in Health Psychology (1994), the William James Fellow Award from the American Psychological Society (2001), and the Distinguished Scientific Contribution Award from the American Psychological Association (1996).

John C. Turner is Professor of Psychology at the Australian National University. He obtained his PhD at the University of Bristol, United Kingdom, in 1975. He developed social identity theory with Henri Tajfel and subsequently originated self-categorization theory. Recent publications include, with S. A. Haslam "Social Identity, Organizations and Leadership" (2001; in M. E. Turner [Ed.], *Groups at Work: Advances in Theory and Research* [pp. 25–65]. Hillsdale, NJ: Lawrence Erlbaum Associates), and with K. J. Reynolds, "The Social Identity Perspective in Intergroup Relations: Theories, Themes and Controversies" (2001; in R. Brown & S. Gaertner [Eds.], *Handbook of Social Psychology. Vol 4. Intergroup Processes* [pp. 133–152]. Cambridge, MA: Blackwell). He was awarded the Henri Tajfel Memorial Medal by the European Association of Experimental Social Psychology in 1999.

Tom R. Tyler is University Professor of Psychology at New York University. His research explores authority dynamics in groups, organizations, and societies. His books include *The Social Psychology of Procedural Justice* (1988), *Why People Obey the Law* (1990), *Social Justice in a Diverse Society* (1996), and *Cooperation in Groups* (2000).

Robin Vallacher is a professor of psychology, Florida Atlantic University, and a research affiliate at the Center for Complex Systems, Warsaw University. He has been a visiting scholar at the University of Bern, Switzerland, and the Max-Planck-Institute for Psychological Research in Munich. Dr. Vallacher has investigated a wide variety of topics, from principles of social cognition, action identification, and self-concept, to issues in social justice and social change. His current work, employing experimentation and computer simulations, centers on identifying the invariant properties underlying these otherwise diverse phenomena. Dr. Vallacher has published five books, including two with Andrzej Nowak that develop the implications of dynamical systems for social psychology.

Rick van Baaren is assistant professor of social psychology at the University of Nijmegen. He received his PhD at the University of Nijmegen in 2003. His recent articles in the *Journal of Personality and Social Psychology* and *Psychological Science* address the prosocial nature of mimicry. His further research interests include social influence and advertising.

Eric van Dijk studied both economics and social psychology. In 1993 he received a PhD in social psychology for his dissertation on asymmetric social dilemmas. He is now a professor of social psychology at Leiden University. His main interest is in social decision making, and in particular in how the presentation (framing) of situations affects the decisions that people make. Research topics include bargaining and reluctance to trade, social dilemmas, emotions, and fairness. He teaches social psychology and economic psychology.

Paul Van Lange is a professor of social psychology at the Free University at Amsterdam, the Netherlands, as well as a professional fellow on societal conflicts in the Department of Social and Organizational Psychology at the University of Leiden. His research interests focus on differences in prosocial, individualistic, and competitive orientations; forgiveness, sacrifice, and generosity; trust and misunderstanding in social interaction; and interdependence and taxonomic approaches to social psychology. Also, he was a coauthor of a book entitled *Atlas of Interpersonal Situations* (Cambridge) by Kelley and others. He has held a number of positions in the field, including being scientific director of the Kurt Lewin Institute (an interuniversity graduate school for social psychology and its applications), associate editor of the *Journal of Personality and Social Psychology* and the *European Journal of Social Psychology*, and member of the Policy Advice Committee of the Dutch Organization of Scientific Research.

Frans van Winden graduated in economics (with additional training in social psychology and sociology) at the University of Amsterdam, and obtained his PhD at Leiden University (1981). Since 1983 he has been a full professor of economics at the University of Amsterdam. He is also director of CREED—the Center for Research in Experimental Economics and Political Decision Making. His main research interests concern political economics, experimental economics, and the economic significance and modeling of emotions. He has published widely in these areas. He is one of the founding directors of the Tinbergen Institute, former president of the European Public Choice Society, research fellow of the Tinbergen Institute and CESifo, and coordinator of ENABLE, the international research network on behavioral economics.

J. Mark Weber is an assistant professor at the Rotman School of Management, University of Toronto. He earned his doctorate in management and organizations at the Kellogg School of Management, Northwestern University. His research interests include social dilemmas, cooperation, trust, negotiations, and the role of values in decision making. Some of his most recent work has appeared in *Personality and Social Psychology Review, Research in Organizational Behavior,* and *Trust and Distrust Across Organizational Contexts: Dilemmas and Approaches.*

Lioba Werth is a researcher and lecturer at the University of Würzburg. She was recently awarded the Bavarian Habilitation Prize. Her research interests are implicit and explicit processes in applied social psychology.

Michael West is a professor of organizational psychology and Director of Research at Aston Business School. He graduated from the University of Wales in 1973 and received his PhD in 1977 (the psychology of meditation). He then spent a year working in the coal mines of South Wales. He has authored 16 books and over 150 scientific and practitioner articles and book chapters. He is a fellow of the British Psychological Society, the American Psychological Association (APA), and the Royal Society for the Encouragement of Arts, Manufactures, and Commerce. His areas of research interest are team and organizational innovation and effectiveness.

Tim Wildschut received his PhD in psychology from the University of North Carolina at Chapel Hill in 2000 and is currently an associate professor of social and personality psychology at the University of Southampton. His main research interests are in the study of intergroup relations and self-conscious emotions. He is a recipient of the 2003–2004 Gordon Allport Intergroup Relations Prize.

Vincent Yzerbyt took his PhD in 1990 from the Catholic University of Louvain at Louvain-la-Neuve, Belgium, where he is now a professor of psychology. He has written and edited several books dealing with social cognition, stereotyping, and intergroup relations and authored a great number of articles on such issues as the black sheep effect, the ingroup overexclusion effect, social judgeability, stereotype change, entitativity, essentialism, causal attribution, and social emotions. Recipient of the 1994 Belgian 5-yearly award for early career in psychology, he served as associate editor on the *British Journal of Social Psychology* and the *Personality and Social Psychology Bulletin* and contributes to the editorial board of several prominent outlets in the field. He is currently president of the European Association of Experimental Social Psychology.

Mark P. Zanna is Professor, Department of Psychology, University of Waterloo. He received his Ph.D. in 1970 from Yale University. His research focuses on overcoming resistance to change.

Author Index

Subject Index